Where the Brook
and
River Meet

A Literature-Based Unit Study
of the Victorian Era

Margie Gray

ISBN O-9652511-5-2

First printing, 1999. Second printing, 2004.

All quotes from *The Annotated Anne of Green Gables* by L.M. Montgomery, edited by Wendy E. Barry, Margaret Anne Doody, and Mary E. Doody Jones. Copyright © 1997 by Oxford University Press, Inc. Used by permission of Oxford University Press, Inc.

All quotes from *The Selected Journals of L.M. Montgomery,* Volume I, 1889–1910, page 358, edited by Mary Rubio and Elizabeth Waterston, © 1985 University of Guelph. Used with permission.

Published by Cadron Creek Christian Curriculum
4329 Pinos Altos Road, Silver City, New Mexico 88061

About the Cover Photo

Lauren Ciarrone, age 10, has always been homeschooled. She has three younger brothers. Her interests are ballet, piano, and reading *Anne of Green Gables*. The photographer was her mother, Maureen Ciarrone.

⇒ Acknowledgments ⇐

I would like to thank the Lord who has enabled me to do more than I thought possible. He is the great Provider. He has given me an encouraging, helpful husband, as well as friends and acquaintances who have counseled me. I am grateful to the numerous homeschoolers across the country who gave me feedback and encouragement during this work.

This work would not have materialized without the help of my editors, Mei Leslie and Julie Bowen, or without the encouragement of and help from my daughter, Janell. Once again her love for reading has encouraged me to challenge her reading abilities.

The second edition was improved by the input of many home educators who completed the first edition and with the faithful and encouraging assistance of my editor, Barb Saxton.

I am also grateful for the professional and dedicated service of Laura Howell of Howell Graphics and her assistant, Sarah Johnson.

⇒ About the Author ⇐

Margie Gray was born on a Navajo Indian reservation in Arizona where her parents taught school. When Margie was eight, the family moved to Barstow, California, where she finished high school. Although she had many exceptional teachers, Margie began to see the "social agenda" of the educational system. Seeing the problems her parents faced within their profession, she chose a nursing degree. After college, Margie moved to Mountain Pass, California, where in 1983, she met and married her husband, Owen, a heavy equipment operator.

In 1990 Owen and Margie moved their family of six to Arkansas to be nearer to relatives. Margie's grandmother lived with them the last three years of her life. After she died, Owen and Margie longed to move west.

So in 1997, with hopes of employment nearer to home and a better climate, the Gray family moved to Silver City, New Mexico. Owen and Margie have always homeschooled their five girls, ages 21, 18, 16 (twins), and 10, and plan to continue with their son 5. The academic benefits of homeschooling have been wonderful, but greater joy has been in the strengthening of family relationships. Because of this, Margie participates actively in the leadership of local home school groups to encourage the hearts of parents toward their children.

Where the Brook and River Meet is the second of two literature-based unit study curricula Margie has authored and self-published. The first, *The Prairie Primer,* was published in 1993. She is the major contributing editor for another literature-based unit study, *Further Up and Further In,* and she compiled and edited *Anne's Anthology.* Look for her next book soon, another unit study, based on the book, *Endurance.*

⟐ About the Illustrators ⟐

Trisha Lynn McKenzie was born in October of 1986 in Louisiana and has been a source of joy for her family ever since. She came to know Jesus as her Savior when she was 13 and has been homeschooled since seventh grade, now being ready to complete high school using *Where the Brook and River Meet*. Trish loves working with her hands (Proverbs 31:13), chiefly: crocheting, hugging, and handshaking. And she loves the Holy Word of God. She now resides in the backwoods of Mississippi with her parents—Ricky and Susie—and her siblings —Kristopher and Joshua—enjoying wildlife and nature walks. She hopes to, one day, marry a Christian man and homeschool their children in the ways of the Lord (Deuteronomy 11:19). "The LORD is the strength of my life . . ."

Born in San Diego, California, in 1986, Alexis Gray has been home-schooled from birth. She has gone from finger paints to oil paints; from 1, 2, 3 to geometry. She will graduate from high school soon and plans to go to college. Before her younger siblings were born, when her mother had more time, Alexis remembers many of the things she did with her mom at a young age. Though she has been taught to work independently since then, Alexis has always known her mother has been there for her.

⤖ Editor's Note ⤗

From the practical to the poetic, *Where the Brook and River Meet* takes students on a journey through the Victorian Era. Through varied, thought-provoking activities that stimulate interest and inquiry, they will explore the events and thinking of the time. Combining elements of the classical education of Anne's day—dictation, recitation, memorization, essay writing—with the interdisciplinary approach of today—use of primary documents, field trips, hands-on projects—this study will challenge students to reflect on the historical issues of the Victorian day as well as the personal challenges of growing up.

While following the lively, imaginative Anne into young womanhood, students will be led to look at their own journey into maturity. From discussions of self-acceptance, appearance, friendship, and romance, they will move beyond to reflect on character-building questions. What does it take to be a good friend? What should be the topic of our conversations? What are the effects of unforgivingness? For, at the heart of this study is the author's desire to see young women grow into the grace of womanhood and the fruitfulness of the Lord.

It has been my honor to edit *Where the Brook and River Meet* and to see the clear call to a higher standard it sets forth.

Standing, with reluctant feet,
Where the brook and river meet,
Womanhood and childhood fleet!
—*Longfellow*

Table of Contents

Introduction

Grace and peace be multiplied unto you through the knowledge of God, and of Jesus our Lord, according as his divine power hath given unto us all things that pertain unto life and godliness, through the knowledge of him that hath called us to glory and virtue: whereby are given unto us exceeding great and precious promises; that by these ye might be partakers of the divine nature, having escaped the corruption that is in the world through lust. And besides this, giving all diligence, *add to your* faith *virtue; and to* virtue, *knowledge; and to* knowledge, *temperance; and to* temperance, *patience; and to* patience, *godliness; and to* godliness, *brotherly kindness; and to* brotherly kindness, *charity. For if these things be in you, and abound, they make you that ye shall neither be barren nor unfruitful in the knowledge of our Lord Jesus Christ.* II Peter 1:2–8 (KJV)

What do I want to teach my children?

Anne of Green Gables is the treasured story of a vivacious, lovable orphan girl who becomes a dutiful, thoughtful, selfless woman. Countless readers have witnessed Anne's humorous and touching struggles and victories and have loved her as she grows and changes into a strong young woman. While growing in stature, Anne also grows in character and wisdom. *Where the Brook and River Meet* is a unit study based on *Anne of Green Gables* which aspires to promote that same growth in your child.

While writing this unit study, I asked myself, "What do I want to teach my children?" I knew academics and facts were important, but of learning there is no end. So what, specifically, do I want to impart? The answer is partially contained in *Where the Brook and River Meet*. I want to prepare my daughters with skills needed for both singleness and married life. I want them to have knowledge and skills that would benefit them as a wife and mother, as well as in the working world. But foremost, I want them to grow in the knowledge of the Lord. I want them to develop discernment. These are the same goals Marilla has for Anne.

Where the Brook and River Meet has been written to help parents raise children to be fruitful in the knowledge of the Lord. It is also a tool to encourage a productive exchange between parents and their children in academic subjects and godly development. *Anne of Green Gables* provides a springboard for learning a Biblical world view in the setting of the Victorian era in Canada.

This study has also been developed with an independent student in mind. Much of the work can be done with minimal oversight, guidance, and assistance from the parent. Suggestions can, and probably will, be changed by the parent. Of course, if parental time permits and the student needs or wants more parental involvement, there are a number of opportunities in this study for interactive learning.

Using *Where the Brook and River Meet*

Scheduling Time

There are nine units in *Where the Brook and River Meet*, each one corresponding to four or five chapters of *Anne of Green Gables*. A Unit may take four weeks out of a school year of 36 weeks, depending on the depth to which the student researches each subject and the amount of time you choose to allot to each subject. Two of my girls have completed *Where the Brook and River Meet*. One took two years and the other took almost as long. They both worked diligently. Countless other families have completed *Where the Brook and River Meet* in just a year. *It is emphasized that you should follow a plan best suited to your family's pace.*

It is a good idea to skim through the entire curriculum at the beginning of the year to set priorities and to decide which of the suggested materials you want to purchase to enhance the study. Skimming will also help you preview the field trips, allowing you to group some together; to schedule others in the appropriate season; and to be on the watch for certain once-a-year community activities to incorporate into your individual program.

By popular demand, this revised edition of *Where the Brook and River Meet* has daily lesson plans. These lesson plans are for the student wishing to complete the study in one year. They are placed after each Chapter Planning Guide. They are a guideline and may be tailored to individual needs.

Notice that while not all subjects have daily or even weekly assignments, all subjects will have adequate attention in the overall course of the year. Also, some of the assignments are placed under two subject categories, most frequently writing and another subject. This is to show the distribution of written assignments.

It is suggested that the parent/instructor sit down with the student, pick the activities which are to be done, and put the approximate amount of time anticipated for the Activities. The suggested time for a student to spend daily on a Unit is one to two hours reading and researching the chosen Activities and at least half an hour for writing, part of which will include the dictation exercise. Thirty minutes a day should be spent in handwork to complete the long range craft project. *2-3 hr day*

Adapting this Curriculum

The needs of students will be different according to their age, abilities, and the family's particular goals in using this curriculum. While providing both a comprehensive structure and materials, *Where the Brook and River* is designed to allow you to meet those individual needs. Feel free to supplement, omit, and tailor assignments and activities for your family. Resources and research topics are suggested and, again, can be modified, used, or not used as appropriate.

Choose those activities, research topics, and resources that are age, ability, and interest appropriate for your student.

Some students will require more time for reading while others will need more time for writing assignments. Others may become absorbed in research. Many assignments may take more than one day to complete well. There will be activities that should be only be skimmed, while others should be explored in more depth. Please allow the student some flexibility.

The poetry selections may be challenging for younger students and older ones who have not been accustomed to reading poetry. Use your judgment as to which of these assignments the student needs to do alone, which will require your assistance, and which you will need to simplify or simply forego. Also, watching plays, movies, or reading abridged versions may be substituted for the required literature sources.

You may want to go over some of the history writing assignments orally. If writing is tedious for your student, instruct her to print out her favorite Web page on the topic and highlight the important and interesting segments. These pages can be filed in the History notebook in place of the written reports. *Remember to adapt to time available, age, ability, and interest.*

Additional Curricula for Junior/Senior High Students

- A separate science course. Due to the depth and progression of the sciences at the upper grade levels, science is not covered extensively in *Where the Brook and River Meet.*
- A separate mathematics program.
- A separate grammar course, particularly if the student is not proficient in grammar. (Latin is an excellent way to improve grammar.)
- A separate Latin course. In keeping with the classical education Anne herself follows, a one-year Latin course should be included in your curriculum. This course can be as simple as *English from the*

Roots Up or as in-depth as *Artes Latinae.* (See the *Appendix of Resource* for vendors who carry these programs.)
- If spelling is problematic, then *Spelling Power* is the suggested program of choice.

Earning High School Credits

The following discusses two methods for earning high school credits with *Where the Brook and River Meet.* One method is based on the amount of material covered and the other, on time spent.

The first method was designed by Beverly Adams-Gordon, author of *Home School, High School, and Beyond.* To use this method, the majority of activities should be completed in the category for each subject area in which you want to obtain credit. If you are utilizing *Where the Brook and River Meet* for Bible, then you should do the majority of Bible Activities. If you do not want to obtain credit for a particular subject, for instance Health, then you may omit all the health projects.

The method Gordon uses to calculate these credits is described in her book, *Home School, High School, and Beyond.* A complete year of high school consists of six credits. Notice the credits in the list below for *Where the Brook and River Meet* based on Gordon's system total more than six credits.

Subject	Credits
Bible/Religion/Character	1.0
Literature/Language Arts	1.0
Social Studies (majority is World History)	1.0
Economics	.25
Fine Arts	.25
Occupational Education	.5
Physical Education	.5
Health	.5
Subtotal	5.0
Add subjects from other studies:	
Math	1.0
Latin	1.0
Science	1.0
Total	8.0

The second method of earning high school credits is more time consuming, but offers greater flexibility. It is explained in detail in "How Do We Earn High School Credits?" by Ellen Davis in *The Elijah Company Catalog, 1998/1999*, pages 166–167. The following information is quoted from her article:

About Credits

"Most states have the following minimal number of high school credits required for graduation:

Subject	Credits
Language Arts	3.0–4.0
Math	2.3–3.0
Fine Arts or Language	1.0
American Government	$1/2$
Physical Education (includes Health)	2.0
Science	2.0
Social Studies	2.0–3.0
Economics	$1/2$
U.S. History & Geography	1.0
World History & Geography	1.0
Electives	7.0–9.0

"What do these credits mean? Usually one credit in a particular subject (for example, one credit in Language Arts) means that a class was offered in that subject for 50 minutes each school day for a year (180 days), and that the student attended that class for 165 of the 180 days it was offered, and performed work in that class to the teacher's satisfaction.

"First, let's examine the concept of a high school credit in more detail. Let's say your child needed one high school credit in Language Arts. If we multiply 50 minutes (the length of class time each day) by 150 days (the number of days the student actually attended the class, assuming the student was allowed 15 absences a year and another 15 classroom periods were spent with assemblies, pep rallies, substitute teachers, non-learning activities, etc.) we get 126 hours of actual class time for that credit. However, we know that in a typical classroom, less than

half of the time is spent in learning activities. The other half is spent settling down the class, discussing assignments, taking up or giving out papers, dealing with trouble-makers, and so on.

"This means that out of that year of class time in Language Arts, teaching (and presumably learning) was actually occurring for less than 63 hours. Add 20 minutes of homework in that class three days a week and that adds another 36 hours of learning time. So a high school credit actually reflects roughly 100 hours of work in a particular subject, if that much. (When we have talked to former school teachers, they agree that 100 hours is a generous estimate.)...

"Because our student is earning a course credit based on spending 100 hours of time, this 100 hours can be spread over two weeks, two months, or two years. When and how the credit is earned is not the issue; covering the material is. We could even design the course so that it provides only half a credit. In high schools with a semester system, courses are often only given for one semester, so they count for half a credit each."

Utilizing the above method, the instructor and student can pick and choose which activities need to be done. The student times herself performing the activity and writes the amount of time next to each completed activity (minus any dawdling, interruptions, becoming side-tracked, etc.). The time listed under each educational heading, e.g. Literature, Health, etc., is then added up and credits or fractions of credits are assigned to each subject.

Grading

Frequently instructors will be referred to an Assessment Rubric for grading writing assignments. However, instructors are free to establish their own guidelines. One way to grade is on the effort expended and quality of the papers and discussion. Objective criteria would be: write or give within a nine-week period, 10 reports for an A; 8 reports for a B; 6 reports for a C.

For high school transcripts, *Where the*

Brook and River Meet needs to be broken down into subject categories.

The following chart is a suggested method of grading for those teachers who are keeping grades or preparing a transcript.

A Suggested Method of Grading

Bible & Character
25% Contract Reading
25% Memory
25% Notebook and Activities
25% Quizzes and Test

Fine Arts
75% Notebook and Activities
25% Quizzes and Test

Health
75% Notebook and Activities
25% Quizzes and Test

History and Geography
50% Notebook and Activities
25% Contract Reading
25% Quizzes and Test

Literature
25% Contract Reading
25% Daily Reading and Vocabulary
25% Notebook and Activities
25% Quizzes and Test

Occupational Education
75% Notebook and Activities
25% Contract Reading

Contract Reading

If you look at the suggested grading table above, you will see under most of the subject headings Contract Reading comprises 25% percent of the overall subject grade. The Contract Reading assignments for each letter grade are given in the Contracts. The student must read all of the assignments for not only the grade she desires to earn, but also for each grade below that. Before the coursework begins, the student selects the grade she desires to earn and makes a "Contract" to read all of the books or segments of books that are listed in the Contract for that grade level and each one below it.

Contract assignments for each subject may be found on page 10 and following. Only four of the six academic subjects—Bible, History, Occupational Education, and Literature—have Contract Reading as part of the overall subject grade.

Remember: The Contract Reading assignments are chosen before course work begins and are determined by the letter grade the student selects.

Note: Younger students and slower readers may, with parental permission, listen to some of the books on tape.

Required Resources

Where the Brook and River Meet is an in-depth study and many resources are required. You will, however, only need to purchase the books in Anne's Daily Pack, which are the four resources listed below. (See the *Appendix of Resources* for suggested vendors.) Most other assigned reading books, including those for Contract Reading, may be obtained at your local library, from your local homeschool support group, your church library, or the Internet. You will need access to the Internet or a good set of encyclopedias, a dictionary, a Bible, a Bible concordance, and a thesaurus. (Note that scriptures used in this study are taken from the King James Version of the Bible.) A world history textbook may be helpful for some research. The Web sites mentioned are optional resources.

The page numbers referred to in *Where the Brook and River Meet* correspond with the 1987 Bantam Classic paperback edition of the *Anne of Green Gables* series and *The Annotated Anne of Green Gables* 1997 edition. When reference is made to page numbers only, the passage is to be found in the Bantam Classic edition of *Anne of Green Gables*.

✓ • *Anne's Anthology* compiled and edited by Margie Gray. Cadron Creek Christian Curriculum, 2000. ISBN 0-9652511-2-8.

✓ • *The Annotated Anne of Green Gables* by L.M. Montgomery. Edited by Wendy E. Barry, Margaret Anne Doody, and Mary E. Doody Jones. Oxford University Press, 1997. ISBN 0-19-510428-5. This book contains the complete text of *Anne of Green Gables*. This is a beautiful, useful resource, but the authors have a definite feminist slant in their commentaries. They do not present a Christian world view. Discussion between the instructor and student regarding content is encouraged.

✓ • *The Green Gables Letters from L.M. Montgomery to Ephraim Weber 1905–1909* edited by Wilfrid Eggleston. Borealis Press, 2001. ISBN 0-88887-932-6.

✓ • *Writers INC* written and compiled by Patrick Sebranek, Dave Kemper, and Verne Meyer. Houghton Mifflin Co., 2001. ISBN 0-669-47186-0. This is used daily.

While not required to be purchased, a number of other resources with vendors are listed in the *Appendix of Resources* for your information.

Web Sites

Where the Brook and River Meet may be completed without using a computer, although using the Internet to do research will help develop research skills and make it easier to obtain information. If you do not have access in your home, you may be able to use the Internet on a friend's computer or at your public library. Usually a library will allow you to print Web pages for later study at home. Because Web sites frequently change addresses, servers go down, etc., updated Web sites can be found at CadronCreek.com. If a particular site cannot be found, use the search engines to find other sites on the topic. To improve and maintain the links offered in this study, please e-mail

CadronCreek.com when a Web site does not work or if you find a new one that is beneficial in your study. Even if the text does not refer you to <www.cadroncreek.com> for a research project, you may want to check for new listings as useful links for research topics will be added on an ongoing basis. It is important to monitor your child while research is being done on the computer due to the fact that pornography and witchcraft may be encountered on the Web.

✎ Notebook

The assignments in this Unit Study are best kept organized in a three-ring binder divided into the following sections:

Bible

Dictation/Writing: For all writing not pertaining to other subject areas.

Fine Arts: A separate sketchbook may be used in place of this section.

Health

History: Pages should be loose leaf. All history pages should have the date of the event boldly written in the upper right hand corner of the page. As events are written about, the student will place them in chronological order in her notebook. Because *Anne of Green Gables* does not survey literature or history sequentially, the student will need to use the notebook as a timeline to place events in order.

Literature: Pages should be loose leaf so written material can be organized for easy reference. You may want subsections for poetry, literary terms, and periods of literature or for other topics you find useful.

Occupational Education

Vocabulary

For all work other than History, write the date and the Chapter number to which the work corresponds in the upper right hand corner of the page.

The Unit Study

The Planning Guide

At the beginning of each Unit is a Planning Guide which lists the information and items you need to gather for one week of study. Suggested resources for the information and items are given as well as videos and field trips. Space is also is provided at the bottom of the Planning Guide for your own notes and suggestions. Use this page(s) to prepare for the Unit ahead.

Some Units will list an optional Group Activity. Group Activities add much needed spice, variety, energy, and enthusiasm to your schooling. These Activities can be done informally with siblings or may include neighbors, other homeschoolers, or families who are using *Where the Brook and River Meet*.

Assignment Tables

These were added to the study to assist the parent and student in breaking down the Chapters into daily lessons. Please go through each table with your student to select those assignments that you do not wish to cover during the Chapter study. If you are taking over a year to complete the study you may want to allow an additional week for finishing assignments, reading the contract reading assignments, or working on occupational education projects.

Study Guide

At the beginning of each Chapter, a reading assignment is given from *Anne of Green Gables*. Following the reading assignment, the Study Guide is divided into Reading Comprehension Questions, Vocabulary, and Activities. A week in *Where the Brook and River Meet* consists of four days of assignments. Use the fifth day of the week for Recitation, Field Days, and Field Trips. This is also a good day for incorporating suggested movies or Group Activities.

Comprehension Questions

Reading Comprehension questions may be done orally or in writing, but should always be answered in complete sentences. Let the dialogue with your student during this time be relaxed and enjoy getting to know her opinion and her skills in logic and observation. The answers to most of the questions are given in the *Answer Appendix*.

Vocabulary

Learning the vocabulary is the first step in increasing the student's comprehension of *Anne of Green Gables* and the Victorian era. Sometimes fill in the blank sentences are given. (The vocabulary word may or may not be used in the same context as Montgomery uses it in her text.) At other times the student is asked to write her own sentences or to find the vocabulary word in the context of Montgomery's writing. The latter is most easily accomplished using an online text of *Anne of Green Gables* and the find command on your computer. Although it is more difficult visually skimming the text for a vocabulary word, this can be a beneficial skill to develop. Besides the vocabulary in *Anne of Green Gables*, students will learn vocabulary from the poetry they will be reading.

Activities

A wide variety of Activities expand and deepen understanding of *Anne of Green Gables* as well as the Victorian Era and related topics. Activities are vital in increasing your student's comprehension. These sections cover academic, Bible, and vocational studies as well as hands-on activities that relate to the chapters or pages read. A subject category is given in the margin next to each Activity assignment to help you choose, record, or balance your student's studies. Many of the Activities may take more than one day to complete, depending on your family's interest and time. Make note of any Activity that is inappropriate due to the season of the year or the readiness of your family and plan to complete it when the time and conditions are appropriate.

For the ease of the student, many of the Activity questions have answers, hints, or explanations. These helps will decrease the student's research time.

A comprehensive list of topics covered in *Where the Brook and River Meet* is categorized by subject areas and found in the *Topics Covered Appendix*.

Bible: As Anne encounters difficulties and challenges while maturing into adulthood, hope and encouragement are given to the student in her own walk with God. As students this age begin to question what they believe, they are taught Christian doctrines such as the attributes of God and they are able to see the lives of great men and women of God.

English/Dictation: A daily dictation text is suggested. Begin by having the student copy the passage, then dictate with pre-study. Finally advance to dictation without pre-study. This may be handled in one of two ways: the student may read the required passage into a tape recorder, then take dictation from the recording; or a family member may read the text to the student. Use one passage until it is written perfectly from dictation. This may take several days of copying, comparing with the original, correcting, rewriting and so on.

Anne had daily dictation in school. It developed speed and accuracy in writing, improved spelling, and served as a good way to review for grammatical errors. These dictations should be corrected first by the student, then reviewed by the parent. Once it is seen that the student is careful in catching her errors, she may correct her work independently. A follow-up activity will be given to increase understanding of punctuation, grammar, or a literary technique. *Writers INC,* a student handbook for writing and learning, will be used almost daily as a reference for these and other activities.

Fine Arts: Just as Anne's life is enhanced by the arts, an introduction to opera and painting is given to the students.

Health: Prevention, care, and understanding of diseases and injuries are learned, as well as an attitude of service to the sick or injured.

History: The History assignments are derived from both the reading of *Anne of Green Gables* and the poetry selections. The Victorian time period comes alive by intertwining historical events with the literature of the day. The *Background Information Appendix* contains a wide variety of important resources including some primary documents on subjects of debate of the time. Students will be tested on the material.

Geography is also included in the History Credits. In Unit 2, Chapter 5, Activity 11, students are directed to begin marking locations of significant events they are studying. Students should continue this activity throughout the Study, even when not specifically directed to do so.

Literature: In addition to *Anne of Green Gables*, the student will be exposed to a wide variety of literature. The instructor may decide to have the student read some of the literature in its original form, while in other cases an abridged version, video, or a play may be a better choice.

Occupational Education: The goal of Occupational Education is to expose the student to a variety of vocational fields, including homemaking. Students are directed to evaluate how these occupations may benefit their future family. Just as Montgomery weaves into *Anne of Green Gables* the different philosophies of a woman's role in society, *Where the Brook and River Meet* explores these roles in today's modern setting.

Students will also do a number of hands-on projects and crafts, many of which are drawn from the Victorian Era. They will be directed to undertake a long-term project to work on throughout the study, either an afghan, rag rug, or patchwork quilt.

Recitation: Beginning in Unit 2, students will give a weekly recitation of literary selections and memorized Scripture. The goal of these recitations is to develop the student's ability to communicate clearly while holding the audience's attention with an engaging presentation. They will also add depth to the student's appreciation of both Scripture and the literary selections.

Writing: Numerous assignments are given which cover all types of writing. Only

through frequent writing can a student improve her skills.

⏰ *Unit Quiz and Test*

At the end of each Unit there is a Unit Quiz. Parents/instructors may want to assist students in studying for the Quiz by letting them know the specific items they should study. These items are marked in each Chapter by a ⏰ icon.

The quizzes are to be seen as another learning tool. Each quiz has different point values for each subject. It is suggested that points for all the quizzes in each subject be totaled and then a percentage given for that subject.

A final exam has been provided that may be given at the end of this Study. It covers information from all the reading, plus ⏰ marked activities.

Key to Activity Icons

The following icons will be used in the Activities to help in planning and carrying out the different tasks.

✎	write
♡	memorize
✖	discuss
📖	read
🔑	look up
∞	watch video or listen to tape
✋	hands-on activity or draw
✦	map skill

Reading Contract
for the subject of Bible

For Bible I plan to make a reading contract for a/an _____ grade. This grade will make up 25% of my overall grade in the subject of Bible. To earn my _____ grade I will read the following as listed in Contract Reading Assignments in *Where the Brook and River Meet*:

C grade

started _____ finished _____ A biography of George Mueller (Unit 1)

started _____ finished _____ Job (Unit 1)

started _____ finished _____ *The Christian's Secret of a Happy Life* by Hannah Whithall Smith (Unit 5)

started _____ finished _____ Assigned portions of *How Should We Then Live? The Rise and Decline of Western Thought and Culture* by Francis A. Schaeffer (Units 3, 7, and 8)

B grade

The above books plus:

Circle one: *Pilgrim's Progress* by John Bunyan (Unit 3)

                               In His Steps by Robert Sheldon (Unit 4)

                               The Beautiful Side of Evil by Johanna Michaelsen (Unit 7)

started _____ finished _____

A grade

The above books plus:

started _____ finished _____ *The Normal Christian Life* by Watchman Nee (Unit 6)

started _____ finished _____ *Passion and Purity: Learning to Bring Your Love Life Under Christ's Control* by Elisabeth Elliot and Joshua Harris (Unit 7)

Circle one: *Mere Christianity* by C. S. Lewis (Unit 9)

                               Essential Truths of the Christian Faith by R. C. Sproul (Unit 9)

                               That's Why They Call It Grace!, Audiocassette, by Diana Waring (Unit 9)

started _____ finished _____

Signature _____ Date _____

Reading Contract
for the subject of History

For History I plan to make a reading contract for a/an ____ grade. This grade will make up 25% of my overall grade in the subject of History. To earn my ____ grade I will read the following as listed in Contract Reading Assignments in *Where the Brook and River Meet*:

C grade

started _____ finished _____ A biography of Napoleon (Unit 2)

started _____ finished _____ *What in the World's Going on Here?: A Judeo-Christian Primer of World History,* Volumes I & II, by Diana Waring (Unit 2)

started _____ finished _____ *Whatever Happened to Penny Candy?: A Fast, Clear and Fun Explanation of the Economics You Need for Success in Your Career, Business and Investments* by Rick Maybury and Richard J. Maybury (Unit 6)

B grade

The above books plus:

started _____ finished _____ *Are You Liberal? Conservative? or Confused?* by Rick Maybury and Richard J. Maybury (Unit 4)

A grade

The above books plus:

started _____ finished _____ A biography of Queen Victoria (Unit 5)

Signature _____ Date _____

Reading Contract
for the subject of Literature

For Literature I plan to make a Reading Contract for a/an _____ grade. This grade will make up 25% of my overall grade in the subject of Literature. To earn my _____ grade I will read the following as listed in Contract Reading Assignments in *Where the Brook and River Meet*:

C grade

started _____ finished _____ *Anne of Green Gables*

B grade

The above books plus:

Circle one: ✓ *King Arthur and His Knights* by Richard Lancelyn Green (Unit 1)

Alice in Wonderland by Lewis Carroll (Unit 2)

✓ A "Pansy" book (Unit 3)

Ben Hur: A Tale of the Christ by Lew Wallace (Unit 7)

started _____ finished _____

A grade

The above books plus:

started _____ finished _____ ✓"The Snow Queen" by Hans Christian Anderson (Unit 1)

Circle one: *Great Expectations* by Charles Dickens (Unit 1)

✓ *Oliver Twist* by Charles Dickens (Unit 1)

started _____ finished _____

started _____ finished _____ *Marmion* by Sir Walter Scott (Unit 6)

Signature _____ Date _____

Reading Contract
for the subject of Occupational Education

For Occupational Education I plan to make a Reading Contract for a/an _____ grade. This grade will make up 25% of my overall grade in the subject of Occupational Education. To earn my _____ grade I will read the following as listed in Contract Reading Assignments in *Where the Brook and River Meet*:

C grade

started _____ finished _____ *The Hidden Art of Homemaking* by Edith Schaeffer (Units 1, 4, 5, and 7)

started _____ finished _____ *The Way Home: Beyond Feminism, Back to Reality* by Mary Pride (Units 4, 7, and 8)

B grade

started _____ finished _____ *Laurel's Kitchen Caring: Recipes for Everyday Home Caregiving* by Laurel Robertson (Unit 5)

A grade

Circle one: *Do I Vacuum or Dust First?: And 99 Other Nitty Gritty Housecleaning Questions* by Don Aslett (Unit 2)

Another book on cleaning by Don Aslett or other author

started _____ finished _____

Signature _____ Date _____

To the Students who undertake this Study:

It is my prayer that Where the Brook and River Meet
*will cause you to be fruitful in the knowledge of the Lord; that
through the challenging study of* Where the Brook and River Meet
*you will work diligently to add to your foundation of faith;
that you will be called to work diligently because of the "exceedingly
great and precious promises" which He has given to each of us.*

*As you join Anne in her journey through maidenhood, may you
make every effort to add to your faith the virtue to which Anne aspired.
May you be inspired and encouraged by her desire and struggles to be good.*

*To this virtue, may you add knowledge, so that like Anne,
you learn how to do household tasks, how to behave in social situations,
how to gain academic knowledge, and, finally, to learn who God is.*

*To progress in your journey, may you follow Anne
in applying self-control—to curb imagination, to be attentive to tasks,
or to master whatever habits may be stumbling blocks for you.*

*And, to self-control may you add the perseverance of Anne
as she pursues her studies with faithfulness despite distractions
and difficult subjects; and as she persists in forgiving Josie Pye
despite her ongoing spiteful and disparaging remarks.*

*To perseverance, may you add godliness—
the knowledge and acquisition of His character.*

*May brotherly kindness be added to godliness, demonstrating love,
even as Anne, to the critical Mrs. Lyndes in your life.*

*To this kindness, adding love—not only
the love of gratefulness, but of self-sacrifice—
of putting aside one's own cherished plans to meet the needs of others.*

*And, knowing He has given you "all things that pertain to life and
godliness," that with Anne, you may look with confidence to the road ahead.
May you also share her delight in the mystery of the "bend in the road."*

———◆———

✦ Planning Guide

Gather These Items:

1. The 1987 Bantam Classic paperback edition of *Anne of Green Gables* or *The Annotated Anne of Green Gables* by L. M. Montgomery. Edited by Wendy Barry, Margaret Anne Doody, and Mary Doody Jones. Oxford University Press, 1997.** ISBN 0-19-510428-5.*

2. *The Anne of Green Gables Treasury* by Carolyn Collins and Christina Wyss Eriksson. Viking Press, 1991. ISBN 0-670-82591-3. (This is out of print, but may be found on the Internet or at a used book store.)

3. Pattern and yarn for a knitted or crocheted afghan or directions and rags for making a braided rag rug.

4. *Writers INC* written and compiled by Patrick Sebranek, Dave Kemper, and Verne Meyer. Houghton Mifflin Co., 2001.** ISBN 0-669-47186-0.*

5. *The Green Gables Letters from L. M. Montgomery to Ephraim Weber 1905–1909* edited by Wilfred Eggleston. Borealis Press, 2001.** ISBN 0-8887-932-6.*

6. *Anne's Anthology* compiled and edited by Margie Gray. Cadron Creek Christian Curriculum, 2000. ISBN 0-9652511-2-8.*

7. A biography of George Mueller for an "A" grade in Contract Reading — Bible.
   —*George Mueller: Man of Faith and Miracles* by Basil Miller. Bethany House Publishers, 1972. ISBN 0-87123-182-4.
   —*Answers to Prayer: From George Mueller's Narrative* by George Mueller. Moody Classics Series. Moody Publishers, 1984. ISBN 0802405657.

This resource is used during each unit but will not be mentioned again under "Gather These Items."
**This edition should be used in order to assure that the page numbers given in the study correlate to those in your book.*

Research Topics:

Resources listed are only suggested; please feel free to substitute or gather your own.

1. Prince Edward Island

. . . .

2. Oceanic climates

. . . .

3. Jacques Cartier

. . . .

4. The French and Indian War, also known as the Seven Year War

. . . .

5. The expansion of the railroads
   —*Railway Age* by L. W. Cowie. Silver Burdett Press, 1984. ISBN 0-382-06296-5.
   —*Railway Pathfinders* by Pierre Berton. Bt Bound, 1999. ASIN 0613012240.
   —*Steel Across the Shield* by Pierre Berton. McClelland & Stewart, 1994. ASIN 0771014228.
   —*The Railways,* Discovering Canada Series, by Robert Livesay and A. G. Smith. Stoddart Publishing, 1997. ISBN 0-7737-5901-8.
   —"Railroads." *edu.Scapes.* Feb. 2001. Annette Lamb and Larry Johnson. Aug. 1998 <http:www.42explore2.com/railroad.htm>.

. . . .

6. Plant identification
   —*Wildflowers of Prince Edward Island* by Katherine Clough. Ragweed Press, 1992. ISBN 0-921-55627-6. (This is out of print, but may be found on the Internet or at a used book store.)

. . . .

Suggested Videos:

Suggested Field Trips:

1. Visit a modern day orphanage. (See Activity 14)

Memory Work:
Hebrews 13:1–8

Notes:

Assignments — Chapter I

Contract Reading

	A Grade	B Grade	C Grade
Bible	❏ The book of Job ❏ A biography of George Mueller	❏ The book of Job	❏ The book of Job
History			
Literature			

Weekly

Quiet Time Reading Book: A biography of George Mueller; the book of Job
Independent Project: Afghan or rag rug
Memory Work: Hebrews 13:1–8

	Literature	History	Bible	Health	Occu. Education	Fine Arts	Grammar & Writing
M	Read Chap. I AGG, Reading Comp.	#4	#11		#10		#1, #2, #11
T	Vocab., #3	#6	#12				#1, #3, #6, #12
W	#5	#7	#13				#1, #9
Th	#15	#8	#15				#1, #8, #15
F	#16				#14 Field Trip		

AGG — *Anne of Green Gables*

❧ Study Guide

Read Chapter I
Reading Comprehension:

1. How did the positioning of the Cuthbert house differ from the others in Avonlea? Why?

2. How did Marilla keep her yard? Her kitchen?

3. Why did Marilla agree to adopt Anne despite her misgivings?

4. What effect did Mrs. Lynde's visit have on Marilla?

5. List at least three of the four community projects in which Mrs. Lynde was involved.

Match the words and phrases with the appropriate character.
There will not be an even number of each.

A. Matthew

B. Marilla

C. Rachel

6. _____ deftly

7. _____ shy

8. _____ placidly

9. _____ briskly

10. _____ disapprovingly

11. _____ worthy

12. _____ tall, thin

13. _____ pessimism

14. _____ Job's comforting

15. _____ narrow experience

16. _____ rigid conscience

Vocabulary Words:

alder*

ladies' eardrops* (see note in *The Annotated Anne*)

gauntlet

placidly*

Lombardies

decorum*

wont

strychnine*

ferreted

dint

Vocabulary:

☞ Look up the vocabulary words in a dictionary or encyclopedia. Fill in the blanks using the vocabulary words.

17. A type of tree that likes moist land is called an _____.

18. He _____ entered the room.

19. To speak and behave with _____ is essential to good breeding.

20. The police _____ out the vagrants from their hiding place.

21. A _____ is a large iron glove with fingers covered with small plates, formerly worn by cavaliers, armed at all points.

22. Passover was a yearly solemn feast she was _____ to observe.

Extra credit:

1. Words become a part of speech by the way they are used in context. Some words can be used as more than one part of speech. Identify each vocabulary word marked with an asterisk as either a noun (n),

verb (v), adjective (adj), or adverb (adv) as they are used in the above
sentences.

2. 🖐 Draw ladies' eardrops in your sketchbook or in the Fine Art section
of your notebook or show a photograph or professional sketch to your
instructor. (Ladies' eardrops are also called jewelweed or wild touch-
me-not.)

 Activities:

1. Anne has daily dictation in school. It develops speed and accuracy in   **Dictation**
writing, improved spelling, and serves as a good review for grammati-
cal errors. Enter all dictation exercises in the Writing/Dictation section of your notebook. The following method will be used to learn the
art of taking dictation. Read all the instructions first before beginning
the dictation assignment.

✎ To begin learning how to take dictation, carefully copy into the Writing/
Dictation section of your notebook the following passage from page 2 of
Anne of Green Gables:

> There are plenty of people, in Avonlea and out of it, who can
> attend closely to their neighbor's business by dint of neglect-
> ing their own; but Mrs. Rachel Lynde was one of those
> capable creatures who can manage their own concerns and
> those of other folks into the bargain. —*Anne of Green Gables*, page 2

It may take several days of copying, comparing with the original,
correcting, and rewriting before the student advances to having the
selection dictated to her. Once the student is able to accurately copy
the selection, she may proceed with the actual dictation.

The dictation may be handled in one of two ways: the student may
read the required passage into a tape recorder, then take dictation
from the recording or a family member may read the text to the student. Repeat the same passage until the student can write it perfectly
from dictation.

Dictations should be corrected first by the student then reviewed by
the instructor. Once it is seen that the student is careful in catching
her errors, she may be independent in this. A follow-up activity is given
to increase understanding of the punctuation or the literary technique
used in the dictation.

2. After your student completes the dictation, have her check   ⚘ Follow-up
her spelling and punctuation against the original. Correct any
errors. Circle the semicolon.

⚷ Look up the uses of a semicolon in *Writers INC*.

🕸 With your instructor answer these questions:
  a. Why is a semicolon used in the above dictation? *See answer in
     Answer Appendix.*

       b. Commas are used to enclose explanatory words or phrases. What is the explanatory phrase in the above dictation? *See answer in Answer Appendix.*

Literature   3. Is this book fiction or nonfiction? *See answer in Answer Appendix.*

    📖 Read *The Anne of Green Gables Treasury,* pages 3–6 and/or *The Annotated Anne of Green Gables,* pages 3–21.

    📖 In *Writers INC,* read the section on page 168, "Writing Guidelines: Story Writing." Pay special attention to "Pre-Writing." Is it any wonder that there are so many similarities between Anne and L.M. Montgomery? The town of Avonlea is based on the author's childhood home, Cavendish.

    📖 Read pages 35–36 from *The Green Gables Letters from L.M. Montgomery to Ephraim Weber 1905–1909.* How does Montgomery pick ideas for stories?

    ✎ In the Literature section of your notebook:
List the similarities mentioned between Montgomery and Anne.

☀ **History**   4. ✦ Locate the following on a map: Gulf of St. Lawrence, Bright River, Avonlea, and Nova Scotia. The real orphan asylum in Nova Scotia was in the Halifax-Dartmouth area. Hopetown was a fictitious name. See page 7 of *The Anne of Green Gables Treasury.*

    📖 Also read *The Annotated Anne of Green Gables* pages 415–418.

    ✦ Latitude is the angular distance north or south from the earth's equator. Longitude is the distance, east or west, of any place on the globe from a given meridian.

    ✎ In the History section of your notebook answer these questions:
a. What effect does latitude have on a location's temperature?
b. What is an oceanic climate?
c. Draw a map of Prince Edward Island and the surrounding area and mark its latitude and longitude on the map.

☀ **Literature**   5. 📖 Read "Study-Reading Skills," pages 357–366, in *Writers INC.* Calculate the reading rate (pages per day) you will need in order to finish your Contract Reading assignments.

    ✎ In the Literature section of your notebook:
Write a schedule to complete the reading assignments for your Contract Reading for this week.

History   6. 📖 Read about the history of Prince Edward Island in *The Anne of Green Gables Treasury,* pages 19–20.

    📖 Also read *The Annotated Anne of Green Gables,* pages 418–421.
Study the life and explorations of Jacques Cartier. As a minimum, read about him and his travels in the encyclopedia.

✥ In the History section of your notebook:
Draw a map of Canada and highlight the region Cartier explored.

There is a long history of conflict between the French and Scottish settlers of Prince Edward Island. In 1758 the British won the Island from France. The battle between the British and the French over the island is known to Americans as the French and Indian War; the Canadians called it the Seven Year War. After the war, England re-named the island, the Isle St. Jean (St. John). Not until 1799 did it finally become Prince Edward Island. Using texts and encyclopedias, study this war. You may want to further investigate this time period by reading some historical fiction such as *The Last of the Mohicans* by James Fennimore Cooper.

✎ In the History section of your notebook:
Make a timeline page for the Seven Year War and include information you learned about the war, using methods from *Writers INC*, pages 359–364.

---

7. Are there previous names for the state, province, or town in which you live? How did they get their name(s)?   History

⚇ With your instructor:
Discuss the origins of the names you discovered with your instructor.

---

8. In 1877, Anne arrives on Prince Edward Island by train. The Prince Edward Island Railway had opened two years earlier. The Canadian Pacific Transcontinental Railway was completed in 1885, whereas the last spike for the U.S. Transcontinental was put in place in 1869.   History

✎ In the History section of your notebook:
Make a timeline page for and write about the westward expansion of the railroad in your country.

⚇ With your instructor:
Discuss what political and geographic factors differed between the United States and Canada to effect the completion times of each country's transcontinental railway. *See answer in Answer Appendix.*

---

9. 📖 Read page 38 from *The Green Gables Letters from L.M. Montgomery to Ephraim Weber 1905–1909*. What advice about writing does Montgomery give? Read about "Clustering" in *Writers INC*, pages 10 and 43.   Writing

✎ Pretend you are Marilla. Brainstorm for a few minutes and then write down your thoughts about what it would be like to have an orphan come to stay with you using clustering.

✎ In the Literature section of your notebook:
Write for ten minutes without stopping based on your clustering ideas. (Instructor, grade this on thought content, not writing mechanics.)

Occupational Education	10. Mrs. Lynde knits cotton warp quilts. Cotton warp yarn was sold in stores and identified as such on the label. It was soft and was principally used for weaving. As a choice of a long-term project, knit or crochet an afghan, make a rag rug, or patchwork quilt. (See Chapter XII & XIII, Activity 3)
Bible	11. In her conversation with Marilla, Mrs. Lynde offers what is called "Job's comforting." Set a schedule to read the book of Job during this Unit. How does Mrs. Lynde compare to Job's friends? ✎ In the Bible section of your notebook: After the completion of reading Job, you will be expected to explain the comparison between Mrs. Lynde and Job's friends.
Bible	12. One aim of Montgomery's stories about children is to present children as worthy of value simply because they are children. She attempts to dispel the prevalent attitude of the day that viewed orphans and poor children only as cheap labor. 📖 Read about orphans in *The Annotated Anne of Green Gables*, pages 422–428. 🔑 Use a concordance and look up scriptures in the Bible about orphans. ✖ With your instructor: Discuss what you have learned about the Biblical view of orphans. 📖 Set a schedule to read a biography of George Mueller prior to reading Chapter V in *Anne of Green Gables*. (This is a requirement for an "A" grade in your Contract Reading for Bible.) Mueller observed that orphans were not being cared for, so with God's faithfulness, he met this need. 🔑 What other organizations have arisen to help orphans? 📖 ✍ Read "Writing a Book Review" in *Writers INC*, pages 221–226. Pay careful attention to page 224. When you have completed reading the biography of George Mueller, write a one page review of the book. After grading, file the review in the Literature section of your notebook.
Bible	13. 📖 George Mueller took God's words to heart. ♡ Read Hebrews 13:1–8 and commit it to memory.
Field Trip	14. ✍ Visit a modern day orphanage. To find an orphanage, inquire at churches that sponsor orphanages (e.g., the Methodist Church in Mississippi has an orphanage in Jackson). You might also want to talk to a social worker at Lutheran Social Services or Catholic Social Services about adoption. ✖ With your instructor: Compare today's treatment of orphans with Anne's adoption/orphanage experience. Compare the orphanage conditions of the late 1800's with

the conditions in modern orphanages in this country and in other parts of the world.

---

15. ⚷ Use your concordance and look up scriptures on being a talebearer (gossip).

  📖 Read about "Writing a Paraphrase" in *Writers INC* on page 402 and on pages 256–257.

  ✎ In the Bible section of your notebook:
List at least four scriptures about being a talebearer, then paraphrase what the Bible says about being one.

Bible

---

16. ⚷ Read the definition of a novel. This can be found in a dictionary or on page 238 of *Writers INC*. The elements of a novel are characters, setting, and plot. Look up the definitions of these elements in the "Literary Terms" section of *Writers INC,* pages 233–234.

  ⚘ With your instructor:
Discuss the characters and setting of *Anne of Green Gables*.

Literature

——◆——

🙢 Planning Guide

Gather These Items:

1. *King Arthur and His Knights of the Round Table* by Richard Lancelyn Green. Reissue edition. Puffin Classics, 1995. ISBN 0140366709. This is for an "A" or "B" grade in Contract Reading Choice — Literature.

2. Items to make a small chain maille piece.

3. Recipes and food for a medieval feast.

Research Topics:

1. Knights, feudalism, serfs

. . . .

2. Chain maille and how to make chain maille
   —The Internet gives terrific directions, but all sites should be previewed by a parent and no links should be followed without parental permission. Here are two sites:
   <http://www.alleycatscratch.com/lotr/Armor/ChainS.htm>
   <http://www.chainmail.com/chainmall/cteach2.htm>

. . . .

3. Greek myths and Artemis ("Diana" to the Romans)
   —Encyclopedia
   —*D'Aulaire's Book of Greek Myths* by Ingri D'Aulaire, Edgar Parin D'Aulaire. Bantam Doubleday Dell Publishing Group, 1980. ISBN 0440406943.

. . . .

Suggested Videos:

1. *How Should We Then Live?* by Francis Schaeffer. Videocassette set. Gospel Communications Int'l, 2001.

2. *Faith Lessons on the Early Church* by Ray Vander Laan. Videocassette set. Focus on the Family and Zondervan, 1999.

Suggested Field Trips:

1. Go to a Renaissance Fair if one is held in your area. (See Activity 6)

Memory Work:
Ephesians 6:10–18

Notes:

Assignments — Chapter II

Contract Reading

	A Grade	B Grade	C Grade
Bible	❏ The book of Job	❏ The book of Job	❏ The book of Job
History			
Literature	❏ Choice: *King Arthur and His Knights of the Round Table*	❏ Choice: *King Arthur and His Knights of the Round Table*	

Weekly

Quiet Time Reading Book: *King Arthur and His Knights of the Round Table*
Independent Project: Afghan or rag rug
Memory Work: Ephesians 6:10–18

	Literature	History	Bible	Health	Occu. Education	Fine Arts	Grammar & Writing
M	Read Chap. II AGG, Reading Comp.		#10			#3	#1, #2, #10
T	Vocab., #4	#5			#6		#1, #5
W	#8	#5, #8	#7				#1, #8
Th		#5, #9	#9		#6 Field Trip	#9	#1, #9
F		#5 Medieval Feast & Mock Joust					

🐉 Study Guide

Read Chapter II
Reading Comprehension:

1. Why did Matthew dread all women except Marilla and Mrs. Lynde?

2. What was harder than "bearding a lion out of his den" for Matthew? (This reference comes from the poem *Marmion, A Tale of Flodden Field* by Sir Walter Scott. A section of *Marmion* under the title "The Parting of Marmion and Douglas" is in the *Fifth Royal Reader*. The *Royal Readers* were the Canadian equivalent of *McGuffey's Reader* in the United States. All school children read them.)

3. Did Matthew enjoy Anne's talkativeness?

4. Matthew dreaded informing Anne she would not have a home with them. To what act did he compare this disclosure?

Match the words and phrases with the appropriate character.
There will not be an even number of each.

A. Matthew

B. Anne

5. _____ shuffled

6. _____ slower intelligence

7. _____ peculiarly clear sweet voice

8. _____ long iron-gray hair

9. _____ ungainly figure

10. _____ brisk mental processes

11. _____ freckled

Vocabulary Words:

wincey

alabaster

crocus

ruminated

eccentric

ludicrously

vivacity

rapturously

rapt

loquacious

Vocabulary:
⚷ Look up the vocabulary words in a dictionary, encyclopedia, or plant book. Fill in the blanks using the vocabulary words.

12. As the clown walked to the circus tent for his performance, he _____ made faces at the lions.

13. The vase was made from _____.

14. To depart from that which is regular is to be _____.

15. Anne's attractiveness sprang from her _____.

16. The ballet captured everyone's _____ attention.

17. The ballet instructor gazed _____ at her student's flawless performance of Swan Lake.

18. The President _____ over his decision to bomb the struggling third world country.

19. The _____ speaker put his audience to sleep.

Extra credit:

✋ In your sketchbook or the Fine Arts section of your notebook, draw a crocus or balsamy fir or show a photograph or professional sketch to the person who evaluates your work.

🍂 Activities:

---

1. ✎ Write the following passage from dictation: Dictation

> In the evening when little Kay was at home and half undressed, he crept up onto the chair by the window and peeped out of the little hole. A few snowflakes were falling, and one of these, the biggest, remained on the edge of the window box. It grew bigger and bigger, till it became the figure of a woman dressed in the finest white gauze, which appeared to be made of millions of starry flakes. She was delicately lovely, but all ice—glittering, dazzling ice. She was still alive. Her eyes shone like two bright stars, but there was no rest or peace in them. She nodded to the window and waved her hand. The little boy was frightened and jumped down off the chair, and then he fancied that a big bird flew past the window. —Hans Christian Anderson, "The Snow Queen"

---

2. ✎ If there is not enough space on a line to complete a word without extending into the margin, words may be divided by syllables and separated by a hyphen. Divide the vocabulary words into syllables. Use the dictionary to check if you have any questions. *See answers in Answer Appendix.*   ☼ Follow-up

---

3. 📖 Read the description of Anne on page 11 (*The Annotated Anne of Green Gables*, page 51).   Fine Arts

✋ From the description, draw your interpretation of Anne in your sketchbook or the Fine Arts section of your notebook.

---

4. According to *The Annotated Anne of Green Gables*, page 458:   ☼ Literature

> The American poets quoted within the narrative seem all to serve a positive function. They are as a group associated with statements about growth and possibility, helpers in dealing with change and development. . . . The American poets cited here—Lowell, Whittier, Longfellow—seem to record the inward and tender, combined with a poignant need for experience, acceptance, and growth. Lowell's "The Vision of Sir Launfal," offers the mood appropriate for the June day of

Anne's arrival, a day not just of spring but of spiritual challenge and renewal.

📖 Read "The Vision of Sir Launfal." It is in *Anne's Anthology.*

According to the mythology of the Romance poets the "San Greal," or the "Holy Grail," was the cup from which Jesus partook of the Last Supper with His disciples. It was said to have come to England and those who had charge of it were required to be chaste in thought, word, and deed. As the legend goes, one of the keepers broke this condition and the Holy Grail disappeared. It was then a favorite enterprise of the knights of Arthur's court to go in search of it. Sir Galahad was at last said to be successful in finding the Holy Grail; his story is in the seventeenth book of the *Romance of King Arthur.* Tennyson has made Sir Galahad the subject of one of his greatest poems, "Holy Grail."

History
5. The vision of "Sir Launfal," *Marmion,* and "Elaine" all take place during the period of time when England had knights.

📖 In the *Background Information Appendix,* read about knights and feudal society. Continue your study of knights, feudalism, and serfs by using other sources.

✎ In the History section of your notebook write about knights, feudalism, and serfs.

✋ End your week long study by dressing in appropriate clothing for knights and damsels, having a medieval feast, and holding a mock joust.

Occupational Education
6. ✋ Read about chain maille. Work on a small piece of chain maille.

✋ Go to a Renaissance Fair if one is held in your area.

Bible
7. Armor was very important in medieval times. Without it, a knight would be injured or killed easily by his opponent. Even the horses sometimes had armor to protect them during battle.

♡ While working on your chain maille, memorize Ephesians 6:10–18.

With your instructor:
Discuss how you can increase the strength of your spiritual armor and make a plan to do so.

History
8. 📖 If you have chosen to read *King Arthur and His Knights of the Round Table* for your Contract Reading, do so.

✎ In *Writers INC,* pages 221–223, read how to write a book review. Write a book review of this book. After it is graded, submit your review to Amazon.com.

9. Matthew thinks that the name "Diana" is heathenish. As a Victorian   Bible/History
   Christian, Matthew would have been well acquainted with the Biblical
   view of idolatry. The pagan Ephesians worshipped a goddess called
   Diana.

📖 Read about the Ephesian Diana in Acts 19:24–35. Many goddesses
   were named "Diana." The goddess that the Ephesians called Diana had
   some of the same characteristics of the Greek and Roman goddess but
   lacked others—namely youth and virginity. One trait of polytheistic
   religions is their gods and goddesses change names and attributes.
   The Christian God is always the same.

👓 The video series, *How Should We Then Live?* by Francis Schaeffer, and
   the video series, *Faith Lessons on the Early Church* by Focus on the
   Family, have segments on the church in Ephesus. These segments talk
   about the oriental goddess Diana. Watch one or both of these videos.
   The Temple to Diana in Ephesus is considered one of the Seven Wonders of the World.

📖 The Romans based their deity Diana on the Greek goddess Artemis.
   Read about Artemis in *D'Aulaire's Book of Greek Myths*.

✎ In the Literature section of your notebook:
   Write a paragraph about the goddess Diana.

✋ Draw a picture of the Greek Diana and one of the Ephesian Diana
   mentioned in the Bible.

🔑 Look up references to idolatry in a Bible concordance.

✎ In the Bible section of your notebook:
   Write a persuasive paragraph against idolatry from a Biblical perspective. You can read about persuasive paragraphs in *Writers INC*,
   page 98.

📖 With your instructor:
   Discuss whether you think it is of any spiritual significance that
   Montgomery chooses Diana for the name of Anne's best friend.

10. Anne can not decide whether it was better to be angelically   Bible
    good or beautiful.

🔑 What does the Bible say about beautiful women? Use a
   concordance to look up specific scriptures about beauty.

📖 Read about writing poetry in *Writers INC*, pages 179–184.

✎ In the Bible section of your notebook:
   Write a poem about beauty.

✤ Planning Guide

Gather These Items:

1. *Oliver Twist* or *Great Expectations* by Charles Dickens (any edition) for an "A" grade in Contract Reading Choice — Literature.

2. *The Hidden Art of Homemaking* by Edith Schaeffer. Tyndale House Publishers, 1985. ISBN 0842313982.

3. Chocolate-caramel candies.

4. A simple gown pattern and an old sheet for material.

5. "The Economics of Child Labor." *Scientific American* October 2003. (This may be found at your local library.)

Research Topics:

1. Foster care system

2. Charles Dickens

3. The effect of sugar on the human body

4. The meaning of names
   —A baby name book
   —Do an Internet search with your favorite search engine using the terms "meanings," "Bible," and "names"

5. Thomas Edison, his life and works

6. Child labor laws (See Activity 12)

Suggested Videos:

1. *Young Tom Edison* (1940). Perf. Mickey Rooney. Warner Studios, 1993. ASIN 6302922941.

Suggested Field Trips:
1. Visit someone who does foster care or a social worker who works with foster children. (See Activity 7)

Memory Work:
Continue Ephesians 6:10–18

Notes:

Assignments — Chapter III

Contract Reading

	A Grade	B Grade	C Grade
Bible	❏ The book of Job	❏ The book of Job	❏ The book of Job
History			
Literature	❏ Choice: *Oliver Twist* or *Great Expectations*		

Weekly

Quiet Time Reading Book: *Oliver Twist* or *Great Expectations*
Independent Project: Gown, afghan or rag rug
Memory Work: Continue Ephesians 6:10–18

	Literature	History	Bible	Health	Occu. Education	Fine Arts	Grammar & Writing
M	Read Chap. III AGG, Reading Comp., #9		#5		#11	#3	#1, #2, #9
T	Vocab., #5	#4			#11		#1, #5
W	#6	#7, #8		#10	#11		#1, #7, #8, #10
Th	#9	#12	#12		#11		#1, #12
F		#4			#7 Field Trip		

❧ Study Guide

Read Chapter III
Reading Comprehension:

1. How did Anne find out about the "mistake" of a girl being sent from the orphanage?

2. What were Marilla's three choices for where Anne could spend the night?

3. Who said, "We might be of some good to her"?
   What does this statement show about the speaker's character?

Match the words and phrases with the appropriate character.
There will not be an even number of each.

A. Matthew   4. _____ briskly   8. _____ odd little figure

B. Marilla   5. _____ meekly   9. _____ stray waif

C. Anne   6. _____ deliberately   10. _____ eager luminous eyes

            7. _____ depths   11. _____ smile, rather rusty
                of despair   from disguise ᵘˢᵉ

Vocabulary Words:

deprecate

breach

romantic

perturbation

predilection

Vocabulary:

🗝 Look up the vocabulary words in a dictionary, encyclopedia, or a plant book. Fill in the blanks using the vocabulary words.

12. Knowing it would cause conflict, Jill chose not to _____ her sister's decision.

13. Because her mother always dressed her in crinoline and lace, she had a _____ for finer clothing.

14. *The Three Musketeers* is a wild, _____ tale of valor and chivalry.

15. His selling of half the shares was a _____ of contract.

16. Tapping one's foot, rolling one's eyes, and sighing can all be signs of _____.

❧ Activities:

Dictation

1. ✎ Write the following passage from dictation:

When Marilla had gone, Anne looked around her wistfully. The whitewashed walls were so painfully bare and staring that she thought they must ache over their own bareness. The floor was bare, too, except for a round braided mat in the middle such as Anne had never seen before. —*Anne of Green Gables*, page 27

2. The commas before and after "too" are used to enclose an explanatory word.

Personification is a literary device in which the author speaks of or describes an animal, object, or idea as if it were a person. This was used in the dictation when Anne thinks the walls must "ache." Find another personification on page 22 of *Anne of Green Gables* (*The Annotated Anne of Green Gables*, page 64). Discuss how this example illustrates personification with your instructor.

3. Marilla appears to have an underdeveloped sense of creativity. Read chapters 1, 2, and 5 from *The Hidden Art of Homemaking* by Edith Schaeffer. What do you feel like doing after reading these chapters?

Fine Arts

With your instructor:
See if any of the ideas you got from the homemaking book can be pursued.

4. Notice on page 26 of *Anne of Green Gables* that Marilla is using candlelight. Anne came to Green Gables in 1877. Thomas Edison invented the light bulb in 1879. Electric lights were introduced to Prince Edward Island at Charlottetown in 1885.

History

Study the life and experiments of Thomas Edison.

Watch the video, *Young Tom Edison,* starring Mickey Rooney.

5. God, the original author, demonstrated in the Bible that names frequently have symbolic meanings in literature.

Literature

In the Bible section of your notebook write the meaning of each of the following names: Jacob, Israel, Ichabod, Hannah, Issachar, Hephzibah, Matthew. *See answers in Answer Appendix.*

Many authors choose a character's name to symbolize certain qualities or to allude to the historical, mythical, literary, or Biblical meaning behind the name. The names of Charles Dickens' characters always hold some deeper meaning, for example.

Montgomery also uses names to add deeper meaning to her story. In *Anne of Green Gables,* Anne makes a strong point about the exactness of her name. She makes her point by saying, "Anne with an 'e'." (It is interesting to note that Lucy Maud Montgomery preferred to be called Maud and distinctly disliked putting the "e" at the end of her name.) Despite her insistence on the correct spelling of it, Anne is unhappy with her own name and wishes to be called Cordelia, Elaine, Rosamond, or Geraldine. These names have literary and historical allusions that reveal much about Anne's character. Cordelia, for example, is a character in Shakespeare's play *King Lear*. Cordelia is the innocent youngest daughter of King Lear. She is murdered because of her father's weaknesses. Cordelia's example of true filial devotion (to the death) would be a perfect reason for the orphan Anne to want to be known by that name. Anne may be trying to tell Matthew and Marilla that she is like Cordelia and would be a true and loyal child if given the chance.

✎   In the Literature section of your notebook:
Describe the significance of Matthew and his name to his character and his place in the story.

Literature   6. In Anne's day, non-Christians are more familiar with the Bible than many present-day believers because it was considered essential to one's education to read the Bible as great literature. Montgomery frequently quotes Scripture throughout her books.

📖   Read Leviticus 20:3, then read about Matthew smoking on page 28 of *Anne of Green Gables* (*The Annotated Anne of Green Gables*, pages 72–73).

🔑   Look up **allusion** in the *Writers INC* index. Then turn to the page specified and read about it.

🕸   Discuss with your instructor:
What phrase is taken from Scripture? What is alluded to about Marilla's relationship with her house?

History   7. Instead of going into an orphanage, today's children in the United States and Canada often enter the foster care system.

🔑   Find out about the foster care system. What is the primary reason children enter the foster care system? What precautions are taken to ensure the safety and well being of the children in the foster care system?

✋   If possible, interview a foster parent and a caseworker for foster children and discover their observations about the foster care system. Prior to the interviews, make a list of questions for each person to answer.

History   8. Montgomery is not the only writer inspired by the plight of orphans. Orphans were frequent characters in Charles Dickens' books.

📖   Read about Charles Dickens and his work.

📖   In *Writers INC,* read pages 403 and 404 on "Writing a Summary."

✎   Write a one page summary on Charles Dickens. Place it in the History section of your notebook in correct chronological order.

Literature   9. 📖 If you chose to read *Oliver Twist* or *Great Expectations* for your Contract Reading, do so.

Health

10. Anne remembers she once had a chocolate-caramel two years ago. Imagine rarely eating anything sweet. Eat no desserts or candy for a week, then eat a chocolate-caramel.

🔑   In the early 1800's, the average sugar consumption was 12 pounds per person annually. This increased to 124 pounds in 1980 and to 152 pounds in 1997. Research the effects sugar has on health.

✎ Outline a paper summarizing the results of your research on sugar, then write a one page paper. File this paper in the Health section of your notebook.

---

11. ✋ Pick a very simple gown pattern for yourself, a sibling, or a friend. Use an old sheet to make a gown. Make sure that the pattern for the gown fits the amount of cloth you have available.

Occupational
Education

---

12. Charles Dickens and L.M. Montgomery were both concerned with the plight of orphans. In *Oliver Twist* and Anne's day, orphans were often used as cheap or unpaid labor. What Matthew and Marilla wanted from the orphanage was a boy to do work cheaply for them in return for room, board, and clothing. The practice of low paid child labor persists to this day.

📖 Read James 1:27. What does James say is our Christian duty to orphans?

📖 Read the article, "The Economics of Child Labor," in the October 2003 edition of the *Scientific American* magazine. To help you find the article, read *Writers INC*, pages 344–345, on "Finding Articles in Periodicals." This article may also be purchased on the *Scientific American* Web site, <www.sciam.com>.

✎ Take notes on this information in the History section of your notebook.

🗝 Look up information on child labor laws in your country on the Internet or call your local department of labor. The department of labor will be listed in your phone book in the government section. The United States Department of Labor has much information on child labor on its Web site as well. The U.S. Department of Labor's Web address is <www.dol.gov>. Write some of what you find out from your research in the History section of your notebook.

📖 Read *Writers INC*, pages 105–114, "Writing Expository Essays." Also read the "Reference List: Overview" on page 289 of *Writers INC*.

✎ Write an expository paper on child labor using the magazine article as a reference at least once. Make a reference list for your paper. Edit your draft using the Assessment Rubric on page 114 of *Writers INC*. Correct and rewrite your paper and then have your instructor grade your paper using the Assessment Rubric. File this paper in the History section of your notebook.

👥 With your instructor:
Discuss what you found out about child labor and the ethics of using products produced by child labor based on what you have learned from your research and from James 1:27. Discuss changes needed in the treatment of chidren and ways your family can help bring about these changes.

👁 History/Bible

🦋 Planning Guide

Gather These Items:

1. Items to grow scented geraniums.

2. "The Snow Queen" by Hans Christian Anderson for an "A" grade in Contract Reading — Literature. This fairy tale may be found in a book of Hans Christian Anderson's fairy tales. (Warning: This story contains magic and may not be appropriate for some families.)

3. *What in the World's Going on Here?: A Judeo-Christian Primer of World History,* Volumes 1 & 2, by Diana Waring. Audiocassette set. History Alive!, 1996. ISBN 1930514026. These tapes are for a "C" or better grade in Contract Reading — History.

4. A clock or watch with a second hand.

Research Topics:

1. Growing scented geraniums

. . . .

2. The health benefits of exercise

. . . .

Suggested Videos:

1. A movie version of Hans Christian Anderson's fairy tale, "The Snow Queen" *(1959)*

2. 'Oliver'

Suggested Field Trips:

1. Tour a plant nursery or visit a botanical garden in your area. (See Activity 13)

Memory Work:

Psalm 30, especially verse 5

Notes:

Assignments — Chapter IV

Contract Reading

	A Grade	B Grade	C Grade
Bible	❏ The book of Job	❏ The book of Job	❏ The book of Job
History	❏ *What in the World's* tapes	❏ *What in the World's* tapes	❏ *What in the World's* tapes
Literature	❏ "The Snow Queen"		

Weekly

Quiet Time Reading Book: *Oliver Twist,* "The Snow Queen"
Independent Project: Afghan or rag rug
Memory Work: Psalm 30, especially verse 5

	Literature	History	Bible	Health	Occu. Education	Fine Arts	Grammar & Writing
M	Read Chap. IV AGG, Reading Comp.	#8	#4	#9, #10	#3		#1, #2
T	#5	#8	#5				#1
W	#6	#8					#1, #6
Th	#7, #11	#8	#7, #11				#1, #12
*F	#7				#13 Field Trip		

Note: This is an easier week. Use the extra time to finish all assignments from previous weeks.

*On Friday, at the end of each Unit, review and take the Unit Quiz in the *Test Appendix.*

❧ Study Guide

Read Chapter IV

Reading Comprehension:

1. In what season does this chapter take place? Write down phrases that illustrate the season.

2. What did Anne say about sorrows?

3. What did Marilla find more frustrating than a man who would not talk back?

Match the words and phrases with the appropriate character.
There will not be an even number of each.

A. Matthew   4. _____ curtly   9. _____ reverie

B. Marilla   5. _____ deftly   10. _____ muttered

C. Anne   6. _____ martyr   11. _____ grimly

                  7. _____ distrustfully   12. _____ uncomfortable ignorance

                  8. _____ looking wistful

❧ Activities:

Dictation   1. ✎ Write the following passage from dictation:

> "I never in all my life saw or heard anything to equal her," muttered Marilla, beating a retreat down cellar after potatoes. "She is kind of interesting, as Matthew says. I can feel already that I'm wondering what on earth she'll say next. . . . I wish he was like other men and would talk things out. A body could answer back then and argue him into reason. But what's to be done with a man who just looks?" —*Anne of Green Gables*, page 35

Follow-up   2. ✎ Circle the quotation marks in your paper with blue. Quotation marks show when someone is speaking. Periods and commas are always inside quotation marks. Circle the apostrophes in red. All the apostrophes in this section are used to show that one or more letters have been left out of a word to form a contraction. Which two words form the word "she'll"? An ellipsis (three periods) is used to show that one or more words have been omitted in a quotation. In the above quotation the words are omitted after the end of a sentence and the ellipsis are placed after the period, so there are four periods in a row.

Occupational
Education   3. ✋ Grow a scented geranium. A scented geranium, or pelargonium, was a kitchen herb; its leaves were sometimes used for flavoring. These plants are not as beautiful as what we commonly think of as a gera-

nium. Scented geraniums are available from specialty stores and plant nurseries. Regular geraniums are named in the poisonous plant list. See the *Appendix of Resources* for places to obtain scented geraniums.

✎ In the Occupational Education section of your notebook write: What type of soil do geraniums like? What type of lighting? How much water? How are they started?

---

4. After her "tragical evening," Anne wakes up joyous.   Bible

♡ Read Psalm 30 and commit it to memory, especially verse five. Complete this by the end of Unit 2.

---

5. Lucy Maud Montgomery took the phrase, "howling wilderness," (page 32) from Scripture.   Bible

📖 Read Deuteronomy 32:10.

📖 Review the meaning of allusion in *Writers INC*.

🗣 Discuss with your instructor: What do you think the author was alluding to when she wrote of the "howling wilderness"?

---

6. The phrase, "kindred spirit," is from the well-known poem by Thomas Gray, "Elegy Written in a Country Churchyard," which was found in the *Fifth Royal Reader* or *McGuffey's Sixth Reader*. Almost all school children used these readers in the course of their education and would have been familiar with this poem. (The *Royal Reader* was the predominately used reader in Canada. It was similar to the *McGuffey's Reader* in the United States.)   Literature

📖 Read "Elegy Written in a Country Churchyard" in *Anne's Anthology*.

> Thomas Gray, 1716–1771, wrote this simple yet highly finished and beautiful poem. It is the best known of all his writings. It was finished in 1749—seven years from the time it was commenced. Probably no short poem in the English language ever received or deserved more praise. Gray was born in London; his father possessed property, but was indolent and selfish; his mother was a successful woman of business, and supported her son in college at Eton and Cambridge from her own earnings. He declined the honor of poet laureate; but in 1769 was appointed Professor of History at Cambridge. —*McGuffey's Sixth Eclectic Reader*, page 108

✎ In the Literature section of your notebook:
a. Write a paragraph about what friend you think was gained by the speaker of the poem.
b. Why do you think Anne likes this poem?

---

7. Anne calls a tree "The Snow Queen." This is the title of a story by Hans Christian Anderson. His fairy tales were first translated into English   Literature

in 1846. Read *The Annotated Anne of Green Gables,* page 82, to learn how "Hans Anderson's tales were a perennial joy" for Montgomery.

📖 Read this story for an "A" grade in Literature or watch a video of the story of "The Snow Queen."

History   8. ✇ Listen to Diana Waring's tape set, *What in the World's Going on Here?* Volumes 1 and 2. This is a requirement for a "C" or better grade in history. The tapes will give you a good background for the historical information in this study.

Health   9. Gardening is the second most popular form of exercise in Canada, attracting 72% of Canadian adults. It is second only to walking. Numerous studies have shown that regular physical activity reduces risk of premature death, heart disease, obesity, high blood pressure, adult-onset diabetes, osteoporosis, stroke, depression, and colon cancer. Gardening and yard work contribute to healthy living. They require all three types of physical activity—endurance, flexibility, and strength. Heavy yard work like raking and carrying leaves contributes to both endurance and strength, while all those stretches and contortions in the garden can help increase and maintain flexibility.

🖐 Make a plan for the next four months to spend at least half an hour three times a week gardening or doing some other cardiovascular exercise such as brisk walking, bicycling, or ballroom dancing. The type of exercise you do may change due to the time of year or other factors, but make sure you keep exercising in some cardiovascular way. Write your plan in the Health section of your notebook. *(The Duke)*

✏ One way to determine if exercising is benefiting you is to track your resting heart rate. This is how fast your heart beats when you are resting. The rate should become lower as you exercise regularly, indicating a healthier heart. Make a "Resting Heart Rate" page in the Health section of your notebook. Record your resting heart rate once a week for four months.

To find your resting heart rate do the following:
The night before you plan to measure your resting heart rate, put a clock or watch with a second hand near your bed where you can see it. Before you get up the following morning, count the number of times your heart beats in one minute. Do this by putting your index and middle fingers in the groove in your neck that is to one side of your trachea (windpipe). The pulse you feel is the carotid artery. (Do not use your thumb to take a pulse because it has its own pulse and will confuse the results.) When you can feel your pulse beating, look at the clock or watch with a second hand and count how many times your heart beats in one minute. This is your resting heart rate. Write this number, along with the date, on the "Resting Heart Rate" page in the Health section of your notebook.

To exercise safely and effectively, you should make sure your heart is beating within the range of your target heart rate. Your target heart rate is how many times per minute your heart should beat during exercise. If you are just starting out, it is important to stay at the low end of the target heart rate range so that you do not injure yourself. For the beginning exerciser your target heart rate should be 50–75% of your maximum heart rate. After you have been exercising for a while (six months) you can exercise with your heart rate up to 85% of the maximum.

Now calculate your target heart rate range:

220 minus your age now = your maximum heart rate

(220 minus your age now) x .5 = the low number in your target heart rate range

(220 minus your age now) x .75 = the high number in your target heart rate range

For example if you are 16 years old:

(220 − 16) x .5 = 102.4, your target heart rate low number

(220 − 16) x .75 = 153, your target heart rate high number

While exercising, measure the pulse rate at your neck for one minute using a clock or watch with a second hand. Make sure you are reaching your target heart rate range. If you have not been exercising regularly, it is very important to start slowly and not overexert yourself.

There are many good Web sites on exercise and health including the American Heart Association's Web site. For more information on finding your heart rate or on exercise, do an Internet search using words like "target heart rate" or "heart health."

Caution: Some health conditions make it dangerous to engage in certain exercise programs. Consult your physician before you begin.

---

10. ❈ With your instructor: Health
    Schedule a time after four months of regular cardiovascular exercise to discuss the changes in your resting heart rate and your overall health.

---

11. ❈ With your instructor: Literature
    Discuss Mrs. Lynde's, "Job's comforting," as referred to in Chapter 1, Activity 11.

---

12. ✎ Review writing a book review In *Writers INC* on pages 221–223.   Literature
    Write a book review of *Oliver Twist* or "The Snow Queen" (see Activity 7) and, after parental correction (parents see page 226), submit your

review to Amazon.com. Finish this project by the time you are done with Chapter IV of *Anne of Green Gables* unless you and your instructor believe an extension of time is warranted.

Occupational Education	13. ✋ Tour a plant nursery or visit a botanical garden in your area.
🔔 Quiz	14. Review and take Unit 1 Quiz in the *Test Appendix*.

✦ Planning Guide

Gather These Items:

1. Large map of Europe, velcro and contact paper, or poster stick-um.

2. *What in the World's Going on Here?: A Judeo-Christian Primer of World History,* Volumes 1 and 2, by Diana Waring. Audiocassette set. History Alive!, 1996. ISBN 1930514026.

3. A biography of Napoleon for a "C" or better grade in Contract Reading — History.
—*The True Story of Napoleon—Emperor of France* by Anthony Corley. Children's Press, 1964. (This book is currently out of print but may be found through the library system or in a used book store.)
—*The Importance of Napoleon Bonaparte* by Bob Carroll. Lucent Books, 1994. ISBN 1560060212.

4. Muslin and directions for a set of curtains.

5. Favorite family poems and materials to make an anthology book.

6. *American Dictionary of the English Language* (1828 Edition) by Noah Webster.

7. *The Columbia Granger's Index to Poetry* by Grangers, William F. Bernhardt, and Edith Granger. Columbia University Press, 1994. ASIN 0231062761. (This book may be found in the reference section of your library.)

Research Topics:

1. Napoleon

. . . .

2. Canadian government

. . . .

3. Adoption of the Canadian Constitution

. . . .

4. British Commonwealth

. . . .

5. John Greenleaf Whittier

. . . .

6. Salem witch trials
   —*Puritans vs. Witches: Christian Controversies in American History*
   by Paul Jehle. Audiocassette or CD. Vision Forum, 2002. ISBN
   1-929241-66-6.

. . . .

7. Fever—definition, cause, treatment

. . . .

8. Diseases prevalent in the 1800's
   —The cause, spread, symptoms, treatment, and mortality rate of
   diseases such as smallpox, malaria, diptheria, cholera, typhoid fever,
   typhus, and yellow fever
   —The 1889 world-wide outbreak of influenza
   —The polio epidemic of 1893 in the United States, the first known polio
   outbreak

. . . .

Suggested Videos:

Suggested Field Trips:

Memory Work:
Continue Psalm 30

Notes:

Assignments — Chapter V

Contract Reading

	A Grade	B Grade	C Grade
Bible			
History	❏ A biography of Napoleon	❏ A biography of Napoleon	❏ A biography of Napoleon
Literature			

Weekly

Quiet Time Reading Book: A biography of Napoleon
Independent Project: Afghan or rag rug; poetry book
Memory Work: Psalm 30
Health: Continue your cardiovascular exercise program initiated in Unit 1, Chapter IV,
    Activity 9

	Literature	History	Bible	Health	Occu. Education	Fine Arts	Grammar & Writing
M	Read Chap. V AGG, Reading Comp.	#8	#17			#24	#1, #2, #8
T	Vocab., #4, #12, #13	#9	#18		#25		#1, #3, #15, #18
W	#5 (long-term), #14	#10, #11		#26		#5 (long-term)	#1, #5 (long-term), #10
Th	#6, #15, #16	#19	#23				#1, #19
F	#7 Recitation, #20	#22	#21				

Worksheet

Crossword Puzzle
For Chapter V • Poetry Terms

Constructed using Crossword Weaver

Across

2 regular or random occurrence of sound
4 two unstressed syllables
7 six feet
8 eight-line stanza
12 four feet
13 anapestic
14 pattern of unstress and stressed syllables

Down

1 similarity or likeness of sound
3 one foot
5 stressed followed by unstressed
6 five feet
7 seven feet
9 eight feet
10 two unstressed followed by stressed
11 four-line stanza

🌺 Study Guide

Read Chapter V

Reading Comprehension:

1. Of what did Anne's parents die? How old was she when they died?

2. Describe the different places Anne had lived.

3. What love of her life did Anne reveal in this chapter?

4. What fault did Marilla find with Anne?

Vocabulary:

📖 Look up the vocabulary words in a dictionary or encyclopedia. Fill in the blanks using the vocabulary words.

5. The outer rear edge of the wing of a bird, containing the primary feathers is called the _____.

6. The testimony was given to the lawyer _____.

7. An unloving person can be _____ when attempting to correct someone.

8. A place of retreat and security is considered an _____.

9. Our Savior _____ in his followers humility and forgiveness of injuries.

10. That is a _____ observation.

11. Thousands of people seek to _____ to the United States every year.

12. The _____ did not know where their final destination would be, they just knew they had to escape the religious persecution in their own country.

Vocabulary Words:

confidentially

inculcates

reproachful

asylum

shrewd

pinion

emigrants

immigrate

🍂 Activities:

1. ✎ Write the following passage from dictation.

   "Don't you just love poetry that gives you a crinkly feeling up and down your back? There is a piece in the Fifth Reader—'The Downfall of Poland'—that is just full of thrills." —*Anne of Green Gables*, page 41

2. A dash is used to show a sudden break in thought; in place of parentheses to set off an explanatory or amplifying matter that is very abrupt; to indicate interrupted speech; to show that words or lett

are missing; or to emphasize a word, series, or clause. Check all punctuation in the dictation against the original.

📖 Look up the sections on the dash, quotations, and capitalization in *Writers INC* and read them. The punctuation marks before and after "The Downfall of Poland" may look like apostrophes, but they are not. They are called single quotation marks. A quotation within a quotation should be enclosed within single quotation marks. Quotation marks should be used to enclose direct quotations, actual thoughts, certain titles including shorter poems, and to distinguish a word that is being discussed. In your dictation, check for capitalization in proper names, titles, and at the beginning of sentences. Words in titles are capitalized, although small words like "of" or "a" are not unless they are the first word in the title.

✖ With your instructor discuss:
a. The reason the dash was used in the above dictation.
b. The reason the author used single quotations in this text.
c. The reasons for capitalization in the above dictation.

Follow-up   3. Divide the vocabulary words into syllables and place accent marks above stressed syllables. If you cannot hear the stressed syllables, look up the words in a dictionary and check the pronunciation guide immediately following the word. The *American Dictionary of the English Language* (1828 edition) by Noah Webster does not contain diacritical pronunciations. Copy the pronunciation guides, including the accent marks, and say the words. This will help you begin to hear the stressed syllables. *See answer in Answer Appendix.*

Literature   4. In this chapter, Anne's love of literature shines through. Lucy Maud Montgomery, herself very well-read, intersperses her text with numerous direct and indirect literary references and quotes. On page 38, Anne's quote, "A rose by any other name would smell as sweet," is from Act II, Scene 1 of Shakespeare's *Romeo and Juliet*. Even at age eleven, Anne is familiar with the works of William Shakespeare. In this chapter she lists several poems she knows in their entirety or in part. Anne's familiarity with great literature mirrors the trend in education in the 1800's towards mental training through memorization. Montgomery wrote the Anne books for children and many of the literary references are ones with which her young audience was well acquainted. These classics are not readily available to us today; for this reason, *Anne's Anthology* was compiled.

📖 Read the "Reading Poetry" section on page 366 of *Writers INC*.

📖 Familiarize yourself with the "Poetry Terms" in the sections on pages 242–243 in *Writers INC*.

📖 From *Anne's Anthology* or *The Annotated Anne of Green Gables,* pages 467, 471–472, read "The Battle of Hohenlinden" and "The Downfall of Poland."

Thomas Campbell, 1777–1844, was the author of both "The
Battle of Hohenlinden" and "The Downfall of Poland." He
entered the university in his hometown of Glasgow, Scotland
at age thirteen. His translations of Greek tragedy were considered without parallel in the history of the university. He
then moved to Edinburgh and adopted literature as his profession. Here "Pleasures of Hope" was published in 1799, and
achieved immediate success. He traveled extensively on the
Continent, and during his absence wrote "Lochiel's Warning,"
"Hohenlinden," and other minor poems. In 1826 he was chosen
Lord Rector of the University of Glasgow. During the last years
of his life he produced little of note. He died in Boulonge, France.
During most of his life money was tight, and ill-health and
family afflictions cast melancholy over his later years. His
poems were written with much care, and are uniformly
smooth and musical. —*McGuffey's Sixth Eclectic Reader*, page 211

Many of the poems referred to in *Anne* reflect the situations of
the Scottish immigrants to Canada. The first poems that
Anne mentions—"The Battle of Hohenlinden," "Edinburgh
after Flodden," and others . . . reflect the unhappy state of a
homeless expatriate. It seems almost subversive . . . for these
emigrants to teach these poems and legends to their children
in a country within the British Commonwealth. Like the
thousands of emigrants expelled from their native country,
when we first see her Anne is a homeless waif. Unwelcome
and unwanted, she must make a new home for herself in a
strange new place, much as Montgomery's ancestors had. "The
Battle of Hohenlinden" and "Edinburgh after Flodden" are re-
minders to the schoolchildren who learned them in their *Royal
Readers* of the defeat and oppression the Scots suffered at the
hands of the English. Later in the novel, Anne is identified with
Mary, Queen of Scots, when she recites the poem of that name
by Henry Glassford Bell. . . . It is natural, however, for red-
haired Anne to be identified with the Queen of Scotland, for she
does in a sense, become queen of this island of expatriated Scots.
Before the end of the novel, Anne can say with Scott's Rob Roy
that "her foot is on her native heath" not only in the subject of
English but on P.E.I. as well. —*The Annotated Anne of Green Gables*, pages 457–458

5. In this chapter Anne lists some of her favorite poems.   Litera

Collect your favorite poems from your previous studies and reading.
Include your parents' and siblings' favorite poems.

Print out or write your poems neatly to make pages for an anthology of
poetry. Hint: By doing a search on the Internet you can find your favorite poems to copy into your word processing program for formatting.

Illustrate your poetry anthology, if desired, by hand or with graphics
from the Internet.

Make a nice cover and back page for your anthology. Punch uniform holes in the left-hand side of your cover and in the pages of your anthology and then stack them with the cover on top. Thread ribbon through the holes back to front and tie it off to put your book together.

Literature	6.	Because poetic references in *Anne of Green Gables* may only include a few lines, given without authors' names and sometimes without titles, finding a complete poetic work requires some research in the reference section of the library.

☞ *The Columbia Granger's Index to Poetry* lists poems by title, first line, and by author. At your library, use the *Granger's Index* to find an author or the title, using only the first line of a poem referred to in *Anne of Green Gables*. Then, find a complete copy of the poem. After finding the author of a poem, look for an anthology of his/her work. You may also check the table of contents or index of each multi-author anthology. Although most libraries prohibit patrons from checking out reference books, it is possible to photocopy needed material. In some libraries, the Reference Desk Assistance may have all the poems contained within anthologies in their computer system.

Literature	7.	Reserve time every Friday throughout this Unit for recitation. Choose a favorite poem from this lesson and read it aloud several times.

☞ Use the tips on page 366 in *Writers INC* to enhance your presentation. Look up the pronunciation of any words of which you are unsure.

After you have practiced and have assembled your audience, give your recitation. Unless required by your teacher, it is not necessary to memorize your poetry selection. You should, however, be comfortable enough with the poem to be able to look up from the page frequently and to make eye contact with the audience.

Quote Psalm 30 to your instructor.

History	8.	In 1800 Napoleon renewed his military campaign against Austria. The Battle of Hohenlinden was fought on December 3, 1800. Napoleon's army under Moreau completely defeated the Archduke John, who had been appointed to take the place of his brother Charles. The French then advanced to Linz. Another army, under MacDonald, advanced in Tyrol and in January, 1801, Brune, with the army of Italy, crossed the Adige and began the invasion of Austria from the south. A near defeat was turned into a victory for Napoleon. Austria agreed to sign a peace treaty on February 9, 1801, at Luneville.

📖 For an overview of this time period, read in a history text or an encyclopedia about Napoleon. Also read the section of the *Royal Reader* in the *Background Information Appendix* titled "George III," which gives a summary of the events during this king's reign.

⌒ᴑ Follow-up your reading by listening to Tape 1 of Volume 2 of Diana Waring's *What in the World's Going on Here?*.

✦ On the map of Europe:
Mark "The Battle of Hohenlinden." (Refer to Activity 11 for further instructions.)

✎ For a "C" or better grade in Contract Reading for History, read a biography of Napoleon) and write a two-page paper on this historical figure. Write an outline for your paper before you start. There are example outlines on page 108 in *Writers INC*.

---

9. 📖 Read the following information to help you understand more about "The Downfall of Poland." Kosciusko, 1746–1817, was a celebrated Polish patriot who had served in the American Revolution. His forces were besieged at Warsaw in 1794 by a large force of Russians, Prussians, and Austrians. After the siege was raised, he marched against a force of Russians much larger than his own and was defeated. He himself was severely wounded and captured. "Sarmatia" is the ancient name for a region of Europe which embraced Poland, but was of greater extent.

⏰ History

---

10. 📖 Read pages 31–33 in *The Anne of Green Gables Treasury*. When Anne is one year old and living with Mr. & Mrs. Thomas, Laura Ingalls Wilder, author of the Little House books, was born. Whereas the Little House books stop when Laura is 22, the *Anne of Green Gables* series continues on to the end of World War I when Anne is 53 years old. Also, it is interesting that Anne was born years earlier than Lucy Maud Montgomery. Montgomery paralleled the conception of Canada with the conception of Anne and the meeting of the first legislature, to the birth of Anne. The adoption of a Canadian Constitution and the convening of the first Canadian legislature were significant events. Although Canada remained part of the Commonwealth, the Constitution made Canadians more self-governing.

⏰ History

📖 Read "Attachment to the Queen" in the *Background Information Appendix*.

📖 Read in an encyclopedia or textbook about the government of Canada.

✎ In the History section of your notebook write:
a. Why did Canada want to remain tied to the British Commonwealth?
b. Why did Australia want to remain a colony?
c. What event in the United States caused Canada to limit the power of the Canadian provinces and give all remaining powers to the centralized federal government?

Geography   11. ⟡ On the map of Europe:

Attach small pieces of velcro to Glasgow, Boulonge, Edinburgh, London, Iser (a significant river in the Czech Republic), Austria, and Warsaw. Cut out quarter-sized circles of paper and, as you study, write or draw something representative of an event that occurred in each city or country. Cover the circles with contact paper and attach velcro to the opposite side. Let this be an on-going project. There may be more than one circle for each city. Each time another circle needs to be attached to the same location, remove the previous one and place it to the side or on top of the other. In lieu of using laminated circles with velcro you may use poster stick-um.

Literature   12. 📖 Read "Poetry Terms" on pages 242–243 of *Writers INC*.

✎ Pay special attention to and copy down into the Literature section of your notebook, the following terms and their definitions:

couplet
foot
meter
rhyme
rhythm
stanza
verse

Rhyme and **rhythm** are two elements of language you can feel and hear, especially in poetry.

Rhythm is the regular periodic beat in a poem, the pattern of accented (stressed) syllables with the unaccented. This is also known as meter. A common form of meter with which you will be familiar is the limerick. Here is an example :

> "There **wás** an Old **Mán** with a **beárd**,
>
> Who **sáid**, "It is **júst** as I **feáred**!—
>
> Two **Ówls** and a **Hén**, four **Lárks** and a **Wrén**
>
> Have **áll** built their **nésts** in my **beárd**."

—Edward Lear (1812–1888)

📖 All limericks have the same pattern of sounds. Review the definition and types of a "foot" on page 242 in *Writers INC* and try to determine what type of foot a limerick uses. (Hint: Emphasize the words in bold.) *See answer in Answer Appendix.*

Rhyme is the regular pattern of similar sounds, usually occurring at the end of lines. In poetry a pattern of rhyme is called the "rhyme scheme" of the poem. To find the rhyme scheme of a poem, label rhyming words using letters. The following example is from "The Vision of Sir Launfel."

Over his keys the musing organist, (A—"organist")
  Beginning doubtfully and far away, (B—"away")
First lets his fingers wander as they list, (A—rhymes with "organist")
  And builds a bridge from Dreamland for his lay: (B—rhymes with "away")
Then, as the touch of his loved instrument (C, new word—"instrument")
  Gives hopes and fervor, nearer draws his theme, (D, new word—"theme")
First guessed by faint auroral flushes sent (C—rhymes with "instrument")
  Along the wavering vista of his dream. (D—rhymes with "theme")

The above section of poetry has a rhyme scheme of ABABCDCD.

✎ **A stanza** is a division of poetry named for the number of lines it contains. The above excerpt is a stanza with eight lines called an "octave." Review the definition of stanza on page 243 in *Writers INC*. In the Literature section of your notebook write down the terms used for stanzas with different numbers of lines. For example: couplet—a two line stanza; triplet—a three line stanza, etc.

✎ As a review of the information that you have learned in this activity, complete the Poetry Terms Crossword Puzzle worksheet that is located following the Assignment page for Chapter V. *See answer in Answer Appendix.*

---

13. ✎ Using the information you learned about poetry, answer the following questions in the Literature section of your notebook: Literature
    a. Which lines rhyme in "The Battle of Hohenlinden"? What is the rhyme scheme for the first stanza? *See answers in Answer Appendix.*
    b. Compare the rhyme scheme of the first stanza of "The Battle of Hohelinden" with the other stanzas in the poem. Compare this rhyme scheme with the rhyme scheme of "The Downfall of Poland." Is it the same? If not, what is the rhyme scheme of the "The Downfall of Poland"? *See answers in Answer Appendix.*
    c. A couplet consists of two lines of verse with the same meter that usually rhyme. Look at "The Downfall of Poland." Does it contain couplets? *See answer in Answer Appendix.*

⚷ Review *Writers INC* for what each different type of stanza is called.
    d. What type of stanza is used in "The Battle of Hohenlinden"? *See answer in Answer Appendix.*

---

14. 📖 Review "foot" and "verse" on page 242–243 of *Writers INC*.   Literature

✄ **A stress** on a syllable is shown with an accent above or to the right of that syllable. In poems, syllables are stressed in the same way they would be in normal speech. To help you understand stressed and unstressed syllables look at the pronunciation guides next to the words in a dictionary. Open your dictionary to the word "syllable." The word "syllable" will be used in the following example. Your dictionary entry should begin with something like the following:

syllable (sil'e-bel)

In the pronunciation guide there is an accent mark after the first syllable. This means the accent or stress is on the first syllable. You pronounce the word "**syll**able" with the emphasis on the capitalized bold letters. Now look up the word "tomorrow" in your dictionary.

tomorrow (te-mor′o)

Look at the pronunciation guide. This is how "to**mor**row" is normally said with the stress on the second syllable. You would not stress the third syllable, tomor**row**. It would sound ridiculous.

With your instructor:

Say your vocabulary words a few times putting the emphasis on different syllables. Here is an example. Emphasize the letters in bold.

beautiful

beau**ti**ful

beauti**ful**

Check pronunciation guides to help you emphasize certain syllables in the words. Then discuss how the words sound when they are said with the wrong syllable emphasized.

Literature   15.   Review the meaning of "foot" and "verse" on pages 242–243 of *Writers INC*. The type of verse used in Shakespeare's plays is iambic pentameter. Iambic means the stress is on the second syllable, i.e. good-**bye**′. Remember: an accent mark above or to the right of a syllable means it is the stressed syllable. Pentameter indicates the line has five "feet"; in this case, repeating units of two syllables each. The "feet" in poetry are separated by a vertical line or a backslash. So a verse of iambic pentameter can be marked as follows:

"But **soft**′/ what **light**′/ through **yon**′/ der **win**′/ dow **breaks**′..."

                                —*Romeo and Juliet*, Act II, Scene 1, line 44

With your instructor:

Look at the limerick in Activity 12. The stressed and unstressed syllables are marked in each word. Study this example and it will help you to answer the following questions about "The Battle of Hohenlinden."

Look at the first line of "The Battle of Hohenlinden":

"On Linden, when the sun was low, . . ."

a. Mark each word with stressed and unstressed syllables.
b. What is the smallest repeated pattern or foot?
c. How many feet are in this verse? In traditional poetry, variations are permissible in writing verse; feet may be interchanged, and unaccented syllables may be added if the thought or word demands them. The author keeps the same variety of feet in each stanza. Check the other verses within the same stanza. Are they the same? *See answers in Answer Appendix.*

16. Marilla says Anne does not speak rudely or use slang.   Literature

📖 Read about "Diction" in *Writers INC* on page 234. What is slang?

With your instructor:
Give some examples of slang which are popular today.

___

17. In the beginning of Chapter 5, Marilla replies mercilessly to Anne   Bible
about her staying, yet later on we see pity stirring in Marilla's heart
and, by the end of the chapter, she is determined to keep the child.

📖 Read Proverbs 21:1 which speaks of God being able to turn a king's
heart. In this chapter we see it happening to Marilla.

___

18. Some people today may think Marilla is saying something odd when   Bible
she states, "She's lady like. It's likely her people were nice folks." She
attributes Anne's good character to her parents. Her biological parents
had only raised her for three months while her subsequent environment had been abusive. Marilla's statement expresses the belief that
character is inherited. For years there has been a controversy
over heredity versus environment and their effects on human
development.

📖 Read Genesis 3. What did mankind inherit as a result of Adam and
Eve's sin?

📖 Read Exodus 20:5 and Numbers 14:18.

🗝 Look up the word "iniquity" in the 1828 *Dictionary* or a Bible dictionary. What is the difference between iniquity and sin?

🗝 Use a concordance to find more verses about the inheritance of iniquity. Although we may have a propensity toward certain sins, we do
have a hope.

📖 Read Isaiah 53:4–6.

✎ In the Bible section of your notebook:
a. Write the difference between iniquity and sin.
b. Give examples from the Bible of sons committing the same sins
as their fathers.

___

19. 📖 Read about John Greenleaf Whittier. Begin by reading the informa-   History
tion in the *Background Information Appendix,* then expand your
knowledge by reading other sources. Knowing the writer and the times
he lived in will develop breadth of view.

✎ In the History section of your notebook:
Write half a page about John Greenleaf Whittier and his work.

___

20. On page 41 of *Anne of Green Gables* (*The Annotated Anne of Green*   Literature
Gables, page 89), "woodsy and wild and lonesome" is set off with quotation marks. This shows Montgomery is quoting someone's work. She is
quoting John Greenleaf Whittier's "Cobbler Keezer's Vision."

Read "Cobbler Keezer's Vision" in *Anne's Anthology*. Warning: This poem contains subject matter that may not be appropriate for some students. A discussion of the Biblical response to occult practices and witchcraft, as well as numerous Bible references, are in Activity 21.

Both cults and occult practice are anti-Christian and very dangerous. To understand the descriptions of some of the men listed below, look up the words "cult" and "occult" in a dictionary. Please do not research any of the historical figures or practices mentioned in the following definitions section without the guidance of a strong Christian adult and appropriate Christian explanatory literature.

Use the following definitions to add to your understanding of the poem.

fish-ward: someone who watches over the fish

waxed ends: a kind of shoemaker's thread that has been lubricated and protected from the elements by waxing it

Teuton: a member of any of the peoples speaking a Germanic language, especially a German

goodwife's reckoning: The "goodwife" is the lady of the house. "Reckoning" means a bill or tab, so the expression refers to the money the cobbler owed the lady of the house.

Brocken: The Brocken is the highest peak of Germany's Harz Mountain Range. The "tales that haunt the Brocken" were about a ghost or "spectre." The "Spectre of the Brocken" appeared when a low sun was behind a climber who was looking down from a ridge or peak into the mist below. The sun would shine brightly and a "glory" or bright spot would form in the mist below the climber. This "glory" would have the shadow of the climber cast on it, making a dim human shape in the mist. The shadow in the mist with the bright spot around it was thought to be a ghost. The following Web site currently has a picture of the Brocken Spectre: <http://www.sundog.clara.co.uk/droplets/globrock.htm>.

lapstone: a shoemaker's tool; a stone the cobbler holds in his lap and upon which he beats the leather or soles of shoes in order to give them a contoured shape; also used when pounding down folded edges or seams with a flat-faced hammer

Mormon's goggles: "magic goggles" worn by Joseph Smith, the founder of the cult of Mormonism, by which only he would be able to translate a new "Gold Bible" revealed to him by the "angel" Moroni. Smith was born in Vermont in 1805 and was a contemporary of John Greenleaf Whittier. The Mormon cult is also known by the name of "The Church of Jesus Christ of Latter-day Saints." This cult is especially dangerous because members claim to be Christians when their true beliefs are based on false doctrine.

Doctor John Dee: the Astrologer to Elizabeth I in the 1600's. He was heavily involved in occult practices and possessed numerous "magical" objects.

Cornelius Agrippa: a contemporary of Martin Luther who resurrected the occult philosophy of Cabalism in the 1500's. He was described as a "knight, doctor, and by common reputation, a magician." Cabalism is anti-Christian in that it questions God's words and motives and reinterprets scripture and prophetic revelations.

Nettesheim: Agrippa's residence.

Minnesingers: poets or musicians of the Minnesang tradition in Germany, active during the 12th through the 15th centuries. Originally members of the high nobility, minnesingers later came from the emerging middle class and had an economic as well as social interest in singing.

garner: a storage building for grain

beeves: an old English plural of the word beef; applicable to all ruminating animals except camels, and especially to the Bovidae, or horned cattle

fête: feast

flagon: a large metal or pottery vessel with a handle and spout used to hold alcoholic beverages, usually wine

Rhenish: from the Rhineland. The Rhineland is the home of most German wines, which were highly regarded in Whittier's day.

✎ Write the answers to these questions in the Literature section of your notebook.
   a. The cobbler was an early settler of the Merrimac Valley. Where did he come from originally? Write each line which alludes to the cobbler's country of origin. (See stanzas 4, 5, 17, 18, 23.)
   b. What did the cobbler forsee the next 50 years would bring the Valley? Name at least three things.
   c. Did the cobbler practice occultism?
   d. What did Whittier say happened to witches?
   e. Why do you think the cobbler laughed?

---

21. 📖 What does the Bible say about witchcraft? Read Deuteronomy 18:10; II Kings 17:17–18; II Kings 21:6; II Kings 23:24 (Amplified); Leviticus 19:31 (Amplified); Leviticus 20:6–7 (Amplified); Deuteronomy 18:11 (Amplified); 1 Samuel 28:3–10 (Amplified); II Chronicles 33:6 (Amplified); Isaiah 8:19–21 (Amplified); and Acts 13:6.   Bible

There are three sources of knowledge:
—God given knowledge. See Exodus 35:31–35; Psalm 94:10; Proverbs 1:7; and Proverbs 2:6.
—Knowledge which man gains using the talents God has given him. In the past many mathematicians and chemists were thought to be wizards. They were not, but only used God's laws to discover scientific and mathematical truth.
—Knowledge gained from Satan. The Devil shares his "wisdom" for a price. Read James 3:15. The very first sin originated from the desire

for knowledge that did not come from God. All knowledge must be acquired from a godly source. Read Genesis 3:4. The Devil's tactics have not changed. Knowledge is not our god. Jesus is our savior, not knowledge. We are only to look to Him for our knowledge.

Even some "children's games" are based on getting knowledge from evil sources. Use wisdom in choosing the games that you play.

History	22. 📖 If you are not familiar with the Salem Witch Trials, read in an encyclopedia, listen to *Puritans vs. Witches,* or look up another source about this unusual time in U.S. history.

Bible 23. Anne's memorization of poetry demonstrates the character quality of diligence. As the book progresses, the reader will see Anne applying diligence to other parts of her life. In order to be fruitful in the knowledge of our Lord Jesus Christ, we must have diligence.

📖 Read II Peter 1:2–8.

🗝 Look up "diligence" in The *American Dictionary of the English Language* (1828 edition) by Noah Webster or in a dictionary of your choice.

With your instructor:
Discuss a person whom you think to be diligent and why.

Fine Arts 24. ✋ In your sketchbook or the Fine Arts section of your notebook, draw a picture of the house you lived in when you were born.

Occupational Education 25. ✋ Make muslin curtains. If your house does not have a need for muslin curtains, then find someone who does have a need for them. If you cannot make the curtains, at least discuss with your parent how these curtains would have been made. You may find a pattern online or in a sewing guidebook that you can check out from the library.

Health 26. Anne's parents died of a fever. In the late 1800's and early 1900's, infectious diseases were the most serious threat to a person's health and well-being. During the mid to late 1800's, diseases ranging from malaria, diptheria, typhoid fever, cholera and smallpox, devastated many areas. The most common cause of death was respiratory disease, primarily pneumonia and tuberculosis. The second most common cause of death was the cluster of diarrheal diseases such as cholera and typhoid. Collectively, infectious diseases are known as "communicable" diseases because they are spread by contact with an infected host. In the 1800's and early 1900's, close human contact as well as poor sanitation (especially in the cities) provided the conditions in which diseases spread unchecked. This unchecked spread of disease is called an "epidemic."

Here is a list of some epidemics in the United States:

1860   smallpox, Pennsylvania, U.S.
1861   epidemics, U.S. (Civil War—numerous infectious diseases)
1865   smallpox, U.S.
1865   cholera, U.S.
1865   typhus, U.S.
1868   smallpox, U.S. (lasted 7 years)
1873   cholera, U.S.
1878   yellow fever, Florida, U.S.
1885   typhoid, Pennsylvania, U.S.
1886   yellow fever, Florida, U.S.
1889   influenza, worldwide
1893   polio, U.S. (first known outbreak)

✎ In the Health section of your notebook, make a table and answer the
   questions:
   a. For each of the above diseases find out the cause, how it is spread,
      prevention, symptoms, treatment, and mortality rate. Make a table
      with this information.
   b. What is a fever? Does fever have a purpose in the body? What is the
      appropriate treatment of a fever?
   c. Of the diseases which killed many people in the 1800's, in which
      ones was fever a symptom?

✺ Planning Guide

Gather These Items:
1. *Kings and Queens of England.* Bellerophon Books. ISBN 8388-053-9. (This is a coloring book. It is optional.)

2. *Westminster Shorter Catechism.* (Copies may be found on the Internet.)

3. Posterboard and markers to make a genealogy of your family.

Research Topics:
1. Kings and queens of England, especially from 1483 on
   —*Holinshed's Chronicles of England, Scotland & Ireland* by Raphael Holinshed. Reprint edition. AMS, 1997. ISBN 040403330X. (This is a reference book and may be found in the library.)

2. Erasmus

3. Kings and queens of Scotland
   —*Kings and Queens of Scotland* by W. A. Ross, Patrick Billington, and Jane Dodds. Appletree Press, 2001. ISBN 0862816262.

4. Genealogy as a hobby

5. Thomas Randolph, Earl of Murray

6. Self-acceptance
   —The Institute in Basic Life principles (formerly, Institute in Basic Youth Conflicts) has information on self-acceptance in its Basic Seminar program. See their Web site at <http://www.iblp.org>.

Suggested Videos:

Suggested Field Trips:
1. Visit a farm or dairy and watch a cow being milked. (See Activity 4)

Memory Work:
Memorize questions and answers 1–4 of the *Shorter Catechism*. For extra credit, memorize one verse for each question that best proves the answer. Pick your own or use the suggestions in Activity 12 of this Chapter.

Continue Psalm 30

Notes:

Assignments — Chapter VI & VII

Contract Reading: No new contract reading

Weekly
Quiet Time Reading Books:
Independent Project: Afghan or rag rug; poetry book
Memory Work: Continue Psalm 30; Questions 1–4 of the *Shorter Catechism*
Health: Continue your cardiovascular exercise program initiated in Unit 1, Chapter IV, Activity 9

	Literature	History	Bible	Health	Occu. Education	Fine Arts	Grammar & Writing
M	Read Chaps. VI & VII AGG, Reading Comp.	#6, #8, #9	#7, #11		#4 Field Trip		#1, #2, #3, #8
T	Vocab., #5	#10, #18	#12				#1, #18
W	#16 (ongoing)	#6, #8	#13, #14				#1, #14
Th		#6, #8	#15				#1, #15
F	#19 Recitation		#17				#17

🦁 Study Guide

Read Chapters VI & VII
Reading Comprehension:
Chapter VI
1. Who wanted a girl to help her? What was her reputation?
2. By what attribute was Mrs. Spencer known?
3. Why did Marilla change her mind?
4. What did Matthew think of Anne? What did Marilla want Anne to be?
5. What was the agreement Marilla made with Matthew?
6. Why did Marilla not tell Anne of their decision that night?
7. What symbolism do you see in Mrs. Blewett's name?

Chapter VII
8. What did Marilla find out about Anne? What was her solution to remedy this situation?

Vocabulary Words:

fractious

haunt

ungraciously

gimlet

ottoman

vim

duty

pert

qualm

infinite

glibly

harrowing

catechism

assented

obliged

irreverence

luxurious

Vocabulary:
☞ Look up the vocabulary words in a dictionary or encyclopedia. Fill in the blanks using the vocabulary words.

9. The _____ toddler disrupted church.
10. In order to have _____, one must eat well.
11. The riddle will _____ me until I figure it out.
12. She used a _____ to bore the holes.
13. He _____ refused his hand.
14. At times Shirley Temple acted _____.
15. If the Lord does not want you to do something, frequently you will have a _____ about it.
16. The airplane crash was a _____ experience.
17. She was unable to answer the simplest question in doctrine because she had not studied her _____.
18. The Epicurean sought _____ living.
19. The off-the-cuff remark was given _____.
20. The soloist _____ with yet another encore.
21. Matthew _____ to the plan.
22. _____ toward God is analogous to disrespect toward man.
23. Space is _____.

Extra Credit:
✋ Draw an ottoman in your sketchbook or in the Fine Arts section of your notebook.

🍂 Activities:

1. ✎ Write the following passage from dictation: Dictation

    Marilla looked at Anne and softened at the sight of the child's pale face with its look of mute misery—the misery of a helpless little creature who finds itself once more caught in the trap from which it had escaped. —*Anne of Green Gables,* page 46

2. Did you remember to put the apostrophe in the word "child's"? Whenever you write "s" at the end of a word, read the sentence to make sure whether you are referring to a plural or showing possession.   Follow-up

    📖 Look up and read the section in *Writers INC.* about the use of apostrophes. Did you remember not to put the " ' " in "its"? "It's" is the contraction for "it is," while "its" shows possession. Most possessive words have an apostrophe between the end of the word and the "s." There are, however, a few possessive words that do not use an apostrophe, such as yours, mine, and ours.

    ❊ With your instructor:
    Discuss the reason for the dash in the dictation. *See answer in Answer Appendix.*

3. 📖 Read about speech style in pages 431–432 of *Writers INC.* Become familiar with the terms.   ✓Follow-up

    ✎ In the Literature section of your notebook, write the answers to the following questions:
    a. The sentence in your dictation is an example of what figure of speech? *See answer in Answer Appendix.*   →*Pg. 236 (Writer's INC.)*
    b. Is the statement in the dictation an accurate depiction of Anne's predicament? Give reasons why or why not.

4. ✋ Visit a farm or dairy. Watch a cow being milked. Try milking a cow yourself. Allow the milk to separate so that you can see the cream. Taste the fresh cream. If possible, observe how a creamer works.   Occupational Education

5. 📖 From *Anne's Anthology* (*The Annotated Anne of Green Gables,* pages 467–469), read "Edinburgh After Flodden."   ☀ Literature

    In *Anne's Anthology,* pay particular attention to the footnotes to this poem. These footnotes will help you with this poem and others.

    ✎ Write the vocabulary words from the footnotes with their definitions in the Vocabulary section of your notebook and then memorize them.

✎ Review the poetry terms "rhyme" and "stanza." (See Chapter V, Activity 12) In the Literature section of your notebook, write the answers to the following:
a. What is the rhyme pattern for the first stanza in "Edinburgh After Flodden"?
b. Compare this rhyme scheme with the other verses within the poem.
c. What type of stanza is it? *See answers in Answer Appendix.*

☞ On pages 242–243 of *Writers INC* review the poetry terms "foot" and "verse." Look at the first lines of "Edinburgh After Flodden":

> "News of battle! News of battle!—
>   Hark! 'Tis ringing down the street: . . ."

Note that the second line is indented because it continues the thought of the first line.

✎ In the Literature section of your notebook:
d. Mark each word with stressed and unstressed syllables.
e. What is the smallest repeated pattern or foot?
f. How many feet are in this verse? Check the other verses within the same stanza. Are they the same? *See answers in Answer Appendix.*

History   6. The history of Scotland is filled with conflict with England. Although defeated at Flodden in 1513, Scotland also had its share of victories over England. Two hundred years before Flodden, in 1314, King Robert the Bruce (Robert I) attained a decisive victory over England at Bannockburn. A man named Thomas Randolph (Earl of) Murray, the nephew of Robert I, was instrumental in the Scots' fight against England.

☞ Research Thomas Randolph, Earl of Murray, on the Internet or at your library in books about Scottish history and monarchs. Like many historical figures, Randolph's name may be spelled in various ways in resources. As you search for information, include "Thomas Randolph Murray" or "Moray, Thomas Randolph" in your queries.

After the Battle of Flodden Field, a "Randolph Murray" is the man who delivers the news of the Scottish defeat to Edinburgh. He is the sole survivor of the battle. This "Randolph Murray" is not the same as King Robert the Bruce's nephew, Thomas Randolph, Earl of Murray, although they share a name.

In English and Scottish history, many names were passed down from generation to generation. This passing down of names occurs in many parts of the world. Sometimes children are named after a famous historical figure to honor that person and give the child a distinguished name. We may never know if the Randolph Murray who fought in the Battle of Flodden Field in 1513 was a descendant of the Thomas Randolph, Earl of Murray of the 1300's, but you can trace names that are passed down from generation to generation in your own family.

✎ Look up "genealogy" in an encyclopedia or online. Make a family tree or "genealogy" of your family. Ask your parents about the names of their parents, grandparents, and great-grandparents as far back as they can remember. Write your genealogy on a piece of poster board and hang it in your classroom.

☞ Look up information about how to diagram your genealogy.

---

7. Jesus' genealogy is written in the first chapter of the book of Matthew.   Bible

✎ Answer these questions in the Bible section of your notebook.
   a. How many generations does it include?
   b. Are there any names passed down through the generations? *See answers in Answer Appendix.*

---

8. The poem "Edinburgh After Flodden" speaks of "the Gallant King."   ☀ History

> The Gallant King refers to James IV. He succeeded to the Scottish throne in 1488. In 1503 he married Margaret, daughter of Henry VII of England—an alliance that led to Scotland and England being ruled by the same monarch in 1603. Later, in 1707, the English and Scottish crowns were united. During the lifetime of his father-in-law, James continued on good terms with the English government. But the imperious character of his brother-in-law, King Henry VIII, made it difficult for James to remain peaceful. When Henry engaged in war with France, James took sides with the latter. He encamped on the hill at Flodden. The Earl of Surrey marched against him with an English army. James foolishly allowed the English force to cross and march between him and Scotland without attacking. This fatal blunder lost him the day. The bravest and noblest of Scots formed a ring around King James, and he and they were hewn down where they stood. Before the days of standing armies, each town maintained a company of militia, for its own defense. These men were placed at the king's disposal in time of war and were called the city band. —*Royal Reader No. VI*, 1891

During the Battle of Flodden, the Scots were crushed and King James IV and his son were killed leaving an eighteen-month-old successor to the throne, James V. The Battle of Flodden is significant because with this battle, England changed its tactics in Scotland. Instead of a generalized march of conquest toward Scotland, England began attacking specific targets to achieve its goals.

📖 For more information about this period in English and Scottish history, read in an encyclopedia and in textbooks about the history of Scotland, James IV, Henry VII, and Henry VIII. Mary Queen of Scots was James IV's daughter. *Kings and Queens of England* also contains information about this era. Check your library for information on the kings and queens of England and Scotland.

✎ Make a timeline/flowchart titled "Kings and Queens of England." Make a second timeline titled "Kings and Queens of Scotland" on the same scale.

✎ Write poem titles about specific events or rulers next to that event or ruler on your timelines. (For example: Write "Edinburgh After Flodden" next to the names of James IV and Henry VIII on your timelines.)

Marmion is another poem set in 1513, the year of the decisive defeat of James IV of Scotland by the English.

✎ In the History section of your notebook:
Write at least two pages on this time period and the aforementioned kings. Review "Writing Expository Essays" on pages 105–114 of *Writers INC* before you begin.

Geography   9. ✦ On the map of Europe:
Mark Scotland and Flodden. (See Chapter V, Activity 11)

Geography   10. 📖 In an encyclopedia read about the "northern streamers" or "aurora borealis," as they are more commonly known. In the following quote from *Julius Caesar,* Act II, Scene 2, Shakespeare expresses the superstition that unusual appearances in the heavens foretold the death of great men.

> "When beggars die, there are no comets seen:
> The heavens themselves blaze forth the death of princes."

🕯 Bible   11. On the bottom of page 49 of *Anne of Green Gables (The Annotated Anne of Green Gables,* pages 97–98), Anne states who God is. Is what she says about God true?

✎ In the Bible section of your notebook:
Write at least one scripture for each attribute Anne gives to God. (The online versions of the *Shorter Catechism* have scripture texts for the question, "What is God?" Using these scriptures will make your assignment easier.)

🕯 Bible   12. When Montgomery married she became a Presbyterian preacher's wife. The Presbyterian church has used the *Westminster Shorter Catechism* since 1647 to teach doctrine to its children. The *Shorter Catechism* may be easily found online by typing "Shorter Catechism" into your favorite search engine. Have your parent ask you some of the questions of the *Catechism.* For what percentage of the questions did you already have the correct idea? There are 107 questions. Discuss any answers with which your family disagrees.

♡ Memorize questions and answers 1–4 of the *Shorter Catechism.* For extra credit, memorize one scripture for each question that best demonstrates the answer given. Choose your own or use the suggested scripture choice.

Q. 1. What is the chief end of man?
A. Man's chief end is to glorify God, and to enjoy him forever.

Scripture choice: **Revelation 4:11.** Thou art worthy, O Lord, to receive glory and honour and power: for thou hast created all things, and for thy pleasure they are and were created.

Q. 2. What rule hath God given to direct us how we may glorify and enjoy him?
A. The Word of God, which is contained in the Scriptures of the Old and New Testaments, is the only rule to direct us how we may glorify and enjoy him.

Scripture choice: **2 Timothy 3:15–17.** And that from a child thou hast known the holy Scriptures, which are able to make thee wise unto salvation through faith which is in Christ Jesus. All Scripture is given by inspiration of God, and is profitable for doctrine, for reproof, for correction, for instruction in righteousness: That the man of God may be perfect, thoroughly furnished unto all good works.

Q. 3. What do the Scriptures principally teach?
A. The Scriptures principally teach what man is to believe concerning God, and what duty God requires of man.

Scripture choice: **Micah 6:8.** He hath showed thee, O man, what is good; and what doth the LORD require of thee, but to do justly, and to love mercy, and to walk humbly with thy God?

Q. 4. What is God?
A. God is a Spirit, infinite, eternal, and unchangeable, in his being, wisdom, power, holiness, justice, goodness, and truth.

Scripture choice: **Psalm 104:24.** O LORD, how manifold are thy works! in wisdom hast thou made them all: the earth is full of thy riches.

---

13. 📖 Read in *Anne's Anthology* the selection from the *Peep of Days*.　　Bible

---

14. Anne's character reflects in a comic way upon problems many girls face 　💡 Bible
as they grow up. As with many girls, Anne did not like her hair.

✎ In the Bible section of your notebook, write why Anne had not said prayers. *See answer in Answer Appendix.*

It is essential we see ourselves through God's redeeming perspective. Anne uses flawed judgment when she makes the following points:

Fact A: God created everyone. Fact B: God loves everyone. Fact C: God created and loves me. Therefore, "if what I see in the mirror is an example of God's creativity and love, then how can I trust Him for the future?"

A lack of acceptance of God's creative work in our lives such as Anne's leads to bitterness and shows an inability to trust God. Anne has problems seeing herself through God's eyes; she rejects the way He had made her. Some signs of self-rejection in ourselves and others include being overly concerned with clothes, changing one's hair color, self-criticism, hypersensitivity to criticism, and bizarre actions or statements.

📖 Read Psalm 139:16; Jeremiah 1:5; Isaiah 49:1, 5; Isaiah 44:2, 24; Job 10:8–9; and Isaiah 29:16; 45:9–12; 64:8–9. Is there an area in your life in which you are not accepting God's loving design for you?

📖 Read about each of the following Bible characters and their own unchangeable feature.

Jacob—Genesis 32:31
Paul—II Corinthians 12:7
Moses—Exodus 4:10
Zaccheus—Luke 19:3
Timothy—II Timothy 1:5
Elisha—II Kings 2:23
Jepthah—Judges 11:1
Joseph—Genesis 37:4

✎ In the Bible section of your notebook:
Paraphrase what each Bible character said about his unchangeable feature. If further study is desired, read the "Self-acceptance" bulletin published by the Institute in Basic Youth Conflicts.

Bible   15. Marilla says Anne "was next-door to a perfect heathen." Marilla then formulates a plan to correct this situation. Montgomery demonstrates that orphans, even girl orphans, had a need not only for physical care, but also to come to a saving knowledge of the Lord Jesus Christ.

✎ In the Bible section of your notebook:
a. Write the definition of a heathen.
b. What became Marilla's new purpose in keeping Anne?
c. According to II Peter 1:2–8, we are to have faith in God. Write at least one page on the topic of faith, incorporating the dictionary definition of faith and Biblical scriptures. Be sure to include what faith is and how it is obtained. Verses that should be discussed in your paper include: Ephesians 2:2–9; Hebrews 11:1–12:2; and Romans 1:16–17. Conclude the paper by writing about your own faith in God.

Literature   16. English literature can be divided into categories or time periods.

📖 Read about English literature in an encyclopedia or in a literature text.

✎ In the Literature section of your notebook, write the categories of English literature. Copy the following list or one from your reference, such as an Abeka or a Bob Jones University world literature text. Some experts have slightly different divisions and dates. The differences are minor and the ideas remain the same.

Ancient (900 B.C.–300 B.C.)—e.g. *Iliad; Odyssey*

Old English (500–1100)—e.g. *Beowulf*

Middle English (1100–1485)—e.g. *The Canterbury Tales* by Geoffrey Chaucer

Beginning of Modern English (1485–1603)—e.g. *Common Prayer* by William Tyndale; *The Faerie Queen* by Edmond Spencer; William Shakespeare

Stuarts and the Puritans (1603–1660)—e.g. Sir Francis Bacon; *Paradise Lost* by John Milton

Restoration Literature (1660–1700)—e.g. John Dryden; John Bunyan

Augustan Age or Neoclassical Age (1700–1750)—e.g. *Gulliver's Travels* by Jonathan Swift; Daniel DeFoe; Alexander Pope

Romantic Period (1750–1832)—e.g. *The Rime of the Ancient Mariner* by Samuel Taylor Coleridge; Lord Byron; John Keats; William Wordsworth

Victorian Period (1832–1901)—e.g. Alfred, Lord Tennyson; Matthew Arnold

Students should write the titles of all poetry and books read under the dates they were written. For example, Thomas Campbell, 1777–1844, was the author of both "The Battle of Hohenlinden" and "The Downfall of Poland." Because these poems would have been written during the Romantic Period, the titles of these poems should be listed under the Romantic Period in the Literature section of their notebook. Students should realize that, just as a composer is influenced by styles from previous musical periods, poets are influenced by previous writers.

---

17. In *Anne of Green Gables,* page 44 (*The Annotated Anne of Green Gables,* page 92), the phrase "tender mercies" is used.   Bible

    📖 Read Proverbs 12:10.

    ✎ In the Bible section of your notebook:
    Write a few sentences about what further insight this scripture gives you concerning Marilla's expectations of Mrs. Blewett.

---

18. Marilla tells Matthew if she fails in raising Anne correctly, he can then "put his oar in." This phrase means to interfere or meddle. The image comes from rowing a boat: only one person can row at a time or there is a risk of changing the boat's direction. Erasmus first published this expression in 1500. This is a recurrent metaphor for Matthew's relation to Marilla's raising of Anne. (See *The Annotated Anne of Green Gables,* page 96.)   History

Erasmus of Rotterdam (1466?–1536) helped Martin Luther and the Reformation by producing a Latin translation of the New Testament in 1516 that contained newly discovered texts as well as annotations. He and his followers wanted a limited reform of the church, in contrast to the Reformers who wanted to go back to the church as it originally was, with the Bible as its sole authority.

✎ In the History section of your notebook:
Write a half page describing Erasmus and his work.

Literature   19. Reserve time every Friday throughout this Unit for recitation. Choose a favorite poem from the week's lesson and read it aloud several times.

Quote memorized scriptures to your instructor including the questions and answers 1–4 of the *Shorter Catechism* and Psalm 30.

🌿 Planning Guide

Gather These Items:

1. *Alice in Wonderland* by Lewis Carroll for an "A" or "B" grade in Contract Reading Choice — Literature.

2. *Famous Men of Greece* by Cynthia A. Shearer, A. B. Poland, and John H. Haaren. Greenleaf Press, 1989. ISBN 1882514017. (Try finding this resource at the public library or borrowing it from your homeschooling support network. This book is also available online at The Baldwin Project Web site. Select the book at their site for the author, John H. Haaren, at <http://www.mainlesson.com/displayauthor.php?author= haaren>.)

3. *Do I Vacuum or Dust First?: And 99 Other Nitty Gritty Housecleaning Questions* by Don Aslett. Reprint edition. Signet, 1993. ISBN 0451175697. This book or another of Don Aslett's books is for an "A" grade in Contract Reading Choice — Occupational Education.

4. Items to make a print:
   foam from a well-washed meat or mushroom container
   scissors or a knife
   paint or printing ink
   paper

5. Items to crochet a dishcloth:
   I or J crochet hook
   cotton yarn

Research Topics:

1. Lithographs

   . . . .

2. Printmaking

   . . . .

3. Cleaning

   . . . .

*Beginning in this Chapter, assignments for research include subjects from more than one Chapter. This will spread out the research so as not to overload the student.

4. Socrates, Solon, Lycurgus, Aristides, Cimon*

. . . .

5. The effects of fear and anger on the body

. . . .

6. Attention Deficit Disorder

. . . .

Suggested Videos:

1. A video of a movie or television version of *Alice in Wonderland*
   —*Alice in Wonderland.* A television version produced by Hallmark
   Home Entertainment, 2000. ASIN 6305372837. (This movie also contains some elements of Lewis Carroll's sequel to *Alice in Wonderland*
   called *Through the Looking Glass.)*

Suggested Field Trips:

1. With the approval of your instructor, visit an older woman you know
   who is a good housekeeper. (See Activity 15)

2. Visit an artist in your area who makes prints or lithographs. Have him
   or her demonstrate the process of printmaking or lithography to you.

3. Take a printmaking class. (Optional)

Memory Work:

The Lord's Prayer and I Corinthians 10:13

Continue Psalm 30

Notes:

Assignments — Chapter VIII

Contract Reading

	A Grade	B Grade	C Grade
Bible			
History			
Literature	❒ Choice: *Alice in Wonderland*	❒ Choice: *Alice in Wonderland*	
Occupational Education	❒ Choice: *Do I Vacuum or Dust*		

Weekly

Quiet Time Reading Books: *Alice in Wonderland*
Independent Project: Afghan or rag rug; poetry book; dishcloth
Memory Work: Lord's Prayer and I Corinthians 10:13; continue Psalm 30
Health: Continue your cardiovascular exercise program initiated in Unit 1, Chapter IV,
    Activity 9

	Literature	History	Bible	Health	Occu. Education	Fine Arts	Grammar & Writing
M	Read Chap. VIII AGG, Reading Comp.	See Chap. XII & XIII, #9 Socrates*	#5, #6		#16	#12	#1, #2, #3
T	Vocab., #4	Solon	#7	#11		#12 Field Trip	#1, #4
W	#13	Lycurgus	#8, #10	#10			#1, #13
Th		Aristides	#9			#14	#1, #9
F	#17 Recitation	Cimon	#17		#15 Field Trip		

*Note: Since there is a lot of material to cover in Activity 9, Chapters XII & XIII, begin this study now.

Study Guide

Read Chapter VIII
Reading Comprehension:

1. What would recall Anne to work?

2. Why does one scald a dishcloth?

3. What did Marilla think about imagining things to be different than they are? What do you think?

4. What did Marilla want Anne to learn about obedience?

5. What character qualities did Marilla admire in Diana?

6. At the conclusion of chapter VIII, what does Anne think of herself?

7. Do you give names to inanimate objects? If so, what objects do you name?

Vocabulary Words:

fortnight

desperately

Vocabulary:
☞ Look up the vocabulary words in a dictionary or encyclopedia. Write sentences with each.

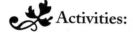 **Activities:**

Dictation	1. ✎ Write the following passage from dictation:
	"If everybody minded their own business," the Duchess said in a hoarse growl, "the world would go round faster than it does." —Lewis Carroll, *Alice in Wonderland*
Follow-up	2. "Their" and "hoarse" each have homophones. Homophones are words that sound alike, but have different spellings, meanings, and origins. Spell the other type of "their" and "hoarse." How do you remember which to use?
Follow-up	3. Did you remember that periods and commas are placed inside quotation marks? Quotation marks are placed before and after direct quotations. Only the exact words quoted are placed within the quotation marks. The comma after "growl" and the small "t" in "the" demonstrate the continuation of the sentence.
Literature	4. Marilla is fond of moral sayings, just like the Duchess in *Alice in Wonderland*. Many books written in the Victorian period were moralistic, to the point of syrupy sweetness. Publishers at first rejected the Anne manuscripts, perhaps because Montgomery's books did not fit the moralistic form of other Victorian literature. Comparing Marilla to the Duchess was a way of taking a jab at the children's literature of the day.

📖 Read the section on "Quotes from the Duchess in *Alice in Wonderland*" in *Anne's Anthology.*

෨ Watch a video of *Alice in Wonderland.*

📖 If *Alice in Wonderland* was chosen for an "A" or "B" grade in Contract Reading — Literature, begin reading this book.

✎ Upon completion of this book, write a book review in the Literature section of your notebook.

---

5. ♡ Memorize "The Lord's Prayer." This is located on page 298 in *Anne's Anthology.*   ☼ Bible

---

6. ⚷ Where is "The Lord's Prayer" located in your Bible? Use your concordance to find two places in the New Testament where "The Lord's Prayer" is quoted. Are these versions of "The Lord's Prayer" the same or different from one another?   Bible

With your instructor:
   Discuss the similarities and differences of the two versions of "The Lord's Prayer" and why you think they were written differently.

---

7. What opinion of Anne does Mrs. Thomas have? *See answer in Answer Appendix.* Instead of just being reproachful, perhaps Mrs. Thomas is ineffectually trying to teach Anne about the sinfulness of man.   Bible

📖 Read Isaiah 53:6 and Jeremiah 17:9.

---

8. With your instructor discuss: ☼ Bible
   What do you do when you meet a seemingly irresistible temptation?

♡ Read and memorize I Corinthians 10:13. This verse will enable you to stand firm in times of testing.

---

9. With your instructor discuss: Bible/Writing
   a. Who were Anne's friends prior to coming to Green Gables?
   b. What type of friend does Anne look for?
   c. Do you have any friends with these characteristics?
   d. Following are some quotes to read over and ponder about friendship:

   He has no friend who has many friends.   —Aristotle, *Eudemian Ethics VII*

   In poverty and other misfortunes of life, true friends are a sure refuge. The young they keep out of mischief; to the old they are a comfort and aid in their weakness, and those in the prime of life they incite to noble deeds.   —Aristotle

   If you have one true friend, you have more than your fair share.   —Thomas Fuller

   One friend in a lifetime is much; two are many; three are hardly possible.   —Henry Adams, *The Education of Henry Adams*

We walk alone in the world. Friends such as we desire are dreams and fables. —Ralph Waldo Emerson, "Friendship"

No receipt openeth the heart but a true friend, to whom you may impart griefs, joys, fears, hopes, suspicions, councils, and whatsoever lieth upon the heart to oppress it, in a kind of civil shrift or confession. —Francis Bacon, "Of Friendship"

A friend loveth at all times, and a brother is born for adversity. Proverbs 17:17

A man who has friends must himself be friendly, but there is a friend who sticks closer than a brother. Proverbs 18:24

Ointment and perfume delight the heart, and the sweetness of a man's friend does so by hearty counsel. Do not forsake your friend or your father's friend, nor go to your brother's house in the day of your calamity; for better is a neighbor nearby than a brother far away. Proverbs 27:9–10

What a great blessing faithful friendship is—the friendship of a true woman on whom one can depend and in whom one can trust. I fear it is a rare thing. Yet I have found some such friends—not many but enough. I do not, since girlhood passed, make friends easily or lightly. But I no longer desire many friends or a superficial popularity. Rather do I wish a few, kin to me of soul, whom I can grapple to my life with bonds not to be broken, on whose honor I can rely, and in whose companionship I can find satisfaction. For such friends I say "Thank God," with all my heart. —Lucy Maud Montgomery

📖 Read "Writing Paragraphs" on pages 95–104 in *Writers INC*.

✎ In the Writing section of your notebook:
Write a paragraph using one of the above sayings as a topic sentence. Be specific. Include examples from personal experience, literature, or the Bible.

⏰ Bible/Health   10. According to Marilla, what is Anne's most serious shortcoming? *See answer in Answer Appendix.* This is a poor habit Anne has allowed herself to develop. It brings her pleasure when little else in her life does, yet it becomes a stumbling block. Today some might wonder if Anne had Attention Deficit Disorder or ADD. If six of the following nine criteria are present in someone, he or she is considered to have ADD. He/she:

1. Often fails to give close attention to details or makes careless mistakes in schoolwork, work, or other activities.
2. Often has difficulty sustaining attention in tasks or play activities.
3. Often does not seem to listen when directly spoken to.

4. Often does not follow through on instructions and fails to finish schoolwork, chores, or duties in the workplace.

5. Often has difficulty organizing tasks and activities.

6. Often avoids, dislikes, or is reluctant to engage in tasks that require sustained mental effort.

7. Often loses things necessary to complete tasks.

8. Is often easily distracted by extraneous stimuli.

9. Is often forgetful in daily activities.

✎ In the Health section of your notebook:
Jot down signs of Anne's inattentiveness.

Just like Anne, we sometimes allow our minds to be inattentive. Search your heart and see if you have allowed the seeds of inattentiveness to grow. If so, then read the following scriptures and helps for rooting out inattentiveness.

📖 Read I Corinthians 10:31; Luke 16:10; James 1:14–15; and Colossians 3:22–23.

These verses will help you to give up the desires that lead to inattentive behavior. We often want to go on to do a more pleasurable activity instead of concentrating on what we are doing right now. We must put off the "desires of the flesh" and do as "unto the Lord."

📖 Read I Peter 1:13–14; Proverbs 1:8–9; and Galatians 3:23.

These passages will help you to increase your attentiveness. Another way to train oneself to concentrate is by setting increasingly longer periods of time for practicing attentiveness.

📖 Read James 1:19 and Luke 8:18.

Anne needs to listen when spoken to directly. Failure to listen is selfishness. This is shown in Philippians 2:3–4; Romans 12:10; and Proverbs 19:20.

📖 The Bible has much to say not only about starting well, but also finishing well. To reinforce this idea, read Galatians 6:9 and Matthew 21:28–32. Because the Apostle Paul applied this principle, he was able to say at the end of his life in II Timothy 4:7, "I have fought the good fight, I have finished the course, I have kept the faith."

📖 Orderliness is also a godly characteristic. Read I Corinthians 14:33, 40. Anne should not allow herself to forget the task at hand until she is finished. Another sign of ADD is losing things necessary for tasks. Everything a person possesses should have a place, and everything must be in its place when it is not in use.

📖 Read Proverbs 18:9; Romans 14:10; and I Corinthians 4:2.

Paraphrased from Rita Jameson's article, "ADHD and the Christian Home." *Nathhan News* Fall 1995: pages 10–12.

Used with permission.

📖 Also refer to Montgomery's advice to Ephraim Weber. (See Chapter I, Activity 9)

Health   11. When we experience anger or fear our body produces epinephrine. Epinephrine causes nervousness, tremor, euphoria, anxiety, coolness of extremities, pallor, heart palpitations, difficulty breathing, and tremors.

✎ In the Health section of your notebook:
Jot down the signs of fear noted in Anne's description on page 53 of *Anne of Green Gables* (*The Annotated Anne of Green Gables,* page 101).

☀ Fine Arts   12. ⚷ Look up the definitions of "printmaking" and "lithography" in a dictionary, an encyclopedia, or on the Internet.

📖 Read notes 4 and 5 on page 104 of *The Annotated Anne of Green Gables.* What is a "chromo"?

Lithography is a type of artwork that is printed using photography to make a design on stone or metal plates.

✋ Make a simple paint print of your own by cutting a design in the back of a well-washed piece of foam from a meat or mushroom container. (For your first print make a very simple design like a heart or a leaf. You can make more complex designs after you have become familiar with the process.)

Lightly cover your design with paint or printing ink. A rolling tool called a "breyer" may be helpful in applying the paint or ink. These may be found in the craft section of stores or at art supply stores. Make sure you do not have an excess of paint on your design as it will smudge the image.

Press your paint-covered design onto a piece of plain white paper. (Or, you can use colored paper and white paint for a different effect.)

This process takes practice. Do not be afraid to make many practice prints on scratch paper before you make your final print. Your foam design can be used over and over so do not be afraid to experiment. Wash the design well between colors and when you are finished.

✋ Visit an artist in your area who makes prints or lithographs. Have him or her demonstrate the process of printmaking to you. You might want to take a printmaking class.

☀ Literature   13. ⚷ Look up the writing term "theme" in the index of *Writers INC,* then turn to the page(s) listed and read the definition of "theme."

✎ What is the theme of *Anne of Green Gables*? Write several sentences about the theme of *Anne of Green Gables* in the Literature section of your notebook. Give reasons to support your answer. *See answer in Answer Appendix.*

In *Anne of Green Gables,* page 56 (*The Annotated Anne of Green Gables,* page 104), Anne looks at a "chromo" entitled, "Christ Blessing the Little Children." How does this picture fit the theme of *Anne of Green Gables?*

14. The Bible tells the story of Jesus blessing the children in Matthew 19:13–15; Mark 10:13–16; and Luke 18:15–17. Read these scriptures. These passages in the Bible have inspired works of art all over the world. Many churches have developed stained glass windows using this theme. If you have online access, do a search for "Jesus Blessing the Children." See if you can find and view the interpretations of this scripture by three or four artists. Either pick your favorite artist's version of the above scriptures and copy it or let the Lord inspire you and draw your own original version of "Jesus Blessing the Children" in your sketchbook or the Fine Arts section of your notebook.	Fine Arts
15. Anne is learning how to clean. Read one of Don Aslett's books on cleaning or a similar book by a different author for an "A" grade in Contract Reading — Occupational Education. If possible, visit an older woman you know who is a good housekeeper. While interviewing her and/or helping her with housework, ask her advice on cleaning. Based on what you learn from your reading and from your visit with an older woman, write three things you can do differently to clean either more efficiently or more effectively in the Occupational Education section of your notebook.	Occupational Education
16. Crochet one or more dishcloths. These may be given away as Christmas gifts to those who have contributed to your education. (See the *Activity Appendix* for further directions.)	Occupational Education
17. Reserve time every Friday throughout this Unit for recitation. Recite passages from *Alice in Wonderland* and sayings of the Duchess. Quote the Lord's Prayer; I Corinthians 10:13; and Psalm 30.	Literature

 # Planning Guide

Gather These Items:
1. *Famous Men of Greece* by Cynthia A. Shearer, A. B. Poland, and John H. Haaren. Greenleaf Press, 1989. ISBN 1882514017. This book is also available online at The Baldwin Project Web site. Select the book at their site for the author, John H. Haaren, at <http://www.mainlesson. com/displayauthor.php?author=haaren>.

2. *A History of Us, An Age of Extremes 1870–1917,* Book 8, by Joy Hakim. Oxford University Press, 1999. ISBN 0-19512774-9.

3. Items to paint an impressionistic painting.

Research Topics:
1. Timoleon, Phocion, Pelopidas, Epaminodas, Agis, Aratus*

. . . .

2. Industrial Revolution

. . . .

3. Impressionism

. . . .

4. How to read poetry
   —*McGuffey's Sixth Eclectic Reader*

. . . .

Suggested Videos:

Suggested Field Trips:
1. Visit an art museum that has impressionistic paintings. (See Activity 14)

Memory Work:
Psalm 15

Complete Psalm 30

Continuing in this Chapter, assignments for research include subjects from more than one Chapter. This will spread out the research so as not to overload the student.

Notes:

Assignments — Chapter IX

Contract Reading: No new contract reading

Weekly
Quiet Time Reading Books:
Independent Project: Afghan or rag rug; poetry book
Memory Work: Psalm 15; complete Psalm 30
Health: Continue your cardiovascular exercise program initiated in Unit 1, Chapter IV,
    Activity 9

	Literature	History	Bible	Health	Occu. Education	Fine Arts	Grammar & Writing
M	Read Chap. IX AGG, Reading Comp., #2	See Chap. XII & XIII, #9 Timoleon				#11	#1
T	Vocab., #3	#8, Phocion	#4			#12	#3
W	#6	#7, #8, Pelopidas	#5			#13	#6, #9
Th		#8, #10, Epaminodas	#9				#10
*F	#15 Recitation	#8, #11, Agis, Aratus				#14 Field Trip	#8

Note: Since there is a lot of material to cover in Activity 9, Chapter XII & XIII, continue working on this study.

*On Friday, at the end of each Unit, review and take the Unit Quiz in the *Test Appendix.*

🙰 Study Guide

Read Chapter IX
Reading Comprehension:

1. What did Mrs. Rachel Lynde think of those who are sick?

2. What had Anne done during her free time at Green Gables? How long was she allowed to roam?

3. When did Marilla not allow Anne to chatter?

4. When Marilla spoke of Anne's positive characteristic, to what did she refer?

5. What was Anne's response to Mrs. Lynde's unkind remark?

6. On the way up the stairs Marilla felt condemned about her own feelings. Why?

7. What event in Marilla's life allowed her to be empathetic with Anne? Has this ever happened to you?

8. What are three reasons Anne should have been respectful?

9. Why was Marilla "troubled in mind" and "vexed in soul"?

Vocabulary Words:

grippe

empathetic

apology

deprecates

vexation

reprehensible

suppositions

fortnight

Vocabulary:

🗝 Look up the vocabulary words in a dictionary or encyclopedia. Fill in the blanks using the vocabulary words.

10. Her poor conduct was _____.

11. "Passions too violent—afford us _____ and pain." —Temple

12. "An _____ is a reason assigned for what is wrong or may appear to be wrong, and it may be either an extenuation or a justification of something by those who are not acquainted with the reasons." —Noah Webster, *American Dictionary of the English Language* (1828 Edition)

13. Mrs. Lynde was not well; she had the _____.

14. Sometimes the Lord has us go through different trials so that we may be _____ and compassionate toward others.

15. The boss commonly _____ his employees.

16. His business took him away for a _____.

17. Evolution is based on unsupported _____.

Activities:

1. Write the following passage from dictation:	Dictation

> Then Marilla suddenly became aware of an uncomfortable and rebuking consciousness that she felt more humiliation over this than sorrow over the discovery of such a serious defect. —*Anne of Green Gables,* page 66

2. Compare your dictation with the original. This is an example of **characterization**. The author is revealing Marilla and her character.	Follow-up

3. On page 69 of *Anne of Green Gables* (*The Annotated Anne of Green Gables,* page 118), the term "Parthian shaft" is used. This is an **allusion**, a literary reference to a familiar person, place, thing, or event. Read the sentence in the book and this definition of Parthian shaft:	Literature

> A parting shot; a telling or wounding remark made on departure, giving one's adversary no time to reply. An allusion to the ancient practice of Parthian horsemen turning in flight, to discharge arrows and missiles at their pursuers. —E. Cobb Brewer, *Brewer's Dictionary of Phrase and Fable,* page 807

✎ In the Literature section of your notebook:
Write the definition of the Parthian shaft followed by an example of the allusion referred to in this Chapter.

4. What character quality does Marilla have with regard to decisions? *See answer in Answer Appendix.*	Bible

🕮 With your instructor discuss:
Do you think this is a good or bad quality to have?

📖 Read Psalm 15 and Luke 9:62.

♡ Memorize Psalm 15.

5. 🕮 With your instructor discuss:	Bible

a. On what quality does Mrs. Lynde pride herself? *See answer in Answer Appendix.*
b. How is this good? How is this bad? *See answers in Answer Appendix.*

📖 Read Proverbs 20:19; 26:28; and 29:25.

🕮 With your instructor:
Discuss how much of what Mrs. Lynde says is not said in love. Give some examples.

📖 Read I Corinthians 13.

Literature   6. 📖 Read "Bingen on the Rhine" by Caroline Norton from *Anne's Anthology* (*The Annotated Anne of Green Gables,* pages 470–471). Although Bingen is a town in Hesse Darmstadt, Germany, and Algiers is on the northern coast of Africa, the spirit of the poem is universal.

Two vocabulary words to know are:

coquetry: flirtation
truant: wandering

📖 This is beautiful poetry to read aloud. *McGuffey's Sixth Eclectic Reader* has 49 pages on reading aloud, including pointers on articulation, inflection, accent and emphasis, reading verse, the voice, and gesture. If you have access to this book, read over the contents and use some of the pointers in your reading aloud. To make the measure of poetry perceptible to the ear, there should be a slight pause at the end of each line, even where the sense does not require it. Notice the long dashes contained within the poem. When it is desired to give a phrase great force of expression, each word, and even the parts of a compound word, is independently emphasized with a long dash. A short pause is often made before or after an emphatic word or phrase.

✏ In the Literature section of your notebook, use the first line of "Bingen on the Rhine" to complete the following activities:

"A soldier of the Legion lay dying in Algiers; . . ."

a. Mark each word with stressed and unstressed syllables. (Review all of the poetry terms used in this section in Chapter V, Activities 12, 13, 14, and 15.) *See answer in Answer Appendix.*
b. What is the smallest repeated pattern or foot? *See answer in Answer Appendix.*
c. How many feet are in this verse? *See answer in Answer Appendix.*
d. **Enjambment** is the running over of a sentence or thought from one line to another. Does this happen in this poem? If so, give an example. *See answer in Answer Appendix.*
e. **Refrain** is the repeating of a line or phrase of the poem at regular intervals, especially at the end of each stanza. Does this poem contain a refrain? If so, give an example. *See answer in Answer Appendix.*

Geography   7. ⬥ On the map of Europe:

Locate Bingen on the Rhine and place a circle tag there. (See Chapter V, Activity 10)

History   8. In this chapter Anne interacts with both Marilla and Matthew throughout the day. Their life illustrates how many lives were before the Industrial Revolution. Prior to the advent of reliable transportation, such as the railroad studied in Unit 1, many things needed to be made locally. When parents began working in the factories, there was a problem of what to do with the children. No longer were they working at their parents' side. Many times the wages made working at the factories were very low, despite great profits being made by the factory owners. In *A History of Us, An Age of Extremes* or other similar book, read about Andrew Carnegie, John Davison Rockefeller, John Pierpont Morgan, and monopolies. Also read in *A History of Us, An Age of Extremes,* chapters 15–17, about producing goods and workers. In this same book, read the chapter, "Telling It Like It Is," which talks about the beginning of child labor laws. Divide this reading between four days.

✎ Write a paragraph contrasting the ideal lifestyle depicted in *Anne of Green Gables* versus that of the families of factory workers.

9. ☛ Use a concordance to find verses and stories about how godly men should treat their employees.   Bible

❁ With your instructor:
Discuss godly treatment of employees.

10. ✎ In the appropriate time period in the History section of your notebook: Pick one of the men studied in Activity 8 above. Write a one page essay about him, highlighting how he treated his workers, spent his money, and helped or hindered society. As an alternative, you could read a biography of Sam Walton and write a one page essay on him. Include in this essay one verse you think fits your topic's character.   History

11. The description of Anne outdoors lends itself to an impressionistic painting. The landscapes of Impressionists almost always had a human presence. The experience of nature was primarily a social one. The ever-changing face of nature sparked their interest in capturing fleeting moments of light and color. They used broken brushwork to convey movement and spontaneity. The Impressionists were not interested in rendering details, but wanted to create an effect as though the scene was perceived in a fleeting glance. Impressionistic paintings differed from the traditional painting of the period in color, brushwork, themes, and the general depiction of nature.   ☀ Fine Arts

☛ This Web site on Impressionism is excellent: <http://www.impressionism. org/>. (This site is very informative. It includes lessons to download and a tour of France at the turn of the century. Warning: There was one nude in the pictures.)

Initially Impressionism was not an accepted painting style. In 1874, the year Montgomery was born, several impressionistic painters put on their own exhibit. Those participating were Claude Monet, Pierre-Auguste Renoir, Paul Cézanne, Edgar Degas, and Alfred Sisley.

☛ Look at paintings done by each of these artists.

❁ Discuss with your instructor which painter is your favorite and why.

☼ Fine Arts   12. Technology and science both played an important role in the develop-
                   ment of Impressionism. The emerging science of color theory was
                   especially significant in this development. Science had shown that the
                   color white is composed of primary colors. Using a palette of only eight
                   to ten colors, the Impressionists were able to achieve many different
                   effects. The art of photography also had an effect on the Impressionists
                   as it motivated them to depict people without mythological or historical
                   exaggeration.

               ✋ In your sketchbook or the Fine Arts section of your notebook, draw a
                  color wheel. Identify which colors are primary and which colors are
                  complementary.

Fine Arts   13. ✋ Using what you have learned about Impressionism and its tech-
                   niques, paint Anne as described in this chapter (*The Annotated Anne
                   of Green Gables,* page 112).

Fine Arts   14. ✋ If possible, go to an art museum that has impressionistic paintings.

Literature   15. ✋ With your instructor:
                   Reserve time every Friday throughout this Unit for recitation.
                   Quote Psalm 15 and recite your favorite poem from your studies in
                   this Chapter.

☼ Quiz   16. Review and take Unit 2 Quiz in the *Test Appendix.*

🐝 Planning Guide

Gather These Items

1. *Pilgrim's Progress* by John Bunyan for a "B" or better grade in Contract Reading Choice — Bible.

2. *How Should We Then Live? The Rise and Decline of Western Thought and Culture* by Francis A. Schaeffer. Crossway Books, 1983. ISBN 0-89107-292-6.

3. Items to make the hat listed on pages 96-97 in *The Anne of Green Gables Treasury* by Carolyn Collins and Christina Wyss Eriksson. Viking Press, 1991. ISBN 0-670-82591-3. (This is out of print, but may be found on the Internet or at a used book store.)

4. Items to make a flower pounding. Directions are included in the *Activity Appendix*.
   flowers, leaves and/or grass
   masking tape
   muslin fabric
   small embroidery hoop
   clear printer transfers or calligraphy tools

5. *American Dictionary of the English Language* (1828 Edition) by Noah Webster.

6. *Famous Men of Rome* by John H. Haaren, Robert G. Shearer, and A. B. Poland. Greenleaf Press, 1989. ISBN 1882514033. This book is available online at The Baldwin Project Web site. Select the book at their site for the author, John H. Haaren, at <http://www.mainlesson.com/displayauthor.php?author=haaren>.

7. *Famous Men of Greece* by John H. Haaren, Robert G. Shearer, and A. B. Poland. Greenleaf Press, 1989. ISBN 1882514033. This book is also available online at The Baldwin Project Web site. Select the book at their site for the author, John H. Haaren, at <http://www.mainlesson.com/displayauthor.php?author=haaren>.

Research Topics:

1. Restoration of the monarchy in England in 1660

. . . .

2. Glorious Revolution of England

. . . .

3. The French Revolution
   —*Liberty, Equality, Fraternity: Exploring the French Revolution* by authors and editors Lynn Hunt of UCLA and Jack Censer of George Mason University. Center for History and New Media, George Mason University and the American Social History Project, City University of New York. © 2001 <http://chnm.gmu.edu/revolution/>. (With over 600 primary documents, images, maps, and other information, this site on the French Revolution looks like it could be very helpful.)

. . . .

4. Leonidas, Philopoemen, Numa Pompilius, Servius Tullius, Lucius Junius, Fabricius*

. . . .

Suggested Videos:

Suggested Field Trips:

Memory Work:
Proverbs 29:22

Notes:

Continuing in this Chapter, assignments for research include subjects from more than one Chapter. This will spread out the research so as not to overload the student.

Assignments — Chapter X & XI

Contract Reading

	A Grade	B Grade	C Grade
Bible	☐ Choice: *Pilgrim's Progress*	☐ Choice: *Pilgrim's Progress*	
History			
Literature			

Weekly

Quiet Time Reading Books: *Pilgrim's Progress*
Independent Project: Afghan or rag rug; poetry book
Memory Work: Proverbs 29:22
Health: Continue your cardiovascular exercise program initiated in Unit 1, Chapter IV, Activity 9

	Literature	History	Bible	Health	Occu. Education	Fine Arts	Grammar & Writing
M	Read Chap. X & XI AGG, Reading Comp., #2	See Chap. XII & XIII, #9 Leonidas, Philopoemen	#3				#1, #2
T	Vocab., #5, #8	Numa Pompilius	#4		#11		#5, #8
W	#7, 10	#7, #9, Servius Tullius	#12				#6, #7, #9
Th	#13	Lucius Junius	#15			#14	
F	#16 Recitation	Fabricius					

Worksheet

Crossword Puzzle
For Chapter X & XI • Vocabulary

Across
- 3 be sorry for
- 5 armored cavalry units
- 9 pious
- 10 remorseful
- 14 rotations
- 17 degradation
- 19 requesting earnestly
- 20 flounce on a garment

Down
- 1 necessary
- 2 proud
- 4 satin-like cotton
- 5 tobacco-like
- 6 willful
- 7 feather
- 8 disheartened
- 11 mournful
- 12 wearily
- 13 unruly
- 15 atoned
- 16 unwanted services
- 18 contributor

🐉 Study Guide

Read Chapters X & XI
Reading Comprehension:
Chapter X

1. When was the last time Matthew had been upstairs? What brought him up there this time?

2. What did Marilla see in Anne's apology that Mrs. Lynde did not?

3. What did Mrs. Lynde care for less than one with a temper?

4. How did Anne describe being forgiven? Have you ever experienced this?

5. What effect did Anne holding Marilla's hand have on Marilla?

Chapter XI

6. L.M. Montgomery initially wrote *Anne of Green Gables* as a serial for Sunday School papers. What message did she give in this Chapter to the teachers and to the girls in the Sunday School class?

Vocabulary

⚷ Look up the vocabulary words in a dictionary or encyclopedia. Do the crossword puzzle using these words. *See answers in Answer Appendix.*

Extra Credit:

✋ In your sketchbook or in the Fine Arts section of your notebook, draw the following. As an alternative, show a photograph or professional sketch to your instructor.
June lilies, also known as narcissi
buttercups
fuchsia
birches

Vocabulary Words:

refractory

repent

obdurate

abasement

smote

wanly

vain

benefactor

plaintive

plume

officious

snuffy*

sateen

dejected

penitent

behoove

askew

beseechingly

furbelows

gyration

devout

squadrons

Midians

*Note: "Snuffy-colored" refers to the yellowish or brown color of snuff or powdered tobacco.

Activities:

Dictation	1. ✎ Write the following from dictation:

"It gives you a lovely, comfortable feeling to apologize and be forgiven, doesn't it? Aren't the stars bright tonight?" —*Anne of Green Gables*, page 76

Follow-up	2. Did you remember to use question marks instead of periods? Sometimes it is easy to be inattentive and put periods at the end of sentences that are really questions. Did you remember your apostrophes to show the missing letters? Lastly, if you forgot the comma after "forgiven," put the rule number from your handbook above the space for the comma. Notice the two sentences have nothing in common. L.M. Montgomery uses the technique of free writing to show Anne's inattentiveness and to give the feeling of free flow conversation.

⚷ Look up free writing in the index of *Writers INC* and read about this technique.

Bible	3. In the dictation, Anne describes the lightness associated with forgiveness. Have you ever experienced this lightness?

📖 Read I John 1:9. When you ask the Lord to forgive you of your sins, isn't it a great feeling to know that the Lord does forgive you?

Bible	4. 📖 Read Revelation 3:2–3, the text for the sermon which Anne hears at church. Anne tells Marilla, "It was a very long text. If I was a minister I'd pick the short, snappy ones." (*The Annotated Anne of Green Gables*, page 132) Do you agree with Anne that this is "a very long text" on which to build a sermon?

✎ In the Bible section of your notebook:
Do some brainstorming. Jot down questions that could be asked about this text, then do a study to find the answers. Pretend you are answering a question on this text for a friend or that you are responsible for a study group.

Writing	5. ⚷ Look up "vain" in the *American Dictionary of the English Language* (1828 Edition). According to this definition, is Anne vain?

📖 Review writing paragraphs on pages 95–104 in *Writers INC*, especially the section on persuasive paragraphs. Then read "Writing Persuasive Essays" in *Writers INC* on pages 115–123. This section provides more details on persuasive writing. (Parents, the "Assessment Rubric" for persuasive essays is on page 123.)

✎ In the Writing section of your notebook:
Write two paragraphs. The first should be an expository paragraph, explaining what the word "vain" means. The second should be persuasive, giving reasons why Anne was or was not vain.

6. Anne gives descriptive names to places surrounding her house. For example, she calls the Avenue, "White Way of Delight," and the Barry's pond, "Lake of Shining Waters."

Writing

✎ In the Writing section of your notebook:
Write descriptive names for places surrounding your house and town.

7. On page 74, the phrase, "valley of humiliation," is used. This is an allusion to *Pilgrim's Progress,* the allegorical masterpiece by John Bunyan. An **allusion** in literature is a reference to a familiar person, place, thing or event; an **allegory** is a story in which the characters and/or events represent an idea or generalization about life. Allegories often have a strong moral lesson. *Pilgrim's Progress* is the story of Christian's pilgrimage to the Celestial City, a journey beset with trials and temptations and sprinkled with incidental encouragements. One place Christian must travel through is the Valley of Humiliation. This is a "must read" book. It has been reprinted and translated more often than any other book except the Bible. In the 1700's it was used as a textbook in many schools. Lucy Montgomery knew this allusion would spark the desired image of Anne's suffering to readers who were familiar with *Pilgrim's Progress.*

☼ Literature/ History

This book was written during the Restoration period of literature. John Bunyan was born in 1628 in Elstow, England. His father was a tinker. In 1647 John Bunyan married a grown orphan. She led her husband to the Lord and he was baptized. Bunyan soon began to preach, but was arrested and thrown into prison for preaching without receiving permission from the established Church in 1660. He remained there for twelve years, during which time he wrote *Pilgrim's Progress.* He was imprisoned again in 1675. John Bunyan died in 1688.

📖 Read *Pilgrim's Progress* if this is your choice for a "B" or better grade in Contract Reading — Bible.

📖 Read Activity 9 and do further reading about this time period.

✎ In the History section of your notebook, in the appropriate time period:
a. Keep notes from your reading.
b. Do more research into the life of John Bunyan.
c. Write about the events in England which caused him to become a political prisoner.

8. In *Let Us Highly Resolve,* David and Shirley Quine state that during the 1600's revelation was considered the ultimate source of truth and knowledge. God revealed himself to man through Scripture. The Biblical world view was understood to give man both adequate and sufficient answers to the basic questions of life. Reason and emotion were under the umbrella of divine revelation. Revelation given in the Scripture was the gauge by which reason and feelings were measured.

☼ Literature

Although the ability to reason is God-given, the 1700's abandoned revelation and enthroned reason as the goddess to worship. When man reasons apart from God and His Word, it leads to confusion and empty speculations. Adam and Eve, reasoning apart from God's Word, ushered humanity into this state of confusion. During the 1700's man was left alone to find for himself all he needed to know. However, because man is not all-knowing, he is unable to see the complete picture.

Reason was toppled during the 1800's and Romanticism rose to the top. Man sought escape from reason and turned to feelings and experience. However, since feelings and experiences are as changing as the tide, these also failed as an adequate standard of truth.

✎ In the Literature section of your notebook:
Based on this explanation of revelation, reason, and romanticism, explain how *Pilgrim's Progress* is representative of literature written during the 1600's. Use a persuasive paragraph to answer this question.

☼ History   9. The Puritan leader of England, Oliver Cromwell, died in 1658. His son could not handle the affairs of government and in 1660 George Monk, a general who served under Cromwell, overthrew the government. A new Parliament, elected in 1660, restored the monarchy under Charles II.

📖 Read about the Restoration.

In 1685 Charles II died and his Catholic brother, King James II, became king. He wanted to restore Catholicism and absolute monarchy to England. Many people demanded the abdication of James from the throne. Leading politicians invited William of Orange, who was the husband of the daughter of James II and ruler of the Netherlands, to invade England with Dutch forces and restore English liberties. In 1688 William landed in England. King James II fled to France, giving up his throne in what is called the Glorious Revolution.

📖 Read further about the Glorious Revolution.

📖 Read a comparison of the Glorious Revolution and the French Revolution in chapter 6 of *How Should We Then Live?* by Francis A. Schaeffer.

✎ In the appropriate time period of the History section of your notebook, write about the Restoration and the Glorious Revolution. Include the factors which contributed to this being a "bloodless revolution."

Literature ✓10. 📖 In *Anne's Anthology* or *The Annotated Anne of Green Gables,* page 472, read "The Dog at his Master's Grave."

✎ In the Literature section of your notebook write:
a. Do you think the Sunday School class would have enjoyed this poem?
b. Is it a romantic idea that a dog would mourn the loss of his master for so long?
c. Compare the death of the dog with the death of a Christian.

11. ✋ Make Anne's Sunday School hat listed on pages 96–97 in *The Anne of Green Gables Treasury* by Carolyn Collins and Christina Wyss Eriksson. | Occupational Education

12. The lines, "Quick as the slaughtered squadrons fell / in Midian's evil day," were from a hymn written by John Morrison of Aberdeen which he based upon Judges 8 and Isaiah 9. | Bible

📖 Read Judges 8 and Isaiah 9, the Bible texts from which this hymn originated. Montgomery remembers being thrilled by these lines when she was only nine.

13. "Handsome is as handsome does," is from *The Vicar of Wakefield*, written in 1766 by Oliver Goldsmith. On page 74 of *Anne of Green Gables* (*The Annotated Anne of Green Gables*, page 123) it says, "Marilla had plumed herself." This means prided herself, especially in regards to something trivial. This is an allusion to "The Jay in Peacock's Feathers" by Aesop. Read this tale: | Literature

The Jay in Peacock's Feathers
A Jay ventured into a yard where Peacocks used to walk. There were a number of feathers which had fallen from the Peacocks when they were molting. He tied them all to his tail and strutted down towards the Peacocks. When he came near them they soon discovered the cheat, and striding up to him pecked at him and plucked away his borrowed plumes. So the Jay could do no better than go back to the other Jays, who had watched his behavior from a distance; but they were equally annoyed with him, and told him:
"It is not only fine feathers that make fine birds."

With your instructor, discuss your thoughts about these two phrases Montgomery uses in *Anne of Green Gables*. Tell what you think Montgomery means by each of them. Compare what each of them says about pride and vanity. Express what you learned from them.

14. ✋ See the flower pounding directions in the *Activity Appendix*. Flower pounding items may be used as Christmas tree decorations, wall hangings, or gifts. | Fine Arts

15. Anne displays a bad temper. Do you have a bad temper? Read the following and discuss it with your instructor: | Bible

There once was a little girl who had a bad temper. Her mother gave her a bag of nails and told her that every time she lost her temper, she must hammer a nail into the back of the fence. The first day the girl had driven 37 nails into the fence. Over the next few weeks, as she learned to control her anger, the number of nails hammered daily gradually dwindled down. She discovered it was easier to hold her temper than to drive nails into the fence. Finally the day came when the girl didn't lose her temper at all. She told her mother about it and the mother suggested that the girl now pull out one nail for each day that she was able to hold her temper. The days passed and the young girl was finally able to tell her mother that all the nails were gone.

The mother took her daughter by the hand and led her to the fence. She said, "You have done well, my daughter, but look at the holes in the fence. The fence will never be the same. When you say things in anger, they leave a scar just like this one. You can put a knife in a person and draw it out. It won't matter how many times you say 'I'm sorry,' the wound is still there. A verbal wound is as bad as a physical one. Friends are very rare jewels, indeed. They make you smile and encourage you to succeed. They lend an ear, share words of praise and they always want to open their hearts to us." —unknown

♡ Memorize Proverbs 29:22.

Literature   16. ❈ With your instructor:
Reserve time every Friday throughout this Unit for recitation. Quote the Lord's Prayer; I Corinthians 10:13; Psalm 15; and Proverbs 29:22.

———◆◆———

🦢 Planning Guide

Gather These Items:

1. Items to make homemade ice cream, preferably with a hand-crank freezer. There are recipes listed in the *Activity Appendix*.

2. *Famous Men of Rome* by John H. Haaren, Robert G. Shearer, and A. B. Poland. Greenleaf Press, 1989. ISBN 1882514033. This book is available online at The Baldwin Project Web site. Select this book at their site for the author, John H. Haaren, at <http://www.mainlesson. com/displayauthor.php?author=haaren>.

3. *D'Aulaire's Book of Greek Myths* by Ingri D'Aulaire, Edgar D'Aulaire, and Edgar Parin D'Aulaire. Reprint ed. Yearling Books, 1992. ISBN 0440406943.

4. Material and pattern to make a skirt, either modern or Victorian era.

5. Material and pattern to make a patchwork quilt. (This is optional. See Activity 3)

Research Topics:

1. Cooking with chocolate

. . . .

2. Planning a small flower garden
   —*Square Foot Gardening* by Mel Bartholomew. VHS Videocassette. ASIN B00004TRZM.

. . . .

3. The art of hair work—hair braiding and jewelry
   —*Art of Hair Work: Hair Braiding and Jewelry of Sentiment* by Mark Campbell, Jules Kliot, and Kaethe Kliot. Lacis, 1996. ISBN 0-916896-31-5.
   —I really like this site: <http://www.morninggloryantiques.com/ collectHair.htm>.

. . . .

4. Victorian fashions, especially children's clothing
   —*Authentic Victorian Dressmaking Techniques* by Kristina Harris. Dover, 1999. ISBN 0486404854.
   —*Victorian Fashions and Costumes from Harper's Bazar: 1867–1898* by Stella Blum. Dover, 1974. ISBN 0486229904.

. . . .

5. Murals of Apollo and the Graces which appear in the Library of Congress. See the Web site, <http://www.vanderbilt.edu/AnS/Classics/classical_traditions/#libraryofcongress>.

. . . .

6. Sandro Botticelli's famous painting of the Graces, "La Primavera."

. . . .

7. Apollo or Phoebus, Camillus, Virgil, Homer, Pope, Hamlet, Othello, Monimia (heroine of Otway's tragedy, *The Orphan*), Belvidera (heroine of Otway's tragedy, *Venice Preserved*), Mantuan, Muses' Hill, Earl of Chesterfield, Cincinnatus, Scipio, Cato, Brutus, Carthage-Regulus.

. . . .

Suggested Videos:

To understand the allusions in the poem, "Winter," it is suggested students watch videos of the plays, *Hamlet* and *Othello*. Julia Stiles has performed in many good Shakespearean remakes. Our family definitely does **not** recommend *O,* a modern adaptation of *Othello,* by Timark Home Entertana 2002.

Suggested Field Trips:

1. Visit a chocolate factory where they make chocolate or fudge; they sometimes have these in malls. (See Activity 18)

2. Visit a garden shop, botanical garden, horticultural specialist at a community college, or attend a garden club meeting. (See Activity 5)

Memory Work:

Memorize Hebrews 12:4–8

Notes:

Assignments — Chapter XII & XIII

Contract Reading: No new contract reading

Weekly
Quiet Time Reading Books: *Pilgrim's Progress*
Independent Project: Sew a skirt
Memory Work: Hebrews 12:4–8
Health: Continue your cardiovascular exercise program initiated in Unit 1, Chapter IV,
     Activity 9

	Literature	History	Bible	Health	Occu. Education	Fine Arts	Grammar & Writing
M	Read Chap. XII & XIII AGG, Reading Comp.	Camillus	#19		#3, #17		#1, #2
T	Vocab., #7	#9, #13, Scipio	#6	#8	#4, #5 Field Trip		
W	#10	#9, #13, Cincinnatus			#14		#12
Th		#11, Cato			#16		#15
F	#20 Recitation	Carthage-Regulus			#18 Field Trip		

 # Worksheet

Who Am I?
For Chapters XII & XIII • Activity 11 • "Winter"

Choose from the following:

Apollo

Aristides the Just of Veii

Cato the Censor

Cimon

Cincinnatus

Hamlet

Homer

Lycurgus

Belvidera

Brutus

Camillus

Monimia

Othello

Pope

Scipio

Socrates

Solon

1. I drank Hemlock for my death sentence.

2. I wrote of the gods of love and war.

3. I am a fictitious Shakespearean character whose father's ghost charged me to avenge his death.

4. I am a fictitious Shakespearean character who killed my wife in a fit of jealousy and killed myself in a fit of sadness.

5. I am the Greek god of the sun.

6. I erased the debts of the Athenians and gave all Athenians the right to vote. I established a more just legal system.

7. I was a prince of Sparta who gave all Spartans the right to vote and developed Sparta into a powerful military state.

8. I helped beat the Persians and was entrusted with money to restore Athens.

9. I was in charge of the Athenian fleet, which comprised the finest sailors in all of Greece.

10. I am a Senate appointed dictator. To end a seven year siege, I dug a tunnel under the city of Veii.

11. My name means curly-haired. I was appointed dictator of Rome.

12. I was given command of the Roman army, and we fought and defeated the Carthaginians. I was elected to the council.

13. I led an army against the Spanish rebellion. Then I went to Greece and defeated Antiochus in the pass of Thermopylae. I thought that the luxury and extravagance of the rich were taking away the strength of Rome. I passed a high tax on carriages to encourage people to walk.

14. I helped banish King Tarquin.

15. I am a Catholic, English satirist.

16. I am in Otway's tragedy of *The Orphan*. Sir Walter Scott says, "More tears have been shed for the sorrows of me, than for those of Juliet and Desdemona."

17. I am in Otway's *Venice Preserved*. Sir Walter Scott says, "More tears have been shed for the sorrows of me and Monimia than for those of Juliet and Desdemona."

🪬 Study Guide

Read Chapters XII & XIII
Reading Comprehension:
Chapter XII

1. How did Marilla keep on track in her discipline of Anne?

2. Why was Anne so excited to go with Marilla for the skirt pattern?

3. Why did Mrs. Barry want a playmate for Diana?

4. How did Matthew know Anne liked chocolates?

5. What good character quality did Marilla note in Anne?

6. What did Marilla not like in a man?

Chapter XIII

7. What character flaw in Anne needed to be overcome before she could cook?

8. Why did Anne not like patchwork?

9. In what one way did Anne see Diana as not being perfect?

10. What event was Anne excited about?

Vocabulary:

🗝 Look up the vocabulary words in a dictionary or encyclopedia. Fill in the blanks using the vocabulary words.

Vocabulary Words:
sarcasm
deprecatory
staccato
dolefully
dubious

11. "He saved others, but he cannot save himself," is an example of _____.

12. She _____ cried about the loss of her dog.

13. To some, the Vietnam War was a _____ war.

14. The _____ speech grabbed the attention of the class.

Extra Credit:

Use each of the different forms of deprecate correctly in a sentence:

    a. deprecate *vt*   b. deprecatingly *adv*   c. deprecation *n*

    d. deprecatory *adj*   e. deprecatorily *adv*

Activities:

Dictation	1. ✎ Write the following passage from dictation:

> Then he began to go forward; but Discretion, Piety, Charity, and Prudence, would accompany him down to the foot of the Hill. So they went on together, reiterating their former discourses, till they came to go down the Hill. Then said Christian, as it was difficult coming up, (so far as I can see), it is dangerous going down. Yes, said Prudence, so it is; for it is a hard matter for a man to go down into the Valley of Humiliation, as thou art now, and to catch no slip by the Way; therefore, said they, are we come out to accompany thee down the Hill. So he began to go down, but very warily; yet he caught a slip or two.
>
> —John Bunyan, *Pilgrim's Progress*, "Part the First"

Follow-up	2. ▯ Read about parentheses on page 471 in *Writers INC*.

     ▯ Circle each comma in the dictation exercise. Read about comma usage on pages 457–461 and pages 83–84 in *Writers INC*.

     ▯ Circle the semicolons. Read about semicolon usage on pages 461–462 in *Writers INC*.

     ✎ In the Dictation section of your notebook:
     a. Identify which rule applies to each comma.
     b. Do the same for the semicolons.
     c. Compared to those in the past, authors today usually use clear, succinct sentences. Long sentences can be confusing to read. Rewrite the dictation section with shorter sentences and use formal punctuation for the dialogue with quotation marks and paragraphing. *See answer in Answer Appendix.*

Occupational Education	3. ✋ If you have not already done so, begin a daily sewing time. An idea for the first project is a patchwork quilt. Contrary to Anne's opinion, there is "scope for the imagination" in quilting.

     Perhaps you may want to make a friendship quilt. Have several friends make a block for your quilt. Or, you can try scanning illustrations of your favorite book or family on to fabric squares.

Occupational Education	4. ✋ Do some research on some of the flowers listed on page 87 (*The Annotated Anne of Green Gables*, pages 139–140). Find out which ones will grow in your area, their height, color, and blooming time. Use the information to plan a small garden for growing them. Research prices and estimate the cost for buying the flowers as well as for fertilizer. Save the plans and, if it is economically feasible and you have the time, plant your garden.

Field Trip	5. ✋ Visit a garden shop, botanical garden, horticultural specialist at a community college, or attend a garden club meeting to increase your knowledge of plants.

6. What are the two different types of swearing referred to on page 87 (*The Annotated Anne of Green Gables,* pages 139–140)? *See answer in Answer Appendix.* What does the Bible say about swearing?

Bible

  Read Leviticus 19:12; Exodus 20:7; Deuteronomy 6:13; and Jeremiah 4:2.

7.   Read another of Anne's favorite poems, "Winter," from *The Seasons* by James Thomson in *Anne's Anthology.* "Winter" was the best known of all his works.

 Literature

James Thomson (1700–1748), the son of a clergyman, was born in Scotland. He studied at the University of Edinburgh and intended to enter the clergy, but never did. Instead, in 1724 he went to London where he spent most of the rest of his life. He had shown some poetic talent as a boy and he published "Winter" in 1726. He was also a playwright, but none of his plays achieved any success. In the last year of his life he published *The Castle of Indolence,* the most famous of his works except for *The Seasons.*

Both *The Castle of Indolence* and *The Seasons* suggest Thomson's interest in the sources of human feeling and demonstrate his efforts to use traditional verse forms to record fresh perceptions. Sensitive to the aesthetic and philosophic implications of the natural world, Thomson nonetheless does not find in nature an adequate solution to all problems. He seems to be searching for an adequate value system. *The Castle of Indolence* is in some ways a particularly poignant record of personal conflict. Notice that the endings of the lines do not rhyme and the stanzas are of different lengths. Read about free verse and blank verse in *Writers INC.* Remember that personification is a literary device in which the author speaks of or describes an animal, object, or idea as if it were a person.

  In the Literature section of your notebook:
  a. Write the definitions of both free verse and blank verse.
  b. Which one better fits this poem?
  c. Prose is especially distinguished from poetry by its greater irregularity and variety of rhythm and its closer representation of the everyday patterns of speech. What makes "Winter" poetry rather than prose? *See answer in Answer Appendix.*
  d. Find an example of personification in "Winter."

8.   Read the following information regarding consumption:

 Health

In the past, most uses of the word "consumption" referred to tuberculosis, a lung disease which was fatal prior to antibiotics. It was characterized by night sweats and a general wasting away of the individual. Frequently doctors would send patients to warm, dry climates in the hope of improving their condition. Later on, in the early 1900's, infected people were placed in sanatoriums to limit the spread of the disease. Sometimes people were misdiagnosed with tuberculosis when they actually had other diseases with the same symptoms. Tuberculosis can be dormant and asymptomatic for years, then, during times of stress, poor nutrition, etc., will begin to manifest itself. Tuberculosis is spread by droplet contamination, but sunlight quickly kills the germs. Therefore places that have many people indoors much of the time with poor nutrition, such as an asylum, would tend to be more of a breeding ground for the bacteria that cause tuberculosis. Because of routine screening and treatment of those with tuberculosis, the disease is not as common today as it once was.

History   9. The poem, "Winter," has many references to notable Greeks and Romans. The poet uses allusions with which his contemporaries would have been familiar. Parts of "Winter" were included in the readers of Anne's day both in the United States and Canada. Even though this poem was written a century before Anne, through her classical study these allusions would have been understood.

It is assumed you have learned about many of these interesting men in prior years of study. This is a great time to review what you have learned about them. Read a biographical sketch of each of these men in a textbook, Greenleaf Famous Men Series, or encyclopedia. If you have not studied them, make this a long term project, or, when you have completed *Where the Brook and River Meet*, you may want to learn about these men in more detail. A complete list of the references is included below:

Solon	Philopoemen	Belvidera
Lycurgus	Numa Pompilius	Apollo or Phoebus
Leonidas	Servius Tullius	Philip Dormer Stanhope,
Aristides the	Lucius Junius	fourth Earl of Chesterfield
Just of Veii	Camillus	Othello
Cimon	Fabricius	Hamlet
Timoleon	Cincinnatus	Homer
Pelopidas	Carthage-Regulus	Brutus
Epaminondas	Scipio	Pope
Phocion	Cato	Socrates
Agis	Virgil	Muses' Hill
Aratus	Monimia	Mantuan

Literature   10. The poem, "Winter," mentions many famous authors, works of literature, and characters. Pope, Hamlet, Othello, Monimia, Belvidera, Phoebus, Mantuan, Muses' Hill, Chesterfield, Virgil, and Homer are all mentioned. Use the footnotes in *Anne's Anthology* to aide your study.

In the Literature section of your notebook, write each of the above proper nouns. Then, next to each one, write two or three sentences about it. Here is an example:

Alexander Pope was an English poet of the eighteenth century, known for his satiric wit and insistence on the values of classicism in literature: balance, symmetry, and restraint. His best known poems are "The Rape of the Lock," "An Essay on Criticism," and "An Essay on Man."

(Parents: This is a difficult project. Although some will be easy, it is not expected that information on all of these people and characters will be found. The student may need to go to the library to continue her research. In looking up these words, please remember spelling was not standard in the 1700's.)

∞ For improved comprehension of "Winter," view Shakespeare's *Hamlet*   *w/Mel Gibson*
and *Othello* on video. Please be mindful that Shakespeare was a talented artist, but his dramas were tragic.

To save time, you can pin your skirt pattern on your material, cut it out, and iron seams while watching the movies.

Extra Credit: Read about Apollo and the Graces from *D'Aulaire's Book of Greek Myths*. Add what you have learned to the above assignment. You may want to find pictures of statues of Apollo and the Graces. Warning: Many of the statues are of nude figures.

⚷ Find pictures of the murals of Apollo and the Graces that appear in the Library of Congress.

⚷ Find a photograph of Sandro Botticelli's famous painting of the Graces, "La Primavera."

11. Complete "Winter" worksheet which is found after the Assignment page for this Chapter. *See answers in Answer Appendix.*	History
12. ✎ In the Literature section of your notebook, write about the poem, "Winter," by choosing one of the following options: 　a. Answer the question, "What does the season of winter have to do with any of the characters listed in Activity 9 or 10?" 　b. Write background information on the characters, tying it in with what James Thomsom said about each one.	Writing
13. ✦ Continue to place circles on your map for each geographical site you study. Be sure to include Rome and Greece and the important characters from these countries.	Geography
14. ✋ Make homemade ice cream with an ice cream maker, preferably a hand-crank one. See the *Activity Appendix* for homemade ice cream recipes.	Occupational Education
15. ✎ Imagine never having been at a picnic! What a picture this draws for the reader of Anne's previous life! Do you remember a time in your life when you were anticipating going to an exciting event which was quite new to you? Write a paragraph describing the anticipation and dreaming which surrounded this event. Did you think looking forward to the event was half the pleasure?	Writing

Occupational
Education

16. ☞ Marilla's brooch had hair braiding in the setting. There are some beautiful examples of hair work online. Look for some of these examples by using a search engine such as Google and typing in "braided hair pins."

Hair braiding jewelry is a lost art from the Victorian age. However, there are some instructional books available currently available. See the *Appendix of Resources*. The following is a review of one of the sources:

> Hair work and braiding at its height of sophistication is detailed in this republication of the 1875 edition. Much akin in technique to Kumi-Himo, these braids rely on openness and texture rather than color. Supplemented by material from Godey's Lady's Book from years 1850–1859. Should appeal to craft person, historian, jeweler and collector. —Mark Campbell, *Art of Hair Work: Hair Braiding and Jewelry of Sentiment*

✋ If you enjoy this type of craft, you may want to try making a small piece of jewelry for your mother.

Occupational
Education

17. ☞ It is assumed that Marilla goes to Diana's to borrow a skirt pattern for Anne. The fashion industry has changed the way skirts look throughout the years. To see some of the other changes in fashion, do some research online to find pictures of fashions from the Victorian era.

✋ After looking at some of the fashion of the day, choose whether you would like to sew a skirt from Anne's time period or one from our own time period.

Occupational
Education

18. 📖 Read about making and working with chocolate.

✋ Visit a chocolate factory.

Bible

19. In these chapters we see Marilla and Matthew both enjoying Anne and Anne's dreams coming true. Marilla, however, does not let this enjoyment distract her from correcting Anne's behavior and teaching her about such things as punctuality. Although Anne was not doing anything wrong while she was being tardy, Anne was tardy. Marilla kindly brings Anne back in line.

📖 Read Hebrews 12:1–12.

♡ Memorize Hebrews 12:4–8.

Thank God that you are His child and that he disciplines you.

Literature

20. 📖 With your instructor:
Reserve time every Friday throughout this Unit for recitation. Quote Hebrews 12:4–8 and other scriptures you have memorized.

🐚 Planning Guide

Gather These Items:
1. *Tales from Shakespeare* by Charles Lamb and Mary Lamb. Reissue ed. Puffin, 1995. ISBN 0140366776.

2. Ribbon to make a Scottish snood.

3. Peas to shell. (This is a seasonal activity.)

4. *American Dictionary of the English Language* (1828 Edition) by Noah Webster.

Research Topics:
1. Sir Walter Scott
   —<http://www2.sjsu.edu/depts/english/ten.htm>

   . . . .

2. *The Lady of the Lake* summary
   —Do a search online for *"The Lady of the Lake* Sir Walter Scott"
   —Look up a summary in the appropriate volume of *Masterplots,* which can be found in the reference section of most libraries

   . . . .

3. The song, "Hail to the Chief"
   —<http://lcweb2.loc.gov/cocoon/ihas/loc.natlib.ihas.200000009/default.html>

   . . . .

4. Capital punishment

   . . . .

Suggested Videos:
To understand Anne's affinity for the name "Cordelia," it is suggested students watch a video of the play, *King Lear.*

Suggested Field Trips:

Memory work:
Luke 9:62

Notes:

Assignments — Chapter XIV

Contract Reading: No new contract reading

Weekly
Quiet Time Reading Books:
Independent Project: Continue sewing skirt
Memory Work: Luke 9:62
Health: Continue your cardiovascular exercise program initiated in Unit 1, Chapter IV,
    Activity 9

	Literature	History	Bible	Health	Occu. Education	Fine Arts	Grammar & Writing
M	Read Chap. XIV AGG, Reading Comp.		#3				#1, #2
T	Vocab., #4				#9		#4
W	#5	#7			#6		#5, #7
Th	#10	#8					
F	#11 Recitation						

🐉 Study Guide

Read Chapter XIV
Reading Comprehension:

1. What did Anne see as one good thing about herself?

2. What block did Anne refer to on page 97?

3. What did Marilla think was worse than fits of temper?

4. Who was slow to lose faith in Anne?

5. Why did Marilla feel she could not go to Mrs. Lynde for advice?

6. What had happened to Marilla's brooch? Why did Anne confess?

Vocabulary:

🔑 Look up the vocabulary words in a dictionary or encyclopedia. Fill in the blanks using the vocabulary words.

7. The _____ was quick, insensitive, and turned my own words against me.

8. The dress the princess wore was _____.

9. The banquet was _____.

Vocabulary Words:

retort

scrumptious

sublime

🌿 Activities:

1. ✎ Write the following passage from dictation: "It's a fearful responsibility to have a child in your house you can't trust." —*Anne of Green Gables*, page 98	Dictation
2. What two contractions were used in this sentence? What two words were combined in each contraction to make one word?	Follow-up
3. On page 101, Marilla said, "I've put my hand to the plough and I won't look back." She was referring to the commitment of raising Anne. 📖 Read Luke 9:57–62. 👥 With your instructor: Discuss whether or not you think this quotation applies to the situation. ♡ Memorize Luke 9:62.	Bible

Literature

4. Anne frequently refers to Cordelia, who was the youngest of the king's three daughters in the play, *King Lear,* by William Shakespeare. At first King Lear thinks Cordelia is ungrateful to him because she refuses to flatter him as her sisters do; he soon finds out she is the only one of the three who genuinely cares for him. Perhaps by referring to this character, Anne is saying that given the chance, she will be a devoted daughter. Why do you think Anne refers to Cordelia?

📖 If you have time, read or watch this play. An alternative to reading the original work is to read *King Lear* in *Tales from Shakespeare.* Charles and Mary Lamb have written delightful short narratives of many of Shakespeare's most famous works, *King Lear* being one.

✏ Read pages 215–220 in *Writers INC.* Write a response to the play, *King Lear,* in the Literature section of your notebook.

💡 Literature

5. Anne mentioned she had read *The Lady of the Lake* by Sir Walter Scott. Published in 1810, this poem was an instant success, selling 25,000 copies in eight months. The adventurous plot, full characterization, and popularity quickly spawned at least three play productions. In 1812, a New York production of the poem used the music, "Hail to the Chief," from the British production. The Library of Congress has more information on the history of "Hail to the Chief."

📖 Although *The Lady of the Lake* was extremely popular in the 1800's, by today's standards it is a long and somewhat daunting poem. Prior to reading a difficult poem or story, it is helpful to have an overview of the main characters and the plot. Look online for an overview or summary of the poem. If you do not have online access, ask a parent for permission to use a computer at the library or at a friend's. You can also find a summary in a set of books called *Masterplots.* Libraries frequently have these books in their reference section. *Anne's Anthology* has what was included in the *Sixth Royal Reader* of the *The Lady of the Lake.* Sections of *The Lady of the Lake* are abridged in this version. Read Part I of this poem. The Internet has the complete poem online, if you would prefer to read that version.

✏ In the Literature section of your notebook, write each of the footnotes in Part I of *The Lady of the Lake.* Knowing these words will help you understand this poem as well as ones you read in the future.

Also look up the definition of **canto** under "Poetry Terms" in your *Writers INC.* Write this definition in your Literature notebook.

✏ In the Literature section of your notebook, write a one paragraph summary of the events in Part I. Copy your favorite line(s) from Part I onto your paper. My favorite lines are from Canto I, Stanza 31: "Sleep the sleep that knows not breaking, / Morn of toil nor night of waking."

6. Read this definition:

> **Snood:** a headband worn by maidens in Scotland to bind up the hair. The Scottish snood was a narrow circlet or ribbon fastened around the head and worn primarily by unmarried women, as a sign of chastity. The word "snood" used referring to a hairnet is a 20th century misunderstanding; a snood originally was a type of hair ribbon.

✋ Using plaid ribbon, make a Scottish headband.

Occupational Education

---

7. 📖 In *Writers INC,* read about "Viewing Web Sites" on page 453 and "Researching on the Net," pages 332–334. Also read pages 50 and 51, "A Closer Look at Prewriting" and "Forming Your Thesis Statement."

🗝 Read in the encyclopedia about Sir Walter Scott, his writing, and his life. Also do an online search for more information about this important author.

✎ In the History section of your notebook, in the appropriate time period: Write half a page about Sir Walter Scott and his work.

History

---

8. ✎ Answer these questions in the History section of your notebook:
   a. What type of capital punishment (if any) is used in your state? Alberta
   b. Which type of punishment seems the most humane?
   c. What crimes are punishable by the death penalty?
   d. According to the Bible, what crimes are punishable by death and what conditions have to be met before the death penalty is used?
   e. Find articles on capital punishment, at least one each for the pro and con arguments.

History

---

9. ✎ Shell peas. (This is a seasonal activity.) To save time, you can do this activity while watching *King Lear.*

Occupational Education

---

10. Anne mentions it was Marilla's duty to punish her. Duty was a common theme in Victorian literature. Read the definition of duty in Webster's 1828 *Dictionary*. Has the concept of duty changed over the years?

Literature

Read and discuss these quotes with your parent. Which one is your favorite and why?

> To do my duty in that state of life unto which it shall please God to call me. —*Book of Common Prayer*

> A brave endeavor
> To do thy duty, whate'er its worth,
> Is better than life with love forever
> And love is the sweetest thing on earth.
>
> —James Jeffrey Roche, "Sir Hugo's Choice"

For never anything can be amiss,
When simpleness and duty tender it.

—Shakespeare, *A Midsummer Night's Dream*

The eternal difference between right and wrong does not fluctuate. It is immutable. And if the moral order does not change, then it imposes on us obligations toward God and man. Duty, then, requires the willingness to accept responsibility and to sacrifice one's desires to a higher law. —Patrick Henry

With nations as with individuals our interests soundly calculated will ever be found inseparable from our moral duties.

—Thomas Jefferson

Fear God, and keep his commandments; for this is the whole duty of man. Ecclesiastes 12:13

Duty is ours; results are God's. —John Quincy Adams

Let us have faith that right makes might; and in that faith let us to the end, dare to do our duty as we understand it.

—Abraham Lincoln, Address at Cooper Union

Not once or twice in our rough-island story
The path of duty was the way to glory.

—Alfred Tennyson, "Ode on the Death of the Duke of Wellington"

There is no duty we so underrate as the duty of being happy. By being happy we sow anonymous benefits upon the world.

—Robert Louis Stevenson

Make it a point to do something every day that you don't want to do. This is the golden rule for acquiring the habit of doing your duty without pain. —Mark Twain

---

Literature   11. ✠ With your instructor:

Reserve time every Friday throughout this Unit for recitation. Pick your favorite part of a poem from this week's lesson. Read it aloud several times, utilizing as many reading tips as you know. Be sure to look up the pronunciation of any words you are reading of which you are unsure. After you have practiced and assembled your audience, give your recitation. Unless required by your teacher, it will not be necessary to memorize your poetry selection, but you should be familiar enough with the passage you do not stare at the page constantly.

Quote Hebrews 12:4–8; Luke 9:62; and other scriptures you have memorized.

❧ Planning Guide

Gather These Items

1. A "Pansy" book by Isabella Alden née MacDonald. This is an
   optional reading choice for a "B" or better grade in Contract
   Reading — Literature.
   —*A Christmas Surprise.* (Mantle Ministries)
   —*Ester Reid* (Mantle Ministries)

2. Spruce gum, the congealed sap of spruce trees. (Anne used this, but
   others have described it as horrible.)

3. "The Three Sillies"
   —Type "The Three Sillies" into your favorite online search engine.

4. Items to make a bead ring. Directions are included in the *Activity
   Appendix.*
   2–3 inches 18 gauge round wire
   2–3 inches 22–28 gauge round wire
   one or two beads
   wire cutters
   jeweler's files
   round nosed pliers
   flat nosed or bent nosed pliers
   rawhide hammer
   ring mandrel

5. *American Dictionary of the English Language* (1828 Edition) by
   Noah Webster.

Research Topics:

1. Cicero

. . . .

Suggested Field Trips:

1. Some bead shops give lessons. Check with your local bead shop to see if
   they have any interesting lessons.

Suggested Videos:

Memory Work:
Psalm 139:13–14

Notes:

Assignments — Chapter XV

Contract Reading

	A Grade	B Grade	C Grade
Bible			
History			
Literature	❏ Choice: "Pansy" book	❏ Choice: "Pansy" book	

Weekly
Quiet Time Reading Books: "Pansy" book
Independent Project:
Memory Work: Psalm 139:13–14
Health: Continue your cardiovascular exercise program initiated in Unit 1, Chapter IV,
  Activity 9

	Literature	History	Bible	Health	Occu. Education	Fine Arts	Grammar & Writing
M	Read Chap. XV AGG, Reading Comp.		#15				#1, #2
T	Vocab., #10	#13	#4, #14		#12		#10
W	#3, #11		#5				#3, #5, #6
Th	#7, #9		#8				#9
*F	#16 Recitation						

*On Friday, at the end of each Unit, review and take the Unit Quiz in the *Test Appendix*.

🦁 Study Guide

Read Chapter XV

Reading Comprehension:

1. How long is a generation?

2. Marilla responded sharply to Anne's description of her teacher. What was the tone of Anne's response? What does this tell about Anne? Think of other tones she could have used.

3. What positive physical characteristic did Anne have?

4. Tell about Gilbert Blythe. Why was he behind others that were his age in school?

5. What did Anne find a little humiliating?

6. What did Anne do wrong in school?

7. What was Anne's response to discipline?

8. What was one difference between Anne and Diana?

9. From whom did Marilla seek counsel?

10. What amazed Matthew?

11. Explain the saying: "If you must borrow trouble, for pity's sake borrow it handier home."

Vocabulary:

☞ Look up the vocabulary words in a dictionary or encyclopedia. Fill in the blanks using the vocabulary words.

12. The _____ reproduces by spores.

13. "He strides _____, and with haughty cries /
To single fight the fairy prince defies." —Tickell

14. "I could a tale unfold, whose lightest word /
Would _____ up thy soul." —Shakespeare

15. The _____ of Red Skelton had everyone laughing.

16. "I am _____ enough to repel force by force." —Dryden

Vocabulary Words:

drollery

indignant

vindictive

harrow

bracken

Extra Credit:

1. Harrow has two meanings. Use the other definition of "harrow" in a sentence.

2. ✍ Draw a spruce and a gum tree in your sketchbook or in the Fine Arts section of your notebook or show a photograph or professional sketch to your instructor.

3. The term "pick a chew" referred to spruce gum formed by the congealed sap of a spruce tree. If this is available in your area, you may want to try this treat.

🍂 Activities:

Dictation

1. ✎ Write the following passage from dictation:

Anne, starting out alone in the morning, went down Lover's Lane as far as the brook. Here Diana met her, and the two little girls went on up the lane under the leafy arch of maples—"maples are such sociable trees," said Anne; "they're always rustling and whispering to you," until they came to a rustic bridge. —*Anne of Green Gables,* page 106

☀ Follow-up

2. What inanimate object is personified in the dictation? Did you remember the apostrophe, showing possession, in "Lover's Lane"? Did you remember the apostrophe, showing a contracted word, in "they're"? The word "there" has two homophones, words that sound alike but mean something different. Name them. *See answer in Answer Appendix.*

✎ In the Vocabulary section of your notebook:
Write each homophone in the dictation and its correct usage. Also write any helpful clues. (For example: "There" contains the word "here," which refers to a place. "Their" contains "i" and "I" can own items.)

🔑 Read over pages 491–500 in *Writers INC.* Pick five sets of words which are particularly confusing for you. Write them down in your Literature notebook along with their explanation.

Did you capitalize the proper nouns?

🔑 If not, refer to page 477 in *Writers INC.*

🔑 If you missed the commas that set off the nonrestrictive clause, refer to page 459 in your handbook.

The long dashes are used to indicate a sudden break or change in the sentence.

Literature

3. 📖 Read *The Lady of the Lake,* Part II.

✎ In the Literature section of your notebook, write each of the footnotes in Part II. Remember this is from the *Sixth Royal Reader* and Anne and Gilbert are only in the *Fourth Royal Reader.*

✎ In the Literature section of your notebook, write a one paragraph summary of the events in Part II. Copy your favorite line(s) from Part II onto your paper. These are some of my favorites from the original, unabridged poem:

Some feelings are to mortals given
With less of earth in them than heaven.

—*The Lady of the Lake,* Canto II, Stanza 22

Like the dew on the mountain,
Like the foam on the river,
Like the bubble on the fountain,
Thou art gone, and forever!

—*The Lady of the Lake,* Canto II, Stanza 16

---

4. 📖 Using a concordance, read what the Bible says about winking and   Bible
the one who winks.

✎ In the Bible section of your notebook write:
   a. What you have learned, including the verses from which you learned
      these things.
   b. What does Anne think about Gilbert winking?

---

5. Anne's response to discipline is shame, anger, and humiliation. This   Bible
shows Anne is prideful. How does God feel about pride?

📖 Read Proverbs 6:16–17; Proverbs 8:13; Proverbs 16:5; Proverbs 21:4;
I Samuel 15:23; Psalm 5:5; and Psalm 101:5; 138:6.

The discipline Anne received does not cause her to admit her sin and
turn from it.

📖 Read Proverbs 9:8; Proverbs 12:1; Proverbs 13:10; and James 4:6.

Peace is just within reach.

📖 Read I John 1:9.

📖 Read Matthew 25:21. Anne says she will do anything for Diana, even
have her body "torn limb from limb," but she will not forgive Gilbert.
God wants us to be faithful in the little things of life even before He
expects the big things. It is a romantic notion, but if Anne cannot bring
her will into subjection to forgive Gilbert, how can she voluntarily
allow herself a torturous martyr's death? Pride is consumed with itself
and what it wants. It tends to its own needs before those of others.
Pride can be consumed with meeting the needs of others, such as being
willing to be torn limb from limb, but does so for self-centered reasons
like self-esteem and approval.

✎ After reading the above verses, write down your thoughts about them
in an informal journal fashion in the Bible section of your notebook.
How do these scriptures apply to what you are studying? An example
of a journalistic comment would be, "I Samuel 15:23 HEAVY! That was
my reaction on reading arrogance is like the evil of idolatry."

---

6. 🔑 Look up "pride" in the dictionary, preferably the *American Dictio-*   Writing
nary of the English Language, 1828 edition.

📖 Read pages 208–210 in *Writers INC,* "Essay of Definition."

✎ In the Bible section of your notebook:
Write a paragraph about pride using the dictionary definition of pride
and the Bible verses listed in Activity 5. (Parents, the "Assessment
Rubric" for grading this paper is on page 213.)

| Literature | 7. ⌐ Look up "Gilbert" and "Blythe" or "Blithe" in the dictionary and in a name book. What do they mean? From his name, what would you expect Gilbert to be like? |

| Bible | 8. 📖 When Anne refers to the "iron entering her soul" after her teacher spells her name without the "e," she is quoting Psalm 105, verse 18. Read this verse. Note: This verse reads differently in today's versions, even the King James Version. Anne's reference makes more sense if you know she is probably familiar with the translation in the *Common Psaltery* which reads, "Whose feet they hurt in the stocks: the iron entered into his soul." See the note in *The Annotated Anne of Green Gables* on page 168. |

| ☼ Literature | 9. 📖 The "Pansy" books were written by Isabella Alden, née Macdonald (1841–1930). She wrote about 120 books, mainly for girls. The books stress religion in action. Alden admires self-reliance and energy in her heroines. Read further about her from the *Background Information Appendix*. You may want to visit bookstores dealing in old and rare books to see if you can locate one of these books. Mantle Ministries has republished this author. This is an optional reading choice for a "B" or better grade in Contract Reading — Literature. |

📖 If this is your choice for reading in Literature, then read pages 215–220 in *Writers INC* when you are done.

✎ Write a journal entry giving your response to this novel in the Literature section of your notebook.

📖 Read what Montgomery has to say about the "Pansy" books in *The Green Gables Letters from L.M. Montgomery to Ephraim Weber 1905–1909*, page 67.

| Literature | 10. The title of this chapter, "Tempest in the School Teapot," is from the expression, "storm in a teapot," derived from the author, Cicero. |

📖 Read about Cicero and his works.

✎ In the History section of your notebook, in the appropriate time period: Write half a page about Cicero and his work.

| Literature | 11. 📖 The story of Anne being worried about Diana's marriage reminds me of one of my favorite stories, "The Three Sillies." This may be readily found online by typing "The Three Sillies" into a search engine. It is an English Fairy Tale. Enjoy! |

| Occupational Education | 12. ✋ Anne was able to wear a bead ring. Make a bead ring using the directions in the *Activity Appendix*. |

✋ Take lessons in beading or making jewelry with beads.

13. 📖 Although Anne and Gilbert are older, they are only in the *Fourth Royal Reader* book. Read "Education on P.E.I." in *The Annotated Anne of Green Gables,* pages 430–434.   History

 Discuss with your instructor the differences in education then and now.

14. 📖 Twice in this chapter, Anne mentions boys. First she sees herself as one with whom no one would want to be coupled. Later, she expands on this thought, concluding that Diana will marry and she will be left alone.   Bible

 Anne, however, likes the idea of love. She, too, has probably seen the "way of a man with a maiden." Read Proverbs 30:18. Finding a husband is in the hand and the timing of the Lord. Read Song of Solomon 2:7. Take time now to pray for faith to wait for God's timing. Realize your self-worth is not dependent on the interest, or lack of interest, of a young man.

 📖 Read Matthew 10:30–31; I Peter 3:4; and II Thessalonians 3:5.

15. Anne is complimented on her nose. Sometimes when we are complimented it makes us feel awkward. Remember to turn the compliment to God.   Bible

 ♡ Memorize Psalm 139:13–14. Thank Him for the way He made you.

16. With your instructor: Literature
 Reserve time every Friday throughout this Unit for recitation. Pick your favorite part of a poem from this week's lesson. Read it aloud several times, utilizing as many reading tips as you know. Be sure to look up the pronunciation of any words you are reading of which you are unsure. After you have practiced and assembled your audience, give your recitation. Unless required by your teacher, it will not be necessary to memorize your poetry selection, but you should be familiar enough with the passage you do not stare at the page constantly.

 Quote memorized scripture to your teacher: I Corinthians 10:13; The Lord's Prayer; Psalm 30; Hebrews 12:4–8; Luke 9:62; and Psalm 139:13–14.

17. Review and take Unit 3 Quiz in the *Test Appendix.*   Quiz

Unit 4
Chapters XVI – XIX

🎋 Planning Guide

Gather These Items:

1. Items for a tea party:
   tea and teapot
   recipe and ingredients to make raspberry cordial (See *Activity Appendix*)
   recipe and ingredients to make cake (Anne had fruitcake.)
   items to make place cards (See *Activity Appendix*)

2. Recipe and ingredients to make plum pudding and pudding sauce.
   —Internet (Check several recipes, there are quite an assortment)

3. Make chocolate mice for a centerpiece when serving the pudding sauce.
   (See *Activity Appendix*)

4. *The Hidden Art of Homemaking* by Edith Schaeffer. Tyndale House
   Publishers, 1985. ISBN 0842313982.

5. *The Way Home: Beyond Feminism, Back to Reality* by Mary Pride.
   Good News Publishers, 1985. ISBN 0-89107-345-0.

6. *In His Steps* by Charles Sheldon. Reprint ed. Fleming H. Revell Co.
   ISBN 0800786084. (Full text available at several different sites
   online.) This is a choice book for a "B" or better grade in Contract
   Reading — Bible.

Research Topics:

1. Catholic religious doctrine and religious order
   —Encyclopedia

. . . .

2. Protestant religious doctrine
   —Encyclopedia

. . . .

3. Teatime
   —Go to <www.cadroncreek.com> for a list of Internet sites to visit.

. . . .

4. The pros and cons of immunizations
—Information from the public health department (pro)
—"How to Make Wise Decisions About Immunizations." *Basic CARE Bulletin 17: Series One*. Medical Training Institute of America.
—"Journey Through God's Word Concerning Vaccinations" by Alan and Jill Bond. *Home School Digest: Simple Living; Simply Trusting* Volume 10: Number 2, pages 19–23.
—"Be Informed before Immunizing" by Michael Dye. *Back to the Garden* Spring/Summer 1999, Issue 18, pages 14–16.

6. Smallpox
—Internet
—<http://www.bt.cdc.gov/training/smallpoxvaccine/reactions/smallpox.html>
—<http://dermatology.about.com/cs/smallpox/a/smallpoxhx.htm>

Suggested Video:

1. *Outbreak*. Perf. Dustin Hoffman and Rene Russo. Warner Studios, 1999. ASIN 0790740265. R: View only with parental approval. Not all parents will approve of this.

2. 1945 Academy Award winning film, *The Lost Weekend*. Perf. Academy Award winner Ray Milland and Jane Wyman. Universal Studios, 2002. ASIN: 6301005740. NR

Suggested Field Trips:

1. If you are Protestant, attend a Catholic Church service. OR, if you are Catholic, attend a Protestant church service. (See Activity 8)

2. Schedule a visit with an infection control nurse at your local hospital. (See Activity 16)

3. Go to an old graveyard where many people are buried who died during a smallpox outbreak or other epidemic. (See Activity 16)

Group Activities:

1. Plan and have a tea party.

Bible Memory:

Titus 1:7–10

Notes:

Assignments — Chapter XVI

Contract Reading

	A Grade	B Grade	C Grade
Bible	❑ Choice: *In His Steps*	❑ Choice: *In His Steps*	
History			
Literature			

Weekly
Quiet Time Reading Books: *In His Steps*
Independent Project:
Memory Work: Titus 1:7–10
Health: Continue your cardiovascular exercise program initiated in Unit 1, Chapter IV, Activity 9

	Literature	History	Bible	Health	Occu. Education	Fine Arts	Grammar & Writing
M	Read Chap. XVI AGG, Reading Comp., #2		#13, #18				#1, #2
T	Vocab., #3		#7, #8 Field Trip				#3, #7
W			#5	#11, #12	#4		#5, #11
Th		#10	#9	#14, #15	#6		#9, #14
F	#19 Recitation			#16 Field Trip	#17		#16

❦ Study Guide

Read Chapter XVI

Reading Comprehension:

1. What sense was not developed in Marilla?

2. What two things happened because of Anne's inattentiveness while preparing and caring for food?

3. What did Anne believe God was incapable of doing?

4. What two changes are occurring in Marilla?

5. What did Matthew haul to the vessels? (Note: This is still a major export in the Maritimes.)

6. What made Mrs. Barry suspicious of Anne?

7. What fault did Marilla see in Diana?

Vocabulary Words:

aesthetic

addlepated

wont

cloister

mortifications

nun

pathetic

woe

prepense

Vocabulary:

☛ Look up the vocabulary words in a dictionary or encyclopedia. Fill in the blanks using the vocabulary words.

8. The _____ worked as a nurse in the Catholic hospital.

9. The political refugees were found hiding in the _____.

10. Researchers found that if a physician's office had an _____ appeal, the patients were calmer.

11. The _____ song moved the audience to tears.

12. In charity to all mankind, bearing no _____ or ill-will to any human being, and even compassionating those who hold in bondage their fellow-men, not knowing what they do.

—John Quincy Adams, Letter to A. Bronson, July 30, 1838

13. "It is one of the vexatious _____ of a studious man to have his thoughts disordered by a tedious visit." —L'Estrange

14. "They were _____ to speak in old time saying" II Samuel 20

15. "They weep each other's _____." —Pope

Extra credit:

✎ "Mortifications" has two other meanings besides the one used in the above sentence. Write a sentence for each of the other meanings.

 Activities:

1. ✎ Write the following passage from dictation: Dictation

> Beloved, do not avenge yourselves, but rather give place to
> wrath; for it is written,
>> "Vengeance is Mine, I will repay," says the Lord.
>> "Therefore if your enemy hungers, feed him;
>> If he thirsts, give him a drink;
>> For in doing so you will heap coals of fire on his head."
> Do not be overcome by evil, but overcome evil with good.
>
> Romans 12:19–21

2. It is all right if your formatting (the spacing of the words on the page)   Follow-up
is not identical to that of the dictation passage. The quotes are inset so
as to call attention to them. The quotation within this passage is from
the book of Proverbs.

✎ Circle any punctuation discrepancies in your dictation, then place
chronological numbering beside each mistake. Use *Writers INC* and
find the omitted rules of punctuation. At the bottom of your dictation
write the number and the missed rule.

3. 📖 Read *The Lady of the Lake,* Part III, from *Anne's Anthology.*   Literature

✎ In the Literature section of your notebook, write each of the footnotes
in Part III.

✎ In the Literature section of your notebook, write a one paragraph
summary of the plot of Part III of this poem.

4. What does Anne think about cooking? Unlike Anne, Lucy Montgomery   Occupational Education
the author said, "If I had not been a poor devil of an author I think I
would have made an excellent cook."

📖 Read Chapter 8 in *The Hidden Art of Homemaking* by Edith Schaeffer.

📖 Read Chapter 14 in *The Way Home* by Mary Pride.

✦ With your instructor, discuss what you learned from these readings
and what you think about the ideas presented.

5. On page 128 (*The Annotated Anne of Green Gables,* page 187), Anne   Bible
quotes a verse from "The Song of Deborah" in Judges 5. Reflecting on
this verse and the reference to Proverbs on page 126 (*The Annotated
Anne of Green Gables,* page 185), do you think Marilla is doing a good
job educating the "heathen orphan"?

📖 Read Judges 5. In this Chapter we see that Anne is increasing in the
knowledge of the Lord and of Scripture. We are to ". . . add to our faith,
virtue, and to virtue, knowledge." (See II Peter 1:2–8.)

📖 Read Proverbs 1:7; 2:3–6; and 9:10.

✎ In the Bible section of your notebook:

a. Write out the entire verse from which this phrase is excerpted: ". . . the stars in their courses fight against . . ."

b. Figuratively speaking, hot coals are heaped upon Anne's head. How? From what scripture does this phrase come? Bible commentators disagree on the meaning of this phrase. The New Geneva Bible says, "This (heaping coals) may lead to conversion or at least to such a sense of shame that evil behavior is modified." Other commentaries think that heaping coals is giving a recognized blessing. For instance, if your fire went out, you would go to your neighbor's house to obtain hot coals with which to restart your fire. These you would carry home in a pot on your head. It may also refer to something soothing like a heating pad for a headache. However, other commentators view hot coals on the head as something painful, but purifying, for the recipient. Write what you think this verse means.

c. Define "knowledge" according to the dictionary. Then incorporate scriptures into the definition of knowledge and how it is obtained. Conclude by writing about your knowledge of the Lord. Write at least one page.

📖 Read pages 53–54 of *The Green Gables Letters from L.M. Montgomery to Ephraim Weber 1905–1909*. What did Montgomery have to say about the Bible?

✎ You may wish to comment on her reflections and jot down your reactions to them in a journal type fashion in the Bible section of your notebook.

Occupational Education

6. 📖 Read *The Anne of Green Gables Treasury* pages 55–59 and page 76.

🖐 Go to <www.cadroncreek.com> for a link to assist you in planning a tea party.

🖐 Plan and have a tea party. Make a cake for the tea party as well as raspberry cordial. See the *Activity Appendix* for a raspberry cordial recipe and directions for a Pressed Flower Place Card.

Bible

7. 📖 Read about the doctrines of the Catholic and Protestant denominations. Study the history of the two churches. We have seen some of the political strife between these two religions through the life of John Bunyan. Begin your study by reading from an encyclopedia.

✎ In the Bible section of your notebook:

a. Write about the differences and the similarities between the two denominations.

b. Describe each church hierarchy.

With your instructor, compare the beliefs of both Catholics and Protestants to the Apostles' Creed. Note any similarities and differences, if any, in the beliefs of both denominations to the Apostles' Creed. (See the Apostles' Creed in Activity 18.)

Field Trip

8. 🖐 After you have done extensive research for Activity 7, attend a church service for the denomination that is different from your own. (If

you are a Protestant, attend a Catholic Church service; if Catholic, attend a Protestant service.)

✎ In the Bible section of your notebook write:
a. What are the differences between the services?
b. Are the churches different architecturally? How?

---

9. ⚷ In this chapter we see two Christians with different beliefs about drinking alcoholic beverages. Interview your parents and find out what they think about drinking and why. Use a Bible concordance and look up words such as wine, ale, and drunkard. What does Scripture say about this? Marilla was saving the wine for medicinal purposes. For what maladies does the Bible say wine can be used? | Bible

📖 Read pages 195–197 of *Writers INC*, "An Essay of Argumentation."

✎ In the Bible section of your notebook:
Write an essay of argumentation on the topic of drinking.

---

10. ⚷ For further study, you may want to investigate Prohibition. What laws are present in your state to control the drinking of alcoholic beverages? | History

---

11. ⚷ Although alcohol in moderation may have some positive side effects, it has a very ugly side. Look up about cirrhosis of the liver, pancreatitis, fetal alcohol syndrome, domestic abuse and alcohol, and delirium tremens. | ☼ Health

📖 Read pages 109–113 in *Writers INC* on expository essays.

✎ Write an expository essay about alcoholism. (Teachers, for grading, look at the "Assessment Rubric" on page 114.)

---

12. 👓 Watch the 1945 Academy Award winning film about alcoholism, *The Lost Weekend*, by Universal Studios and starring Academy Award winner Ray Milland. | Health

---

13. 📖 *In His Steps*, written in 1896 by Charles Sheldon, delves into some of the problems brought about by alcohol addiction and poverty. This is a choice book for a "B" or better grade in Contract Reading — Bible. It is available free online. | Bible

---

14. Anne was daydreaming about Diana having smallpox. Smallpox is a highly contagious, often fatal viral disease. The virus that causes the disease is present in the nose and throat of the infected person, in the blisters on his skin, and in his excretions throughout the course of the disease. Its most noticeable symptom is the appearance of blisters and pustules on the skin. The incubation period is generally 12 days, although it may vary from 7–21 days. The first symptoms of smallpox are severe headache, chills, and high fever. Children may suffer from vomiting and seizures. Within 3–4 days, a rash of small red pustules appears, first on the face, then on the arms, wrists, hands, and legs. In a day or two the spots become blisters and fill with clear fluid. Over | Health

the next week, the fluid turns into a yellowish, pus-like substance and begins to dry up, leaving a crust or scab on the skin. These scabs fall off after three to four weeks, leaving disfiguring pits in the skin, particularly on the face. There is no cure for smallpox. Smallpox has many of the same symptoms as the better known chicken pox, but everything is worse with smallpox. The scars are larger, the mortality rate higher, and the duration of the disease longer. Only the symptoms can be treated. Smallpox has become rare in most parts of the world because of widespread immunization. See if either of your parents have a smallpox vaccination scar. They no longer vaccinate for this disease in the United States because the risks incurred by immunization are greater than the risk of contracting the disease. In 2003, however, the government briefly vaccinated first responders due to a perceived threat of biological warfare during Operation Iraqi Freedom.

☞ Before there were immunizations, how did people attempt to stop the spread of smallpox? *See answer in Answer Appendix.*

📖 Research the pros and cons of immunization.

✎ In the Health section of your notebook:
Present both sides of the immunization debate.

Health   15. 👓 Other than AIDS, which is not nearly as infectious as smallpox, this generation has not seen widespread death from infections. The movie *Outbreak* is based on a hypothetical modern day infectious epidemic. It is very intense. If your parents approve, you may want to watch this movie. Notice what measures are taken to isolate those who are infected with the disease.

Health/   16. ✋ Arrange a visit with an infection control nurse at your local hospital.
Field Trip   Learn the different types of isolation used for patients with infectious diseases. What is universal infection control policy versus respiratory control policy? What different devices are used for infection control? What type of soap is used? What diseases require quarantine today? What special precautions are taken in the nursery or surgery to prevent the spread of disease? How can you apply what you learned to improve the health of your family? If you are interested in health care as a profession, you may want to ask the infection control nurse the questions on the Apprentice Worksheet. (The Worksheet may be found in the *Activity Appendix.*) For an extended field trip, ask to shadow the person for an hour or two as they perform their job. Permission for this may be more difficult to obtain.

✎ In the Health section of your notebook:
After the field trip, write a follow-up report as well as a thank you note. Be sure to include specifics from your conversations so the nurse will know you were listening and her time was appreciated.

✋ Go to an old graveyard where many people are buried who died during a smallpox outbreak or other epidemic.

17. ✋ Make plum pudding and pudding sauce. Serve it to your family and explain what happened to Marilla's plum pudding. Have a centerpiece with chocolate mice. (See *Activity Appendix* for chocolate mice recipes)

Occupational Education

---

18. ♡ Memorize Titus 1:7–10.

🕎 Bible

Tell your instructor how this verse describes what you have learned in this chapter.

The Apostles' Creed is a trustworthy message and has been taught through the ages. It was developed to refute apostasy.

> I believe in God, the Father Almighty,
>   the Creator of heaven and earth,
>   and in Jesus Christ, His only Son, our Lord:
>
> Who was conceived of the Holy Spirit,
>   born of the Virgin Mary,
>   suffered under Pontius Pilate,
>   was crucified, died, and was buried.
>
> He descended into hell.
>
> The third day He arose again from the dead.
>
> He ascended into heaven
>   and sits at the right hand of God the Father Almighty,
>   whence He shall come to judge the living and the dead.
>
> I believe in the Holy Spirit, the holy catholic* church,
>   the communion of saints,
>   the forgiveness of sins,
>   the resurrection of the body,
>   and life everlasting.
>
>   Amen.

*The word "catholic" refers not to the Roman Catholic Church, but to the universal church of the Lord Jesus Christ.

---

19. With your instructor:

Literature

Each Friday from now on during this Unit will be used for recitation. Pick your favorite part of the poem from this week's lesson. Read it aloud several times, utilizing as many tips as you know. Be sure to look up the pronunciation of any words of which you are unsure. After you have practiced and assembled your audience, give your recitation. Unless required by your teacher, it will not be necessary to memorize your poetry selection, but you should be familiar enough with the passage that you do not stare at the page constantly.

Quote memorized scripture to your teacher: I Corinthians 10:13; The Lord's Prayer; Psalm 30; and others from previous Chapters.

Planning Guide

Gather These Items:

1. Materials for props and costumes. (See Activity 4)

2. Floral catalog from which to cut a large picture of a flower to laminate. (See Activity 5)

3. Crochet thread and crochet hook or items for tatting and directions for making lace. (See Activity 6)

4. Items to make autograph books. (See Activity 12)
   —Internet search, "bookmaking"

5. Items for a casual afternoon tea. (See Activity 12)

Research Topics:

1. Jacques-Louis David and his artwork

. . . .

2. Geometry

. . . .

3. Euclid

. . . .

4. Lord Byron
   —<http://englishhistory.net/byron/images.html>
   —*A History of the English-Speaking Peoples: The Great Democracies*, Vol. 4, by Winston Churchill. Dodd Mead, 1958: pp 32, 70. ASIN 0396082718.

. . . .

Suggested Videos:

Suggested Field Trips:

Group Activities:

1. Plan and have a casual afternoon tea and autograph book signing.

Memory Work:

Proverbs 10:17

Notes:

Assignments — Chapter XVII

Contract Reading: No new contract reading

Weekly
Quiet Time Reading Books: *In His Steps*
Independent Project: Lace
Memory Work: Proverbs 10:17
Health: Continue your cardiovascular exercise program initiated in Unit 1, Chapter IV,
      Activity 9

	Literature	History	Bible	Health	Occu. Education	Fine Arts	Grammar & Writing
M	Read Chap. XVII AGG, Reading Comp.		#14			#5	#1, #2
T	Vocab., #3	#10	#13		#4		#3, #13
W		#7			#6	#9	#9
Th	#11	#8			#12		#11
F	#15 Recitation						

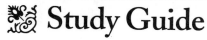 # Study Guide

Read Chapter XVII
Reading Comprehension:
 1. What did Diana say that surprised Anne?

 2. What had happened to Katie Maurice and Violetta?

 3. Had Mrs. Lynde been right about Anne staying out of school?

 4. What had the other students missed about Anne?

 5. What was Anne's relationship with Gilbert?

 6. Why did Anne progress despite a poor teacher?

 7. Why did Anne find it hard to stay sad?

Vocabulary Words:

stanchly*

muse

dolefully

effusion

ostentation

annexed

perquisites

tenacity

Vocabulary:

⚷ Look up the vocabulary words in a dictionary or encyclopedia. Fill in the blanks using the vocabulary words.

 8. Sir William Wallace fought for his rights with _____.

 9. In lieu of an annual salary he received _____.

10. We did not want our neighborhood to be _____ to the city, because then we could no longer have livestock.

11. "He knew that good and bountiful minds are sometimes inclined to _____." —Atterbury

12. Her lip quivered as she _____ replied.

13. "He was filled with admiration and deep _____ to hear of things so high and strange." —Milton

14. "For by grace are we saved" is an _____ of the Holy Spirit.

15. The widow _____ visited the grave of her husband on the anniversary of his death.

*Note: "stanchly" is spelled without a "u" here as that is the correct spelling for the Victorian Era.

 Activities:

Dictation   1. ✎ Write the following passage from dictation: (Note: The instructor needs to identify for the student when each new line begins.)

> And Santa Croce wants their mighty dust;
> Yet for this want more noted, as of yore
> The Caesar's pageant, shorn of Brutus' bust,
> Did but of Rome's best son remind her more:
> Happier Ravenna! on thy hoary shore,

Fortress of falling empire! honour'd sleeps
The immortal exile;—Arqua, too, her store
Of tuneful relics proudly claims and keeps,
While Florence vainly begs her banish'd dead and weeps.

—Lord Byron, *Childe Harold's Pilgrimage*, Canto IV, Stanza 59

2. Did you correctly punctuate the three possessive words? Explain why the apostrophe is prior to the "s" in Caesar, but after the "s" in Brutus. If you do not know the rule, copy it from *Writers INC*. Notice the new line is capitalized although it is still part of the same sentence. This is the format of most traditional poetry.	Follow-up
3. 📖 Read *The Lady of the Lake*, Part IV, from *Anne's Anthology*. ✎ In the Literature section of your notebook, write each of the footnotes in Part III. 📖 Read pages 174–177 of *Writers INC*. ✎ The poem, *The Lady of the Lake*, inspired several plays. Take your favorite part of the poem and write dialogue for at least two people. The dialogue should last 2–5 minutes only. Use as much of the original dialogue as you want or you can update the language.	Literature
4. ✋ Make simple costumes and props for the skit you have written and present it. Have fun!	Occupational Education
5. ✋ Make a desk decoration like the one Ella May gives Anne on page 133 (*The Annotated Anne of Green Gables*, page 194). Finish it with contact paper or laminate it to make it last longer.	Fine Arts
6. ✋ Learn how to make lace by tatting or crocheting. Use it to trim an apron, socks, or pillowcases.	Occupational Education
7. 📖 It was said Anne met her Waterloo. Anne learned about Napoleon and Waterloo at school. The *Sixth McGuffey's Reader* has a poem by Lord Byron which is called, "Battle of Waterloo." It is actually an excerpt from *Childe Harold's Pilgrimage*, Canto III, Stanzas XXI, XXII, XXIV, XXVI, XXVII, and XXVIII. Read these stanzas in *Anne's Anthology*. With your instructor, discuss reasons you think *McGuffey's* left out stanzas XXIII and XXV of Byron's poem.	History
8. 📖 Read in the *Background Information Appendix* about the "The Character of Napoleon Bonaparte." This oratory was in the *Sixth McGuffey's Reader* of Anne's day. ✎ Circle any of the words for which you do not know either the pronunciation or the meaning. Learn these words, writing them in the Literature section of your notebook. Work on this piece for Friday's recitation.	History

Fine Arts   9.   🔑 The oration on Napoleon mentions Jacques-Louis David, French Neoclassical painter, 1748–1825. He was best known as the court painter of Napoleon. One of my favorite paintings of his is "Bonaparte Crossing the Alps." Find this painting and read about this interesting artist and his work. Warning: A few of his paintings contain nudity or partial nudity. Please have your parent do a preview.

   ✏️ Write a one-half page summary about Jacques-Louis David and his work. Include a copy of your favorite painting and a brief explanation of the painting and why you like it. If you have a computer, you may want to have the painting as a background on your desktop for awhile.

Math   10. 🔑 If your math book has a geometry section, begin it now. Or do a cursory examination of geometry by reading about it in an encyclopedia.

Literature   11. According to *The Annotated Anne of Green Gables,* page 459:

> The English poets perform a function somewhat different from American ones in *Anne.* If allusions to American poets evoke moral sympathy and quiet effort, allusions to English poets draw vivid representations of triumph and disaster.

The English poets Byron and Scott were among Montgomery's favorite poets. On page 134 (*The Annotated Anne of Green Gables,* page 195), while Anne and Diana are forbidden to see each other, Montgomery uses a quote from Byron's *Childe Harold's Pilgrimage,* Canto IV, Stanza 59, to underscore how disastrous this separation is for the girls.

   📖 Today's dictation is taken from Canto IV of *Childe Harold's Pilgrimage* by Lord Byron. The word, "Childe," is the ancient term for a young noble awaiting knighthood. Byron's poem, however, is not about a gallant knight on a lofty pilgrimage. Rather, his poem is a travelogue, narrated by a melancholy, passionate, well-read, and eloquent tourist. The first two Cantos were written while Byron was on tour in Spain, Portugal, Albania and Greece. He published them in 1812 and immediately became famous. Canto III, published in 1816, relates travels through Belgium, up the Rhine, and to Switzerland and the Alps. Canto IV, published in 1818, describes the great cities and monuments of Italy. In the first three Cantos, Byron insisted the narrator, Childe Harold, was a fictitious character. The world insisted on identifying the character of the protagonist with Byron, so in Canto IV he abandons the third person and speaks out with the first person voice. According to *The Norton Anthology of English Literature,* page 491:

> . . . the result is like seeing Europe by flashes of lightning, for everything is presented not as it is in itself but as it affects the violent sensibility, the Romantic Man of Feeling. It turns a tourist's record of scenes into a dramatic and passionate experience by using shock tactics of apostrophes, exclamations, hyperbole, and abrupt changes in subject, pace, and mood.

Byron had a great reputation as a poet during his life time. He lived from 1788 to1824. In religion, he was a skeptic. Throughout his short life he practiced the pursuit of temporary pleasures. He was handsome; married only once, had a child out of wedlock, and had many sexual partners. Some of his writings helped kindle European enthusiasm for Greek classical revival and, in turn, the Greek political cause. Because of this, as well as his exhaustion and boredom with promiscuity, Byron organized and led an expedition to assist the Greeks in their war of independence from the Turks. While fighting for this cause, Byron died after a series of feverish attacks and just after his thirty-sixth birthday. This man, who lived by an Epicurean philosophy, died defending the society with an Epicurean history.

✎   In the History section of your notebook:
  a. Write a definition of Epicureanism.
  b. Read more about George Gordon, Lord Byron, and write a brief biography. Be sure to include his political leanings.

---

12. ✋ Make an autograph book for yourself and a few for your friends. Ask your friends to memorize a favorite friendship or autograph verse from the past. Invite your friends over for a tea and to exchange autograph verses. There is an example of this type of verse in this chapter of *Anne* and one in chapter XVIII.
 | Occupational Education

> When twilight drops her curtain down
> And pins it with a star
> Remember that you have a friend
> Though she may wander far.
>
> *—The Annotated Anne of Green Gables,* page 194

> If you love me as I love you
> Nothing but death can part us two.
>
> *—The Annotated Anne of Green Gables,* page 209

---

13. 📖 When Anne returns to school, many people give her gifts. Read Proverbs 19:6. | Bible

✎   In the Bible section of your notebook, write your thoughts about this verse and how you think it relates to Anne's experience upon returning to school.

---

14. Diana is obedient to her mother. She appeals to her mother, but she does not disobey her mother. Anne understands and respects this. | Bible

📖 Read Deuteronomy 5:16 and Colossians 3:20. Does Colossians 3:20 have any qualifier, such as obeying parents only when they are right? The first chapter of Romans talks about the depravity of man. In Romans 1:30 it lists "disobey their parents" as an example of man's depravity. Both Anne and Diana strove to do the right thing.

Read Proverbs 10:17 and Proverbs 28:10. Have you ever been guilty of encouraging someone to disobey their parents? If so ask God for forgiveness.

✎ In the Bible section of your notebook, write your thoughts about this subject.

♡ Memorize Proverbs 10:17.

Literature   15. ❀ With your instructor:

Continue with recitation each Friday during this Unit. Recite the oratory discussed in Activity 8 of this Chapter, "The Character of Napoleon Bonaparte." Pick your favorite poem or part of a poem from this week's lesson to recite.

Quote memorized scriptures to your teacher: Proverbs 29:22; Hebrews 12:4–8; Luke 9:62; Psalm 139:13–14; Titus 1:7–10; and Proverbs 10:17.

Planning Guide

Gather These Items:

1. Items to make taffy.

2. *Are You Liberal? Conservative? or Confused?* by Rick Maybury, Richard J. Maybury, and Jane A. Williams. Bluestocking Press, 1995. ISBN 0942617231. This book is for a "B" or better grade in Contract Reading — History.

3. "Across My Desk" by Mary Pride. *Practical Homeschooling* Volume 18:16. (See Activity 10)

4. Canning jars, directions, and other items to make plum preserves or other favorite jelly.

5. Items to make orange biscuits.
   —For recipes, see the Internet
   —*Aunt Maud's Recipe Book: From the Kitchen of L.M. Montgomery* by L.M. Montgomery, Elaine Crawford with Kelly Crawford and Eline Crawford. Moulin Publishers, 1997. ISBN 1896867014.

6. Items to trim socks: crochet thread, crochet hook, and a pair of cuff socks.
   —For directions, see a crochet book or the Internet

7. Items for China painting (See *Appendix of Resources*)
   —real china, paints, pattern
   —Creativity for Kids Activity Kit: Paint and Pretend Mini Tea Set

Research Topics:

1. James V

2. Felicia Dorothea Hemans

3. Canadian Premier

4. Woman's suffrage
   —<http://www.pbs.org/stantonanthony/wherearewe/index.html?body=women_politics.html>

—<http://www.archives.gov/digital_classroom/lessons/woman_suffrage/woman_suffrage.html>
—<http://www.rochester.edu/SBA/history.html>

. . . .

5. Voting records of Congress and state legislatures

. . . .

6. Ottawa

. . . .

7. Victorian china patterns

. . . .

8. Robert Lewis Dabney
—<http://www.pointsouth.com/csanet/greatmen/dabney/dab-bio.htm>

. . . .

Suggested Videos:

Not For Ourselves Alone: The Story of Elizabeth Cady Stanton and Susan B. Anthony. Videocassette. PBS. The PBS Web site listed below has extensive video clips of this video.
—<http://www.pbs.org/stantonanthony/wherearewe/index.html?body=women_politics.html>

Suggested Field Trips:

1. Attend a political rally. (See Activity 9)

2. Go to an antique shop to look at Victorian china patterns. (See Activity 20)

3. As an optional activity, take china painting lessons. (See Activity 20)

Group Activities:

1. Make taffy with some friends. (See Activity 7)

Memory Work:

Choose either Ephesians 3:20; Proverbs 17:27–28; or James 3:13, 17 (See Activity 5)

Notes:

Assignments — Chapter XVIII

Contract Reading

	A Grade	B Grade	C Grade
Bible			
History	❏ *Are You Liberal? Conservative? or Confused?*	❏ *Are You Liberal? Conservative? or Confused?*	❏ *Are You Liberal? Conservative? or Confused?*
Literature			

Weekly

Quiet Time Reading Books: *Are You Liberal? Conservative? or Confused?*
Independent Project: Trim a pair of socks
Memory Work: Ephesians 3:20; Proverbs 17:27–28; or James 3:13, 17
Health: Continue your cardiovascular exercise program initiated in Unit 1, Chapter IV,
   Activity 9
Since there are a number of Activities in this Chapter which require research and writing, the assignment schedule is extended an additional week.

	Literature	History	Bible	Health	Occu. Education	Fine Arts	Grammar & Writing
M	Read Chap. XVIII AGG, Reading Comp., #2		#5				#1, #2
T	Vocab.	#10	#14	#6			#3, #10
W	#19	#4					#4
Th		#8			#11		#8
F		#9 Field Trip			#7		
M	#12				#20		#12
T	#15		#13		#21		#13
W		#16					
Th		#17, #18					#18
F	#22 Recitation				#20 Field Trip		

✾ Study Guide

Read Chapter XVIII
Reading Comprehenson:

1. What kept Anne studying diligently instead of reading the book she wanted to read?

2. What made the roads red?

3. What was Ruby Gillis' idea of courting? What do you think about it?

4. What was Anne's approach to resisting temptation?

5. How did Anne heap coals of fire on Mrs. Barry's head?

6. Anne was not the only person up all night; Matthew was as well. What did he offer to do for Anne?

7. Notice once again how Montgomery points out the value of children. Anne, herself a child, saved a child's life. Matthew drove all over the country looking for a doctor for Minnie May. At the same time, what did Anne note about how adults typically treated her?

Vocabulary Words:

russets

buxom

indulgently

Vocabulary:

☞ Look up the vocabulary words in a dictionary or encyclopedia. Fill in the blanks using the vocabulary words.

8. The _____ girl sometimes had trouble finding a dress that fit comfortably.

9. The _____ were a blessing to the poor family.

10. "You may stay up till ten," her mother said _____.

Note: In the story, Anne went to the cellar to get russets to eat. Russets in Canada are a round apple about the size of a large plum with a textured peel. Their name is derived from their reddish brown color.

 Activities:

Dictation   1. ✎ Write the following passage from dictation:

> "Oh, Matthew, isn't it a wonderful morning? The world looks like something God had just imagined for His own pleasure, doesn't it? The trees look as if I could blow them away with a breath—pouf! I'm so glad I live in a world where there are white frosts, aren't you? And I'm so glad Mrs. Hammond had three pairs of twins after all. If she hadn't I mightn't have known what to do for Minnie May. I'm real sorry I was ever cross with Mrs. Hammond for having twins."

—Anne of Green Gables, page 144

2. 📖 Read pages 77, 82, and 522–523 in *Writers INC*. With what part of speech does each sentence begin? Is there variety in the length of Mrs. Montgomery's sentences? What different types of sentences are used in this part of the paragraph?

   Onomatopoeia is the use of a word the sound of which suggests its meaning. Write "onomatopoeia" under your dictation writing and give examples of this term. Find them in the above dictation paragraph.

   Once again the flow of the paragraph gives a conversational feel, rather than one that strictly follows a topic sentence.

   ✎ Circle any punctuation discrepancies. Then place chronological numbering beside any mistakes. Use *Writers INC* and find the omitted rule of punctuation. At the bottom of your dictation write the number and the missed rule.

   Follow-up

---

3. Pick one of your essays where the sentences lack variety. Rewrite your essay using the skills learned in *Writers INC* to improve the variety in your sentences.

   Literature

---

4. From the footnotes in *Anne's Anthology,* we have learned that the main character of *The Lady of the Lake* is James V.

   📖 Read further about James V.

   ✎ In the History section of your notebook, in the appropriate time period: Write a half page summary about James V. Utilize sentence variety techniques learned in the "Follow-up" exercise.

   ☀ History

---

5. Anne does not think God is capable of changing Mrs. Barry's mind. What does Anne learn about God through the situation with Mrs. Barry?

   📖 Read **Ephesians 3:20**. Is there a time in your life that you have experienced the truth of this verse?

   📖 Read Romans 8:28. How does this verse apply to Anne's situation?

   📖 Read Proverbs 12:18 and **Proverbs 17:27–28**. Anne also is careful in her reply to Mrs. Barry.

   Not only is Anne up all night, so too is Matthew. Yet he does his chores as well as Anne's without complaint and with a humble heart.

   📖 Read Matthew 16:24; Philippians 2:3–9; and **James 3:13, 17**.

   ♡ Choose one of the scriptures in bold to memorize.

   Bible

---

6. Croup is not a disease in itself, but a group of symptoms of varied origin. It can originate from an allergy, foreign object obstruction, infection, or a tumor. Croup has the following general characteristics:

   1. Obstruction of the upper respiratory tract, usually at the level of the larynx or just below the trachea. In a book of human anatomy, identify these parts.
   2. Hoarseness.

   ☀ Health

3. A resonant cough, usually described as "barking."
4. A croaking sound, called stridor, during respiration.

A typical attack of croup usually begins at night and is often precipitated by exposure to cold air. The onset is sudden, with a hoarse, "croupy" voice or cough, and with what seems like difficult breathing. Spasms of choking that seem close to strangulation follow. With today's medical treatment croup is rarely fatal.

To care for one suffering from croup, warm moist air should be provided by heating water on a stove or using a vaporizer. High humidity liquefies the secretions and reduces the spasms of the laryngeal muscle. A cool mist vaporization, unavailable in Anne's day, would have been preferable for those patients with a fever. While providing an atmosphere of high humidity, it is important to keep the patient dry and comfortable and prevent chilling. A calm presence helps the child relax.

What is syrup of ipecac? The main use for syrup of ipecac is for emergency use in poisoning. It is a medicine that can be purchased in any pharmacy without a prescription which, when given to a child or an adult, will cause vomiting. An emetic, such as syrup of ipecac, may reduce laryngeal spasms. Give water after the syrup. Syrup of ipecac induces vomiting within 30 minutes in 90% of patients; the average time is less than 20 minutes. Sometimes small portions of the intestinal wall may be seen in the emesis. SYRUP OF IPECAC MUST NEVER BE USED BEFORE CALLING YOUR FAMILY PHYSICIAN OR THE POISON CONTROL CENTER.

Note: In a new policy statement, "Poison Treatment in the Home," the American Academy of Pediatrics (AAP) recommends that syrup of ipecac no longer be used routinely as a home treatment strategy. Until recently, the AAP advised that parents keep a 1-ounce bottle of syrup of ipecac in the home to induce vomiting if it was feared a child had swallowed a poisonous substance. For more about syrup of ipecac, see the *Background Information Appendix*.

With your instructor:
Determine if you have syrup of ipecac in your home. If so, identify the location in your house and review the indications and directions for administration for this medicine.

Look up the number for the Poison Control Center in your area and write it an emergency number list.

Occupational Education	7. Invite friends over and make taffy. There is a recipe for taffy on page 209 of *The Annotated Anne of Green Gables*.
History	8. The First Minister of the Crown is a term still used for the head of the Canadian government. The Prime Minister referred to in this chapter is probably Sir John A. MacDonald (1815–1891), who twice served as Conservative Prime Minister (1867–1873, 1878–1891). MacDonald did visit Prince Edward Island in 1890, but would not have chosen to do so

in the winter because of the danger of having the Strait freeze and not being able to get out. Most English speaking people on the island would have been on the Premier's side politically. Marilla's reference to the Premier's nose reinforces the idea that they were referring to Mr. MacDonald. His nose was famous and prominent in character.

📖 On the Internet, read about some of Sir John MacDonald's policies.

✎ In the History section of your notebook write:
   a. What is a Canadian ~~Premier~~? *Prime Minister*
   b. For what is the Canadian city of Ottawa known?
   c. Write about Sir John MacDonald's policies.

9. ✋ Attend a political rally or a town meeting with a local legislator.	Field Trip

10. 📖 Read *Are You Liberal? Conservative? or Confused?* by Rick and Richard Maybury. An additional source is an article by Mary Pride titled, "Across My Desk," *Practical Homeschooling,* Volume 18:16.	History

✎ In the History section of your notebook:
   a. Write an article explaining why you are a conservative or a liberal.
   b. If you have questions left unanswered when you have finished reading the Mayburys' book, write them a letter. Send it after both you and your instructor have proofread it.

11. ✋ Marilla serves Anne plum preserves. She had probably made them with Anne. Make plum preserves or some other type of jam or jelly. Montgomery thought an orange biscuit served with plum preserves a special treat. Make orange biscuits.	Occupational Education

12. Anne says, when she gives the last drop of ipecac, "This is the last lingering hope and I fear 'tis a vain one." This is a quote from the poem, *The Siege of Valencia.*	Literature

📖 Read *The Siege of Valencia* by Felicia Dorothea Hemans. How does the line from this poem quoted in the text relate to both the story and the poem?

Felicia Dorothea Hemans has the distinction of having achieved wider recognition and popularity among her contemporaries than any other woman poet in the English language. She had five sons between 1812 and 1818. Following the birth of the last son, her husband separated from her and went to Rome until after her death. Felicia supported herself and children from the writing of her poetry. Some literary contemporaries did not take her seriously as a poet or dramatist. She drew most of her inspiration from the Enlightenment and therefore her poetry was closer to Pope and Cowper than to that of her contemporaries, Wordsworth, Byron, Scott, and Shelley. Neatness and polish of the verse and clarity of syntax and diction are attributes of this inspiration. Her poetry does not reflect the struggle of self-discovery that characterizes poems of growth such as *Childe Harold* by Lord Byron.

📖 Read more about this author.

✎ In the History section of your notebook, in the appropriate time period: Write a brief biography of Felicia Hemans.

Bible   13. Maturity is characterized by three elements: self-control, wisdom, and responsibility. We see in this chapter Anne shows self-control by not reading the book she desperately wants to. According to II Peter 1:2–8, we are to add ". . . to knowledge, self-control."

✎ In the Bible section of your notebook:
Define self-control according to the dictionary. Incorporate scriptures about self-control and how to improve one's self-control in your definition. Conclude by writing about a time in which you demonstrated self-control.

Bible   14. 📖 Anne is not a fair-weather friend. Diana is blessed to have a friend like Anne. Read Proverbs 17:17 and Ecclesiastes 4:10. Being a good friend can be an important task. Frequently our friends are people who we enjoy being around. There are times, however, when these same people may need us around and it will not be fun.

☀ **Literature**   15. 📖 Read "Woman's Rights" in the *Background Information Appendix*. This article, from the time period, is a response to the woman's rights movement. It is from *Godey's,* which was one of the most popular lady's magazines of the century. Each issue contained poetry, beautiful engraving, fashion illustrations, and articles by some of the most well known authors in America.

✖ Discuss this article with your instructor.

☀ **History**   16. Robert Lewis Dabney was born March 5, 1820 and died on Monday, January 3, 1898. He was a Presbyterian of the Old School. Because he was not only a contemporary, but also a Presbyterian, it is likely Montgomery had read some of Dabney's writings. At the very least, she was aware of the controversy in the Presbyterian Church about woman's suffrage.

As a preacher, Dabney was in a league of his own. It was said his sermons were crammed full of thought.

> His speeches in the courts of the church were always weighty in logic—and on occasions when he deemed the truth or the church to be in danger from the policy or intrigue of mistaken men, the torrent of argument and passion flowed, fused like the iron and the white heat from the crucible of a furnace.
> He was a Calvinist. His biographer says of him, ". . . he was not only a Calvinist in name, but in fact, that he knew why he was a Calvinist."

—John Thomas Cripps, "A Biography of R. L. Dabney," A Lecture given November 1994 anno Domini

During the Civil War he was Jackson's adjutant as well as a chaplain and a soldier. One of Jackson's officers remarked on how Dabney filled these roles: "The parson isn't scared of Yankee bullets and he preaches like hell." Most importantly, he was a mighty man of God and a mighty preacher of the Gospel.

After the Civil War, Dabney was a seminary professor. During this time he continued his battle against northern ideals with his pen. His words were spoken about and quoted. He wrote, "It is only the atheist who adopts success as the criterion of right." He also wrote a prophetic article entitled "Women's Rights Women." Read some excerpts of this article in the *Background Information Appendix*.

Discuss these questions with your parent:
1. What did Dabney say about Conservatisim?
2. Where did he think the woman's suffrage movement would lead?

17. Watch the PBS video, *Not For Ourselves Alone: The Story of Elizabeth Cady Stanton and Susan B. Anthony*.   History

With your instructor:
Discuss the reasons given in the video for women wanting the right to vote.
Video: The Canadians: Emily Murphy

18. At this point in history, women were not allowed to vote in either Canada or America. Study about the movement to give women the right to vote in your country. (In America the woman's suffrage movement culminated in the passage of the Nineteenth Amendment. Mothers, wives, or sisters of men in active duty obtained the right to vote in Canada in 1917.) Present the information you have learned as an oral report. Use visual aids.   History

In *These Happy Golden Years* by Laura Ingalls Wilder, Mrs. McKee felt giving women the right to vote would end anti-family policies. This has not proved true, as is seen by the legalization of abortion, anti-homeschooling laws, child care tax credits to accredited agencies, taxing married couples at a higher rate, etc. It is interesting to note that both Mrs. Lynde in Canada and Mrs. McKee in America shared many of the same opinions. Both pre-teen Anne and teen Laura noted their opinions.

Research the voting record of Congress or your state legislature on a family issue which is important to you, e.g. abortion, child care tax credit versus dependent tax credit, homosexual rights. Did males and females vote differently? If so, which group best represented your viewpoint?

In the History section of your notebook, write:
a. The findings of your research.
b. Do you think Dabney's futuristic conclusions were correct? Why or why not?

Literature	19. ☞ From *Writers INC,* read page 239 on **point of view**. Now reread the first page of *Anne of Green Gables*. What point of view does Montgomery use?

Occupational Education	20. ✋ Mrs. Barry serves Anne on her best china. Go to an antique store to look at Victorian china patterns. If you were Mrs. Barry, which pattern would you choose?

Victorian china painting reached its peak during the Victorian Era primarily because the chief art forms available and acceptable for women were needlework and china painting. Boat loads of white porcelain and china would arrive in the New World from Europe and the Orient, at which time ladies would pick a pattern and start to work. Often they used the same kiln that made the bricks for their homes.

📖 From books or the Internet, read about china painting.

✋ If this is something you would like to try, there are several classes and books listed on the Internet. Perhaps there is a class in your area.

Occupational Education	21. ✋ Diana teaches Anne a new crochet stitch which they are not to share with anyone. Frequently clothing was embellished by crocheting. Trim a pair of socks for yourself or as a gift.

Literature	22. ✠ With your instructor:

Continue with recitation each Friday during this Unit. Pick a favorite poem or part of a poem from this week's lesson to recite.

Quote memorized scriptures to your teacher. Choose either Ephesians 3:20; Proverbs 1:27–28; or James 3:13, 17.

⚜ Planning Guide

Gather These Items:

1. Clear contact paper or laminate for making a bookmark. (See Activity 8)

2. Items to make a fresco. (See Activity 9)
   plaster
   powdered tempera paint
   eggs
   Masonite or wood

3. Knitting needles, yarn, and instructions or an instruction book for learning how to knit. (See Activity 11)

4. Flip board. (See Activity 14)

5. Dictionary of quotes or other reference in which you can look up quotations and the origins of quotations. (See Activity 7)
   —Go to <www.cadroncreek.com> for a list of Internet sites to visit.

Research Topics:

1. Sir Walter Scott's writing style

. . . .

2. Oliver Cromwell

. . . .

3. Fresco painting

. . . .

4. Pompadour hairstyle directions
   —<www.flinc.net/vell/articlehair.htm>
   —<www.erasofelegance.com/hairstyles.html>
   —<www.geocities.com/rockhog.geo/hairstyles.html>
   —*Hairstyles and Headdresses of the Victorian, Edwardian, and Ragtime Eras.* Vintage Victorian, 2001.
   —*Victorian & Edwardian Beauty: Hairstyles and Beauty Preparations,* Vintage Living Series, by Daniela Turudich. Streamline Press, 2003. ISBN 193006411X.

. . . .

5. Heliograph

. . . .

Suggested Videos:

1. *Brother Against Brother—The English Civil War.* Videocassette. Kultur Video, 2001. NR*

[handwritten: epl.ca ?] 2. *Cromwell.* Videocassette. Columbia/Tristar Studios, 1998. Rated G*

[handwritten: w/Richard Harris, Alec Guinness 1987]

Suggested Field Trips:

1. Visit an elderly lady with whom a kindred spirit relationship may develop. (See Activity 6)

Group Activities:

1. Have a friend spend the night. (See Activity 10)

2. Go on a sleigh ride.

Memory Work:

Proverbs 14:24

Notes:

*I have not personally seen this.

Assignments — Chapter XIX

Contract Reading: No new contract reading

Weekly
Quiet Time Reading Books: *Are You Liberal? Conservative? or Confused?*
Independent Project: Knitting project
Memory Work: Proverbs 14:24
Health: Continue your cardiovascular exercise program initiated in Unit 1, Chapter IV,
   Activity 9

	Literature	History	Bible	Health	Occu. Education	Fine Arts	Grammar & Writing
M	Read Chap. XIX AGG, Reading Comp., #2				#6 Field Trip		#1, #2
T	Vocab., #3	#4	#12		#11	#9	#4, #5
W	#7		#8		#8	#9	
Th	#14	#13				#14	
*F	#15 Field Trip, #16 Recitation				#10 Field Trip		

*On Friday, at the end of each Unit, review and take the Unit Quiz in the *Test Appendix.*

🐉 Study Guide

Read Chapter XIX

Reading Comprehension:

1. What did Anne use to clean the floor?

2. What did Anne want to do? What were Marilla's objections to this?

3. How did Anne do in school the day of the concert?

4. Why did Carrie Sloan cry?

5. How did Anne conquer her jealousy of Diana's clothes?

6. What was Anne's response to Gilbert when he quoted one of her favorite poems?

7. What happened after the concert at the Barry's? What were the repercussions from it?

8. After talking to Mrs. Lynde, what did Anne do?

Vocabulary Words:

moral

crescendo

pompadour

valise

mortal

sagely

pensive

dire

contrite

Vocabulary:

🔑 Look up the vocabulary words in a dictionary or encyclopedia. Fill in the blanks using the vocabulary words.

9. "A broken and _____ heart, O God, thou wilt not despise."

Psalm 51

10. "The _____ is the first business of the poet." —Dryden

11. "Of that forbidden tree whose _____ taste /
Brought death into the world, and all our woe." —Milton

12. The grandmother _____ gave advice to her granddaughter.

13. "_____ was the tossing, deep the groans." —Milton

14. All paragraphs should be structured as a _____ rising to a climactic last sentence.

15. The _____ was made more distinguished by adding ringlets by the face.

16. Seeing the depth of her despair, he grew _____.

17. You should be able to pack for overnight in the _____.

Extra Credit:

✋ Demonstrate crescendo on a musical instrument.

✎ Write the dictionary pronunciation of "crescendo," then pronounce it correctly aloud to your instructor.

Activities:

1. ✎ Write the following passage from dictation:

   "I think you ought to let Anne go," repeated Matthew firmly. Argument was not his strong point, but holding fast to his opinion certainly was. Marilla gave a gasp of helplessness and took refuge in silence. —*Anne of Green Gables*, page 150

   Dictation

2. **Characterization** is the method an author uses to reveal or describe characters and their various personalities. In the dictation, what did you learn about Matthew's character?

   ✎ Circle any punctuation discrepancies and then place chronological numbering beside each mistake. Use *Writers INC* and find the omitted rule of punctuation. At the bottom of your dictation, write the number and the missed rule.

   Follow-up

3. 📖 From *Anne's Anthology* (*The Annotated Anne of Green Gables*, pages 473–474) read "Curfew Must Not Ring Tonight."

   ✎ In the Literature section of your notebook write:
   a. The refrain in this poem.
   b. How many lines are contained in each stanza?
   c. What kind and number of feet compose each verse? Refer to pages 242 and 243 in *Writers INC*.

   Literature

4. ☞ The poem, "Curfew Must Not Ring Tonight," refers to the Puritan, Oliver Cromwell. Study about this man.

   ✎ In the History section of your notebook, at the appropriate time period: Write a one page biography about Cromwell and his role in England's history.

   ⏱ History

5. ✎ Based on your reading of *The Lady of the Lake*, answer these questions in the Literature section of your notebook:
   a. What ideology does Sir Walter Scott promote in his writings?
   b. What view of God does he display through his writings?
   c. What view of authority?
   d. According to the previous definition of Romanticism (Unit 3, Chapter X & XI, Activity 8), does Sir Walter Scott's writing belong in the Romantic period? Why or why not?

   ⏱ Writing

6. ✋ Make friends with an elderly lady with whom a "kindred spirit" relationship may develop, preferably with someone who is not in a nursing home. Diana's aunt was lonely, but she was not in a nursing home. Less than 5 percent of the elderly live in nursing homes, so going strictly to nursing homes can give a skewed view of the elderly.

   Occupational Education

Literature	7. ☞ What reason does Mrs. Lynde suggest for Anne getting in trouble? What is Anne's reason for not applying Mrs. Lynde's advice? Mrs. Lynde talks about "looking before you leap." This is a popular saying dating back to the 1600's. Go to <www.cadroncreek.com> for a list of Internet sites to visit to assist in finding the origins of commonly quoted sayings. Another way to access a helpful site is to go to a search engine, type in "quotes," and scan down to "Bartlett." Once at the site, type in "leap." Look up the origins of several other common quotes.
	✎ In the Literature section of your notebook: Write the different quotes found on the Bartlett Web site, identifying the author of each.

Bible/ Occupational Education	8. Anne thinks not being impulsive would spoil the fun in life.
	📖 Read Proverbs 13:19 and Proverbs 26:11. Impulsiveness can be dangerous.
	📖 Read Proverbs 17:12. As Mrs. Lynde says, a wise man reflects and thinks, while a fool is impetuous.
	📖 Read Proverbs 13:16; 18:2; 14:24; 24:9, and 22:15. We see from Proverbs 22:15, children are foolish and they must be taught to grow in wisdom. We see Anne making foolish choices on one hand, yet beginning to grow in knowledge and wisdom on the other.
	✋ Make a bookmark that will remind you of the danger of foolishness. Laminate it or use contact paper to protect it. Punch holes around the edge. Starting from the center of the bottom of the bookmark, whip stitch the edges together with colored embroidery thread. When you have finished with the edge stitching, make a tassel with the thread at the bottom of the bookmark.

☼ Fine Arts	9. "Fresco" is the Italian word for fresh. A true fresco is a painting on moist plaster with water colors or pigment such as tempera. The paint is mixed with egg so it is absorbed by the plaster and becomes part of the wall itself. Among the most celebrated frescoes of the Renaissance are the decorations of the Sistine Chapel in the Vatican by Michelangelo. A German artist, Peter von Cornelius, revived interest in fresco painting during the 1800's.
	📖 Read about frescoes in an encyclopedia.
	👁 Show your instructor pictures of at least four frescoes.
	✋ Draw a sketch for a miniature fresco you would like to paint. Mix plaster by putting 1 cup water in a bowl, then adding powdered plaster until the plaster comes to the surface. Stir until the plaster is the consistency of cold cream. Apply it $1/16 - 1/4$ inch thick to a scrap piece of wood or scored Masonite, then paint the moist plaster with the water-colors or tempera mixed with egg. (Note: Water is easier to use.) It is a very good idea to put your dark colors down first. Start at the top and

go down from there. Remember the wetter the plaster, the longer it takes to dry.

10. ✋ Have a friend over to spend the night. Spend time experimenting with the pompadour or other Victorian hairstyle. For directions, see the Web sites and books listed under "pompadour hairstyle directions" in "Research Topics" for this Chapter.	Field Trip
11. ✋ Learn the basics of knitting: casting on, casting off, and one or two basic stitches. If you have never knitted before, knit a neck scarf for a doll. If you know how to knit, knit a hand muff or cap.	Occupational Education
12. ☞ On page 214 of *The Annotated Anne,* Marilla states, "I wash my hands of it." See if you can find the Biblical story to which this refers. Use a concordance to find the answer. *See answer in Answer Appendix.*	Bible
13. 📖 Anne and Diana worked out a sort of heliograph, which was a wire-free telegraph used extensively in the West. The military used Morse code to communicate messages up to 50 miles away. Briefly read about this method of communication. ✋ You may want to experiment with this method of communication with a neighbor.	History
14. 📖 Read "How Sockery Set a Hen" from *Annotated Anne of Green Gables,* pages 474 and 475. This is difficult because it is written as if the person is speaking English with a strong German accent. ✋ Once you are familiar with the overall plot of the story, make large illustrations of the plot on a flip board. After dinner one evening, entertain your family with reading this piece and showing your illustrations.	Literature
15. ✋ Dress warmly and go on a sleigh ride. How would you describe it?	Field Trip
16. ✸ With your instructor: Continue with recitation each Friday during this Unit. Present "How Sockery Set a Hen" as described in Activity 14 above. Pick a favorite poem or part of a poem from this week's lesson to recite. Quote memorized scriptures to your teacher: I Corinthians 10:13; Proverbs 29:22; Hebrews 12:4–8; Luke 9:62; Psalm 139:13–14; Titus 1:7–10; Proverbs 10:17; Proverbs 14:24; and your choice of either Ephesians 3:20; Proverbs 1:27–28; or James 3:13, 17.	Literature
17. Review and take Unit 4 Quiz in the *Test Appendix.*	⏰ Quiz

Alexandria
Gray

Planning Guide

Gather These Items:

1. A biography of Queen Victoria is required for an "A" grade for Contract
   Reading — History.
   —*Queen Victoria,* World Leaders Past & Present. Chambers Harrap
   Publishers Ltd., 1991. ASIN 0245601023.
   —*At Her Majesty's Request: An African Princess in Victorian England*
   by Walter Dean Myers. Scholastic, 1999. ISBN 0590486691.

Research Topics:

1. Mayflower (*Epigaea repens*) photo and information
   —Internet search, "mayflowers"

   . . . .

2. Victorian era architecture, art, furniture, dress
   —*Victoria and Her Times* by Jean-Loup Chiflet and Alain Beaulet.
   Henry Holt and Company, Inc., 1997. ASIN 0805050841.

   . . . .

3. News stories about daring

   . . . .

4. An overview of the play *Julius Caesar* and the character Mark Anthony

   . . . .

5. Great Exhibition

   . . . .

Suggested Videos:

sapl   *Victoria & Albert*

Suggested Field Trips:

1. Tour homes built during the Victorian era.

Group Activities:

1. Have a party celebrating Queen Victoria's birthday. (See Activity 7)

Memory Work:

Proverbs 17:12

Notes:

Assignments — Chapter XX

Contract Reading

	A Grade	B Grade	C Grade
Bible			
History	❏ A biography of Queen Victoria		
Literature			

Weekly

Quiet Time Reading Books:
Independent Project:
Memory Work: Proverbs 17:12
Health: Continue your cardiovascular exercise program initiated in Unit 1, Chapter IV, Activity 9

	Literature	History	Bible	Health	Occu. Education	Science & Fine Arts	Grammar & Writing
M	Read Chap. XX AGG, Reading Comp., #2						#1, #2
T	Vocab., #3, #4	#5	#8				#5
W	#9	#6, #10	#12			#10, #11	
Th	#13						
F	#15 Recitation	#7 Queen's Party, #6 Field Trip				#14 Field Day	

🦢 Study Guide

Read Chapter XX
Reading Comprehension:

1. What quality did Anne seem to admire the most in people?

2. What did Anne discover about imagination?

Vocabulary:

🔑 Look up the vocabulary words in a dictionary or encyclopedia. Fill in the blanks using the vocabulary words.

Vocabulary Words:

capricious

limpid

sarcastic

inexorable

reveries

3. A _____ and sarcastic boss is hard to work for.

4. The _____ stream was beautiful.

5. "What a fierce and _____ reprehension would this have drawn from the friendship of the world." —South

6. "There are _____ and extravagances which pass through the minds of wise men as well as fools." —Addison

7. The _____ prisoner finally escaped his captor.

Extra Credit:

✋ Draw some mayflowers in your sketchbook or in the Fine Arts section of your notebook. As an alternative, show a photograph or professional sketch of these flowers to your instructor.

🍂 Activities:

1. ✎ Write the following passage from dictation: (Note: The instructor needs to identify for the student when each new line begins.)

   Dictation

   Good friends, sweet friends, let me not stir you up
   To such a sudden flood of mutiny.
   They that have done this deed are honourable:
   What private griefs they have, alas, I know not,
   That made them do it; they are wise and honourable,
   And will, no doubt, with reasons answer you.

   —William Shakespeare, *Julius Caesar*, Act III, Scene 2

2. ✎ Circle any punctuation discrepancies. Place chronological numbering beside each mistake. Use *Writers INC* to find each omitted rule of punctuation. At the bottom of your dictation, write the number and the missed rule.

   Follow-up

Literature	3. 📖 Read the selection from *Julius Caesar* in *Anne's Anthology*. In this scene, Shakespeare uses repetition. Read an overview of the play and of Mark Anthony's life.

📖 Read the definition of **repetition** in *Writers INC* on page 129. Besides adding a sense of balance, the repetition of the phrase causes the reader to question the statement.

With your instructor:
  a. Tell which phrase was repeated frequently in this scene.
  b. Discuss the overview of the play and of Mark Anthony's life.

Literature   4. 🔑 In the Literature section of your notebook:
From which Shakespearian play is Mr. Phillips quoting when he says, "sweets to the sweet"? Look it up on the Bartlett Web site.

History   5. Queen Victoria was born on May 24, 1819 and died in 1901. Her 64-year reign was the longest in British history. She reigned during a good portion of Lucy Montgomery's life. Victoria showed herself a hard-working monarch concerned with the welfare of her people and she gained their affection and admiration. Although Canada had a Constitution, it remained part of the British Commonwealth during Queen Victoria's reign.

📖 In the *Background Information Appendix,* read more about Queen Victoria, the events of her reign, and her personal life. For an "A" grade in Contract Reading — History, read a biography of this important monarch.

📖 In the above *Background Information,* the Great Exhibition is mentioned briefly. Read further about the Great Exhibition. What did this Exhibition accomplish?

📖 Read pages 85 and 86, "Writing Clear Sentences," in *Writers INC* and utilize this information in the following writing assignment.

✎ In the History section of your notebook, in the appropriate time period: Write a summary of what you have learned about Queen Victoria and her reign.

History/   6. 🔑 Research Victorian architecture, furniture, dress, and art. You may
Field Trip   want to tour homes built during the Victorian era.

History   7. ✋ Canada still celebrates Queen Victoria's birthday as a holiday. Plan a party for the Queen's birthday. Make Victorian style invitations. Dress in Victorian era clothing. Wear your hair in a pompadour. Either save your plans until May 24 or plan an alternate date to culminate your study of Queen Victoria.

Bible   8. 📖 Anne decides she should be content with the commonplace. She learns that planting an imaginary thought can bring forth undesirable real life consequences. By not controlling her imagination, she allows strongholds to be built. Read II Corinthians 10:4–6; Romans 1:20, 21;

and Jeremiah 23:16, 17. Of what should Anne have been thinking? Read Philippians 4:8.

---

9. 🔑 Anne sung the praises of mayflowers. Find pictures and information about this flower. It is the Massachusetts state flower. *Nova Scotia provincial flower.*

✎ Draw a picture of this flower and write a several sentences about it.

📖 John Greenleaf Whittier also sung the praises of the mayflower in a poem by that title. Read "The Mayflowers" in the *Background Information Appendix.*

Literature

---

10. 📖 The students sang "My Home on the Hill" by W.C. Baker. I could not find this song online, but I found other songs by Baker. In the *Annotated Anne of Green Gables,* look at the musical score and words for this song. If you play an instrument, try playing it.

History/ Fine Arts

---

11. 🗫 With your instructor discuss:
    a. What is the first sign of spring in your area?
    b. When do the first signs of spring occur in your area?

Science

---

12. The students dare each other to do many different things. Ask your parents to recall a time in which a person was dared to do something and the results were catastrophic or find an article online about such an incident. Daring can be folly.

📖 Read Proverbs 5:23; 15:4, 21; and Proverbs 17:12.

♡ Memorize Proverbs 17:12.

Bible

---

13. 🗫 With your instructor, discuss:
    a. What happened to Anne a year ago?
    b. What important events do you keep up with besides birthdays?

Literature

---

14. ✋ Each Friday from now on during this Unit will be used as a field day. Study the plants, flowers, and birds native to your area. Begin by identifying all the plants on your property. As time allows, increase the area. Take a camera or a sketch pad as well as plant and bird identification books. After a plant is identified, take a picture of it and place it in your Fine Arts notebook or draw it in your sketchbook and label it.

Science

---

15. 🗫 With your instructor:
    Continue with recitation each Friday during this Unit. Choose a favorite portion of the section of *Julius Caesar* which you studied to recite.

    Quote memorized scriptures to your teacher: Proverbs 10:17; Titus 1:7–10; Hebrews 12:4–8; Luke 9:62; Psalm 139:13–14; The Lord's Prayer; I Corinthians 10:13; Shorter Catechism verses; Psalm 15; Psalm 30, especially verse 5; and Proverbs 17:12.

Literature

🙵 Planning Guide

Gather These Items:

1. Items to make a centerpiece for your table. (See Activity 4)

2. Items to make jellied chicken. (See Activity 8)
—See "Chicken Mould" in *Aunt Maud's Recipe Book: From the Kitchen of L.M. Montgomery* by L.M. Montgomery, Elaine Crawford with Kelly Crawford and Eline Crawford. Moulin Publishers, 1997. ISBN 1896867014.

3. Items to make cold tongue. (Not to be confused with cold shoulder!) (See Activity 8)

4. Items to make lemon pie. (See Activity 8)
—See "Maud's Lemon Pie" in *Aunt Maud's Recipe Book*.

5. Items to make biscuits. (See Activity 8)
—See "Baking Powder Biscuits" in *Aunt Maud's Recipe Book*.

6. Balloons and baking powder. (See Activity 10)

7. *The American Dictionary of the English Language* (1828 Edition) by Noah Webster.

8. *The Hidden Art of Homemaking* by Edith Schaeffer. Tyndale House Publishers, 1985. ISBN 0842313982.

9. Handkerchief and embroidery thread, lace or crochet thread for making decoration and/or trim. (See Activity 16)

10. Lavender linen water. Either buy or make your own. (See Activity 16)

11. Items to make a collage. (See Activity 17)
blue muslin or muslin and blue dye
miniature roses
felt
paint

12. *The Christian's Secret of a Happy Life* by Hannah Whitall Smith. Whitaker House, 1983. ISBN 0883681323. This is Contract Reading — Bible for a "C" or better grade. (The Internet has the full text. See <http://www.ccel.org/s/smith_hw/secret/secret.htm>.)

Research Topics:

1. Your church's doctrinal statement.
   —Churches often give this out to new people

2. Rules of etiquette for a tea

3. Information about plants, flowers, and birds in your area
   —Check with the local Department of Agriculture Extension office
   —Check with local native plant and/or garden societies
   —Go to the Audubon Web site

4. Food poisoning: signs, symptoms and prevention (Activity 14 has some information)

5. Aluminum sources in diet and possible links with diseases

6. The difference between fresh and day old bread

7. Formal and informal place settings
   —Internet
   —<http://www.replacements.com/piecetype/crystal_formal.htm>

8. Storage of poisons in the home
   —Internet search, "Storage of poisons in the home"
   —<www.pharmacy.arizona.edu/centers/apdic/household.shtml>

Suggested Videos:

Suggested Field Trips:

1. Tour a florist shop. (See Activity 5)

2. Take a floral arrangement class at a local hobby shop or community college. (See Activity 4)

Group Activities:

1. Invite your pastor's or Sunday School teacher's family for dinner and serve some of the items Marilla served on page 172 of *Anne of Green Gables* (*The Annotated Anne of Green Gables,* page 238).

   Use the centerpiece you make in Activity 4.

Memory Work:
Lamentations 3:22–23

Notes:

Assignments — Chapter XXI

Contract Reading

	A Grade	B Grade	C Grade
Bible	❐ *The Christian's Secret of a Happy Life*	❐ *The Christian's Secret of a Happy Life*	❐ *The Christian's Secret of a Happy Life*
History			
Literature			

Weekly

Quiet Time Reading Books: *The Christian's Secret of a Happy Life*
Independent Project: Handkerchief project
Memory Work: Lamentations 3:22–23
Health: Continue your cardiovascular exercise program initiated in Unit 1, Chapter IV, Activity 9

	Literature	History	Bible	Health	Occu. Education	Science & Fine Arts	Grammar & Writing
M	Read Chap. XXI AGG, Reading Comp., #2		#3, #21		#14, #16, #18		#1, #2, #3
T	Vocab.		#6, #19		#4	#17	#6
W	#13		#7	#22	#8 Dinner		#7
Th	#15	#11	#20	#12	#9, #10		#11
F	#24 Recitation				#5 Field Trip	#23 Field Day	#5

🐉 Study Guide

Read Chapter XXI
Reading Comprehension:

1. Who left and who arrived in Avonlea?

2. Why did Mrs. Lynde have several items returned to her that night?

3. How did the church at Avonlea pick a preacher?

4. What was special about the way Mr. Allan prayed?

5. What change did Mrs. Allan make in Anne's Sunday School class?

6. What new kindred spirit did Anne find?

7. What happened to Anne's cake? How could this have been prevented?

8. What made Anne want to be a Christian?

9. What did Anne like about tomorrow?

Vocabulary:

☞ Look up the vocabulary words in a dictionary or encyclopedia. Fill in the blanks using the vocabulary words.

10. The chubby baby had such cute _____.

11. The Greeks spoke of a _____ in the woods.

12. The rain _____ the heat.

13. To look at today's antacid commercials, you'd think that there are many _____ people in society.

14. The Scriptures are profitable to teach _____.

15. "Natural _____ is the knowledge we have of God from his works, by the light of nature and reason." —Webster

16. The Indian told Mr. Ingalls of his _____ that the winter would be a bad one.

17. "To soothe the sorrows of her _____ son." —Dryden

18. The _____ was next to the church.

19. This silver dollar has been _____.

20. "Yet have they many baits and guileful spells /

    To _____ and invite the unwary sense." —Milton

Vocabulary Words:

dyspeptic

dryad

inveigle

adulterated

dimples

plaintive

manse

dissipated

doctrine

theology

presentiment

Activities:

Dictation	1. ✎ Write the following passage from dictation:

> "Mrs. Barry had her table decorated," said Anne, who was not
> entirely guiltless of the wisdom of the serpent, "and the minis-
> ter paid her an elegant compliment."   —*Anne of Green Gables,* page 174

Follow-up	2. 📖 Read pages 125–131, "Writing with Style," in *Writers INC.* Lucy Montgomery had an effective writing style.

    With your instructor, discuss some examples of Montgomery's style which you think are particularly effective.

    ✎ Circle any punctuation discrepancies. Place chronological numbering beside each mistake. Use *Writers INC* to look up each omitted rule of punctuation. At the bottom of your dictation, write the number and the missed rule.

Bible	3. 📖 What tactic of the serpent does Anne use on Marilla (*Annotated Anne,* page 241)? See Matthew 10:16 and Genesis 3:1.

    ✎ In the Bible section of your notebook:
Write an explanation of the origin of the reference in Matthew.

Occupational Education	4. 📖 Read chapter 7, "Flower Arrangements," from *The Hidden Art of Homemaking* by Edith Schaeffer.

    ✋ Make a centerpiece for your table. Take a floral arrangement class.

    Montgomery wrote in June 1905 to Mr. Weber regarding bouquets.

    📖 Read pages 33–34 of *The Green Gables Letters from L.M. Montgomery to Ephraim Weber 1905–1909.*

Field Trip	5. ✋ Arrange a visit with a florist. Assemble pertinent questions prior to the visit. How can what you learned be applied to your family? If you are interested in being a professional florist you may want to ask questions on the Apprentice Worksheet in the *Activity Appendix.* For an extended field trip, ask to shadow the person performing his or her job for an hour or two.

    ✎ In the Occupational Education section of your notebook:
After the field trip, write a follow-up paper as well as a thank you note. Be sure to include specifics from your conversations so the florist will know you were listening and his or her time was appreciated. Remember to proofread your note.

Bible	6. 🔑 In Mrs. Lynde's opinion, what makes a good combination for a minister's family? Is this scriptural? Use a concordance to look up scriptures pertaining to leadership or teaching positions in the church. After writing this book, Maud Montgomery became a preacher's wife.

✎ In the Bible section of your notebook, write an answer to this question: Do you think Montgomery agreed with Mrs. Lynde?

7. 📖 Study your church's doctrine.	Bible/Writing

✎ In the Bible section of your notebook:
Write what you believe about the Lord.

📖 Read "Avoiding the Ailments of Style" on page 132 of *Writers INC*. "Cure" any sentences that lack an effective style.

8. ✋ Invite your pastor's or Sunday School teacher's family for dinner. Serve some of the items Marilla served on page 172 (*The Annotated Anne of Green Gables,* page 238). Use the centerpiece made in Activity 4.	Occupational Education

⚷ Learn about formal and informal dinner place settings.

9. ⚷ Research, then discuss, the difference between fresh and day old bread. (Staleness is not the answer.)	Occupational Education

10. What does baking powder do in foods? Baking powder is a fine white powder used to make cakes and biscuits leaven or rise. Chemicals in baking powder react with air and a liquid, usually water or sweet milk, to form carbon dioxide (CO_2). Bubbles of carbon dioxide trapped in the flour mixture expand when they are heated and make the mixture rise.	Occupational Education

All baking powders contain starch, baking soda (sodium bicarbonate), and acid forming ingredients. Starch keeps the powder dry and prevents it from acting until a liquid is added. Baking soda reacts with the acid-forming ingredient to produce carbon dioxide. Different baking powders contain different acids. There are tartrate, phosphate, sulfate, and combination baking powders. Sulfate powders contain sodium aluminum. Baking powders differ in speed of reaction. Sulfate powder is the slowest; it does not react until fully heated. Tartrate and phosphate powders are the fastest, reacting as soon as they are mixed with a liquid.

From previous cooking you may have noticed that when sour milk, buttermilk, lemon juice, or vinegar are used in a recipe, soda is used instead of baking powder. Why? Baking soda reacts with the acid in these foods so the acid contained in baking powder is not needed.

When does baking powder lose its ability to work? To demonstrate baking powder's loss of carbon dioxide in the presence of moisture and its resulting loss of potency, gather some tartrate or phosphate baking powder and a previously inflated and deflated balloon. (The inflation and deflation of the balloon breaks it in and makes it easier to inflate again.) Place 2 tablespoons of tartrate or phosphate baking powder into the balloon. Add ¼ cup water, quickly tie the balloon, and then shake. For another experiment, add 2 tablespoons baking soda and ¼ cup water to a different balloon, tie immediately and shake. Or, add 2 tablespoons baking soda to ¼ cup lemon juice or vinegar, quickly tie and shake.

✂ Discuss with your instructor the results of the experiment or experiments and your observations.

Commercial baking powder was an important innovation in the 1800's, becoming

> . . . a feature of modern North American life in the last two decades of the nineteenth century. Before that time, women had had to make their own mixes, blending soda with cream of tartar, to ensure the rising of baked goods. . . . The commercial product combined and standardized everything that was needed. . . . Rival companies—often local pharmacies—boasted of their own product and spread alarm about those of others. In short, housewives at the end of the century tended to talk a lot about baking powders. Hence, we can understand Anne's seemingly ridiculous remark when confronted with the horrible taste of her cake: "It must have been the baking powder" (p. 241) . . . but in this instance the baking powder had visibly done all that it could be asked to do and the cake has risen beautifully; it is indeed "light and feathery as golden foam" (p. 280)—a phrase that could have come out of an advertisement. . . .   —*The Annotated Anne of Green Gables,* page 447

History/Writing 11. 📖 Read pages 98 and 99 in *Writers INC* about "Types of Paragraphs—Persuasive" and "Paragraph Unity."

In her concern about her cake, Anne worries about the baking powder and quotes Mrs. Lynde to Marilla:

> "And Mrs. Lynde says you can never be sure of getting good baking powder nowadays when everything is so adulterated. Mrs. Lynde says the Government ought to take the matter up, but she says we'll never see the day when a Tory Government will do it."   —*The Annotated Anne of Green Gables,* page 240

✎ In the History section of your notebook:
Imagine a typical conversation among women in Victorian society about the quality of baking powder. Pretend you are concerned about this issue and write a persuasive paragraph about the lack of consistent quality in baking powder and whether the government should make laws regarding the quality of this product. Use the knowledge gained through reading *Are You Liberal? Conservative? or Confused?* by the Mayburys.

Health 12. Which type of baking powder does your family use? Some researchers think there is a relationship between Alzheimer's disease and the intake of aluminum. Certain baking powders, processed cheeses such as Velveeta, some antacids, and fiber powders contain aluminum. Cooking acidic foods in aluminum pots and pans or placing aluminum foil over acidic foods for storage can cause aluminum to leech into the foods.

❀ With your instructor or parent:
Find sources of aluminum in your home. If you can not find any, go to the store and read the labels on some of the products mentioned above to identify which brands have aluminum.

☛ Do some research to find the answer to this question: Is aluminum a nutrient utilized in your body or is it a possible toxin?

❀ Discuss your findings with your instructor.

---

13. At the tea for the Allans, Marilla serves both pound cake (the traditional English recipe—rich in butter and eggs) and the new layer cake recipe which displays the North American style of making tall cakes with elaborate icings or fillings. While tall cakes became quite popular in North America, women in England, Australia, and New Zealand did not abandon traditional cake baking methods until after World War II. They continued to use eggs and egg whites to make cakes rise, but cakes made this way had become dull to North Americans well before that time. (See *The Annotated Anne of Green Gables,* page 447.)

    Literature

    ☛ So far in our reading we have encountered English and American influence in both poetry and cooking. As you are reading *Anne of Green Gables,* look for other comparisons and instances of the blending of these two cultures.

---

14. Marilla serves jellied chicken. Mishandling poultry can be a cause of food poisoning. Poultry and egg products can carry salmonella. Food poisoning from salmonella can cause symptoms ranging from mild to severe diarrhea. Other symptoms are nausea, stomach cramps, fever, and headache. The infection is acquired by ingestion of contaminated food or water. The incubation period is 8 to 48 hours after exposure and the acute illness lasts from 3 to 21 days. Bacteria are shed in the stool for months in some treated patients.

    ☀ Occupational Education/ Health

    Since bacteria can not move by themselves, it is important to prevent the transmission of salmonella bacteria. To protect your food at the grocery store, make sure the clerk bags raw meat and poultry separately from other foods. At home, store meats separately in your refrigerator so blood does not drain onto other foods. Wash your hands, knives, cutting boards, and counter surfaces before and after handling raw meats. Use either bleach or a disinfectant and rinse with water. The best cutting boards for meats have nonporous surfaces such as marble or glass. Wood is very hard to disinfect. Never put cooked meat on an unwashed plate on which raw meat has been placed. Cook food thoroughly. The flesh of the chicken should be white, not pink. It is best not to stuff poultry. Thaw and marinate meat in the refrigerator, not on the counter top. Always keep hot foods at 60° C (140° F) or above and store cold foods below 5° C (41° F).

✂ With your instructor:
Check the temperature of your refrigerator to make sure it is no more than 5° centigrade.

Literature

15. "All went marry as a wedding bell" is a quote from Lord Byron's *Childe Harold's Pilgrimage,* Canto III, Stanza 21. This was read in Unit IV, during the study of Napoleon.

Once again Montgomery demonstrates her love for poetry and her familiarity with it. Notice the ease and flow of Montgomery's use of quotes from poetry within her writing.

📖 Read page 258 in *Writers INC,* "Using Quoted Material."

📖 You may want to read Canto III of *Childe Harold's Pilgrimage* in its entirety.

Occupational Education

16. ✋ Anne brings a handkerchief to class. Before the days of Kleenex tissue it was common to carry a nice handkerchief. Buy a plain handkerchief and either decorate it by embroidering your favorite flower studied this year or by putting an edging on it. You can trim it with lace you purchase or make by crocheting. Carry it in your purse. You might be surprised at how frequently it is used. Victorians frequently ironed their linens with fragrant water. Buy or make some lavender water to use in ironing your handkerchief.

Fine Arts

17. ✋ Make a collage of Mrs. Allan arriving at the railroad station in her beautiful blue muslin dress with puffed sleeves.

Occupational Education

18. ✋ Anne is afraid she might forget the flour. A cook needs to be attentive while cooking. While you are making your cake, look at the difference in the batter between batter with flour and batter without flour.

Bible

19. Mrs. Allan is very kind, discreet, and joyful. During this chapter we see religion in shoes.

📖 Read Psalm 5:11; Psalm 9:2; Psalm 40:16; Psalm 68:3; Psalm 118:24; Romans 15:13; Galatians 5:22; and I Thessalonians 5:16. Christians are to be joyful in the Lord. If you are not joyful, pray Psalm 51:12 and Psalm 90:14.

📖 Read *The Christian's Secret of a Happy Life* by Hannah Whitall Smith published in 1870. She and her husband, Robert Pearsall Smith, formed an evangelistic team that awakened both England and the United States to the joys of the "deeper life" in the Christian experience. This book is Contract Reading — Bible for a "C" or better grade.

✎ After reading Mrs. Smith's book, answer these questions in the Bible section of your notebook:
a. What is the spiritual "secret" she wants to share with her readers? Are there one or two sentences in the book that sum up the "secret"?

What are two or three key scriptures she quotes which reveal the "secret"?

    b. Did reading this book awaken in you the thirst for the "deeper life"? If so, how does Smith's writing help you follow that thirst to a new depth in your Christian experience?

20. 📖 Anne is mortified to think others would find out about her putting liniment in the cake. Read the following verses Proverbs 11:13; Proverbs 11:22; Proverbs 16:28; and Titus 2:5. Mrs. Allan is a discreet woman.

        Bible

21. Anne is unhappy about the mistakes she has made, but she looks forward to starting the next day with a clean slate.

 📖 Read Psalm 30:5 about joy in the morning. Also read Lamentations 3:22–23 and I John 1:9.

 ♡ Memorize Lamentations 3:22–23.

        Bible

22. Marilla had put a non-edible liquid into the vanilla bottle. The anodyne liniment was not poisonous, but it definitely was not tasty.

 📖 Read about the storage of poisons in the home.

 ✎ In the Health section of your notebook, list the poisons found in your house and garage.

 ✋ Make a poster illustrating factors that contribute to poisoning or how to poison proof your home. One factor which contributes to poisoning is storing poisonous products in food or drink containers.

        ☼ Health/ Occupational Education

23. 🌿 Continue to use Friday as a field day. Study the plants, flowers, and birds native to your area. Begin by identifying all the plants on your property. As time allows, increase the area. Take a camera or a sketch pad as well as plant and bird identification books. After a plant is identified, take a picture of it and place it in your Fine Arts notebook or draw it in your sketchbook and label it.

 🔑 Look up information about the plants, flowers, and birds in your area. For sources, see the suggestions under "Research Topics" in this Chapter.

        Science

24. 🎭 With your instructor:
Continue with recitation each Friday during this Unit. Choose a favorite portion of a poem from this week's lesson to recite.

Quote memorized scriptures to your teacher: Proverbs 10:17; Titus 1:7–10; Hebrews 12:4–8; Luke 9:62; Psalm 139:13–14; The Lord's Prayer; I Corinthians 10:13; Shorter Catechism verses; Psalm 15; Psalm 30, especially verse 5; Proverbs 17:12; and Lamentations 3:22–23.

        Literature

❧ Planning Guide

Gather These Items:
1. *American Dictionary of the English Language* (1828 edition) by Noah Webster.

Research Topics:
1. Robert Browning

. . . .

2. Sampling of Montgomery's poetry
   —Go to <www.cadroncreek.com> for a list of Internet sites to visit.
   —*The Poetry of Lucy Maud Montgomery* selected and introduced by John Ferns and Kevin McCabe. Fitzhenry & Whiteside, 1987. ISBN 88902-931-8.

. . . .

3. Etiquette, contemporary and in the Victorian Era
   —*Etiquette in Society, in Business, in Politics and at Home* by Emily Post. Funk & Wagnalls Company, 1922. ISBN 1-58734-039-9. (This is available on the Internet at <http://www.bartleby.com/95/>.)

. . . .

4. Opium Wars
   —"China: The Opium Wars." *The British Empire*. Ntl Group Ltd. 2004 <http://homepage.ntlworld.com/haywardlad/chinaopium.html>.
   —"The Opium Wars: Wason Collection" *Explorecornell.edu*. Cornell University © 2003 <http://www.explore.cornell.edu/scene.cfm? scene=wason%20collection&stop=WC%20-%20Narrative%20Opium& view=allViews#v_3>.

. . . .

5. Opium, its effects on the body and on society

. . . .

Suggested Videos:

Suggested Field Trips:

Group Activities:
1. Have a tea for a younger girl. (See Activity 12)

Memory Work:
Romans 5:19

Notes:

Assignments — Chapter XXII

Contract Reading: No new contract reading

Weekly
Quiet Time Reading Books: *The Christian's Secret of a Happy Life*
Independent Project:
Memory Work: Romans 5:19
Health: Continue your cardiovascular exercise program initiated in Unit 1, Chapter IV,
     Activity 9

	Literature	History	Bible	Health	Occu. Education	Science & Fine Arts	Grammar & Writing
M	Read Chap. XXII AGG, Reading Comp., #2		#8, #9				#1, #2
T	Vocab., #7		#5		#10		
W	#3	#3	#4		#12		#3, #13
Th	#6	#14	#6, #11	#14	#13		#6, #14
F	#16 Recitation				#12 Tea	#15 Field Day	

🌸 Study Guide

Read Chapter XXII
Reading Comprehension:

1. What was Anne excited about in this chapter?

2. Why did Marilla worry about Anne not taking things calmly? Why should she not have worried about this?

3. Anne stated that she wanted to become a minister's wife. Why did she want to become one?

4. Can someone be nice and not a kindred spirit?

5. What did Mrs. Lynde think was a dangerous innovation?

Vocabulary Words:

seraph

demure

deportment

pithy

saffron

trebled

organdy

waif

Vocabulary:

🗝 Look up the vocabulary words in a dictionary or encyclopedia. Fill in the blanks using the vocabulary words.

6. _____ is an expensive spice.

7. "The _____ speech prevailed and all agreed." —Dryden

8. Compound interest _____ my debt.

9. A _____ is an angel of the highest order.

10. Queen Victoria's _____ countenance lasted an extended time after the death of Prince Edward. *Albert*

11. Her _____ made us believe she was the daughter of a King.

12. The _____ curtains cast a shimmering glow in the dining room.

13. We picked through the _____ on the shore to find what we wanted.

🍂 Activities:

Dictation

1. ✎ Write the following passage from dictation:

> For Anne to take things calmly would have been to change her nature. All 'spirit and fire and dew,' as she was, the pleasures and pains of life came to her with trebled intensity. —*Anne of Green Gables,* page 178

💡 Follow-up

2. A **simile** is comparison of two unlike things using the words "like" or "as."

📖 Read about "similes" on pages 138 and 236 of *Writers INC*. What was the simile in the dictation?

"Spirit and fire and dew" was placed in quotation marks to show Montgomery was quoting something or someone. She was quoting from the poem, "Evelyn Hope," by Robert Browning.

✎ Write five original similes in the Literature section of your notebook.

✎ Circle any punctuation discrepancies and place chronological numbering beside each one. Use *Writers INC* to look up each omitted rule of punctuation. At the bottom of your dictation, write the number and the missed rule.

---

3. Robert Browning, 1812–1889, received most of his education at home in London. He was an extremely bright child and a voracious reader. He admired Elizabeth Barrett's poetry and contrived to meet her. Although she was an invalid, the two married and moved to Florence, Italy. She wrote of her growing love for Robert in *Sonnets from the Portuguese*. He often called her "my little Portuguese." In 1855, he in turn dedicated *Men and Women* to her. "Evelyn Hope" was in this collection.

👁 Literature

In the 1850's, Robert Browning visited Paris and London and developed friendships with literary and artistic figures of the day, including Dante Gabriel Rossetti, Charles Kingsley, and Alfred, Lord Tennyson. During her life Elizabeth was more famous, but sympathy for Robert after her death in 1861 helped the critical reception of his later poetry. Although he lived and wrote actively for another twenty years, the late 1860's were the peak of his career. His poetry is known for its rough verse pattern and rapid movement. According to World Book Encyclopedia, his verse "expresses a spiritual and bodily vitality."

Perhaps Montgomery had just finished reading this poem.

📖 Read "Evelyn Hope" in *Anne's Anthology*.

💬 With your instructor, discuss what insight into Robert Browning's spiritual beliefs this poem gives. Consider the following in your discussion: Basing his hope on the belief that after death we pass through a series of lives and worlds "not a few" [line 10], the middle-aged lover says his time will "come for taking" [line 32] the sixteen-year-old Evelyn; though he is sitting by her dead body now, and she never did love him, "perhaps she had scarcely heard my name" [line 10]. God will see to it that each passion is requited, even if it takes several afterlives to reach that consummation. This is a remarkable example of optimism. Being the romantic that he was, Browning's "optimism" in the face of death, this belief that love may somehow blossom in another life, is a very appealing solution to an untimely demise. As a romantic poet, Browning seeks to supersede all notions of the bonds of time, and the cultural and doctrinal ideas of eternal life, to place the fulfillment of love and passion as the highest goal and purpose of God. This is a hopeful scenario to him; the girl's name is intended to allude to this "hope." In romantic poetry, religious ideas/doctrines of the time were often cast off or merely used as "structures" on which to hang a passionate interpretation of how the world ought to be.

✏ Write the answers to these questions about the poem in the Literature section of your notebook:
a. Tell what strikes you as " Victorian" about this poetry.
b. What is the rhyme pattern of this poem?

✦ On your map, mark Robert Browning's country of origin.

✏ In the History section of your notebook, in the appropriate time period: Write a brief biography of Robert Browning's life from your reading and research.

📖 Read Hebrews 9:27. Browning's optimistic hope of living several lives was scripturally unfounded.

Bible   4. 📖 Read pages 38–39 of *The Green Gables Letters from L.M. Montgomery to Ephraim Weber 1905–1909*. In this section Montgomery writes that reincarnation is an appealing idea. Belief in reincarnation may seem appealing, but remember God set forth the universe and its laws.

📖 Read Proverbs 14:12. Although reincarnation is a popular belief, it is not Biblically based and therefore "it ends in the way of death."

📖 Read I John 2:15–17 and Matthew 16:24–27. These verses demonstrate that a love of the world and the pleasures of the world are not of the Father, but of the world.

📖 Read II Corinthians 5:1–7. Unlike Montgomery and her acquaintance, the Apostle Paul believes our souls yearn to be present with the Lord.

Bible   5. What solid advice does Marilla give about manners?

📖 Read II Timothy 3:2–4 and John 12:43. A prideful attitude is consumed with self. A prideful person strives to be admired.

📖 Read Proverbs 29:25; James 3:14; and Philippians 2:3. A person who demonstrates humility is consumed with God and others.

📖 Read Matthew 16:24. Humility draws attention to God. Read I Corinthians 10:31; I Corinthians 11:1. Anne realizes Marilla is right.

Literature   6. 📖 Read Proverbs 19:20. Look up "pride" and "humility" in the *American Dictionary of the English Language* (1828 edition).

📖 Read about writing poetry, pages 179–184, in *Writers INC*.

📖 In *The Green Gables Letters from L.M. Montgomery to Ephraim Weber 1905–1909*, page 34, read what Montgomery has to say about writing her poem, "The Choice."

The Poetry of Lucy Maud Montgomery contains "The Choice," as well as other poetry written by Montgomery. Or, for a "Sampling of Montgomery's Poetry," go to the link at <www.cadroncreek.com>.

✎ In the Bible section of your notebook:
Write a poem about either pride or humility.

---

7. The mention of Miss Muriel Stacy is an example of **foreshadowing**. | Literature

📖 Read in *Writers INC* about "foreshadowing."

---

8. Mrs. Lynde says Anne is full of "original sin." Original sin is the doctrine that humankind is innately depraved as the result of Adam's fall. | 💡 Bible

📖 Read these verses which refer to original sin: Psalm 51:5; Romans 5:12–21; and I Corinthians 15:21–22. Original sin is different from actual sin (Romans 3:23), which refers to sins committed by the individual.

♡ Memorize Romans 5:19.

---

9. Anne believes some people were naturally good. | Bible

✗✗ Discuss with your instructor whether or not you think this is true.

---

10. Etiquette shows you ways to think of other people rather than yourself. It is a good base from which to build our relationships with people. However, we have to remember the foundation of etiquette, the command to love our neighbors as ourselves. The goal is not to slavishly follow etiquette, but to use it as a guide on how to treat others. A good hostess has the manners to make guests feel comfortable, regardless of etiquette protocol. | Occupational Education

There is a wonderful story about Queen Elizabeth II that may or may not be true. The Queen was hosting a dinner of leaders of state, as she often does. The guest of honor was the leader of a distant nation where customs are different from our own. When the soup course was served, the leader picked up his bowl of soup and loudly started to drink from it! The other guests, aghast, looked to Queen Elizabeth to see her reaction to this breach of English manners. The Queen, understanding true manners, immediately and without showing that she saw anything amiss, picked up her own bowl of soup and began to drink it just as her guest had done, whereupon the other guests did the same and all was fine.

She was probably able to respond quickly this way because she had heard the story of Queen Victoria. One of Queen Victoria's dinner guests, unfamiliar with formal etiquette, drank the water from the finger bowl! The Queen, to make sure her guest was not dishonored, followed suit and drank from her own bowl as well.

Finger bowls provide a source of confusion to many. If a finger bowl is presented one should simply dip the tips of the fingers in the bowl, barely touching the lemon slice that is floating there, and then dry the fingers on the napkin.

With your instructor, discuss how she uses manners to make people feel comfortable.

Bible 11. The downfall of some dear hope or plan plunges Anne into "deeps of affliction." Notice the quotation marks around "deeps of affliction." It appears this saying may have had its origin in Christian circles. In the King James Version of the Bible there are four verses which have the word "deeps": Nehemiah 9:11; Psalm 88:6; Psalm 148:7; and Zechariah 10:11. In his commentary on Psalm 130:1–2, John Owen, used the phrase, "deeps of affliction." Part of this text may be found in the *Background Information Appendix*. John Owen, 1616–1683, was a Presbyterian writer who served Oliver Cromwell in England.

Occupational Education 12. Emily Post, 1873–1960, was born into a wealthy American family. She was an American authority on etiquette. She has advice on giving a tea.

Read her advice in the *Background Information Appendix*.

Have a tea for a younger girl. Make it as special as you can. What kind of things can you do to make her feel special?

History 13. Different times and different places have different rules of etiquette. To assume that all places must be the same is a false assumption. The saying, "When in Rome do as the Romans do," is very true of etiquette.

Read the following interesting samples of turn of the century etiquette:

THE VISIT OF EMPTY FORM

Not so many years ago, a lady or gentleman, young girl or youth, who failed to pay her or his "party call" after having been invited to Mrs. Social-Leader's ball was left out of her list when she gave her next one. For the old-fashioned hostess kept her visiting list with the precision of a bookkeeper in a bank; everyone's credit was entered or cancelled according to the presence of her or his cards in the card receiver. Young people who liked to be asked to her house were apt to leave an extra one at the door, on occasion, so that theirs should not be among the missing when the new list for the season was made up, especially as the more important old ladies were very quick to strike a name off, but seldom if ever known to put one back.

HOW TO ENTER A DRAWING-ROOM

To know how to enter a drawing-room is supposed to be one of the supreme tests of good breeding. But there should be no more difficulty in entering the drawing-room of Mrs. Worldly than in entering the sitting-room at home. Perhaps the best instruction would be like that in learning to swim. "Take plenty of time, don't struggle and don't splash about!" Good manners socially are not unlike swimming, not the "crawl" or "overhand," but smooth, tranquil swimming. (This advice is quite probably the source of the expression, "in the swim"!) Before actually entering a room, it is easiest to pause long enough to see where the hostess is. Never start forward and then try to find her as an afterthought. The place to pause is on the threshold, not half-way in the room. The way *not* to enter a drawing-room is to dart forward and then stand awkwardly bewildered and looking about in every direction. A man of the world stops at the entrance of the room for a scarcely perceptible moment, until he perceives the most unencumbered approach to the hostess, and he thereupon walks over to her. When he greets his hostess he pauses slightly, the hostess smiles and offers her hand; the gentleman smiles and shakes hands, at the same time bowing. A lady shakes hands with the hostess and with every one she knows who is nearby. She bows to acquaintances at a distance and to strangers to whom she is introduced.

HOW TO SIT GRACEFULLY

Having shaken hands with the hostess, the visitor, whether a lady or a gentleman, looks about quietly, without hurry, for a convenient chair to sit down upon, or drop into. To sit gracefully one should not perch stiffly on the edge of a straight chair, nor sprawl at length in an easy one. The perfect position is one that is easy, but dignified. In other days, no lady of dignity ever crossed her knees, held her hands on her hips, or twisted herself sideways, or even *leaned back in her chair*! To-day all these things are done; and the only etiquette left is on the subject of how not to exaggerate them. No lady should cross her knees so that her skirts go up to or above them; neither should her foot be thrust out so that her toes are at knee level. An arm a-kimbo is *not* a graceful attitude, nor is a twisted spine! Everyone, of course, leans against a chair back, except in a box at the opera and in a ballroom, but a lady should never throw herself almost at full length in a reclining chair or on a wide sofa when she is out in public. Neither does a gentleman in paying a formal visit sit on the middle of his backbone with one ankle supported on the other knee, and both as high as his head.

The proper way for a lady to sit is in the center of her chair, or slightly sideways in the corner of a sofa. She may lean back, of course, and easily; her hands relaxed in her lap, her knees together, or if crossed, her foot must not be thrust forward so as to leave a space between the heel and her other ankle. On informal occasions she can lean back in an easy chair with her hands on the arms. In a ball dress a lady of distinction never leans back in a chair; one cannot picture a beautiful and high-bred woman, wearing a tiara and other ballroom jewels, leaning against anything. This is, however, not so much a rule of etiquette as a question of beauty and fitness. A gentleman, also on very formal occasions, should sit in the center of his chair; but unless it is a deep lounging one, he always leans against the back and puts a hand or an elbow on its arms.

—Emily Post, *Etiquette in Society, in Business, in Politics and at Home*

With your parent discuss any similarities between etiquette then and now.

Practice sitting gracefully. I have two Victorian chairs. The backs have been broken several times by people using them in a manner for which they were not designed, lounging. Victorians did not lounge.

History/Health   14.   In the Background Information on Queen Victoria, the Opium Wars are briefly mentioned. Read about the Opium Wars.

If you find the information on the Internet, print what you read and found informative and put it into the History section of your notebook in the appropriate time period.

Briefly study about the problems opium has on the body and on society.

If you find the information on the Internet, print what you read and found informative and put it into the Health section of your notebook.

Pretend you are an enraged British citizen and write a letter to the editor opposing the Opium Wars or pretend you are a member of the House of Commons and write a speech you will give against the Opium Wars.

Science   15.   Continue to use Friday as a field day. Study the plants, flowers, and birds native to your area. Begin by identifying all the plants on your property. As time allows, increase the area. Take a camera or a sketch pad as well as plant and bird identification books. After a plant is identified, take a picture of it and place it in your Fine Arts notebook or draw it in your sketchbook and label it.

Literature   16.   With your instructor:

Continue with recitation each Friday during this Unit. Choose a favorite portion of a poem from this week's lesson to recite.

Each Friday quote memorized scriptures to your teacher: I Corinthians 10:13; The Lord's Prayer; Psalm 30; Romans 5:19; and your choice of Ephesians 3:20; Proverbs 17:27–28; or James 3:13, 17.

❧ Planning Guide

Gather These Items:

1. *Laurel's Kitchen Caring: Recipes for Everyday Home Caregiving* by Laurel Robertson. Ten Speed Press, 1997. ISBN 0-89815-951-2. This book is required for a "B" or better grade in Contract Reading — Occupational Education.

2. *American Dictionary of the English Language* (1828 edition) by Noah Webster.

3. Balance beam: either a 2" x 4" with blocks of wood attached underneath to elevate slightly or a real balance beam.

4. Items to make a goodie basket for a sick person:
   basket
   book or video (just for loan)
   nutritional goodie
   get well card

Research Topics:

1. Spinal cord and spinal cord injury (See Activities 3 and 4 for some information)

   . . . .

2. Fainting (See Activity 5 for some information)
   —*American Medical Association Family Medical Guide,* Third Edition, by American Medical Association. Random House, 1994. ISBN 0679412905.

   . . . .

3. First aid treatment
   —What to do and not do in cases of injury and accident
   —First aid kits for home and auto

   . . . .

4. Nutritional treatment for bone fractures
   —*The Natural Healing Cookbook: Over 450 Delicious Ways to Get Better and Stay Healthy* by Mark Bricklin and Sharon Claessens. Rodale Press, 1991. ASIN 0878573380.
   —*Prescription for Nutritional Healing: A Practical A–Z Reference to Drug-Free Remedies Using Vitamins, Minerals, Herbs, and Food*

Supplements, Third Edition, by James Balch, M.D. and Phyllis Balch, C.N.C. Avery Penguin Putnam, 2000. ISBN 1583330771.

5. Oliver Wendell Holmes

6. A picture of the tibia, fibula, and the talus, or ankle bone

7. Potato famine

8. The effects of bitterness and unforgivingness on health

Suggested Videos:

Suggested Field Trips:

1. Call your local nursing home or assisted living facility and ask if you can help any of the residents by reading or writing letters. (See Activity 18)

2. Visit someone who is sick or injured. (See Activity 19)

3. Take a first-aid class that includes instruction on how to handle the injured.

Group Activities:

Memory Work:
Memorize: Proverbs 25:27

Notes:

Assignments — Chapter XXIII

Contract Reading

	A Grade	B Grade	C Grade
Bible			
History			
Occupational Education	❏ *Laurel's Kitchen Caring*	❏ *Laurel's Kitchen Caring*	

Weekly

Quiet Time Reading Books: *Laurel's Kitchen Caring: Recipes for Everyday Home Care*

Independent Project:

Memory Work: Proverbs 25:27

Health: Complete your cardiovascular exercise program initiated in Unit 1, Chapter IV, Activity 9

	Literature	History	Bible	Health	Occu. Education	Science & Fine Arts	Grammar & Writing
M	Read Chap. XXIII AGG, Reading Comp., #2		#14	#3			#1, #2
T	Vocab., #9			#4, #15	#8		#10
W	#13	#20	#11	#5, #16			#11
Th	#17		#12, #17	#6, #7, #8	#18		
*F	#22 Recitation				#19 Field Trip	#21 Field Day	

*On Friday, at the end of each Unit, review and take the Unit Quiz in the *Test Appendix*. On quiz days parents and students may want to opt to reduce or eliminate Field Day and Recitation.

🐉 Study Guide

Read Chapter XXIII
Reading Comprehension:

1. Name some small mishaps that have occurred since Anne put the liniment in the cake.

2. What factor led to the girls daring each other?

3. What caused Anne's downfall?

4. When Marilla saw Mr. Barry carrying Anne, what revelation did she have?

5. What wish of Anne's came true? What did she think about it afterward?

6. Why would Marilla have stayed on the ground?

7. What were the consequences of Anne's foolishness?

8. What did Anne think was one good thing about being laid up?

9. What dark burden would Josie have been carrying if Anne had died?

Vocabulary Words:
unconscious

shrewish

Vocabulary:
🗝 Look up the vocabulary words in a dictionary or encyclopedia. Write sentences using each of the vocabulary words.

🌿 Activities:

Dictation   1. ✎ Write the following passage from dictation:

> At that moment Marilla had a revelation. In the sudden stab of fear that pierced to her very heart she realized what Anne had come to mean to her. She would have admitted that she liked Anne—nay, that she was very fond of Anne. But now she knew as she hurried wildly down the slope that Anne was dearer to her than anything on earth. —*Anne of Green Gables,* page 186

☀ Follow-up   2. Notice the use of strong, colorful words.

📖 From *Writers INC,* read about word choice on pages 22, 24, 78, and 130–131.

✎ Give examples of L. M. Montgomery's choice of a strong noun, a vivid verb, an active verb, a verb that shows. Pick one of your previous papers which would benefit from improvement in word choice. Write the improved words above the old ones.

Discuss the changes with your instructor:
   a. Did the changes help the paper or were they just changes?
   b. What depth did the changes add to your paper?

Circle any punctuation discrepancies and place chronological numbering beside each one. Use *Writers INC* to look up each omitted rule of punctuation. At the bottom of your dictation, write the number and the missed rule.

---

3. What causes one to become unconscious?   ☀ Health

Unconsciousness refers not only to a coma, but also to a state in which a person is drowsy, confused, and unable to respond to others. It may be precipitated by brain damage from head injury or stroke, loss of blood, lack of oxygen in the blood from drowning or other causes, or chemical changes caused by drugs or disease, as in a diabetic coma. If a person shows any of these signs of unconsciousness, contact 911.

Then, unless you suspect spinal cord damage, move the victim into the recovery position. In recovery position, the patient should be lying on his side, with his head forward so he can breathe freely and liquids can drain freely from the mouth. Arms and legs should be placed so they support the patient's body in a stable position.

---

4. When Anne fell she could have broken her back and damaged her   ☀ Health
spinal column. Before picking up someone after a fall what precautions should be taken?

Always check for signs of spinal injury. If the person has severe pain in the neck or spine, any tingling or loss of feeling or control in his arms or legs, or any loss of bladder or bowel control, the spinal column may be fractured or dislocated. If the patient is unconscious, especially from an accident, take spinal cord precautions. In such cases, do not move the person unless his life is in immediate danger or he is vomiting or choking. If the person must be moved, keep his body straight, and do not bend the back or neck or twist the body. Move the person's body in a straight line, preferably placing him on a rigid surface such as a door or ironing board.

Look up more information about spinal injury, recognizing the signs of possible spinal injury, and cautions as well as measures to take if you suspect spinal injury. Also, research more about what to do in case of injury and accident. You might want to take a first aid or other type of emergency care course. These are offered by various organizations like the Red Cross and local health offices.

With a friend or your instructor, review the description of the recovery position in Activity 3 and practice placing each other in that position. Also practice the first response to a person with possible spinal column injury and how to move them if you must.

Health

5. Fainting is the temporary loss of consciousness due to lack of oxygen to the brain. It may be a nervous reaction stemming from fear, hunger, pain, or any emotional shock. If a person who is about to faint or has fainted is starting to fall, try to steady them and control the fall. Establish a hold on the trunk of the person while keeping your own body in line to prevent injury to yourself. They should be made to lie down with the legs somewhat elevated and clothing should be loosened. If this is not possible and the person is conscious, he should sit with his head between his knees for about five minutes. Aromatic spirits of ammonia may be held under his nose until he revives. Prolonged loss of consciousness indicates a condition more serious than simple fainting and should be treated by a physician. Fainting was common among women in the Victorian era because of the tight corsets they wore. They even had fainting couches.

Make a poster demonstrating what to do for someone fainting.

Find out what a first aid kit should contain. Determine if aromatic spirits of ammonia and splints should be included in first aid kits.

In the Health section of you notebook, make a list of all the items home and auto first aid kits should contain.

With your instructor, make first aid kits for your home and automobiles. If you already have first aid kits, check them. Make sure they have all the items needed, they have a sufficient amount of each item, and all medicines have a current expiration date.

Review with your instructor how to handle the items in the kit as well as how and when to use each of the items.

Health

6. Anne breaks her ankle. The ankle joint is a hinge joint formed at the junction of the tibia, fibula, and the talus or ankle bone. The bones are cushioned by cartilage and connected by a number of ligaments, tendons, and muscles which strengthen the joint and enable it to be moved.

A fracture is a broken bone. Immediate first aid consists of splinting the bone. It should be supported in such a way that the injured part will remain steady and will resist jarring if the victim is moved. A fracture is "set" by reduction, which means the broken ends are pulled into alignment and the continuity of the bone is reestablished so healing can take place and the bones made whole. Once the reduction is accomplished, the bone is immobilized by the application of a cast or by exerting traction on the distal end of the bone.

Read about nutrition and nutritional healing, especially for someone with bone fractures.

In the Health section of your notebook:
a. Write about the type of nutrition and/or nutritional supplements which should be given to someone with broken bones to promote healing.

b. Draw and label a picture of the tibia, fibula, and the talus, or ankle bone.

---

7. Anne breaks her ankle. You are to bring dinner to help the family.

⏰ Health

✎ In the Health section of your notebook:
Plan a meal that would promote healing nutritionally.

---

8. People visit Anne while she is sick.

⏰ Occupational Education/ Health

📖 Read Matthew 25:35–45. From the *Background Information Appendix,* read John Wesley's sermon 98, "On Visiting the Sick." When is the last time you heard a sermon on visiting the sick?

📖 Read these rules of etiquette for visiting hospital patients:
1. Never sit on the bed; it cramps the patient.
2. Only stay a few minutes to wish the patient well.
3. If the nurse or doctor has to do something, be polite and leave the room.
4. If the patient wants to go for a walk with you, check with the nurse first to see if it is all right. Walking is usually very good for surgical patients, but be sure to watch the patient for any sign of tiredness or dizziness.
5. Be polite and stand if there are not enough chairs.
6. If you do take food, even if the patient has asked for it, check with the nurses to see if the patient can eat it
7. Be quiet while you are visiting. Others will be sleeping.

WHEN CARDS MUST BE LEFT

Etiquette absolutely demands that one leave a card within a few days after taking a first meal in a lady's house; or if one has for the first time been invited to lunch or dine with strangers, it is inexcusably rude not to leave a card upon them, whether one accepted the invitation or not.

One must also unfailingly return a first call, even if one does not care for the acquaintance. Only a real "cause" can excuse the affront to an innocent stranger that the refusal to return a first call would imply. If one does not care to continue the acquaintance, one need not pay a second visit. . . .

It seems scarcely necessary to add that anyone not entirely heartless must leave a card on, or send flowers to, an acquaintance who has suffered a recent bereavement. *One should also leave cards of inquiry or send flowers to sick people.* (Emphasis added.) —Emily Post, *Etiquette in Society, in Business, in Politics and at Home*

📖 *Laurel's Kitchen Caring: Recipes for Everyday Home Caregiving* by Laurel Robertson has nourishing, soothing, comforting dishes for anyone who is not well. In addition to giving recipes, it comforts and gives advice to the caregiver. This book is required for a "B" or better grade in Contract Reading — Occupational Education.

Literature   9. "A Morning Visit" seems to refer to a dialogue which is similar to "The Society for the Suppression of Gossip" and is mentioned in the next chapter. (For the full text of "The Society for the Suppression of Gossip," see *Anne's Anthology* or *The Annotated Anne of Green Gables,* pages 477–480.)

There is a poem called "The Morning Visit," written by the American poet, Oliver Wendell Holmes, which fits Anne's situation in that it humorously describes the bad behavior of doctors to patients.

📖 Read "The Morning Visit" in *Anne's Anthology,* then study about Oliver Wendell Holmes. This accomplished man was a lawyer, a physician, a medical professor, a poet, and the father of Supreme Court Justice Oliver Wendell Holmes, Jr.

Discuss with your instructor:
a. What was the target audience of this poem?
b. Do you think it was an effective teaching tool? Give the reasons for your opinion.

On your map, mark Oliver Wendell Holmes' country of origin.

Writing   10. 📖 Read about dialogue writing in *Writers INC.* See the sections, "Dialogue," on page 175, and "Placement of Punctuation," on page 468.

✎ In the Writing section of your notebook:
Create your own dialogue entitled "A Morning Visit." Use specific nouns and vivid verbs. You may want to write about a hypothetical visit between Tennyson and Browning.

Bible/Writing   11. Anne realizes her fall is because of pride. This is an experience which increases her hatred of sin and pride and decreases her willingness to sin. Through this experience she develops fear of the Lord and, therefore, her knowledge of the Lord increases.

📖 Read Proverbs 16:18; Proverbs 18:12; II Chronicles 32:25; Daniel 4:37; and Proverbs 1:7.

✎ In the Bible section of your notebook:
Write an acrostic poem on pride. (Acrostic poems are easy to write. Using all capital letters, write the word "pride" vertically on a piece of paper. Now think of a word that describes pride which begins with a "P" and write it beside the "P." Continue in this fashion, writing a word for each of the remaining letters: "R," "I," "D," and "E.")

Health   12. Bitterness and unforgivingness affect health. Use your concordance to find the effect they have on health. Anne is unwilling to forgive whom?

Find information on how bitterness and unforgivingness affect health.

✎ Record your findings in the Bible section of your notebook.

13. A **foil** is someone who serves as a contrast or a challenge to another character.

⌘ Discuss with your instructor:
Who is a foil for Anne?

— —

Literature

14. 📖 Read the definition of "honor" in the *American Dictionary of the English Language* (1828 edition).

Was Anne's honor truly at stake when Josie dared her to walk a ridge-pole? How does Proverbs 25:27 apply to this situation?

📖 Read Psalm 62:6–8; Psalm 71:20–21; Proverbs 3:13–17; Proverbs 15:32–33; and Proverbs 21:21.

✎ Write your thoughts about these verses in the Bible section of your notebook. Tell which teachings made an impression on you.

♡ Memorize Proverbs 25:27.

Bible

15. ✋ Walk on a balance beam and then perform the following:
   a. Balance on one foot, with your hands at your side. Now raise your arms out like an airplane. Finally, bend at the waist until your back is parallel with the beam.
   b. Walk the beam heal-to-toe.
   c. Walk the beam without looking at your feet.
   d. Walk sideways on the beam.
   e. Stoop down and pick something up off the beam.
   f. Duck walk forward.
   g. Duck walk sideward.
   h. Slowly skip the length of the beam.
   i. Kneel on one knee. Come to an erect position. Repeat, using the other leg.

Physical Education

16. ✋ Mark how far you can hop on one foot without putting your other foot down. Can you hop to your neighbor's house?

Physical Education

17. It was hard for Anne to think of Mr. Bell as a young boy.

📖 Read "An Old Lady's Poem" in the *Background Information Appendix*.

📖 Read Leviticus 19:32 and Proverbs 23:22.

⌘ With someone your parents' age or older, ask questions about their youth. Ask them if they ever hurt themselves and how they took care of their injury. Find out if the injury was their fault or someone else's.

Ask the older person if they have ever felt disdained because of their age. Do they feel people only see the elderly as they are currently, without a youth or past of any kind?

📖 Read Job 30:1 and Lamentations 5:12.

⌘ Discuss with your instructor how we treat the elderly today.

Literature/Bible

Occupational Education	18. ✋ Call your local nursing home or assisted living facility and ask if you can help any of the residents by reading or writing letters.
Occupational Education	19. ✋ Visit someone who is sick. Prepare an attractive basket for them. Include some nutritional goodies and a get well card you have made. If they like to read or watch television, loan them a book, video, or cassette tape to help them occupy their time. Be sure to pray with them.
History	20. 📖 In the *Background Information Appendix* on Queen Victoria, the potato disease and famine are mentioned. Read about the Potato Famine. ✏ If you find the information on the Internet, print what you read and found informative and put it into the History section of your notebook, in the appropriate time period.
Science	21. ✋ Continue to use Friday as a field day. Study the plants, flowers, and birds native to your area. Begin by identifying all the plants on your property. As time allows, increase the area. Take a camera or a sketch pad as well as plant and bird identification books. After a plant is identified, take a picture of it and place it in your Fine Arts notebook or draw it in your sketchbook and label it.
Literature	22. 👥 With your instructor: Continue with recitation each Friday during this Unit. Choose a favorite portion of a poem from this week's lesson or the dialogue you wrote to recite. Quote memorized scriptures to your teacher: I Corinthians 10:13; The Lord's Prayer; Psalm 30; Romans 5:19; Proverbs 25:27; and your choice of Ephesians 3:20; Proverbs 17:27–28; or James 3:13, 17.
💡 Quiz	23. Review and take Unit 5 Quiz in the *Test Appendix*.

———◆———

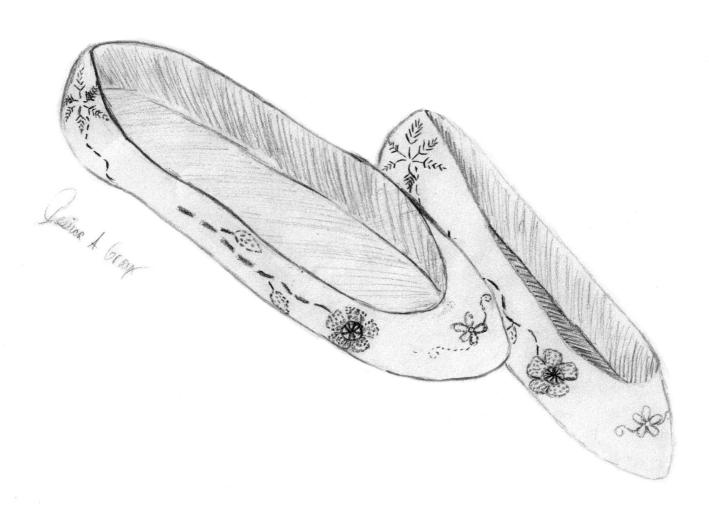

🦋 Planning Guide

Gather These Items:

1. Camera with film.

2. Costume and props for a *tableau vivant*. (See Activity 14)

Research Topics:

1. Mary, Queen of Scots

. . . .

2. Red Cross
   —American Red Cross Web site, <www.redcross.org>

. . . .

3. Crimean War
   —"The Crimean War." *A History of the English-Speaking Peoples: The Great Democracies,* Vol. 4, by Winston Churchill. Dodd Mead, 1958. ASIN 0396082718.

. . . .

4. Florence Nightingale
   —"Florence Nightingale." *Adventures in History.* Album AH-2, Tape H-17. Audiocassette. Your Story Hour, Christian Family Services, <http://www.headthirst.com/cfs/cfsyourstoryhour.shtml>

. . . .

5. Benefits of physical education

. . . .

6. History of the Canadian flag

. . . .

7. *Tableau vivant*
   —<http://norman.walsh.name/2004/02/08/images/letter>
   —<http://www.latinschool.org/scrapbook/lower/art_show/ tableau_vivant/>

. . . .

8. Pictures of P.E.I. during different seasons
   —Do a Web search for images with your favorite search engine and/or find some books on P.E.I. with pictures

. . . .

Suggested Videos:
1. *Mary of Scotland* (1936). Videocassette. Perf. Katharine Hepburn and Fredric March. Turner Home Entertainment, 1991. ASIN 6301278429. NR.

Suggested Field Trips:
1. Visit your local Red Cross. (See Activity 8)

Group Activities:
1. Plan and present a *tableau vivant*.

Memory Work:
I Corinthians 13:13

Notes:

Assignments — Chapter XXIV

Contract Reading: No new contract reading

Weekly
Quiet Time Reading Books:
Independent Project:
Memory Work: I Corinthians 13:13

	Literature	History	Bible	Health	Occu. Education	Science & Fine Arts	Grammar & Writing
M	Read Chap. XXIV AGG, Reading Comp.	#11	#15			#12	#1, #2
T	Vocab., #5	#3, #4				#14	#3, #5
W		#6	#9	#7			#6, #7
Th		#10		#8 Field Trip			#10, #13
F	#17 Recitation					#16 Field Day	

🪶 Study Guide

Read Chapter XXIV

Reading Comprehension:

1. How did Anne describe Miss Stacy?

2. What did Anne recite?

3. What did Anne dearly want to be?

4. Why did Anne not see herself as being able to be a foreign missionary?

5. Why was Matthew glad he did not have to bring up Anne?

6. What did Matthew add to Anne's life?

Vocabulary words:

laudable

gadding

vivacious

Vocabulary:

🗝 Look up the vocabulary words in a dictionary or encyclopedia. Classify the words according to their parts of speech: noun, verb, adverb, or adjective. Use each word in a sentence. *See answers in Answer Appendix.*

 Activities:

Dictation	1. ✎ Write the following passage from dictation. (Note: The instructor will need to indicate the beginning of each line to the student.)
	The swords are drawn, the daggers gleam, the tears and words are vain— The ruffian steel is in his heart, the faithful Rizzio's slain! Then Mary Stuart dashed aside the tears that trickling fell: "Now for my father's arm!" she cried; "my woman's heart farewell!" —Henry Glassford Bell, "Mary, Queen of Scots"
Follow-up	2. ✎ Compare your copy with the original. Correct any mistakes.
☀ History	3. 📖 Read about Mary, Queen of Scots. ✎ In the History section of your notebook, in the appropriate time period: Write half a page about this queen. What do you think was her Achilles' heel? 🧭 On your map, mark the birthplace of Mary, Queen of Scots, and the place from which she ruled. Mark any other places of significance in her life and reign.
History	4. 👓 Watch the video, *Mary of Scotland,* (1936), with Katharine Hepburn and Fredric March.
Literature	5. 📖 From *Anne's Anthology* (*The Annotated Anne of Green Gables,* pages 475–477), read the poem, "Mary, Queen of Scots."

With your instructor discuss:
1. What is the rhyme pattern of this poem?
2. What happens in this poem?

On your map, mark some of the important places in this poem.

Look up information on the author of this poem, Henry Glassford Bell.

In the History section of your notebook, in the appropriate time period:
Write a paragraph about the life of this author.

---

6. Read about Florence Nightingale or study the early beginnings of
the American Red Cross and its founder, Clara Barton.

History

In the History section of your notebook, in the appropriate time period:
Write about how Florence Nightingale changed nursing OR write
about Clara Barton and the American Red Cross.

On your map, mark some of the important places in the life of the
person you chose to study.

---

7. Read about the benefits of physical education.

Health

In the Health section of your notebook:
a. Describe how physical education improves gracefulness and promotes good digestion.
b. Were these benefits widely recognized in the 1870's?
c. Describe your physical education program. Write about what you are
doing to increase your strength, flexibility, and endurance.

---

8. Visit your local Red Cross. Find out what they do both between and
during times of crisis. What are the qualifications for volunteer workers? If there is no Red Cross office in your community, and if you have
access to the Internet, visit the American Red Cross Web site,
<www.redcross.org>.

Field trip

In the Health section of your notebook:
Print the information you gathered and highlight the answers to the
questions or write a summary of your findings.

---

9. Marilla opposes concerts and practices because she considers them to
be "gadding about."

Bible

Read Charles Spurgeon's sermon, "Gadding About," in the *Background
Information Appendix*. This sermon was published in 1906. Remember
Anne of Green Gables was not published until 1907. Could the voracious reader, Montgomery, have read this sermon and included reference to it in her book?

If concerts and practices are "gadding about," then Marilla would be
justified in opposing them. What is wrong with "gadding about"?

Read Proverbs 31 and Titus 2:3–5.

※ Discuss your thoughts and opinions regarding "gadding about" with your instructor. Include your answers to the following questions in your discussion:
  a. Were the concerts and practices Anne attended "gadding about" or were they an important educational opportunity?
  b. If educational, what skills was Anne learning while she was enjoying herself?

☀ History   10. ☞ Learn about the Crimean War. What were the causes of it, who fought in it, who won it, and what effect did the war have on history?

✎ In the History section of your notebook, in the appropriate time period: Write at least one paragraph about the Crimean War. At the bottom of the page, draw a map of the area in which it was fought.

✥ Mark where this war occurred on your world map.

☀ History   11. ☞ Research the evolution of the Canadian flag.

✎ In the History section of your notebook, write:
  a. What does the Canadian flag look like today?
  b. What would it have looked like during Anne's youth?
  c. What events precipitated changes to its design?
  d. Draw a picture of what the flag looks like today, what it looked like in Anne's youth, and what it looked like after any significant changes.

Science   12. We have been through all four seasons, gloriously described. What season sounds the most appealing during which to visit P.E.I.?

📖 From the *Annotated Anne of Green of Gables,* read pages 434–438, "Gardens and Plants."

☞ Find some pictures of P.E.I. which show what the area looks like in the different seasons.

Literature   13. ✎ Write a composition about a remarkable person.

Fine Arts   14. "And we're to have a tableau at the last—*Faith, Hope* and *Charity.*" (See page 262, *The Annotated Anne of Green Gables.*) The word, "tableau," is

> . . . a short form of *tableau vivant,* literally "living picture." A tableau is a representation of a personage, character, scene, incident, or such, or of a well-known painting or statue, by one person or group of people in suitable costumes and attitudes, who remain silent and motionless. Faith, hope, and charity are traditional Christian virtues: "And now abideth faith, hope, charity, these three; but the greatest of these is charity" (Corinthians I 13:13).
> —*The Annotated Anne of Green Gables,* page 263

✋ Plan and present a *tableau vivant*. See the *Activity Appendix* for directions. Be sure to take pictures.

15. What character has hope for Anne? What character or characters have love for Anne?   Bible

📖 What does the Bible say about love and hope? Read I Corinthians 13. What does verse 7 say about hope?

♡ Memorize I Corinthians 13:13.

16. ✋ Continue to use Friday as a field day. Study the plants, flowers, and   Science
birds native to your area. Begin by identifying all the plants on your property. As time allows, increase your observation area. Take a camera or a sketch pad as well as plant and bird identification books. After a plant is identified, take a picture of it and place it in your Fine Arts notebook or draw it in your sketchbook and label it.

17. 🎭 With your instructor: Literature
Continue with recitation each Friday during this Unit. Recite "Mary, Queen of Scots."

Quote memorized scriptures to your teacher: I Corinthians 10:13; The Lord's Prayer; Psalm 30; Romans 5:19; Proverbs 25:27; I Corinthians 13:13; and your choice of Ephesians 3:20; Proverbs 17:27–28; or James 3:13, 17.

Planning Guide

Gather These Items:

1. *American Dictionary of the English Language* (1828 edition) by Noah Webster.

2. Items to make Christmas decorations. See *Activity Appendix* for directions. (See Activity 8)
   large sleigh bells
   strap to sew the bells on
   key chain ring
   pink and white tissue paper
   green florist tape
   construction paper
   paper doilies
   glue stick

3. An inexpensive pair of pastel leather or satin slippers. Check at yard sales or at thrift stores like Goodwill. (See Activity 9)
   beads
   satin bows
   buckles
   fabric glue or hot glue gun with glue sticks
   needle and thread

4. *The Normal Christian Life* by Watchman Nee. Kingsway Publications, 1961. This book is required for an "A" grade in Contract Reading — Bible. The entire text of the 1961 edition of this book is online at <http://www.ccel.org/n/nee/normal/normal.htm>. (Note: There are a number of editions and publishers of this book.)

5. *Whatever Happened to Penny Candy?: A Fast, Clear and Fun Explanation of the Economics You Need for Success in Your Career, Business and Investments,* 4th edition, by Rick Maybury, Richard J. Maybury, and Nancy Bixler. Bluestocking Press, 2000. ISBN: 0942617312. This book is required for a "C" or better grade in Contract Reading — History.

Research Topics:

1. Beaded shoes
   —Do an Internet search for "beaded shoes"

   . . . .

2. Exchange rate, Canadian to US dollars
   —<http://www.x-rates.com/calculator.html>

   . . . .

3. Price of flags
   —<http://store.yahoo.com/united-states-flag/outdoorflags.html>

   . . . .

4. Inflation

   . . . .

5. Irony
   —Dramatic irony: <http://wwwksu.edu/english/baker/english320/
   cc-dramatic_irony.htm> and <http://www.kippax.org.au/sermons/
   19981122.htm>
   —Verbal irony: <http://www.ksu.edu/english/baker/english320/
   cc-verbal_irony.htm>
   —Irony of situation

   . . . .

Suggested Videos:

Suggested Field Trips:

Group Activities:

Memory Work:
Romans 8:5–8

Notes:

Assignments — Chapter XXV

Contract Reading

	A Grade	B Grade	C Grade
Bible	❑ *The Normal Christian Life*		
History	❑ *Whatever Happened to Penny Candy?*	❑ *Whatever Happened to Penny Candy?*	❑ *Whatever Happened to Penny Candy?*
Literature			

Weekly

Quiet Time Reading Books: *The Normal Christian Life; Whatever Happened to Penny Candy?*
Independent Project:
Memory Work: Romans 8:5–8

	Literature	History	Bible	Health	Occu. Education	Science & Fine Arts	Grammar & Writing
M	Read Chap. XXV AGG, Reading Comp.		#3				#1, #2
T	Vocab., #5	#10	#4			#8	#4, #10
W			#6		#9		#6
Th			#7				#7
F	#12 Recitation					#11 Field Day	

🪲 Study Guide

Read Chapter XXV
Reading Comprehension:

1. After much consideration, what did Matthew see as different about Anne?

2. What was a matter of conscience with Matthew?

3. How did Matthew solve the dilemma of purchasing a dress with puffed sleeves?

4. Mrs. Lynde saw Marilla as making what mistake in raising Anne?

5. What kind of Christmas were the people in Avonlea looking for?

6. What gift did Diana bring that was providential?

7. What gave Anne courage for the performance?

8. How old was Anne?

9. Was Marilla proud of Anne's performance? Did she tell her? Did Matthew?

10. What did Matthew think needed a lot of thinking over? What does this say about his personality?

Vocabulary:

🗝 Look up the vocabulary words in a dictionary or encyclopedia. Classify the words according to their parts of speech: noun, verb, adverb, or adjective. Use each word in a sentence.

Vocabulary Words:

cogitation

ingratiatingly

deprecatory

Activities:

1. ✎ Write the following passage from dictation: "I suppose she's trying to cultivate a spirit of humility in Anne by dressing her as she does; but it's more likely to cultivate envy and discontent. I'm sure the child must feel the difference between her clothes and the other girls'. But to think of Matthew taking notice of it! That man is waking up after being asleep for over sixty years." —*Anne of Green Gables,* pages 199–200	Dictation
2. "She's" and "I'm" are contractions for what words? Did you remember the apostrophe? What type of sentence is the one which speaks about "Matthew"? Could you tell by the reading that an exclamation mark belonged there? There is an apostrophe after "girls," but there is no noun following. Why?	Follow-up

☼ Bible

3. Had Anne demanded a dress with puffed sleeves, she could have pointed out they were wealthy enough to buy her such a dress, but she does not. Anne also could have felt slighted and resentful she does not have puffed sleeves, but she does not. Anne is thankful for what she does have. In our devotion time we accomplish much more by rejoicing and surrender than by pleading and asking. It is one of the weapons of our warfare as Christians (II Corinthians 10:3–5). We begin to break through when we **rejoice** in the midst of adversity. God delights to turn things around and bring forth miracles when we rejoice (Acts 16:25–26). When we rejoice we learn patience, experience hope, and grow in Christ. When we react in anger, guilt, fear, or anxiety, we enter a vicious cycle of misery, defeat, and self-destruction.

Paraphrased from Otto Koning's sermon, "The Weapons of Our Warfare"

📖 Read and ponder what Paul wrote in Romans 8:5–8.

♡ Memorize Romans 8:5–8.

☼ Bible

4. Anne wants to be a model girl, but then what happens? Anne finds ". . . somehow it's hard to carry out your resolutions when irresistible temptations come."

Two of Satan's weapons against us are deception and temptation, but our spiritual weapons are more than adequate to overcome Satan's lies. One weapon of our warfare is **resisting**.

Paraphrased from Otto Koning's sermon, "The Weapons of Our Warfare"

📖 Read I Peter 5:8–9. Good verses for Anne to have memorized are I Corinthians 10:13 and James 4:6–10.

📖 Anne describes the same conflicts Paul did in Romans 7 and 8. Read these two chapters.

📖 Read in *Writers INC* about writing paraphrases, pages 256–257 and 402.

✎ In the Bible section of your notebook:
Write a paraphrase of Romans 7 and 8.

📖 For an "A" grade in Contract Reading — Bible, read the Christian classic which addresses Romans 7 and 8, *The Normal Christian Life,* by Watchman Nee.

☼ Literature

5. 📖 From *Anne's Anthology* or *The Annotated Anne of Green Gables,* pages 477–480, read "The Society for the Suppression of Gossip."

✎ In the Literature section of your notebook write:
a. What role do the characters' names play in the dialogue?
b. What views of males are expressed by the characters in "The Society for the Suppression of Gossip"?
c. What views of females are expressed by the characters?
d. To what do you think the author of the dialogue is alluding regarding the differences or similarities between males and females?

Read about **irony** in *Writers INC,* page 237. In the *Background Information Appendix,* read the sermon on dramatic irony.

There are three different kinds of irony:
dramatic irony: It is ironic that Gilbert picks up the rose that fell from Anne's hair.
verbal irony: "It's nothing to me what that person does," said Anne loftily. "I simply never waste a thought on him, Diana."
irony of situation: It is ironic the Cuthberts want a boy who can work for them and get a girl who they want to send to college. When Anne finally faints, she finds it is much less romantic than imagined.

What type of irony can you find in the dialogue, "The Society for the Suppression of Gossip"? Give examples. Find examples of the gossip which they are attempting to suppress. Pay attention to the names of the characters. How similar are they to their names?

Montgomery uses irony frequently in the *Anne of Green Gables* books. As you continue in *Anne of Green Gables,* look for further examples of irony. Briefly describe each instance in the Literature section of your notebook, explaining the irony and noting the type of irony exemplified.

---

6. Use your concordance and look up three scriptures on gossip.   Bible
    What does the Bible say about gossip?

In the Bible section of your notebook:
From the *American Dictionary of the English Language* (1828 edition), write the definition of "gossip." Then write an essay of definition about gossip. Identify gossip in the dialogue in Activity 5 above. In their book, *Are You Liberal? Conservative? or Confused?,* the Mayburys write that conservatives want to legislate morality. "The Society for the Suppression of Gossip" is a hilarious example of what happens when people try to legislate morality.

---

7. Anne perseveres in being nice to Josie Pye, even though she feels Josie   Bible
    would rejoice at her failures.

Reread II Peter 1:2–8. It takes self-control to develop perseverance.

In the Bible section of your notebook:
Write a definition of perseverance derived from a combination of the dictionary definition and Scripture. For the conclusion, include situations you have read in *Anne of Green Gables* where characters demonstrate perseverance.

Read Proverbs 24:17–18. As we see Gilbert continuing to "turn the other cheek" towards Anne, we see Anne doing the same towards Josie. "As the bird by wandering, as the swallow by flying, so the curse causeless shall not come" (Proverbs 26:2).

Fine Arts	8. ✋ Make Anne-like Christmas decorations. See *Activity Appendix* for directions. Lacy Paper Fans Pink and White Tissue Roses Matthew's Sleigh Bell Door Chimes

Occupational Education	9. ✋ Anne receives "kid slippers, with beaded toes and satin bows and glistening buckles" from Diana's aunt. Make beaded slippers by decorating an inexpensive pair of leather or satin slippers. For ideas, look at several varieties of beaded shoes on the Internet. Sew and glue beads, satin bows, and buckles on in a beautifully creative pattern. Make both slippers match.

💡 History   10. Diana states they probably "made as much as ten dollars" from the concert.

✎ Was this a good amount of money to raise for a flag? To help answer this question, determine how much ten dollars is worth in today's currency. Start by finding out what ten dollars in Canadian money would be in U.S. dollars. Look up the current exchange rate and multiply that number by $10.00. Then convert that amount into today's value by using Consumer Price Index (CPI) Conversion Factors. Round your answer to the nearest dollar. (See the *Background Information Appendix*.) Compare your answer to the estimate in the *Answer Appendix*. Answers will vary due to exchange rates. For those of you living in other countries this can be done the same way using your monetary standard.

🔑 Look at the price of your country's flag. Would the amount they collected (converted into today's value) have been enough to buy a flag appropriate for a school?

🔑 Learn about inflation. Be able to name at least three causes of inflation. What causes the rise and fall of the U.S. dollar in the world market?

✎ In a couple of paragraphs, write what you have learned from your research in the History section of your notebook.

📖 Read *Whatever Happened to Penny Candy?*. It is a remarkably easy and fun explanation of investment cycles, velocity, business cycles, recessions, inflation, the demand for money, and more. This book is Contract Reading — History for a "C" or better grade.

Science   11. ✋ Continue to use Friday as a field day. Study the plants, flowers, and birds native to your area. Begin by identifying all the plants on your property. As time allows, increase your observation area. Take a camera or a sketch pad as well as plant and bird identification books. After a plant is identified, take a picture of it and place it in your Fine Arts notebook or draw it in your sketchbook and label it.

12. ❋ With your instructor: Literature

Continue with recitation each Friday during this Unit. Recite some of
your favorite poems or a portion of the dialogue, "The Society for the
Suppression of Gossip."

Quote memorized scriptures to your teacher: I Corinthians 10:13; The
Lord's Prayer; Psalm 30; Romans 5:19; Proverbs 25:27; I Corinthians
13:13; Romans 8:5–8; and your choice of Ephesians 3:20; Proverbs
17:27–28; or James 3:13, 17.

🜨 Planning Guide

Gather These Items:
1. *Hamlet* by William Shakespeare, either an online or a hard copy from the library.

Research Topics:
1. Dwight L. Moody

   . . . .

2. Charles Spurgeon

   . . . .

3. Shorthand

   . . . .

4. Songs written by Ira Sankey
   —Hymnal
   —<http://www.cyberhymnal.org/bio/s/a/sankey_id.htm>

   . . . .

5. Ira Sankey
   —<http://www.wholesomewords.org/biography/biorpsankey.html>
   —<http://www.silentwordministries.org/devotion/50.htm>

   . . . .

6. Creative writing contests
   —Do a search on the Internet

   . . . .

7. George Eliot

   . . . .

Suggested Videos:
1. *The Mill on the Floss.* Videocassette. Perf. Emily Watson. WGBH Boston Video, 1997. ASIN B00005JHBS. (Parents please preview this film!)

Suggested Field Trips:

Group Activities:
1. Begin a Story Club as described by Anne. Have weekly or bimonthly meetings and read aloud stories you have written. There are also homeschool online writing clubs. Remember to follow all Internet safety rules, even if it is a homeschool club.

Memory Work:
Psalm 15

Notes:

Assignments — Chapter XXVI

Contract Reading: No new contract reading

Weekly
Quiet Time Reading Books:
Independent Project:
Memory Work: Psalm 15

	Literature	History	Bible	Health	Occu. Education	Science & Fine Arts	Grammar & Writing
M	Read Chap. XXVI AGG, Reading Comp., #2		#15				#1, #2
T	#11	#3	#7, #8				#3, #8
W	#12, #13		#4				#5, #13
Th	#14, #16, #17		#6				#6, #9
F	#19 Recitation					#18 Field Day	#10

❧ Study Guide

Read Chapter XXVI
Reading Comprehension:

1. What effect did the concert have on the residents of Avonlea? Who fought for Anne's reputation?

2. What was Anne's response to people confessing their past sins? What was Mrs. Lynde's response?

3. What did Marilla think of the story club?

 Activities:

Dictation

1. ✎ The following dictation is considerably longer than usual. It is excerpted from a sermon by Charles Spurgeon. When he preached, Spurgeon would speak for forty minutes from only one page of notes. His sermons were recorded in shorthand and then published in the newspaper. Although he would speak many times in a week, only one sermon per week was printed. For this reason, the tradition of his sermons being printed in the newspaper continued long after his death until all the sermons were printed.

Many famous writers developed and improved their own style of writing by copying whole books by their favorite authors.

"They shall speak of the glory of thy kingdom, and talk of thy power." Psalm 145:11

You have only to look at the preceding verse, and you will discover, in a single moment, who are the people here spoken of who shall speak of the glory of God's kingdom, and talk of his power. They are the saints: "All thy works shall praise thee, O Lord, and thy saints shall bless thee. . . ."

Possibly some will ask, "Well, sir, how can we talk about religion? Upon what topic shall we converse? How are we to introduce it? It would not be polite, for instance, in the company with which we associate, to begin to say anything about the doctrines of grace, or about religious matters at all." Then, beloved, be not so polite; that is all I have to say in reply to such a remark as that. If it would be accounted contrary to etiquette to begin talking of the Saviour, cast etiquette to the winds, and speak about Christ somehow or other. The Christian is the aristocrat of the world; it is his place to make rules for society to obey,—not to stoop down, and conform to the regulations of society when they are

contrary to the commands of his Master. He is the great
Maker of laws; the King of kings, and the Lord of lords; and
he makes his people also to be kings. Kings make rules for
ordinary men to obey; so must Christians do. They are not to
submit to others; they must make others, by worth of their
principles, and the dignity of their character, submit to them.
It is speaking too lightly of a Christian's dignity when we say
that he dare not do the right, because it would not be fashionable. We care nothing for that, for "the fashion of this world
passeth away," "but he that doeth the will of God abideth
forever. . . ."

First, here is A SUBJECT FOR CONVERSATION: "They
shall speak of the glory of thy kingdom, and talk of thy
power." Here are two subjects; for God, when he puts grace
into the heart, does not lack a subject upon which we shall
converse.

First, we are to converse concerning *the glory of Christ's
kingdom*. The glory of Christ's kingdom should ever be a
subject of discourse to a Christian; he should always be
speaking, not merely of Christ's priesthood or his prophesying,
but also of his kingdom, which has lasted from all eternity; and
especially of that glorious kingdom of grace in which we now
live, and of that brighter kingdom of millennial glory, which
soon shall come upon this world, to conquer all other kingdoms, and break them in pieces. —Charles Spurgeon, "Christian Conversation"

---

2. ✎ Compare your copy with the original. Circle mistakes in red, including spelling. Then have someone else compare your copy to see if he or
she finds any additional errors.

📖 Read about shorthand; look at samples of shorthand. (*Writers INC* has
a section on shorthand on page 396.) What are the uses and advantages of shorthand?

Follow-up

---

3. Anne's classmate, Moody Spurgeon, is named after two contemporary
evangelists. Interestingly, Charles Spurgeon was English, while
Dwight L. Moody was American. The two men knew and respected
each other. Dwight L. Moody taught at Spurgeon's church during an
evangelistic campaign in England.

☀ History

Charles Haddon (C. H.) Spurgeon was born June 17, 1834. At the age
of six he read *Pilgrim's Progress* for the first time. He is said to have
read this book more than a hundred times prior to his death in 1892.
Some of his notable evangelical acquaintances were George Mueller
and Hudson Taylor. As a compelling speaker, Spurgeon said he had but
one solitary purpose: "I take my text and make a bee-line to the cross."
A single burning desire filled his heart—to see people come to Jesus
Christ by faith. "Saving faith is an immediate relation to Christ, accepting, receiving, resting upon Him alone, for justification, sanctifica-

tion, and eternal life by virtue of God's grace," Spurgeon explained. Devoted to the Scriptures, to disciplined prayer, and to godly living, Spurgeon exemplified Christian commitment when he stood in the pulpit. It was the power behind his preaching. As a Baptist preacher, Spurgeon's most controversial sermon was "Down Grade," which spoke against Charles Darwin's theory of evolution and the liberal theology which threatened to downgrade the church. Spurgeon also frequently spoke out against slavery.

📖 Read more about Charles Spurgeon.

✏️ In the History section of your notebook, in the appropriate time period: Write half a page about this powerful man of God. Do you think Queen Victoria ever heard this man preach?

Dwight Lyman (D. L.) Moody was born February 5, 1837 in Northfield, Massachusetts. He started as a shoe salesman, then became a preacher. Just ten years before his death in 1889, he founded the Chicago Bible Institute, later called the Moody Bible Institute. He founded religious schools and wrote hymns. He said, "I am only one, but I am one. I cannot do everything, but I can do something. And that which I can do, by the grace of God, I will do." With that simple commitment, God used him to bring revival to England and America. One of his closest friends, R. A. Torrey, thought God used D. L. Moody because he was (1) fully surrendered, (2) a man of prayer, (3) a student of the Word of God, (4) a humble man, (5) free from love of money, (6) consumed with a passion for the lost, and (7) possessed a definite endowment of power from on high.

Dwight Moody visited England. Guess what two men he really wanted to visit! Hint: They lived in England; we have studied about them this year.

📖 Read more about this dynamic evangelist.

✏️ In the History section of your notebook, in the appropriate time period: Write half a page about this man and his accomplishments.

🔑 Find songs written by Ira Sankey for D. L. Moody's ministry. Sing them or play them on a musical instrument.

📖 Read about Ira Sankey's life.

✏️ In the History section of your notebook, in the appropriate time period: Write one paragraph about this man and his accomplishments.

Bible   4. Ruby Gillis thinks of nothing but beaus. When she marries, what will she think of then? What else should girls think of?

📖 Finish reading the rest of the sermon, "Christian Conversation," from the *Background Information Appendix*. Make it a goal to daily speak of the glory of God's kingdom and His power. Write in your journal daily about God's glory.

5. In *Writers INC,* read about note taking on pages 392–396 and about making an outline on page 108.

Literature

✎ Charles Spurgeon was an organized, effective speaker. Outline one of his sermons. Two of his sermons are included in the *Background Information Appendix.*

6. Anne refers to "just a few things proper to talk about on Sundays." During this period, Sundays were modeled after and frequently called, the Sabbath. People did little work, attended church, and spent time reading the Bible and memorizing Scripture. The focus was meant to be on spiritual things. In America, some states had "blue laws" restricting the consumption or selling of either nonedible items or alcohol on Sundays.

🎇 Bible

📖 Read Exodus 20:8–11; Deuteronomy 5:12–15; Psalm 92; Isaiah 56:6–7; and Mark 2:27–28.

📖 The following is from *A Puritan Catechism, With Proofs,* compiled by C. H. Spurgeon, "Heir of the Puritans":

Q. 49. Which is the fourth commandment?
A. The fourth commandment is, "Remember the Sabbath day, to keep it holy. Six days shalt thou labour, and do all thy work: but the seventh day is the Sabbath of the Lord thy God: in it thou shalt not do any work, thou, nor thy son, nor thy daughter, thy manservant, nor thy maidservant, nor they cattle, nor thy stranger that is within thy gates. For in six days the Lord made heaven and earth, the sea, and all that in them is, and rested the seventh day: wherefore the Lord blessed the Sabbath day and hallowed it."

Q. 50. What is required in the fourth commandment?
A. The fourth commandment requires the keeping holy to God such set times as he has appointed in his Word, expressly one whole day in seven, to be a holy Sabbath to himself (Lev. 19:30; Deut. 5:12).

Q. 51. How is the Sabbath to be sanctified?
A. The Sabbath is to be sanctified by a holy resting all that day, even from such worldly employments and recreations as are lawful on other days (Lev. 23:3), and spending the whole time in the public and private exercises of God's worship (Ps. 92:1–2; Isa. 58:13–14), except so much as is taken up in the works of necessity and mercy (Matt. 12:11–12).

D. L. Moody made the following appeal in regard to the Sabbath:

There has been an awful letting-down in this country regarding the Sabbath during the last twenty-five years, and many a man has been shorn of spiritual power, like Samson, because he is not straight on this question. Can you say that you observe the Sabbath properly? You may be a professed

Christian: are you obeying this commandment? Or do you neglect the house of God on the Sabbath day, and spend your time drinking and carousing in places of vice and crime, showing contempt for God and His law? Are you ready to step into the scales? Where were you last Sabbath? How did you spend it?

I honestly believe that this commandment is just as binding today as it ever was. I have talked with men who have said that it has been abrogated, but they have never been able to point to any place in the Bible where God repealed it. When Christ was on earth, He did nothing to set it aside; He freed it from the traces under which the scribes and Pharisees had put it, and gave it its true place. "The Sabbath was made for man, not man for the Sabbath." It is just as practicable and as necessary for men today as it ever was—in fact, more than ever, because we live in such an intense age.

The Sabbath was binding in Eden, and it has been in force ever since. The fourth commandment begins with the word remember, showing that the Sabbath already existed when God wrote this law on the tables of stone at Sinai. How can men claim that this one commandment has been done away with when they will admit that the other nine are still binding?

I believe that the Sabbath question today is a vital one for the whole country. It is the burning question of the present time. If you give up the Sabbath the church goes; if you give up the church the home goes; and if the home goes the nation goes. That is the direction in which we are traveling.

The church of God is losing its power on account of so many people giving up the Sabbath, and using it to promote selfishness.

✎ In the Bible section of your notebook, write:
How does your family "honor the Sabbath"? Also, respond to Moody's statement that "people giving up the Sabbath" are promoting selfishness.

Bible   7. What does Anne consider to be her besetting sin?

📖 Read about besetting sins in Hebrews 12:1 and then consider this devotional, "More Than Conquerors," by Charles Spurgeon:

"Nay, in all these things we are more than conquerors through him that loved us." Romans 8:37

We go to Christ for forgiveness, and then too often look to the law for power to fight our sins. Paul thus rebukes us, "O foolish Galatians, who hath bewitched you, that ye should not obey the truth? This only would I learn of you, Received ye the Spirit by the works of the law, or by the hearing of faith?

are ye so foolish? having begun in the Spirit, are ye now made perfect by the flesh?" Take your sins to Christ's cross, for the old man can only be crucified there: we are crucified with him.

The only weapon to fight sin with is the spear which pierced the side of Jesus. To give an illustration, you want to overcome an angry temper, how do you go to work? It is very possible you have never tried the right way of going to Jesus with it. How did I get salvation? I came to Jesus just as I was, and I trusted him to save me. I must kill my angry temper in the same way? It is the only way in which I can ever kill it. I must go to the cross with it, and say to Jesus, "Lord, I trust thee to deliver me from it." This is the only way to give it a death-blow. Are you covetous? Do you feel the world entangle you? You may struggle against this evil so long as you please, but if it be your besetting sin, you will never be delivered from it in any way but by the blood of Jesus. Take it to Christ. Tell him, "Lord, I have trusted thee, and thy name is Jesus, for thou dost save thy people from their sins; Lord, this is one of my sins; save me from it!"

Ordinances are nothing without Christ as a means of mortification. Your prayers, and your repentances, and your tears—the whole of them put together—are worth nothing apart from him. "None but Jesus can do helpless sinners good;" or helpless saints either. You must be conquerors through him who hath loved you, if conquerors at all. Our laurels must grow among his olives in Gethsemane.

---

8. Montgomery writes to Mr. Weber on her view of Christ. Read *The Green Gables Letters from L.M. Montgomery to Ephraim Weber 1905–1909*, pages 35 and 67. Montgomery's beliefs stated on these pages are contrary to what the Bible says about Christ. Pretend that L.M. Montgomery wrote you these passages.   Bible

✎ In the Bible section of your notebook write:
Your return letter to her. Utilize your concordance to help you find scriptures that support your view.

---

9. 📖 From *Writers INC*, read the section on "Personal Writing" on pages 143–153. Pay particular attention to "reminiscence writing," which is writing that focuses on a memorable past experience.   Writing

✎ In the Writing section of your notebook:
Write a composition on "A Winter's Walk in the Woods." (Instructors, the "Assessment Rubric" for grading is on page 154 of *Writers INC*.)

---

10. 📖 From *Writers INC*, read the "Creative Writing" sections on pages 167–178. This will give you various approaches to creative writing.   Writing

✎ Use these suggestions to write a short story.

☝ Begin a Story Club as described by Anne. Have weekly or bimonthly meetings and read aloud stories you have written. Each week write a new story, the continuation of a previous one similar to Charles Dickens' serial stories for the newspapers, or write an improved, edited version of one of your previous stories. There are also homeschool online writing clubs. Remember to follow all Internet safety rules, even if it is a homeschool club.

☝ Enter your story in a creative writing contest.

Literature   11. After the concert, things seem "weary, flat, stale, and unprofitable." This phrase was taken from *Hamlet,* Act I, Scene 2.

📖 Read Act I until you find this phrase.

✎ In the Literature section of your notebook, write:
a. What caused Hamlet to feel this way?
b. Why does Anne feel this way?

☀ **Literature**   12. Anne's story is called "The Jealous Rival, or In Death Not Divided." The phrase, "in death not divided," originally came from II Samuel 2:23.

📖 Read II Samuel 2:23. To what two characters does this phrase refer?

Anne's story has an ending similar to George Eliot's story, *The Mill on the Floss,* in which Tom and Maggie drown in a flood and are buried in one grave with the tombstone reading, "In Death They Were Not Divided." This book has been described as a Victorian soap opera. Anne, a voracious reader, frequently enhances her imagination with plots from books she has read.

📖 For those who are interested, this book, *The Mill on the Floss,* is available online.

George Eliot was a pseudonym for Mary Ann (or Marian) Evans, 1819–1880. She was raised in a Christian home, but later, to the dismay of her loving father and family, rejected her belief in the deity of Jesus Christ and, therefore, His teachings. She became an outcast in her family by living with a married man for twenty-four years. Throughout her adult life, Mary Ann battled with bouts of deep depression. In 1876 she was regarded as the greatest living English novelist. She is especially known for great character development.

👓 You may want to watch the video, *The Mill on the Floss.* It is a powerful, emotional story about the choice between love and loyalty. Knowing what you know about George Eliot's life, do you think the characters in her story choose love or loyalty?

Literature   13. Until printing became more widespread, the main book most people owned and read was the Bible. Another was *Pilgrim's Progress.* These two books were highly prized and caused many to grow spiritually. Marilla, typical of the practical women of her day, thinks reading any other material is frivolous. Anne attempts to justify her own writing by including morals in her stories. Perhaps this is L.M. Montgomery's way of taking a jab at the writers of her day who, at the expense of good literature, packed their books with moral lessons to the point of being trite.

✎ Write in the Literature section of your notebook:
What are your criteria for good/acceptable reading materials? How does your reading compare with the Biblical principles listed in Philippians 4:8?

---

14. ⚇ With your instructor, reminisce about some of your most exciting memories. | Literature

---

15. ♡ Read and memorize Psalm 15. Which person in Avonlea emulates this scripture? *See answer in Answer Appendix.* | Bible

Who in this chapter fits Proverbs 18:6? *See answer in Answer Appendix.*

📖 Why do you think the students were involved in "trifling frictions" after the concert? Read James 3:16 and Galatians 5:25–26.

⚇ Discuss with your instructor whether you have seen this to be true.

---

16. ⚇ Ask your parents and several others to tell their story of how they became engaged. Which stories are romantic? Which ones were similar to Susan Gillis'? Which ones were full of thought and creativity? | Literature

---

17. Montgomery once again uses irony in this chapter. Anne tells how Josephine Barry finds the Club's stories amusing and how "That kind of puzzled us because the stories were all very pathetic and almost everybody died." What do you know that Anne does not realize? | Literature

---

18. ✋ Each Friday during this Unit will be used for a field day. Study the plants, flowers, and birds native to your area. Begin by identifying all the plants on your property. As time allows, increase your observation area. Take a camera or a sketch pad as well as plant and bird identification books. After a plant is identified, take a picture of it and place it in your Fine Arts notebook or draw it in your sketchbook and label it. | Science

---

19. ⚇ With your instructor: | Literature

Continue with recitation each Friday during this Unit. Recite some of the writings of D. L. Moody or Charles Spurgeon you studied in this Chapter.

Quote memorized scriptures to your teacher: I Corinthians 10:13; The Lord's Prayer; Psalm 30; Romans 5:19; Proverbs 25:27; I Corinthians 13:13; Romans 8:5–8; Psalm 15; and your choice of Ephesians 3:20; Proverbs 17:27–28; or James 3:13, 17.

Planning Guide

Gather These Items:

1. Overview of the poem, *Marmion,* by Sir Walter Scott. For an "A" grade in Contract Reading — Literature, read the entire poem, *Marmion.*
   —<http://www.walterscott.lib.ed.ac.uk/biography/poet.html>
   —<http://www.walterscott.lib.ed.ac.uk/works/poetry/marmion.html>
   —<http://www.mindspring.com/~boba4/Marmion.html>
   —*Masterplots*

2. "The Gift of the Magi" by O. Henry, either an online or a hard copy from the library.
   —<http://www.auburn.edu/~vestmon/Gift_of_the_Magi.html>

3. Directions for a Victorian snood, either crocheted or fabric, and items for making the snood of your choice.
   —McCalls pattern #8449 for a snood (a nifty hair net)

Research Topics:

1. Nutrients for healthy hair

2. Locks of Love (See Activity 10)
   —

3. Newspaper or magazine articles on "gifts of hair" (See Activity 10)

4. Snood
   —Internet site for Victorian Trading Post

5. Home alone safety advice

6. Vows of a Catholic nun
   —<http://www.cptryon.org/ask/ask/vows.html>

7. Abbess
   —Online Catholic Encyclopedia

8. Dangers of Tylenol or acetaminophen
   —<http://www.detnews.com/2003/health/0302/28/h06-94303.htm>
   —<http://www.torahview.com/bris/html/tylenol.html>

. . . .

9. Functions of the liver

. . . .

Suggested Videos:

1. *Little Women.* There are several versions available.

Suggested Field Trips:

1. Visit a cosmetology school or a beauty college to watch someone having their hair dyed. (See Activity 4)

2. Visit a beautician. Learn about her trade, especially what she knows about hair dyes. Use the Apprentice Worksheet in the *Activity Appendix.* (See Activity 4)

Group Activities:

1. Continue writing stories to read aloud at meetings of the Story Club you started in Chapter XXVI, Activity 10.

Memory Work:

I Peter 3:17

Notes:

Assignments — Chapter XXVII

Contract Reading

	A Grade	B Grade	C Grade
Bible			
History			
Literature	❏ *Marmion*	❏ *Marmion*	❏ *Marmion*

Weekly

Quiet Time Reading Books: *Marmion*
Independent Project: Snood
Memory Work: I Peter 3:17

	Literature	History	Bible	Health	Occu. Education	Science & Fine Arts	Grammar & Writing
M	Read Chap. XXVII AGG, Reading Comp.		#3	#14	#16		#1, #2
T	Vocab., #8	#9	#5		#7		#5
W	#6	#15	#13				#13
Th	#10, #18	#18	#17, #18	#11, #12	#11		#17
*F	#20 Recitation				#4 Field Trips	#19 Field Day	

*On Friday, at the end of each Unit, review and take the Unit Quiz in the *Test Appendix*. On quiz days, parents and students may want to opt to reduce or eliminate Field Day and Recitation.

🎋 Study Guide

Read Chapter XXVII
Reading Comprehension:

1. What were Marilla's expectations upon arriving home? What greeted her instead?

2. Anne was not to let the Italian peddlers in the house, so as not to encourage them. How had Anne followed the rule, while disregarding the intention of it?

3. Besides Matthew and Marilla, who knew Anne's fatal secret? Did she ever tell?

4. What made losing her hair even more tragic for Anne?

5. List several consequences of Anne's vanity. What did Anne learn about vanity through this experience?

6. Whom did Anne consider to be good?

7. What does Marilla now think of Anne's chattering?

Vocabulary:

☞ Look up the vocabulary words in a dictionary or encyclopedia. Classify the words according to their parts of speech: noun, verb, adverb, or adjective. Use each word in a sentence.

*Note: "Snood" has two meanings. In Scotland, whose culture Anne is closely tied to, a snood was a distinguishing hairband used by unmarried women. (See Chapter XIV, Activity 6) The other meaning, further removed in time, refers to the medieval fashion of wearing a hairnet or a fabric bag to hold the hair.

Vocabulary Words:

veracity

vexation

snood*

implicitly

 Activities:

1. ✎ Write the following passage from dictation:

> Prayer does not mean that I am to bring God down to my thoughts and my purposes, and bend His government according to my foolish, silly, and sometimes sinful notions. Prayer means that I am to be raised up into feeling, into union and design with Him; that I am to enter into His counsel and carry out His purpose fully. —Dwight L. Moody

Dictation

| Follow-up | 2. ✎ Compare your copy with the original. Correct any mistakes. |

| Bible | 3. 📖 Read Ecclesiastes, chapter 1, in the King James Version of the Bible. The title of this chapter in *Anne of Green Gables* is a phrase derived from the first chapter of Ecclesiastes. |

✎ In the Bible section of your notebook:
Write the verse from which the title of the chapter in *Anne of Green Gables* originated. Why does it make a good title for this chapter?

Anne is vexed by the mistake she makes. Montgomery had experienced this in her own life, although perhaps not in such a comical manner.

📖 Read *The Green Gables Letters from L.M. Montgomery to Ephraim Weber 1905–1909*, pages 29–30.

| ☀ Occupational Education | 4. Hair dyes have improved greatly since Anne's days. It is most likely that the dye Anne uses mixed with copper in the water. Anne's hair probably turns green by oxidizing, just as copper roofs turn green. |

✋ Visit a cosmetology school or a beauty college. Watch someone having their hair dyed. What are the risks and the benefits?

✋ Visit a beautician. Learn about her trade, especially what she knows about hair dyes. Use the Apprentice Worksheet in the *Activity Appendix*.

| Bible | 5. 🗝 Marilla thought Rachel would "pick faults in the Angel Gabriel himself." Find verses about this angel using your concordance. Start with Daniel 9:21 and Luke 1:19–38. |

✎ In the Bible section of your notebook:
Write a short paragraph about this angel.

| ☀ Literature | 6. Marilla's attitude while coming home and Marilla's attitude upon arriving home are placed in **juxtaposition**. |

📖 Read about this literary term in *Writers INC*. What does the juxtaposition add to the story line?

| Occupational Education | 7. Anne pays for the hair dye with her portion of the chicken money. Raising and selling chickens is a small business which provides good experience for Anne. Because of it, she can associate work with profit and is able to calculate profit after the cost of production or overhead. How do you make money? Does your money-making venture involve upfront costs? What is your profit after costs? |

| ☀ Literature | 8. "What a tangled web we weave when first we practice to deceive!" is quoted from Sir Walter Scott's poem, *Marmion*, Canto Sixth, "The Battle," Stanza XVII. |

📖 *Marmion* is a challenging poem to read. Sometimes it is helpful to know an overview of the plot of a difficult work. Read the following summary of *Marmion*. Other more in-depth overviews may be found online or in the reference section of your library.

Basically the prefaces to each Canto are letters to friends describing the changing seasons at Ashestiel, the castle where Sir Scott was living. The last Canto describes Christmas. Additionally, the introduction to the first Canto is full of political compliments.

The whole poem narrates the events that lead up to the Battle of Flodden Field where "all was lost but our honor." The English army inflicted heavy losses on the Scots, killing King James IV and most of his nobles.

Lord Marmion, a friend of King Henry VIII, desires to have the wealthy heiress, Clara de Clare, but she is betrothed to her beloved Sir Ralph De Wilton. Marmion devises a plan to falsely accuse DeWilton of treason. He enlists the help of his past mistress, Constance de Beverly, who is now a nun. Constance is willing to do this in hopes of getting Marmion back. (What was she thinking!) Marmion abandons Constance who is condemned to death for breaking her vows!

DeWilton challenges Marmion in a duel, but loses and is banished abroad. Clare takes refuge in a convent. DeWilton returns to Scotland disguised as a holy Palmer. (A Palmer wears two crossed palm leaves as a sign of his pilgrimage to the Holy Land.) Before being put to death, Constance clears DeWilton's name by signing documents she gives to the Abbess.

DeWilton tracks down Marmion, who is serving as an ambassador for King Henry VIII. Meanwhile, the Abbess finds DeWilton in Edinburgh and gives him the documents clearing his name. DeWilton uses these documents to show Marmion's host, the Earl of Angus, the truth. Angus gives DeWilton armor and readmits him to the order of knighthood. The Battle of Flodden Field is fought before DeWilton can get his revenge against Marmion. During this battle, Marmion is killed. In the end DeWilton and Clare marry. His honor and his estates are returned to him.

📖 Read Canto Sixth of Sir Walter Scott's *Marmion* or, for an "A" grade in Contract Reading — Literature, read the entire poem.

---

9. 🔑 What vows do nuns take and what do they mean? What is an abbess? Was it common for nuns to be put to death for breaking their vows?

History

Discuss with your instructor what you have learned.

---

10. In this chapter, Anne refers to losing one's hair from fever or selling it as a good deed. A famous literary example of selling one's hair is in Louisa May Alcott's *Little Women,* written in 1868.

Literature

∞ Obtain the video of this movie. (There are at least two versions available, an older Katharine Hepburn version, and a newer one with Susan Sarandon.)

O. Henry's, "The Gift of the Magi," is another story which tells of a woman who sells her hair. *Pat of the Silver Bush* and *On the Shores of Silver Lake* tell of girls who lose their hair from fever. In the latter, Mary Ingalls loses her hair from scarlet fever.

Read the short story, "The Gift of the Magi," which was printed in 1904. This story is a classic example of irony. What type of irony is it?

Occupational Education/ Health	11. Hair and nails are dead, hardened structures that are chemically very similar to the surface layer of your skin. Hairs grow in follicles, which are pits of actively dividing cells that occur in varying numbers in your skin.

Look up information on nutrients necessary for healthy hair and factors that have an adverse effect on hair.

Hair loss may follow any major stress, surgery, illness, or accident, but generally the hair grows back in the following weeks or months. Some forms of cancer treatment, particularly radiation or chemotherapy, can cause thinning or hair loss. The hair usually grows back after treatment. Have you met anyone who has lost his or her hair as a result of infection? This is rare today because of antibiotics; our bodies have not undergone the stresses necessary to combat infections serious enough to cause hair loss.

Read the following description of the organization, Locks of Love, which helps children who suffer from hair loss:

> Locks of Love is a non-profit organization that provides hairpieces to financially disadvantaged children under age 18 suffering from long-term medical hair loss. We meet a unique need for children by using donated hair to create the highest quality hair prosthetics. Most of the children helped by Locks of Love have lost their hair due to a medical condition called alopecia areata, which has no known cause or cure. The prostheses we provide help to restore self-esteem and confidence, enabling them to face the world and their peers. —<http://www.locksoflove.org/>

Go to the Locks of Love Web site. Print the requirements for donating hair.

Do an Internet search and read newspaper and magazine articles about people who have donated hair.

Health	12. The average body temperature taken orally is 98.6 degrees Fahrenheit (F) or 37 degrees Centigrade (C). Because people's temperatures vary slightly, a temperature of 100° F (37.7° C) orally or 101° F (38.3° C) rectally is generally considered a fever.

Take your temperature. Have your parent demonstrate how to use a thermometer if you do not know how to use one.

Fever is a warning sign that there is some disturbance within the body. It almost always accompanies infectious disease and infected cuts, burns, or other wounds. Some medical scientists consider fever a protective device of the body because certain disease-causing organisms are destroyed when fever is present. It is also believed that the increased metabolic rate associated with fever increases the immune function of the cells. Fever brings discomfort, weakness or tiredness, and sometimes pain, causing the patient to rest and conserve his energy to battle against disease.

A prolonged or extremely high fever is likely to cause dehydration, so the patient should be encouraged to drink plenty of fluids. Generally, unless a fever is over 102° F (38.9° C), it is enough to make sure the patient drinks plenty of fluids and is clothed comfortably. From 102–104° F (38.9–40° C), Tylenol or the generic acetaminophen may be used if the patient is miserable. If the temperature remains elevated, Motrin or the generic ibuprofen may be used simultaneously with the Tylenol. You may find it necessary to lower the body temperature and the patient may need to be sponged with tepid water. It is important not to allow the temperature to drop too rapidly. If, in spite of medication, the patient's temperature continues to rise over 104° F, a physician should be called. Damage to the cells begins at 106° F (41.1° C) and death will occur within hours if the temperature is allowed to remain at 110° F (43.3° C). Sometimes children will have febrile seizures. If this is in the child's medical history, steps should be taken to decrease the child's temperature earlier.

Many people mistakenly think over-the-counter medicines are safe because they are available without a prescription. This is not true. Just as with prescription drugs, there are the dangers of overdose and overuse. The side-effects can be deadly. Like any other medicine, Tylenol or the generic acetaminophen, must be used with caution. Three causes of Tylenol overdose are:

1. Two people medicating the same child. Always check to make sure no one else has given a child medication or, if someone has, determine what kind of medication has been given and the dosage.
2. Not realizing Tylenol has several different dosage strengths.
3. Combining two medications with the active ingredient, acetaminophen.

Research the dangers associated with the use of Tylenol or the generic acetaminophen.

Make a warning poster regarding Tylenol or the generic acetaminophen and place it on the inside of your medicine cabinet.

In the Health section of your notebook:
a. Identify normal body temperature and fever.
b. Name the steps one can and should take for fever.
c. Name seven functions of the liver.

Bible	13. Diane keeps Anne's secret. Anne would not have profited by others knowing the cause of her hair loss. Diane could gossip about her friend, but she does not. She truly is a good friend.

📖 Read Proverbs 11:13; Proverbs 16:28; 17:9; and 20:19.

✏️ In the Bible section of your notebook:
Jot down any thoughts you have on your ability to be a good friend and the value of trustworthiness in a friendship.

Health	14. Anne does not allow a stranger into the house while Marilla is gone, but she goes outside with him. This too could be dangerous.

✂️ With your instructor and your parents:
Read and discuss safety with strangers. What rules do you have for when you are home alone?

☀️ History	15. ✎ Using the Consumer Price Index (CPI) Conversion Factors in the *Background Information Appendix,* convert the prices of the dye, $.75 and $.50, into U.S. money and then convert them into today's money. How much was the peddler asking in today's money? *See answers in Answer Appendix.* How much did Anne pay? Go to the grocery store. What do the hair dyes in the grocery store cost? How much does it cost to have one's hair dyed at a beauty shop?

Occupational Education	16. 🔑 View Victorian snoods on the Internet or look up pictures in books.

✋ Make a Victorian snood. Choose whether you want to crochet one or make one out of fabric. Find a pattern or devise your own.

Bible	17. Anne suffers through Josie's comments about her hair.

📖 Read I Peter 3:14–17 and I Peter 4:14–16. Have you ever suffered for Christ or has your suffering been the result of disobedience?

✎ Write your thoughts on these verses in a journalistic style in your notebook.

♡ Memorize I Peter 3:17.

Literature/Bible	18. Anne states she knew she was doing something slightly wicked in dyeing her hair. She says she had counted the cost. Scripture tells us to count the cost in following God. I do not know how one can count the cost of evil. It is wrong of Anne to disobey Marilla's wishes regarding dyeing her hair. It is wrong of her to trade with a peddler despite Marilla's objections. Montgomery once again uses irony. What type of irony does Montgomery use in this chapter? What does Anne miss about her hair once it is gone? Slowly we see Anne learning lessons which make her appreciate how God has made her.

Science	19. ✋ Continue to use each Friday for a field day. Study the plants, flowers, and birds native to your area. Begin by identifying all the plants

on your property. As time allows, increase your observation area. Take a camera or a sketch pad as well as plant and bird identification books. After a plant is identified, take a picture of it and place it in your Fine Arts notebook or draw it in your sketchbook and label it.

---

20. With your instructor: Literature

Continue with recitation each Friday during this Unit. Recite some of your favorite passages from *Marmion* or from other poems you have studied in previous Chapters.

Quote memorized scriptures to your teacher: I Corinthians 10:13; The Lord's Prayer; Psalm 30; Romans 5:19; Proverbs 25:27; I Corinthians 13:13; Romans 8:5–8; Psalm 15; I Peter 3:17; and your choice of Ephesians 3:20; Proverbs 17:27–28; or James 3:13, 17.

---

21. Review and take Unit 6 Quiz in the *Test Appendix*.   Quiz

🐚 Planning Guide

Gather These Items:

1. *The Hidden Art of Homemaking* by Edith Schaeffer. Tyndale House Publishers, 1985. ISBN 0842313982.

2. *Passion and Purity: Learning to Bring Your Love Life Under Christ's Control* by Elisabeth Elliot, Joshua Harris, and Ruth Bell Graham. Fleming H Revell Co., 2002. ISBN 0800758188. This is for an "A" grade in Contract Reading — Bible.

3. Trout preparation tips and recipes and trout (fishing pole and bait suggested).

Research Topics:

1. Boat safety
   —"Boating Safety: Sidekicks," *National Safe Boating Council* Web site, <http://www.boatingsidekicks.com/index1024.html>.

   . . . .

2. Duck hunting boats
   —"Duck Boats 101," *duckboats.net,* <http://www.duckboats.net/duckboats101.htm>.

   . . . .

3. Trout buying and storing tips

   . . . .

4. Health benefits of omega fatty acids

   . . . .

5. Alfred, Lord Tennyson

   . . . .

Suggested Videos:

Suggested Field Trips:

1. Go to a lake or large pond where you can row a boat. Plan a picnic lunch; don't forget your umbrella or sunscreen! You may want to do this as a group and have races.

2. If you are in boats frequently, check into taking a boat safety class.

3. Go trout fishing. Have someone teach you how to fly fish.

4. If you do not know how to swim, take swimming lessons. If you do know how to swim, consider taking the training to become certified as a Red Cross lifeguard.

Group Activities:

1. Continue writing stories to read aloud at meetings of the Story Club you started in Chapter XXVI, Activity 10.

2. Plan a dramatization of a favorite ballad, dialogue, poem, or play studied in *Where the Brook and River Meet.* Consider forming a Drama Club or including drama presentations in your Story Club. (See Activity 7)

Memory Work:
Proverbs 4:23

Notes:

Assignments — Chapter XXVIII

Contract Reading

	A Grade	B Grade	C Grade
Bible	❏ *Passion and Purity*	❏ *Passion and Purity*	❏ *Passion and Purity*
History			
Literature			

Weekly

Quiet Time Reading Books: *Passion and Purity*
Independent Project:
Memory Work: Proverbs 4:23

	Literature	History	Bible	Health	Occu. Education	Science & Fine Arts	Grammar & Writing
M	Read Chap. XXVIII AGG, Reading Comp., #2		#5	#11		#7	#1, #2
T	Vocab., #3, #4		#8	#12	#13 Field Trip	#6, #7	
W	#17	#17	#9	#15		#7	#17
Th			#10		#14	#7	
F	#20 Recitation			#16 Field Trip		#7, #19, #18 Field Day	

❧ Study Guide

Read Chapter XXVIII
Reading Comprehension:

1. How was Anne's hair changing?

2. What had happened to Idlewild?

3. What was more fascinating about the pond?

4. Anne wanted to be the principal character, yet what made her think it was impossible?

5. What happened to Anne's boat?

6. What limited view of God did Anne have as her boat was sinking?

7. Who rescued Anne?

8. What did Matthew want Anne to keep a little of?

Vocabulary Words:

presentiment

jaunty

pall

samite

procured

haughtily

parsed

Camelot

Vocabulary:

☞ Look up the vocabulary words in a dictionary or encyclopedia. Fill in the blanks.

9. "The more we raise our love, / The more we _____ and cool and kill his ardor." —Dryden

10. The ballerina made several _____ leaps.

11. She confirmed my _____ about her character.

12. Marco Polo brought back _____ from the Orient.

13. During the siege Mother _____ the unobtainable.

14. The spoiled child _____ addressed her mother.

15. During English we _____ ten sentences.

16. Arthur and Guinevere reigned in _____.

Extra Credit:

17. Write a sentence utilizing a different definition of "pall."

Note: Bridge piles are the pillars of a bridge.

 **Activities:**

1. ✎ Write the following passage from dictation:

> "I've learned a new and valuable lesson to-day. Ever since
> I came to Green Gables I've been making mistakes, and
> each mistake has helped to cure me of some great short-
> coming. The affair of the amethyst brooch cured me of med-
> dling with things that didn't belong to me. The Haunted
> Wood mistake cured me of letting my imagination run away
> with me. The liniment cake mistake cured me of carelessness
> in my cooking. Dyeing my hair cured me of vanity. I never
> think about my hair and nose now—at least, very seldom.
> And today's mistake is going to cure me of being too
> romantic." —*Anne of Green Gables, page 227*

2. ✎ Compare your copy with the original. Correct any mistakes.

📖 From *Writers INC*, read "Modeling Sentences," page 92.

✎ Using your life, write your own version of the dictation paragraph
imitating it part by part. As a side note, this section of the dictation
paragraph was arranged in chronological order of Anne's life at
Avonlea. Make sure yours is chronological as well.

3. The phrase, "Lily Maid," in the title of this chapter is from "Lancelot
and Elaine" in Alfred, Lord Tennyson's poem, *Idylls of the King*. In this
poem, Elaine dies of hopeless love for Lancelot, a knight who is attached to Queen Guinevere, the wife of King Arthur. Montgomery
writes in her journal: "I detest Tennyson's Arthur! . . . Lancelot—he is
just as unbearable in another way." (*The Annotated Anne of Green
Gables*, page 293 quoting *The Selected Journals of L.M. Montgomery*,
Vol. I, 1889–1910, edited by Mary Rubio and Elizabeth Waterson,
University of Guelph, page 358.) Note: Because of the adulterous
undertones, some parents may not approve of the content of this poem.

The students in Anne's class ". . . had analyzed it and parsed it and
torn it to pieces. . . ."

✄ With your instructor:
Discuss the negative and positive aspects of literary analysis. **Literary analysis** is the exercise of breaking down and examining literature to better understand it. It is the process of making correlations
and connections within the material by highlighting cause and effect
and comparison and contrast between characters or events. In *Writers
INC*, read pages 227–243.

Literature   4. 🕮 Read "Lancelot and Elaine" from *Anne's Anthology* aloud to your instructor.

🕮 With your instructor discuss the following.
   a. What does Lancelot do that awakes Elaine's love for him? Is this intentional?
   b. Elaine is described as willful. How does this willfulness affect her life?

Bible   5. 📖 As young ladies and women it is important to guard our hearts. Read *Passion and Purity: Learning to Bring Your Love Life Under Christ's Control* by Elisabeth Elliot and Joshua Harris for an "A" grade in Contract Reading — Bible.

Elaine needed to guard her heart against awakening love prematurely.

♡ Memorize Proverbs 4:23.

Fine Arts   6. What was Mrs. Lynde's opinion of playacting?

📖 From *The Hidden Art of Homemaking*, read about drama in chapter 10.

🕮 With your instructor:
Discuss your opinion of drama and acting.

Fine Arts   7. ✋ Pick your favorite ballad, dialogue, poem, or play studied in *Where the Brook and River Meet* and act it out. You may need to include friends and/or siblings in your dramatization.

✋ Consider forming a Drama Club or including drama presentations in your Story Club.

📖 In *Writers INC*, read the definition of dramatic monologue and soliloquy.

Bible   8. What romantic act between Anne and Gilbert is lost because of unforgivingness? Why does Anne almost recant? Anne reacts with contempt to Gilbert because he called her "Carrots." She strengthens a wrong emotional focus toward him by continually reviewing his offensive action in her mind. Anne is trying to be a good person, but because of pride she is not obeying Ephesians 4:30–32. Bitterness has a direct and devastating effect upon our bones.

📖 Read Ephesians 4:30–32 and then read Psalm 32:3; Proverbs 17:22; Proverbs 14:30; Proverbs 12:4; and Ezekiel 32:27. The spiritual consequences of bitterness are found in I John 4:20, 21 and Matthew 6:12. While Anne is mired in anger and bitterness, Gilbert is using the weapon of **love**, forgiveness in action.

📖 Read Matthew 5:44 and I Corinthians 13:5–8.

Anne needed to guard her heart against bitterness.

9. In the paragraph chosen for dictation, Anne is using the "weapon" of **rejoicing**.

   Read Romans 5:3–5 and I Thessalonians 5:18. When confronted with a problem she is in distress, but by rejoicing she learns patience and experiences hope which result in growth in Christ. According to Otto Koning in his sermon, "The Weapons of Our Warfare," the weapon of rejoicing is best used when circumstances are bad. It will increase your faith and frequently may end in a miracle.

   Read Acts 16:25–26.

☼ Bible

---

10. As Christians we are to use the weapon of **prayer** always. It is dependence in action. We are told to pray in His name (John 14:13–14); with thanksgiving (Philippians 4:6); in the Spirit (Ephesians 6:18); and in His will (I John 5:14–15).

   Read these verses and write them at the top of a prayer journal. If you do not have a prayer journal, start one. Divide your prayer list into two pages. The first page is for those we pray for daily such as our family, pastor, missionaries, and the president. The second page is for specific requests. For a specific request, pray only once or until you have the peace of God, then check it off and thank Him for what He is doing or will do in time.   —Paraphrased from Otto Koning's sermon, "The Weapons of Our Warfare"

   Anne feels the only way God can save her is for her to get close to the bridge piles. She could pray believing this. He answers her prayer in this way, but in the time of crisis she forgets God is all powerful and He can answer her prayer in an unusual way. She is also doing God's thinking for Him, as if He were not capable of devising a way to save her. She could have shown complete dependence on Him by simply asking Him to save her, period. No conditions; no directions.

☼ Bible

---

11. It is assumed Anne does not know how to swim.

   If you do not know how to swim, arrange to take swimming lessons. If you do know how to swim, this may a good time to become certified as a Red Cross lifeguard.

Health

---

12. If you have Internet access, spend some time looking at the boating safety information on the *National Safe Boating Council* Web site suggested in the "Research Topics." The information for child safety is the most important for this study.

   The Canadian Coast Guard has the following requirements for canoes, kayaks, rowboats, and rowing shells (not over 6 meters in length):

☼ Health

Minimum Required Safety Equipment
Personal Protection Equipment
1. One Canadian-approved personal flotation device or lifejacket of appropriate size for each person on board
2. One buoyant heaving line of not less than 15 meters in length

Boat Safety Equipment
3. One manual propelling device OR an anchor with not less than 15 meters of cable, rope or chain in any combination
4. One bailer or one manual water pump fitted with or accompanied by sufficient hose to enable a person using the pump to pump water from the bilge of the vessel over the side of the vessel

Navigation Equipment
5. A sound-signaling device or a sound-signaling appliance
6. Navigation lights that meet the applicable standards set out in the Collision Regulations if the pleasure craft is operated after sunset and before sunrise or in periods of restricted visibility

—Canadian Coast Guard, January 1999

✍ If you are in boats frequently, check into taking a boat safety class.

✍ If you have a boat, make sure that you have the minimum required safety equipment.

Of the above safety devices, what would have been helpful for Anne to have?

Which boats are the most dangerous? Why do you think they are the most dangerous?

> When fatalities on different types of boats are "normalized" by exposure (per million hours of operation), the results are somewhat surprising: Canoes and kayaks have the highest fatality rate, double the rate of personal watercraft and almost four times higher than open motorboats. Measured in deaths per million hours, the numbers are: canoes, 42; personal watercraft, 24; rowboats, 20; inflatables, 17; open motorboats, 14; sailboats, 12; cabin motorboats, .07.

—"The National Recreational Boating Survey," commissioned by the U.S. Coast Guard

For what did Mr. Barry use his boat?

🔑 Briefly look up information on duck hunting boats.

Why do people use boats?

> And why were all these boaters out there on the water in 1998? The survey found that fishing was the primary activity for 63% of boaters, closely followed by cruising (52%) and waterskiing (24%) and swimming/diving (21%). The majority

of boaters reported using their primary craft on lakes (59%),
the next most common venue was rivers and creeks (19%),
coastal (11%), the ocean (6%) and the Great Lakes (4%).

—"The National Recreational Boating Survey," commissioned by the U.S. Coast Guard

---

13. Many ponds in the U.S. are catfish ponds. Unless they are cold spring-
fed, the water in the ponds is too warm for trout. The survival range
for trout is published at 35–75° F (2–23° C). And the optimum feeding
range for most trout species is between about 50 and 68° F (10–20° C).
Trout require cold, well oxygenated water and are highly sensitive to
excessive silt loads, increased water temperatures, and lowered oxygen
levels.

✋ Go trout fishing. If possible have someone teach you how to fly fish.

Occupational
Education

---

14. ✋ Look through different recipes on cooking trout. Decide on the one
that sounds the best to you. Cook trout for your family.

Occupational
Education

---

15. ☞ Look up the health benefits of eating trout. Trout has omega fatty
acids. Specifically, what are the benefits of these fatty acids?

✎ Write what you have learned in the Health section of your notebook.

⏰ Health

---

16. ✋ Go to a lake or large pond where you can row a boat. Plan a picnic
lunch; don't forget your umbrella or sunscreen! Perhaps you may want
to do this as a group and have races.

Physical
Education

---

17. 📖 Read about Alfred, Lord Tennyson and his writing.

✎ Write one page about this author and his works. Put this in the appropriate time period section of your History notebook.

⏰ History

---

18. ✋ Continue to use each Friday for a field day. Study the plants, flowers, and birds native to your area. Begin by identifying all the plants
on your property. As time allows, increase your observation area. Take
a camera or a sketch pad as well as plant and bird identification books.
After a plant is identified, take a picture of it and place it in your Fine
Arts notebook or draw it in your sketchbook and label it.

Science

---

19. ✋ You may want to track changes in some of the plants on your property. Keep records of such things as when they bloom, when they go
dormant, and which are the first ones to blossom and leaf out in
spring. If you choose to add this kind of observation, make a list of
changes and the plants you want to track. Make predictions as to what
you think will happen and when. You could also add some experiments
to your observations, such as comparing results of different ways of
caring for the same plant. For example, you could water one rose plant
by soaking and one by sprinkling.

Science

✎ If you choose to do any of these activities, make a plan with a schedule so you can start them as soon as possible. It may be practical for you to do these activities during your weekly Field Day.

Literature 20. ✖ With your instructor:

Continue with recitation each Friday during this Unit. Recite some of your favorite passages from "Lancelot and Elaine" or from other poems you have studied in previous Chapters.

Quote memorized scriptures to your teacher: I Corinthians 10:13; The Lord's Prayer; Psalm 30; Romans 5:19; Proverbs 25:27; I Corinthians 13:13; Romans 8:5–8; Psalm 15; I Peter 3:17; Proverbs 4:23; and your choice of Ephesians 3:20; Proverbs 17:27–28; or James 3:13, 17.

———◆———

✥ Planning Guide

Gather These Items:

1. Items to paint a picture. (See Activity 3)

2. Works of Aristotle.

3. Cassette tape, CD, or record of a late nineteenth century opera, preferably one by Verdi or Wagner.

4. Chicken for broiling. (See Activity 7)

5. *How Should We Then Live? The Rise and Decline of Western Thought and Culture* by Francis A. Schaeffer. Crossway Books, 1983. ISBN 0-89107-292-6.

6. *The Beautiful Side of Evil* by Joanna Michaelsen. Dearborn Resources, 1984. ISBN 0-89081-322-1. This is Contract Reading Choice — Bible for a "B" or better grade.

Research Topics:

1. Aristotle

. . . .

2. Opera composer Verdi or Wagner
   —"The Story of Verdi In Words and Music." *An Introduction to the Classics.* Audiocassette. Vox Music Masters.
   —"The Story of Wagner In Words and Music." *An Introduction to the Classics.* Audiocassette. Vox Music Masters.
   —*The Ring and the Fire: Stories from Wagner's Nibelung Operas* by Clyde Robert Bulla. Thomas Y. Crowell Co., 2000. ASIN 0690702523.

. . . .

3. Emma Lajeunesse or Madame Albani
   —Go to <www.cadroncreek.com> for a list of Internet sites to visit

. . . .

4. Opera
   —Encyclopedia

. . . .

5. Odin
   —Encyclopedia

. . . .

6. Tantallon Castle
   —Internet

. . . .

7. Gambling
   —*Citizen Link,* Focus on the Family, <http://www.family.org/cforum/fosi/gambling/>

. . . .

8. How hot air balloons work

. . . .

Suggested Videos:

Suggested Field Trips:

1. Attend a county or state fair. Enter a project.

2. Attend an opera.

3. Go to a hot air balloon festival or a place which gives balloon rides.

4. Take a thirty mile bicycle ride.

Group Activities:

1. Continue writing stories to read aloud at meetings of the Story Club you started in Chapter XXVI, Activity 10.

2. Continue the Drama Club you started in Chapter XXVIII, Activity 7.

Memory Work:
James 1:2–4

Notes:

Assignments — Chapter XXIX

Contract Reading

	A Grade	B Grade	C Grade
Bible	❏ Choice: *The Beautiful Side of Evil*	❏ Choice: *The Beautiful Side of Evil*	
History			
Literature			

Weekly

Quiet Time Reading Books: *Passion and Purity; The Beautiful Side of Evil*

Independent Project:

Memory Work: James 1:2–4

Science: If you have chosen to track changes in some of the plants on your property and/or do some experiments as suggested in Chapter XXVIII, Activity 19, continue following your schedule for these activities

	Literature	History	Bible	Health	Occu. Education	Science & Fine Arts	Grammar & Writing
M	Read Chap. XXIX AGG, Reading Comp., #2		#4, #20			#3	#1, #2
T	Vocab., #5	#5	#8	#17		#11, #19 Field Trip	
W		#6	#6, #10		#14 Field Trip	#12	#6
Th	#15, #18	#16	#9			#13	#13
F	#22 Recitation				#7	#12 Field Trip, #21 Field Day	

🐉 Study Guide

Read Chapter XXIX
Reading Comprehension:

1. Despite Anne's good imagination, what could she not guess?

2. Of what did Anne need to repent?

3. How was Anne guarding her heart from disappointment?

4. Why did Marilla now make Anne's dresses fashionably?

5. How did Anne feel in the luxury of Aunt Josephine's house?

6. When did Anne realize how much she liked Mrs. Lynde?

7. What did Anne think was the worst part of growing up?

8. What was Miss Barry's relationship with most people? How was Anne different?

Vocabulary Words:

epoch

prosaic

abomination

Vocabulary:

🔑 Look up the vocabulary words in a dictionary or encyclopedia. Write a sentence with each.

 Activities:

Dictation

1. ✎ Write the following passage from dictation:

> . . . Anne followed them dreamily, repeating aloud the battle canto from *Marmion*—which had also been part of their English course the preceding winter and which Miss Stacy had made them learn off by heart—and exulting in its rushing lines and the clash of spears in its imagery. When she came to the lines:
>
> > "The stubborn spearsmen still made good
> > Their dark impenetrable wood,"
>
> she stopped in ecstasy to shut her eyes that she might the better fancy herself one of that heroic ring. —*Anne of Green Gables,* page 229

Follow-up

2. 📖 In *Writers INC,* review page 258, "Using Quoted Material—Quoting Poetry." Both the way suggested in *Writers INC* and the one used by Montgomery in *Anne of Green Gables* are acceptable for quoted material. Writing styles for formal papers vary, however, and each instructor sets his or her own requirements. It is very important, therefore, to ascertain and follow the style guidelines of each instructor who gives you writing assignments. The two major style manuals are published

by the Modern Language Association and the American Psychological Association. (For further information, see pages 259 and 285 in *Writers INC.*)

📖 In *Writers INC,* read pages 462–463 regarding colons. How was the colon used in the dictation?

---

3. ✋ Paint a picture of the opening scene on page 229.   Fine Arts

---

4. Why is Anne "glad that [she] felt glad" Josie Pye took first place in knitted lace? *See answer in Answer Appendix.*   Bible

📖 Read I John 2:1–14. What does Anne know has occurred in her life?

---

5. The poetry lines in the dictation are the third quotation from Canto Sixth of *Marmion* Montgomery uses in *Anne of Green Gables.* In this chapter and in chapter XXVII, she has Anne quote specific lines from the Canto; in chapter II, Montgomery uses a phrase from the poem in her description of one of Matthew's dilemmas. For an overview of the poem, see Chapter XXVII, Activity 8.   👁 Literature/ History

📖 *Marmion* opens at the beginning of August and concludes with the defeat of Flodden on September 9, 1513. Read the Introduction to Canto Sixth from *Marmion.* Use the footnotes in the poem to increase your understanding of this piece.

Odin: chief god of Norse mythology.

📖 Read further about Odin in the encyclopedia or in a book of myths.

🔑 Look up information on Tantallon Castle.

✋ In the Literature section of your notebook:
Draw the scenes the Introduction to the Canto Sixth describes.

✳ With your instructor:
    a. Retell the story found within Canto Sixth.
    b. Explain the terms vassal, tenant, serf, and baron.
    c. Find the lines Anne quotes in this chapter.
    d. Tell what Anne likes about this poem. Do you share her opinion?
    e. Notice the alliteration in Canto Sixth, section II. Which sound is used for the alliteration? How does this sound add to the experience of reading this poem?
    f. Recite eight or more of your favorite lines from this poem by memory.

---

6. "Virtue has its own reward" is a quote from Aristotle. Aristotle (384–322 B.C.) was a famous Greek philosopher whose writings were banned from universities by Pope Urban IV but accepted by Thomas Aquinas (1225–1274). Aquinas used the teachings of Aristotle to elevate human reason, thus putting it on equal footing with religious revelation. As a result, philosophy was gradually separated from   👁 History/Bible

revelation—and from the Bible—and philosophers began to think in an independent, autonomous manner. (See *How Should We Then Live? The Rise and Decline of Western Thought and Culture* by Francis A. Schaeffer, page 52.)

Read the outcome of mixing Aristotelian philosophy with Christianity on pages 52–56 in *How Should We Then Live? The Rise and Decline of Western Thought and Culture*. Also read about its effect on science on pages 130–131.

In the History section of your notebook, in the appropriate time period:
a. Write a half-page biographical sketch of Aristotle.
b. Write some of your favorite quotes from Aristotle below the biographical sketch.

Occupational Education	7. Cook broiled chicken.

Bible	8. Anne has to get up early in the morning to go to Charlottetown, but she "counted it all joy."

Use your concordance to find this scripture reference.

Copy the entire scripture reference in the Bible section of your notebook.

Memorize James 1:2–4.

Bible	9. While she and Diana are at the horse races, Diana suggests a small wager, but Anne ". . . refused to bet, because . . . it's always wrong to do anything you can't tell the minister's wife." She is also glad she did not bet because she would have lost the money.

Read Proverbs 22:6 in *The Message*.

Go to *Citizen Link* at the Focus on the Family Web site to view "Focus on Social Issues: Gambling." (See <http://www.family.org/cforum/fosi/gambling/>.) Read a few of the articles. Be sure to read "Gambling: A Biblical Perspective" and, on the same page, "Gambling and the Bible: A General Overview." Also read the "Consequences of Gambling" and some of the other articles under that heading.

Print the most convincing and informative article you read. Put it in the Bible section of your notebook.

Bible	10. Anne is worried about gambling at a horse race, but she goes to a fortune-teller, otherwise known as a medium or spiritist. Yet the Bible says fortune-telling is an abomination.

It was quite fashionable in the Victorian age to consult a fortune-teller, an act similar to consulting a psychic today. Perhaps because the fortune-teller is not called a medium or spiritist, Anne does not see the correlation with the scripture she had read. Or perhaps because she thinks this man has no power, and the fortune is just a lark, there is nothing wrong with this activity.

Read I Samuel 28; Leviticus 19:31; Leviticus 20:27; Deuteronomy 18:9–12; I Chronicles 10:13–14; II Kings 21:6; 23:24; and Isaiah 8:19.

If you have chosen to read *The Beautiful Side of Evil* for Contract Reading — Bible, do so now.

---

11. A prima donna is a female opera star. Madame Selitsky is a fictitious name. Montgomery is probably referring to Emma Lajeunesse (1847–1930), a Canadian opera star who, during this time period, called herself "Madame Albani." She sang for Queen Victoria and later sang at her funeral. In all of her world tours she never forgot her native land and gave a number of recitals in Canada. (See *The Annotated Anne of Green Gables,* page 310.)   **Fine Arts**

To find out more about Madame Albani, go to <www.cadroncreek.com> for a list of Internet sites to visit.

---

12. Read about opera.   **Fine Arts**

In the Fine Arts section of your notebook, define these terms: libretto, aria, bel canto, coloratura, ensemble, opera buffa, opera seria, recitative, score, singspiel, leitmotif, and verismo.

Read the libretto of an opera you wish to attend.

With your instructor:
Attend an opera.

---

13. Study about nineteenth century opera composer Verdi or Wagner.   **Fine Arts**

In the History section of your notebook, in the appropriate time period: Write a half-page biographical sketch of Verdi or Wagner.

With your instructor:
Listen to music by the composer about whom you chose to write.

---

14. Attend a county or state fair. Enter a project.   Occupational Education

---

15. Read the footnote in *The Annotated Anne of Green Gables,* page 304, regarding weddings. Look at photos from your parents' wedding. Where were they married? Have you ever attended a wedding?   Literature

---

16. Nine miles an hour is the average speed of a trotting horse. How long would it take to go the 30 miles to Charlottetown? To what city in your area could you travel by car in that amount of time?   History

---

17. If you are in good enough shape, ride a bicycle 30 miles. How long did it take you? Many people ride a 100 miles a day on bicycles.   Physical Education

Literature	18. What is "something that Anne and Diana dated from for years?" What does this statement mean? Is there a time in your life from which you date events?

Science	19. ✋ Go to a hot air balloon festival or a place which gives balloon rides. Watch the hot air balloons take off. Find out how hot air balloons work.

Bible	20. Anne wisely states it is far too early to look for a husband. 📖 Remember to keep reading *Passion and Purity: Learning to Bring Your Love Life Under Christ's Control* by Elisabeth Elliot and Joshua Harris.

Science	21. ✋ Continue to use each Friday for a field day. Study the plants, flowers, and birds native to your area. Begin by identifying all the plants on your property. As time allows, increase your observation area. Take a camera or a sketch pad as well as plant and bird identification books. After a plant is identified, take a picture of it and place it in your Fine Arts notebook or draw it in your sketchbook and label it.

Literature	22. 🗣 With your instructor: Continue with recitation each Friday during this Unit. Recite eight lines from *Marmion* and other passages from poems you have studied in previous Chapters. Quote memorized scriptures to your teacher: I Corinthians 10:13; The Lord's Prayer; Psalm 30; Romans 5:19; Proverbs 25:27; I Corinthians 13:13; Romans 8:5–8; Psalm 15; I Peter 3:17; Proverbs 4:23; James 1:2–4; and your choice of Ephesians 3:20; Proverbs 17:27–28; or James 3:13, 17.

❧ Planning Guide

Gather These Items:

1. A sheep heart. Contact a slaughter house, butcher shop, or Home Training Tools, 1-800-860-6272.

2. *Ben Hur: A Tale of the Christ* by Lew Wallace. Signet, 2003. ISBN 0451528743 for a "B" or better grade in Contract Reading Choice — Literature.

3. *The Way Home: Beyond Feminism, Back to Reality* by Mary Pride. Good News Publishers, 1985. ISBN 0-89107-345-0.

4. *What's a Girl to Do?: How to Wisely Invest Your Daughter's Time* by Doug Phillips. CD or Audiocassette. The Vision Forum, Inc., 2003. ISBN 1929241704.

5. "Young Women Content At Home" by Brook Tingom. *Home School Digest: Seeing the World Through God's Eyes* Volume 9: Number 4, pages 10–13. This article may be found in the *Background Information Appendix*.

6. "What About College?" by Ellen Davis. *The Elijah Company Catalog* 1998/1999, pages 168–169. This article may be found in the *Background Information Appendix*.

7. Items to make a framed verse. (See Activity 23)
   picture frame
   wide lace
   material scraps
   calligraphy paper

Research Topics:

1. Tuition as well as room and board at a college or university you might attend

   . . . .

2. The heart and its function
   —Go to <www.cadroncreek.com> for a list of Internet sites to visit

   . . . .

3. Causes, signs, and symptoms of a heart attack
   —Go to <www.cadroncreek.com> for a list of Internet sites to visit

   . . . .

4. Planting zones
   —Internet
   —For an excellent map of planting hardiness zones, see the following
   page at the Web site for The United States National Arboretum:
   <http://www.usna.usda.gov/Hardzone/ushzmap.html>
   —Gardening book or catalog

. . . .

5. Blooming dates
   —See the following page at the Web site for The United States National
   Arboretum: <http://www.usna.usda.gov/Education/blooming.html>

. . . .

6. Jewelweed

. . . .

7. Crackerberries

. . . .

Suggested Videos:

1. Watch the movie, *Ben Hur*. There are three versions of this movie.
   The one starring Charlton Heston is probably best known, but you
   might want to see the same one Montgomery did which starred
   Raymond Novarro.

Suggested Field Trips:

1. Become CPR certified. Check with the Red Cross, fire department, or
   with your local hospital for certification programs.

2. Visit a cardiac rehabilitation center. (See Activity 18)

3. Visit a local university. (See Activity 19)

4. Take an aptitude test. Check with your local high school or university.
   Also, Crown Financial Ministries sells one called *Career Direct Guidance System*. (You may view a sample of this test online at their Web
   site, <http://www.crown.org>.)

Group Activities:

1. Continue writing stories to read aloud at meetings of the Story Club
   you started in Chapter XXVI, Activity 10.

2. Continue the Drama Club you started in Chapter XXVIII, Activity 7.

Memory Work:
Colossians 1:10

Notes:

Assignments — Chapter XXX

Contract Reading

	A Grade	B Grade	C Grade
Bible			
History			
Literature	❏ Choice: *Ben Hur: A Tale of the Christ*	❏ Choice: *Ben Hur: A Tale of the Christ*	

Weekly

Quiet Time Reading Books: *Ben Hur: A Tale of the Christ*

Independent Project:

Memory Work: Colosians 1:10

Science: If you have chosen to track changes in some of the plants on your property and/or do some experiments as suggested in Chapter XXVIII, Activity 19, continue following your schedule for these activities

	Literature	History	Bible	Health	Occu. Education	Science & Fine Arts	Grammar & Writing
M	Read Chap. XXX AGG, Reading Comp., #2		#5, #9		#9, #20		#1, #2, #9
T	Vocab., #3		#7	#15	#10		
W	#4, #6		#8	#16	#11, #13		#6
Th	#21		#22		#12, #14	#23	#22
F	#25 Recitation			#17, #18 Field Trip	#19 Field Trip	#24 Field Day	

🦎 Study Guide

Read Chapter XXX
Reading Comprehension:

1. How did Anne deal with Marilla being critical? Why was Marilla so critical?

2. What was Anne's opinion of thinking about boys all the time?

3. Name the two things Anne had done wrong when she read *Ben Hur* during class time.

4. Anne had ignored Gilbert for years. What was she finding out now?

5. How did Anne pass her days?

6. What did Mrs. Lynde admit to being wrong about?

Vocabulary words:

contritely

rue

Vocabulary:

🗝 Look up the vocabulary words in a dictionary or encyclopedia. Write a sentence with each. Skim the chapter or use the word search in the online edition of *Anne of Green Gables* and write the sentence in which the word is used in the story.

 Activities:

Dictation

1. ✎ Write the following passage from dictation:

> The two gazed at each other. We know what Esther presented—a beautiful woman, a happy mother, a contented wife. On the other side, it was very plain that fortune had not dealt so gently with her former rival. The tall figure remained with some of its grace; but an evil life had tainted the whole person. The face was coarse; the large eyes were red and pursed beneath the lower lids; there was no color in her cheeks. The lips were cynical and hard, and general neglect was leading rapidly to premature old age. Her attire was ill chosen and draggled.   —Lew Wallace, *Ben Hur,* page 429

☀ Follow-up

2. ✎ Anne speaks of "poetical justice" in reference to the chariot race in *Ben Hur*. The concept of **poetical** or **poetic justice** stems from Aristotle's belief that the good characters in literary works should succeed and the bad be punished. Note that the dictation from *Ben Hur* contains another example of poetic justice. Identify and explain that example.

Literature

3. ∾ Watch the movie *Ben Hur*. According to *The Annotated Anne of Green Gables,* page 316, Montgomery went to watch the version star-

ring Raymond Novarro in 1926. She wrote in her journal it was: "About the only movie of a book I have not been disappointed in. The chariot race was still amazing." (Quoted from *The Selected Journals of L.M. Montgomery,* Vol. I, 1889–1910, edited by Mary Rubio and Elizabeth Waterson, University of Guelph, page 358.)

📖 If this is your choice for a "B" or better grade in Contract Reading — Literature, read *Ben Hur: A Tale of the Christ* by Lew Wallace.

---

4. In speaking of the rivalry between Gilbert and Anne, Montgomery refers to Gilbert as a "foeman worthy of her steel." This is a quote from *The Lady of the Lake* by Sir Walter Scott.

Literature

With your instructor:
Show this line in the poem to your instructor.

---

5. To what incident is Anne referring when she states, ". . . I had tasted the bitterness of death"?

Bible

📖 Read I Samuel 15:32 and Matthew 16:28.

Despite her disappointment that Diane is not in the Queen's class, Anne recognizes the truth of Mrs. Lynde's statement, ". . . we can't have things perfect in this imperfect world." When things do not go as we had hoped, we need to remember, as Isaiah reminds us in chapter 55, verse 8, God's ". . . thoughts are not your thoughts, neither are your ways My ways." He has ". . . plans to prosper you and not to harm you, plans to give you hope and a future." (Jeremiah 29:17) While His plans may not be the same as ours, we can always know ". . . that in all things God works for the good of those who love Him." (Romans 8:28)

---

6. Miss Stacy does not want Anne to read unwholesome books. As a girl, Marilla was not allowed to read novels. Hudson Taylor, a missionary to China during this time period, wrote to his sister warning her to stay away from novels (The dictation for Chapter XXXI is an excerpt from this letter.) Another missionary from the same time period, David Livingstone, wrote while working in Africa:

Literature/
Writing

> I read in this way classical authors, and knew Virgil and Horace better at sixteen than I do now. In reading, everything that I could lay my hands on was devoured *except novels* (emphasis added). Scientific works and books of travel were my delight; though my father, believing with many of his time who ought to know better, that the former were inimical to religion, would have preferred to have seen me poring over the "Cloud of Witnesses" or Boston's "Fourfold State."

With your instructor:
a. What unwholesome book does Miss Stacy catch Anne reading?
b. What kinds of books today might be called unwholesome?

✎ In the Literature section of your notebook:
Write a persuasive paper on what type of writings one should and should not read.

Bible   7. Anne is anxious to please Miss Stacy. She delights in doing things to please her. If this is true of Anne's relationship with Miss Stacy, should it also be true of our relationship to God?

📖 Read John chapter 14.

Bible   8. ⚒ Discuss with your instructor:
   a. What are some good habits to form for the rest of your life?
   b. What habits are you forming now?
   c. Which are good ones? Which are not?

Occupational Education/ Bible   9. 📖 Read page 244 of *Anne of Green Gables* (*The Annotated Anne of Green Gables,* page 320).

✎ In the Occupational Education section of your notebook:
Describe each of the girls' plans after finishing school at Avonlea. Why were those who were going on to Queen's pursuing higher education?

Mr. Allan had said, "Everyone must have a purpose in life and pursue it faithfully."

⚒ Discuss with your instructor what you think is your purpose in life.

📖 Read I Corinthians 10:31; Ephesians 2:10; Colossians 1:10; and Colossians 3:23–24.

♡ Memorize Colossians 1:10.

Occupational Education   10. 📖 Read Chapters 11, 12, 13 of *The Way Home* by Mary Pride.

📖 To better understand the point of view of Diana's parents, read the article, "Young Women Content At Home," by Brook Tingom. This article may be found in the *Background Information Appendix.*

👓 Also you may want to listen to the CD or audiocassette, *What's a Girl to Do?*, by Doug Phillips.

⚒ With your instructor:
Discuss what you have read and listened to.

Occupational Education   11. On page 242, Marilla says, "When Matthew and I took you to bring up we resolved we would do the best we could for you and give you a good education. I believe in a girl being fitted to earn her own living whether she ever has to or not."

📖 From the *Background Information Appendix,* read "What About College?" by Ellen Davis.

12. ✍ Colleges or high schools frequently have aptitude tests. These are interesting to take if you have not previously done so. Also, Larry Burkett's Crown Financial Ministries has an aptitude test. (See information in the "Suggested Field Trips" section of the Planning Guide.)

Occupational Education

13. 🗝 Find out how much each class hour costs and the expense of room and board on campus at a college or university you are interested in attending. How much would one semester cost? The main cost of attending Queen's was not the cost of academic hours, but of paying room and board in the city.

If you are interested in a trade school, research the cost of these as well.

✎ In the Occupational Education section of your notebook:
Write your findings.

Occupational Education

14. ⚛ With your instructor:
Discuss the aptitudes with which God has endowed you to make a living and to be a helpful, informed wife. If you have chosen training in a career, do you think the skills you learn will be a valuable asset to bring into a marriage as your husband's helpmate?

Occupational Education

15. Matthew is having problems with his heart.

📖 Read about the heart and its function. Go to <www.cadroncreek.com> for a list of Internet sites to visit or find books to read about heart disorders.

💡 Health

16. ⚛ With your instructor:
Procure a sheep heart from a slaughter house, your local butcher, or from Home Training Tools at 1-800-860-6272. A sheep's heart is closer in size to a human heart. Dissect the heart in half lengthwise. Observe the heart chambers. Locate and discuss the upper and lower chambers, the openings through which the blood flows, and the muscle and blood vessels on the heart exterior. Compare the sheep heart to a diagram of a human heart. How are they alike?

💡 Health

✎ In the Health section of your notebook:
a. Draw a picture of the heart, including the ascending and descending vascular structure. Label at least fifteen different parts of the heart with correct terminology.
b. Define cholesterol. Include the difference between fat and cholesterol and how they are interrelated.
c. Define angina.
d. Describe a heart attack. What are the symptoms? What occurs in the body when a person has a heart attack?
e. What can you do to decrease your chance of a heart attack?
f. What are risk factors that you cannot change?

Health	17. ✋ Become CPR certified. Check with the Red Cross, fire department, or with your local hospital for certification programs. You can join a group that is taking the training or gather your own group.
Health	18. ✋ Visit a cardiac rehabilitation unit. Find out what this type of unit does for people with cardiac problems and what types of programs and advice are offered for maintaining healthy hearts.
Occupational Education	19. 📖 From *Annotated Anne of Green Gables* read pages 430–434, "Education on P.E.I." ✋ Visit your local university. Find out what type of training is required for government school teachers in your state.
Occupational Education	20. As noted on page 315 of *The Annotated Anne of Green Gables*, crackerberries are ". . . the berries of the jewelweed or ladies' ear drops that burst with a loud pop or crack when you press them." For years jewelweed has been used as a treatment for poison ivy. The crackerberry is supposedly rather tasteless. Do they have crackerberries where you live? 🔑 Research jewelweed and crackerberries on the Internet. Look at pictures of the plants and compare them. Are they the same plant? 🔑 Look at a map of planting zones. What planting zone are you in? Look at blooming dates for different plants. Remember, plants will bloom at different times at different latitudes and elevations. ✖ Tell your instructor about your observations of different blooming times in your area and give examples.
Literature	21. Moody Spurgeon "blushed uncomfortably every time he thought of it." Has this ever happened to you? ✖ Have your instructor share a time when she was carried away by her feelings and was embarrassed afterward. In turn, share your story of such an incident.
Bible	22. Marilla has noted positive changes in Anne. She now describes her as being steady and reliable. Anne also realizes she is growing, both physically and mentally. With a mixture of excitement and wistfulness, she looks forward to the time when she trades the shorter dresses of a girl for the long skirts of a lady. 📖 Read I Corinthians 13:8–12 and Philippians 1:6. ✎ In your journal or the Bible section of your notebook, reflect on what it means to "put away childish things."

23. ✋ Pick your favorite verse from this week's Bible reading. Type it into the computer, print it onto nice paper, and cut it out. You may want to singe the edges, but only do this with parental supervision and using appropriate safety measures. Make a collage using Victorian style lace, scraps of material, and your Bible verse. Place this into your frame.

Fine Arts

24. ✋ Continue to use each Friday for a field day. Study the plants, flowers, and birds native to your area. Begin by identifying all the plants on your property. As time allows, increase your observation area. Take a camera or a sketch pad as well as plant and bird identification books. After a plant is identified, take a picture of it and place it in your Fine Arts notebook or draw it in your sketchbook and label it.

Science

25. ✸ With your instructor:

Literature

Continue with recitation each Friday during this Unit. Recite your favorite lines from *Lady of the Lake* and passages from *Ben Hur*.

Quote memorized scriptures to your teacher: I Corinthians 10:13; The Lord's Prayer; Psalm 30; Romans 5:19; Proverbs 25:27; I Corinthians 13:13; Romans 8:5–8; Psalm 15; I Peter 3:17; Proverbs 4:23; James 1:2–4; Colossians 1:10; and your choice of Ephesians 3:20; Proverbs 17:27–28; or James 3:13, 17.

Planning Guide Chapter XXXI

Gather These Items:
1. Items to make a flounce skirt:
   pattern
   material
   notions

Research Topics:
1. Henry Wadsworth Longfellow

. . . .

2. Alexander Pope

. . . .

3. Ralph Waldo Emerson

. . . .

4. Medical practices of the 1800's

. . . .

5. Women in the church, then and now
   —"What Does the Bible Teach About Women's Ministry?" by
   Graham Truscott (pro)

. . . .

6. Entrance exam tests

. . . .

Suggested Videos:

Suggested Field Trips:
1. Visit a medical museum or the medical section of a museum.

Group Activities:
1. SAT or ACT preparation course.

Memory Work:
Galatians 6:9

Notes:

Assignments — Chapter XXXI

Contract Reading: No new contract reading

Weekly
Quiet Time Reading Books: *Ben Hur*
Independent Project: Flounce skirt
Memory Work: Galatians 6:9
Science: If you have chosen to track changes in some of the plants on your property and/or do
some experiments as suggested in Chapter XXVIII, Activity 19, continue following your
schedule for these activities.

	Literature	History	Bible	Health	Occu. Education	Science & Fine Arts	Grammar & Writing
M	Read Chap. XXXI AGG, Reading Comp., #2	#9 Field Trip	#10		#15		#1, #2, #10, #13
T	Vocab., #3	#4	#5	#8	#12, #15		#4, #13
W	#7	#7	#6		#14, #15		#7, #13
Th	#11	#11			#15		#11, #13
*F	#17 Recitation					#16 Field Day	

*On Friday, at the end of each Unit, review and take the Unit Quiz in the *Test Appendix*. On quiz days parents
and students may want to opt to reduce or eliminate Field Day and Recitation.

❧ Study Guide

Read Chapter XXXI

Reading Comprehension:

1. Why did Marilla allow Anne so much freedom during her summer vacation?

2. What improved Anne's alertness, spring in her step, and zest?

3. At the end of the summer, what "good friends" did Anne retrieve?

4. What effect did Rachel have on both Marilla and Anne? What was good about Rachel?

5. What did Anne find about growing up?

6. What caused Anne to do even better academically?

7. What did Marilla notice about Anne besides her growth in height? What brought forth this change in Anne?

8. Why did Anne expand socially?

9. What had happened to the story club?

10. What was Anne's stumbling block? Moody Spurgeon? Who is missing from the list?

11. What did Anne think she could not bear? Is there something that you think you could not bear?

Vocabulary Words:

theology

shirks

flounce

trustees

elopement

Vocabulary:

🗝 Look up the vocabulary words in a dictionary or encyclopedia. Write a sentence with each. Skim the chapter or use the word search in the online edition of *Anne of Green Gables* to find the sentence in which the word is used in the story. Write each sentence.

🌿 Activities:

☀ Dictation

1. ✎ Copy the following letter from renowned missionary, Hudson Taylor, to his sister, Louisa:

> There is one thing I would specially warn you against. One of the greatest curses I believe of the present day—the practice of novel reading. If you value your mind and soul, avoid it as you would a dangerous serpent. I cannot tell you what I would give to be able to forget certain novels I have read and to efface their influence from my memory. And I firmly believe, though some would deny it, . . . that no Christian ever did or ever will read them without injury, . . . very serious injury too, if the habit is indulged in. It is like opium-

smoking, and begets a craving for more than must be supplied. Better books are neglected, and no one can estimate
the mischief that results. Few, I believe, could honestly ask
God's blessing upon the reading of a novel, and few would
venture to assert that they read them to the glory of God. I
dread them for you especially as a temptation to which you
are constitutionally disposed. . . . For you and I resemble one
another very much as to temperament. . . . The only safety
lies in avoiding them as one of Satan's most dangerous
snares.

   I often fear that while I may be remembered by you as your
brother the missionary in China, you will not feel towards me
as to one who has a deep, a constant, and increasing interest
in your welfare. May God bless you, my dearly-beloved and
often prayed-for sister, and make you all that He Himself
would have you be. Good-night, my oil
is done.
   Once more, God bless you.

   —Dr. and Mrs. Howard Taylor, *Hudson Taylor in Early Years: The Growth of a Soul,* page 378

---

2. ✎ Compare your copy with the original. Correct any mistakes.   **Follow-up**

📖 Review *Writers INC,* "Modeling Sentences," page 92.

✎ Write your own version of several sentences by imitating them part
by part.

---

3. 📖 From *Anne's Anthology,* read "Maidenhood" by Henry Wadsworth   ☼ **Literature**
Longfellow.

   The title of this chapter in *Anne of Green Gables* is taken from a line
   from the poem, "Maidenhood." How does this poem reinforce the plot of
   this chapter? In chapter 30, in what setting did Miss Stacy discuss the
   girls growing up?

---

4. Longfellow is a famous American poet. "Maidenhood" is one of his   ☼ **History**
shorter works.

📖 Read more about this poet. You may want to read other works by him.

✎ In the History section of your notebook, in the appropriate time period:
Write a half-page biographical sketch of Longfellow. Include a paragraph about his poetry.

---

5. Anne wonders why there are not any women preachers.   ☼ **Bible**

🗝 What does the Bible say about a woman's role within the church? Use
your concordance to find out.

🗝 What is your church's belief about women preachers? Find out if you
do not know.

📖 In the *Background Information Appendix,* read 19th century Presbyterian leader R. L. Dabney's view on women preaching in public.

✹ With your instructor:
Discuss what you have learned about the role of women in the church, any differences found, and your own view.

☼ Bible   6. This chapter alludes to an increase in Anne's knowledge of the Bible. Montgomery uses Biblical phrases at least three times.

✎ In the Bible section of your notebook:
Skim the chapter to see if you can find these Biblical phrases and then use your concordance to locate at least one reference. *See answers in Answer Appendix.*

☼ Literature   7. "Hills peeped o'er hills and Alps on Alps arose" is set apart in the text to show Montgomery is quoting from a literary work. Sometimes Montgomery sets a quote apart while at other times she just weaves the reference or allusion into the text. This quote is taken from Alexander Pope's "An Essay on Criticism."

Alexander Pope was born in London on May 21, 1688 to a Roman Catholic family. Catholics at this time were severely restricted in their liberty and ownership of property by the English government. Pope had tuberculosis of the bone, probably contracted from his wet nurse. At 12 he suffered from a tubercular spinal infection. As a result of this illness he only grew to a height of four feet, six inches and developed a hunched back. This left him permanently deformed and very sensitive about his appearance.

He was barred from an English university education because of his religion, but he continued his education at a Catholic institution and supplemented his learning with extensive reading of Greek and Latin authors. He began writing verse by verse translations of these and imitations and adaptations of other authorss such as Chaucer, Waller, and Cowley.

Pope attained fame at the age of twenty-three upon the publication of "An Essay on Criticism." He was considered the greatest English poet of the early 1700's. Known for brilliant verse satires which ridiculed many kinds of human folly, his biting wit made him one of the most feared writers of his time in England. He wrote in couplets of ten syllables each. His verse was polished, concise, and demonstrated a keen sense of sound. He has become one of the most often quoted poets. "An Essay on Criticism" contains two well-known lines: "A little learning is a dangerous thing" and "To err is human; to forgive, divine." His most famous work, "The Rape of the Lock," satirizes the frailties of fashionable people and ridicules the battle between the sexes: "Oh! If to dance all night, and dress all day / Charm'd the smallpox, or chased old age away."

📖 Read "An Essay on Criticism" from *Anne's Anthology*.

✎ In the Literature section of your notebook write:
   a. What do the Alps symbolize in this poem?
   b. How does the stanza from which the quote was taken fit Anne?
   c. What is the definition of **satire**?

✎ In the History section of your notebook, in the appropriate time period:
   a. Write a brief biographical sketch of Alexander Pope.
   b. At the conclusion, write three or four quotable couplets from
      Pope's work.

---

8. ⚕ With your instructor: Health
   a. Discuss the advice the physician from Spencervale gives to Marilla
      about Anne.
   b. What effect does his advice have on Marilla and, in turn, Anne?
   c. During your school breaks, what do you do to be out in the open air?
   d. From the book of Ecclesiastes, tell what effect Solomon thought too
      much study would have.

---

9. ⚷ Briefly research the medical practices of the nineteenth century.   History
   What training did doctors need to have? How much did they charge for
   their services?

✋ Visit a medical museum or the medical section of a museum.

---

10. In II Peter 1:2–8 we are directed to add **godliness** to perseverance.   Bible
    Godliness is having the attributes of God's character. We cannot have
    attributes of His person, such as omnipresence and omniscience, but
    we can have attributes of His character.

✎ In the Bible section of your notebook:
   Write examples that show how Anne is developing godliness.

♡ Memorize Galatians 6:9.

---

11. "I feel just like studying with might and main" is an unusual state-   ☼ Literature/
    ment. The 1913 Webster defines the phrase, "might and main" as   History
    "with all one's strength; with violent effort." This phrase was used
    in chapter III, "Wealth," in *The Conduct of Life* by Ralph Waldo
    Emerson (1803–1882). The entire chapter may be found easily on
    the Internet at several different Web sites. The following is an excerpt
    from the chapter:

> The subject of economy mixes itself with morals, inasmuch
> as it is a peremptory point of virtue that a man's indepen-
> dence be secured. Poverty demoralizes. A man in debt is so
> far a slave; and Wall-street thinks it easy for a *millionaire* to
> be a man of his word, a man of honor, but, that, in failing
> circumstances, no man can be relied on to keep his integrity.
> And when one observes in the hotels and palaces of our
> Atlantic capitals, the habit of expense, the riot of the senses,
> the absence of bonds, clanship, fellow-feeling of any kind, he

feels, that, when a man or a woman is driven to the wall, the chances of integrity are frightfully diminished, as if virtue were coming to be a luxury which few could afford, or, as Burke said, "at a market almost too high for humanity." He may fix his inventory of necessities and of enjoyments on what scale he pleases, but if he wishes the power and privilege of thought, the chalking out his own career, and having society on his own terms, he must bring his wants within his proper power to satisfy.

The manly part is to do with *might and main* (emphasis added) what you can do. The world is full of fops who never did anything, and who have persuaded beauties and men of genius to wear their fop livery, and these will deliver the fop opinion, that it is not respectable to be seen earning a living; that it is much more respectable to spend without earning; and this doctrine of the snake will come also from the elect sons of light; for wise men are not wise at all hours, and will speak five times from their taste or their humor, to once from their reason. The brave workman, who might betray his feeling of it in his manners, if he do not succumb in his practice, must replace the grace or elegance forfeited, by the merit of the work done. No matter whether he make shoes, or statues, or laws. It is the privilege of any human work which is well done to invest the doer with a certain haughtiness. He can well afford not to conciliate, whose faithful work will answer for him. The mechanic at his bench carries a quiet heart and assured manners, and deals on even terms with men of any condition. The artist has made his picture so true, that it disconcerts criticism. The statue is so beautiful, that it contracts no stain from the market, but makes the market a silent gallery for itself. The case of the young lawyer was pitiful to disgust, —a paltry matter of buttons or tweezer-cases; but the determined youth saw in it an aperture to insert his dangerous wedges, made the insignificance of the thing forgotten, and gave fame by his sense and energy to the name and affairs of the Tittleton snuffbox factory.

In the *Background Information Appendix,* read about Emerson's life, philosophy, and works in the two articles by Ruth Nourse from the series, "Hijacking American Education." Also read briefly about Emerson on the Internet.

In the History section of your notebook:
Write about the far reaching effects Emerson's philosophy has had in our modern world.

| Occupational Education | 12. Who does Anne list as people who will help her grow up successfully? Besides your parents, who do you have to help you grow up successfully? What attributes make these people important in your development? |

13. ✎ Have you, like Anne, found growing up is fun, ". . . but it's not the kind of fun I expected. . . ."? Write a story about your unexpected experiences in growing up. Use Miss Stacy's techniques to improve your creative writing: write simply with short words and only about things that might happen in your own life in your town.

Writing

14. ⚷ What tests do you need to pass in order to go to the school of your choice? What can you do to prepare?

Occupational Education

✋ List the things you would like to do to prepare for these tests and make a plan for accomplishing them.

⚸ Discuss your plan with your instructor.

15. ✋ Make a flounce skirt.

Occupational Education

16. ✋ Continue to use each Friday for a field day. Study the plants, flowers, and birds native to your area. Begin by identifying all the plants on your property. As time allows, increase your observation area. Take a camera or a sketch pad as well as plant and bird identification books. After a plant is identified, take a picture of it and place it in your Fine Arts notebook or draw it in your sketchbook and label it.

Science

17. ⚸ With your instructor:

Literature

Continue with recitation each Friday during this Unit. Recite your favorite lines from "Maidenhood," Pope's "An Essay on Criticism," and other passages from works you have studied in previous Chapters.

Quote memorized scriptures to your teacher: I Corinthians 10:13; The Lord's Prayer; Psalm 30; Romans 5:19; Proverbs 25:27; I Corinthians 13:13; Romans 8:5–8; Psalm 15; I Peter 3:17; Proverbs 4:23; James 1:2–4; Colossians 1:10; Galatians 6:9; and your choice of Ephesians 3:20; Proverbs 17:27–28; or James 3:13, 17.

18. Review and take Unit 7 Quiz in the *Test Appendix*.

☼ Quiz

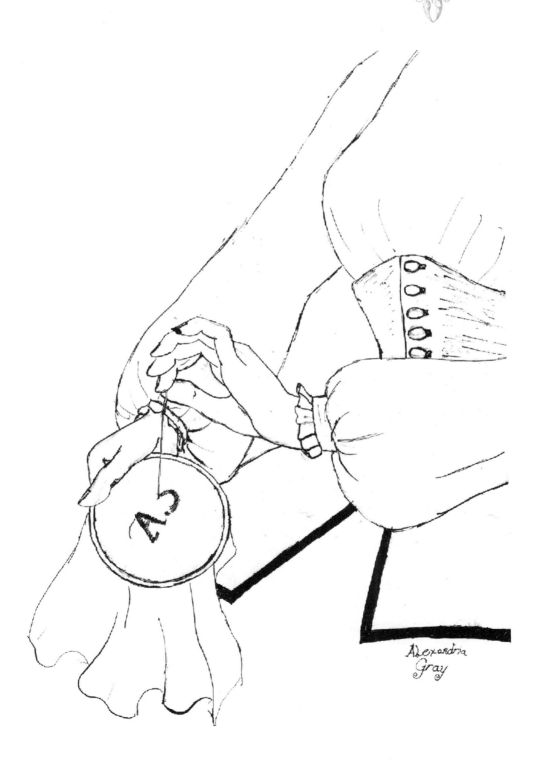

Alexandria
Gray

Planning Guide

Gather These Items:
1. Stamped pillowcase, embroidery thread, and embroidery hoop. These are available at Wal-Mart, a fabric store, or a hobby store.

Research Topics:
1. ACT or SAT exam.

. . . .

2. Requirements for entrance and scholarship information for the school of your choice

. . . .

Suggested Videos:

Suggested Field Trips:

Group Activities:

Memory Work:
Jeremiah 9:23–24

Notes:

Assignments — Chapter XXX II

Contract Reading: No new contract reading

Weekly
Quiet Time Reading Books:
Independent Project: Pillowcase
Memory Work: Jeremiah 9:23–24
Science: If you have chosen to track changes in some of the plants on your property and/or do some experiments as suggested in Chapter XXVIII, Activity 19, continue following your schedule for these activities.

	Literature	History	Bible	Health	Occu. Education	Science & Fine Arts	Grammar & Writing
M	Read Chap. XXXII AGG, Reading Comp., #2				#7		#1, #2
T	Vocab.		#3		#5		#3
W			#4		#5		
Th			#6		#5		
F	#9 Recitation					#8 Field Day	

🐲 Study Guide

Read Chapter XXXII
Reading Comprehension:
1. What sage advice did Miss Stacy give for the night before the exam?

2. What unkind words did Josie say to Anne prior to the first day of the exam?

3. Why was Ruby in hysterics when Anne reached the boarding house?

4. What was Anne's presentiment?

5. For what was the Tory political party blamed?

6. Tell how Diana showed herself to be a true and good friend.

Vocabulary:
🗝 Look up the vocabulary words in a dictionary or encyclopedia. Write a sentence with each. Compare your sentence to the one in which it is used in *Anne of Green Gables*. Skim the chapter or use the word search in the online edition of the book to find the sentence, then write it below your sentence.

Vocabulary Words:

composed

recite

languished

lamented

sibilant

aspiration

conjugations

reverent

 Activities:

1. ✎ Write the following passage from dictation:

   > That night Anne, who had wound up a delightful evening by a serious little talk with Mrs. Allan at the manse, knelt sweetly by her open window in a great sheen of moonshine and murmured a prayer of gratitude and aspiration that came straight from her heart. There was in it thankfulness for the past and reverent petition for the future; and when she slept on her white pillow her dreams were as fair and bright and beautiful as maidenhood might desire. —*Anne of Green Gables,* page 264

   Dictation

2. ✎ Compare your copy with the original. Correct any mistakes.

   Follow-up

   What is the adjective modifying pillow? What does the color symbolize?

   The last sentence of the paragraph is reminiscent of the lines from the poem, "Maidenhood," by Longfellow: "Deep and still, that gliding stream / Beautiful to thee must seem, / As the river of a dream."

   ✎ Imagine what her dreams are. Write your thoughts about Anne's dreams in your journal.

Bible	3. Anne is truly thankful for her blessings. She has worked hard, but she is not prideful.

    ♡   Read and memorize Jeremiah 9:23–24.

    ✎   In the Bible section of your notebook write:
What is God's attitude toward those who are thankful and those who are not? Give examples from people in the Bible as well as verses that teach about thankfulness. Write at least one page. Use your concordance as necessary.

Bible	4. Moody Spurgeon says he is leaving early from the examination because it is easier to be a carpenter than a minister.

    ✎   In the Bible section of your notebook write:
Who in the Bible was first a carpenter and then became a preacher?

Occupational Education	5. The examination Anne and her fellow students take is comparable to the college entrance exams, ACT and SAT. Many colleges and universities require their own competency exam as well as the ACT or SAT. The results are no longer printed in the paper, but are sent out individually.

    ⚷   Find out from a university or college which test or tests they prefer and what they have set as the minimum score for entrance without remedial work. Moody Spurgeon was accepted on the condition he take extra history courses or do remedial work in history. Secondly, find out if the college or university gives scholarships for students who attain high test scores. If so, what are those scores? Find out the cost and procedure for taking these tests, when the tests are given, and what age or grade is recommended for taking them the first time.

    ✿   With your instructor:
Discuss your findings and decide if and when you should take these exams. There are textbooks to help prepare for ACT or SAT as well as online help. Go to <www.cadroncreek.com> for a list of Internet sites to visit.

Bible	6. 📖 Diana rejoices with Anne, although if Anne had not passed she would have remained in Avonlea. She wants what Anne wants. Everyone else who loves Anne rejoices with her. Read Romans 12:15 and I Corinthians 12:26.

        Think of a time when a friend or family member achieved something they really wanted. How did everyone rejoice?

Occupational Education	7. ✋ "Anne slept on her white pillow." Many people during the Victorian age embroidered their pillowcases. Find a pillowcase stamped with a simple, but striking embroidery pattern. Work on this project during your sewing and/or spare time. Be sure you use a variety of stitches, including French knots, the chain stitch, and the satin stitch.

8. ✋ Continue to use each Friday for a field day. Study the plants, flowers, and birds native to your area. Begin by identifying all the plants on your property. As time allows, increase your observation area. Take a camera or a sketch pad as well as plant and bird identification books. After a plant is identified, take a picture of it and place it in your Fine Arts notebook or draw it in your sketchbook and label it.

Science

9. 📖 With your instructor:

Literature

Continue with recitation each Friday during this Unit. Recite your favorite lines from "Maidenhood," and other passages from works you have studied in previous Chapters.

Quote memorized scriptures to your teacher: I Corinthians 10:13; The Lord's Prayer; Psalm 30; Romans 5:19; Proverbs 25:27; I Corinthians 13:13; Romans 8:5–8; Psalm 15; I Peter 3:17; Proverbs 4:23; James 1:2–4; Colossians 1:10; Galatians 6:9; Jeremiah 9:23–24; and your choice of Ephesians 3:20; Proverbs 17:27–28; or James 3:13, 17.

Planning Guide

Gather These Items:

1. *How Should We Then Live? The Rise and Decline of Western Thought and Culture* by Francis A. Schaeffer. Crossway Books, 1983. ISBN 0-89107-292-6.

2. Recipes and items to make chicken salad.

3. Prices for each item used to make chicken salad.

Research Topics:

1. Alfred Noyes
   —"Poetry Exhibits: Alfred Noyes." *Poets.org*. 24 Jul 2001. The Academy of American Poets. © 1997–2004 <http://www.poets.org/ poets/ poets.cfm? prmID=691>.
   —"Alfred Noyes: The Highwayman." 5 Jan. 2003. *Historique.net*. © 2003 <http://litterature.historique.net/noyes.html>.

2. Artist Raphael
   —Internet
   —*What Makes a Raphael, a Raphael?* by Richard Muhlberger. Bt Bound, 1999. ASIN 0785721045.
   —*How Should We Then Live? The Rise and Decline of Western Thought and Culture* by Francis A. Schaeffer. Crossway Books, 1983. ISBN 0-89107-292-6.

3. Artist Tiziano Vecellio or Titian (Warning: Many of his subjects are nude.)
   —*Titian's Women* by Rona Goffen. Yale University Press, 1997. ISBN 0-300-06846-8.

4. Pre-Raphaelites
   —"The Pre-Raphaelites and the New Romantic Tradition" by Terri Windling. *Gallery of Mythic Arts*. The Endicott Studio. © 1997–2004 <http://www.endicott-studio.com/galprb.html>.

5. John Waterhouse
   —*jwwaterhouse.com* at <http://www.jwwaterhouse.com/>

. . . .

6. Dante Rossetti

. . . .

7. John Millais

. . . .

8. How to find and use your most flattering colors through the study of skin tone, eye pattern, and personality
   —Internet search, "colors to wear"
   —*Color My Wardrobe* at <http://www.colormywardrobe.com/>
   —Internet

. . . .

9. "Dress for Success"

. . . .

10. The symbolic meaning of flowers (See Activity 5)

. . . .

Suggested Videos:

Suggested Field Trips:
1. Visit an art museum and view paintings by Raphael, Titian, and the Pre-Raphaelites.

Group Activities:
1. Work with your local hospital auxiliary to raise money for the hospital.

Memory Work:
Ephesians 1:17–18 and II Timothy 1:7

Notes:

Assignments — Chapter XXXIII

Contract Reading: No new contract reading

Weekly
Quiet Time Reading Books:
Independent Project: Pillowcase
Memory Work: Ephesians 1:17–18 and II Timothy 1:7
Science: If you have chosen to track changes in some of the plants on your property and/or do some experiments as suggested in Chapter XXVIII, Activity 19, continue following your schedule for these activities.

	Literature	History	Bible	Health	Occu. Education	Science & Fine Arts	Grammar & Writing
M	Read Chap. XXXIII AGG, Reading Comp., #2				#14		#1, #2
T	Vocab., #3	#3, #7	#13		#16	#7	#3, #7
W	#4	#4	#11		#10	#8	#4, #8
Th	#5, #6		#15		#12	#9	#15
F	#18 Recitation					#8 Field Trip, #17 Field Day	

Worksheet

Poetry
For Chapter XXXIII • "The Highwayman"

Write the definition and an example from "The Highwayman" for each of the following:

1. Alliteration:

2. Metaphor:

3. Onomatopoeia:

4. Simile:

5. How does your favorite poetic technique used contribute to the "mental picture" seen by the person reading the poem?

🐉 Study Guide

Read Chapter XXXIII
Reading Comprehension:

1. Describe how the east gable had changed over the past four years?

2. Where did Anne go and why?

3. What was Diana's reputation?

4. Why was Anne forever debarred from wearing wild-rose pink?

5. What did Diana do for Anne?

6. Describe Billy.

7. What scared Anne? What helped Anne get over her stage fright?

8. Why did Anne say they were rich?

9. Why was Anne happy with her pearls?

Vocabulary Words:

debarred

elocutionist

dint

unpropitious

scrutinized

languidly

lithe

limpid

rustic

staunchly

pallid

burnished

conniving

encore

scoffed

amateur

ballads

Vocabulary:

🗝 Look up the vocabulary words in a dictionary or encyclopedia. Fill in the blanks using the vocabulary words.

10. The _____ tavern had bullet holes in the wall.

11. The _____ gave a moving soliloquy.

12. She _____ the food and found a black hair.

13. She _____ recommended her friend for the position.

14. A _____ ballet dancer is a delight to watch.

15. The couple walked _____ down the beach.

16. The doctor wrote in a _____ style.

17. She succeeded by _____ of hard work.

18. Because of her past she was forever _____ from the club.

19. President Clinton's aides ensure that he will not arrive at an _____ time.

20. The haughty businessman _____ at the job applicant.

21. The audience made an _____ to bring back Ballet Magnificant.

22. The pans were _____ beautifully.

23. The _____ girl became ill as the day passed.

24. The _____ legislator failed to take action against the abortion bill.

25. The _____ cyclist could not keep up with Lance Armstrong.

26. Music in the 1970's contained more _____ than current music.

Activities:

1. ✎ Write the following passage from dictation: Dictation ✓

> At this unpropitious moment her name was called. Somehow, Anne—who did not notice the rather guilty little start of surprise the white-lace girl gave and would not have understood the subtle compliment implied therein if she had—got on her feet, and moved dizzily out to the front. —*Anne of Green Gables*, page 271

2. ✎ Compare your copy with the original. Correct any mistakes.   Follow-up ✓

✎ What was inferred in this text? Choose one of the above dictation sentences and write your own version, imitating it part-by-part.

3. "One moonbeam from the forehead to the crown" is a quotation from   Literature ✓
Aurora Leigh (Book 4, l. 1013), written by Elizabeth Barrett Browning. This 350 page novel in blank verse tells the life story of a fictional woman poet. Born in Italy of an Italian mother and an English father, Aurora, whose name means "the dawn," is orphaned by the age of thirteen. She goes to England to be cared for and educated by her father's sister. This aunt is a convention-bound woman; she imposes on Aurora an education intended to prepare her to be an ordinary, middle-class wife. The girl studies religion, languages, a little math and science, and some music and art. Feeling like a caged bird, Aurora keeps her inner life to herself while outwardly training to be a humble wife. She decides to become a poet. Her aunt's cousin, Romney Leigh, proposes marriage to her. He is dedicated to social service and wishes Aurora to help him in his political career, but she rejects him in favor of her own vocation as a poet. Romney then decides to marry a lower-class woman, Marian Earle, but she is discouraged from the marriage by an aristocratic lady, who is a rival for Romney's love. Sent away to France, Marian is trapped and raped, becoming pregnant as a result. She and her child are later rescued by Aurora. The three set up a home together in Italy, where Romney later appears. He has been blinded by an accident and has been somewhat softened by experience. Meanwhile, Aurora has learned the value of love from living with Marian and her child. She marries Romney in a new spirit of modest self-effacement. While not giving up poetry, she will write in service to the ideas of her husband. Thus Elizabeth Barrett Browning closes with a compromise between the artist's drive for self-expression and the Victorian wife's role of submissive service.

Paraphrased from the Web site: <http://www.vanderbilt.edu/ AnS/english/English151W-03/auroraleigh.htm>

✎ In the History section of your notebook, in the appropriate time period: Write a half-page report on the life and poetry of Elizabeth Barrett Browning.

🔆 Literature   4. Anne does not recite "The Highwayman," as she does in the movie version of *Anne of Green Gables,* but "The Maiden's Vow." According to *The Annotated Anne of Green Gables,* page 351, there are at least two possible candidates for this poem, "The Maiden's Vow" by Caroline Oliphant and "Mars La Tour, or, The Maiden's Vow," by Stafford MacGregor. Because of the theme and imagery of the latter poem, the authors think it a more likely candidate. If you would like to read this poem, it may be found in *The Annotated Anne of Green Gables,* pages 481–482. The former poem may be found online.

Personally I think Montgomery could have been inspired by the poem, "The Highwayman." She was a voracious reader who obviously loved poetry. "The Highwayman," published in 1907, was written by Alfred Noyes. His work shows a clear influence of the romantic poets such as Wordsworth. For your enjoyment, "The Highwayman" is included in the *Background Information Appendix.*

✎ Write one paragraph about the poet, Alfred Noyes. Place it in the correct place in the History section of your notebook. What clues do you find in your research that suggest some of Alfred Noyes' beliefs and values?

✎ Complete the Poetry Worksheet found after the Assignment page.

🔆 Literature   5. White lilies adorn Miss Stacy's picture in Anne's room. This, too, is probably an allusion to the poem "Maidenhood" by Longfellow.

> Gather, then, each flower that grows,
> When the young heart overflows,
> To embalm that tent of snow.
>
> Bear a **lily** in thy hand;
> Gates of brass cannot withstand
> One touch of that magic wand.

☞ Look up the symbolic meaning of flowers.

✎ In this or other chapters, find three instances where Montgomery uses flowers as a symbol to enhance her meaning. Write the meaning of these symbols in the Literature section of your notebook.

Literature   6. ✎ In the Literature section of your notebook:
Write the descriptive terms used of both Anne's and the elocutionist's recitation. Can the same be said of your recitation?

🗣 With your instructor:
Decide which element of elocution you will work on for this Friday's recitation.

7. Mrs. Allan thinks Anne looks like the Madonna when her hair is parted a certain way. Who is the Madonna? The Madonna has been painted numerous ways by numerous artists, but Raphael is one of the most famous.

☞ Look up information about the life and works of Raphael and Titian.

☞ View some of Raphael's paintings.

☼ Fine Arts

> Raphael also painted "The School of Athens" (c. 1510). This fresco is in the Vatican. Plato, Aristotle's student, has one finger pointing upward, which is an indication that he pointed toward absolutes or ideals. In contrast, he portrayed Aristotle with his finger spread wide and thrust down to earth, indicating he emphasized particulars."
>
> —Francis Schaeffer, *How Should We Then Live? The Rise and Decline of Western Thought and Culture*, page 52

Anne is described as having Titian hair. Titian, too, has painted the Madonna. Perhaps Titian is not as well known for his paintings of hair as he is for his enduring fascination with the theme of beautiful woman. His paintings have an erotic appeal. For instance, his mythological images represent a use of the female body to demonstrate "divine" craftsmanship. His devotional images introduce the paradox of subject matter with a sexual component that both stimulates and inhibits. Through his paintings Titian invites the viewer to respond to female emotions.

☞ View some paintings by Titian. (Warning: Some of these will have nudes.)

📖 For a chronological survey of the arts read, *How Should We Then Live? The Rise and Decline of Western Thought and Culture*, pages 57–78 and 97–104.

✎ In the History section of your notebook, write in the appropriate time period:
   a. A half-page biography each of Titian and Raphael. Include what made "a Raphael a Raphael" and what made "a Titian a Titian."
   b. Include at the end of each biography the names of at least two of your favorite paintings and describe why you like them.
   c. After viewing some of Titian's paintings, describe what "Titian hair" is and which paintings are the best examples of "Titian hair."
   d. How does man's philosophical outlook affect art?

8. As I read this chapter in *Anne of Green Gables,* it evoked images of Pre-Raphaelite paintings. The Pre-Raphaelites

☼ Fine Arts

> . . . were a brotherhood of English painters and poets formed in 1848 in protest against the low standards of British art. The principal founders were Dante Rossetti, William Holman Hunt, and John Millais. In poetry as well as in painting, the Pre-Raphaelites turned away from the growing materialism

of industrialized England. They sought refuge in the beauty of the medieval world. In the works of the Italian painters prior to Raphael, they found a style that they tried to imitate. The paintings of the Pre-Raphaelites are characteristically nostalgic in tone, bright in color and mannered in style. —<http://users.telenet.be/gaston.d.haese/drossetti.html>

📖 In *Writers INC,* read about writing a summary on pages 403–404. Use this technique as you write about the artists in the following assignment.

The Pre-Raphaelite movement was intended to redefine art, and indeed it helped pave the way for our modern era.

✎ In the History section of your notebook, in the appropriate time period:
a. Write at least a half-page biography each of Dante Rossetti, John Waterhouse, and John Millais. Be sure to include what each of Rossetti's portraits of women have in common and why this was so.
b. Include at the bottom of your biography the names of at least two of your favorite paintings and describe why you like them.
c. Choose one for the wallpaper of your computer.

✋ Visit an art museum and view paintings by Raphael, Titian, and the Pre-Raphaelites.

Fine Arts   9. Leonardo da Vinci (1452–1519), Italian Renaissance painter, sculpture, architect, and engineer, compared painting to poetry:

Although the poet has as wide a choice of subjects as the painter, his creations fail to afford as much satisfaction to mankind as do paintings . . . if the poet serves the understanding by way of the ear, the painter does so by the eye, which is the nobler sense.

✋ Pick one of the paintings by an artist studied in this chapter and copy it to the best of your ability.

Occupational Education   10. 🔑 Because of her coloring Anne could not wear pink. Find out which colors look best on you.

Bible   11. ". . . the white-lace girl kept talking audibly to her next neighbour about the 'country bumpkins' and 'rustic belles' in the audience, languidly anticipating 'such fun' from the displays of local talent . . ."
a. What type of attitude do the comments of the "white-lace girl" portray about her character?
b. How do these comments affect Anne?
c. Have you been on the receiving end of similar comments?
d. Have you been guilty of saying similar comments?

📖 Read Job 41:34; Psalm 18:27; Psalm 101:5; Proverbs 6:16–17; Proverbs 16:18; Proverbs 21:4; and Isaiah 13:11.

12. Have you ever arrived somewhere and felt either over or under dressed?

⚷ Look up information on appropriate dress. There are several Internet "Dress for Success" sites. Most of these are for interviews and the job world, but much of the information can carry over to other situations.

✋ Make a poster demonstrating a positive and negative rule of "Dressing for Success."

Occupational Education

13. Normally the best performer is saved until last. Anne feels acutely intimidated following the talented, professional elocutionist. This is poor planning on the part of the concert committee. Several times through the evening Anne wishes she were ". . . back in the white room at Green Gables." Many times we do not do things because of fear. As we see in I Corinthians 2:3–5, the Apostle Paul was fearful yet he persevered. His words in II Timothy 1:7 have been a source of encouragement for many. Although Anne was not necessarily promoting the gospel with her speech, she was using her God given talent for the good of those around her. We need not be immobilized by fear.

♡ Memorize II Timothy 1:7.

Bible ✓

14. The girls think it would be fun to eat chicken salad everyday.

✋ Over the next couple of weeks, try two or three different chicken salad recipes. Pick the one you like the best. Pretend you are starting a restaurant; figure the cost per serving of making your favorite chicken salad recipe. How much would you need to charge to break even serving this dish?

Occupational Education

15. As the book progresses, we continue to see Anne happier and happier in her daily life in Avonlea.

📖 Read I Timothy 6:6 and Ephesians 1:3–23.

✎ In the Bible section of your notebook:
Paraphrase the section from Ephesians. You may want to review the sections on paraphrasing in *Writers INC*.

♡ Memorize Ephesians 1:17–18.

Bible

16. ✋ Inquire what your hospital auxiliary is planning to do to raise money for your local hospital. See if there is anything you can do to help. What is their need for money?

Occupational Education

17. ✋ Continue to use each Friday for a field day. Study the plants, flowers, and birds native to your area. Begin by identifying all the plants on your property. As time allows, increase your observation area. Take a camera or a sketch pad as well as plant and bird identification books. After a plant is identified, take a picture of it and place it in your Fine Arts notebook or draw it in your sketchbook and label it.

Science

Literature   18. ✠ With your instructor:

Continue with recitation each Friday during this Unit. Recite your favorite lines from *Aurora Leigh,* one or both of the "The Maiden's Vow" poems, and "The Highwayman."

Quote memorized scriptures to your teacher: I Corinthians 10:13; The Lord's Prayer; Psalm 30; Romans 5:19; Proverbs 25:27; I Corinthians 13:13; Romans 8:5–8; Psalm 15; I Peter 3:17; Proverbs 4:23; James 1:2–4; Colossians 1:10; Galatians 6:9; Jeremiah 9:23-24; Ephesians 1:17–18; II Timothy 1:7; and your choice of Ephesians 3:20; Proverbs 17:27–28; or James 3:13, 17.

———◆———

 Planning Guide

Gather These Items:

1. *How Should We Then Live? The Rise and Decline of Western Thought and Culture* by Francis A. Schaeffer. Crossway Books, 1983. ISBN 0-89107-292-6.

2. Items to make a homesick basket. (See Activity 10)

Research Topics:

1. History and development of the telephone

. . . .

2. Virgil
   —Encyclopedia
   —*How Should We Then Live? The Rise and Decline of Western Thought and Culture* by Francis A. Schaeffer. Crossway Books, 1983. ISBN 0-89107-292-6.

. . . .

3. Onomatopoeia

. . . .

Suggested Video:

Suggested Field Trips:

Group Activities:

Memory Verse:
Matthew 5:44–45

Notes:

Assignments — Chapter XXXIV

Contract Reading: No new contract reading

Weekly
Quiet Time Reading Books:
Independent Project: Pillowcase
Memory Work: Matthew 5:44–45
Science: If you have chosen to track changes in some of the plants on your property and/or do
    some experiments as suggested in Chapter XXVIII, Activity 19, continue following your
    schedule for these activities.

	Literature	History	Bible	Health	Occu. Education	Science & Fine Arts	Grammar & Writing
M	Read Chap. XXXIV AGG, Reading Comp., #2		#7				#1, #2
T	Vocab., #4		#8				#3
W	#5	#5					#5
Th	#9	#6			#10		#6, #9
F	#12 Recitation					#11 Field Day	

Study Guide

Read Chapter XXXIV
Reading Comprehension:

1. How did Anne demonstrate her affection to Matthew and Marilla? What did Marilla wish when Anne did this?

2. What did Matthew see in Anne?

3. To what did he attribute Anne's coming to Green Gables?

4. How did Diana and Marilla respond to Anne's leaving? What did each of them do?

5. Why does Anne decide not to board with Miss Josephine Barry?

6. What did Anne think about having Gilbert in class?

7. Anne wondered who would be her friend. From outward appearances, what did Anne think about the girls? What attracted her to each? Have you ever done this?

8. Explain the different ways Josie Pye insults Anne during their visit. Compare Josie's comments with those of Jane's.

9. What did Anne say about ambition?

Vocabulary:

☞ Look up the vocabulary words in a dictionary or encyclopedia. Write a sentence with each.

Vocabulary Words:

preposterous

scorned

ambition

pinnacle

aspiration

 Activities:

1. ✎ Write the following passage from dictation: Dictation ✓

   "My foot is on my native heath, and my name is MacGregor."

   —Sir Walter Scott, *Rob Roy*, Chapter 34

2. ✎ Compare your copy with the original. Correct any mistakes.   Follow-up ✓

   Montgomery uses the term "native heath" in a sentence on page 281 regarding the Avery scholarship.

   ✎ In the Literature section of your notebook:
   Write your own sentence incorporating a quote from a piece of literature you have read during this study.

Writing		3. ✎ In the Literature section of your notebook: Write a "Valentine" letter to someone in your family who needs to know how much you care. Put your feelings into words. For examples, reread the letter from Hudson Taylor to his sister and Anne's words to Marilla.

Literature 4. "Kerwollops" is an example of **onomatopoeia**, a word invented to imitate a sound.

✎ In the Literature section of your notebook:
Write other examples of onomatopoeia.

Literature 5. Jane says she should be studying Virgil. She was referring to the *Aeneid* written by Publius Vergilius Maro or Virgil (70–19 B.C.). In *How Should We Then Live?* by Francis Schaeffer, read pages 22 and 58 about Virgil. Also, read about Virgil in the encyclopedia.

✎ In the History section of your notebook, in the appropriate time period:
Write a page about Virgil and his writings.

History 6. Note that there are telephone lines outside Anne's window.

✎ In the History section of your notebook, in the appropriate time period:
Write about the history and development of telephones. Include examples of specific technologies that have improved the telephone.

Bible 7. Some people have difficult personalities; Josie Pye is one of them. How does Anne deal with Josie Pye?

With your instructor, discuss a person who you find has a difficult personality. Discuss some strategies for dealing with this difficult person.

📖 Read Matthew 5:38–39; Matthew 5:44–45; Proverbs 25:4; and Psalm 5.
♡ Memorize Matthew 5:44–45.

Bible 8. Anne has ambition. Ambition is not wrong, only selfish ambition.

📖 The Apostle Paul had ambition. Read Romans 15:20.

With your instructor discuss:
What goals do you have?

📖 We can make plans, but we must remember that God takes us on adventures we cannot foresee. Read Isaiah 55:9.

Literature 9. ✎ Have you ever been out of your home, away from family for an extended period of time, and developed homesickness? Write a paper describing this event. What made you feel better? What made it worse? If you have been away, but have not experienced homesickness, write why you think you were not homesick.

10. Marilla packs Anne goodies which have ". . . the real Avonlea flavour."   Occupational
                                                                                     Education

   With your instructor discuss:
   What foods remind you of home?

   Each year more of your friends may be leaving home to pursue their
   goals. Design a homesick basket to give them before they leave.

11.   Continue to use each Friday for a field day. Study the plants, flow-   Science
   ers, and birds native to your area. Begin by identifying all the plants
   on your property. As time allows, increase your observation area. Take
   a camera or a sketch pad as well as plant and bird identification books.
   After a plant is identified, take a picture of it and place it in your Fine
   Arts notebook or draw it in your sketchbook and label it.

12.   With your instructor: Literature

   Continue with recitation each Friday during this Unit. Recite your
   favorite lines from poems and other passages from works you have
   studied in previous Chapters.

   Quote memorized scriptures to your teacher: I Corinthians 10:13; The
   Lord's Prayer; Psalm 30; Romans 5:19; Proverbs 25:27; I Corinthians
   13:13; Romans 8:5–8; Psalm 15; I Peter 3:17; Proverbs 4:23; James
   1:2–4; Colossians 1:10; Galatians 6:9; Jeremiah 9:23-24; Ephesians
   1:17–18; II Timothy 1:7; Matthew 5:44–45; and your choice of
   Ephesians 3:20; Proverbs 17:27–28; or James 3:13, 17.

Planning Guide

Gather These Items:
1. *Aeropagitica* by John Milton. (The full text may be found online.)

Research Topics:
1. John Milton, his works and life

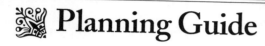

Suggested Videos:

Suggested Field Trips:

Group Activities:

Memory Verse:
II Peter 1:2–8

Notes:

Assignments — Chapter XXXV

Contract Reading: No new contract reading

Weekly
Quiet Time Reading Books:
Independent Project:
Memory Work: II Peter 1:2–8
Science: If you have chosen to track changes in some of the plants on your property and/or do
some experiments as suggested in Chapter XXVIII, Activity 19, continue following your
schedule for these activities.

	Literature	History	Bible	Health	Occu. Education	Science & Fine Arts	Grammar & Writing
M	Read Chap. XXXV AGG, Reading Comp.		#6				#1, #2
T	Vocab., #3				#7		
W	#4						#4
Th	#5						#5
*F	#9 Recitation					#8 Field Day	

*On Friday, at the end of each Unit, review and take the Unit Quiz in the *Test Appendix*. On quiz days parents
and students may want to opt to reduce or eliminate Field Day and Recitation.

❧ Study Guide

Read Chapter XXXV
Reading Comprehension:

1. With whom was Gilbert walking home, carrying her satchel? What did Anne think about this?

2. Which did Anne think were the best and dearest hours in the whole week?

3. What positive character qualities did Anne now see in Gilbert? Why did Ruby not seem Gilbert's kind of girl?

4. Were Anne's first impressions of her two female classmates correct?

5. How did each one at Avonlea make a mark of distinction at Queen's?

6. What helped Anne keep the examinations in perspective?

7. How did Anne respond to Josie's comment?

Vocabulary Words:

eddy

chaplet

commencement

immortal

Vocabulary:

☞ Look up the vocabulary words in a dictionary or encyclopedia. Write a sentence with each.

❧ Activities:

Dictation	1. ✎ Write the following passage from dictation:	

"I've done my best and I begin to understand what is meant by the 'joy of the strife.' Next to trying and winning, the best thing is trying and failing." —*Anne of Green Gables,* page 287

Follow-up	2. ✎ Compare your copy with the original. Correct any mistakes.

Literature	3. In this chapter we see numerous references to literature. The references further convince the reader that Anne is diligently pursuing the Avery scholarship. Notice the quotation marks around "mist of green" on page 285. This is an excerpt from Alfred, Lord Tennyson's, "The Brook." In this poem, Lawrence Aylmer returns home after an absence of twenty years. He wanders by the brook and recalls the past and the rhyme about the brook written by his brother Edward.

📖 Tennyson is the prevailing poet of *Anne of Green Gables.* Read pages 460–461 of *The Annotated Anne of Green Gables.*

📖 From *Anne's Anthology,* read "The Brook" by Alfred, Lord Tennyson.

4. On page 287, there are single quotation marks around 'joy of the strife.' This is a quote from the poem, "The Woman on the Field of Battle" by Felicia Hemans.

📖 From *Anne's Anthology,* read "The Woman on the Field of Battle" by Felicia Hemans.

✎ After reading this poem, in the Literature section of your notebook write:
What you think the phrase, "joy of the strife," means.

⚹ Discuss with your instructor:
a. What was the purpose of the poem "The Woman on the Field of Battle"?
b. What is Anne's battlefield?

☉ Literature

5. Anne's ambitions and dreams combine to create visions of her future, ". . . each year a rose of promise to be woven into an immortal chaplet." The context of this allusion, the following quote from Milton's *Aeropagitica,* adds even more to the sense of battle and perseverance in Anne's pursuit of the scholarship:

> I can not praise a fugitive and cloistered virtue, unexercised and unbreathed, that never sallies out and sees her adversary, but slinks out of the race, where that immortal garland is to be run for, not without dust and heat.

📖 The full text of Milton's essay, *Aeropagitica* (also spelled *Areopagitica*) may be found online. Read this essay.

⚲ Look up information on the life and works of John Milton.

✎ Write several paragraphs about this writer and his works.

Literature

6. 📖 Read Galatians 6:9. What is the key to persevering? How does Anne demonstrate perseverance?

♡ Memorize II Peter 1:2–8.

Bible

7. The girls discuss what they will wear to commencement. From your studies of Victorian fashion and the descriptions of dresses in previous chapters, create some mental pictures of appropriate attire.

✋ In the Occupational Education section of your notebook or in your sketchbook, draw pictures of dresses you think the girls might wear to commencement.

Occupational Education

8. ✋ Continue to use each Friday for a field day. Study the plants, flowers, and birds native to your area. Begin by identifying all the plants on your property. As time allows, increase your observation area. Take a camera or a sketch pad as well as plant and bird identification books. After a plant is identified, take a picture of it and place it in your Fine Arts notebook or draw it in your sketchbook and label it.

Science

Literature	9. With your instructor: Continue with recitation each Friday during this Unit. Recite your favorite lines from the poems, "The Brook" and "The Woman on the Field of Battle" or the essay, *Aeropagitica*. Quote memorized scriptures to your teacher: I Corinthians 10:13; The Lord's Prayer; Psalm 30; Romans 5:19; Proverbs 25:27; I Corinthians 13:13; Romans 8:5–8; Psalm 15; I Peter 3:17; Proverbs 4:23; James 1:2–4; Colossians 1:10; Galatians 6:9; Jeremiah 9:23–24; Ephesians 1:17–18; II Timothy 1:7; Matthew 5:44–45; II Peter 1:2–8; and your choice of Ephesians 3:20; Proverbs 17:27–28; or James 3:13, 17.
Quiz	10. Review and take Unit 8 Quiz in the *Test Appendix*.

Unit 9
Chapters XXXVI – XXXVIII

Planning Guide

Gather These Items:
1. *American Dictionary of the English Language* (1828 Edition) by Noah Webster.

Research Topics:
1. Eyeglasses

. . . .

2. History of retirement
  —Internet search, "History of Retirement"
  —"A Brief History of Retirement." *Re-VisioningRetirement.com*. AIG SunAmerica. <http://www.google.com/search?q=cache:fxF6IKXXfFoJ: www.re-visioningretirement.com/PDF/history.pdf+&hl=en>.

. . . .

3. Empathy
  —"The Empathy Quotient Quiz." *Guardian Unlimited*. Guardian Newspapers Limited. © 2003 <http://www.guardian.co.uk/ life/flash/ page/0,13249,937836,00.html>.

. . . .

4. William Wordsworth, his life and works

. . . .

Suggested Videos:
✓1. *Secondhand Lions*. Perf. Michael Caine and Robert Duvall. Videocassette. New Line Home Video, 2004. ASIN B0000YTP0C. Rated PG (With parental approval only.)

✓2. *It's a Wonderful Life* (1947). Perf. Jimmy Stewart and Donna Reed. Videocassette. Republic Studios, 2002. ASIN 630289915X.

Suggested Field Trips:
1. Visit an optometrist.

Group Activities:

Memory Work:
Matthew 19:19

Notes:

Assignments — Chapter XXXVI

Contract Reading: No new contract reading

Weekly
Quiet Time Reading Books:
Independent Project:
Memory Work: Matthew 19:19
Science: If you have chosen to track changes in some of the plants on your property and/or do some experiments as suggested in Chapter XXVIII, Activity 19, continue following your schedule for these activities.

	Literature	History	Bible	Health	Occu. Education	Science & Fine Arts	Grammar & Writing
M	Read Chap. XXXVI AGG, Reading Comp., #2		#11		#5		#1, #2
T	Vocab.	#8	#3				#3
W	#4	#4					#4
Th	#6, #7			#9 Field Trip			
F	#13 Recitation	#10				#12 Field Day *Plants*	

❧ Study Guide

Read Chapter XXXVI
Reading Comprehension:

1. What caused Anne to feel a sickening pang of defeat?

2. What was Jane to do? Who won the Avery?

3. How did the boys congratulate Gilbert? How was Anne congratulated?

4. When Anne came home, what did she notice about Matthew and Marilla?

5. What were her plans?

6. How did Matthew want to die?

Vocabulary:

☞ Look up the vocabulary words in a dictionary or encyclopedia. Write a sentence using each word.

Vocabulary Words:

infatuated

sanctifying

oculist

nominal

❧ Activities:

1. ✎ Write the following passage from dictation:

   For we pay a price for everything we get or take in this world; and although ambitions are well worth having, they are not to be cheaply won, but exact their dues of work and self-denial, anxiety and discouragement. —*Anne of Green Gables,* page 288

   Dictation

2. ✎ Compare your copy with the original. Correct any mistakes.

   Follow-up

   ✎ In the Literature section of your notebook:
   Write examples of the "dues" Anne pays for her ambitions.

3. What does Josie tell Diana? The following quotes are from the author, Mark Twain:

   Bible

   "It is by the goodness of God that in our country we have those three unspeakably precious things: freedom of speech, freedom of conscience, and the prudence never to practice either of them."

   "It takes your enemy and your friend, working together, to hurt you to the heart; the one to slander you and the other to get the news to you." —*Following the Equator*

   "He gossips habitually; he lacks the common wisdom to keep still that deadly enemy of man, his own tongue."

   —*Letters from the Sandwich Islands*

☞ Look up "discretion" in the 1828 *Dictionary.*

✎ In the Bible section of your notebook:
Write an essay of definition on discretion.

Literature

4. The chapter title, "The Glory and the Dream," is taken from William Wordsworth's poem, "Ode: Intimations of Immortality from Recollections of Early Childhood."

📖 Read this poem in *Anne's Anthology*.

🗝 Do research to learn about William Wordsworth's life and poetry.

✎ In the Literature section of your notebook:
a. Explain what the theme of this poem has to do with this chapter and the rest of the book.
b. Tell what the poem says about vision. How is vision discussed in this chapter of *Anne of Green Gables?*

✎ In the History section of your notebook:
Write half a page about William Wordsworth and his poetry.

Occupational Education

5. What is Mrs. Lynde's attitude about higher education for girls? What is Marilla's?

With your instructor:
Discuss the advantages and disadvantages of higher education for women.

Literature

6. ✎ In the literature section of your notebook:
a. Look up the literary term **foreshadowing** in *Writers INC*. Write the definition.
b. Note what is foreshadowed in this chapter.
c. Of what are the faded June lilies symbolic?

Literature

7. In reply to her concern about him working too hard, Matthew tells Anne ". . . I'd rather drop in the harness." This statement is similar to one in *Secondhand Lions* where the uncles say they want to die with their boots on.

👓 If you have time, watch this movie.

History

8. Matthew does not mention retiring.

🗝 Do research to learn about the history of retirement. It is a twentieth century phenomena.

Health

9. ✋ Visit an optometrist. How do optometrists check vision? How do they check the vision of those who cannot verbally communicate with them? What eye conditions can eyeglasses help?

History

10. 👓 *It's a Wonderful Life* has a subplot which portrays the struggles a bank went through to stay in business. Watch this classic movie, paying attention to the bank's struggles. What are the causes of the bank's struggles?

11. We see Anne looking at the needs and condition of both Matthew and   Bible
    Marilla. This shows Anne using her power of observation for a practi-
    cal purpose. She is empathizing. Also notice that Marilla knows Anne
    likes flowers and leaves a "flowering house-rose" on the window sill of
    her room for her homecoming.

    ✋ You may want to take "The Empathy Quotient Quiz" online at <http://
    www.guardian.co.uk/life/flash/page/0,13249,937836,00.html>.

    Empathy is, at heart, following the commandment to love your neigh-
    bor as yourself.

    ♡ Memorize Matthew 19:19.

    Anne not only notices a problem, she plans to help with the problem.
    She takes one day for herself and then plans to help Marilla.

12. ✋ Continue to use each Friday for a field day. Study the plants, flow-   Science
    ers, and birds native to your area. Begin by identifying all the plants
    on your property. As time allows, increase your observation area. Take
    a camera or a sketch pad as well as plant and bird identification books.
    After a plant is identified, take a picture of it and place it in your Fine
    Arts notebook or draw it in your sketchbook and label it.

13. ✖✖ With your instructor: Literature

    Continue with recitation each Friday during this Unit. Recite your
    favorite lines from the poem, "Ode: Intimations of Immortality from
    Recollections of Early Childhood," as well as from other literary works
    you have read in this study.

    Quote memorized scriptures to your teacher: I Corinthians 10:13; The
    Lord's Prayer; Psalm 30; Romans 5:19; Proverbs 25:27; I Corinthians
    13:13; Romans 8:5–8; Psalm 15; I Peter 3:17; Proverbs 4:23; James
    1:2–4; Colossians 1:10; Galatians 6:9; Jeremiah 9:23–24; Ephesians
    1:17–18; II Timothy 1:7; Matthew 5:44–45; II Peter 1:2–8; Matthew
    19:19; and your choice of Ephesians 3:20; Proverbs 17:27–28; or
    James 3:13, 17.

 # Planning Guide

Gather These Items:

1. For an "A" grade in Contract Reading Choice — Bible at the high school level, students should choose either:
   —*Mere Christianity* by C. S. Lewis. Harper San Francisco, 2001. ISBN 0060652926.
   —*Essential Truths of the Christian Faith* by R. C. Sproul. Tyndale House Publishers, 1998. ISBN 0842320016.
   —*That's Why They Call It Grace! 20 Centuries of Church History* by Diana Waring. Audiobook on Cassette. History Alive!, 2003. ISBN 1930514247.

2. Roses for transplanting.

3. Obituaries from the newspaper

4. "Pending Notification of the Next of Kin" by Jim and Bonnie Ferguson. *Home School Digest: Higher, Higher* Volume 11, Number 3.

Research Topics:

1. Banking

   . . . .

2. History of bank failures

   . . . .

3. Transplanting roses

   . . . .

4. Gambia

   . . . .

5. English Imperialism
   —*The Norton Anthology of English Literature: The Victorian Age,* Vol. 2B, edited by M. H. Abrams. W. W. Norton & Company, 2003. ISBN 0-393-15108-5. (This may be available in the reference section of your public library.)
   —"The Victorian Age in Britain (1837–1914)." *ukstudentlife.com.* UK Student Life © 2002–2004 <http://www.ukstudentlife.com/Britain/History/Victorian.htm>.

   . . . .

6. Grief and the grieving process

. . . .

7. Joe-Pye Weed

. . . .

8. James Whitcomb Riley, his life and works

. . . .

Suggested Videos:

Suggested Field Trips:
1. Visit a bank. (See Activity 5)

2. Visit a funeral home or cemetery.

Group Activities:

Memory Work:
Psalm 116:15

Notes:

Assignments — Chapter XXXVII

Contract Reading

	A Grade	B Grade	C Grade
Bible	❏ Choice: *Mere Christianity* or *Essential Truths of the Christian Faith* or *That's Why They Call It Grace!*		
History			
Literature			

Weekly

Quiet Time Reading Books: *Mere Christianity, Essential Truths of the Christian Faith,* or *That's Why They Call It Grace!*

Independent Project:

Memory Work: Psalm 116:15

Science: If you have chosen to track changes in some of the plants on your property and/or do some experiments as suggested in Chapter XXVIII, Activity 19, continue following your schedule for these activities.

	Literature	History	Bible	Health	Occu. Education	Science & Fine Arts	Grammar & Writing
M	Read Chap. XXXVII AGG, Reading Comp., #2		#3, #4				#1, #2, #3
T	Vocab., #12	#5	#13				#14
W	#8		#8, #15	#7 Field Trip	#6		#8, #9
Th	#8, #10	#9, #10	#17	#11	#16		#4, #10, #17
F	#19 Recitation	#5 Field Trip				#18 Field Day	#5

❧ Study Guide

Read Chapter XXXVII

Reading Comprehension:

1. What sudden shock contributed to Matthew's death?

2. What did Anne drop when she grabbed for Matthew? Do you think this was symbolic? If so, of what?

3. What kind of flowers surrounded Matthew? How was this fitting?

4. How did Anne and Marilla respond "out of character" to Matthew's death?

5. What did Anne find out about Marilla? With Matthew's death, what happened to Marilla and Anne's relationship?

6. What did Anne find sad and almost shameful after Matthew's death?

7. What reminded Marilla of her previous beau?

Vocabulary Words:

thronged

vigil

convolutions

Vocabulary:

⚷ Look up the vocabulary words in a dictionary or encyclopedia. Write a sentence using each word.

❧ Activities:

1. ✎ Write the following passage from dictation:	Dictation

For the first time shy quiet Matthew Cuthbert was a person of central importance; the white majesty of death had fallen on him and set him apart as one crowned. —*Anne of Green Gables*, page 295

2. ✎ Compare your copy with the original. Correct any mistakes.	Follow-up

✎ In the Literature section of your notebook:
Write several descriptive phrases from this chapter which you especially like. Example: "white majesty of death."

3. ✎ In the Bible section of your notebook, write: a. What is the seal of the Great Presence? b. According to the Bible, what is death? What does God think about the death of his saints?	Bible

4. 📖 For an "A" grade in Contract Reading Choice — Bible, high school students should choose either *Mere Christianity* by C. S. Lewis, *Essential Truths of the Christian Faith* by R. C. Sproul, or *That's Why They Call It Grace!* by Diana Waring.	Bible

✎ In the Bible section of your notebook:
Write a book report on the book of your choice. Include a summary of
Christian beliefs about death.

History   5. ☞ Research the banking industry, past and present, in your country.

What causes banks to fail? What are the ramifications (or effects) of
bank failures? What protection is there now to prevent what happened
to Matthew?

✋ After your research, visit a local bank and tour the facility. If you are
interested in banking as a profession, you may want to ask questions
from the Apprentice Worksheet in the *Activity Appendix*. As an extended field trip, which may be more difficult to arrange, ask if you
may "shadow" a bank employee for an hour or two.

Fri: Field Trip?

✎ After the field trip, write a follow-up paper on what you have learned
as well as a thank you note. Be sure to include specifics from your
conversations so the person will know you were listening and that his
or her time was appreciated.

Occupational Education   6. 📖 Read about how to care for roses and how to transplant them.

✋ Grow or transplant roses.

Health   7. In *Letters from the Earth,* Mark Twain, a contemporary of
Montgomery's, said this of funerals: "When a blood relative sobs, an
intimate friend should choke up, a distant acquaintance should sigh, a
stranger should merely fumble sympathetically with his handkerchief."

👥 With your instructor:
Discuss how the community gathers around Anne and Marilla. What
do they do for them? Has someone in your family died? What was done
for your family? What things helped? What comments did not help? In
what did you find comfort? If no one in your family has died, have you
ever had a chance to be of comfort to someone whose loved one has
died? What did you do? If not, discuss what you could do that would be
helpful. Also note how family-oriented the funeral was: Matthew's body
is kept at the house instead of at a mortuary.

📖 Read the article, "Pending Notification of the Next of Kin," by Jim and
Bonnie Ferguson. It is about a modern family who chooses to have the
funeral service and burial at home.

✋ You may want to ask your local funeral parlor for a tour of their facility. Specifically, ask how they assist grieving families and find out what
they do that cannot be done at home.

Literature   8. "Loss in all familiar things" is a quote from John Greenleaf Whittier's
poem, *Snow-bound: A Winter Idyll* (1866). The following is an excerpt
from Whittier's introduction to *Snow-bound:*

"The inmates of the family at the Whittier homestead who are referred to in the poem were my father, mother, my brother and two sisters, and my uncle and aunt, both unmarried. In addition, there was the district school master who boarded with us. The 'not unfeared, half-welcome guest' was Harriet Livermore, daughter of Judge Livermore, of New Hampshire, a young woman of fine natural ability, enthusiastic, eccentric, with slight control over her violent temper, which sometimes made her religious profession doubtful. . . .

"In my boyhood, in our lonely farm-house, we had scanty sources of information; few books and only a small weekly newspaper. Our only annual was the almanac. Under such circumstances story-telling was a necessary resource in long winter evenings. My father when a young man had traversed the wilderness to Canada, and could tell of his adventures with Indians and wild beasts, and of his sojourn in the French villages. My uncle was ready with his record of hunting and fishing, and, it must be confessed, with stories which he at least half believed, of witchcraft and apparitions. My mother, who was born in Indian-haunted region of Somersworth, New Hampshire, between Dover and Portsmouth, told us of the inroads of the savages, and the narrow escape of her ancestors. She described strange people who lived on the Piscataqua and Cocheco among whom was Bantam the sorcerer."

When Whittier wrote *Snow-bound,* only one was left of all that circle that used to gather round the homestead hearth; and to this one, his brother, he dedicated the poem. He outlived his brother, too, by many years; outlived Longfellow and Hawthorne and Bayard Taylor and Garrison and Lowell, and almost all the other poets and story-tellers and public men who had been the fellow-workers and the friends of his life.

—"An Introduction to John Greenleaf Whittier"

📖 Read *Snow-bound: A Winter Idyll* in *Anne's Anthology.*

🔑 Look at the footnotes in *Anne's Anthology.* These footnotes will help you understand the poem.

✎ In the Literature section of your notebook:
   a. Read a stanza of *Snow-bound* and give it a title.
   b. Cite three examples of the narrative portions of the poem.
   c. Cite three examples of purely descriptive portions.
   d. Cite three examples of lyrical portions which voice personal opinion and feeling.
   e. If you have enjoyed reading this poem, tell what part appealed to you the most.
   f. Where is Dartmouth College? How near is it to Whittier's home?
   g. What is meant by the phrase, "low green tent," found in the description of his elder sister?

h. What view of death does the poet give? Give quotes to support your remarks.

i. Where does Whittier think he will get his satisfaction for writing this poem?

✎ In the Bible section of your notebook:

a. Gather together the passages containing references to religion or religious feeling and from them construct a statement about Whittier's religious beliefs.

b. Who was Calvin? What religious denomination did he found? For what does the acronym T.U.L.I.P. stand?

With your instructor:

a. Name the meter of *Snow-bound. See answer in Answer Appendix.*

b. Discuss the tie between this poem and *Anne of Green Gables.*

History   9. ↝ *Snow-bound* mentions the West African colony of Gambia. Briefly learn more about Gambia. Then learn more about English Imperialism in Africa, India, Hong Kong, and Ireland.

✎ In the History section of your notebook, in the appropriate time period: Write briefly about English Imperialism in the Victorian Era.

Literature   10. The poem which Montgomery alludes to through Mrs. Allan portrays death both optimistically and vividly.

📖 From *Anne's Anthology,* read James Whitcomb Riley's poem, "Away" (1884).

📖 Read about James Whitcomb Riley and his poetry.

✎ In the History section of your notebook: Write half a page about James Whitcomb Riley and his poetry.

Health   11. Montgomery writes to Weber regarding one of her first experiences with death and grief. Read about this account in *The Green Gables Letters from L.M. Montgomery to Ephraim Weber 1905–1909,* page 24. Grief is handled differently in different cultures, but it is still grief.

📖 Read about grief and the grieving process. The loss process can last anywhere from three months to three years. The five stages of grief— denial, bargaining, anger, despair, and acceptance—can occur in either the sequence as listed or in any variety of sequences. One stage can last a long time. Grief is very individual.

Literature   12. Marilla brought to light the connection between Josie Pye's name and herbs. In eastern North America, "Joe-Pye Weed" has tiny, purple, and fuzzy flowers growing in flattish clusters.

↝ Look up information about "Joe-Pye Weed."

With your instructor: Compare the character of a wild plant with Josie Pye and her family.

13. Throughout *Anne of Green Gables,* Anne increases in brotherly kind-ness.

✎ In the Bible section of your notebook:
Give examples of Anne's increasing kindness.

Bible

---

14. 📖 Examine some obituaries in the newspaper.

✎ Write an obituary article for Matthew Cuthbert.

Literature

---

15. ♡ Memorize Psalm 116:15.

Bible

---

16. ⚇ Discuss with your instructor:
   a. What the needs of the Cuthbert family might be after Matthew's death.
   b. How people meet those needs.
   c. What is frequently done in today's society for the families of those who have died?

Occupational Education

---

17. 🔑 Using your Bible concordance, look up the word "mourned."

✎ Write what the scriptures you found teach about grief and mourning.

Bible

---

18. ✋ Continue to use each Friday for a field day. Study the plants, flow-ers, and birds native to your area. Begin by identifying all the plants on your property. As time allows, increase your observation area. Take a camera or a sketch pad as well as plant and bird identification books. After a plant is identified, take a picture of it and place it in your Fine Arts notebook or draw it in your sketchbook and label it.

Science

---

19. ⚇ With your instructor:
Continue with recitation each Friday during this Unit. Recite your favorite lines from the poems, *Snow-bound* and "Away," as well as lines from other literary works you have read in this study.

Quote memorized scriptures to your teacher: I Corinthians 10:13; The Lord's Prayer; Psalm 30; Romans 5:19; Proverbs 25:27; I Corinthians 13:13; Romans 8:5–8; Psalm 15; I Peter 3:17; Proverbs 4:23; James 1:2–4; Colossians 1:10; Galatians 6:9; Jeremiah 9:23–24; Ephesians 1:17–18; II Timothy 1:7; Matthew 5:44-45; II Peter 1:2–8; Matthew 19:19; Psalm 116:15; and your choice of Ephesians 3:20; Proverbs 17:27–28; or James 3:13, 17.

Literature

 # Planning Guide

Gather These Items:

1. "Part Four: Back to Homeworking," *The Way Home: Beyond Feminism, Back to Reality* by Mary Pride. Good News Publishers, 1985. ISBN 0-89107-345-0. (If you do not have a copy of this book, try to obtain one from the public or home school support library.)

2. Items to make a pop-up book or card.

3. *How to Make Pop-Ups* by Joan Irvine, illustrated by Barbara Reid. Toronto: Kids Can Press, 1987. ISBN 0921103360. This edition is out of print in Canada. It is available in a U.S. edition, published by William Morrow, 1988, ISBN 0688079024.

Research Topics:

1. The eye and disorders of the eye
   —*The American Medical Association Family Medical Guide,* Third Edition, by American Medical Association. Random House, 1994. ISBN 0-679-41290-5.

. . . .

2. How to make pop-ups
   —*How to Make Pop-Ups* by Joan Irvine, illustrated by Barbara Reid. Toronto: Kids Can Press, 1987. ISBN 0921103360. This edition is out of print in Canada. It is available in a U.S. edition, published by William Morrow, 1988, ISBN 0688079024.
   —*How to Make Super Pop-Ups* by Joan Irvine, illustrated by Linda Hendry. Toronto: Kids Can Press, 1992. ISBN 1550740695. This edition is out of print in Canada. It is still available in a U.S. edition, published by Beech Tree Books, William Morrow, 1992, ISBN 0688115217.
   —Irvine, Joan. "How to Make a Pop-Up." February 2002 <http://www.makersgallery.com/joanirvine/howto.html>.

. . . .

3. Marietta Holley, her life and works

. . . .

Suggested Videos:
1. *Anne of Green Gables.* There are three versions available on videocassette: 1934, 1985, and 1986.

Suggested Field Trips:
1. Visit an ophthalmologist. (See Activity 10)

Group Activities:

Memory Work:
Philippians 1:6 and Romans 8:28

Notes:

Assignments — Chapter XXXVIII

Contract Reading: No new contract reading

Weekly
Quiet Time Reading Books:
Independent Project:
Memory Work: Philippians 1:6 and Romans 8:28
Science: If you have chosen to track changes in some of the plants on your property and/or do
some experiments as suggested in Chapter XXVIII, Activity 19, continue following your
schedule for these activities.

	Literature	History	Bible	Health	Occu. Education	Science & Fine Arts	Grammar & Writing
M	Read Chap. XXXVIII AGG, Reading Comp., #2			#9			#1, #2
T	Vocab., #3, #4, #7		#11				#3, #4, #7, #11
W	#5	#5			#6		#6
Th	#8, #14		#15			#13	#8, #12
*F	#17 Recitation			#10 Field Trip		#16 Field Day	#10

*On Friday, at the end of each Unit, review and take the Unit Quiz in the *Test Appendix*. On quiz days parents
and students may want to opt to reduce or eliminate Field Day and Recitation. Following the Unit Quiz, after
review, take the Final Exam in the *Test Appendix*.

 Study Guide

Read Chapter XXXVIII

Reading Comprehension:

1. Why was Marilla distraught?

2. What advice and hope did the eye doctor give Marilla?

3. What did Mr. Sadler want?

4. What did Anne decide she would do to help Marilla?

5. What did the people in Avonlea think of Anne's decision? Anne cared about Mrs. Allan's opinion. What did Mrs. Allan think about Anne's decision? What was Mrs. Lynde's reason for agreeing with it? Do you think Gilbert agreed?

6. How did Anne find out she had the job at Avonlea?

7. What was her response toward Gilbert?

8. What did Anne think about her future?

9. Montgomery's writing appeals to the senses. What can be smelled in this chapter?

Vocabulary Words:

thwarted

destiny

hues

congenial

hollyhock

mule

Vocabulary:

⚷ Look up the vocabulary words in a dictionary or encyclopedia. Write a sentence using each word.

Extra credit:

1. 🖐 Draw a picture of a hollyhock.

2. 🖐 Draw a picture of a mule. In a caption, describe the difference between a mule, a horse, and a donkey.

🌿 Activities:

1. ✎ Today's dictation is full of **local color**. The spelling is purposely improper, demonstrating the speaker's lack of formal education. Copy the following:

💡 Dictation

> Says I, "We won't argue long on that point, for I would overwhelm you if I approved of overwhelmin'. But I merely ask you to cast your right eye over into England, and then beyond into France. Men have ruled exclusively in France for the last 40 to 50 years, and a woman in England: which realm has been the most peaceful and prosperous?"
>
> He sighed twice. And he bowed his head upon his breast, in a sad, almost meachin' way. I nearly pitied him, disagreeable as he wuz. When all of a sudden he brightened up; and says he,—

"You seem to place a great deal of dependence on the Bible. The Bible is against the idee. The Bible teaches man's supremacy, man's absolute power and might and authority."

"Why," says I, "the one great theme of the New Testament,—the redemption of the world through the birth of the Christ,—no man had anything to with that whatever. Our divine Lord was born of God and woman."

—Josiah Allen's Wife, *Sweet Cicely*

Follow-up   2. ✎ Compare your copy with the original. Notice that each speaker's words form a new paragraph.

🔑 Look up the definition of "local color" in *Writers INC*.

❈ With your instructor:
Find another piece of literature in which the author utilizes local color.

Literature   3. "A haunt of ancient peace" is a line taken from one of Montgomery's favorite poets, Alfred, Lord Tennyson.

📖 Read Tennyson's "The Palace of Art" (1832), from *Anne's Anthology*. Locate the line, "a haunt of ancient peace," in the poem.

This poem is about finding "redemption in one's own intellectual constructs." Tennyson describes the palace rooms filled with love of beauty, nature, philosophy, religions, and literary figures. But all these provide vain comfort—the soul is perpetually struggling against loneliness and isolation. His soul has constructed a "place" wherein he rules as god—and "like God" he is alone. The soul, "she," realizes that this is "part of the package" of being one's own lord. The soul knows this state is imperfect, but she, the soul, cannot reconcile why and does not relinquish her rule. The soul's pride brings forth the soul's confusion, followed by the soul's self-hatred and doubts; the soul is lifeless. In isolation the soul even denies the existence of God, which leads to total despair. Finally the soul sees some hope and cries, "What is it that will take away my sin, / And save me lest I die?" Yet in the end, although she leaves her palace, she retains it: "Perchance I may return with others there / When I have purged my guilt."

📖 From *The Annotated Anne of Green Gables,* page 461, read about the use of this poem in the text.

Tennyson's plan was to introduce both painting and sculpture into "The Palace of Art," (*Memoir,* I, *119*). He was often successful at painting pictures in verse. The lesson is valuable, depicting the soul's pride and blindness, which we can learn from even though the soul, in its isolation, does not. But the imagery, more than the moral, is the poem's primary achievement.

✎ In the Literature section of your notebook:
a. Choose and copy a couple of the stanzas which present a vivid picture to your mind.

b. Refer to David and Shirley Quine's explanation of literature periods in Unit 3, Chapter X & XI, Activity 8. How does the moral of "The Palace of Art" fit their explanation of literature?

✎ In the Bible section of your notebook:
Describe the effect the knowledge of the soul's plight has upon you.

---

4. "God's in his heaven, all's right with the world" is a quote from Robert Browning's *Pippa Passes* (1841), Part 1, "Morning," lines 227–228.   Literature

📖 Read the portion of *Pippa Passes* in *Anne's Anthology*. (Due to the inappropriateness of this poem, only a part of the poem is included in the *Anthology*.)

📖 From *The Annotated Anne of Green Gables,* pages 461–462, read about the use of this poem.

✎ In the Literature section of your notebook:
Note parallels between the characters, Pippa and Anne.

---

5. Anne mentions not overdoing women's rights as "Josiah Allen's wife."   ☼ Literature

📖 For more information about the character from the book by this name and about its author, read the article, "Marietta Holley: Best Selling Writer," in the *Background Information Appendix* and the dictation for this Chapter.

In the section used for dictation, Josiah Allen's wife is debating a congressman about the right of women to vote. As a side-note, to which English monarch is she referring? *See answer in the Answer Appendix.*

📖 You may want to look for one of Josiah Allen's wife's* books in old libraries or in a bookstore which sells old books. I located a copy for $10.

*Note: "Josiah Allen's Wife" is the pseudonym for the author, Marietta Holley. "Josiah Allen's wife" or Samantha is the main character in Holley's books.

---

6. A common theme in *Anne of Green Gables* is woman's role in society.   Occupational Education

📖 Read "Part Four: Back to Homeworking" from Mary Pride's *The Way Home.*

✎ In the Occupational Education section of your notebook:
a. Tell what each of the characters in *Anne of Green Gables* thinks about a woman's role in society.
b. Summarize what Mary Pride thinks about a woman's role in society.

---

7. Lucy Montgomery wants her readers to enjoy *Anne of Green Gables*. In addition to the enjoyment of reading this book, what message(s) do you think Montgomery communicates with her writing?   Literature

✎ In the Literature section of your notebook:
Write the message(s) Lucy Montgomery tries to impart to her readers.

Literature 8. ✎ Lucy Montgomery has been termed a "feminist." Define "feminist" and then write a persuasive paper stating whether Montgomery was or was not a "feminist." Give specific examples.

Health 9. Marilla is having difficulty with her eyes.

📖 Read about the eye and conditions of the eye.

✎ In the Health section of your notebook:
a. Draw and label the parts of a healthy eye. At the bottom of the page, explain briefly the process of seeing an object.
b. Describe the condition and treatment of: scleritis, trachoma, cataracts, glaucoma, macular degeneration, diabetic retinopathy, and retinal detachment.
c. Which of these conditions has symptoms most closely resembling Marilla's symptoms? What is the recommended treatment today?

Health 10. ✋ After your research, you may want to visit with an ophthalmologist. If you are interested in health care as a profession, you may want to ask questions on the Apprentice Worksheet in the *Activity Appendix*. As an extended field trip, ask to shadow an ophthalmologist for an hour or two. After the field trip, write a follow-up paper as well as a thank you note. Be sure to include specifics from your conversations so the ophthalmologist will know you were listening and that his or her time was appreciated.

Bible 11. Anne continues to grow spiritually. Increased diligence and attentiveness is evident in the improvements in her homemaking skills. Her thoughts of giving up on being nice to Josie Pye can be seen not only as resignation, but also as a willingness to accept the things she cannot change. She finally responds to Gilbert's example of perseverance and self-sacrifice by expressing her forgiveness and seeking reconciliation.

Lastly, we see Anne herself able to be self-sacrificing. Throughout the earlier part of *Anne of Green Gables,* Anne is attracted to the romantic idea of sacrifice, but does not have the spiritual maturity to see the sacrifices she might realistically make. As she has grown in stature, she has also grown in spiritual maturity. From spiritual maturity, she is able to love. She makes the decision to not continue her formal education so she can assist Marilla. While she receives the approval of her heroine, Mrs. Allan, she makes this selfless decision entirely on her own.

📖 Read chapter 16 of *The Way Home* by Mary Pride.

✎ In the Bible section of your notebook:
a. Write about Mary Pride's vision of "charity beginning at home." Then, from *Anne of Green Gables,* give examples of each point of charity Mary Pride describes.
b. Write a definition of the word "love" that utilizes both references from Scripture and a dictionary definition. Also include the effect Christ's love has on us.

📖 Read Philippians 1:3–11, especially Philippians 1:6. Imagine Marilla extracting these words and writing them to Anne. In the beginning of the story, Anne feels desperately wicked and thinks she never can be as good as Mrs. Allan, yet she is in the Father's hand as He carries His work on to completion. Just as we see goodness in Anne all along, so our Heavenly Father sees us clothed in His righteousness.

♡ Memorize Philippians 1:6.

---

12. "She had looked her duty courageously in the face and found it a friend—as duty ever is when we meet it frankly."	Writing ✓
✎ Write a poem or essay on the subject of "duty."	

---

13. ✋ Make a pop-up book or card, using something from *Anne of Green Gables* as the "pop-up." For example, you could make Anne's Sunday hat, a flower, or even the words of a favorite line from a poem.	Fine Arts *- Model House ?*

---

14. 👓 Watch the movie *Anne of Green Gables*. There are several versions available.	Literature *'Anne of Green Gables' Party w/ Raspberry Cordial*
⚎ With your instructor: Compare the movie with the book. How are they similar? Different? What things were lost by utilizing the media of film instead of the written word?	

---

15. Trials may make you better or bitter. Anne chooses better. Read Lamentations 3:25; Nahum 1:7; and Proverbs 14:22.	Bible ✓
♡ Memorize Romans 8:28.	

---

16. ✋ Review the observation notes, pictures, and sketches from your native plant and bird studies.	Science
⚎ With your instructor: Discuss what you have learned about the plants, flowers, and birds of your area.	

---

17. ✋ Select some of your favorite poems or portions of poems from this study and prepare a special presentation of them along with a selection of your favorite scriptures. Tell why you selected each of them, what they mean to you, and something about how they relate to *Anne of Green Gables*.	Literature

---

18. Review and take Unit 9 Quiz in the *Test Appendix*. Study "☀" marked activities to prepare for the Final Exam. The Exam is at the end of the *Test Appendix*. Ask your instructor to give you the Exam when you think you are prepared.	☀ Test

Background Information Appendix

Table of Contents

The articles in the *Background Information Appendix* give more in-depth information about the time periods, the authors, and the topics studied in *Where the Brook and the River Meet*. A number of these articles are primary documents and are invaluable for the presentation of some of the views and thoughts on the issues and events of the times. Students are encouraged to read the articles reflectively, giving attention to the views expressed, weighing and evaluating them, and discussing them with their instructor. Since the information in this *Appendix* is important for under-standing, students will be tested on many of the facts presented.

While the purpose of these articles is to give insight into the thinking as well as the events of the times, it is not to advocate any particular viewpoint or belief and the views expressed in the articles are not neces-sarily the views of the author of this study.

------◆------

Knights, Chivalry, and Feudal Society

Before the Middle Ages, soldiers on horseback were not effective fighters. It was not until invaders from central Asia introduced Europeans to the stirrup that the horse soldier's ability in combat was improved to the point where he was effective in battle. Attached to a horse's saddle, the stirrup would hold the rider's feet and enable him to sit firmly. Now he could charge against a line of foot soldiers and be less likely to be unhorsed by long spears.

Another innovation that made battle using horses as mounts possible was the horseshoe. Made of iron and nailed into the horse's hooves, horseshoes helped the horse maintain his footing in soft ground and to gallop longer over hard ground. Now the horse could carry a heavy load such as an armored horse warrior and not damage its hooves. As the horse warriors gained importance in the fighting of battles, they also began to be called "knights." These two terms became synonymous after the Norman Conquest.

The warhorse was almost as important as the knight during battle and was the result of improved breeding. These animals were costly and only wealthy nobles could provide riding equipment, training for battle, and expensive armor—all of which were required by knights.

With the medieval knight's evolution as an honored and feared warrior, a code of conduct developed known as chivalry. "Chivalry" is derived from the French words "cheval" (horse) and "chevalier" (mounted warrior). At first, chivalry was military and secular; it referred to a loose fellowship among the warrior class, where king and knight were equal. It emphasized courage, loyalty to one's superior, and devotion to military duty.

Today we may think of chivalry as referring to a moral quality rather than to its origin with mounted horse warriors. However, the qualities of early chivalry were originally connected to fighting. Bravery, even to the point of absolute recklessness, was expected of the true knight. The slightest insult was to be avenged and no knight could afford any suspicion of cowardice or treachery. Honor required that he never fail his lord or avoid a challenge.

In battle, the true knight disdained all tricks and engaged the enemy as an equal. He would not strike an unarmed or unprepared foe. If defeated or captured, he expected honorable treatment until he was ransomed. A knight was rarely killed in battle due to his protective armor and to the fact that a live knight was more valuable for ransom than a dead one. While chivalry emphasized loyalty and truthfulness, it accepted war as a fact of life.

By the twelfth century, when society was more sophisticated, the Christian church encouraged that the rules of chivalry include such ideas as courtesy towards women and protection of the defenseless. Although many knights did not live up to all of the rules, in time it would become a guide to behavior.

Over time, the Church also used its influence to add to the definition of chivalry the idea that Christian knights swear to defend the faith against enemies, especially the Moslems.

Despite additions to the code of new social mores, chivalry remained a way of living in which physical prowess was of utmost importance and was frequently demonstrated. The battle trumpet sounded the theme of the secular Middle Ages. War was a normal condition. Knights made private war against knights, coalitions of lords fought other lords, lords against kings, and often churchmen fought on both sides.

Knights kept themselves in training for war with mock combats which were often violent and fatal. They practiced their skills in tournaments which were imitation battles. Sometimes they fought in enclosures before an audience. Other times teams of knights would participate in battles covering the countryside. The object was not to kill one another but to capture the opponent. Jousts and tournaments were held to celebrate holidays and important events in the life of a noble family. Jousts were tests of a knight's strength and endurance.

During jousts, mounted knights rode full speed at each other holding lances; the object was for a knight to unseat the other by striking his opponents' shield with the force of the lance. Sometimes legal disputes would be settled after the contestants had asked God to grant victory to the righteous. If fighting was a knight's main occupation, the tournament was one of his favorite amusements along with hunting wild game and falconry.

By the fourteenth century, knights in armor no longer provided the most efficient fighting force. Armor was made obsolete by the development of firearms. The new age of warfare allowed the striking down of the bravest knight from a distance. The knights' military importance declined as a result. Eugene F. Rice, Jr. in *The Foundation of Early Modern Europe* states that "gun power hastened the decay of chivalry" (16).

Knights were no longer able to fight according to a personal code of honor. The feudal nobles could only continue to maintain their chivalrous traditions through tournaments and ceremonies. The glamour of knighthood was translated into the song and story of heroic and virtuous men. The legacy of chivalry as a code of behavior would become the ideal for good manners in polite society and translate into the concept of the gentleman.

Women and Childhood

The feudal system structured early medieval society in an orderly fashion with its main activities of fighting, farming, and praying delegated to people in specific social groups with specific hierarchies. In the feudal world, loyalty and service were used to connect people from the king, to the Church lords, to the lowest serf.

The Feudal Age was a male dominated society. It was a commonly held belief at the time that due to women's physical inferiority their place was in the home and that they owed strict obedience to the male. But in practice, even without a political voice, women played an important economic and social role in society.

Women were primarily regarded as necessary housekeepers and breeders of children. Marriages among the nobility were for the most part arranged for land and dowries and not as a result of love. Women were often married by age twelve, and since there was a high mortality rate among women, remarriage was common. If by age twenty-one a woman was not married, she could expect to stay single and sometimes, would retire to a cloister to become a nun.

The position of women improved during the Middle Ages due to the church's influence on chivalry. Medieval religious devotion to Mary, Mother of Christ, also helped to raise the status of women.

There is no doubt that noble women had influence in the family and the community. Because of their role as mistresses on larger estates, women exercised considerable influence depending upon their ability, personality, dowry, and family connections. While lords and knights were away on crusades or pilgrimages, it was the wives who ran the affairs of the castle or manorial estates, often for years at a time.

The lady of the manor ran the household, supervising the training of young girls living in the castle. She was also often the nurse that tended to the sick and ill of the household. Because of her many duties, a noble woman had to know about cooking, spinning, embroidering, and medicine. Upper class women also knew how to read and write and often were better educated than their noble husbands.

The development of towns also had an effect upon the status of women. Daughters often learned their fathers' craft along with their brothers. In the towns, many women received an education and some qualified for the skilled professions or creative arts. More and more, women came to be regarded as individuals.

There was no place for what we consider a "childhood" in the medieval world; children were considered small adults. There was no such thing as children's literature. For the most part, the literature of the day dealt with war and quests, male stories of knights and lords, and not with children or family. Children were a result of the duty of procreation and the necessity to breed laborers. Loyalty, for king, God, and religion, was the substitute for family attachments; even the guild system with its control over economic and political life caused the family to be second in importance.

Children were prepared at an early age to fulfill their adult role in society as noble, serf, wife, or craftsman. Medieval clothing did not even distinguish child from adult. The clothing differences that did exist were related to social standing. From birth, children were regarded as small adults in dress, in work and in play.

When the child was able to live without mother or nanny, he belonged to the adult world. At about the age of seven, male and female children were put out to service in the houses of people for seven or nine years. As servants, they performed menial tasks such as waiting tables, making beds and helping in the kitchen; at the same time, they learned manners and practical skills. The *Babees Book* of 1475, concerning medieval manners for the young, cites some rules for table manners:

Stand before the lord until he bids you sit, and be always ready to serve him with clean hands.

Do not hang your head over your dish, or in any way drink with full mouth.

If you eat with another, turn the nicest pieces to him and do not go picking out the finest and largest for yourself.

When you have done, look they that you rise up without laughter, or joking, or boisterous word and go to your lord's table, and there stand, and pass not from him until grace be said and brought to an end.

Then some of you should go for water, some hold the cloth, and some pour water upon his hands.

"All education was carried out by means of apprenticeship. . . . They were sent to another house, with or without a contract, to live and start their life there, or to learn the good manners of a knight, or a trade, or even to go to school and learn Latin." (Philippe Aries, *Centuries of Childhood,* 366.)

The separation from the family did not mean that the parents did not care for their children. In the medieval family the unit was a moral and social one rather than a sentimental unit. The family shared the common experiences of daily living, not just from close physical quarters, but from communal working, praying, and playing together. Family ties remained strong under the leadership of the male parent whose duty was to provide for the family. Parents were interested and attempted to insure a place for their children in society with the knowledge of a craft or in a marriage by arrangement for possible freedom from serfdom. Early separation cut across class lines; poor people's children spent time away from home just as a noble's child would serve as a page in another castle.

George III
60 years (1760–1820)

1. George III, grandson of the late king, came to the throne at the age of 22, and at a time when Britain had become the most powerful nation in the world. During the Seven Year's War with France and Spain, 12 great battles had been won, 25 islands (mostly in the West Indies), nine cities, 40 forts and castles, 100 ships of war, and twelve millions of treasure taken. France and Spain now sought for peace; and the Treaty of Paris was concluded in 1763.

2. In 1765 a dispute arose with the American colonies. The English Government claimed the right of taxing them, although they had no voice in Parliament; and accordingly passed the Stamp Act. This raised such storm of anger that it was repealed: but the right was still claimed; and in spite of the loud warnings of Pitt, Fox, and Burke, taxes were laid on tea and other articles imported to America.

The Americans, however, were in no humour to submit to pay them; and a cargo of tea, sent from England to Boston, was turned overboard in Boston harbor by the enraged inhabitants.

England resolved to enforce submission by the sword. Large bodies of troops were sent out. The Americans raised an army in their own defense, under the command of George Washington, threw off their allegiance to Britain, drew up a Declaration of Independence in 1776, and formed a union of 13 States, under the name of the United States of America.

A desperate struggle was carried on for seven years, during which many bloody battles were fought with various success; but at last Lord Cornwallis with 7000 British troops, being hemmed in at Yorktown by the skillful movements of Washington, was forced to surrender. Another English army, under General Burgoyne, had surrendered some time previously; and now England decided to give up the strife. A treaty was drawn up in 1783, by which the independence of the States was acknowledged; and a general peace with America, France, Spain, and Holland, which had all been united against England, soon followed.

3. England, once more at rest from the din of war, was now enjoying great prosperity at home, and cultivating the arts of peace; but a fresh source of trouble arose in 1789, when a terrible

Revolution broke out in France, which plunged the continent of Europe into the deepest gloom. In Paris a mob, excited by poverty and oppression, rose up against King Louis XVI, whom, with his Queen, they seized and beheaded (1793).

France was declared a Republic, the law was set as naught, and a number of fearful events followed during 22 years, by which nations were shaken to their foundations, thrones overturned, and fertile districts drenched in blood.

4. On the death of the King and Queen of France, war was declared against the new Republic, by Britain, Holland, Spain, Austria, and Prussia. The English took Toulon; but were driven back by the French under Napoleon Bonaparte, a Corsican officer, who soon attracted the attention of all Europe by his skill as a general.

He drove the Austrian forces almost out of Italy, and compelled the German states to sue for peace. After this he sailed across the Mediterranean with a great fleet and army to invade Egypt, intending, if possible, to reach and conquer our Indian empire. After taking possession of Malta on his way, he landed at Alexandria, marched to Cairo, and gained the Battle of the Pyramids.

But his fleet was pursued by Nelson, and utterly defeated in Aboukir Bay, at the famous Battle of the Nile (1798). In this battle, which was fought in the night, nine French admirals, with a crew of 1,000 men, perished. Napoleon then left Egypt and marched to Syria: but here he was defeated by Sir Sidney Smith; and leaving his army, he returned to France, where he was made first consul in 1799, and emperor in 1804.

5. Having now several great armies at his command, he resolved on the conquest of Europe. He at once made preparations for invading England, and collected a number of gunboats to convey his troops; but his plans were so closely watched by Nelson, that the project was given up.

Lord Nelson then attacked the combined fleets of France and Spain off Cape Trafalgar in 1805, and totally defeated them; but lost his life by a bullet fired from the enemy's rigging. His death caused the nation much grief; and to this sad loss was added that of two great statesmen, Pitt (the younger) and Fox, who died the next year.

Whilst the French were defeated by sea, they were victorious on land. In the great Battle of Austerlitz, Napoleon crushed the power of Austria (1805); and in that of Jena, in the next year, defeated the army of Prussia.

6. Napoleon, now Emperor of France and King of Italy, tried to extend his power still further filling the thrones of Europe with his relatives. Having craftily taken the King of Spain prisoner, he claimed the crown for his brother Joseph. At this the Spaniards were so enraged that they rose in arms throughout the country, and called upon England for help.

An army of 10,000 men was sent to Spain, under the command of Sir Arthur Wellesley (afterwards Duke of Wellington), who defeated the French at Vimiera; and thus began the Peninsular War (1808). A great number of battles were fought, in almost all of which the British troops were victorious.

Victory after victory added glory to the English arms. The French armies were step by step driven across the Pyrenees. The last important battle was fought at Vitoria, in Biscay; after which Wellington entered France, and scattered the remains of Soult's army at Toulouse (1814).

7. Meanwhile Napoleon had resolved on an invasion of Russia, and in 1812 marched into that vast country with an army of half a million men. He intended taking up his winter quarters in Moscow; but on arriving at the city his progress was checked by its flames. The inhabitants had set fire to their houses and fled.

He was therefore compelled to retreat. But his provisions were exhausted; the Russian winter had set in; the snow already lay deep upon the ground; and during that terrible march homewards almost the whole of his fine army perished from starvation and the attacks of the Russians.

8. The nations of Europe now united to crush the power of Napoleon; and an army of Russians, Swedes, Germans, Austrians, and Prussians met and defeated him at the Battle of Leipzig, entered Paris, and forced him to resign the throne. He retired to the island of Elba; and Louis XVIII was made King of France in 1814.

Early in the next year, however, he left Elba, landed in France, and marched to Paris, where he was soon surrounded by thousands of his old companions-in-arms, who were ready to lay down their lives in his service. Once more he mounted the throne; but his glory was soon to end. He was met on the plains of Waterloo, near Brussels, by the British and Prussian armies, under the Duke of Wellington and Marshal Blucher, and in a long bloody battle, fought on Sunday, June 18, 1815, was completely defeated.

Napoleon fled the field, but afterwards gave himself up to the English, and was sent a prisoner to the lonely island of St. Helena, where he lingered six years, and died in 1821.

Thus ended a long and terrible war, which in 22 years had cost hundreds of thousands of human lives, and raised the National Debt from 239,000,000 to the frightful sum of 860,000,000. It was happily followed by a peace which was almost unbroken for 40 years.

9. In 1820 died King George III, in the 82nd year of his age and the 60th of his reign—the longest and most remarkable in English history. During the last ten years he had been afflicted with a disordered mind, which had made him unable to fulfill the duties of king; and a Regency had been appointed under his eldest son, George, who now succeeded as George IV.

10. In this reign Captain Cook made three voyages round the world (1767–1779), and was killed at Owhyhee by a native.

In 1797 the seamen in the British navy mutinied, demanding more pay. At Spithead they were easily pacified; but at the Nore, they seized the ships, and did not return duty till the ringleaders were arrested and hanged. The French Revolution, following closely upon the emancipation of the American colonies, had an evil influence on Ireland. Both Protestants and Catholics were dissatisfied with the arbitrary and oppressive methods of government adopted by the English.

They attempted a Rebellion in 1798, but it was speedily put down. This suggested the necessity of binding Ireland more closely to the Empire. After much opposition in Ireland, the Union of the Parliaments was accomplished in 1801. Ireland was to send 32 lords and 100 commoners to the Imperial Parliament.

Sunday schools were founded by Robert Raikes of Gloucester, 1781. Gas was first used to light the streets of London in 1807. The first steam-vessel was launched on the Clyde in 1812. Several important inventions and improvements in machinery were made, amongst which may be named the steam-engine, by James Watt; the "spinning-jenny," by James Hargreaves; a machine called the "mule," by Samuel Crompton; and the power-loom, by Dr. Cartwright. The *Times* was the first newspaper printed by steam-power, 1814.

Royal Reader. No VI. London: Thomas Nelson and Sons, 1891. 354–357.

Attachment to the Queen
Some Explanation of the Colonies' Loyalty to England

Our attachment to the Queen, our own Victoria, is mingled with a tenderness not inconsistent with the sterner sentiment, which it softens and embellishes without enervating. Let her legitimate authority as a constitutional monarch, let her reputation as a woman, be assailed, and not withstanding the lamentation of Burke that the age of chivalry was past, thousands of swords would leap from their scabbards to avenge her. Ay, and they would be drawn as freely and wielded as vigorously and bravely in Canada or in Nova Scotia, as in England. Loyalty! love of British institutions!—they are engrafted on our very nature; they are part and parcel of ourselves; and I can no more tear them from my heart (even if I would, and lacerate all its fibres) than I could sever a limb from my body.

And what are those institutions? A distinguished American statesman recently answered this question. He said: "The proudest Government that exists upon the face of the earth is that of Great Britain. And the great Pitt, her proudest statesman, when he would tell of Britain's crowning glory, did not speak, as he might have done, of her wide-spread dominion upon which the sun never sets. He did not speak of martial achievements, of glorious battle-fields, and of splendid naval conflicts. But he said, with swelling breast and kindling eye, that the poorest man of Great Britain in his cottage might bid defiance to all the force of the Crown. It might be frail, its roof might shake, the wind might blow through it, the storm might enter, the rain might enter; but the King of England could not enter it. In all his forces he dared not cross the threshold of that ruined tenement." Hon. W. Young.

Royal Reader. No VI. London: Thomas Nelson and Sons, 1891. 173–174.

An Introduction to
John Greenleaf Whittier
Written in 1847 to introduce the first general collection of Whittier's *Poems*

It stands there still, the old homestead, just as it stood "that brief December day." There is the long, low house with slanting roof and huge stone chimney up the middle. There is the round well-curb beneath its looming sweep. The bridle-post, a big stone with projecting step, still keeps its seat at the garden gate. And over the way still stands the barn —the big new barn that held treasures of the Whittier farm. It is a lonely spot, as lonely still as can be found, perhaps, in any busy county of New England. It lies in what is called the East Parish of Haverhill, in the valley of Merrimac. Planted here, with not a neighbor roof in sight, where

> *no social smoke*
> *Curled over woods of snow-hung oak,*

five generations of Whittiers had taken up, each in its turn, the work of the farm; and each in its turn, on long winter evenings,
had sat around the homestead hearth. In John Greenleaf Whittier's boyhood, there were, besides his father and mother, his Aunt Mercy and Uncle Moses, and his own young brother, Matthew, and two sisters—Mary, older than himself, and Elizabeth, the youngest of them all.

The Whittiers were strict Quakers, as had been every Whittier beneath that roof. They used the gentle "thee" and "thy" of Quaker speech, eschewed all vanities, and dressed in homespun Quaker gray. Every "First day" they drove to the meeting of the Society of Friends at Amesbury, and that was about as much of the wide world as John Greenleaf knew up to his fifteenth year. Then something happened that ever after he looked back upon as one of the greatest events of his life.

That was the coming of a poet into the house— not a poet, flesh and blood, in coat and breeches, but the mind and the soul of
a poet alive forever in his book. And that poet was a Scotch farmer named Robert Burns. He was very properly introduced, too, being brought in by the schoolmaster himself. Joshua Coffin, teacher of the district school, fresh from Dartmouth College and full of life and fun, used often to come around of an evening, bringing a book to read aloud—a book of travel and adventure, usually; but this particular night, the poems. And he sat down and read page after page, explaining the Scottish dialect as he went. Greenleaf Whittier sat spell-bound listening. He was finding out, that night, another world, or another way of looking at this one, which is quite the same thing, after all. He was still rapt in his vision when the reading stopped and the master, rising, offered to leave the book, if he liked it. Did he like it? He took it out into the hayfield in the morning, he carried it with him all that day and the next, he read it to himself, he read it aloud, he read it to the dog and the brook and the birds; and if the cows in the new barn waited longer that summer for the yield of the early mowing, the fault must be laid to Robert Burns.

But the work of the farm had to go on, and his hand was needed with the rest; for only by "all hands to" could the stubborn soil be made to yield a livelihood. But he thought of Burns, the Scottish farmer, and the songs he made behind the plough.

> *And daily life and duty seemed*
> *No longer poor and common*
> *I saw through all familiar things*
> *The romance underlying*
> *The joys and griefs that plume the wings*
> *Of Fancy skyward flying.*

In short, John Greenleaf Whittier, with an inborn love of rhyming, was beginning to find that he himself was something of a poet, too.

One day, five years later, Whittier was standing by the roadside, helping his father mend a stone wall, when the postman, riding by on horseback, tossed over to them the weekly paper. What was Whittier's surprise when he opened it, to find in its "Poet's Corner" some verses of his own, signed "W."—his sister Mary had filched the poem and sent it off. The paper was a small sheet edition edited at Newburyport by William Lloyd Garrison, who was only two years older than Whittier. And the sequel of the story was that the young editor drove himself to hunt up the young poet (and found the young poet flat on his stomach hunting up a hen's nest under the barn), and the Friend Whittier was urged to release his son from farm work and send him to the academy. "Sir," he sternly replied, "poetry will not give him bread!" But as Whittier was not very strong, he had permission to go, if he could pay his own way. And this he did, by making slippers, and book-keeping, and teaching in vacation time.

There is a good old Eastern proverb that says, "Square thyself for use. The stone that will fit in the wall is not left in the way." By the end of Whittier's school days it was time for him to choose what he would do. He had written many verses, and many of them had been published; but verses were not paid for. He might make a good cobbler, for whom surely there is always much use in the world. But he had "squared" himself for yet a better use, and fate picked him up to meld the understanding of his fellows in yet a better way.

If we were to follow Whittier through the next twelve years, we should find ourselves in first one New England town and then another, and going by stagecoach and boat to Philadelphia or New York; for Whittier was in demand as a newspaper editor. He was, in fact, becoming a public man. At one time he was nominated for Congress, but his health was so poor that the had to withdraw his name before the election. There were three things that, true to his Quaker principles, he used all the weight of his influence against. These were intemperance, war and slavery. He wrote a great deal in both prose and verse on these three subjects, but particularly the last. On this only a very small party of his countrymen at that time agreed with him; and more than once his office was attacked, his papers were burned, mobs followed him when he went to public antislavery meetings, and he narrowly escaped stones and fists, despite his Quaker garb. But he was not to be daunted in anything he believed was right; and it was one very beautiful trait of his character—and one all too rare in this world—that he could firmly disagree with another man's opinion without in the least quarreling with the man. That is probably one reason why he had always warm friends in all parts of the country, whether they were of his way of thinking or not.

Every day was adding to his reputation as "the Quaker poet"; but it was not until ill-health had forced him to settle down quietly at home, that he wrote the greater number of those poems we still delight to read. Meanwhile, the family had sold the old farm and bought a little cottage in Amesbury, and this was the poet's home for the remaining fifty-six years in his life.

If we look at the "Table of Contents" of Whittier's *Poems*—and that is a pretty good way, too, to get some idea of the extent of an author's work—we will find a large group of poems called "legendary." Here, then, is a poet who loved old tales, and, most of all, if we may judge by the titles, tales of the land where he was born. "Telling the Bees," "Abraham Davenport," and "How the Robin Came" are examples of this. Recollections of his own boyhood appear not alone in "Snowbound" but also in "The Barefoot Boy" and in "My Playmate."

Pansy
By Richard "Little Bear" Wheeler

Isabella Macdonald was born November 3, 1841, in Rochester, New York, the youngest of five daughters. Her father, Isaac Macdonald, was a fine upstanding Christian man. Her mother, Myra Spaffold Macdonald, was the daughter of Horatio Gates Spafford (1778–1832), author and inventor. Isabella's uncle, Horatio Gates Spafford Jr., penned the words to "It Is Well With My Soul" after learning that his wife had survived a tragic shipwreck while his four daughters were lost at sea. Isabella was home educated by her father and mother. Her father encouraged her to keep a journal and to develop a natural affection for writing. Under his direction, and endowed with a natural God given talent, she acquired the ability to write while still a young girl.

When she was only ten, the local weekly newspaper published her composition entitled, "Our Old Clock," a story that was inspired by an accident to the old family clock. That first published work was signed Pansy. Isabella acquired that pen name partly because pansies were her favorite flower and partly because of a childhood episode involving decorating a tea party setting with pansies.

Years later, while teaching at Oneida Seminary, from which she had earlier graduated, Isabella wrote her first novel, *Helen Lester,* in competition for a prize. She won fifty dollars for submitting the manuscript that explained the plan of salvation so clearly and pleasantly that very young readers would become Christians.

Isabella wrote or edited more than two hundred published works, including short stories, Sunday school lessons, and more than a hundred novels. She had only one manuscript rejected. At one time her books sold a hundred thousand copies annually, with translations in Swedish, French, Japanese, Armenian and other languages. She usually wrote for a young audience hoping to motivate youth to follow Christianity and the Golden Rule. The themes of her books focused on the value of church attendance; the dangers lurking in popular forms of recreation; the duty of total abstinence from alcohol; the need for self-sacrifice; and, in general, the requirements, tests, and rewards of being a Christian.

Her gifts for telling stories and her cleverness in dreaming up situations held the interest of readers young and old. Isabella was known for developing characters who possessed an unwavering commitment to follow Christ. She portrayed characters and events that anyone might encounter in small town America during the last quarter of the nineteenth century.

A writer in Earth Horizon (1932) acknowledged that whoever on his ancestral book shelves can discover a stray copy of one of the Pansy books will know more, on reading it of culture in the American eighties (1880's) than can otherwise be described. Some of the customs of the times in which Isabella wrote may seem peculiar to readers today. But to better understand the present culture, we need to know the beliefs and practices that have existed in the past.

Throughout her career Isabella took an active interest in all forms of religious endeavors, but her greatest contributions came in her fictional writings. She wanted to teach in story form using precepts and parables the lessons that her husband taught from the pulpit, in Bible class, and in the homes of his parishioners. Her writing was always her means of teaching religious and moral truths as she understood them.

Her husband, Gustavus Rossenberg Alden, was a descendant of John Alden, one of the first settlers in the Plymouth colony. He graduated from Auburn Theological Seminary and was ordained soon after his marriage to Isabella in 1866. He served as a pastor in churches in New York, Indiana, Ohio, Pennsylvania, Florida and Washington D.C. The Aldens moved from place to place for health reasons and to be near their son, Raymond, during his years of schooling and teaching.

Her final years were marked by a series of trials. In 1923, after fifty-seven years of marriage, Mrs. G. R. Alden's husband died. A month later her only son, Raymond, died. About two years later she fell and broke her hip. Although in much pain and discomfort, she continued writing until the end. Her final letters were filled with thoughts of going "Home." Among her last words she spoke were, "Isn't it blessed to realize that one by one we shall gather Home at last to go no more out forever! The hours between me and my call to come Home grow daily less . . ." Mrs. G. R. Alden died August 5, 1930, at the age of eighty-nine in Palo Alto, California, which had been her home since 1901.

Wheeler, Richard "Little Bear." Biography. *A Christmas Surprise.* By Isabella Macdonald Alden, "Pansy," Mrs. G. R. Alden. Bulverde: Mantle Ministries, 1885, reprinted 1997. i–iii. Reprinted by permission of Mantle Ministries.

The Character of Napoleon
Oratory by Charles Phillips

Charles Phillips, 1787–1859, an eminent barrister and orator, was born in Sligo, Ireland, and died in London. Charles was called to the Irish Bar in 1812; active in behalf of Catholic emancipation; called to the English Bar in 1821, and became a leader at the Old Bailey. He gained much of his reputation as an advocate in criminal cases. In his youth he published some verses; later in life he became the author of several works, chiefly of biography. (About 1817)

He is fallen! We may now pause before that splendid prodigy, which towered among us like some ancient ruin, whose frown terrified the glance its magnificence attracted.

Grand, gloomy, and peculiar, he sat upon the throne, a sceptered hermit, wrapped in the solitude of his own originality.

A mind bold, independent, and decisive—a will, despotic in its dictates—an energy that distanced expedition, and a conscience pliable to every touch of interest, marked the outline of this extraordinary character—the most extraordinary, perhaps, that, in the annals of this world, ever rose, or reigned, or fell.

Flung into life, in the midst of a revolution that quickened every energy of a people who acknowledged no superior, he commenced his course, a stranger by birth, and a scholar by charity!

With no friend but his sword, and no fortune but his talents, he rushed into the lists where rank, and wealth, and genius had arrayed themselves, and competition fled from him as from the glance of destiny. He knew no motive but interest—he acknowledged no criterion but success—he worshiped no God but ambition, and with an Eastern devotion he knelt at the shrine of his idolatry. Subsidiary to this, there was no creed that he did not profess, there was no opinion that he did not promulgate: in the hope of a dynasty, he upheld the crescent; for the sake of a divorce, he bowed before the Cross: the orphan of St. Louis, he became the adopted child of the Republic; and with a parricidal ingratitude, on the ruins both of the throne and the tribune, he reared the throne of his despotism.

A professed Catholic, he imprisoned the pope; a pretended patriot, he impoverished the country; and in the name of Brutus, he grasped without remorse, and wore without shame, the diadem of the Cæsars!

Through this pantomime of his policy, fortune played the clown to his caprices. At his touch, crowns crumbled, beggars reigned, systems vanished, the wildest theories took the color of his whim, and all that was venerable, and all that was novel, changed places with the rapidity of a drama. Even apparent defeat assumed the appearance of victory—his flight from Egypt confirmed his destiny—ruin itself only elevated him to empire.

But if his fortune was great, his genius was transcendent; decision flashed upon his counsels; and it was the same to decide and to perform. To inferior intellects, his combinations appeared perfectly impossible, his plans perfectly impracticable; but, in his hands, simplicity marked their development, and success vindicated their adoption.

His person partook the character of his mind—if the one never yielded in the cabinet, the other never bent in the field.

Nature had no obstacles that he did not surmount—space no opposition that he did not spurn; and whether amid Alpine rocks, Arabian sands, or polar snows, he seemed proof against peril, and empowered with ubiquity! The whole continent of Europe trembled at beholding the audacity of his designs, and the miracle of their execution. Skepticism bowed to the prodigies of his performance; romance assumed the air of history; nor was there aught too incredible for belief, or too fanciful for expectation, when the world saw a subaltern of Corsica waving his imperial flag over her most ancient capitals. All the visions of antiquity became common places in his contemplation; kings were his people—nations were his outposts; and he disposed of courts, and crowns, and camps, and churches, and cabinets, as if they were the titular dignitaries of the chess-board!

Amid all these changes he stood immutable as adamant. It mattered little whether in the field or the drawing-room—with the mob or the levee—wearing the jacobin bonnet or the iron crown—banishing a Braganza, or espousing a Hapsburg—dictating peace on a raft to the Czar of Russia, or contemplating defeat at the gallows of Leipsic—he was still the same military despot!

Cradled in the camp, he was to the last hour the darling of the army; and whether in the camp or the cabinet, he never forsook a friend or forgot a favor. Of all his soldiers, not one abandoned him, till affection was useless; and their first stipulation was for the safety of their favorite.

They knew well that if he was lavish of them, he was prodigal of himself; and that if he exposed them to peril, he repaid them with plunder. For the soldier, he subsidized every people; to the people he made even pride pay tribute. The victorious veteran glittered with his gains; and the capital, gorgeous with the spoils of art, became the miniature metropolis of the universe. In this wonderful combination, his affectation of literature must not be omitted. The jailer of the Press, he affected the patronage of letters—the proscriber of books, he encouraged philosophy—the persecutor of authors, and the murderer of printers, he yet pretended to the protection of learning!—the assassin of Palm, the silencer of De Stael, and the denouncer of Kotzebue, he was the friend of David, the benefactor of De Lille, and sent his academic prize to the philosopher of England.

Such a medley of contradictions, and at the same time such an individual consistency, were never united in the same character. A Royalist—a Republican and an Emperor—a Mohammedan—a Catholic and a Patron of the Synagogue—a Subaltern and a Sovereign—a Traitor and a Tyrant—a Christian and an Infidel—he was, through all his vicissitudes, the same stern, impatient, inflexible original—the same mysterious incomprehensible self—the man without a model, and without a shadow.

His fall, like his life, baffled all speculation. In short, his whole history was like a dream to the world, and no man can tell how or why he was awakened from the reverie.

Such is a faint and feeble picture of Napoleon Bonaparte, the first (and it is to be hoped the last) emperor of the French.

That he has done much evil there is little doubt; that he has been the origin of much good, there is just as little. Through his means, intentional or not, Spain, Portugal, and France have arisen to the blessings of a free constitution; superstition has found her grave in the ruins of the inquisition; and the feudal system, with its whole train of tyrannic satellites, has fled for ever. Kings may learn from him that their safest study, as well as their noblest, is the interest of the people; the people are taught by him that there is no despotism so stupendous against which they have not a resource; and to those who would rise upon the ruins of both, he is a living lesson, that if ambition can raise them from the lowest station, it can also prostrate them from the highest.

Notes:

St Louis (b.1215, d. 1270), a wise and pious king of France, known as Louis IX. Napoleon was appointed to the Military School at Brienne, by Louis XVI.

Brutus, Lucius Junius, abolished the royal office at Rome (509 BC) and ruled as consul for two years.

Jacobin Bonnet, The Jacobins were a powerful political club during the first French Revolution. A peculiar bonnet or hat was their badge.

Braganza, the name of the royal family of Portugal. Maria of Portugal, and her father, Charles IV, of Spain, were both expelled by Napoleon.

Hapsburg, the name of the royal family of Austria. Napoleon's second wife was Maria Louisa, the daughter of the Emperor.

Czar, the treaty of Tilsit was agreed to between Bonaparte and the Czar Alexander on the river Memel.

Leipsic, Napoleon was defeated by the allied forces, in October, 1813, at this city.

Palm, a German publisher, shot, in 1806, by order of Napoleon, for publishing a pamphlet against him.

DeStael, a celebrated French authoress, banished from Paris in 1802 by Napoleon.

Kotzebue, an eminent German dramatist.

DeLille, an eminent French poet and professor.

Explanatory notes from *McGuffey's Sixth Eclectic Reader*, 145–146.

David, Jacques-Louis, early in his career he was a leader in the neoclassical movement; later his subjects became more modern and political. David was himself active in the French Revolution as a supporter of Robespierre and is sometimes called the chief propagandist for the Revolution; after the Reign of Terror ended he was briefly imprisoned for his actions under the moderate Directory and saved by the intervention of his estranged wife. The painting, "Intervention of the Sabine Women," symbolized this. When Napoleon took power, David became his court painter and created several grand canvasses of the Emperor, including the heroic "Napoleon Bonaparte Crossing the Alps" (1801) and the enormous "Coronation of Napoleon and Josephine" (1807). David also painted "Napoleon in His Study" (1812), with its famous image of Napoleon with one hand tucked inside his vest. After Napoleon's ouster, David went in exile to Brussels, where he remained until his 1825 death.

Explanatory notes from <http://www.artchive.com/artchive/ftptoc/david_ext.html>.

Phillips, Charles. "The Character of Napoleon." *The World's Famous Orations* Ed. William Jennings Bryan. New York: Funk and Wagnalls, 1906.

Syrup of Ipecac

Syrup of ipecac is for emergency use in poisoning. It is a medicine that can be purchased in any pharmacy without a prescription that, when given to a child or an adult, will cause vomiting.

SYRUP OF IPECAC MUST **NEVER** BE USED BEFORE CALLING YOUR FAMILY PHYSICIAN OR THE POISON CONTOL CENTER .

Normally syrup of ipecac should **not** be given **at home** if:
1. The patient is less than one year old or
2. Corrosives (lye, drain cleaners, oven cleaners, automatic dishwasher detergent, or other strong acids or bases) have been taken or burns are seen around or in the mouth or
3. A petroleum distillate-containing product (kerosene, gasoline, paint thinner, furniture polish, etc.) has been taken or
4. The patient is lethargic (sluggish), asleep, or comatose (unconscious) or
5. The patient is convulsing

Directions:
For children over one year and adults
1. Give **one tablespoonful** (15 ml, one half ounce) of syrup of ipecac.
2. Immediately give 8–16 oz of any fluid **except** milk (kool-aid, soda pop, fruit juice, etc.).
3. Vomiting should occur in approximately 15–20 minutes.
4. IF vomiting has not occurred in 20 minutes, administer an additional tablespoonful of syrup of ipecac. **Never give more than two table-spoonfuls.**

Woman's Rights
By Haddie Lane

"HADDIE," said my Aunt Debbie, laying aside the stocking she had been knitting, and interrupting me in a most animated discussion with Cousin Tom. "Haddie, what do you mean by the words 'Woman's Rights'? They have passed your lips at least a dozen times within the last ten minutes."

"Why, auntie, I was just wishing to exercise my 'rights' as Tom's physician, and I was vowing to give him such a dose of ratsbane as would rid the world for ever of such a pest."

"I am sorry, my Haddie, to hear you speak jestingly on such a grave subject; but get your bonnet, and join me in a walk through the village, and you will find, I hope, before we return, that you have numerous and noble rights. You will learn that which will make you tremble for yourself, lest you should misuse your talents."

Greatly wondering what Aunt Debbie could mean, I was soon equipped, and found her waiting in the hall. As we descended the steps together, I noticed a shade of sadness on her brow, her lips had lost their usual smile, and there was a slight tremor in her voice when she spoke.

"Here, Miss Haddie, I shall want your help: which will you carry, the basket or the bundle?"

"Neither, Aunt Debbie," I replied, snatching up the basket, however. "Where are you going to take me, aunt?" I asked, after we had gone some distance. "This basket is not as light as it might be, and the bundle is of a respectable size."

My aunt answered by leading the way into a narrow lane, which I immediately recognized as leading to the cottage of Widow Green, whose daughter was one of my old playmates.

"Really, aunt, things seem so changed since I went to school. I have not heard from Mary Green this many a long day. I expect she is married—the bride of some rustic Ichabod or Peter."

"Haddie, can you—will you be grave for the next five minutes? I promised to tell you of woman's rights, and you should be serious."

She knocked at the door; a feeble voice bade us enter. I followed Aunt Debbie, who walked to a corner of the room. There, on a low bed, lay a wasted form, in whose dark eyes lurked a lingering resemblance to her who was once the village beauty. It was with difficulty that I checked the exclamation of surprise that sprang to my lips; but a glance from Aunt Debbie warned me, and I sat down silently by the bedside. Could that be Mary Green? The rosy cheeks, the laughing glances were gone. "So young to die!" I murmured. "Just my age."

"Come here, Haddie," said Aunt Debbie, cheerfully; "here is an old friend."

A sweet smile hovered on the sick girl's lips, as I bent over her.

"Changed—sadly changed!" she said.

"Yes, Mary, changed," said Aunt Debbie; "but gladly changed, from a thoughtless, giddy girl, to a true Christian; from a proud girl to a humble sufferer."

"True—most true, I trust," Mary answered. "Haddie, dear, I spoke only of my face. I am about to die, Haddie—I am in dreadful agony sometimes—yet, believe me, I would not be as I once was for all the wealth of worlds. I am far happier now than even in those merry days when we used to run races to the school-house, and wonder if queens were as gay as we. Your aunt, Haddie, has made me a Christian—has told me of my God."

A violent cough interrupted her. I feared that the spirit had flown as she fell back heavily on the pillow; but her eyes gently unclosed, and she was about to proceed, when Aunt Debbie spoke—

"Another time, Mary; not now."

She acquiesced.

Tearfully, but silently, I watched my aunt, now arranging the pillows, now holding a cup of water to Mary's parched lips; then, unbarring the window, she let in a glorious stream of sunlight to the room. Seating herself by the bedside, and taking one thin hand between her own, she read a chapter from the Bible. The words were simple, but they spoke of hope beyond the grave, of the glorious heaven where Mary so soon would be. My tears flowed fast; when my aunt, closing the book, knelt down on the earthen floor, motioning to me to do the same. The golden sunlight seemed to rest like a halo on my aunt's head, as her calm, clear voice uttered the words of prayer.

The thought flashed across my mind, this then is one of woman's duties—of woman's rights.

Noble—truly noble! A glorious right, to smooth the thorny pillow of the dying, to point out the way of life to the troubled spirit, to cheer the fainting soul with words of hope.

We left the cottage as noiselessly as we had entered it. We walked on and on till we came to the last house in the village. Aunt Debbie opened the gate, scattering a flock of chickens who had taken up their quarters for the night thereon. What was that dirty object in the doorway? I always considered myself passionately fond of children; but I confess my heart revolted at the view of that unsightly object. Its face begrimed with dirt and tears, its uncombed curls in frightful confusion, it ran screaming to its mother; while Aunt Debbie, seeing my lip curl, whispered, "Shrink not here, Haddie; another of woman's rights."

A woman now came forth to greet us, whose distressed countenance was a sufficient appeal to our sympathies. Three or four little urchins were clinging to her skirts. I coaxed an acquaintance with the cleanest of them, while my aunt was occupied with the mother.

The poor woman's story was briefly told. Once possessed of affluence, she had been reduced to poverty by the failure of a bank, in which all her funds were vested. Sickness and death following close on the heels of poverty, she had been reduced to her present condition. Strangers in the village, they had been literally famishing, when a poor woman, herself a recipient of Aunt Debbie's bounty, brought information of them to my charitable aunt.

My basket was soon opened; the children gathered around it, and they made terrible inroads on the cold chicken and bread and butter. When their enormous appetites seemed somewhat appeased, which was not until the basket was completely lightened, Aunt Debbie opened her bundle.

"We must make these little ones look a little more respectable," said she.

The mother blushed as she told us that trouble had made her forget everything.

"Oh, never mind," said Aunt Debbie; "a little soap and plenty of fresh water will work wonders. Haddie will take charge of that little fellow with the long curls."

It was a tiresome task. I scrubbed, and rubbed, and pulled hair most unmercifully, but the rogues bore it all quietly; and when it was over, and they were arrayed in clean, whole dresses, what beauties they were! Their mother looked almost happy, with seeing her children look so bright; and when, at parting, Aunt Debbie promised to procure employment for her, and to take the eldest girl under her own care, I thought there would be no end to the "God bless you!"

My heart swelled as we turned homeward.

"Certainly, Aunt Debbie," said I, "this right makes you feel very happy; though I attribute part of my present feelings to joy at being rid of that basket."

Descending the hill, we came to the school-house. I caught sight of an old acquaintance through the window.

"Is Amy Henry the teacher, Aunt Debbie? That saucy girl, who used to play at tit-tat-toe on her slate instead of doing her sums, and make such comical little heads on her copy-book; and"—

"Hush my dear; Amy is graver now, and would probably not relish hearing of her youthful follies. Shall we go in?"

"O no! I could never keep my countenance to hear Amy lecturing the class. We will stand here; they will not see us."

Amy was bending over a slate, while a little girl stood by her side with a terribly puzzled countenance. There was something so comic in her woe-begone visage, that Amy burst into a hearty laugh, and so did I. Of course, we were discovered, and forced in to occupy that post of honor, the visitors' seat. I watched her carefully, as she moved quietly among her scholars. Their bright glances showed how much they loved her; and I did not wonder at it, so patiently and kindly did she smooth away difficulties, so gently did she correct their faults, and her smile of approval was so sweet. She called up her class to recite; and they proved, by their answers, that her labor had not been lost. A brighter set of boys I never saw before.

When the school was dismissed, the scholars passed noiselessly from the room, so carefully had they been trained; but when they assembled on the green, there arose a tremendous shout. I stepped to the door to learn the cause. They were hurrahing for Miss Amy and Aunt Debbie.

My aunt spoke truly—another noble right, to gain the love, the almost adoration of those little hearts; to rouse the slumbering fires of genius; to mold their minds at her will—a glorious right, yet a fearful one.

We left the pale teacher in her now quiet school-room. I wanted her, nay, I urged her to walk home with me; but she smilingly refused, pointing to a huge bundle of quills to be mended, a large pile of copies to be set.

"Duty, duty—all right," said Aunt Debbie; "and then comes the pleasure of a visit from you, Amy, on Saturday, when the children will have a half holiday."

"Yes, Haddie, think of Saturday; and till then, good-by."

"Now, Haddie, for a race to the top of the hill," said Aunt Debbie.

I soon attained the summit, and called to my aunt to follow. We had stood there some time, drinking in the splendid sunset, when we heard voices in the adjoining wood.

"The wood-cutters, John Holm and his son, I suppose," said my aunt.

The sounds, which had at first been those of cheerful conversation, now became louder and angry.

"Oh! aunt, they are quarreling," I exclaimed.

Aunt Debbie stepped boldly into the forest. Guided by the sounds, we soon emerged from the tangled thicket into an open glade. There stood the two disputants. The old man's countenance was crimson with rage; the son stood with uplifted arm and quivering lip. His glittering ax shone in his hand. In an instant, Aunt Debbie was between them, a hand on the arm of each.

"Are ye men!" said she. "Would you sully this bright glade with an act of violence? Old man, would you strike your son—that boy who was once your pride? Your white hairs should have taught you wisdom. Do not stir up his anger, lest he be too sorely tempted. Son, would you stain your gleaming ax with your father's blood? Remember that he is your father. That word alone should secure your respect. But he has toiled for you; his frame has been bent with labor, his hair has whitened with toil for you—for you, his ungrateful son."

The young man's arm relaxed its hold, and his ax fell to the earth. But the old man still grasped his, and his face wore a sterner frown.

"John," my aunt continued, "can you imagine your sainted wife looking down from heaven, and beholding you with arm uplifted against her son, her living image?"

At the mention of his wife, the old man burst into a flood of tears; and, sitting down on the newly-fallen tree, he buried his face in his hands and wept bitterly.

"Now go to him," said Aunt Debbie, touching the young man's arm; "go tell him you are penitent; ask his forgiveness, and all will be well."

He walked towards his father, and we left them. As we threaded our way through the thicket, now blinded by a branch from some impertinent tree, now scratched by a briar, now starting at a squirrel, I thought to myself—"Still another right—a peace-maker. Who but woman, helpless, unresisting woman is so formed to glide in gently among angry men, to calm their ruffled spirits, to weaken the strong arm and the hand heavy with passion? Who but woman can show them the noblest revenge—the revenge of kindness? A right so fearful must make every true woman tremble at the thought. Heaven send us strength to use it!"

As we descended the hill, I recognized the long avenue of cedars on our right, as leading to the house of Squire Carlton, as the magistrate was called. I had many a fine race down that avenue with Fanny Carlton; but I had not seen or heard anything of her for two years. True, before I left my native village for a fashionable boarding-school in a distant city, we two had plighted a solemn promise never to forget each other, and to write a long letter once a week; but amid the busy life of a school-girl and the excitement of new faces and new friends, I had forgotten, and Fanny was too proud to intrude her letters where she deemed herself neglected. My aunt, in answer to the question which fell fast from my lips, informed me that Mr. Carlton had been for a long time afflicted with the gout; that his temper, never remarkable for urbanity, had now become very irritable; that Fanny had given up her friends, her studies, and her amusements, devoting her whole time to her father, who repaid this devotion with reproofs and harshness.

"I see them, Aunt Debbie," I cried, "there on the lawn."

It was, indeed, Fanny; but my playmate was greatly altered—she had grown tall. Her complexion was exquisitely clear; and her hair, instead of falling to her waist in those careless curls which seemed like a gleam of sunshine floating through the air, was turned smoothly back from her forehead, and gathered into a knot behind. Her slight figure bent under the weight of the stately old man who leaned on her arm. They had observed us, and were coming slowly to meet us.

"We will wait for them here at the gate," said Aunt Debbie; "it is too late to go in."

I assented, and was stooping to gather some of the white violets with which the ground was covered, when an exclamation from my aunt startled me. Fanny and her father had approached nearly to where we stood, when the old man's foot struck against some obstacle in the path. He with difficulty suppressed a loud cry of pain; but, lifting his arm quickly, gave his daughter a blow so heavy that she reeled forward, and would have fallen but for a friendly cedar which stood near. She had been hastening towards us, her face beaming with pleasure; but at this shameful blow her color faded; an expression of pain crossed her face, and, bending upon me a look in which disappointment was mingled with mortification, she waved her hand and turned towards the house. We stood in silence, as if rooted to the spot. Mr. Carlton walked as fast as his foot would allow, muttering curses and imprecations; while Fanny seemed to have forgotten the blow, so tenderly did she support the old man, and so skillfully did she direct his steps.

"Wait a minute," said Aunt Debbie, after they had entered the house; "Fanny will soon be back, I fancy." And scarcely had the words passed her lips, when Fanny was at our side.

After the usual greetings, she reverted to her father's fall, blaming her own carelessness, but without mentioning her blow. She held her handkerchief to her forehead to hide the swelling. Aunt Debbie pressed her to spend the following day with us; but she declined, pleading an engagement.

"But you will come soon to see me?" said I; "on Saturday I shall expect you."

"I am afraid, dear Haddie," said she, confusedly, "that I cannot come at all; my father's indisposition requires my constant attention. I am doing penance, Haddie; I used to be such a rover. But my father likes me near him; and he has so few enjoyments, that I am glad I can help him to forget his sufferings."

A servant now came to inform Fanny that Mr. Carlton requested to see her immediately. With a smile and a half-suppressed sigh, she left us.

"Can this be one of woman's rights, Aunt Debbie?" I exclaimed.

"Yes, Haddie. Fanny is learning a lesson of self-denial, of patience; and though it may seem an unenviable right to you to be able to 'bless them that curse you,' we must think of 'the great reward' which Fanny will obtain in heaven."

We had now arrived at the gate of a small frame house. It was a perfect picture of cleanliness and order. A bright wood fire was crackling and sparkling on the hearth, and the burnished tins that lined the walls were glowing in the blaze. The little tea-table was set: my mouth watered at the sight of the bread, light as a snow-flake, the golden butter, and the dish of strawberries smothered in cream. In the doorway stood a young man, whose dress betokened him a laborer, who was tossing a laughing baby to the very ceiling. His wife, a rosy, good-humored lassie, was removing the newly-washed clothes from the line where they had been sunning themselves all day, and was placing them in a large basket at her side. They smiled their simple greeting, while my aunt said a few kind words to the young mother, and praised the laughing urchin.

"Rural felicity, is it not, aunt?" I asked, as soon as we were out of hearing.

"Yes, indeed, Haddie. And what will you say when I tell you this was all brought about through the agency of a darned stocking? I once heard a very learned lady say, with a sneer on her proud lip, 'To stay at home and darn your husband's stockings—phaw!—the aim of woman's existence!' "

"Oh, tell me all about it, aunty; I am in prime humor for a story."

"It will be but short, my dear. When Henry and Ellen Stuart were married, every one spoke of the excellent match—such a fine young man. The village seemed delighted with itself; but its congratulations did not last long. Soon it began to be whispered that Henry frequented the tavern; he was several times seen reeling home; and at last it became evident to every one that he was a confirmed drunkard. I expostulated, your grandfather lectured him severely, but with no effect. Their furniture piece by piece, was sold to gratify the cravings of his appetite. His wife's clothes and his own went one after another, and at last little remained but the bare walls. In spite of all this, Ellen managed to keep up appearances; she was always neatly and cleanly dressed, and tried to speak cheerfully of the future.

"One morning, after a greater debauch than usual, Henry Stuart lay on the heap of straw which served them as a couch, their bed having been sold long before. His heart was heavy; his conscience was busy, yet he lay there quietly. His wife, after arranging the room, sat down on a broken chair, and quietly began darning a very old and worn stocking. His pride was roused. This was not wont to be so. He watched her as he patiently drew the glittering needle through the

fearful chasms Time had made; he looked at her dress—composed of the coarsest material—her face, its rosy freshness gone, and the sunny smile succeeded by a look of anxiety that made her seem almost old; the room bare of all its former comforts; and all this change he had wrought. He rose from the bed, signed the pledge, resumed his work with energy, and now behold him! By hard work and prudence, he has regained his former standing; and he still keeps the darned stocking, considering it as the dearest legacy he can leave to his daughter; and whenever he is tempted, he looks at it for a few minutes, and self is conquered. Which would you rather be, the proud, wealthy woman, sneering at household duties, and endeavoring wildly to revolutionize the world; or Ellen Stuart, humble and hard-working though she be, rejoicing in the thought that her patient forbearance and the blessed old stocking have wrought this change?"

"Not the virago, for the wealth of worlds."

As we passed through the village, the lights began to twinkle from the windows, and at the door of one small cottage, I could not resist the temptation to peep in. A young girl was seated by a small table, bending over some sewing. Her fingers flew; and well they might, for they were helping to bar the door against poverty. An old man sat in the chimney corner smoking a pipe; while his wife, with spectacles on nose, was busied with her knitting. Sweet Lizzie White, thine is indeed a life of toil. "Day in, day out," rain or sunshine, heat or cold, you must sew, sew on from morn till night. By Lizzie's labor the whole family live. She supports her aged parents and a blind orphan nephew. She never knows holiday—never shows her pretty face except at meeting; and yet few are happier. She sings like a bird; and it would be strange, indeed, to pass their humble dwelling and not hear her sweet voice caroling her simple song.

A blessed right it is to labor for those we love. It gives strength to the hands and warmth to the heart. To feel that you are useful, that the lives of others are cheered by your labor, is enough to make the most sluggish blood course quickly through the veins, to rouse the most sullen heart to action. To meet poverty nobly, to wrestle with it bravely, to subdue it gloriously, this, indeed, makes woman seem "a little lower than the angels."

When we reached our home, the hall was deserted; Aunt Debbie went to hunt my father, and I threw myself on a settee—my limbs wearied with my long walk, but my faculties wide awake, and my brain and heart full to overflowing. I heard voices in an adjoining room. It was my little nephew Harry, talking with his mother. She was telling her boy of God. The merry little fellow was hushed into silence by the solemnity of the theme; and when, a short time afterwards, he knelt and repeated his evening prayer—"God bless Harry, make him a good boy; God bless Aunt Haddie and Carlo"—I could restrain myself no longer, but burst into tears. I thought of my own mother, of her gentle counsels to her wayward daughter, of her noble character; and I wept still more. The last and best of woman's rights—a mother's love. To "shadow forth in your example what you wish your child to be," is, indeed, a right—often abused, it is true, and seldom clearly understood, but still a right, and a noble one. The little being who reposes so confidingly on your bosom will become whatever you choose to make him. If you mold his mind to high

and lofty aspirations after truth, if you teach him to know his duty and to perform it, great, exceeding great will be your reward; but if you teach him to submit to passion's away, to sneer at everything that is right and good, to check every noble impulse, the sin be upon your own head.

That night, when Aunt Debbie entered my chamber to bestow the good-night kiss, I accosted her with—

"Aunt Debbie, you did not tell me of woman's rights—one right you omitted."

"What was it, my darling?"

"Hold down your head; I will tell you, if you will promise not to say anything to Tom."

"Well, I promise—only don't strangle me. What is it, my dear?"

"The—the *right of conquest,* aunty."

"Oh, fie! what a naughty girl!" and Aunt Debbie tripped lightly from the room.

Lane, Haddie. "Woman's Rights." *Godey's Lady's Book* April 1850.

Women's Rights Women
By R. L. Dabney

Note: Dabney often used words, punctuation, and spelling not in use today.

In our day, innovations march with so rapid a stride that they quite take away one's breath. The fantastical project of yesterday, which was mentioned only to be ridiculed, is today the audacious reform, and will be tomorrow the accomplished fact. Such has been the history of the agitation for "women's rights," as they are sophistically called in this country. A few years ago this movement was the especial hobby of a few old women of both Sexes, who made themselves the laughingstock of all sane people by the annual ventilation of their crotchet. Their only recruits were a few of the unfortunates whom nature or fortune had debarred from those triumphs and enjoyments which are the natural ambition of the Sex, and who adopted this agitation as the most feasible mode of expressing their spitefulness against the successful; competitors. Today the movement has assumed such

dimensions that it challenges the attention of every thoughtful mind.

If we understand the claims of the Women's Rights women, they are in substance two: that the legislation, at least, of, society shall disregard all the natural distinctions of the sexes, and award the same specific rights and franchises to both in every respect; and that woman while in the married state shall be released from every species of conjugal subordination. The assimilation of the garments of the two sexes, their competition in the same industries and professions, and their common access to the same amusements and recreations, are social changes which the "strong-minded" expect to work, each one for herself, when once the obstructions of law are removed from the other points.

One result of the reflection which we have been able to give this movement, is the conviction that it will prevail in the so-called "United States." This is foreshadowed by the frantic lust for innovation which has seized the body of the people like an epidemic. It is enough with them to condemn any institution, that it was bequeathed us by our forefathers; because it is not the invention of this age, it is wrong, of course. In their eyes no experience proves anything, save the experience which they have had themselves. They do not suppose that our fathers were wise enough to interpret and record the lessons of former experiences. That certain things did not succeed in our forefathers' hands is no proof that they will not succeed in our hands; for we are "cute," we live in an enlightened age, and understand how to manage things successfully. The philosophy of the Yankee mind is precisely that of the Yankee girl who, when she asked for leave to marry at seventeen, was dissuaded by her mother that she "had married very early and had seen the folly of it." "Yes; but, Mamma," replied the daughter, "I want to see the folly of it for myself." Your Yankee philosopher is too self-sufficient to be cautioned from the past. He does not know history; he would not believe its conclusions if he did; he has no use for its lights, having enough "subjective" light of his own. To such a people the fact that a given experiment is too absurd to have been ever tried before, is an irresistible fascination: it is a chance not to be neglected.

The symptoms of approaching success which already exist are such as may well cheer the advocates of the new revolution. They who a few years ago counted their adherents by scores, now have tens of thousands. They are represented by their own press. They have received the support of at least one religious journal, which presumes to call itself Christian and is the organ of a numerous denomination—the *New York Independent*. They receive the obsequious homage of the demagogues of the day. They have already engrafted a part of their ideas upon some State constitutions. Their apostles are invited to lecture before "Christian Associations" (of that peculiar kind which enumerate billiard and card-tables among the means of grace), and before the United States Congress. And last, a kindred cause, that of indiscriminate divorces, is making such progress in many of the States that it will soon be able to lend a strong helping-hand to its sister. Now it is by just such steps that Radicalism grew from its despised infancy in this country. It was just thus that Abolitionism grew. It is thus that all things grow on the American soil which ripen their harvests of evil.

The advocates of these "women's rights" may be expected to win the day because the premises from which they argue their revolution have been irrevocably admitted by the bulk of the people. Now this popular mind may not be consciously or intentionally consistent and logical. It may jump to many conclusions without much analysis of the steps by which they are reached. It may deliberately harbor the most express purpose to be guilty of any logical inconsistency, however outrageous, in pursuing its supposed interests; and may have its mind ever so clearly made up to eat its own words and principles' whenever its convenience prompts that measure. But still the Creator has made man, in spite of himself, a logical animal; and consequences will work themselves out, whether he designs it or not, to those results which the premises dictate. History will write out the corollaries of the theorems whether the projectors wish to stop for them or not. Now, false principles are already firmly planted from which the whole "Women's Rights" claim must follow. If we look at the coarser, more concrete, and popular form in which the consequence is drawn, we find the argument for the popular, Radical mind perfectly unanswerable. "It has been decided that all negro men have a right to vote: is' not a Yankee white woman with her smartness' and education as good as a stupid, ignorant, Southern black?" We should like to see the answer to that logic from that premise which a Northern Radical mind could be made to appreciate. An unanswerable point thus perpetually made upon the mind of the public, will impinge at last.

Or if we examine the argument in its more exact and logical form, we shall find it, after the established (false) premises are granted, equally conclusive for the educated. The very axioms of American politics now are, that "all men are by nature equal," that all are inalienably "entitled to liberty and the pursuit of happiness," and that "the only just foundation of government is in the consent of the governed." There was a sense in which our fathers propounded these statements; but it is not the one in which they are now held by Americans. Our recent doctors of political science have retained these formulates of words as convenient masks under which to circulate a set of totally different, and indeed antagonistic notions; and they have succeeded perfectly. The new meanings of which the "Whigs" of 1776 never dreamed are now the current ones. Those wise statesmen meant to teach that all men are morally equal in the sense of the Golden Rule:

that while individual traits, rights, and duties vary widely in the different orders of political society, these different rights all have some moral basis; that the inferior has the same moral title (that of a common humanity and common relation to a benignant Heavenly Father) to have his rights—the rights of an inferior—duly respected, which the superior has to claim that his very different rights shall be respected. The modern version is that there are no superiors or inferiors in society; that there is a mechanical equality; that all have specifically all the same rights; and that any other constitution is Against natural justice. Next: when our wise fathers said that liberty is an inalienable, natural right, they meant by each one's liberty the privilege, to do such things as he, with his particular relations, ought to have a moral title to do; the particular things having righteous, natural limitations in every case, and much narrower limits in some cases than in others. Radical America now means by natural liberty each one's privilege to do what he chooses to do. By the consent of the governed our forefathers meant each Sovereign Commonwealth's consenting to the constitution under which it should be governed: they meant that it was unjust for Britain to govern America without America's consent. Which part of the human beings living in a given American State should constitute the State, potentially, the populous whose franchise it was to express the will of the commonwealth for all—that was in their eyes wholly another question; to be wisely decided in different States according to the structure which Providence had given them. By "the consent of the governed" it would appeal that Radicalism means it is entirely just for Yankeedom to govern Virginia against Virginia's consent, and that it is not just to govern any individual human being without letting him vote for his governors. The utter inconsistency of the two parts of this creed is not ours to reconcile. It is certain that both parts (consistent or not) are firmly held as the American creed. The version given to the maxim as to individual rights is universally this: that natural justice requires that suffrage shall be coextensive with allegiance, except where the right has been forfeited by some crime (such as that which the men of 1861 committed in presuming to act on the principles of the men of 1776). To these errors the American people are too deeply committed to evade any of their logical applications. For the sake of these dogmas they

have destroyed one Federal and eleven other State constitutions, have committed a half million of murders, and (dearest of all) have spent some seven thousand millions of dollars. Repudiate these maxims now! Never! This would be to dishonor the ghosts of all the slaughtered Union-Savers; to shame the sacrifices of all the "Trooly Lo'il" during the glorious four years, to dim the very crown of martyrdom upon the brow of the "late lamented," and worst of all, to outrage the manes of all those departed dollars.

Now then, when, Mistress Amazona Narragansett steps forward, and having vindicated her claim to have belonged always to the true Israel of the "Unconditional Unionists," demands simple and obvious application of these honored maxims to her own case, how can she be gainsaid? Hitherto the State has governed her without asking her consent at the ballot-box. This is self-evidently against the immortal truth that "all just government is founded on the consent of the governed." The State has restrained her natural liberty of doing as she chose, compelling her to pay a great many dollars in taxes which she would rather have chosen to expend in crinoline, and forbidding her to do a great many other little acts, such as bigamy, etc., which might have been her preference (and therefore her natural right); and all this without even saving the State's credit and manners by asking her consent at the polls to the laws made for her. And last: the State has committed the crowning outrage and inconsistency of not letting her be a man because God made her a woman! What an outrage this to be committed on so frivolous a pretext! Be consoled, Mistress Amazona; it is simply impossible that such abuses can stand much longer in the full light of this reforming age. "The schoolmistress is abroad." That mighty tide of progress which has already swept away the Constitution, and slavery, and State's rights, and the force of contracts public and private, with all such rubbish, will soon dissolve your grievance also. Has not the Radical version of the political gospel said, "All men are by nature mechanically equal?" And "man," Mistress Amazona (as you will know when you acquire the virile right of learning Latin) here means, not vir, but home; the species irrespective of sex. It means that a woman has a natural right to do all the particular things that a man does (if she can), to it on juries and shave her beard, to serve in the army and ride astraddle, to preach sermons and sing bass.

But seriously: a woman is a human being, and a grown woman is an adult. She is treated, and must be treated, by all governments as a citizen owing allegiance and subject to law. On those principles, which are the first principles of Radicalism, it is impossible to deny her right to vote and to participate in all the franchises of men. Her exclusion is a glaring instance of "class legislation"—that odious thing which Radicalism so strongly condemns as contrary to equality. To subject women to these disabilities is even a more glaring injustice than was the exclusion of the negro from American citizenship because he was "guilty of a skin"; for here the exclusion from natural rights is grounded on the sole fact that woman is "guilty of a sex." And especially are all those laws unnatural and inexcusable iniquities which subject the person or property of the wife to any marital authority. What is such marriage but a species of (white) domestic slavery? Nor is it any excuse to say that in America no woman enters the married state save at her own option; for to that state the most commanding instincts of woman's being impel her; and it is but a mocking tyranny to impose this slavery on the married state of woman, and tell her then that she need not submit to the yoke if she chooses to avoid it by sacrificing the chief instincts of her being. Why, it may be even said to the galley-slave: that he need not be a slave, provided he is willing to disregard that other primal instinct, the love of life: suicide will set him free!

Such is the logic of the Women's Rights party, from Radical premises. Its prospect of triumph is greatly increased by this, that its Northern opponents (the only ones who have any power to oppose) have disabled themselves from meeting it by their furious Abolitionism. The premises of that doctrine, to which they are so irrevocably committed, now shut their mouths. It is vain for the rabid negrophilist, Dr. Horace Bushnell, to write a book at this date against Women's Rights as the "Reform against Nature." He cannot consistently oppose it; he has himself naturalized the false principles from which that "reform" will flow. The true principles from which its folly might have been evinced, the principles held by us "Rebels," he has trampled down with the armed heel, and drowned in blood and buried under mountains of obloquy and odium and slander. He cannot resort to those sound pre-mises. To meet the argument of these aspiring Amazons fairly, one must teach, with Moses, the Apostle Paul, John Hampden, Washington, George Mason, John C. Calhoun, and all that contemptible rabble of "old fogies," that political society is composed of "superiors, inferiors, and equals," that while all these bear an equitable moral relation to each other, they have very different natural rights and duties; that just government is not founded on the consent of the individuals governed, but on the ordinance of God, and hence a share in the ruling franchise is not a natural right at all, but a privilege to be bestowed according to a wise discretion on a limited class having qualification to use it for the good of the whole; that the integers out of which the State is constituted are not individuals, but families represented in their parental heads; that every human being is born under authority (parental and civic) instead of being born "free" in the licentious sense that liberty is each one's privilege of doing what he chooses; that subordi-nation, and not that license, is the natural state of all men; and that without such equitable distribution of different duties and rights among the classes naturally differing in condition, and subordination of some to others, and of all to the law, society is as impossible as is the existence of a house without distinction between the founda-tion-stone and the capstones. No words are needed to show hence that should either the voice of God or of sound experience require woman to be placed for the good of the whole society in a subordinate sphere, there can be no natural injustice in doing so. But these old truths, with their sound and beneficent applica-tions, have been scornfully repudiated by Aboli-tionism and Radicalism. The North cannot, will not, avow and appeal to them, because that would be to confess that the injured South was all the time right in its opposition to Abolition; and the conquerors will rather let all perish than thus humble their pride to the poor conquered victims.

It may be inferred again that the present, movement for women's rights, will certainly prevail from the history of its only opponent, Northern conservatism. This is a party which never conserves anything. Its history has been that it demurs to each aggression of the progres-sive party, and aims to save its credit by a respectable amount of growling, but always acquiesces at last in the innovation. What was the resisted novelty of yesterday is today one of the accepted principles of conservatism; it is now conservative only in affecting to resist the next innovation, which will tomorrow be forced upon its timidity; and will be succeeded by some third revolution, to be denounced and then adopted in its turn. American conservatism is merely the shadow that follows Radicalism as it moves forward towards perdition. It remains behind it, but never retards it, and always advances near its leader. This pretended salt hath utterly lost its savor: wherewith shall it be salted? Its impotency is not hard, indeed, to explain. It is worthless because it is the conservatism of expediency only, and not of sturdy principle. It intends to risk nothing serious for the sake of the truth, and has no idea of being guilty of the folly of martyrdom. It always—when about to enter a protest—very blandly informs the wild beast whose path it essays to stop, that its "bark is worse than its bite," and that it only means to save its manners by enacting its decent role of resistance. The only practical purpose which it now sub serves in American politics is to give enough exercise to Radicalism to keep it "in wind," and to prevent its becoming pursy and lazy from having nothing to whip. No doubt, after a few years, when women's suffrage shall have become an accomplished fact, conservatism will tacitly admit it into its creed, and thence forward plume itself upon its wise firmness in opposing with similar weapons the extreme of baby suffrage; and when that too shall have been won, it will be heard declaring that the integrity of the American Constitution requires at least the refusal of suffrage to asses. There it will assume, with great dignity, its final position.

Indeed, as De Tocqueville predicted, innovations in the direction of extensions of suffrage will always be successful in America, because of the selfish timidity of her public men. It is the nature of ultra democracy to make all its politicians time-servers; its natural spawn is the brood of narrow, truckling, cowardly worshippers of the vox populi, and of present expediency. Their polar star is always found in the answer to the question, "Which will be the more popular?" As soon as any agitation of this kind goes far enough to indicate a possibility of success, their resistance ends. Each of them begins to argue thus in his private mind: "The proposed revolution is of course preposterous, but it will be best for me to leave opposition to it to others. For if it

succeeds, the newly enfranchised will not fail to remember the opponents of their claim at future elections, and to reward those who were their friends in the hour of need." Again: it has now become a regular trick of American demagogues in power to manufacture new classes of voters to sustain them in office. It is presumed that the gratitude of the newly enfranchised will be sufficient to make them vote the ticket of their benefactors. But as gratitude is a very flimsy sort of fabric among Radicals, and soon worn threadbare, such a reliance only lasts a short time, and requires to be speedily replaced. The marvelous invention of negro suffrage (excogitated for this sole purpose) sufficed to give Radicalism a new four years' lease of life; but the grateful allegiance of the freedmen to their pretended liberators is waxing very thin; and hence the same expedient must be repeated, in the form of creating a few millions of female votes. The designing have an active, selfish motive for pushing the measure; but its opponents will without fail be paralyzed in their resistance by their wonted cowardice; so that success is sure.

This expectation is greatly confirmed by a review of the history of past innovations. They have all been carried against the better judgment of the class in the country to whom the Constitution committed the power of deciding for or against them. In 1829–1830, the State of Virginia took her first departure from the old principle of freeholders' suffrage. In 1851 she completed that revolution (as well as introduced sundry other Radical features) by extending the right to vote indiscriminately to all white males. In both instances it was hard to find a freeholder, not a demagogue, who could avow a hearty preference for the changes. They were carried against the convictions of the voters by the influences which have been above described. It is most probable that the same thing was true in every State which adopted universal suffrage. The coercive measures of the Federal Government were undoubtedly precipitated against the convictions of the majority of the Northern people. So the war was transmuted into an Abolition measure under the same circumstances. And last: negro suffrage was undoubtedly introduced against the better judgment of nearly all by the selfish arts of the demagogues; and as there was neither party nor statesman that had the nerve to head the almost universal opposition, the decision went by default. Nor will there be, under any future circumstances, either leader or party that will risk the odium of a movement to take away suffrage from the incompetent hands of the blacks, however clearly it may appear that they are using it for the ruin of themselves and the country. Thus it is the destiny of the Yankee people to commit a species of political Hari-kari with its own unwilling hands. The crowning element of despair is in the enforced consolidation of the Government. There are no reserved rights of States. The mad innovation which is adopted by a majority of them is enforced upon all; so that no place of refuge is left in the whole land where the right principles and usages might find sanctuary, and abide as a wholesome example and recuperative power for reform.

What then, in the next place, will be the effect of this fundamental change when it shall be established? The obvious answer is, that it will destroy Christianity and civilization in America. Some who see the mischievousness of the movement express the hope that it will, even if nominally successful, be kept within narrow limits by the very force of its own absurdity. They "reckon without their host." There is a Satanic ingenuity in these Radical measures which secures the infection of the reluctant dissentients as surely as of the hot advocates. The women now sensible and modest who heartily deprecate the whole folly, will be dragged into the vortex, with the assent of their now indignant husbands. The instruments of this deplorable result will be the (so-called) conservative candidates for office. They will effect it by this plea, that ignorant, impudent, Radical women will vote, and vote wrong; whence it becomes a necessity for the modest and virtuous women, for their country's sake, to sacrifice their repugnance and counterpoise these mischievous votes in the spirit of disinterested self-sacrifice. Now a woman can never resist an appeal to the principle of generous devotion; her glory is to crucify herself in the cause of duty and of zeal. This plea will be successful. But when the virtuous have once tasted the dangerous intoxication of political excitement and of power, even they will be absorbed; they will learn to do con amore what was first done as a painful duty, and all the baleful influences of political life will be diffused throughout the sex.

What those influences will be may be learned by every one who reverences the Christian Scriptures, from this fact, that the theory of "Women's Rights" is sheer infidelity. It directly impugns the authority and the justice of these Scriptures. They speak in no uncertain tones. "The husband is the head of the wife" (Eph. v. 23). "Wives, submit yourselves to your own husbands, as to the Lord" (v. 22). "The man is not for the woman, but the woman for the man" (I. Cor. ii. 9). "Let the woman learn in silence, with all subjection: but I suffer not a woman to teach, nor to usurp authority over the man, but to be in silence: for Adam was first formed, then Eve: and Adam was not deceived, but the woman being deceived was in the transgression" (I. Tim. ii: 11–14). They are to be "discreet, chaste, keepers at home, good, obedient to their own husbands," etc. (Titus ii. 5). How utterly opposed is all this to the leveling doctrine of your Radical. Women are here consigned to a social subordination, and expressly excluded from ruling offices, on grounds of their sex, and a divine ordination based by God upon a transaction which happened nearly six thousand years ago! The woman's sphere is expressly assigned her within her home, and she is taught that the assumption of publicity is an outrage against that nature with which she is endowed. Now the politics which denounce all this as a natural injustice and self-evident folly cannot be expected to reverence these Scriptures; they must and will flout their whole authority. We must then make up our minds in accepting Women's Rights to surrender our Bibles, and have an atheistic Government. And especially must we expect to have presiding over every home and rearing every group of future citizens, that most abhorrent of all phenomena, an infidel woman; for of course that sex, having received the precious boon of their enfranchisement only by means of the overthrow of the Bible, must be foremost in trampling upon this their old oppressor and enemy. Its restoration to authority is necessarily their "re-enslavement," to speak the language of their party.

Second: these new excitements and temptations will utterly corrupt the character and delicacy of American women. It is indignantly asked, "Why should politics corrupt the morals of women more than of the 'lords of creation'?" Suppose now we reply: American politics have corrupted the morals of the men? Suppose we argue that the retort is so true and just and the result has actually gone to so deplorable an extent, that were the female side of our social organization as corrupt as the male side has already become, American society would crumble into ruin by its own putrescence? It is better to save half the fabric than to lose all. And especially is it better to save the purity of the mothers who are, under God, to form the characters of our future citizens, and of the wives who are to restrain and elevate them, whatever else we endanger. Is it argued that since women are now confessedly purer than men, their entrance into politics must tend to purify politics? We reply again that the women of the present were reared and attained this comparative purity under the Bible system. Adopt the infidel plan, and we shall corrupt our women without purifying oar politics. What shall save us then?

But there is another reply to this retort. Political excitements will corrupt women tenfold more than men; and this, not because women are naturally inferior to men, but because they are naturally adapted to a wholly different sphere. When we point to the fact that they are naturally more emotional and less calculating, more impulsive and less self-contained, that they have a quicker tact but less logic, that their social nature makes them more liable to the contagion of epidemic passions, and that the duties of their sex make it physically impossible for them to acquire the knowledge in a foreign sphere necessary for political duties, we do not depreciate woman; we only say that nature has adapted her to one thing and disqualified her for the other. The violet would wither in that full glare of midsummer in which the sunflower thrives: this does not argue that the violet is the meaner flower. The vine, left to stand alone, would be hurled prone in the mire by the first blasts of that history. In the case of the Amorites there was also this wise wind which strengthens the grasp of the sturdy oak upon its bed: still the oak may yield no fruit so precious as the clusters of the vine. But the vine cannot be an oak; it must be itself, dependent, clinging, but more precious than that on which it leans or it must perish. When anything, animate or inanimate, is used for a function to which it is not adapted, that foreign use must endamage it, and the more the farther that function is from its own sphere. So it will be found (and it is no disparagement to woman to say it) that the very traits which fit her to be the angel of a virtuous home unfit her to meet the agitations of political life, even as

safely as does the more rugged man. The hot glare of publicity and passion will speedily deflower her delicacy and sweetness. Those temptations, which her Maker did not form her to bear, will debauch her heart, developing a character as much more repulsive than that of the debauched man as the fall has been greater. The politicating woman, unsexed and denaturalized, shorn of the true glory of her femininity, will appear to men as a feeble hybrid mannikin, with all the defects and none of the strength of the male. Instead of being the dear object of his chivalrous affection, she becomes his importunate rival, despised without being feared.

This suggests a third consequence, which some of the advocates of the movement even already are bold enough to foreshadow. "Women's Rights" mean the abolition of all permanent marriage ties. We are told that Mrs. Cady Stanton avowed this result, proclaiming it at the invitation of the Young Men's Christian Association of New York. She holds that woman's bondage is not truly dissolved until the marriage bond is annulled. She is thoroughly consistent. Some hoodwinked advocates of her revolution may be blind to the sequence; but it is inevitable. It must follow by this cause, if for no other, that the unsexed politicating woman can never inspire in man that, true affection on which marriage should be founded. Men will doubtless be still sensual; but it is simply impossible that they can desire them for the pure and sacred sphere of the wife. Let every woman ask herself: will she choose for the lord of her affections an unsexed effeminate man? No more can man be drawn to the masculine woman. The mutual attraction of the two complementary halves is gone forever.

The abolition of marriage would follow again by another cause. The divergent interests and the rival independence of the two equal wills would be irreconcilable with domestic government, or union, or peace. Shall the children of this monstrous no-union be held responsible to two variant coordinate and supreme wills at once? Heaven pity the children! Shall the two parties to this perpetual co-partnership have neither the power to secure the performance of the mutual duties nor to dissolve it? It is a self-contradiction, an impossible absurdity. Such a co-partnership of equals with independent interests must be separable at will, as all other such co-partnerships are. The only relation between the sexes which will remain will be a cohabitation continuing so long as the convenience or caprice of both parities may suggest; and this, with most, will amount to a vagrant concubinage.

But now, what will be the character of the children reared under such a domestic organization as this? If human experience has established anything at all, it is the truth of that principle announced by the Hebrew prophet when he declared that the great aim of God in ordaining a permanent marriage tie between one man and one woman was "that He might seek a godly seed." God's ordinance, the only effective human ordinance for checking and curbing the first tendencies to evil, is domestic, parental government. When the family shall no longer have a head, and the great foundation for the subordination of children in the mother's example is gone; when the mother shall have found another sphere than her home for her energies; when she shall have exchanged the sweet charities of domestic love and sympathy for the fierce passions of the hustings; when families shall be disrupted at the caprice of either party, and the children scattered as foundlings from their hearthstone—it requires no wisdom to see that a race of sons will be reared nearer akin to devils than to men. In the hands of such a bastard progeny, without discipline, without homes, without a God, the last remains of social order will speedily perish, and society will be overwhelmed in savage anarchy.

Last: it would not be hard to show, did space permit, that this movement on the part of these women is as suicidal as it is mischievous. Its certain result will be the re-enslavement of women, not under the Scriptural bonds of marriage, but under the yoke of literal corporeal force. The woman who will calmly review the condition of her sex in other ages and countries will feel that her wisdom is to "let well enough alone." Physically, the female is the "weaker vessel." This world is a hard and selfish scene where the weaker goes to the wall. Under all other civilizations and all other religions than ours woman has experienced this fate to the full; her condition has been that of a slave to the male—sometimes a petted slave, but yet a slave. In Christian and European society alone has she ever attained the place of man's social equal, and received the homage and honor due from magnanimity to her sex and her feebleness. And her enviable lot among us has resulted from two causes: the Christian religion and the legislation founded upon it by feudal chivalry. How insane then is it for her to spurn these two bulwarks of

defense, to defy and repudiate the divine authority of that Bible which has been her redemption, and to revolutionize the whole spirit of the English common law touching woman's sphere and rights? She is thus spurning the only protectors her sex has ever found, and provoking a contest in which she must inevitably be overwhelmed. Casting away that dependence and femininity which are her true strength, the "strong-minded woman" persists in thrusting herself into competition with man as his equal. But for contest she is not his equal; the male is the stronger animal. As man's rival, she is a pitiful inferior, a sorry she-mannikin. It is when she brings her wealth of affection, her self-devotion, her sympathy, her tact, her grace, her subtle intuition, her attractions, her appealing weakness, and places them in the scale with man's rugged strength and plodding endurance, with his steady logic, his hardihood and muscle, and his exemption from the disabling infirmities of her sex, that he delights to admit her full equality and to do glad homage to her as the crown of his kind. All this vantage-ground the "Women's Rights women" madly throw away, and provoke that collision for which nature itself has disqualified them. They insist upon taking precisely a man's chances; well, they will meet precisely the fate of a weak man among strong ones. A recent incident on a railroad train justly illustrates the result. A solitary female entered a car where every seat was occupied, and the conductor closed the door upon her and departed. She looked in vain for a seat, and at last appealed to an elderly man near her to know if he would not "surrender his seat to a lady." He, it seems, was somewhat a humorist, and answered: "I will surrender it cheerfully, Madam, as I always do, but will beg leave first to ask a civil question. Are you an advocate of the modern theory of women's rights?" Bridling up with intense energy, she replied, "Yes, sir, emphatically; I let you know that it is my glory to be devoted to that noble cause." "Very well, Madam," said he, "then the case is altered: You may stand up like the rest of us men, until you can get a seat for yourself." This was exact poetic justice; and it foreshadows precisely the fate of their unnatural pretensions. Men will treat them as they treat each other; it will be "every man for himself, and the devil take the hindmost." There will be of course a Semiramis or a Queen Bess here and there who will hold her own; but the general rule will be that the "weaker vessels" will succumb; and the society which will emerge from this experiment will present woman in the position which she has always held among savages, that of domestic drudge to the stronger animal. Instead of being what the Bible makes her, one with her husband, queen of his home, reigning with the gentle sceptre of love over her modest, secluded domain, and in its pure and sacred retirement performing the noblest work done on this earth, that of moulding infant minds to honor and piety, she will reappear from this ill-starred competition defeated and despised, tolerated only to satiate the passion, to amuse the idleness, to do the drudgery, and to receive the curses and blows of her barbarized masters.

Thus will be consummated that destiny to which so many gloomy prognostics point as the allotment of the North American continent: to be the accursed field for the final illustration of the harvest of perdition, grown from the seeding of the dragon's teeth of infidel Radicalism. God gave the people of this land great and magnificent blessings, and opportunities and responsibilities. They might and should have made it the glory of all lands. But they have betrayed their trust; they have abused every gift: above all have they insulted him by flaunting in his face an impudent, atheistic, God-defying theory of pretended human rights and human perfectibility which attempts to deny man's subordination,

his dependence, his fall and native depravity, his need of divine grace. It invites mankind to adopt material civilization and sensual advantage as their divinity. It assumes to be able to perfect man's condition by its political, literary, and mechanical skill, despising that Gospel of Christ which is man's only adequate remedy. It crowns its impiety by laying its defiling hands upon the very forms of that Christianity, while with the mock affection of a Judas it attempts to make it a captive to the sordid ends of Mammon and sense. Must not God be avenged on such a nation as this? His vengeance will be to give them the fruit of their own hands, and let them be filled with their own devices. He will set apart this fair land by a sort of dread consecration to the purpose of giving a lesson concerning this godless philosophy, so impressive as to instruct and warn all future generations. As the dull and pestilential waves of the Dead Sea have been to every subsequent age the memento of the sin of Sodom, so the dreary tides of anarchy and barbarism which will overwhelm the boastful devices of infidel democracy will be the caution of all future legislators. And thus "women's rights" will assist America "to fulfil her great mission," that of being the "scarecrow" of the nations.

Dabney, Robert L. *Discussions, Philosophical.* Vol. IV. Reprint edition (first published in 1897). Harrisonburg, VA: Sprinkle Publications, 1984. 489–505.

Queen Victoria
1837 A.D.

1. **Queen Victoria** ascended the throne, June 20, **1837**, in the nineteenth year of her age. Her Majesty is the daughter of the late Duke of Kent, who was the brother of William IV, and fourth son of George III. She was born at Kensington Palace, May 24 **1819**, and crowned at Westminster in 1838.

In **1840** Her Majesty married her cousin, Albert of Saxe-Coburg-Gotha. She had three sons, Albert Edward Prince of Wales, Alfred, and Arthur; and four daughters, Victoria the Princess-Royal, Helena, Louisa, and Beatrice. One son. Leopold, and one daughter Alice, have died.

2. At the Queen's accession **Hanover** became a separate kingdom, as, by Salie law, no woman could wear that crown; and Ernest, Duke of Cumberland, fifth son of George III, became its king.

Between the years **1839** and **1849** a war raged in Afghanistan, Sinde, and Punjaub, by which a vast extent of territory was added to our Indian Empire.

War also broke out between Turkey and Egypt, which greatly interfered with our Black Sea trade; and the Sultan having asked aid of Britain, a fleet was sent to his assistance, which bombarded the strong town of **Acre**, in Syria, and brought the Pacha of Egypt to terms, and the war to a close in **1840**.

3. In the same year a dispute with **China** about the importation of opium, a drug which the Chinese love to smoke and chew. The emperor, wishing to put an end to this dangerous habit, ordered that none should be imported; and seized and destroyed many cargoes which our merchants tried to smuggle into the Chinese ports from India, where it is cultivated. He also imprisoned several British subjects.

War was declared. British troops captured several large towns, and compelled the Chinese to open four ports to our trade, to pay a large sum of money, and to give up the island of Hong Kong, which has ever since belonged to Britain.

4. The year **1846** is memorable for the **Repeal** of the **Corn Laws**. High duties had been charged on all corn imported from abroad. This made bread dear; and Richard Cobden proposed that the duties should be removed. The farmers called loudly for protection; but through the eloquent speeches of Mr. Cobden in Parliament and of Sir Robert Peel, who joined him, the cause of Free Trade triumphed; and the duty on wheat was fixed at a shilling per quarter.

5. The year **1848** was a very stormy one throughout Europe. A third Revolution took place in France. King Louis-Philippe escaped to England, and France was once more a Republic. Louis Napoleon was chosen resident, and afterwards emperor—a dignity he retained until **1876**.

In England, the Chartists raised great riots, and, with Feargus O'Connor at their head, caused much excitement through the nation. A Rising also took place in Ireland under Smith O'Brien and others. The leaders were taken and condemned to death; but the sentence was changed to transportation.

6. In **1851** the **Great Exhibition** was built in Hyde Park, from designs by Sir Joseph Paxton. The grand idea of International Exhibitions was first stated by Prince Albert. This exhibition was opened by Her Majesty and Prince Albert, May 1, **1851**, and closed in October. The building was afterwards taken down and rebuilt in Sydenham. It is now known as the Crystal Palace.

7. In **1854** war was declared by England and France against Russia, in defense of the Sultan of Turkey, whose land had been invaded and his provinces north of the Danube seized by the Russian army. The Turks had, by a number of gallant efforts driven the Russians back, when 5,000 Turks were massacred by the Russian fleet at Sinope.

The English and French fleets then sailed to the Black Sea, bombarded Odessa, blew up the powder magazines, and captured thirteen ships laden with war stores. The Russians besieged Silistria, a Turkish town on the Danube; but failed to take it, and lost 30,000 men in the attempt.

8. The Allies now invaded **Crimea**; and a battle was fought on the banks of the little river **Alma**, in which they gained a great victory over the Russians. They then laid siege to **Sebastopol**, the great Russian stronghold on the Black Sea. During the siege the Russians made a desperate attack on the Allies in the valley of **Balaklava**, but without success, though they gained some advantages; and very shortly followed the terrible and bloody battle of **Inkermann**, which lasted twelve hours, and which 8000 English and 6000 French defeated 50,000 Russians.

Lord Raglan having died, General Simpson took the command of the British forces; and he was soon succeeded by Sir W. Codrington.

The next battle was fought in the valley of **Tchernaya**, in the summer of **1855**. The Sardinians, who had joined the allies with an army of 15,000 men, were attacked by the Russians in great force; but, being assisted by the French, repulsed them with great slaughter. The Russians left 3000 men dead on the field.

9. Meanwhile the siege of Sebastopol had been slowly by surely carried on; and now the final bombardment began. Day after day shot and shell were poured into the town from the batteries of the allied armies, setting fire to buildings, blowing up powder-magazines, and slaughtering the enemy to the number of a thousand per day; until one night, under cover of darkness, the Russian general, Prince Gortschakoff, drew off his troops in fine order, set the town on fire, destroyed the bridge across the river, and sunk all the vessels of war in the harbour. The allied armies took possession of the town the next day, but found little else than a heap of blackened ruins.

It is said that during this terrible siege, which lasted nearly a year, there fell, of Russians,

English, French, and Sardinians, no fewer than 100,000 men. The fleets also did their part in the war, by bombarding several Russian forts on the Baltic and Black Seas. Russia now sought for peace; and a treaty was signed at Paris in **1856**.

10. In **1857** the British rule in India was almost overturned by a general **Mutiny** which broke our in Bengal amongst the Sepoys, our native soldiers—great numbers of whom are trained and employed by Great Britain for the protection of the East Indian Empire. These, at a given signal, rose in revolt, overpowered the British troops, took possession of Delhi and other places, and at Cawnpore savagely murdered great numbers of English gentlemen, ladies, and children, after treating them in a most brutal manner.

The rebels were, however, after a long and desperate struggle, brought to submission by the brave and good Sir Henry Havelock, and Sir Colin Campbell, afterwards Lord Clyde. Havelock lost his life in the conflict. The government of India has been brought under the Crown; and the East India Company is no more.

11. In **1859** Lord Palmerston was made Premier, and fears of invasion were set at rest by the enrollment of **Rifle Volunteers**—a movement by which England has been put into a state of defense unknown in former years.

The year **1861** was a year of mourning and sadness on account of the death of the **Prince Consort**, "Albert the Good." Never in the history of our nation has the death of a royal prince caused such deep and universal grief.

12. The **Fenian** Conspiracy in Ireland assumed serious dimensions in **1865**, and in **1866** the Habeas Corpus Act was suspended in that island.

13. In **1867** a new **Reform Bill** was passed, under a Tory ministry, Mr. Disraeli being Premier. This Bill greatly increased the number of voters, enfranchised certain towns of greater population, and disfranchised others of less. Six members were added to the representatives of Scotland.

14. In **1867** a British army was sent from India for the invasion of Abyssinia, and the release of a number of English captives whom Theodore, king of that country, refused to give up. The expedition was successful. The town of Magdala was besieged and taken (April 13, **1868**), and the prisoners released. The king shot himself. Sir Robert Napier, the commander of the expedition, was rewarded with the title of Lord Napier of Magdala.

15. In the end of **1868** Mr. Disraeli resigned during the recess, when he saw that his appeal to the country left him in the minority. He was succeeded by Mr. Gladstone, with Lord Granville as foreign Secretary and leader of the House of Lords.

The session following (**1869**) was occupied with a measure for the disestablishment and disendowment of the **Irish Church**, which ceased to exist as a State Church on 1st January **1871**.

The **Irish Land Act**, putting the relations of landlord and tenant on a more satisfactory basis, was passed in **1870**. The same year produced an **Elementary Education Act** for England and Wales.

In the end of **1871** the **Prince of Wales** passed through the crisis of an almost fatal fever, which caused intense anxiety to the nation, and called forth many demonstrations of loyalty. In March following, the Queen, accompanied by the Prince and Princess of Wales, attended a public **Thanksgiving Service** at St. Paul's Cathedral.

In **1872**, **Vote** by **Ballot** in parliamentary elections was introduced experimentally for a period of eight years; and an Act was passed providing a system of **National Education** in Scotland. The Ballot Act was renewed in **1880**.

16. The **Ashantees**, near the west coast of Africa, interfered with other tribes in their trade with Great Britain. In **1874**, a small army was sent to Ashantee, under Sir Garnet Wolseley. The natives were defeated; Coomassie, their capital, was burned to the ground; and their king was glad to make peace, and to promise all that the British required.

Early in **1874** Mr. Gladstone suddenly dissolved Parliament. A Conservative majority was returned, and Mr. Disraeli again became Prime Minister.

17. The Eastern question was reopened by a new war between **Russia** and **Turkey** in **1877**, in which Turkey was beaten. In June 1878 a convention or defensive alliance, between Great Britain and Turkey was signed at Constantinople. The other Powers did not interfere till the war was concluded. Then they met at Berlin and made a treaty of peace. On this occasion Russia was the gainer, and Turkey had to give up several large Provinces (July).

18. A new **Afghan War** then commenced (**1878**). The Indian Government was alarmed

because the ruler of Afghanistan seemed to favour the Russians more than the British. A British army marched into the country from India and took Cabul, the capital. After peace had been made, the English Envoy, Sir Louis Cavignari, was cruelly murdered, and the fighting began again.

But the English people did not approve of the war. Lord Beaconsfield (Mr. Disraeli) appealed to the country, which declared for the Liberals, and Mr. Gladstone returned to power (**1880**). The Afghan War was then as soon as possible brought to an end (**1881**).

19. In **1878** a war broke out in South Africa between the English and the Zulus, whose king had refused to disarm his soldiers. The English suffered terribly in the battle of Isandlhana; but in the end they were victorious, and the Zulu king was taken prisoner.

A year or two later the colonists of Transvaal, in South Africa, revolted and set up a Free State (**1880**). This led to another war, in which the colonists gained some successes; but they submitted to Great Britain, after being promised the right to govern themselves under British control.

20. More recently the affairs of **Egypt** have given England a great deal of trouble. A military revolt in **1882**, headed by Arabi Pasha, overthrew the Government. The British stepped in to restore order. The fleet, under Admiral Seymour, destroyed the forts at Alexandria; the army, under Sir Garnet Wolseley, gained a great victory at Tel-el-Kebir. The Khedive, or ruler of Egypt, was then restored to his throne.

21. Then a revolt of the native tribes in **Soudan** caused a fresh disturbance. The revolt was headed by a fanatical chief who called himself Mahdi; and its avowed object was to drive the Egyptians out of the Soudan.

Osman Digna, one of Mahdi's lieutenants, occupied the Nubian Desert north of Abyssinia, and the coast of the Red Sea. A British force, under General Sir Gernard Graham, was detached to Suakim, to protect the Red Sea coast, and to relieve the Egyptian garrisons at Tokar and other places. The British succeeded in relieving Tokar, and in breaking up the native force for the time (**1884**). . . .

30. A new **Penny Postage** was adopted, chiefly through the efforts of Rowland Hill, in **1840**. Great distress in Ireland arose from the potato disease in **1845**, which by death and emigration lessened the population by nearly two million. A Submarine Telegraph was laid from Dover to Calais in **1851**. In **1852** the renowned Duke of Ellington died, and was buried in St. Paul's Cathedral, where the great Nelson also lies. A Bill for the admission of Jews into Parliament was passed in 1858, when Baron Rothschild took his seat as member for London. A treaty of Commerce between England and France was arranged by the Emperor Napoleon and Mr. Cobden in **1860**. His Royal Highness the Prince of Wales married the Princess Alexandra of Denmark in 1863. In **1866** the great design of uniting Europe and America by a **Submarine Telegraph Cable** was successfully completed, two previous attempts (**1858** and **1865**) having proved failures.

Royal Reader. No. VI. London: Thomas Nelson and Sons, 1891. pp 360–365.

The Mayflowers
By John Greenleaf Whittier

The trailing arbutus, or mayflower, grows abun-
dantly in the vicinity of Plymouth and was the
first flower that greeted the Pilgrims after their
fearful winter. The name "mayflower" was famil-
iar in England, as the application of it to the
historic vessel shows, but it was applied by the
English, and still is, to the hawthorn. Its use in
New England in connection with Epigaea repens
dates from a very early day, some claiming that
the first Pilgrims so used it, in affectionate memory
of the vessel and its English flower association.

Sad Mayflower! watched by winter stars,
And nursed by winter gales,
With petals of the sleeted spars,
And leaves of frozen sails!

What had she in those dreary hours,
Within her ice-rimmed bay,
In common with the wild-wood flowers,
The first sweet smiles of May?

Yet, "God be praised!" the Pilgrim said,
Who saw the blossoms peer
Above the brown leaves, dry and dead,
"Behold our Mayflower here!"

"God wills it: here our rest shall be,
Our years of wandering o'er;
For us the Mayflower of the sea
Shall spread her sails no more."

O sacred flowers of faith and hope,
As sweetly now as then
Ye bloom on many a birchen slope,
In many a pine-dark glen.

Behind the sea-wall's rugged length,
Unchanged, your, leaves unfold
Like love behind the manly strength
Of the brave hearts of old.

So live the fathers in their sons,
Their sturdy faith be ours,
And ours the love that overruns
Its rocky strength with flowers.

The Pilgrim's wild and wintry day
Its shadow round us draws;
The Mayflower of his stormy bay,
Our Freedom's struggling cause.

But warmer suns erelong shall bring
To life the frozen sod;
And through dead leaves of hope shall spring
Afresh the flowers of God!

A Practical Exposition Upon Psalm CXXX
By John Owen
(excerpted from the book of the same title)

Verse 1. Out of the depths have I cried unto thee, O LORD.

2. Lord, hear my voice; let thine ears be attentive to the voice of my supplications.

3. If thou, LORD, shouldest mark iniquities, O Lord, who shall stand

4. But there is forgiveness with thee, that thou mayest be feared.

5. I wait for the LORD, my soul doth wait, and in his word do I hope.

6. My soul *waiteth* for the Lord more than they that watch for the morning: *I say, more than* they that watch for the morning.

7. Let Israel hope in the Lord: for with the LORD *there* is mercy, and with him *is* plenteous redemption.

8. And he shall redeem Israel from all his iniquities.

A Paraphrase
Verses 1, 2—O Lord, through my manifold sins and provocations, I have brought myself into great distresses. Mine iniquities are always before me, and I am ready to be overwhelmed with them, as with a flood of waters; for they have brought me into depths, wherein I am ready to be swallowed up. But yet, although my distress be great and perplexing, I do not, I dare not, utterly despond and cast away all hopes of relief or recovery. Nor do I seek unto any other remedy, way, or means of relief; but I apply

myself to thee, Jehovah, to thee alone. And in this my application unto thee, the greatness and urgency of my troubles makes my soul urgent, earnest, and pressing in my supplications. Whilst I have no rest, I can give thee no rest. Oh, therefore, attend and hearken unto the voice of my crying and supplications!

Verse 3—It is true, O Lord, thou God great and terrible, that if thou shouldst deal with me in this condition, with any man living, with the best of thy saints, according to the strict and exact tenor of the law, which first represents itself to my guilty conscience and troubled soul; if thou shouldst take notice of, observe, and keep in remembrance, mine, or their, or the iniquity of any one, to the end that thou mightst deal with them, and recompense unto them according to the sentence thereof, there would be, neither for me nor them, any the least expectation of deliverance. All flesh must fail before thee, and the spirits which thou hast made, and that to eternity; for who could stand before thee when thou shouldst so execute thy displeasure?

Verse 4—But, O Lord, this is not absolutely and universally the state of things between thy Majesty and poor sinners; thou art in thy nature infinitely good and gracious, ready and free in the purposes of thy will to receive them. And there is such a blessed way made for the exercise of the holy inclinations and purposes of thy heart towards them, in the mediation and blood of thy dear Son, that they have assured foundations of concluding and believing that there is pardon and forgiveness with thee for them, and which, in the way of thine appointments, they may be partakers of. This way, therefore, will I, with all that fear thee, persist in. I will not give over, leave thee, or turn from thee, through my fears, discouragements, and despondencies; but will abide constantly in the observation of the worship which thou hast prescribed, and the performance of the obedience which thou dost require, having great encouragements so to do.

Verse 5—And herein, upon the account of the forgiveness that is with thee, O Lord, do I wait with all patience, quietness, and perseverance. In this work is my whole soul engaged, even in an earnest expectation of thy approach unto me in a way of grace and mercy. And for my encouragement therein hast thou given out unto me a blessed word of grace, a faithful word of promise, whereon my hope is fixed.

Verse 6—Yea, in the performance and discharge of this duty, my soul is intent upon thee, and in its whole frame turned towards thee, and that with such diligence and watchfulness in looking out after every way and means of thy appearance, of the manifestation of thyself, and coming unto me, that I excel therein those who, with longing desire, heedfulness, and earnest expectation, do wait and watch for the appearance of the morning; and that either that they may rest from their night watches, or have light for the duties of thy worship in the temple, which they are most delighted in.

Verses 7, 8—Herein have I found that rest, peace, and satisfaction unto my own soul, that I cannot but invite and encourage others in the like condition to take the same course with me. Let, then, all the Israel of God, all that fear him, learn this of me, and from my experience. Be not hasty in your distresses, despond not, despair not, turn not aside unto other remedies; but hope in the Lord: for I can now, in an especial manner, give testimony unto this, that there is mercy with him suited unto your relief. Yea, whatever your distress be, the redemption that is with him is so bounteous, plenteous, and unsearchable, that the undoubted issue of your performance of this duty will be, that you shall be delivered from the guilt of all your sins and the perplexities of all your troubles.

General Scope of the Whole Psalm

The design of the Holy Ghost in this psalm is to express, in the *experience* of the psalmist and the working of his faith, the state and condition of a soul greatly in itself perplexed, relieved on the account of grace, and acting itself towards God and his saints suitably to the discovery of that grace unto him—a great design, and full of great instruction.

And this general prospect gives us the parts and scope of the whole psalm; for we have—

I. *The state and condition of the soul* therein represented, with his deportment in and under that state and condition, in verses 1, 2:

"Out of the depths have I cried unto thee, O LORD. Lord, hear my voice; let thine ears be attentive to the voice of my supplications."

II. *His inquiry after relief* and therein are two things that present themselves unto him; the one whereof, which first offers the consideration of itself to him in his distress, he deprecates, verse 3:

"If thou, LORD, shouldest mark iniquities, O

Lord, who shall stand?"

The other he *closeth withal,* and finds relief in it and supportment by it, verse 4:

"But there is forgiveness with thee, that thou mayest be feared."

Upon this, his discovery and fixing on relief, there is the acting of his faith and the deportment of his whole person:

1. Towards God, verses 5, 6:

"I wait for the LORD, my soul doth wait, and in his word do I hope. My soul waiteth for the Lord more than they that watch for the morning: I say, more than they that watch for the morning."

2. Towards the saints, verses 7, 8:

"Let Israel hope in the LORD: for with the LORD there is mercy, and with him is plenteous redemption. And he shall redeem Israel from all his iniquities."

All which parts, and the various concernments of them, must be opened severally.

And this also gives an account of what is my design from and upon the words of this psalm— namely, to declare the perplexed entanglements which may befall a gracious soul, such a one as this psalmist was, with the nature and proper workings of faith in such a condition; principally aiming at what it is that gives a soul relief and supportment in, and afterward deliverance from, such a perplexed estate.

The Lord in mercy disposes of these meditations in such a way and manner as that both he that writes and they that read may be made partakers of the benefit, relief, and consolation intended for his saints in this psalm by the Holy Ghost!

The state and condition of the soul represented in the psalm—the two first verses opened.

The state and condition of the soul here represented as the *basis* on which the process of the psalm is built, with its deportment, or the general acting of its faith in that state, is expressed in the two first verses:

"Out of the depths have I cried unto thee, O LORD. Lord, hear my voice: let thine ears be attentive to the voice of my supplications."

I. *The present state of the soul* under consideration is included in that expression, "Out of the depths."

Some of the ancients, as Chrysostom, suppose this expression to relate unto the depths of the *heart* of the psalmist: [—GREEK—] not from the mouth or tongue only, [—GREEK—]

[—GREEK—], "but from the depth and bottom of the heart;" [—GREEK—] [—GREEK—], "from the deepest recesses of the mind."

And, indeed, the word is used to express the depths of the hearts of men, but utterly in another sense: Ps lxiv. 6, "The heart is deep."

But the obvious sense of the place, and the constant use of the word, will not admit of this interpretation: "E profundis"; from P [—HEBREW—], "profundus fuit," is [—HEBREW—] in the plural number, "profunditates," or "*depths.*" It is commonly used for valleys, or any deep places whatever, but especially of waters. Valleys and deep places, because of their darkness and solitariness, are accounted places of horror, helplessness, and trouble: Ps. xxiii. 4, "Though I walk through the valley of the shadow of death"; that is, in the extremity of danger and trouble.

The moral use of the word, as expressing the state and condition of the souls of men, is metaphorical. These depths, then, are difficulties or pressures, attended with fear, horror, danger, and trouble. And they are of two sorts:

1. *Providential,* in respect of outward distresses, calamities, and afflictions: Ps. lxix. 1, 2, "Save me, O God; for the waters axe come in unto my soul. I stick in the mire of the deep, and there is no standing. I am come, [—HEBREW—], into the depths of waters, and the flood overflows me." It is trouble, and the extremity of it, that the psalmist complains of, and which he thus expresseth. He was brought by it into a condition like unto a man ready to be drowned, being cast into the bottom of deep and miry waters, where be had no firm foundation to stand upon, nor ability to come out; as he farther explains himself, verse 15.

2. There are *internal depths*—depths of conscience upon the account of sin: Ps. lxxxviii. 6, "Thou hast laid me in the lowest pit, in darkness, in the deeps." What he intends by this expression, the psalmist declares in the next words, verse 7, "Thy wrath lieth hard upon me." Sense of God's wrath upon his conscience upon the account of sin, was the deep he was cast into. So, verse 15, speaking of the same matter, saith he, "I suffer thy terrors;" and verse 16, "Thy fierce wrath goeth over me;" which he calls water, waves, and deeps, according to the metaphor before opened.

And these are the deeps that are here principally intended. "Clamat sub molibus et fiuctibus iniquitatem suaxum," says Austin on the place—"He cries out under the weight and waves of his sins."

This the ensuing psalm makes evident. Desiring to be delivered from these depths out of which he cried, he deals with God wholly about mercy and forgiveness; and it is sin done from which forgiveness is a deliverance. The doctrine, also, that he preacheth upon his delivery is that of mercy, grace, and redemption, as is manifest from the close of the psalm; and what we have deliverance by is most upon our hearts when we are delivered.

It is true, indeed, that these deeps do oftentimes concur; as David speaks, "Deep calleth unto deep," Ps. xlii. 7. The **deeps of affliction** awaken the conscience to a deep sense of sin. But sin is the disease, affliction only a symptom of it: and in attending a cure, the *disease* itself is principally to be heeded; the *symptom* will follow or depart of itself.

Many interpreters think that this was now David's condition. By great trouble and distress he was greatly minded of sin; and we must not, therefore, wholly pass over that intendment of the word, though we are chiefly to respect that which he himself, in this address unto God, did principally regard.

This, in general, is the state and condition of the soul managed in this psalm, and is as the key to the ensuing discourse, or the hinge on which it turns. As to my intendment from the psalm, that which ariseth from hence may be comprised in these two propositions:

1. *Gracious souls, after much communion with God, may be brought into inextricable depths and entanglements on the account of sin;* for such the psalmist here expresseth his own condition to have been, and such he was,

2. *The inward root of outward distresses is principally to be attended in all pressing trials; sin, in afflictions.*

If you would like to read the remainder of this work by John Owen, the complete document can be found at the Web site of the Center for Reformed Theology and Apologetics, <http://www.reformed.org/books/owen/vol6/ owen_v6_ps130_v1-2.html>.

Owen, John. *A Practical Exposition Upon Psalm CXXX: The Works of John Owen.* Vol. VI. Ed. William H. Goold. Edinburgh: Banner of Truth Trust, 1967.

Teas and Other Afternoon Parties
By Emily Post

Teas

Except at a wedding, the function strictly understood by the word "reception" went out of fashion, in New York at least, during the reign of Queen Victoria, and its survivor is a public or semi-public affair presided over by a committee, and is a serious, rather than a merely social event.

The very word "reception" brings to mind an aggregation of personages, very formal, very dressed up, very pompous, and very learned, among whom the ordinary mortal can not do other than wander helplessly in the labyrinth of the specialist's jargon. Art critics on a varnishing day reception, are sure to dwell on the effect of a new technique, and the comment of most of us, to whom a painting ought to look like a "picture," is fatal. Equally fatal to meet an explorer and not know where or what he explored; or to meet a celebrated author and not have the least idea whether he wrote detective stories or expounded Taoism. On the other hand it is certainly discouraging after studying up on the latest Cretan excavations in order to talk intelligently to Professor Diggs, to be pigeon-holed for the afternoon beside Mrs. Newmother whose interest in discovery is limited to "a new tooth in baby's head."

Yet the difference between a reception and a tea is one of atmosphere only, like the difference in furnishing twin houses. One is enveloped in the heavy gloom of the mid-Victorian period, the other is light and alluring in the fashion of to-day. A "tea," even though it be formal, is nevertheless friendly and inviting. One does not go in "church" clothes nor with ceremonious manner; but in an informal and every-day spirit, to see one's friends and be seen by them.

The Afternoon Tea with Dancing

The afternoon tea with dancing is usually given to "bring out" a daughter, or to present a new daughter-in-law. The invitations are the same whether one hundred or two thousand are sent out. For instance:

Mrs. Grantham Jones

Miss Muriel Jones

will be at home

on Tuesday, the third of December

from four until seven o'clock

The Fitz-Cherry

Dancing

As invitations to formal teas of this sort are sent to the hostess' "general" visiting list, and very big houses are comparatively few, a ball-room is nearly always engaged at a hotel. Many hotels have a big and a small ballroom, and unless one's acquaintance is enormous the smaller room is preferable.

Too much space for too few people gives an effect of emptiness which always is suggestive of failure; also one must not forget that an undecorated room needs more people to make it look "trimmed" than one in which the floral decoration is lavish. On the other hand, a "crush" is very disagreeable, even though it always gives the effect of "success."

The arrangements are not as elaborate as for a ball. At most a screen of palms behind which the musicians sit (unless they sit in a gallery), perhaps a few festoons of green here and there, and the débutante's own flowers banked on tables where she stands to receive, form as much decoration as is ever attempted.

Whether in a public ballroom or a private drawing-room, the curtains over the windows are drawn and the lights lighted as if for a ball in the evening. If the tea is at a private house there is no awning unless it rains, but there is a chauffeur or coachman at the curb to open motor doors, and a butler, or caterer's man, to open the door of the house before any one has time to ring.

Guests as they arrive are announced either by the hostess' own butler or a caterer's "announcer." The hostess receives everyone as at a ball; if she and her daughter are for the moment standing alone, the new arrival, if a friend, stands talking with them until a newer arrival takes his or her place. After "receiving" with her mother or mother-in-law for an hour or so, as soon as the crowd thins a little, the débutante or bride may be allowed to dance.

The younger people, as soon as they have shaken hands with the hostess, dance. The older ones sit about, or talk to friends or take tea.

At a formal tea, the tea-table is exactly like that at a wedding reception, in that it is a large table set as a buffet, and is always in charge of the caterer's men, or the hostess' own butler or waitress and assistants. It is never presided over by deputy hostesses.

The Menu is Limited

Only tea, bouillon, chocolate, bread and cakes are served. There can be all sorts of sandwiches, hot biscuits, crumpets, muffins, sliced cake and little cakes in every variety that a cook or caterer can devise—whatever can come under the head of "bread and cake" is admissible; but nothing else, or it becomes a "reception," and not a "tea." At the end of the table or on a separate table near by, there are bowls or pitchers of orangeade or lemonade or "punch" (meaning in these days something cold that has fruit juice in it) for the dancers, exactly as at a ball.

Guests go to the table and help themselves to their own selection of bread and cakes. The chocolate, already poured into cups and with whipped cream on top, is passed on a tray by a servant. Tea also poured into cups, not mixed but accompanied by a small pitcher of cream, bowl of sugar, and dish of lemon, is also passed on a tray. A guest taking her plate of food in one hand and her tea or chocolate in the other, finds herself a chair somewhere, if possible, near a table, so that she can take her tea without discomfort.

Afternoon Teas without Dancing

Afternoon teas without dancing are given in honor of visiting celebrities or new neighbors or engaged couples, or to "warm" a new house; or, most often, for a house-guest from another city.

The invitation is a visiting card of the hostess with "to meet Mrs. So-and-So" across the top of it and "Jan. 10, Tea at 4 o'clock" in the lower corner, opposite the address.

At a tea of this description, tea and chocolate may be passed on trays or poured by two ladies, as will be explained below.

Unless the person for whom the tea is given is

such a celebrity that the "tea" becomes a "reception," the hostess does not stand at the door, but merely near it so that anyone coming in may easily find her. The ordinary afternoon tea given for one reason or another is, in winter, merely and literally, being at home on a specified afternoon with the blinds and curtains drawn, the room lighted as at night, a fire burning and a large tea-table spread in the dining-room or a small one near the hearth. An afternoon tea in summer is the same, except that artificial light is never used, and the table is most often on a veranda.

"Do Come in For a Cup Of Tea"

This is Best Society's favorite form of invitation. It is used on nearly every occasion whether there is to be music or a distinguished visitor, or whether a hostess has merely an inclination to see her friends. She writes on her personal visiting card: "Do come in on Friday for a cup of tea and hear Ellwin play, or Farrish sing, or to meet Senator West, or Lady X." Or even more informally: "I have not seen you for so long."

Invitations to a tea of this description are never "general." A hostess asks either none but close friends, or at most her "dining" list; sometimes this sort of a "tea" is so small that she sits behind her own tea-table—exactly as she does every afternoon.

But if the tea is of any size, from twenty upwards, the table is set in the dining-room and two intimate friends of the hostess "pour" tea at one end, and chocolate at the other. The ladies who "pour" are always especially invited beforehand and always wear afternoon dresses, with hats, of course, as distinguished from the street clothes of other guests. As soon as a hostess decides to give a tea, she selects two friends for this duty who are, in her opinion, decorative in appearance and also who (this is very important) can be counted on for gracious manners to everyone and under all circumstances.

It does not matter if a guest going into the dining-room for a cup of tea or chocolate does not know the deputy hostesses who are "pouring." It is perfectly correct for a stranger to say "May I have a cup of tea?"

The one pouring should answer very responsively, "Certainly! How do you like it? Strong or weak?"

If the latter, she deluges it with hot water, and again watching for the guest's negative or approval, adds cream or lemon or sugar. Or, preferring chocolate, the guest perhaps goes to the other end of the table and asks for a cup of chocolate. The table hostess at that end also says "Certainly," and pours out chocolate. If she is surrounded with people, she smiles as she hands it out, and that is all. But if she is unoccupied and her momentary "guest by courtesy" is alone, it is merest good manners on her part to make a few pleasant remarks. Very likely when asked for chocolate she says: "How nice of you! I have been feeling very neglected at my end. Everyone seems to prefer tea." Whereupon the guest ventures that people are afraid of chocolate because it is so fattening or so hot. After an observation or two about the weather, or the beauty of the china or how good the little cakes look, or the sandwiches taste, the guest finishes her chocolate.

If the table hostess is still unoccupied the guest smiles and slightly nods "Good-by," but if the other's attention has been called upon by someone else, she who has finished her chocolate, leaves unnoticed.

If another lady coming into the dining-room is an acquaintance of one of the table hostesses, the new visitor draws up a chair, if there is room, and drinks her tea or chocolate at the table. But as soon as she has finished, she should give her place up to a newer arrival. Or perhaps a friend appears, and the two take their tea together over in another part of the room, or at vacant places farther down the table. The tea-table is not set with places; but at a table where ladies are pouring, and especially at a tea that is informal, a number of chairs are usually ready to be drawn up for those who like to take their tea at the table.

In many cities, strangers who find themselves together in the house of a friend in common, always talk. In New York smart people always do at dinners or luncheons, but never at a general entertainment. Their cordiality to a stranger would depend largely upon the informal, or intimate, quality of the tea party; it would depend on who the stranger might be, and who the New Yorker. Mrs. Worldly would never dream of speaking to anyone—no matter whom—if it could be avoided. Mrs. Kindhart on the other hand, talks to everyone, everywhere and always. Mrs. Kindhart's position is as good as Mrs. Worldly's every bit, but perhaps she can be more relaxed; not being the conspicuous hostess that Mrs. Worldly is, she is not so besieged by position-makers and invitation-seekers. Perhaps Mrs. Worldly, finding that nearly every one who approaches her wants something, has come instinctively to avoid each new approach.

The Every-Day Afternoon Tea Table

The every-day afternoon tea table is familiar to everyone; there is not the slightest difference in its service whether in the tiny bandbox house of the newest bride, or in the drawing-room of Mrs. Worldly of Great Estates, except that in the little house the tray is brought in by a woman—often a picture in appearance and appointment—instead of a butler with one or two footmen in his wake. In either case a table is placed in front of the hostess. A tea-table is usually of the drop-leaf variety because it is more easily moved than a solid one. There are really no "correct" dimensions; any small table is suitable. It ought not to be so high that the hostess seems submerged behind it, nor so small as to be overhung by the tea tray and easily knocked over. It is usually between 24 and 26 inches wide and from 27 to 36 inches long, or it may be oval or oblong. A double-decked table that has its second deck above the main table is not good because the tea tray perched on the upper deck is neither graceful nor convenient. In proper serving, not only of tea but of cold drinks of all sorts, even where a quantity of bottles, pitchers and glasses need space, everything should be brought on a tray and not trundled in on a tea-wagon!

A cloth must always be first placed on the table, before putting down the tray. The tea cloth may be a yard, a yard and a half, or two yards square. It may barely cover the table, or it may hang half a yard over each edge. A yard and a quarter is the average size. A tea cloth can be colored, but the conventional one is of white linen, with little or much white needlework or lace, or both.

On this is put a tray big enough to hold everything except the plates of food. The tray may be a massive silver one that requires a footman with strong arms to lift it, or it may be of Sheffield or merely of effectively lacquered tin. In any case, on it should be: a kettle which ought to be already boiling, with a spirit lamp under it, an empty teapot, a caddy of tea, a tea strainer and slop bowl, cream pitcher and sugar bowl, and, on a glass dish, lemon in slices. A pile of cups and saucers and a stack of little tea plates, all to match, with a napkin (about 12 inches square, hem-stitched or edged to match the tea cloth) folded on each of the plates, like the filling of a layer cake, complete the paraphernalia.

Each plate is lifted off with its own napkin. Then on the tea-table, back of the tray, or on the shelves of a separate "curate," a stand made of three small shelves, each just big enough for one good-sized plate, are always two, usually three, varieties of cake and hot breads.

Things People Eat at Tea

The top dish on the "curate" should be a covered one, and holds hot bread of some sort; the two lower dishes may be covered or not, according to whether the additional food is hot or cold; the second dish usually holds sandwiches, and the third cake. Or perhaps all the dishes hold cake; little fancy cakes for instance, and pastries and slices of layer cakes. Many prefer a simpler diet, and have bread and butter, or toasted crackers, supplemented by plain cookies. Others pile the "curate" until it literally staggers, under pastries and cream cakes and sandwiches of pâté de foie gras or mayonnaise. Others, again, like marmalade, or jam, or honey on bread and butter or on buttered toast or muffins. This necessitates little butter knives and a dish of jam added to the already overloaded tea tray.

Selection of afternoon tea food is entirely a matter of whim, and new food-fads sweep through communities. For a few months at a time, everyone, whether in a private house or a country club, will eat nothing but English muffins and jam, then suddenly they like only toasted cheese crackers, or Sally Lunn, or chocolate cake with whipped cream on top. The present fad of a certain group in New York is bacon and toast sandwiches and fresh hot gingerbread. Let it be hoped for the sake of the small household that it will die out rather than become epidemic, since the gingerbread must be baked every afternoon, and the toast and bacon are two other items that come from a range.

Sandwiches for afternoon tea as well as for all collations, are made by buttering the end of the loaf, spreading on the "filling" and then cutting off the prepared slice as thin as possible. A second slice, unspread, makes the other side of the sandwich. When it is put together, the crust is either cut off leaving a square and the square again divided diagonally into two triangular sandwiches, or the sandwich is cut into shape with a regular cutter. In other words, a "party" sandwich is not the sort of sandwich to eat—or order—when hungry!

The tea served to a lady who lives alone and cares for only one dish of eatables would naturally eliminate the other two. But if a visitor is "received," the servant on duty should, without being told, at once bring in at least another dish and an additional cup, saucer, plate and napkin.

Afternoon tea at a very large house party or where especially invited people are expected for tea, should include two plates of hot food such as toast or hot biscuits split open and buttered, toasted and buttered English muffins, or crumpets, corn muffins or hot gingerbread. Two cold plates should contain cookies or fancy cakes, and perhaps a layer cake. In hot weather, in place of one of the hot dishes, there should be pâté or lettuce sandwiches, and always a choice of hot or iced tea, or perhaps iced coffee or chocolate frappé, but rarely if ever, anything else.

The Etiquette of Tea Serving and Drinking

As tea is the one meal of intimate conversation, a servant never comes to the room at tea-time unless rung for, to bring fresh water or additional china or food, or to take away used dishes. When the tray and curate are brought in, individual tables, usually glass topped and very small and low, are put beside each of the guests, and the servant then withdraws. The hostess herself "makes" the tea and pours it. Those who sit near enough to her put out their hands for their cup-and-saucer. If any ladies are sitting farther off, and a gentleman is present, he, of course, rises and takes the tea from the hostess to the guest. He also then passes the curate, afterward putting it back where it belongs and resuming his seat. If no gentleman is present, a lady gets up and takes her own tea which the hostess hands her, carries it to her own little individual table, comes back, takes a plate and napkin, helps herself to what she likes and goes to her place.

If the cake is very soft and sticky or filled with cream, small forks must be laid on the tea-table.

As said above, if jam is to be eaten on toast or bread, there must be little butter knives to spread it with. Each guest in taking her plate helps herself to toast and jam and a knife and carries her plate over to her own little table. She then carries her cup of tea to her table and sits down comfortably to drink it. If there are no little tables, she either draws her chair up to the tea-table, or manages as best she can to balance plate, cup and saucer on her lap—a very difficult feat!

In fact, the hostess who, providing no individual tables, expects her guest to balance knife, fork, jam, cream cake, plate and cup and saucer, all on her knees, should choose her friends in the circus rather than in society.

The Garden Party

The garden party is merely an afternoon tea out of doors. It may be as elaborate as a sit-down wedding breakfast or as simple as a miniature strawberry festival. At an elaborate one (in the rainy section of our country) a tent or marquise with sides that can be easily drawn up in fine weather and dropped in rain, and with a good dancing floor, is often put up on the lawn or next to the veranda, so that in case of storm people will not be obliged to go out of doors. The orchestra is placed within or near open sides of the tent, so that it can be heard on the lawn and veranda as well as where they are dancing. Or instead of a tea with dancing, if most of the guests are to be older, there may be a concert or other form of professional entertainment.

On the lawn there are usually several huge bright-colored umbrella tents, and under each a table and a group of chairs, and here and there numerous small tables and chairs. For, although the afternoon tea is always put in the dining-room footmen or maids carry varieties of food out on large trays to the lawn, and the guests hold plates on their knees and stand glasses on tables nearby.

At a garden party the food is often much more prodigal than at a tea in town. Sometimes it is as elaborate as at a wedding reception. In addition to hot tea and chocolate, there is either iced coffee or a very melted café parfait, or frosted chocolate in cups. There are also pitchers of various drinks that have rather mysterious ingredients, but are all very much iced and embellished with crushed fruits and mint leaves. There are often berries with cream, especially in strawberry season, on an estate that prides itself on those of its own growing, as well as the inevitable array of fancy sandwiches and cakes.

At teas and musicales and all entertainments where the hostess herself is obliged to stand at the door, her husband or a daughter (if the hostess is old enough, and lucky enough to have one) or else a sister or a very close friend, should look after the guests, to see that any who are strangers are not helplessly wandering about alone, and that elderly ladies are given seats if there is to be a performance, or to show any other courtesies that devolve upon a hostess.

The Atmosphere of Hospitality

The atmosphere of hospitality is something very intangible, and yet nothing is more actually felt—or missed. There are certain houses that seem to radiate warmth like an open wood fire, there are others that suggest an arrival by wireless at the North Pole, even though a much brighter actual fire may be burning on the hearth in the drawing-room of the second than of the first. Some people have the gift of hospitality; others whose intentions are just as kind and whose houses are perfection in luxury of appointments, seem to petrify every approach. Such people appearing at a picnic color the entire scene with the blue light of their austerity. Such people are usually not masters, but slaves, of etiquette. Their chief concern is whether this is correct, or whether that is properly done, or is this person or that such an one as they care to know? They seem, like Hermione (Don Marquis's heroine), to be anxiously asking themselves, "Have I failed to-day, or have I not?"

Introspective people who are fearful of others, fearful of themselves, are never successfully popular hosts or hostesses. If you for instance, are one of these, if you are really afraid of knowing some one who might some day prove unpleasant, if you are such a snob that you can't take people at their face value, then why make the effort to bother with people at all? Why not shut your front door tight and pull down the blinds and, sitting before a mirror in your own drawing-room, order tea for two?

Post, Emily. *Etiquette in Society, in Business, in Politics and at Home.* New York: Funk & Wagnalls, 1922.

On Visiting the Sick
By John Wesley

"I was sick, and ye visited me." Matthew 25:36

1. It is generally supposed, that the means of grace and the ordinances of God are equivalent terms. We commonly mean by that expression, those that are usually termed, works of piety; viz., hearing and reading the Scripture, receiving the Lord's Supper, public and private prayer, and fasting. And it is certain these are the ordinary channels which convey the grace of God to the souls of men. But are they the only means of grace? Are there no other means than these, whereby God is pleased, frequently, yea, ordinarily, to convey his grace to them that either love or fear him? Surely there are works of mercy, as well as works of piety, which are real means of grace. They are more especially such to those that perform them with a single eye. And those that neglect them, do not receive the grace which otherwise they might. Yea, and they lose, by a continued neglect, the grace which they had received. Is it not hence that many who were once strong in faith are now weak and feeble-minded? And yet they are not sensible whence that weakness comes, as they neglect none of the ordinances of God. But they might see whence it comes, were they seriously to consider St. Paul's account of all true believers: "We are his workmanship, created anew in Christ Jesus unto good works, which God hath before prepared, that we might walk therein." (Eph. 2:10)

2. The walking herein is essentially necessary, as to the continuance of that faith whereby we are already saved grace, so to the attainment of everlasting salvation. Of this cannot doubt, if we seriously consider that these are the very words of the great Judge himself: "Come, ye blessed children of my Father, inherit the kingdom prepared for you from the foundation of the world. For I was hungry, and ye gave me meat: Thirsty, and ye gave me drink: I was a stranger, and ye took me in: Naked, and ye clothed me: I was sick, and ye visited me: I was in prison, and ye came unto me." (Matt. 25:34, &c.) "Verily, I say unto you, Inasmuch as ye have done it to the least of these my brethren, ye have done it unto me." If this does not convince you that the continuance in works of mercy is necessary to salvation, consider what the Judge of all says to

those on the left hand: "Depart, ye cursed, into everlasting fire, prepared for the devil and his angels: For I was hungry, and ye gave me no meat: Thirsty, and ye gave me no drink: I was a stranger, and ye took me not in: Naked, and ye clothed me not: Sick and in prison, and ye visited me not. Inasmuch as ye have not done it unto one of the least of these neither have ye done it unto me." You see, were it for this alone, they must "depart" from God "into everlasting punishment."

3. Is it not strange, that this important truth should be so little understood, or, at least, should so little influence the practice of them that fear God? Suppose this representation be true, suppose the Judge of all the earth speaks right, those, and those only, that feed the hungry, give drink to the thirsty, clothe the naked, relieve the stranger, visit those that are in prison, according to their power and opportunity, shall "inherit the everlasting kingdom." And those that do not shall "depart into everlasting fire, prepared for the devil and his angels".

4. I purpose, at present, to confine my discourse to one article of these, —visiting the sick: A plain duty, which all that are in health may practise in a higher or lower degree; and which, nevertheless, is almost universally neglected, even by those that profess to love God. And touching this I would inquire,

I. What is implied in visiting the sick?
II. How is it to be performed? — And,
III. By whom?

I. First, I would inquire, What is the nature of this duty? What is implied in "visiting the sick?"

1. By the sick, I do not mean only those that keep their bed, or that are sick in the strictest sense. Rather I would include all such as are in a state of affliction, whether of mind or body; and that whether they are good or bad, whether they fear God or not.

2. "But is there need of visiting them in person? May we not relieve them at a distance? Does it not answer the same purpose if we send them help as if we carry it ourselves?" Many are so circumstanced that they cannot attend the sick in person; and where this is the real case it is undoubtedly sufficient for them to send help, being the only expedient they can use. But this is not properly visiting the sick; it is another thing. The word which we render *visit,* in its literal acceptation, means to *look upon.* And this, you well know, cannot be done unless you are present

with them. To send them assistance is, therefore, entirely a different thing from visiting them. The former, then, ought to be done, but the latter not left undone.

"But I send a physician to those that are sick; and he can do them more good than I can." He can, in one respect; he can do them more good with regard to their bodily health. But he cannot do them more good with regard to their souls, which are of infinitely greater importance. And if he could, this would not excuse *you:* His going would not fulfil *your* duty. Neither would it do the same good to *you,* unless you saw them with your own eyes. If you do not, you lose a means of grace; you lose an excellent means of increasing your thankfulness to God, who saves you from this pain and sickness, and continues your health and strength; as well as of increasing your sympathy with the afflicted, your benevolence, and all social affections.

3. One great reason why the rich, in general, have so little sympathy for the poor, is, because they so seldom visit them. Hence it is, that, according to the common observation, one part of the world does not know what the other suffers. Many of them do not know, because they do not care to know: they keep out of the way of knowing it; and then plead their voluntary ignorances an excuse for their hardness of heart. "Indeed, Sir," said person of large substance, "I am a very compassionate man. But, to tell you the truth, I do not know anybody in the world that is in want." How did this come to pass? Why, he took good care to keep out of their way; and if he fell upon any of them unawares "he passed over on the other side."

4. How contrary to this is both the spirit and behaviour of even people of the highest rank in a neighbouring nation! In Paris, ladies of the first quality, yea, Princesses of the blood, of the Royal Family, constantly visit the sick, particularly the patients in the Grand Hospital. And they not only take care to relieve their wants, (if they need anything more than is provided for them) but attend on their sick beds, dress their sores, and perform the meanest offices for them. Here is a pattern for the English, poor or rich, mean or honourable! For many years we have abundantly copied after the follies of the French; let us for once copy after their wisdom and virtue, worthy the imitation of the whole Christian world. Let not the gentlewomen, or even the countesses in England, be ashamed to imitate those Princesses

of the blood! Here is a fashion that does honour to human nature. It began in France; but God forbid it should end there!"

5. And if your delicacy will not permit you to imitate those truly honourable ladies, by abasing yourselves in the manner which they do, by performing the lowest offices for the sick, you may, however, without humbling yourselves so far, supply them with whatever they want. And you may administer help of a more excellent kind, by supplying their spiritual wants; instructing them (if they need such instruction) in the first principles of religion; endeavouring to show them the dangerous state they are in, under the wrath and curse of God, through sin; and pointing them to the "Lamb of God, who taketh away the sins of the world." Beside this general instruction, you might have abundant opportunities of comforting those that are in pain of body, distress of mind; you might find opportunities of strengthening the feeble-minded, quickening those that are faint and weary; and of building up those that have believed, and encouraging them to "go on to perfection." But these things you must do in your own person; you see they cannot be done by proxy. Or suppose you could give the same relief to the sick by another, you could not reap the same advantage to yourself; you could not gain that increase in lowliness, in patience, in tenderness of spirit, in sympathy with the afflicted, which you might have gained, if you had assisted them in person. Neither would you receive the same recompense in the resurrection of the just, when "every man shall receive his own reward, according to his own labour."

II. I proceed to inquire, in the Second place, How are we to visit them? In what manner may this labour of love be most effectually performed? How may we do this most to the glory of God, and the benefit of our neighbour?

1. But before ever you enter upon the work, you should be deeply convinced that you are by means sufficient for it; you have neither sufficient grace, nor sufficient understanding, to perform it in the most excellent manner. And this will convince you of the necessity of applying to the Strong for strength; and of flying to the Father of Lights, the Giver of every good gift, for wisdom; ever remembering, "there is a Spirit in man that giveth wisdom; and the inspiration of the Holy One that giveth understanding." Whenever, therefore, you are about to enter upon the

work, seek his help by earnest prayer. Cry to him for the whole spirit of humility, lest if pride steal into your heart, if you ascribe anything to yourself, while you strive to save others you destroy your own soul. Before and through the work, from the beginning to the end, let your heart wait upon him for a continual supply of meekness and gentleness, of patience and longsuffering, that you may never be angry or discouraged at whatever treatment, rough or smooth, kind or unkind, you may meet with. Be not moved with the deep ignorance of some, the dullness, the amazing stupidity of others; marvel not at their peevishness or stubbornness, at their non-improvement after all the pains that you have taken; yea, at some of them turning back to perdition, and being worse than they were before. Still your record is with the Lord, and your reward with the Most High.

2. As to the particular method of treating the sick, you need not tie yourself down to any, but may continually vary your manner of proceeding as various circumstances may require. But it may not be amiss, usually, to begin with inquiring into their outward condition. You may ask whether they have the necessaries of life; whether they have sufficient food and raiment; if the weather be cold, whether they have fuel; whether they have needful attendance; whether they have proper advice, with regard to their bodily disorder; especially if it be of a dangerous kind. In several of these respects you may be able to give them some assistance yourself; and you may move those that are more able than you, to supply your lack of service. You might properly say in your own case, "To beg I am ashamed"; but never be ashamed to beg for the poor; yea, in this case, be an importunate beggar; do not easily take a denial. Use all the address, all the understanding, all the influence you have; at the same time trusting in Him that has the hearts of all men in his hands.

3. You will then easily discern, whether there is any good office which you can do for them with your own hands. Indeed, most of the things which are needful to be done, those about them can do better than you. But in some you may have more skill, or more experience, than them; and if you have, let not delicacy or honour stand in your way. Remember his word, "Inasmuch as ye have done it unto the least of these, ye have done it unto me;" and think nothing too mean to do for Him. Rejoice to be abased for his sake!

4. These little labours of love will pave your way to things of greater importance. Having shown that you have a regard for their bodies, you may proceed to inquire concerning their souls. And here you have a large field before you; you have scope for exercising all the talents which God has given you. May you not begin with asking, "Have you ever considered, that God governs the world—that his providence is over all, and over *you* in particular?—Does any thing then befall you without his knowledge—or without his designing it for your good? He knows all you suffer; he knows all your pains; he sees all your wants. He sees not only your affliction in general, but every particular circumstance of it. Is he not looking down from heaven, and disposing all these things for your profit? You may then inquire, whether he is acquainted with the general principles of religion. And afterwards, lovingly and gently examine, whether his life has been agreeable thereto: whether he has been an outward, barefaced sinner, or has had a form of religion. See next, whether he knows anything of the power; of worshipping God "in spirit and in truth." If he does not, endeavour to explain to him, "without holiness no man shall see the Lord;" and "except a man be born again, he cannot see the kingdom of God." When he begins to understand the nature of holiness, and the necessity of the new birth, then you may press upon him "repentance toward God, and faith in our Lord Jesus Christ."

5. When you find any of them begin to fear God, it will proper to give them, one after another, some plain tracts, as the "Instructions for Christians," "Awake, thou that sleepest," and the "Nature and Design of Christianity." At the next visit you may inquire, what they have read, what they remember, and what they understand. And then will be the time to enforce what they understand, and, if possible, impress it on their hearts. Be sure to conclude every meeting with prayer. If you cannot yet pray without a form, you may use some of those composed by Mr. Spinckes, or any other pious writer. But the sooner you breakthrough this backwardness the better. Ask of God, and he will open your mouth.

6. Together with the more important lessons, which you endeavour to teach all the poor whom you visit, it would be a deed of charity to teach them two things more, which they are generally little acquainted with—industry and cleanliness. It was said by a pious man, "Cleanliness is next to godliness." Indeed the want of it is a scandal to all religion; causing the way of truth to be evil spoken of. And without industry, we are neither fit for this world, nor for the world to come. With regard to both, "whatsoever thy hand findeth to do, do it with thy might."

III. The Third point to be considered is, By whom is this duty to be performed?

1. The answer is ready: By all that desire to "inherit the kingdom" of their Father, which was "prepared forth from the foundation of the world." For thus saith the Lord, "Come, ye blessed; inherit the kingdom; For I was sick, and ye visited me." And to those on the left hand, "Depart, ye cursed; for I was sick, and ye visited me not." Does not this plainly imply, that as all who do this are "blessed," and shall "inherit the kingdom"; so all who do it not are "cursed," and shall "depart into everlasting fire"?

2. All, therefore, who desire to escape everlasting fire, and to inherit the everlasting kingdom, are equally concerned, according to their power, to practise this important duty. It is equally incumbent on young and old, rich and poor, men and women, according to their ability. None are so young, if they desire to save their own souls, as to be excused from assisting their neighbours. None are so poor, (unless they want the necessaries of life) but they are called to do something, more or less, at whatever time they can spare, for the relief and comfort of their afflicted fellow-sufferers.

3. But those "who are rich in this world," who have more than the conveniences of life, are peculiarly called of God to this blessed work, and pointed out to it by his gracious Providence. As you are not under a necessity of working for your bread, you have your time at your own disposal! You may, therefore, allot some part of it every day for this labour of love. If it be practicable, it is far best to have a fixed hour; (for *any time,* we say, *is no time*) and not to employ that time in any other business, without urgent necessity. You have likewise a peculiar advantage over many, by your station in life. Being superior in rank to them, you have the more influence on that very account. Your inferiors, of course, look up to you with a kind of reverence. And the condescension which you show in visiting them, gives them a prejudice in your favour, which inclines them to hear you with attention, and willingly receive what you say. Improve this prejudice to the uttermost for the benefit of their souls, as well as

their bodies. While you are as eyes to the blind, and feet to the lame, a husband to the widow, and a father to the fatherless, see that you still keep a higher end in view, even the saving of souls from death, and that you labour to make all you say and do subservient to that great end.

4. "But have the poor themselves any part or lot in this matter? Are they any way concerned in visiting the sick? What can they give to others, who have hardly the conveniences, or perhaps necessaries, of life for themselves?" If they have not, yet they need not be wholly excluded from the blessing which attends the practice of this duty. Even those may remember that excellent rule, "Let our conveniences give way to our neighbour's necessities; and our necessities give way to our neighbour's extremities." And few are so poor, as not to be able sometimes to give "two mites"; but if they are not, if they have no money to give, may they not give what is of more value? Yea, of more value than thousands of gold and silver. If you speak "in the name of Jesus Christ of Nazareth," may not the words you speak be health to the soul, and marrow to the bones? Can you give them nothing? Nay, in administering to them the grace of God, you give them more than all this world is worth. Go on, go on, thou poor disciple of a poor Master! Do as he did in the days of his flesh! Whenever thou hast an opportunity, go about doing good, and healing all that are oppressed of the devil; encouraging them to shake off his chains, and fly immediately to Him

Who sets the prisoners free, and breaks
The iron bondage from their necks.

Above all, give them your prayers. Pray with them; pray for them; and who knows but you may save their souls alive?

5. You that are *old,* whose feet are ready to stumble upon the dark mountains, may not you do a little more good before you go hence and are no more seen? O remember,

'Tis time to live, if you grow old
Of little life the best to make,
And manage wisely the last stake!

As you have lived many years, it may be hoped you have attained such knowledge as may be of use to others. You have certainly more knowledge of men, which is commonly learned by dear-bought experience. With what strength you have left, employ the few moments you have to spare, in ministering to those who are weaker than yourselves. Your grey hairs will not fail to give

you authority, and add weight to what you speak. You may frequently urge, to increase their attention,

Believe me, youth; for I am read in cares,
And groan beneath the weight of more than threescore years.

You have frequently been a sufferer yourself; perhaps you are so still. So much the more give them all the assistance you can, both with regard to their souls and bodies, before they and you go to the place whence you will not return.

6. On the other hand, you that are *young* have several advantages that are almost peculiar to yourselves. You have generally a flow of spirits, and a liveliness of temper, which, by the grace of God, make you willing to undertake, and capable of performing, many good works, at which others would be discouraged. And you have your health and strength of body, whereby you are eminently qualified to assist the sick and those that have no strength. You are able to take up and carry the crosses, which may be expected to lie in the way. Employ then your whole vigour of body and mind in ministering to your afflicted brethren. And bless God that you have them to employ in so honourable a service; like those heavenly "servants of his that do his pleasure," by continually ministering to the heirs of salvation.

7. "But may not *women,* as well as men, bear a part in this honourable service?" Undoubtedly they may; nay, they ought; it is meet, right, and their bounden duty. Herein there is no difference; "there is neither male nor female in Christ Jesus." Indeed it has long passed for a maxim with many, that "women are only to be seen, not heard." And accordingly many of them are brought up in such a manner as if they were only designed for agreeable playthings! But is this doing honour to the sex? Or is it a real kindness to them? No; it is the deepest unkindness; it is horrid cruelty; it is mere Turkish barbarity. And I know not how any woman of sense and spirit can submit to it. Let all you that have it in your power assert the right which the God of nature has given you. Yield not to that vile bondage any longer. You, as well as men, are rational creatures. You, like them, were made in the image of God; you are equally candidates for immortality; you too are called of God, as you have time, to "do good unto all men." Be "not disobedient to the heavenly calling." Whenever you have opportunity, do all the good you can, particularly to your poor, sick neighbour. And every one of *you*

likewise "shall receive *your* own reward, according to *your* own labour."

8. It is well known, that, in the primitive Church, there were women particularly appointed for this work. Indeed there was one or more such in every Christian congregation under heaven. They were then termed Deaconesses, that is, servants; servants of the Church, and of its great Master. Such was Phoebe (mentioned by St. Paul, Rom. 16:1), "a Deaconess of the Church of Cenchrea." It is true, most of these were women in years, and well experienced in the work of God. But were the young wholly excluded from that service? No: Neither need they be, provided they know in whom they have believed; and show that they are holy of heart, by being holy in all manner of conversation. Such a Deaconess, if she answered her picture, was Mr. Law's Miranda. Would anyone object to her visiting and relieving the sick and poor, because she was a woman; nay, and a young one too? Do any of you that are young desire to tread in her steps? Have you a pleasing form, an agreeable address? So much the better, if you are wholly devoted to God. He will use these, if your eye be single, to make your words strike the deeper. And while you minister to others, how many blessings may redound into your own bosom! Hereby your natural levity may be destroyed; your fondness for trifles cured; your wrong tempers corrected; your evil habits weakened, until they are rooted out; and you will be prepared to adorn the doctrine of God our Saviour in every future scene of life. Only be very wary, if you visit or converse with those of the other sex, lest your affections be entangled, on one side or the other, and so you find a curse instead of a blessing.

9. Seeing then this is a duty to which we are called, rich and poor, young and old, male and female, (and it would be well parents would train up their children herein, as well as in saying their prayers and going to church) let the time past suffice that almost all of us have neglected it, as by general consent. O what need has every one of us to say, "Lord, forgive me my sins of omission!" Well, in the name of God, let us now from this day set about it with general consent. And I pray, let it never go out of your mind that this is a duty which you cannot perform by proxy; unless in one only case, unless you are disabled by your own pain or weakness. In that only case, it suffices to send the relief which you would otherwise give. Begin, my dear brethren, begin now; else the impression which you now feel will wear off; and, possibly, it may never return! What then will be the consequence? Instead of hearing that word, "Come, ye blessed! For I was sick, and ye visited me"; you must hear that awful sentence, "Depart, ye cursed! For I was sick, and ye visited me not!"

Wesley, John. "Sermon 98." 1872 edition. *Christian Classics Ethereal Library*. Ed. Chris Dinter and George Lyons. General Board of Global Ministries, The United Methodist Church Web Server. 24 Oct. 2000 <http:// gbgm-umc.org/UMhistory/Wesley/ sermons/serm-098.stm>.

An Old Lady's Poem
Anonymous

What do you see, children
what do you see?
What are you thinking
when you're looking at me?

A crabby old woman,
not very wise,
Uncertain of habit,
with faraway eyes?

Who dribbles her food
and makes no reply
When you say in a loud voice,
"I do wish you'd try!"

Who seems not to notice
the things that you do,
And forever is losing a
stocking or shoe. . . .

Who, resisting or not,
lets you do as you will,
With bathing and
feeding, the long day to fill. . . .

Is that what you're thinking?
Is that what you see?
Then open your eyes child:
you're not looking at me.

I'll tell you who I am
as I sit here so still,
As I do at your bidding,
as I eat at your will.

I'm a small child of ten. . . .
with a father and mother,
Brothers and sisters,
who love one another.

A young girl of sixteen,
with wings on her feet,
Dreaming that soon now
a lover she'll meet.

A bride soon at twenty—
my heart gives a leap,
Remembering the vows
that I promised to keep.

At twenty-five now,
I have young of my own,
Who need me to guide, and a
secure happy home.

A woman of thirty,
my young now grown fast,
Bound to each other with
ties that should last.

At forty, my young sons
have grown and are gone,
But my husband's beside me
to see I don't mourn.

At fifty once more,
babies play round my knee,
Again we know children,
my loved one and me.

Dark days are upon me,
my husband is dead;
I look at the future, I
shudder with dread.

For my young are all rearing
young of their own,
And I think of the years
and the love that I've known.

I'm now an old woman. . . .
and nature is cruel;
'Tis jest to make old age
look like a fool.

The body, it crumbles,
grace and vigor depart,
There is now a vagueness
where I once had clarity

But inside this old carcass
a young girl still dwells,
And now and again
my battered heart swells.

I remember the joys,
I remember the pain,
And I'm loving and living
life over again.

I think of the years. . . .
all too few, gone too fast,
And accept the stark fact
that nothing can last.

So open your eyes,
children, open and see,
Not a crabby old woman;
look closer . . . see ME!!

The word "nurse" was changed to "child" for the purpose
of this reading.

Story Behind The Poem: *When an elderly lady
died in the geriatric ward of a small hospital
near Dundee, Scotland, it was felt that she
had nothing left of any value. Later, when the
nurses were going through her meager possessions, they found this poem. Its quality
and content so impressed the staff that copies
were made and distributed to every nurse in
the hospital. One nurse took her copy to
Ireland. The lady's sole bequest to posterity
has since appeared in the Christmas edition
of the* News Magazine *of the North Ireland
Association for Mental Health.*

The Sin of Gadding About
By C. H. Spurgeon

"Why gaddest thou about so much to change thy way!" Jeremiah 2:36

God's ancient people were very prone to forget him, and to worship the false deities of the neighboring heathen. Other nations were faithful to their blocks of wood and of stone, and adhered as closely to their graven images as though they really had helped them, or could in future deliver them. Only the nation which avowed the true God forsook its God, and left the fountain of living waters to hew out for itself broken cisterns which could hold no water. There seems to have been, speaking after the manner of men, astonishment in the divine mind concerning this, for the Lord says "Pass over the isles of Chittim, and see; and send unto Kedar, and consider diligently, and see if there be such a thing. Hath a nation changed their gods, which are yet no gods? but my people have changed their glory for that which doth not profit. Be astonished, O ye heavens, at this, and be horribly afraid, be ye very desolate?" In this same chapter the Lord addresses his people with the question, "Can a maid forget her ornaments? or a bride her attire? Yet my people have forgotten me days without number." And here, in this text, the same astonishment appears, "Why gaddest thou about so much to change thy way?" It most certainly was a most unreasonable thing that a people with such a God, who had dealt out to them so graciously the riches of his love, and had wrought such wonders on their behalf, should turn from him to the worship of Baal or Ashtaroth, mimic gods which had ears but heard not, eyes but saw not, and did but mock the worshippers who were deluded by them. As in a glass I see myself in these people. The spiritual people of God are well imaged in the typical nation; for, alas! waywardness and wandering of heart are the diseases not only of the Israelites of old, but also of the true Israel now. The same expostulations may be addressed to us as to that erring nation of old, for we as perpetually backslide, and as constantly forget the Almighty One, to put our trust in an arm of flesh. He saith to us also, "Why gaddest thou about so much?" For we are, alas! too often false to him, forgetting him, and wandering hither and thither, rather than abiding in close and constant fellowship with God our exceeding joy. I desire to put this question to believers, and then to the unconverted. May the Holy Spirit bless it to each class. If you read this question, taking it in its connection you will see in the first place, that there is a relationship mentioned. The question is asked, "Why gaddest thou about so much?" The inquiry is not made of a traveller, nor of one whose business it is to journey from pole to pole, and to investigate distant lands. It is not asked of a wayfarer lodging for a night, nor of a homeless vagrant who finds a poor shelter beneath every bush; but it is asked by God of his people Israel, describing them under the character of a married wife. He represents the nation of Israel as being married unto himself, himself the husband of Israel, and Israel his bride. To persons bearing that character the question comes with great force, "Why gaddest thou about so much?" Let others wander who have no central object of attraction, who have no house, and no "house-band" to bind them to the spot; but thou, a married wife, how canst thou wander? What hast thou to do in traversing strange ways? How canst thou excuse thyself? If thou wert not false to thy relationship thou couldst not do so? No, beloved, we strain no metaphor when we say that there exists between the soul of every believer and Jesus Christ, a relationship admirably imaged in the conjugal tie. We are married unto Christ. He has betrothed our souls unto himself. He paid our dowry on the cross. He espoused himself unto us in righteousness, in the covenant of grace. We have accepted him as our Lord and husband. We have given ourselves up to him, and under the sweet law of his love we ought to dwell evermore in his house. He is the bridegroom of our souls, and he has arrayed us in the wedding dress of his own righteousness. Now it is to us who own this marriage union, and who are allied to the Lord Jesus by ties so tender, that the Well Beloved says, "Why gaddest thou about so much?" Observe, that the wife's place may be described as a threefold one. In the first place, she should abide in dependence upon her husband's care. It would be looked upon as a very strange thing if a wife should be overheard to speak to another man, and say, "Come and assist in providing for me." If she should cross the street to another's house and say to a stranger, "I have a difficulty and a trouble; will you relieve me from it? I feel myself in great need, but I shall not ask my husband to help me, though he is rich enough to give me any thing I require, and wise enough to direct me, but I come to you a stranger, in whom I have no right to confide, and from whom I have no right to look for love, and I trust myself with you, and confide in you rather than in my husband." This would be a very wicked violation of the chastity of the wife's heart; her dependence as a married woman with a worthy husband, must be solely fixed on him to whom she is bound in wedlock. Transfer the figure, for it even so with us and the Lord Jesus. It is a tender topic; let it tenderly touch your heart and mine. What right have I, when I am in trouble, to seek an arm of flesh to lean upon, or to pour my grief into an earthborn ear in preference to casting my care on God, and telling Jesus all my sorrows? If a human friend had the best intentions, yet he is not like my Lord, he never died for me, he never shed his blood for me, and if he loves me he cannot love me as the husband of my soul can love! My Lord's love is ancient as eternity, deeper than the sea, firmer than the hills, changeless as his own Deity; how can I seek another friend in preference to him? What a slight I put upon the affection of my Saviour!

Spurgeon, C. H. "Sermon No. 3007: The Sin of Gadding About." Metropolitan Tabernacle. 1906.

Divine Dramatic Irony
By Gordon Ramsey

Bible Reading: Luke 23:33–43
When I was at University, studying for an Arts degree, one of my major areas of study was English literature. Specifically, I did a lot of work with Shakespeare's plays. (In fact, from memory, I think I ended up studying about 25 of the 37 plays that he wrote.)

One of the things that Shakespeare uses time and time again in his plays is an idea called "dramatic irony." Essentially, it is when one of the characters in the play says something, but the audience has extra information that shows the person is saying something truer than he thinks.

One example might be if there is a set of twins, who have been separated for years and years, and then one twin comes back, disguised as someone else. In a conversation, the first twin might say, "Oh my life would be much more complete, if only my twin brother were here." (Shakespeare would say it in a much more poetic way than that!)

The audience knows something that the character doesn't—that the twin IS here. And **that** is the dramatic irony.

During this past week, I was having a conversation with someone about today's Luke passage, and the person was telling me how hard they found it to relate to the concept of Christ as "King"—not only because in Australia the concept of a "King" is a foreign concept (literally) but also because the times that the passage talks about Christ as a "King" it is done in a mocking way, an unrealistic way.

The sign is put above the cross to be sarcastic—the Jews did *not* have a king.

The soldiers and the onlookers jeer at Jesus on the cross—a "king" (messiah) would never get caught in a situation like this and if he did, he would use his kingly power to get out of it.

How can we presume to call Christ a "King" when the passage points out so strongly the way Jesus and "kingship" **don't** go together.

Now I have some sympathy with the notion that "kingly" terminology has some weaknesses in Australian thought and faith. Probably that owes something to the fact that I have republican tendencies but that's another matter altogether!

But when it comes to the issue of the sarcasm and mocking way in which the crucifixion passages refer to the "kingship" of Christ, I really think we have to stick with the passages quite closely.

Because what is happening is a great instance of Divine Dramatic Irony: We are supposed to get a feeling of disjunction when it comes to the idea. Luke **wants** us to realize that we know something that the characters there did not know. The gospel is written, we must remember, after Easter, and reflects a post-resurrection Christian stance.

Christ is indeed "King" of the Jews—and more.

But what Luke is pushing our way, with all the ironic skill he can muster, is that the concept of a "King" has been misunderstood.

It is **not true** that Christ is not a **real king.**

Instead it is that Christ is the **only true** king and **every other expression** of monarchy throughout the world, throughout the ages has been flawed.

Again Jesus, through his life and death, is holding a mirror to us in regard to the way power is used, the way we may seek to influence other people and the way we may choose to impact on the life of the world.

People who misunderstand power would say "If you are a King, then save yourself."

But Jesus' actions demonstrate that power is not about saving **yourself.**

Readers of the gospel are already meant to understand that Christ's life was to save **others** and that life is meant to be given for others.

People who misunderstand power would say: "If you were powerful, you would summon your subjects and grab a mighty victory." But Jesus' actions demonstrate that his "subjects" are those who so often are trapped by life's circumstances, and who are not free to confront worldly powers and authorities. Readers of the gospel—especially Luke's gospel with its high concern for the lowly and outcast—have been steeped in the idea that Jesus identifies with people in the harshest of times and to mount an escape would be denying the reality of where so many people live.

People who misunderstand power would say "If you are a King, then seek to **defeat** the others—build an empire by having other people of power submit to you." But Jesus' actions demonstrate that power is not about having people submit but bringing people to reconciliation and forgiveness.

As Paul wrote in his letter to the Colossians, the life of Christ was to bring things together:

All the broken and dislocated pieces of the universe—people and things, atoms and animals—get properly fixed and fit together in vibrant harmonies all because of his death—his blood that poured down from the Cross.

To celebrate "Christ the King," we are also celebrating the Reign of Christ—the ongoing event, not just a statement about the person.

Celebrating the Reign of Christ brings us under that same way of life: seeking to save others, and not ourselves; living in solidarity with those forgotten by life, rather than those who can assist us in our living; seeking to bring people and things together in reconciliation rather than encouraging them to "submit" to a way of life, or a principle or a force.

Today is a day of celebration: Celebrating the Divine Dramatic Irony that opens up new ways of living, new ways of relating with God and new hope for the future.

So as we celebrate, why not pray in thanks and in openness to the only true King that the world has ever seen:

**Christ is King,
and broken hangs
in mortal pain
Christ is king—
the poor on earth
a kingdom gain
Christ is king
scorned by the mob
like a sideshow
Christ is king
and those who mourn
new comfort know
Christ is king
with wooden throne
that's not esteemed
Christ is king
the meek inherit
an earth redeemed
Christ is king
while the death squad
gamble with dice
Christ is king
a thirsty soul
finds paradise
Christ is king
and at the end
dies an outcast
Christ is King.
The pure in heart
see God at last!**

Ramsey, Gordon. "Sermon: Divine Dramatic Irony." Sunday Service. Kippax Uniting Church, Canberra, Australia. 22 Nov. 1998 <http://www.kippax.org.au/sermons/19981122.htm>. Reprinted with the permission of Gordon Ramsey. Copyright © Bruce Prewer 1996.

Consumer Price Index (CPI)
Conversion Factors 1800 to estimated 2014
to Convert to Dollars of 2003
By Robert C. Sahr

To convert dollars of any year to dollars of the year 2003 (estimated), divide the dollar amount from that year by the conversion factor (CF) for that year. For example, $1000 dollars of 1925 = $10,526 dollars of 2003 ($1000 / 0.095).

Data series since 1912 have changed periodically, so numbers are not all precisely comparable. Therefore, it is recommended that numbers be rounded to no more than three decimal places. For example, $10,526 in the example above becomes $10,500. For years prior to 1913, using two decimal places is recommended, e.g. $10,526 becomes $11,000 (two decimals).

Note: To reverse the process, that is, to determine what a 2003-dollar amount would be in dollars of another year, simply multiply the 2003 amount by the conversion factor of that year. For example, $1000 2003 dollars would be $76 in 1940 ($1000 x 0.076 = $76), again rounded to 3 or 2 decimal places.

Year	CF	
1870	0.074	
1871	0.069	
1872	0.069	
1873	0.068	
1874	0.065	
1875	0.062	
1876	0.061	
1877	0.059	Anne arrives by train on P.E.I
1878	0.057	Performance
1879	0.057	
1880	0.058	
1881	0.058	
1882	0.058	
1883	0.057	
1884	0.055	
1885	0.055	
1886	0.053	
1887	0.054	
1888	0.054	
1889	0.052	
1890	0.051	

Year	CF	
1891	0.051	
1892	0.051	
1893	0.051	
1894	0.048	
1895	0.048	
1896	0.048	
1897	0.047	
1898	0.047	
1899	0.047	
1900	0.048	
1901	0.048	
1902	0.048	
1903	0.050	
1904	0.051	
1905	0.050	
1906	0.051	
1907	0.053	
1908	0.052	*Anne of Green Gables* published

For the complete chart, go to the Web site listed in the citation below.

Sahr, Robert C. "Consumer Price Index (CPI) Conversion Factors 1800 to estimated 2014 to Convert to Dollars of 2003." *Political Science Department*. 1 Mar 2004. Corvallis, Oregon State University. <http:// oregonstate.edu/Dept/pol_sci/fac/sahr/cv2003.pdf>.

Christian Conversation
By C. H. Spurgeon

"They shall speak of the glory of thy kingdom,
and talk of thy power." Psalm 145:11

You have only to look at the preceding verse, and you will discover, in a single moment, who are the people here spoken of who shall speak of the glory of God's kingdom, and talk of his power. They are the saints: "All thy works shall praise thee, O Lord; and thy saints shall bless thee. *They* shall speak of the glory of thy kingdom, and talk of thy power." A saint will often be discovered by his conversation. He is a saint long before he knows it; he is a saint as being set apart unto salvation by God the Father in the covenant decree of election from all eternity; and he is a saint as being sanctified in Christ Jesus, and called. But he is more especially a saint as being sanctified by the quickening influence of the Holy Ghost, which renders him truly sanctified by making him holy, and bringing him into conformity with the image of our Lord and Saviour Jesus Christ. Yet it is not at all times easy to discern a saint except by Scriptural marks and evidences. There is nothing particular about the countenance or dress of a saint to distinguish him from his fellows. The saints have faces like other men; sometimes, they are sadly marred and furrowed by cares and troubles which worldlings do not know. They wear the same kind of garments as other men wear; they may be rich or they may be poor; but, still, there are some marks whereby we can discern them, and one of the special ways of discovering a saint is by his conversation. As I often tell you, you may know the quality of the water in a well by that which is brought up in the bucket; so may we tell a Christian by his conversation.

It is, however, much to be regretted that true children of the Lord often talk too little of him. What is the conversation of half the professors of the present day? Honesty compels us to say that, in many cases, it is a mass of froth and falsehood, and, in many more cases it is altogether objectionable; if it is not light and frivolous, it is utterly apart from the gospel, and does not minister grace unto the bearers. I consider that one of the great lacks of the Church, nowadays, is not so much Christian preaching as Christian talking—not so much Christian prayer in the prayer-meeting, as Christian conversation in the parlour. How little do we hear concerning Christ! You might go in and out of the houses of half the professors of religion, and you would never hear of their Master at all. You might talk with them from the first of January to the last of December; and if they happened to mention their Master's name, it would be, perhaps, merely as a compliment to him, or possibly by accident. Beloved, such things ought not to be. You and I, I am sure, are guilty in this matter; we all have need to reproach ourselves that we do not sufficiently remember the words of Malachi, "Then they that feared the Lord spake often one to another: and the Lord hearkened, and heard it, and a book of remembrance was written before him for them that feared the Lord, and that thought upon his name."

Possibly some will ask, "Well, sir, how can we talk about religion? Upon what topic shall we converse? How are we to introduce it? It would not be polite, for instance, in the company with which we associate, to begin to say anything about the doctrines of grace, or about religious matters at all." Then, beloved, do not be polite; that is all I have to say in reply to such a remark as that. If it would be accounted contrary to etiquette to begin talking of the Saviour, cast etiquette to the winds, and speak about Christ somehow or other. The Christian is the aristocrat of the world; it is his place to make rules for society to obey—not to stoop down, and conform to the regulations of society when they are contrary to the commands of his Master. He is the great Maker of laws; the King of kings, and Lord of lords; and he makes his people also to be kings. Kings make rules for ordinary men to obey; so must Christians do. They are not to submit to others; they must make others, by the worth of their principles, and the dignity of their character, submit to them. It is speaking too lightly of a Christian's dignity when we say that he dare not do the right, because it would not be fashionable. We care nothing for that, for "the fashion of this world passeth away," "but he that doeth the will of God abideth for ever."

Another says, "What could I speak of? There are so few topics that would be suitable. I must not speak upon doctrinal subjects, for it would offend one of the party. They might hold different views; one might be a Wesleyan, one might be a Baptist, one might be an Independent, one a Calvinist, one an Arminian;—how could I talk so as to please all? If I spoke of election, most of them would attack me at once; if I began to speak of redemption, we should soon differ on that subject, and I would not like to engender controversy." Beloved, engender controversy rather than have wrong conversation; better dispute over truth than agree about lies. Better, I say, is it to dispute concerning good doctrine, far more profitable is it to talk of the Word of God, even in a controversial manner, than to turn utterly away from it, and neglect it.

But, let me tell you, there is one point on which all Christians agree, and that is concerning the person, the work, and the blessed offices of our Saviour. Go where you will, professors, if they are genuine Christians, will always agree with you if you begin to talk about your Saviour; so you need not be afraid that you will provoke controversy; but supposing the mention of your Saviour's name does provoke dispute, then let it be provoked. And if your Master's truth offends the gentlemen to whom you speak of it let them be offended. His name we must confess; of his glory we will continually talk, for it is written in our text, "They shall speak of the glory of thy kingdom, and talk of thy power."

Now, then, first, here is a *subject for conversation:* "they shall speak of the glory of thy kingdom and talk of thy power." Secondly, we will try to find out *some causes why Christians must speak concerning this blessed* subject and then, thirdly, I will very briefly refer *to the effect of our talking more of Christ's kingdom and power.*

I. First, here is A SUBJECT FOR CONVERSATION: "They shall speak of the glory of thy kingdom, and talk of thy power." Here are two subjects; for God, when he puts grace into the heart, does not lack a subject upon which we shall converse.

First, we are to converse concerning *the glory of Christ's kingdom.* The glory of Christ's kingdom should ever be a subject of discourse to a Christian; he should always be speaking, not merely of Christ's priesthood or his prophesying, but also of his kingdom, which has lasted from all eternity; and especially of that glorious kingdom of grace in which we now live, and of that brighter kingdom of millennial glory, which soon shall come upon this world, to conquer all other kingdoms, and break them in pieces. The psalmist furnishes us with some divisions of this subject, all of which illustrate the glory of Christ's kingdom. In the 12th verse he says, "To make known to the sons of men his mighty acts." The glory of a kingdom depends very much on the achievements of that kingdom; so, in speaking of the glory of Christ's kingdom, we are to *make known his mighty acts.* We think that the glory of Old England—at least, our historians would say so—rests upon the great battles she has fought, and the victories she has won. We turn over the records of the past, and we see her, in one place, vanquishing thousands of Frenchmen at Agincourt; at another period, we see the fleets of the Spanish Armada scattered by the breath of God. We turn to different battles, and we trace victory after victory, dotted along the page of history, and we say that this is the glory of our kingdom. Now, Christian, when you speak of the glory of your Master's kingdom, you must tell something of his great victories—how he routed Pharaoh, and cut the Egyptian Rahab, and wounded the dragon of the Nile; how he slew all the firstborn in one night; how, at his command, the Red Sea was divided; how the children of Israel crossed over in safety, and the chivalry of Egypt was drowned in the flood. Talk ye also of how God overcame Amalek, and smote Moab; how he utterly cut off those nations that warred against Israel, and caused them to pass away for ever. Tell how Babylon and Nineveh were made to rue the day when God smote them with his iron hand. Tell ye to the world how God hath crushed great nations and overcome proud monarchs; how Sennacherib's hosts were left dead within their camp, and how those that have risen up in rebellion against God have found his arm too mighty for their strength and prowess. Tell of the terrible acts of our Saviour's kingdom; record his victories in this world; nor cease there. Tell how our Saviour routed the devil in the wilderness when he came to tempt him. Tell how he—"All his foes to ruin hurled, / Sin, Satan, earth, death, hell, the world." Tell how he hath bruised the head of Satan. Tell how death has lost his prey. Tell how hell's deepest dungeons have been visited, and the power of the prince of darkness utterly cut off. Tell ye how antichrist himself shall sink like a millstone in the flood. Tell how false systems of superstition shall flee away, like birds of night when the sun rises too brightly for their dim sight to bear. Tell ye all this, tell it in Askalon and in Gath; tell it the wide world over, that the Lord of hosts is the God of battles; he is the conqueror of men and of devils; he is Master in his own dominions. Tell ye the glory of his kingdom, and rehearse "his mighty acts." Christian, exhaust that theme if thou canst.

Then, in speaking of the glory of Christ's kingdom, the next thing we talk of is *its glorious majesty*. The psalmist further says, in the 12th verse, that the saints shall not only "make known God's mighty acts, but also the glorious majesty of his kingdom." Part of the glory of England consists, not in her achievements, but in the state and majesty which surround her. In ancient times especially, monarchs were noted for the great pomp with which they were surrounded. Thousands of houses must be razed to the ground to find a site for one dwelling for a king. His palace must be gorgeous with riches; its halls must be paved with marble, and its walls set with jewels; fountains must sparkle there; there must be beds of eider on which monarchs may recline; music, such as other ears do not hear, wines from the uttermost regions of the earth, and all manner of delights, are reserved for kings; precious stones and gems adorn their crowns; and everything that is rich and rare must be brought to deck the monarch, and increase the majesty of his kingdom.

Well, Christian, when speaking of Christ's kingdom, you are to talk of its majesty. Tell of your Saviour's glorious majesty; speak of the many crowns that he wears upon his head. Tell of the crown of grace which he wears continually; tell of the crown of victory which perpetually proclaims the triumphs he has won over the foe; tell of the crown of love wherewith his Father crowned him in the day of his espousals to his Church—the crown which he has won by ten thousand hearts which he has broken, and untold myriads of spirits which he has bound up. Tell to all mankind that the glory of your Saviour's majesty far exceeds the glories of the ancient kings of Assyria and India. Tell that, before his throne above, there stand, in glorious state, not princes, but angels; not servants in gorgeous liveries, but cherubs, with wings of fire, waiting to obey his mighty behests. Tell that his palace is floored with gold, and that he has no need of lamps, or even of the sun, to enlighten it, for he himself is the light thereof. Tell ye to the whole world what is the glorious majesty of his kingdom.

But once more, Christians, in speaking of the glory of Christ's kingdom, you must talk of its duration, for much of the honour of the kingdom depends upon the time it has lasted. In verse 13, the psalmist says, "Thy kingdom is an everlasting kingdom, and thy dominion endureth throughout all generations." If one should say to you, concerning an earthly monarch, "Our king sits upon a throne which his ancestors have occupied for many generations"; tell him that a thousand years are to your King but as one day. If another tells you that his king has crowns which were worn by kings a thousand years ago, smile in his face, and tell him that a thousand years are as nothing in Christ's sight. When they speak of the antiquity of churches, tell them that you belong to a very ancient Church. If they talk to you of the venerable character of the religion which they profess, tell them that you believe in a very venerable religion, for yours is a religion which was from everlasting. Christ's kingdom was set up long before this world was brought forth; when as yet neither sun, nor moon, nor stars, had been created, Christ's kingdom was firmly established. I wish Christians would more often talk about the glory of their Master's kingdom with regard to the time it has lasted. If you would begin to talk of the past history of God's Church, you would never have to exclaim, "I have said all that can be said about it, and I have nothing more to say." You would need eternity to keep on going back, back, back, until you came to God alone; and then you might say, "In his mighty breast I see, / Eternal thoughts of love to me."

Then you may speak concerning the future duration of your Master's kingdom. I suppose, if you were to talk much about the second coming of Christ, you would be laughed at, you would be thought diseased in your brain; for there are so few nowadays who receive that great truth, that, if we speak of it with much enthusiasm, people turn away, and say, "Ah! we do not know much about that subject, but Mr. So-and-so has turned his brain through thinking so much about it." Men are, therefore, half-afraid to speak of such a subject; but, beloved, we are not afraid to talk of it, for Christ's kingdom is an everlasting kingdom, and we may talk of the glory of the future as well as of the past. Some say that Christ's Church is in danger. There are many churches that are in danger; and the sooner they tumble down, the better; but the Church of Christ has a future that shall never end; it has a future that shall never become dim; it has a future which shall eternally progress in glory. Her glory now is the glory of the morning twilight; it soon shall be the glory of the blazing noon. Her riches now are but the riches of the newly-opened mine; soon she shall have riches much more abundant and far more valuable than any she has at present. She is now young; by-and-by, she will come, not to her dotage, but to her maturity. She is like a fruit that is ripening, a star that is rising, a sun that is shining more and more unto the perfect day; and soon she will blaze forth in all her glory, "fair as the moon, clear as the sun and terrible as an army with banners." O Christian, here is a topic worthy of thy conversation! Talk of the glory of thy Master's kingdom. Often speak of it while others amuse themselves with stories of sieges and battles; while they are speaking of this or that or the other event in history, tell them the history of the monarchy of the King of kings; speak to them concerning the fifth great monarchy in which Jesus Christ shall reign for ever and ever.

But I must not forget briefly to hint at the other subject of the saints' conversation: "*and shall talk of thy power.*" It is not simply of Christ's kingdom of which we are to speak, but also of his power. Here, again, the psalmist gives us something which will help us to a division of our subject. In the 14th and 15th verses, mention is made of three kinds of power of which we ought to speak: "The Lord upholdeth all that fall, and raiseth up all those that be bowed down. The eyes of all wait upon thee; and thou givest them their meat in due season."

First, the Christian should speak of *Christ's upholding power.* What a strange expression this is, "The Lord upholdeth all that fall"! Yet remember John Bunyan's quaint old saying,

He that is down needs fear no fall;
He that is low, no pride;
He that is humble, ever shall
Have God to be his guide.

So David says, "The Lord upholdeth all that fall."

What a singular expression! How can he hold up those that fall? Yet those that fall, in this sense, are the only persons that stand. It is a remarkable paradox; but it is true. The man who stands on his feet, and says, "I am mighty, I am strong enough to stand alone"; down he will go; but he who falls into Christ's arms, he who says, "But, oh! for this no power have I, My strength is at thy feet to lie"; that man shall not fall. We may well talk, then, of Christ's upholding power.

Tell it to Christians; tell how he kept you when your feet were going swift to hell; how, when fierce temptations did beset you, your Master drove them all away; how, when the enemy was watching, he compassed you with his mighty strength; how, when the arrows fell thickly around you, his mighty arm did hold the shield before you, and so preserved you from them all. Tell how he saved you from death, and delivered your feet from falling by making you, first of all, fall down prostrate before him.

Next, talk of *his exalting power:* "He raiseth up all those that be bowed down." Oh, how sweet it is, beloved, sometimes to talk of God's exalting power after we have been hewed down! I love to come into this pulpit, and talk to you as I would in my own room. I make no pretensions to preaching at all, but simply tell you what I happen to feel just now. Oh, how sweet it is to feel the praisings of God's grace when you have been bowed down! Cannot some of us tell that, when we have been bowed down beneath a load of affliction, so that we could not even move, the everlasting arms have been around us, and have lifted us up? When Satan has put his foot on our back, and we have said, "We shall never be raised up any more," the Lord has come to our rescue. If we were only to talk on that subject in our conversation with one another, no Christian need have spiritless conversation in his parlour. But, nowadays, you are so afraid to speak of your own experience, and the mercy of God to you, that you will talk any stuff and nonsense rather than that. But, I beseech you, if you would do good in the world, rehearse God's deeds of raising up those that be bowed down.

Moreover, talk of God's *providing power:* "The eyes of all wait upon thee; and thou givest them their meat in due season." We ought often to speak of how God provides for his creatures in providence. Why should we not tell how God has taken us out of poverty, and made us rich; or, if he has not done that for us, how he has supplied our wants day by day in an almost miraculous manner! Some persons object to such a book as Huntington's "Bank of Faith," and I have heard some respectable people call it "The Bank of Nonsense." Ah! If they had ever been brought into Huntington's condition, they would see that it was indeed a bank of faith, and not a bank of nonsense; the nonsense was in those who read it, in their unbelieving hearts, not in the book itself. And he who has been brought into many straits and trials, and has been divinely delivered out of them, would find that he could write a "Bank of Faith" as good as Huntington's if he liked to do so; for he has had as many deliverances, and he could rehearse the mighty acts of God, who has opened his hands, and supplied the wants of his needy child. Many of you have been out of a situation, and you have cried to God to furnish you with one, and you have had it. Have you not sometimes been brought so low, through painful affliction, that you could not rest? And could you not afterwards say, "I was brought low, and he helped me"? Yes; "I was brought low, and he helped me out of my distress"? Yes; I see some of you nodding your heads, as much as to say, "We are the men who have passed through that experience; we have been brought into great straits, but the Lord has delivered us out of them all." Then do not be ashamed to tell the story. Let the world hear that God provides for his people. Go, speak of your Father. Do as the child does, who, when he has a little cake given to him, will take it out, and say, "Father gave me this." Do so with all your mercies; go and tell all the world that you have a good Father, a gracious Father, a heavenly Provider; and though he gives you a hand-basket portion, and you only live from hand to mouth, yet tell how graciously he gives it, and that you would not change your blest estate for all the world calls good or great.

II. I must be brief in speaking upon THE CAUSES WHICH WILL MAKE CHRISTIANS TALK OF THE GLORY OF CHRIST'S KING-DOM AND HIS POWER.

One cause is, that *it is the kingdom of their own King.* We do not expect French people to talk much about the victories of the English; and I suppose there is no Russian who would pay very many compliments to the prowess of our arms; but they will all talk about their own monarchs. Well, that is the reason why a Christian should speak of the glory of his Master's kingdom, and tell of his power, because it is the kingdom of his own King. Jesus Christ may be or may not be another man's King; but, certainly he is mine; he is the Monarch to whom I yield absolute submission. I am no longer an alien and a stranger, but I am one of his subjects; and I will talk concerning him, because he is my King.

Secondly, the Christian must talk of the King's victories, *because all those victories were won for him;* he recollects that his Master never fought a battle for himself, never slew an enemy for himself. He slew them all for his people. And if

for me—a poor abject worm—my Saviour did this, shall I not talk of the glory of his kingdom, when he won all that glory for me? Will I not speak of his power, when all that power was exercised for me? It was all for me. When he died, he died for me; when he suffered, he suffered for me; and when he led captivity captive, he did it for me. Therefore, I must and will speak of his dear name. I cannot help testifying to the glory of his grace in whatever company I may be.

Again, the Christian must talk of it, *because he himself has had a good share in fighting some of the battles.* You know how old soldiers will "shoulder their crutch, and tell how fields were won." The soldier, home from the Crimea, when he reads the accounts of the war, says, "Ah! I know that trench; I worked in it myself. I know the Redan; I was one of the men who attacked it." He is interested because he had a share in the battle. "*Quorum pars magna fui,*" said the old soldier, in the days of Virgil; so we, if we have had a part in the battle, like to talk concerning it. And, beloved, it is this which makes our battles dear to us; we help to fight them. Though there was one battle which our great Captain fought alone, and "of the people there was none with him," yet, in other victories, he has permitted his people to help to crush the dragon's head. Recollect that you have been a soldier in the army of the Lord; and that, in the last day, when he gives away the medals in heaven, you will have one; when he gives away the crowns, you will have one. We can talk about the battles, for we were in them; we can speak of the victories, for we helped to win them. It is to our own praise as well as to our Master's when we talk of his wondrous acts.

But the best reason why the Christian should talk of his Master is this, *if he has Christ in his heart, the truth must come out;* he cannot help it. The best reason in all the world is the woman's reason, who said she should do it because she would do it. So it often happens that the Christian cannot give us much reason why he must talk about his Saviour, except that he cannot help it, and he will not try to help it. It is in him, and it must come out. If God has put a fire inside a man's heart, do you think it can be kept down? If we have grace in our souls, will it never come out in conversation! God does not put his candles in lanterns through which they cannot be seen, but he sets them on candlesticks; he does not build his cities in valleys, but he puts them on hills, so that they cannot be hid. So he will not allow his grace to be concealed. A Christian man cannot help being discovered. None of you ever knew a secret believer, a secret Christian. "Oh!" you say, "I am sure I have known such a man." But, look you, he could not have been a secret believer if you knew him, he could not be wholly secret; the fact that you knew him proves that he could not have been a secret Christian. If a man says that nobody knows a thing, and yet he knows it, he contradicts himself. You cannot, then, know a secret believer, and you never will. There may be, indeed, some who are secret for a time, but they always have to come out, like Joseph of Arimathaea, when he went and begged the body of Jesus. Ah! there are some of you sitting in your pews who fancy I shall never discover you; but I shall see you in the vestry by-and-by. Some of you keep on coming Sunday after Sunday, and you say, "Well, I must go by-and-by, and make a profession of faith." Yes, you will not be able to sit there long; if you have the grace of God within you, you will be obliged to come out, and put on the Lord Jesus Christ by being baptized in his name. Why not do so without further delay? If you love your Lord's name, come out at once, and own it.

III. Lastly, WHAT WOULD BE THE EFFECT OF OUR TALKING MORE OF CHRIST'S KINGDOM AND POWER?

The first effect would be *that the world would believe us more.* The world says, "What a parcel of hypocrites Christian people are!" And they are about right concerning a good many of you. The world says, "Why, just look at them! They profess a deal of religion; but if you hear them talk, they do not speak differently from other people. They sing loudly enough, it is true, when they go to church or chapel; but when do you hear them sing at home? They go to the prayer-meeting; but have they a prayer-meeting at their own family altar? Believe them to be Christians? No! Their lives give the lie to their doctrines, and we do not believe them." If we oftener talked of Christ, I am sure the world would think us to be better Christians, and they would, no doubt, say so.

Again, if our conversations were more concerning Christ, *we, as Christian men, should grow faster, and be more happy.* What is the reason of the bickerings and jealousies between Christians? It is this, because they do not know one another. Mr. Jay used to tell a story about a man going out, one foggy morning, and seeing something coming in the fog; he thought it was a monster. But, by-and-by, as he came nearer, he exclaimed, "Oh, dear me! that's my brother John!" So it often happens, when we see people at a distance, and hold no spiritual conversation with them, we think they are monsters. But when we begin to talk together, and get near to one another, we say, "Why, it is brother John, after all!" There are more true brethren about us than we dream of. Then, I say, let your conversation, in all companies, wherever you may be, be so seasoned with salt that a man may know you to be a Christian. In this way, you would remove bickerings better than by all the sermons that could be preached, and be promoting a true Evangelical Alliance far more excellent and efficient than all the alliances which man can form.

Again, if we oftener talked of Christ like this, *how useful we might be in the salvation of souls!* O beloved, how few souls have some of you won to Christ! It says, in the Canticles, "There is not one barren among them"; but are not some of you barren, without spiritual children? It was pronounced as a curse upon one of old that he should die childless. Oh! methinks that, though the Christian is always blessed, it is half a curse to die spiritually childless. There are some of you who are childless to-night. You never were the means of the conversion of a soul in all your lives. You hardly remember having tried to win anyone for the Saviour. You are good religious people so far as your outward conduct is concerned. You go to the house of God, but you never concern yourselves about winning souls for Jesus. O my God, let me die when I can no longer be the means of saving souls! If I can be kept out of heaven a thousand years, if thou wilt give me souls as my wages, let me still speak for thee; but if there be no more sinners to be converted— no more to be brought in by my ministry—then let me depart, and be "with Christ, which is far better."

Oh, think of the crowns that are in heaven! "They that be wise shall shine as the brightness of the firmament; and they that turn many to righteousness as the stars for ever and ever." So many souls, so many gems! Have you ever thought what it would be to wear in heaven a starless crown? All the saints will have crowns, but those who win souls will have a star in their crown for every soul. Some of you, my friends, will wear a crown without a star; would you like that? You will be happy, you will be blessed, you will be satisfied, I know, when you will be there;

but can you bear the thought of dying childless—of having none in heaven who shall be begotten unto Christ by you, never having travailed in birth for souls, never having brought any to Christ? How can you bear to think of it? Then, if you would win souls, beloved, talk about Jesus. There is nothing like talking of him, to lead others to him. I read of the conversion of a servant, the other day. She was asked how she came to know the Lord, "Well," she said, "my master, at dinner, happened to make some simple observation to his sister across the table." The remark certainly was not addressed to the servant; and her master had no notion that she was listening; yet his word was blessed to her. It is well to talk behind the door that which you do not mind hearing afterwards in the street; it is good to speak that in the closet which you are not ashamed to listen to from the housetop, for you will have to listen to it from the housetop by-and-by, when God shall come and call you to account for every idle word you have spoken.

Souls are often converted through godly conversation. Simple words frequently do more good than long sermons. Disjointed, unconnected sentences are often of more use than the most finely polished periods or rounded sentences. If you would be useful, let the praises of Christ be ever on your tongue; let him live on your lips.

Speak of him always; when thou walkest by the way, when thou sittest in thy house, when thou risest up, and even when thou liest down, it may be that thou hast someone to whom it is possible that thou mayest yet whisper the gospel of the grace of God. Many a sister has been brought to know the Saviour by a sister's pleadings that were only heard in the silence of the night. God give you, beloved, to fulfil our text! "They shall speak of the glory of thy kingdom, and talk of thy power." They *shall* do it, mark you; God will make you do it if you are his people. Go and do it willingly. Begin, from this time forth, and keep on doing it for ever. Say, concerning other conversation, "Begone far hence! avaunt! Thus shall be my constant and only theme." Be like the harp of old Anacreon, which would never sound any other note but that of love. The harpist wished to sing of Cadmus, and of mighty men of wisdom, but his harp would resound of love alone. Be, then, like Anacreon's harp,—sing of Christ alone! Christ alone! Christ alone! Jesus, Jesus only! Make him the theme of your conversation, for "they shall speak of the glory of thy kingdom, and talk of thy power." God give you grace so to do, for Christ's sake! Amen.

Spurgeon, C. H. "Sermon No. 2695: Christian Conversation." Lord's-day Evening Sermon. Metropolitan Tabernacle. Newington. Autumn, 1858.

Young Women Content at Home
By Brook Tingom

Many families today are realizing God has something special in mind for a young lady's training—namely, to prepare and aim for Godly womanhood. There are hundreds of young women who have chosen not to take the well-beaten path toward an independent life out in the world, but instead have chosen a hidden path, trod by only a few in recent years. These young women have set their sights on becoming keepers at home, wives and mothers glorifying God while serving their families. In light of such a noble goal, one pleasing to God, but so very different from the world's, these young women and their families are rethinking the training needed for this calling. They are recognizing the special qualities and character traits these young women will need as homemakers of tomorrow, skills and experiences that will be useful, and a way of life that will prepare them for Godly womanhood.

The training of young women to be Godly keepers at home is such a different one than the world's training, for the desired end result is altogether different. Just as a girl wanting to be a seamstress needs to learn the skills of sewing, and not the skills of carpentry, so a young woman aiming toward being a keeper at home needs to learn the ways of home duties, and not the preparations for independence, career, and a life serving her own self. Not only is it a waste of the time spent in preparation, but it is also harmful, for the two are opposites. One works toward fulfilling God's design for women as He created them, the other toward rejecting God's plan and claiming the right to do as one pleases.

Our culture looks down at those who would, as they see it, "waste" their time and energy on menial tasks at home. They see only the drudgery of the work, and miss the homemaker's joy in the wondrous task of training her children to be Godly, and the power she has to create peace and love in the home. They miss the beautiful relationships this keeper of the home weaves throughout her family. They miss the blessings of grace and honor that are bestowed on her, the refinement of her character; indeed, they miss the loveliness of that life glorifying God.

What are your views? Do you see the homemaker's duties as degrading "slavery" or an uplifting service? Do you see the common tasks of the household to be below her dignity, or do you see them as a way the woman of God can minister to her family? Do you see her role as important and glorious as God sees it? If we don't see it as God does, then we must change our outlook. Train your heart to want what God wants. As much as you are able, catch a glimpse of His heart through the Scriptures. Desire to fulfill God's will for you as a Godly woman.

To be a woman of God at home is a high calling; and it is to this calling that young women need to prepare. The training involved will require many years, daily learning the character of Christ, and learning how to bring the family closer together.

The best place for this training is in your present home! It is there that God wants young women, and there that they can best learn the duties and responsibilities of keeping a home. It is in relation to her own family that the girl will best be trained in the virtues of Godly womanhood, just a few of which are submission, dependence, and servanthood.

Coming from a family where my parents and grandparents had gone to college, it was naturally expected that I, too, would attend college upon completing homeschooling. It wasn't until four or five years ago that my family started to reevaluate this decision when we began learning that God's design for women is different than His purpose for men. Where the training of a man needs to aim toward his being a provider and protector, a young woman's training needs to be in nurturing, caring, and supporting. Therefore, a young lady needn't train to be independent in spirit, and aggressive for the fast-paced career world. We began to see that God wants to see some specific traits in women, and that young women need to be taught those traits to help them on their way to Godly womanhood. Seen in this light, taking a detour such as learning the duties of men, seems ridiculous. If young women are to become the keepers at home, the wives and mothers of tomorrow, the nurturers, the helpmeets, the emblem of grace and honor, they must work toward attaining the virtues in which God delights. We began to see that girls need to learn, not the duties of men, but the duties of women as God created them to be.

Go For The Gold, Not The Glitter

We really began to see some goals and ways to get there when we focused on the life of a virtuous woman. We had lots of questions. What does God want a lady to be? How should a young girl train to get there? How should young women spend their time? How should they prepare for life?

As we sought to let God direct us, He began teaching us more about the place of women in the home. If women were to be "keepers at home" then it would seem the best training for my life, as a young woman, would be in preparation for a role as homemaker, wife, and mother. Most significantly, we saw it was important to develop a spirit of submission, and to maintain that submission intact and alive until the girl is given in marriage, when she would become submissive to her husband.

Submission to authority doesn't come naturally for anyone, but if young women learn submission and obedience to parents while they are young, they will find it much easier to be submissive to their husbands when they are older. Young women at home have a special opportunity to practice submission to their parents. Though the world asserts that young people ought to demand their independence and make their own decisions, God's view holds a better plan. It includes blessings for parents and daughters, a guard from evil and disaster, and is an example of the beautiful relationship that is to exist later, between the wife and her husband. This is part of God's excellent plan for the family (the daughter in particular), designed to protect and guide her, so that she will be free from worries and hindrances to do what is right, and to form her heart in a manner pleasing to God.

As my family began considering this element of the Godly wife, we noticed a sharp variance to the accepted ways of young women. I'm sure you are all familiar with it: the girl graduates from high school, and at the tender age of eighteen when, shall I add, most youth are very much prone to conforming to the pressures of those about them, they move, generally to another state to sit under the teachings of, often times, an ungodly professor. Mother and father are far away, and unable to direct and guide their daughter, so, she becomes quite independent. After college, she pursues a career, and lives a life following her own whims, until she perhaps marries. After so many years of living by her own rules, fancies, and way of life, it is often difficult for her to change her whole outlook and live under her husband.

By living away from her family's influences, a young woman becomes independent in spirit and lifestyle. When she is out in the world, she will begin making more and more decisions not based on her parents' guidance and counsel, but on her own preference. Now I do know that there are some who are able to follow this accepted way of life (college and career) and live the way their parents would approve, and later have no trouble submitting to their husbands. My point remains, however, that the very nature of this course of life breeds independence.

At a time in life when many youth demand "freedom" from their parents' authority, and are breaking down morally and making unwise decisions, following God's plan for children's obedience and submission to parents will reap many blessings. The protection and guidance of one's parents gives the girl freedom, not restriction as so many assume. When a girl's parents oversee and help form her character, place limits on her activities, set specific rules of conduct and behavior, it is not to bind the girl so that she cannot do anything for herself. Rather, it is for the girl's very best that she is given parents who care for her so much as to desire to train her in the way she should go. This authority of parents makes it possible for a girl to have the freedom to do what is right, and not as she might want, and points her to living a life pleasing to God.

An independent life and spirit is not a lifestyle a young woman should desire to develop; as it is completely opposite of the virtues of the woman upheld in the Scriptures, it ought to be avoided, and instead a young woman's focus should be on learning the skills and character of the Godly woman. All that would hinder that growth and development should be seriously weighed in all areas of life, so that anything that wars with the making of Godly womanhood may be weeded out.

The life led by many young women who are out from under their parents' direction, or out following the world's path, instead of God's, will often begin to quickly form opinions, attitudes and occupations that lower themselves from the high position God wishes women to have. It is when women forget that God has made them to be different than men that a lie takes control of their lives—when they try to prove they are equal to men, when the very way of life God had in mind for them is rejected for what seems to them a more appealing lifestyle.

It is much like glitter, with no real value or substance. On the outside, college and a career look bright and successful—full of promise. It looks like the way to go—the way to happiness. But is it? No. God's ways are so much higher than man's ways. We can compare it to real gold. The life that is comparable to gold might not always appear very nice, and in fact, to the unseeing eye, it can appear downright dull. But it is when we follow God's plan that we find the life of true gold. The blessings God pours on those seeking to live for Him, and the hidden joys of Godly womanhood are worth more than all the success the world has to offer. The gold—the true joy for most of God's women—lies in the duties at home. It is only when we seek God's best for our lives that we receive true contentment and peace, no matter how many "glittery" pleasures and attainments we may be called to give up. When we seek God's will, He is faithful to fill us with a joyfulness and fulfillment that only He can give.

Don't go after what appears "brightest." Go after what God says is best. How loving a God is He, Who makes known to us what He desires of us as young women! By placing an outline for Godly womanhood in Proverbs 31, we can know what our goal is.

Young women, we need to train to be Godly women, keepers at home. I'd like to call each of you to this training. Will you be committed to growing to Godly womanhood? Will you commit yourself to train and prepare to be a keeper at home? The homes and families of tomorrow are in need of just such women. Don't lose sight of your goal, even when the way is rough, and all around seem not to understand. Let us make our pace sure and steady, toward the role to which God has called us.

Is your vision to be a Godly woman, patterned after the Scriptures? Then it is time to begin your training! What a beautiful path it is! Not always appealing, but beautiful in knowing how in practical life we can glorify God, and beautiful in knowing that our Creator has made a special role in life just for us. Start on this road to Godly womanhood now, and seek to walk on it, ever following Christ. If doing something will help you grow in Godliness, then by all means, do it! If something will hinder your way to Godliness, avoid it, taking no account of the price this decision will cost you, for it will not merely waylay you on your way to Godliness, but ultimately tear you down.

Young Women Need To Serve

Young women need to get in the habit of serving others. Christ commanded us to put others before self. As the life of the Godly woman is spent serving others, it would be well if we young women learned early to think not of ourselves, but of others. First, we need to change our attitude from one of "me first" to "others first." If we have our hearts right in this area, the manifestation of it will naturally follow. This attitude of selflessness is one of the greatest preparations for being a keeper of the home.

Because of the uniqueness of this time in life, girlhood affords a wonderful opportunity to serve others. Before she becomes enmeshed in the cares, responsibilities and duties of the wife, mother, and homemaker, the young woman can be a great source of blessing to others.

Ministry At Home

The primary ministry of the young woman needs to be in her own home. The home can be a place for great ministry. If we cannot learn to serve in our own homes, we cannot expect to be able to serve outside of our own homes. We can help lift the workload of mother's duties, and care for younger siblings by playing with them, and be an example of a helper. We can help father by obeying him, and by attending to the jobs he assigns. Be a companion to mother, and be a source of joy to all in your family. Help your mother make home a peaceful, happy place, looking for ways to grace your home with beauty

and add comfort for everyone. When mother can only manage to make the main dish, why don't you make a salad and muffins? When mother needs a rest, why don't you keep the children busy helping with chores, or reading a book together? A girl who looks about her to do such things for her family will be a sunbeam in her home. A sour attitude so quickly tears down the family, but a sweet, giving attitude can lift and edify your family. Girls, do be "sunbeams" in your family! By making our homes our primary ministry, we are focusing our attention where it ought to be. Even if we someday minister outside the home, we must still keep home number one.

Let me introduce a friend of mine to you, whom I shall call Sarah. Sarah is the eldest of seven brothers and sisters. At twenty years of age, Sarah has had many experiences and lessons. When she was fourteen, she began a bread-baking business, which she enjoyed for a year. The following year she, along with her entire family, ministered to the folks at a nursing home, where Sarah met and learned from a few "grandmothers." Since then, Sarah has graduated from the family homeschool, and has, for the past 2 1/2 years, been helping her mother at home. With her large family, Sarah is kept busy sewing garments for her growing siblings, helping with the weekly cooking and baking, completing most of the housework, and helping here and there with her siblings' studies. One day a week, when she is not needed at home, Sarah volunteers at the church office, and another afternoon each week she does secretarial work for a medical ministry. The world would scream, "Oh, what a waste of her youth!" But is it a waste?

You see, Sarah feels God has placed her in her own family for a reason. She is trusting God to give her all the lessons she needs to build character, and believes that the tasks He has placed in front of her are the things in which she can be most useful in her service to God, in her service to others, and in the preparation of her life and cultivation of her heart.

Would the world consider her to be "unsuccessful"? Yes, it probably would. But Sarah doesn't measure her worth by worldly standards (career, riches, fame and independence)—rather, she sees herself directed by God. She knows she is successful when she obeys God in doing what He has given her to do; success is not in earning worldly success. For the time being, God's usefulness for her is to be a servant to her family, and those she comes into contact with. Though it has not always been easy for Sarah to see it so clearly, and she has had times of discouragement, the lessons she has learned in giving of herself and her own pleasures to minister to the needs of her family have been well worth it. She can look back and see God building in her a true joy in the service set before her. Sarah has learned one of the most difficult lessons of the Christian life: how to be a servant.

Well, now that you've all grown to love my friend Sarah, I suppose I must confess she is part imagined. Nevertheless, her life, her ideals, her lessons, and sweet attitude are very real, and echo the hearts of many such young women.

Though the world might label us unsuccessful, what should that matter? We are not seeking the world's approval, but God's approval.

Certain young ladies, including myself, will find they are not needed to devote all, or even most of their time to keeping the home. I do not have any young brothers or sisters, and my mother is able to manage our home by herself, without much help. Still, I think it is important that we look at our homes as the first priority in ministry. How foolish it would be if we went out to minister to others while we were needed in our own homes!

So, after thus considering the ministry in your home, you might venture to use your time for the service of others. Bathe your decision in prayer, keeping in mind your goal to be under your parents' protection and guidance, and growing spiritually.

Personal Growth At Home

Some will find, after completing their family's requirements for graduation that they just want to continue homeschooling! That is the wonderful thing about home education, learning (such an important element in life!) is upheld as a privilege and joy, and some will find they just don't want to stop! You young ladies who have been home educated are, no doubt, creative enough to come up with your own studies. This sounds very appealing to me, as I have at least two dozen books I'd like to read and study. This course of life might be for those who want a looser learning style, enabling the student to pick up an interest, learn as little or as much as she likes, and then go on to something new. Since you are responsible for your work, and the amount of

time that you devote to it, you can make your schedule fit around other duties or ministries, and spend more time learning in weeks that allow for study, and do less when other duties take priority.

Those wanting a bit more structured study might consider college alternatives. When my family and I first began to feel convicted that I could best please God by staying at home under my parents' protection and guidance, we still wanted to find a way for me to obtain a college degree. Our search led to a Christian correspondence college. The correspondence college is a means to formally study and earn a degree right at home where the amount of time spent studying can be controlled to fit the family's schedule. I love to study, and, if God didn't give me so many other things to do, I would like to spend most of my time in a book. As it is, however, God has filled most of my days with other work in the publishing field (for which I'm most thankful!) and in the last year, I have only been able to complete 1 1/2 courses. At this point, I'm not sure if I will have the time to complete more college courses—it depends on what God has in store for me! I do think it is a wonderful way for young women to continue "homeschooling" in a sense, and at the same time earn a college diploma.

Many homeschooled young women have, upon completion of high school, gone on to apprentice under an experienced craftsman or skilled artisan. Through an apprenticeship, a young lady can learn a trade or skill that she can use as a money-earning venture, a ministry or, later in life, if needed, as a supplement to her husband's income. Again, since women can be most effective in the home, it would be well to consider learning a skill that can be done there. Along the same lines, a skill in a particular area may be used as a "job," if necessary, for supplemental income. An example of a useful skill might be proficiency in a musical instrument, or art, and the ability to give lessons to children (something which can most often be done right in the home). You could learn, in preparation for the possible necessity of earning an income, a home-based work that is self-taught. After gaining experience you may be able to offer your services as a seamstress to other families.

Considering A Ministry

First, when considering a young lady's ministry out of the home, the family must seek God's will in the matter, for the decision may have far-reaching impact for good or for bad. Let God lead in this matter, placing the direction in His hands. Next, also seek to know if the present time is the right time for such a ministry. Is God giving you an interest in serving in a particular field now, or as a preparation signal?

It is important that a young lady not begin ministering outside her home by herself before she is ready. So often girls are sent out too soon, all in the name of "service." Is it a service, though, when the young lady is placed in situations or places of responsibility she is not yet capable of handling? There is no rush. When she has come to a maturity where her parents feel she makes wise decisions, and can behave correctly, there will be plenty of opportunity for ministering. Some situations that had best be avoided now, might, in a few years when the girl has grown in foresight, and learned more skills, be fine. For example, a girl who is inexperienced taking care of children should probably not offer her service to care for children for long periods of time alone. Placing the girl in such a place of responsibility would not be considered wise, nor safe for all involved. A few years down the road, however, after the young lady has gained experience and grown in responsibility, the very same situation would be considered an act of service and a blessing to all involved. Sometimes the ministry in mind just needs to be put "on hold" for a while until the young woman is ready.

Above all, the spiritual maturity of the young lady must be considered when choosing a ministry. Be mindful that spiritual well-being comes first, and if a particular service will hinder or corrupt growth in Christ, it ought to be completely avoided. There can never be any excuse for the hindrance of spiritual growth.

There are some ministries that will prove spiritually rewarding for some, while for others it would tear down their faith. This is because each person has different struggles and different weaknesses. However, there are some ministries that should be avoided altogether. These ministries are ones that place the young lady in situations where it is easy to compromise standards and convictions, where evil is not rebuked, where a young lady is influenced for wrong, and where her parents' authority is undermined. Such a place is not for any young lady—whether spiritually strong or weak. Protection of the spiritual welfare of young women is always to be valued over serving in a ministry. The spiritual comes first. God calls for pureness of heart, not mere deeds.

The beauty of a young woman at home is that she is able to serve God right where she is by being a servant to her family, honoring her parents, and growing in wisdom, with a pure heart. Don't tarnish that pure heart by placing yourself in harmful situations.

The young lady needs to have proven by her obedience and submission to her parents that she's trustworthy before going from her parents' direct oversight. If the parents cannot yet trust their daughter to have Godly character or actions, then she shouldn't be out from their immediate care and direction. The family's standards should be the young woman's standards. Too many girls are sent out before they are spiritually prepared to be of service only to find that, little by little, their inexperience or weakness of character allowed them to compromise "just a little." Oh, what grief have such parents, knowing they might have better sheltered and guided their daughter!

Are you prepared to be useful? When considering a service, think about whether you are ready to help others. Many tasks in a ministry might be something you've done since the time you were very little; others may take an in-depth study in that particular skill. Learn all you can to be useful in service.

A young lady must develop a servant's heart. This seems so obvious, but is one of the most necessary traits to successfully serving others. A servant's attitude will make the girl content with her tasks, no matter how lowly she might otherwise esteem them, and will even give her joy as she gives of herself to bless others. What a beautiful thing is a servant's heart! It is refreshing to all it blesses, and can turn other's thoughts to God.

The family of the young lady will need to consider all the interruptions and effects the ministry of their daughter will have on the rest of the family. Transportation, for instance, might prove to be difficult. Each family will need to consider different factors before making a decision.

There is a lot to consider when choosing a young woman's ministry! One thing I hope to have stressed here, and let me repeat it, is that the young lady must be ready before serving outside of her home. For some, this might be at the age of fifteen, for others, it might be twenty-five. This isn't a contest! We all grow at a different pace, and have different lessons to learn. Some won't even need to consider this since their main ministry will be right in the home.

Be Faithful In The Little Things

Now I'm going to perhaps surprise you by saying don't go looking for a way to serve—let God bring it to you. Before you wonder at this, let me quickly add that I do believe we should have our eyes open to ways that we can serve others, and that we ought to be ready, as much as we are able, to help carry the burdens of another. However, my point is that if a young lady has been faithful in the little things at home, and if God doesn't direct her full-time ministry to be in the home, then He will bring another ministry into her life. God's Word tells us "He who is faithful in a very little thing is faithful also in much. . . ." (Luke 16:10a)

Lessons in faithfulness come in the home, and it is there that this important lesson is best learned. Faithfulness in little things is learned bit by bit, for it is in part a way of thinking, part instilling a habit, and part just getting down and doing it. This lesson, especially when applied to the home life, is also a trial in giving up one's own rights for the benefit of another. I'm sure you young women are well acquainted with it—while rummaging for a pair of scissors you notice the sewing corner really ought to be straightened. A little tugging at your conscience says, "It would be rather nice, you know, if you put this area in order for your mother." If you are like most girls, you'll probably locate your scissors, and make your way out of the room. But young ladies! We are not to be "like most girls," we are to be different, following Christ's example of sacrificing self! As we notice little jobs around the home, let us forsake our plans to do something more enjoyable, and do that little job. When you see the laundry half-folded, give of your time, and finish the folding; when mother's ironing lies in heaps, help her out by lowering that mountain; when the dishes are overflowing the sink, save someone else the job, and wash them yourself. In this way, we can be faithful in the little things. If we cannot serve our own families right at home, with those little time-consuming tasks, why do we ever think we are suited to serve other people at greater tasks? Serving our families at home comes first; it is

here that we learn the lessons of giving up our own rights for the benefit of others; here that we learn what it means to be faithful in doing the small jobs; and here that we can, even in such seemingly small ways, glorify God and bless our families.

Do you want to be a good wife, mother, and keeper of the home? Then your training will begin in the little things of your home now. As John Angell James wrote in 1868 in *Female Piety: A Young Woman's Guide,* "It is in the home of her parents that a young female is trained for a home of her own: and generally speaking what she was in the former, that, in full maturity and expansion, she will be in the latter; the good wife and judicious mother, looking well to the ways of her household, being the full-blown rose of which the good girl at home was the bud of promise and hope."

Don't feel obligated; but take joy in serving others, even when it calls you to do something you find unpleasant. Oh, girls! Do you see? It is not a list of "do this, and do that," it is an opportunity to focus the work of our hands on others, a lesson in giving of ourselves, even when we'd rather not. Make it your joy, your habit, to do these little tasks. God rewards faithfulness in little things by entrusting you with more. What a blessing it is to be able to serve the Lord in greater things!

Well, I'll tell you outright this time, Ruth is another "part-imagined" friend; she doesn't exist in real life, but her life is the patchwork of many real lives, and her faithfulness something we can each imitate.

Ruth was thirteen, and striving to learn to be diligent in even the small areas. To help her achieve this end, and to give her an area in which to become more responsible, her parents gave a new task to her—to cook dinner once a week. Ruth was happy to do so and set upon her new task with zeal. As the weeks wore on, however, the newness of the job wore off, and Ruth accidentally forgot her duty a few times, and just remembered at the last minute other days. As she practiced more and more, though, Ruth became quite regular in her attention to the little things. No longer did her meals lack one or two items, and they even began to taste good, too. One Sunday after Ruth had been cooking for several years, she heard of a family at church whose mother was very ill. An idea came to her that she had not thought of before.

Why, she could help that family by cooking a meal for them! With her parents' permission, Ruth planned and prepared a meal, and was able to be a blessing to that family. God sent more needy people to Ruth's attention, and as she saw a need, she sought to do all she could to help. Today, Ruth spends the time that she is not needed at home, in the homes of families who need help due to an illness. God is able to take faithfulness in little things—the perfect training for greater things—and turn them into an area for wonderful service.

If we're faithful in serving in the little mundane tasks at home, and if we have our eyes focused on following God, we needn't worry about finding an area of ministry. God will see to it that the opportunities and circumstances are placed right in front of us. Through our diligence in doing what we can to serve, God will bring about the ministry He has for each of us.

Content At Home

My final point is that young women need to be content at home. Once you and your parents have decided to pursue training in Godliness at home (or as we've discussed, in a ministry) the next step is to be content at home. We need to rest in the decision we and our families have made, and not plague ourselves with worries that we aren't doing anything important enough. We need, after purposing to grow in Godly womanhood at home, to be at peace with the decision.

Make your family and home your life. Take joy in the duties of homemaking, anticipating needs, and learning creativity in fulfilling them. Instead of mulling over all the things you have to do, enjoy doing them. Teach yourself to have a good time even in the tasks you find unpleasant.

In the same way, enjoy your family! What a lovely position we have in families as daughters and sisters! We have parents to guide us, protect us, and help us live life more fully for Christ. What a privilege! Don't shun this time by looking too much to the future. Enjoy the future when it comes, but until then, soak in the enjoyment of your parents. How good it is to have their counsel, to learn from the wisdom they've gained over many years. Enjoy your brothers and sisters. Delight in the camaraderie you share, and take part in each other's joys and sorrows.

Oh, the comforts of the happy home! They are many, and very sweet; should I list them all, it would take many pages. Let me just say, in these simple words: Do be content with home; take joy in your family. They are a gift from God for this time in your life. Be open to God's direction and open to receive His blessings.

Another area we need to be content with is this time in life. Be happy with the time God has given you right now. Sometimes we young women tend to look forward to the future so much, that we lose sight of today. The future can appear so rosy—the delights of the wife and mother, the keeper at home. It isn't wrong to look with joyful anticipation to all the Lord may give, but let it not dampen your view of today. Let your view of the future not make today seem dull, nor make you discontent. It is today that we can serve God. We can purpose to serve God in the future, but it is today that we can take captive for God's glory. Let us take our eyes off tomorrow, and place it in God's care. We need only focus on the opportunities we have today to serve God. Look at the blessings of today!

The decision to be content at home must be a deliberate one. If we merely agree, we shall get nowhere and grow discontent the minute things do not go our way. Rather, if we are to be content, we must purpose to be content, and to be happy. When things seem to go awry, or when it seems being cheerful is extra hard, pull out your purpose to be content, and look not on your own discomfort but at the chance to serve others. There will be times of discouragement when it seems no one else holds to these same ideals. Friends, neighbors, and relatives will kindly and sometimes not so kindly, let you know what they think of your family's decision. It isn't necessary that they understand your reasons, but it is necessary that you do. If we don't have a solid belief that we are glorifying God through what we are doing, the first storm that comes along will knock us down.

We need to have a clear vision of where we are headed, so that we can stand strong in our convictions. What's our plan? Are we just going to stay home? Often our idea of staying home is rather vague, but if we are going to be able to have this view in mind, we need to seek a clearer vision of where God is directing us. If we try to get as clear a vision as we can of this goal, we will be able to hold onto what we believe is right, without having that vision shatter when friends ask, "And what are you doing?" (And you will be asked this! Don't become discouraged when they haven't the foggiest idea what you are saying!)

This is a different time in life—a little scary when it is hard to see around the corner! It is exciting, though, to see more young women who are devoted to God's leading, and to see what marvelous things He can do with yielded lives.

When we have very few examples of young women at home, and thus far, many of those stories are largely yet untold, it can be easy to become discouraged. Don't be, though! The young women walking this different path need to put their trust in God. Know that God's way for women is best, and trust that His plan for us is preparation at home. Trust that God will use your preparation for His glory, and your good. He is a God to trust! Though not easy, trusting Him with the outcome of our lives, with the preparation of our lives, is the most wonderful way. It will take courage to stand separate. It takes courage to do what is right in the face of discouragement, to take a stand that is so very different than what we see around us. Be courageous, young women! Trust your all to God's loving care.

Ah! Dear young women at home—forget not the beauty of serving your family in the day-to-day duties. Let not the humble responsibilities dim your eyes to the nobler work of the keeper at home. It is to you that I offer this encouragement, that you may continue to focus on glorifying God, as you serve Him at home.

Brook was home educated from Kindergarten through 12th grade. She is now married and has one son. Brook is a regular columnist for the Home School Digest *and* An Encouraging Word *magazines.*

Tingom, Brook. "Young Women Content At Home." *Home School Digest: Seeing the World Through God's Eyes* Volume 9, Number 4, 10–13. Reprinted by permission of Wisdom's Gate, P.O. Box 374, Covert, MI 49043. <http://www.wisgate.com>. All rights reserved by Israel & Brook Wayne.

What About College?
By Ellen Davis

Many home schooling parents are not sure their children should go to college. One of the reasons is the cost, which can easily run more than $15,000 a year for room, board, and tuition. Another reason is that most colleges nurture world views and behaviors that are in conflict with all that Christian home schooling parents try to instill in their children. It doesn't make sense to spend eighteen years instructing a child and then send that child to a place that undermines all you have taught. A third reason is that graduating from college no longer means that a person is highly educated. More than half of all college seniors fail general knowledge tests of basic history and literature. Also, a college education no longer guarantees financial success, nor is a degree essential in getting a good job. Seventy percent of all the jobs in the United States require only on-the-job training or another form of alternative education. None of the twenty career fields listed by the U.S. Department of Labor as the fastest growing occupations require a four-year degree. For these and other reasons many home schooling families are considering alternatives to college.

Harvey Unger in *But What If I Don't Want to Go to College* says there are really only two good reasons to send a child to a traditional four-year college: First, the child has a deep desire to study academic subjects such as history, literature, or philosophy. Second, he has a deep commitment to career goals that require a four-year degree (such as medicine or law). Parents should think twice before sending a child to college if the child is unclear about his future plans because statistics show 50% of college students take six years to get their four-year degree. Some of these students take longer to graduate because they are working their way through, but many of them take an extra two years to finish because they have no clear idea of their future plans and so they keep changing majors along the way. This means the parents are paying an extra ten to thirty thousand dollars or more because the child has no clear idea why he is going to college. Statistics also show that fewer than 25% of those who earn college degrees actually find themselves working in their degree field. This is another reason to think twice before sending a child to college.

What are the alternatives to college? The most obvious choice is to simply get a job.

A job may take the form of an internship, temporary work, working at home, self-employment, or free lancing. *What Color is Your Parachute* can help your student create a picture of his ideal job. Another resource is *Your Career in Changing Times* from Larry Burkett's Christian Financial Concepts (Crown Ministries). This program will help your student identify his gifts, talents, and interests.

A second option is to get specialized training. Alternative education is available through community colleges, vocational-technical schools, on-the-job training, etc. The book *But What If I Don't Want to Go to College* lists the eleven types of alternative education available, gives the advantages and disadvantages of each, and includes guidelines for evaluating any program you might find locally.

A third option is to home school through college. This is not as difficult as it sounds. *Bear's Guide to Non-Traditional Degrees* lists many universities requiring little or no residency. You can also design your own course of study and get college credit for your course work because many colleges now give credits for life experiences and allow course exemptions based on high scores on advanced placement tests.

The fourth option is to help your young person start his own business. Several home schooling leaders suggest that launching your child into business is a better investment than paying for four years of college tuition. If the typical college education costs upward of fifty thousand dollars, would a wiser use of that money be to invest in a business for your child, or better still, simply to invest the money? One of the astonishing things about investments is that investing over the long term (30 to 40 years) can result in much more money than the average person will have earned in the same period of time. A similar option to launching your child into business would be to use college money to buy income-generating property, such as rental housing, duplexes, or apartments that your child can manage. This way he or she will not only have a place to live, but will also have an ongoing source of income.

The final alternative is apprenticeship. Apprenticeship traditionally consisted of four stages. The *novice* observed an expert while generally assuming the role of a servant. He learned the technology and mastered the techniques of the craft. (A college education used to provide this stage for training but no longer does because it lacks any practical application of work.) The *journeyman,* so called because this stage originally involved travel, worked in several shops to master special applications of basic skills. The medical student in internship and residency is a good example of this stage. The *craftsman* owned his own business, and, in direct proportion to his ability to train others, became a *master.* Choosing apprenticeship is a way to enter a profession without getting a standard four-year degree.

Davis, Ellen. "What About College?" *The Elijah Company Catalog* 1998/1999: 168–169. Reprinted by permission of Ellen Davis.

Women Preachers
(The Public Preaching of Women)
by R. L. Dabney

In this day we find a rapid advancement of new ideas. The unbelievable suggestion of yesterday, entertained only by a few fanatics, and only mentioned by the conservatives to be ridiculed, is today the bold reform, and tomorrow will be the accepted practice. Novelties are so numerous and so wild and rash, that in even conservative minds the feeling of wonder is exhausted and the instinct of righteous resistance fatigued. A few years ago the preaching by women was universally condemned among all conservative denominations of Christians. Now the idea is being presented to the churches, and female preachers are knocking at our doors. We are already told that public opinion is being swayed because of the boldness and reasonableness of the claims of these woman preachers, that even our own ministers are hesitant to speak out against the movement. These remarks show that a discussion of woman's proper place in the Christian Church is greatly needed.

The arguments advanced by those who profess reverence for the Bible, yet are in favor of this unscriptural practice, are as follows:

1. They profess to appeal to the sacred history of the prophetesses, Miriam, Deborah, Huldah, and Anna, as proving that sex was not a sufficient barrier to the public preaching by women in the church.

But the critical answer is, that these holy women were inspired. Their call to publicly proclaim God's Word was exceptional and supernatural. There can be no fair reasoning from the exception to the ordinary rule. Elijah, in his civic relationship to the northern kingdom of Israel, would have only been a private citizen without his prophetic calling and divine inspiration. By virtue of this we find him exercising the highest of the noble functions (I Kings 18), administering capital punishment ordained by the law against false prophets and teachers, when he sentenced the priests of Baal and ordered their execution. But it would be a most dangerous inference to argue, therefore that any other private citizen, if moved by religious zeal, might usurp the punitive functions of the civil judge. It is equally bad logic to infer that because Deborah prophesied when the supernatural impulse of the Spirit moved her, therefore any other pious woman who feels only the impulses of ordinary grace may usurp the function of the public preacher. Besides, it must be remembered that all who claim a supernatural inspiration must stand prepared to prove it by supernatural works. If any of our preaching women will work a genuine miracle, then, and not until then, will she be entitled to stand on the ground of Deborah or Anna.

2. A feeble attempt is made to find an implied recognition of the right of women to preach in 1 Corinthians 11:5, which says, "Every woman who prays or prophesies with her head uncovered dishonors her head—it is just as though her head were shaved."

They desire to find here the implication that the woman who feels the call may prophesy or preach in public, as long as she does so with her head covered. But when we turn to the fourteenth chapter, verses 34 and 35, we find the same apostle strictly forbidding public preaching in the churches by women, and commanding silence. No honest reader of Scripture can infer that the Apostle meant by inference to allow the very thing, which, in the same epistle and in the same part of it, he expressly prohibits. It is a wicked thing to represent the Apostle Paul as one who contradicts himself. He did not mean, in chapter 11:5, to imply that a woman could ever preach in public, either with her hat on or off. The learned Dr. Gill, followed by many more recent expositors, believes that in this text the word "prophesy" only means "praise," as it unquestionably does in some places (as in 1 Chronicles 25:2, the sons of Asaph and Jeduthun "prophesied with the harp"), and in many other places in the Old Testament. Thus, the worship service which the apostle is regulating here is not just public preaching, but also the sacred singing of psalms and hymns. And all that he is saying here is, that Christian women, whose privilege it is to join in this praise, must not do so with uncovered heads, in imitation of some pagan priestesses when conducting their sexual and lustful worship, but rather, Christian women must sing God's public praises with their heads covered.

We have no need to resort to this explanation, reasonable though it be. The apostle is about to prepare the way for his categorical exclusion of women from public preaching and teaching. He does so by alluding to the intrusion which had most likely begun, along with many other disorders in the Corinthian churches, and by pointing to its obvious absurdity. Thus he who stands up in public as the herald and representative of the King of Heaven must stand with an uncovered head; the honor of the Sovereign for whom he speaks demands this. But no woman can present herself in public with an uncovered head without sinning against nature and her sex. Therefore no woman can be a public herald of Christ. Thus this passage, instead of implying the authority of woman preachers, really argues the necessary exclusion of women from the pulpit.

3. Another argument is the plea that some Christian women possess every gift claimed by males: zeal, education, holiness, power of speech, and therefore it is asked why these are not qualifications for the ministry in the case of the woman as well as for men.

It is advocated that it is a damaging and a

cruel policy, to deprive the church of the souls that could be won and the good that might be done, which these gifts and graces might procure when exercised in the pulpit by women. Some women claim that they have felt the impulse of both the Spirit and their conscience to proclaim the gospel, which they feel, confirms God's call to the ministry. They say, that they, "must obey God rather than men," and they warn us against opposing their impulses, for they say, "it is possible that we 'will only find ourselves fighting against God.'" They argue that the Apostle Paul himself has told us, in the new creation of grace that, "there is no Greek or Jew, circumcised or uncircumcised, barbarian, slave or free." In Christ, "there is neither Jew nor Greek, slave nor free, male nor female" [Colossians 3:11, Galatians 3:28]. Our answer: if the spiritual kingdom levels all social and earthly distinctions, then its official rights should be equally distributed without any regard to persons—but it is obvious that this is just not the case.

4. Next, it is claimed that God has decided the question by setting His seal of approval on the preaching of some blessed women.

For example, they cite women such as Miss Sarah Smiley, who is commonly referred to as "Friend." If the successful results of her ministry are not of God's grace, then we can reasonably discredit all the fruits of the gospel that are displayed by those whose lives have been changed by her preaching. And so they ask triumphantly, "Would God use and honor an agency which he himself has declared to be unlawful?" We reply, "Yes." However, this confident argument is founded on a very obvious mistake.

Surely God does not honor, but he does use agents whom he disapproves of.

Surely God does not approve of a man who "preaches Christ out of envy and rivalry" (Philippians 1:15), yet the Apostle Paul rejoices in the fact that "whether from false motives or true, Christ is preached." There are two very simple truths, which no believer disputes, destroy the whole force of their argument that the "ends justify the means." One is that a truly sincere Christian may go in the wrong direction in one particular area of their life, and our heavenly Father, who is very patient, may withhold his displeasure from the misguided efforts of his child, through Christ's intercession, because, though misguided, he is his still God's

blessed child. The other is, that it is one of God's clearest and most blessed prerogatives to bring good out of evil. Thus who can doubt that it is wrong for a man dead in his sins to intrude into the sacred ministry? Yet God has often employed such sinners to convert souls; not sanctioning their profane intrusion, but glorifying his own grace by overruling it.

This plea for women preachers may be also refuted by another answer.

If the rightfulness of actions is to be determined by their results, then evidently it ought to be by their complete results.

But who is competent to say whether the complete results of one of these devout blunders will be beneficial or harmful? I will grant that a zealous female may convert or confirm several souls by her preaching. But isn't it also possible that she may, by this bad example, in the future introduce an amount of confusion, disturbance, strife, error and scandal which will greatly outweigh the initial limited good? This question cannot be answered until time is ended, and it will require an omniscient mind to judge it. Thus it becomes perfectly clear that present seemingly good results cannot ever be a sufficient justification of conduct, which violates the clear Word of God. This is our only sure guide. Bad results, following a course of action not commanded in the Word, may present a sufficient, even a commanding reason for stopping. Likewise, good results following such action may suggest some probability for continuance, however when the course of action transgresses the command of Scripture then such probability becomes worthless.

Now we will look at some of the arguments against women preachers.

1. When the apostle teaches the equality of everyone in the privilege of redemption, it is obvious he is speaking in general, and not of official positions in the visible church, but of access to Christ and participation in his blessings.

Paul's exclusion of women from the pulpit is as clear and emphatic as his assertion of the universal equality in Christ. Surely he does not intend to contradict himself. Our interpretation is also established by other instances of a similar kind. The apostle expressly excludes "new converts" from the office of preacher and minister. Yet no one dreams that he would have made the newness of their salvation a ground of discrimination against their equal privileges in Christ. Without a doubt the apostle would have been just as ready to assert that in Christ there is neither young nor old, just as in Christ there is neither male nor female. Equally, every rational man would exclude children from the office of pastor in the church, yet no one would belittle their equal standing in Christ. Likewise, the apostle denies Christians who were guilty of polygamy from being a pastor, however sincere their repentance. If, then, the equality of these classes in Christ did not imply their fitness for public office in the church, neither does the equality of females with males in Christ imply it. So we can see that the scope of the apostle in these verses proves that he meant nothing more, for his purpose in referring to this blessed Christian equality is to reveal that all classes of Christians have a right to church membership and that Christian love and communion ought to embrace everyone.

2. Next, we see that when the claim is made that the church must concede the ministerial function to the Christian woman who sincerely believes she has been called to it, we have a dangerous perversion of the true doctrine of calling or being called to the ministry. True, this calling is spiritual, but it is also scriptural.

The same Spirit who truly calls the minister also dictated the Holy Scriptures. When even a godly man says that **he thinks** the Spirit has called him to preach, there may be room for doubt; but there can be no doubt whatever that the Spirit calls no person to do what the word dictated by the Spirit, forbids. The Spirit cannot contradict himself. No persons are entitled to claim a specific call of the Spirit for them individually to do or teach something contrary to or in violation of the Scriptures previously given to the church, unless they can sustain their claim by some miracle. Again, the true doctrine of calling is that the man whom God has intended and qualified to preach discovers his call through the word. The word is the instrument by which the Spirit teaches him, with prayer, that he is to preach. Therefore, when a person professes to have felt this call whom the word distinctly precludes from the work, like the new Christian, the child, the repentant polygamist, or the female, even though we may ascribe her mistake to a well-intentioned zeal, then we absolutely know that she is mistaken; she has confused a human impulse with the Spirit's calling.

3. Next, the scriptural calling comes not only through the heart of the candidate, but also from the Church itself, for the call is never complete until the Church has confirmed it.

But by what rule will the Church be guided in the matter of ordaining ministers? By the simple declaration of any one who assumes to be sincere? Truly not. The Church is expressly commanded not to "believe every spirit, but to test the spirits to see whether they are from God." They have no other rule than Scripture. Who can believe that God's Spirit is the agent of such anarchy as this, where the Church holds in their hands the Word, teaching them that God does not call any woman, and yet a woman insists against them that God has called her? God "is not a God of disorder but of peace. As in all the congregations of the saints." It is on this very subject of calling to public teaching and preaching that the apostle makes this declaration.

4. Next, the argument from the seeming fitness of some women, by their gifts and graces, to edify the churches by preaching, is then useless and false.

When God endows a woman with the ability to understand and teach His Word, it may be safely assumed that he has some wise end in view; he has some area or sphere in which her gifts will come into proper play. But surely it is far from reverent for the creature to decide, against God's Word, that this sphere is the pulpit. God's wisdom is better than man's. The sin involves the presumption of Uzzah. He was right in thinking that it would be a bad thing to have the sacred ark fall into the dirt, and in thinking that he had the physical strength to steady it, just like any Levite; but he was wrong in presuming to serve God in a way that God had not prescribed. So when men lament the "unemployed spiritual power," which they suppose exists in many gifted females, as a great loss to the church, they are reasoning with Uzzah; they are presumptuously setting their human wisdom above God's wisdom.

The argument, then, whether any woman may or may not be a preacher of the word should be primarily one of Scripture.

1. Does the Bible really prohibit it? I assert that it does.

First, the Old Testament, which contained, in seed, all the principles of the New Testament, allowed no regular church office to any woman. When a few women were employed as mouthpieces of God, it was in a purely extraordinary office, and in which they could offer supernatural evidence of their commission. No woman ever ministered at the altar, as either a priest or a Levite. No female elder was ever seen in a Hebrew congregation. No woman ever sat on the throne of the theocracy, except the pagan usurper and murderess, Athaliah.

Now, this Old Testament principle of ministry is carried over to a degree in the New Testament where we find the Christian congregations, with elders, teachers, and deacons, and its women invariably keeping silent in the assembly.

2. Secondly, if human language can make anything plain, it is that the New Testament institutions do not allow the woman to rule or "to have authority over a man." (See 1 Tim. 2:12; 1 Cor. 11:3, 7–10; Eph. 5:22, 23; 1 Peter 3:1, 5, 6.)

As a minimum, in church affairs, the woman's position in the church is subordinate to the man's. And according to New Testament precedent and doctrine, the call to preaching and ruling in the church must go together. Every church elder is not a preacher, but every preacher of the church must be an elder of the church. It is clearly implied in 1 Timothy 5:17 that there were church elders who were not preachers, but never was there a preacher of the church who was not an elder. The scriptural qualifications for preaching, that is, the knowledge, holiness, experience, authority, dignity, purity, were even more exacting qualifications than those listed for elders. Truly, "The greater includes the less." Therefore it is simply inconceivable that a person could experience a true call to the public preaching and teaching of the Word and not also called to be an elder. Therefore, if it is right for the woman to preach, she must also be a church elder. But God has expressly prohibited the latter, and assigned to woman a domestic and social place, in which her demand that she be an elder and a preacher would simply be anarchy.

This argument may be put in a most practical and specific shape, which will reveal its absolute absurdity. Let it be granted, for argument's sake, that here is a woman whose gifts and graces, spiritual wisdom and experience, are so superior to others, that her friends feel that it would be a great loss of power in the church to confine her to silence in the public assembly. Therefore, for that reason, she exercises her public gift and finds great success. She becomes the spiritual parent of many newborn souls. Is it not right then, that her spiritual offspring should look up to her for guidance? How can she, from her position, justify herself in refusing the needs of these newborn babes in Christ? She herself felt properly driven, by the deficiency in the quantity or quality of the male preaching in this church, to break through the restraints of sex and contribute her superior gifts to the winning of souls. Now, to carry this further, if it appears that a similar deficiency of male leadership, either in quantity or quality, exists in the same church, then the same impulse must, by the stronger reason, prompt her to assume the less public and prominent work of church leadership and rule. She ought to take over the responsibilities of a senior elder, and thus preserve the fruits she has planted. She ought to admonish, command, censure, and excommunicate her male converts, including, possibly, the husband she is to obey at home, if the real welfare of the souls she has won requires such action. All this would be absurd and very damaging to the church.

Let us now look at the Word of God concerning the preaching and leadership of the church; we shall find them particularly, even surprisingly, explicit.

First, we have 1 Corinthians 11:3–16, where the apostle discusses the relation and manner of the sexes in the public Christian assemblies; and he assures the Corinthians, verses 2 and 16, that the rules he announces here were universally accepted by all the churches. Two principles are laid down: first, verse 4, that the man should preach (or pray) in public with his head uncovered, because in that capacity he stands as God's herald and representative; and to assume at that time the emblem of subordination, a covered head, is a dishonor to the office and the God it represents; secondly, verses 5, and 13, that, on the contrary, for a woman to appear or to perform any public religious function in the Christian assembly, with her head uncovered, is a glaring impropriety, because it is contrary to the subordination of the position assigned her by her Creator, and to the modesty suitable to her sex; and even nature settles the point by giving her, her long hair as her natural veil. Even as good taste and a natural sense of propriety would protest against a woman going in public without that beautiful emblem and adornment of her sex—her long hair, cut off like a common soldier or a laborer, even so, clearly does nature herself sustain God's law in requiring the woman to appear always modestly covered in the church. The holy angels who are present, as invisible spectators, hovering over the Christian assemblies, would be shocked by seeing women professing godliness publicly display themselves without this appropriate emblem of their position (verse 10).

1. The woman, then, has a right to the privileges of public worship and the Lord's Supper; she may join audibly in the praises and prayers of the public assembly, but she must always do this with her head covered.

The apostle does not, in this chapter, stop to make the distinction, that if every public herald of God, must not have their heads covered, and the woman must never have her head uncovered in public, then she can never be a public herald of the Gospel. But let us wait. He is not done with these questions of order in public worship; he steadily continues the discussion of them through the fourteenth chapter, and he then in time reaches the conclusion he had been preparing, and in verses 34 and 35, expressly prohibits women from preaching, saying, "women should remain silent in the churches. They are not allowed to speak" (in that place), but must be in submission, as the Bible says. "If they want to inquire about something," about some doctrine which they hear discussed but do not comprehend, then "they should ask their own husbands at home; for it is disgraceful for a woman to speak in the church." And in verse 37, he ends the whole discussion by declaring that "if anybody thinks he is a prophet or spiritually gifted," so as to be entitled to challenge Paul's instructions, then "let him acknowledge that what I am writing to you is the Lord's command," and not his mere personal conclusions. So to challenge Paul's clear instructions on such pretensions of spiritual impulse is inevitably wrong and presumptuous. For the unchallengeable Lord does not issue commands in contradictory ways.

The next passage is 1 Timothy 2:11–15. In the eighth verse, the apostle, having taught what should be the tenor of the public prayers and why, says: "I want men everywhere to lift up holy hands in prayer" (referring to the practice which the two sexes publicly prayed together). He then commands, in keeping with the tenor of the passage in 1 Corinthians 11, for Christian women to come to church dressed in the most modest clothing, so as to express the humble modesty of their sex. He then continues: "A woman should learn in quietness and full submission. I do not permit a woman to teach" (context is to teach in public) nor "to have authority over a man; she must be silent. For Adam was formed first, then Eve. And Adam was not the one deceived [by Satan]; it was the woman who was deceived and became a sinner [first]. But women will be saved through childbearing—if they continue in faith, love and holiness with propriety."

In 1 Timothy 5:9–15, a sphere of church ministry is clearly defined for older single women, and for them only, who are widows or have never been married and are without any near relatives. So specific is the apostle that he categorically fixes the limit to those sixty years old, below which the church may not accept. What was this sphere of labor? It was evidently some form of deaconess type work, helping others, and clearly not preaching, because the age, qualifications and connections all point to these private benevolent tasks, and the uninspired history confirms it.

Now, to all the younger women the apostle then assigns their specific sphere of ministry in these words (verse 14), "So I counsel younger women to marry, to have children, to manage their homes and to give the enemy no opportunity for slander," either against Christians or Christianity in general. Here we find strong evidence that Paul assigned no public preaching function to women. In Titus 2:4, 5, women who have not reached old age are "to love their husbands and children, to be self-controlled and pure, **to be busy at home,** to be kind, and to be subject to their husbands, so that no one will malign the word of God." And the only teaching function even hinted at for the older women is found in verse 4, which is that they teach these private domestic virtues to their younger sisters. We can clearly see that the apostle here assigns the **home** as the proper sphere of activity and ministry of the Christian woman. That is her kingdom, and clearly not the secular workplace nor the church. Her duties in her home will basically keep her away from the public functions. She is not to be in authority over men, but a loving subject to her husband.

The grounds on which the apostle rests the divine legislation against the preaching of women make it clear that we have construed it correctly. Bringing together 1 Corinthians 11 with 1 Timothy 2, we find the following: The male was the first creation of God, the female a subsequent one. The female was made from the substance of the male, being taken from his side. The purpose of the woman's creation and existence is to be a helpmate for man, and in a sense in which the man was not originally designed as a helpmate for the woman. Therefore God, from the beginning of man's existence as a sinner, put the wife under the kind and compassionate authority of the husband, making him the head and her the subordinate in domestic society. Then finally, the action of the woman in yielding first to Satanic temptation and aiding to seduce her husband into sin was punished by this subjection, as seen in the curse of Genesis 3:16, where it is declared that the husband will rule over the wife, and the sentence on the first woman has been extended, by imputation, to all her daughters. These are the grounds on which the apostle says the Lord enacted that in the church assemblies the woman shall be the student, and not the public teacher, ruled, and not ruler.

The reasons against the public preaching and teaching by women apply to all women, of all ages and civilizations alike. Such reasons are, indeed, in strong opposition to the radical theories of individual human rights and equality now in vogue with many today. Instead of allowing all human beings a specific equality and an absolute natural independence, these Scripture doctrines assume that there are orders of human beings naturally unequal in their inherited rights, as in their bodily and mental qualities; that God has not ordained any human being to this proud independence, but placed all in subordination under authority, the child under its mother, the mother under her husband, the husband under the church and civil authorities, and these under the law, whose guardian and avenger is God himself.

The inspired commands of Scripture are explicit to every honest listener, as explicit as human language can make it. Yet modern ingenuity has written much to try to explain it away. One is not surprised to find these expositions, even when advanced by those who profess to accept the Scriptures, colored with a lot of error. For a true and honest reverence of the inspiration of Scripture would scarcely try so hopeless a task as the misrepresenting and diffusing of so clear a law. Thus, sometimes we hear these remarks uttered almost as a sneer, "Oh, this is the opinion of Paul, a crusty old bachelor with his head stuffed with those ideas of woman which were current when society considered her an illiterate, a plaything, and a slave." Or, we are referred to the fable of the paintings of the man dominating the lion, in which the man was always the painter, and it is said, "Paul was a man; he is jealous for the authority of his sex. The law would be different if it were uttered through a woman." What is all this except open unbelief and resistance, when the apostle says expressly that this law was the enactment of the Christ who condescended to be born of woman.

Again, one would have us read the prohibition of 1 Corinthians 14:34, as "women are not allowed to 'babble,'" rather than that they are "not allowed to speak."

Therefore they try to show that the verb used here is in the negative sense only, and that the prohibition is that a woman is not allowed to talk nonsense in public, but does not exclude, but rather implies, her right to preach, provided she preaches well and only solid Biblical truth. No expositor will need to reply to such criticism so wretchedly absurd as this. But it may be good to simply point out in refuting such an argument that the opposite of this verb in Paul's own mind and statement is "to be silent." The implied distinction, then, is not here between solid speech and babbling, but between speaking publicly and keeping silent. Again, in the parallel passage (1 Timothy 2:12), the apostle says "I do not permit a woman to teach" where he uses the Greek word "didasko" whose regular meaning means "to teach" in the general sense—any kind of teaching. And the apostle's whole logic in the contexts is directed, not against silly teachings by women, but against any public teaching by women.

Another way they try to dodge the truth of the text is to say that, "Yes, the law is indeed explicit, but it was only temporary."

When woman were, what paganism and the eastern harem had made her, she was indeed unfit for ruling and public teaching; she was only a grown-up child, ignorant, impulsive and rash, like other children; and while she remained so the apostle's exclusion was wise and just. But the law was not meant to apply to the modern Christian woman, lifted up by better institutions into an intellectual, moral and literary equality with the man. No doubt if the apostle were alive today, he himself would have acknowledged it.

This is at least a more decent argument. But as for a proper interpretation of the text it is as unfair and untenable as the other. For, first, it is false to assume that the Apostle's conception of the Christian woman was that of an ignorant grown-up child from the harem. The harem was not a legitimate Hebrew institution. Polygamy was not the rule, but the exception, in reputable Hebrew families; nor were devout Jews, such as Paul had been, ignorant of the unlawfulness of such domestic abuses. Jewish manners and laws were not like the peoples around them, but a glorious exception to the surrounding nations, in the place they assigned woman; and God's Word of the Old Testament had doubtless done among the Jews the same ennobling work for woman which we now claim Christianity does. The competent archeologist and historian know that it has always been the trait of Judaism to assign an honorable place to woman. Accordingly, we never find the apostle drawing a depreciated picture of woman; every allusion of his to the believing woman is full of reverent respect and honor. Among the Christian women who come into Paul's history there is not one who is portrayed after this imagined pattern of childish ignorance and weakness. The Lydia, the Lois, the Eunice, the Phoebe, the Priscilla, the Roman Mary, the Junia, the Tryphena, the Tryphosa, the "beloved Persis" of the Pauline history, and the "elect lady" who was honored with the friendship of the Apostle John, all appear in the narrative as bright examples of Christian intelligence, activity, dignity, and graciousness. It was not left for the pretentious Christianity of our century to begin the liberation of woman. As soon as Christianity conquered a household, it did its blessed work in lifting up the feebler and oppressed sex; and it is evident that Paul's habitual conception of female Christian character in the churches in which he ministered **was at least as favorable** as his estimate of the male members. Thus the state of facts on which this argument rests had no place in Paul's mind; he did not consider himself as legislating temporarily in view of the inferiority of the female Christian character of his day, for he did not think it was inferior. When

this unfounded argument is inspected it unmasks itself simply into an instance of quiet egotism. The women of our day who feel they are called to preach are in effect saying, "I am so elevated and enlightened that I am above the law, which was good enough for those old fogies, Priscilla, Persis, Eunice; and the elect lady." Indeed! This is modesty with a vengeance! Was Paul only temporarily legislating when he termed modesty one of the brightest jewels in the Christian woman's crown?

A second answer is seen to this plea in the nature of the apostle's basis for the law.

Not one of them is personal, cultural, or temporary. Nor does he say that woman must not preach because he regards her as less holy, less zealous, less eloquent, less educated, less courageous, or less intellectual, than man. Those who advocate woman's rights have a continual tendency to confuse the issue, claiming that the apostle, when he says that woman must not do what man does, meant to belittle her sex. This is a sheer mistake. You will search in vain for any belittling of the qualities and virtues of the female sex; and we may also at this point properly disclaim all such intention. Woman is excluded from this masculine task of public preaching by Paul, not because she is inferior to man, but simply because her Creator has ordained for her another work which is incompatible with the public preaching and teaching of the Word.

Further, we can plainly see that the scriptural law was not meant to be temporary, and had no exclusive reference to the ignorant and childish woman of the Eastern harem, because every basis assigned for the exclusion of women preachers is of universal and perpetual application.

They apply to the modern, educated woman in the exact same way as they applied to Phoebe, Priscilla, and Eunice. They do not lose a single grain of force by any change of social practice or feminine culture, rather they are grounded in the facts of woman's origin and nature and the intended role and purpose of her existence. Thus this second argument for women preachers is totally closed. And the argument finds its final deathblow in such passages as 1 Timothy 2:9 and 5:14. As I have mentioned earlier, a few older women of special circumstances are admitted as assistants in the work of the deacons. However, the apostle then clearly assigns the rest of the body of Christian women to the domestic sphere, indicating clearly that any attempts by them to go beyond their assigned role would give the enemy an opportunity for slander. Here, then, we have the clearest proof, in a negative form, that the Apostle Paul did not plan the assigned role of women to be temporary; for it is **for woman as elevated and enlightened by the gospel** that he preached, that he laid down the limits of their ministry.

The justification is not found in any belittling of woman as man's natural inferior, but in the ancient fact: "He created them as male and female." In order to establish human society God saw that it was necessary to create for man's mate, not his exact image, but his counterpart. An identical creature to man would have utterly marred their companionship, and would have been an equal curse to both. Although there is an obvious similarity in the man and woman, yet there are unique differences which clearly reveal that each is fitted for works and duties unsuitable for the other. And it is no more a degradation to the woman, that the man can do some things better than she can, than the fact that the woman has natural superiority in other things.

But it is also stated: "Your Bible doctrine makes man the ruler, and woman the one ruled."

True. It was absolutely necessary, especially after sin had entered the human race, necessary that a foundation for social order would be laid down in a family government. This family government could not be made consistent, peaceful or orderly by having two heads, because basic human weakness, and especially sin, would ensure collision, at least some times, between any two human wills. It was essential for the welfare of both husband and wife and for the offspring that there must be an ultimate head of the family. Now let reason decide, was it necessary that the man be head over the woman, or the woman over the man? Was it right that he for whom woman was created should be subjected to her who was created for him; that he who was stronger physically should be subjected to the weaker; that the natural protector should be the servant of the dependent; that the divinely ordained bread-winner should be controlled by the bread-dispenser? Every honest woman admits that this would have been unnatural and unjust. Therefore God, acting, so to speak, under an unavoidable moral necessity, assigned to the

male the domestic government of the home, regulated and tempered, indeed, by the strict laws of God, by self-interest and by the most tender affection; and to the female the obedience of love. On this order all other social order depends. It was not the plan of Christianity to subvert it, but only to perfect and refine it. No doubt that spirit of willfulness, which is a feature of our native carnality in both man and woman, tempts us to feel that any subordination to another is a hardship. Self-will resents this natural subordination as a natural injustice. But self-will forgets that "order is heaven's first law;" that subordination is the unalterable condition of peace and happiness, and this is true just as much in heaven as on earth; that this subjection was not imposed on woman only as a penalty, but also for her and her children's good; and that to be governed under the wise conditions of nature is often a more privileged state than to govern. God has conformed his works of creation and providence to these principles. In creating man God has provided him with the natural attributes, which qualify him to work outside the home, to subdue dangers, to protect, and to govern. He has given these same qualities in a lesser degree to woman, and in their place has adorned her with the less hardy, but equally admirable, attributes of body, mind and heart which qualify her to yield, to be protected, and to "guide the home." This order is founded, then, in the unchangeable laws of nature. Therefore all attempts to reverse it must fail, and will always result in confusion.

Now, a wise God designs no conflicts between his domestic and his church institutions. He has ordained that the man shall be the head in the family, thus it would cause great confusion to make the woman the leader in the church. We have stated this morning that the right of public teaching and preaching must involve the right of spiritual rule. The woman, who claims she has a right to preach, ought also claim the right to be a ruling elder. But how would it work to have husband and wife, ruler and subject, change places as often as they passed from their home to the church? One could only imagine that this amount of switching roles would result in something close to absolute anarchy.

Again, the duties which natural affection, natural disposition, and considerations of convenience distribute between the man and the woman make it practicable for him

and impracticable for her to pursue the additional tasks of the preacher and evangelist, without their neglect of other assigned duties.

An example would come from the raising and nurturing of children. The elder in the church, the pastor, must be "the husband of one wife." Both the parents have responsibilities to their children; but the appropriate duties of the mother, especially towards little children, are such that she could not leave them, as a pastor must, for his public tasks without criminal neglect and their probable ruin. It may then be argued that this line of reasoning has no application to unmarried women. The answer is, that God contemplates marriage as the normal condition of woman, yet he does not make singleness a crime, but the sphere he assigns to the unmarried woman is also private and domestic.

No doubt some minds imagine a degree of force in the argument, that God has bestowed on some women gifts and graces eminently qualifying them to edify his churches, and since what he does is always perfect and without waste he thereby shows that he plans for such women to preach.

Enough has been already said to show how utterly dangerous such bogus arguments are. God is not accountable to any man. Doesn't he often give the most splendid gift for usefulness to young men whom he then removes by what we call a premature death from the threshold of the pastoral career? Yet "God always does everything perfectly and without waste." It is not for us to surmise how he will utilize those seemingly unproductive gifts. He knows how and where to do it. We must bow to his perfect plan, whether we understand it or not. It is the same situation with respect to his command restricting the most gifted woman from the public preaching of the Word. But there is a more obvious answer. God has assigned to her a private sphere sufficiently important and honorable to justify the whole expenditure of these heavenly gifts—the formation of the character of children. This is the noblest and most important work done on earth. Add to it the efforts of friendship, the duties of the wife, daughter, sister, helper of the poor, and the work of teaching other woman, and we see a field wide enough for the greatest talents and the most holy ambition.

Now the person making the argument for women preachers returns with the complaint that, while the faithful mother rears six, or possibly twelve, children for God, the gifted evangelist may convert thousands?

But that man would not have been the gifted evangelist had he not enjoyed the blessing of the training from a humble Christian mother. Had he been reared in the disorderly environment of a mother who worked outside the home, instead of being the spiritual father of thousands, he possibly would have been an ignorant unbeliever or a disgusting Pharisee. So the worthiness of his public success fully belongs as much to the humble mother as to himself. Again, the instrumentality of the mother's training in the salvation of her children is mighty and decisive; the influence of the minister over his hundreds is slight and non-essential. If he contributes a few grains, in numerous cases, to turn the scales for heaven, the mother contributes tons on the right scales in her few cases. The one works more widely on the surface, the other more deeply; so that the real amount of soil moved by the two workmen is not usually in favor of the preacher. The woman of sanctified ambition has nothing to regret as to the dignity of her sphere. She does the noblest work that is done on earth. However, its **public** recognition is usually more through the children and others who benefit than through her own person, and that is precisely the aspect of her work which makes it most Christ like. It is also precisely the aspect at which a sinful and selfish ambition takes offence.

Lastly, let me say, that the movement towards women preachers does not necessarily spring from the current secular "woman's rights" movement. The preaching of women marked the early Wesleyan movement to some extent, and the Quaker assemblies. But the real answer to those who might claim it is a "woman's right" to preach is found in the correct statement of human rights we have given in the Bible. The woman is not designed by God, nor entitled to all the positions in society to which the male is entitled. God has disqualified her for any such exercise of them by the endowments of body, mind, and heart he has given her, and the duties he has assigned her in her daily life. And since she has no right to assume the masculine positions, so she will find in the attempt to do so only ruin to her own character and to society. For instance, the very traits of emotion and character which make the woman man's cherished and invaluable "helpmate," the traits which she must have in order to fulfill the purpose of her existence, would ensure her unfitness to meet the distinctive temptations of publicity and power. The attempt to do so would corrupt all these lovelier traits, while it would still leave her, as man's rival, "the weaker partner." She would lose everything and gain nothing.

This common movement for "women's rights," and women's preaching, must be regarded, then, as simply pagan. It cannot be honestly upheld without attacking the inspiration and authority of the Scriptures. We are convinced that there is only one safe attitude for Christians and churches to have towards it. This is to utterly disapprove it, as they do any other assault of infidelity on God's truth and kingdom. The church leader who becomes an accomplice of this intrusion certainly renders himself detestable and open to discipline by the church and the Lord.

We close with one suggestion to such women that may be inclined to this new freedom. If they read history, they will find that the condition of woman in Christendom, and especially in America, is most enviable as compared with her state in all other ages and nations. Let them honestly consider how much they possess here, which their sisters have never enjoyed in any other age. What bestowed those special privileges on the Christian women of America? The Bible. Let them beware, then, when they do anything to undermine the reverence of mankind for the authority of the Bible. It is undermining their own protection. If they understand how universally, in all non-Christian lands, the "weaker partner" has been made the slave of man's strength and selfishness, they will gladly "leave well enough alone," lest in grabbing at some impossible prize, they lose the privileges they now have, and fall back into the gulf of oppression from which these doctrines of Christ and Paul have lifted them. Amen.

An audio copy of this sermon, preached by Tony Capoccia, is available on tape Cassette or CD at <www.gospelgems.com>.

Dabney, Robert Lewis. "Women Preachers (The Public Preaching of Women)." October, 1879. *Bible Bulletin Board.* Ed. Tony Capoccia. Columbus, New Jersey. <www.biblebb.com>. Reprinted with permission from Tony Capoccia. This updated and revised manuscript is copyrighted © 2000 by Tony Capoccia. All rights reserved.

Hijacking of American Education: Part 4— Ralph Waldo Emerson
By Ruth Nourse

In this continuing series, we have examined how the Christian influence in American letters was subtly edited from the modern educational curriculum. This month, we will highlight the life and work of Ralph Waldo Emerson—who is celebrated today as a central figure in our literary history.

Ralph Waldo Emerson has emerged in our time as a prominent figure on the 19th century horizon. In high school and college textbooks today he is presented as the virtual patron saint of American literature. It is interesting to note that he has not always been viewed in this favorable light. In fact, Mr. Emerson was treated as an oddity in his day, and his popularity paled in the light of Henry Wadsworth Longfellow—the Christian poet who had captured the American audience with his themes of love, family, and moral courage.

Emerson's fame has waxed in recent years while Longfellow's has waned. We must ask: Is the path which he marked out for America a more propitious one than Longfellow's?

Ralph Waldo Emerson was born in Boston on May 25, 1803. He was the third son of the pastor of "old brick," Boston's First Church. His father, William Emerson was actively involved in the life of the Boston community and later became chaplain of the Massachusetts state senate. Ralph's father died when he was only eight years old, and his already unhappy home life became more painful. Emerson complained all his life about being unable to feel close to people—and his journals were filled with self-criticism, introspection, and conjecture about the looks and actions of those around him.

At age 14 he entered Harvard College and graduated in 1821 as class poet. In the years that followed, young Emerson began a period of questioning about the established tenets of Christianity. He wrote in his journal: "Who is he that shall control me? Why may not I act and speak and write and think with entire freedom? What am I to the Universe, or, the Universe, what is it to me? Who hath forged the chains of wrong and right, of opinion and custom? And must I wear them?"[1]

During this questioning period he returned to Harvard to study for the ministry. Through reading Samson Reed's *Growth of the Mind,* a new doorway opened to Emerson. He would no longer be shackled to the narrow view of the Church or Scripture: he now believed that one may receive truth directly from Nature through human intuition. He began to consider all the common arguments against Christianity, and with these in hand, the young divinity student began to point out all the "erroneous passages" of Scripture to parishioners.

Unaware of Emerson's struggle, the pulpit committee asked him to fill the pulpit at the First Church while the pastor was away. At this same time his numerous health problems became worse. His new wife, Ellen, died only months after their marriage. By 1832 he had clearly made a spiritual turning point: he announced to church leaders that he was unwilling to serve the bread and wine of communion because he felt it unreasonable to believe Jesus meant all generations of his followers were to observe the ordinance. This step could be called symbolic of Emerson's entire rejection of the authority of Scripture and the Church.

Injecting the Spirit of Anti-Christ into New England

The decision became a watershed in his relationship with Christian truth. Up to this point he seemed to acknowledge the ameliorative influence of the Christian Church in the world. As he descended from this point, he testified most often to the emptiness of Christian forms. He began to look to other sources for light and reality.

The leadership at Boston's First Church was unable to accept a pastor who would not serve communion and regretfully called for his resignation. Emerson made it clear that the resignation applied only to his position with the church, not the Christian ministry. He would continue to be a minister, but would insist upon his own defini-

tion of what that entailed. Freedom would be the essence of his faith and "its object simply to make men good and wise."[2]

Ill health required Emerson to travel abroad, and while in Europe he consulted with philosophers and writers such as Samuel Coleridge. It was in Europe that Emerson discovered the message that would become his hallmark. Afterwards he wrote: "You can never come to any peace or power until you put your whole reliance in the moral constitution of man and not at all in historical Christianity."[3] The faith he would preach from now on had a simple tenet: "A man who lives in deepest harmony with the impulses of his own moral being is, as a consequence, truly good."[4]

This then—in Emerson's mind—was the gospel destined to set America free from empty traditions and Puritanical chains. He established himself as a lecturer around Concord and Boston and was welcomed to pulpits by minister friends everywhere. He would eventually travel the Continent spreading his message of reform.

Emerson had gathered around himself a group of like-minded thinkers who came to be known as the Transcendentalists. He published his first book, *Nature,* anonymously in 1836, and it came to be called the "Transcendentalist New Testament." Christianity was called their Old Testament. From it, they developed the notion that spiritual knowledge could be directly received by reason through human intuition.

On this premise, Emerson—now known as "the Concord philosopher"—proposed to build a superior system of thought. One member of the circle called Transcendentalism "a Pentecost of the new gospel," described Emerson as "that new-born bard of the Holy Ghost."[5] It was most definitely a strange gospel. Swedenborgianism, socialism, Oriental religions, German idealism, Hindu sacred writings, phrenology, French eclecticism, even Maya, became the grist from which the Transcendentalists could grind their "Newness" in all shades. Although Emerson clung to shreds of Christian teaching that forbade dabbling in the occult, there were seers and seeresses who held seances where moving tables and knockings in the darkness sent shivers down transcendental spines.

A "National Joke" Is Now Considered American's Greatest Philosopher

Ralph Waldo Emerson was taken seriously by relatively few in his own time. His fame has grown until his enigmatic doctrines are now quoted like scripture in textbooks that make him a dominant historical figure. He was never more famous than today. Van Wyck Brooks, writing in 1936, gave this estimate of the attitudes of Emerson's contemporaries: "Emerson was travelling, on his lecture-tours, further and further westward. He was still an impossible puzzle in the popular mind, even a national joke, a byword of the country paragraphers."[6]

Modern textbooks take pains to define and describe the transcendentalist movement as the movement which emancipated the New England mind "from the shackles of a narrow orthodoxy." Emerson's part in the movement, along with lucid exposition of his sometimes obscure doctrines, is presented favorably in contrast to "the otherworldly philosophy of the Puritans."

Obviously we have here a continuation of the war on Henry Wadsworth Longfellow and the Christian worldview which he represented. Slowly over time, educators and philosophers have removed Longfellow from his place of prominence in American literature, and replaced

him with a man who showed forthright contempt for Christianity and who espoused the "new religion" of humanism which has now become the guiding force behind public education in this country.

Next month we will examine Ralph Waldo Emerson's greatest triumph—the capitulation of Harvard University to the philosophies of the New Age.

[1] Joel Porte, ed., *Emerson in His Journals* (Cambridge, MA: Harvard University Press, 1982), p. 38.

[2] John McAleer, *Days of Encounter* (Boston: Little Brown and Co., 1984), p. 124.

[3] Porte, p. 182.

[4] McAleer, p. 150.

[5] Ibid, pp. 301-302.

[6] Van Wyck Brooks, *The Flowering of New England* (New York: Random House, 1936), p. 535.

Nourse, Ruth. "Hijacking of American Education: Part 4—Ralph Waldo Emerson." Reprinted with permission from Media House International, P.O. Box 362173, Melbourne FL 32936-2173.

Hijacking of American Education: Part 5—Flapjack Turning at Harvard
By Ruth Nourse

When Harvard University was founded in 1636, the school was expressly chartered to train pastors and teachers of the Christian faith. From the earliest days of the colonies and until well after the Civil War, American education was preeminently Christian. Beginning in the early 1800's, there was a growing influence of Unitarian interpretations of biblical truth on education that was foreign to all that had gone before in America. VERITAS (Truth) was and is Harvard's motto. In 1869, the University administration reversed the motto's meaning and in the revolution that followed the school became an enemy of the Church that founded it.

In the late 1850's, young Charles William Eliot, as a member of the Harvard faculty, demonstrated remarkable administrative talent. Innovations he suggested brought a wide range

of improvement in school life. After the Civil War, Eliot found some changes afoot at Harvard. In 1866, the alumni had already elected Ralph Waldo Emerson; the response now was to add Eliot to Harvard's board of overseers. After Eliot's election to the board, the liberal majority voted to elect a new president. The nomination of Eliot brought firm opposition from conservatives; but liberals, including Emerson, held out for him on succeeding ballots until he was confirmed.

Few Bostonians seemed aware of the prospect of change encapsulated in Eliot's inauguration at Harvard in 1869. Others knew what Eliot stood for and heralded the revolution with exultation. Van Wyck Brooks, a leading literary critic, gives this view of innovations at Harvard: "Charles William Eliot had turned Harvard over like a flapjack."

Full significance of the "flapjack turning" at Harvard is best understood in the light of the early history of the oldest school of higher learning in America. In 1636, just six years after Boston was founded, a college was authorized by the General Court of Massachusetts. While the project was in the planning stage there arrived from England a young graduate of Emmanuel College, Cambridge, John Harvard, a Congregational minister, along with his bride of 10 months. The young minister's story is not often a part of contemporary histories of Harvard University. His simple dedication to the cause of Christ seems somehow out of sync these days with the great University that bears his name.

For one hundred years the Congregational Church controlled the school. Small though its beginnings may seem, the little college had no rival in America for 60 years. As the pride and joy of the colonies, Harvard College fulfilled the purpose for which it was founded. Changes did not happen overnight and there were legitimate reasons for them. What is remarkable is that in the midst of justifiable reform, the school was removed from control of the Congregational Church and placed at the disposal of forces hostile to the Christian faith.

Emerson's Influence At Harvard

Ralph Waldo Emerson had muttered into his journal for 30 years or more about new laws, new religion, a new race, and other things equally enigmatic. Emerson's defection from the Christian faith provided a hinge upon which to turn an entire nation. Preaching and lecturing as occasion arose and pocketbook demanded, he spoke in terms that could only be called spiritual:

If there be one lesson more than another which should pierce (the scholar's) ear, it is, The world is nothing, the man is all: in yourself is the law of all nature . . . in yourself slumbers the whole of Reason: it is for you to know all; it is for you to dare all. A nation of men for the first time exist, because each believes himself inspired by the Divine Soul which also inspires all men.

The Concord philosopher was invited by students to address the senior class of the Divinity school. Emerson told students that Christ had come to teach that God was incarnate in man—all men. He suggested that what man has been unable to find in the Church may be found in the soul: "In the soul let redemption be sought." The *Boston Daily Advertiser* carried an article deploring Emerson's address because it rejected the revelation upon which Christianity is based and demonstrated the work of evil forces seeking to draw men from the Church. Emerson's

philosophy clearly struck at the roots of Christianity, denying both experience and tradition. The "Divinity School Address" resulted in his banishment from Harvard for almost 30 years.

In 1854, when a student opened his dormitory room for Emerson's lecture on "Poetry," an investigation was made to discover why the philosopher was on campus. Clearly Harvard administrators, after 14 years, still remembered the "Divinity School Address." A change of climate became evident at Commencement 1866, when Harvard awarded Emerson the LL.D. degree and the alumni elected him to the board of overseers. Harvard was ready to enter the new era.

At the time of Eliot's inauguration, erosion of the old faith had been making way for change at Harvard for more than a generation. Until 1865, Harvard University had administrative ties with the State of Massachusetts. When these ties were cut, selection of the board of overseers fell into the hands of the school's alumni. Some perceived the time had come for Emerson's "American Scholar." With president and governing board ready to work together, a new system was inaugurated at Harvard that required a new kind of educator and a new curriculum.

William Charles Eliot was not a radical. His response to religious formalism reveals perception and sensitivity rather than irreverence and skepticism. He noted that religious teaching and activity seemed to be associated with articles or buildings and felt such religious trappings led to idolatry. Eliot saw in the Church so much show and ritualism that was unrelated to real human problems, and so much pure dogmatism, that he seemed to conclude that there was no basis of truth in Christianity. His was a total rejection of the power of the Church. Christendom, as he saw it, was responsible for oppressing Jews, exploiting the masses, and limiting individual freedom. He envisioned and wrote about a "Religion of the Future"—for he admitted man's need for spirituality, while rejecting the absolute authority of the Bible.

Under Eliot's administration, campus and dormitory regulations were relaxed. The university would no longer take responsibility for moral training. Eliot shared Emerson's faith in the ability of human beings to instinctively know what is good for them. They thought the doctrine of man's inborn bent to evil had been disproved. They believed human nature to be basically good. Young people could achieve more, they believed, if set free to follow their stars. But the new methods and rules were not nearly as significant as the new courses of study and the new faculty brought on to teach them.

Eliot's next step was to appoint new faculty. Eliot's appointees included Oliver Wendell Holmes, Jr., John Fiske, and Charles S. Pierce, but perhaps most notable was Chauncey Wright. Wright was considered by Cambridge colleagues to be a master of the power of analytic intellect and is quoted as saying: "Behind the bare phenomenal facts there is nothing." Wright advanced the theory of evolution and received Charles Darwin's special commendation.

Henry Wadsworth Longfellow appears to have read Wright's articles and made them centerpieces in *The Divine Tragedy* and "Helen of Tyre." Wright was almost certainly the poet's model for Simon Magus the Seer. The inquiring and perceptive reader may wish to consider whether or not the poet had identified the source of Harvard's new education.

In "The Christus," published in 1871, Emerson's philosophy is alluded to in Simon Magus' words: "He who knows himself knows all things in himself." Simon Magus' incantation in the same poem strangely echoes the title of Wright's article, "The Uses and Origin of the Arrangement of Leaves." ("I take this orange bough with its five leaves, each equidistant on the upright stem . . .") In "Helen of Tyre," Longfellow seems to have sounded a warning against deception of a spiritually impoverished culture by a Simon Magus in academic garb. Furthermore, a link between "Helen of Tyre" and Wright's article, "Evolution of Self-Consciousness," is found in Longfellow's notes.

Yet strangely, three volumes of Longfellow's journals, letters and reminiscences edited and published by his brother, Samuel, include nothing to reveal the poets awareness of the great changes afoot at Harvard. This is indeed a puzzle because Longfellow was active until a few days before he died in 1882. It is to be wondered if the new courses and professors at Harvard may have received more attention than the poet's published papers would lead us to believe. Samuel Longfellow was a Unitarian minister, and may conceivably have believed that suppression of his brother's orthodoxy was the better part of loyalty. The Longfellow papers may some day prove a gold mine for modern research on this dimly lighted era of American history.

Was Longfellow really silent except for a few cryptic lines? Perhaps the mystery of his silence will one day be unraveled.

Next month, the profound implications of Harvard's "flapjack turning" will be shown.

Nourse, Ruth. "Hijacking of American Education: Part 4—Flapjack Turning at Harvard." Reprinted with permission from Media House International, P.O. Box 362173, Melbourne FL 32936-2173.

The Highwayman
By Alfred Noyes
© 1906, 1913

Part One
I
The wind was a torrent of darkness among the
    gusty trees,
The moon was a ghostly galleon tossed upon
    cloudy seas,
The road was a ribbon of moonlight, over the
    purple moor,
And the highwayman came riding—
        Riding—riding—
The highwayman came riding, up to the old inn-
    door.

II
He'd a French cocked-hat on his forehead, a
    bunch of lace at his chin,
A coat of the claret velvet, and breeches of brown
    doe-skin;
They fitted with never a wrinkle: his boots were
    up to the thigh!
And he rode with a jewelled twinkle,
        His pistol butts a-twinkle,
His rapier hilt a-twinkle, under the jewelled sky.

III
Over the cobbles he clattered and clashed in the
    dark inn-yard,
And he tapped with his whip on the shutters, but
    all was locked and barred;

He whistled a tune to the window, and who
    should be waiting there
But the landlord's black-eyed daughter,
       Bess, the landlord's daughter,
Plaiting a dark red love-knot into her long black
    hair.

IV

And dark in the old inn-yard a stable-wicket
    creaked
Where Tim the ostler listened; his face was white
    and peaked;
His eyes were hollows of madness, his hair like
    mouldy hay,
But he loved the landlord's daughter,
       The landlord's red-lipped daughter,
Dumb as a dog he listened, and he heard the
    robber say—

V

"One kiss, my bonny sweetheart, I'm after a prize
    to-night,
But I shall be back with the yellow gold before
    the morning light;
Yet, if they press me sharply, and harry me
    through the day,
Then look for me by moonlight,
       Watch for me by moonlight,
I'll come to thee by moonlight, though hell should
    bar the way."

VI

He rose upright in the stirrups; he scarce could
    reach her hand,
But she loosened her hair i' the casement! His
    face burnt like a brand
As the black cascade of perfume came tumbling
    over his breast;
And he kissed its waves in the moonlight,
       (Oh, sweet black waves in the moonlight!)
Then he tugged at his rein in the moonlight, and
    galloped away to the West.

Part Two
I

He did not come in the dawning; he did not come
    at noon;
And out o' the tawny sunset, before the rise o' the
    moon,
When the road was a gipsy's ribbon, looping the
    purple moor,
A red-coat troop came marching—
       Marching—marching—
King George's men came marching, up to the old
    inn-door.

II

They said no word to the landlord, they drank
    his ale instead,
But they gagged his daughter and bound her to
    the foot of her narrow bed;
Two of them knelt at her casement, with muskets
    at their side!
There was death at every window;
       And hell at one dark window;
For Bess could see, through the casement, the
    road that *he* would ride.

III

They had tied her up to attention, with many a
    sniggering jest;
They bound a musket beside her, with the barrel
    beneath her breast!
"Now keep good watch!" and they kissed her.
       She heard the dead man say—
Look for me by moonlight;
       Watch for me by moonlight;
I'll come to thee by moonlight, though hell should
    bar the way!

IV

She twisted her hands behind her; but all the
    knots held good!
She writhed her hands till her fingers were wet
    with sweat or blood!
They stretched and strained in the darkness, and
    the hours crawled by like years,
Till, now, on the stroke of midnight,
       Cold, on the stroke of midnight,
The tip of one finger touched it! The trigger at
    least was hers!

V

The tip of one finger touched it; she strove no
    more for the rest!
Up, she stood up to attention, with the barrel
    beneath her breast,
She would not risk their hearing; she would not
    strive again;
For the road lay bare in the moonlight;
       Blank and bare in the moonlight;
And the blood of her veins in the moonlight
    throbbed to her love's refrain.

VI

Tlot-tlot; tlot-tlot! Had they heard it? The horse-
    hoofs ringing clear;
Tlot-tlot, tlot-tlot, in the distance? Were they deaf
    that they did not hear?
Down the ribbon of moonlight, over the brow of
    the hill,
The highwayman came riding,

Riding, riding!
The red-coats looked to their priming! She stood
   up strait and still!

VII

Tlot-tlot, in the frosty silence! *Tlot-tlot,* in the
   echoing night!
Nearer he came and nearer! Her face was like a
   light!
Her eyes grew wide for a moment; she drew one
   last deep breath,
Then her finger moved in the moonlight,
      Her musket shattered the moonlight,
Shattered her breast in the moonlight and
   warned him—with her death.

VIII

He turned; he spurred to the West; he did not
   know who stood
Bowed, with her head o'er the musket, drenched
   with her own red blood!
Not till the dawn he heard it, his face grew grey
   to hear
How Bess, the landlord's daughter,
      The landlord's black-eyed daughter,
Had watched for her love in the moonlight, and
   died in the darkness there.

IX

Back, he spurred like a madman, shrieking a
   curse to the sky,
With the white road smoking behind him and his
   rapier brandished high!

Blood-red were his spurs i' the golden noon;
   wine-red was his velvet coat,
When they shot him down on the highway,
      Down like a dog on the highway,
And he lay in his blood on the highway, with a
   bunch of lace at his throat.

*   *   *   *   *   *

X

*And still of a winter's night, they say, when the
   wind is in the trees,*
*When the moon is a ghostly galleon tossed upon
   cloudy seas,*
*When the road is a ribbon of moonlight over the
   purple moor,*
A highwayman comes riding—
      Riding—riding—
*A highwayman comes riding, up to the old inn-
   door.*

XI

*Over the cobbles he clatters and clangs in the
   dark inn-yard,*
*And he taps with his whip on the shutters, but all
   is locked and barred;*
*He whistles a tune to the window, and who
   should be waiting there*
But the landlord's black-eyed daughter,
      Bess, the landlord's daughter,
*Plaiting a dark red love-knot into her long black
   hair.*

Marietta Holley: Best Selling Writer
By AAUW

A North Country woman who achieved fame
and a certain notoriety in her satirical books
about women's rights and a woman's proper
place in marriage never actually was married,
but spoke with the voice of experience through
her fictional heroine, Samantha Allen.

Marietta Holley was born in 1836 on her
father's farm near Pierrepont Manor in Jefferson
County, NY. Her formal education ended at age
14, and she gave piano lessons for several years
and cared for her family after her father died
when she was 25. However, she yearned to be a
writer and was always scribbling verses on
whatever scraps of paper she could find. She
wrote both poetry and fiction and attempted to
sell them under a pseudonym.

Once a neighbor reminded her about her duty
to support the fatherless family. She predicted
that Marietta would not earn enough from her
writing to pay for paper and postage. She also
offered to introduce Marietta to a widower who
needed a hired girl to help him with his two
children and 15 cows. The neighbor said that
Marietta could earn three dollars a week, and if
she suited the man he might marry her.

Her style of writing was often compared both in content and popularity with that of the famous Mark Twain. She used wit and gentle satire to pose questions concerning women's lack of rights in a then male-dominated world. Her fictional spokeswoman, Samantha, wife of Josiah Allen, speaks in a rustic dialect to poke fun at all sorts of claims and pretensions. For example, Samantha cannot understand why men are trying so hard to protect women from the effort it takes to walk to the polling booth and slip a piece of paper in a box. She has noticed that these same protective instincts do not apply to churning butter, baking bread, and washing clothes, which she observes take considerably more effort. Samantha Allen challenged the status quo of social and political reality of the times and planted herself squarely on the side of sensible women's rights. She raised questions concerning history's treatment of women and their powerlessness before the law. She insisted that a woman, upon marriage, gave up control of her body, her property, her wages, even her personal possessions. She was not allowed to testify in court, sue, contract, hold title to property, sign papers as a witness, or establish businesses. A wife's will had to be signed by her husband in order to be legal. Husbands, even proven drunkards, had control of children after a divorce, and were generally able to secure a divorce on broader grounds than were women.

Recognition as a writer and financial independence were slow in coming to Marietta Holley. It was not until 1872 that she received $600 (a substantial sum in those days) for her first book, entitled *My Opinions and Betsy Bobbet's.* This launched a series of Samantha Books—ten in all—which were widely read throughout the world. Some were published in England; some were translated into French. In all these she used humor spoken by Samantha to cover all the issues that stirred women to extricate themselves from second-class citizenship and to struggle for equality. She received large advances from her publishers, and sales of at least one of her books, *Samantha at Saratoga,* put her on the better-seller list for the decade of the 1880's.

Flower Memorial Library in Watertown, NY has a full collection of her works in a special Marietta Holley room. Though she eventually became famous and financially comfortable, Holley always lived in or near her ancestral home until her death in 1926, at the age of 89.

NY Branch of the American Association of University Women. *Women of Courage, Ten North Country Pioneers in Profile.* St. Lawrence County: NY AAUW, 1989.

Activity Appendix

Table of Contents

Scented Geraniums
Scented Geraniums Were Stars in Victorian Valentine Bouquets
By Barbara Crookshanks

Scented geraniums' modest flowers are almost invisible among the big blossoms of their flamboyant cousins . . . but their fragrant leaves made them the secret stars of Victorian Valentine bouquets.

"Once no bouquet was deemed complete without a bit of this fragrant foliage," wrote Louise Beebe Wilder in her 1932 classic, *The Fragrant Path*. She suggested using the leaves as "a delightful frill" for a bunch of sweet peas or stocks, or combining rose geraniums and nasturtiums for a stimulating nosegay.

Scented geraniums' aromas range from sweet rose to pungent cinnamon. They had an honored place in Kate Greenaway's *The Language of Flowers* with the rose geranium meaning "preference"; the lemon, "unexpected meeting"; the nutmeg, "expected meeting."

In their 19th-century heyday, scented geraniums (*pelargonium*) were grown in hundreds of varieties. Their scents included rose, lemon, lime, orange, filbert, nutmeg, almond, apple, anise, pine, musk, violet, lavender, balm, oak, and peppermint.

They sailed to England about 1795 from the Cape of Good Hope via the British fleet. England fell in love with them both for their rainbow of fragrances and their practical uses. The rose geranium could mimic the costly attar of roses' famed scent.

Scented geraniums starred in horticultural shows and were ideal to scent sachets and potpourri. The leaves floated gracefully in crystal finger bowls.

The little plants with the sweet leaves soon arrived in the United States and were highly popular well into the early 20th century. In his 780-page *Household Discoveries: An Encyclopaedia of Practical Recipes and Processes,* published in 1908, Sidney Morse advises good housekeepers to use bags of "odorous leaves," including those of scented geraniums, to assist in preserving linens from the attacks of insects.

The "sweet leaves" added delightful and inexpensive flavors to cookery on both sides of the Atlantic. Virginia ladies placed a scented rose geranium leaf in each jelly glass before pouring in the boiling syrup. They also made several flavors of sugar by placing scented geranium leaves in their sugar jars.

As years passed, scented geraniums gradually became as out of style as the pompadour and the wasp waist. Louise Beebe Wilder credited their downfall to the popularity of their large and colorful cousins, the bedding geraniums, which filled flower beds with "solid blocks of red and pink and white."

However, she predicted that her favorite little plants would take their places in the sun again. Her prediction slowly seems to be coming true.

The plants were—and are—easy to grow. Contentment for scented geraniums means fertile, well drained soil, fairly cool temperature, and full sun. They propagate easily from cuttings. Pinch them back during their growing seasons. Found today in specialty nurseries and catalogs, they become house plants during winter months.

Isabel Gordon Curtis featured a recipe for Rose Geranium Cake in *Mrs. Curtis's Cook Book,* which was published in the same huge volume as Mr. Morse's *Household Discoveries.* She was a noted food editress who served on the editorial staffs of *Good Housekeeping, Collier's Weekly, the Delineator* and *Success* Magazine.

Isabel Gordon Curtis's Rose Geranium Cake

Preheat oven to 350 degrees F
Sift flour, salt, and baking powder together
    2 cups flour
    1/4 teaspoon salt
    1 teaspoon baking powder
In another bowl, cream butter and sugar
    1/2 cup butter
    1 cup sugar
Add alternately water and above flour mixture
    2/3 cup water
Add
    4 egg whites

Whip hard 5 minutes. Line loaf pan with buttered paper and rose geranium leaves. Carefully add cake batter. Bake at 350 degrees until tests done (35 to 40 minutes). The geranium leaves can be pulled off with the paper. Note: To intensify the rose flavor, add a few drops of rose extract to the cake batter. You can also use scented geranium leaves when making a standard pound cake recipe.

Crookshanks, Barbara. "Scented Geraniums Were Stars in Victorian Valentine Bouquets." *AnswerPoint.* 4 Feb. 2004. Central Rappahannock Regional Library. <http://www.answerpoint.org/columns2.asp?column_id=926&column_type=feature>.

Crocheted Dishcloth

Materials Needed:
100% Cotton Worsted Weight Yarn: 1³/₄ ounces (50 grams, 85 yards)
Crochet hook, size I (5.50 mm) or J

Terms:
sc: single crochet
ch: chain

Body: ch 40

Row 1 (Right side): Sc in second chain from hook. Only pick up the back ridge of the chain, *chain 1, skip next chain, sc in next ch; repeat from * across: 20 sc.

Rows 2–28: Ch 1, turn; working in back loops only, *chain 1, skip next chain, sc in next ch; repeat from * across: do not finish off.

Edging: Ch 1, turn; working on back loops only, sc in first sc, ch 1, (sc in next sc, ch 1) across; (sc, ch 1) evenly across end of rows; working in back loops only of beginning ch, sc in first ch, ch 1, *skip next ch, sc in next ch, ch 1; repeat from * across; (sc, ch 1) evenly across end of rows; join with slip stitch to first sc.

Rnd 2: Ch 1, do not turn, sc in same st, ch, (sc in next sc, ch 1) around: join with slip st to first sc, finish off.

Flower Pounding

The first step in flower pounding is to choose a flower, grass, or weed. Then tape it to a piece of muslin fabric with the front side of the flower facing down. After all the edges of the flower are taped down, pull off the bottom of the flower and cover the hole with a final piece of tape. Now you are ready to tap the flower with a hammer until you can see the colors from the flower on the other side of the fabric. Make sure you tap gently so the details of the flower will not be lost.

To finish, you can put a favorite Bible verse on it about God's creation using calligraphy or transfers. If you do not have a favorite verse, use one of the verses below.

Use the above technique to make either bookmarks or pictures to hang on your wall. You can finish the edges of the material by using an embroidery hoop and attaching lace to the edge. The material cannot be washed once the flower is imprinted.

> Great are the works of the LORD;
> they are pondered by all who delight in them.
> > Psalm 111:2 (NIV)

> Sing to the LORD with thanksgiving;
> Sing praises on the harp to our God,
> Who covers the heavens with clouds,
> Who prepares rain for the earth,
> Who makes grass to grow on the mountains.
> > Psalm 147:7–8 (NKJV)

For all flesh is as grass,
    and all the glory of man as the flower of grass.
The grass withereth,
    and the flower thereof falleth away:
But the word of the Lord
    endureth for ever.
And this is the word which
    by the gospel is preached unto you.
                    1 Peter 1:24–25 (KJV)

Homemade Ice Cream Recipes

Margaret's Chocolate

Melt in double boiler:
    1 lb. Milky Way bars
    8 oz. chocolate chips
Add:
    6 eggs
    1½ cups sugar
    4 cups whipping cream
Fill with milk.

Owen's Outstanding Vanilla

Put in the mixing container of the ice cream freezer:
    1 egg
    ½ teaspoon vanilla
    1 cup whipping cream
    1 can sweetened condensed milk
    1 can canned milk
    1⅓ cups sugar
    Milk to the fill line.

Toppings:
    Blended kiwi
    Angel food cake buttered then grilled or toasted.

Barbie's Rose Geranium Sour Cherry Ice Cream

3 rose geranium leaves
$\frac{1}{2}$ cup sugar
$1\frac{1}{2}$ cups pitted sour cherries
2 tablespoons Kirsch
$1\frac{1}{2}$ cups heavy cream
6 egg yolks, stirred to combine
3 bittersweet chocolate squares chopped. (Chocolate is optional.)

Marinate cherries in 1 tablespoon Kirsch, 1 tablespoon of the sugar, and 2 rose geranium leaves; stir a few times and let stand a few hours, overnight is even better.

Simmer the cherry mixture over low heat with $\frac{1}{4}$ cup sugar until tender and the juices have thickened slightly (about 15 minutes). Turn into bowl to cool and add remaining 1 tablespoon Kirsch.

Heat cream with remaining sugar and last rose geranium leaf over medium low heat until sugar is dissolved and bubbles form around the edges of the pan. Let steep an hour. Reheat just until bubbles form.

Whisk a little at a time some of the hot cream into the egg yolks and then pour the egg mixture into the saucepan and heat over a low flame, stirring constantly. After the mixture forms a custard, the temperature will be about 160 degrees and it will no longer taste of raw egg. Quickly pour through sieve into the bowl of cherries. Stir well and cover with Saran Wrap right on top of the custard. Chill thoroughly in the refrigerator.

When custard is cold, remove geranium leaves and freeze in ice cream maker. Add chocolate pieces if you want and let the ice cream maker run a few minutes more.

You have a sublime and elegant dessert.

"Barbie's Rose Geranium Sour Cherry Ice Cream." *Scented Geraniums.* No Thyme Productions © 2000–2004 <www.nothyme.com/scentedgeraniums/default.cfm#culinary>.

Bead ring

You'll enjoy making this quick Curly Wire & Bead Ring. Of course, they aren't as quick as instant coffee, but they are pretty easy to make and take only a small amount of wire and a few beads.

You'll need:
2–3 inches 18 gauge round wire
2–3 inches 22–28 gauge round wire
one or two beads
wire cutters
jeweler's files
round nosed pliers
flat nosed or bent nosed pliers
rawhide hammer
ring mandrel

Note about Sizing:
Play around with it, and remember that the wire isn't going completely around a finger since a bead or beads are added in the center.

1. File the ends of your round wire.
2. Wrap the wire around a ring mandrel to shape into a big U.
3. Use round nosed pliers to curl both ends, but do not close the curls yet.
4. Take your other wire and wrap around the U a few times just below one of the curls.

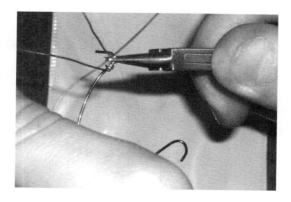

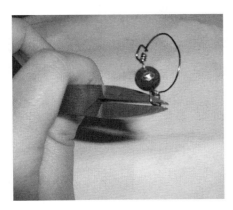

5. Thread the wire through the curl next to it.
6. Thread on your bead or beads.
7. Bring wire down and inside the curl on the opposite end of the ring.
8. Wrap the wire around the U.
9. Use flat or bent nosed pliers to press the ends of the wrapped wire so it is flat against the ring and file a little if necessary so it doesn't poke the wearer.

Colored wire is easy to mark up if you handle the wire too much.

Powley, Tammy. "Curly Wire & Bead Ring." Jewelry Making. © 2004. About, Inc. <http://jewelrymaking.about.com/library/blcrlrng.htm>.

Raspberry Cordial

Real raspberry cordial is prepared by mashing:
  ¹/₂ cup of ripe raspberries (you may substitute blackberries)
  in a stone jar with
  2 tablespoons of white sugar
Pour over them:
  2 tablespoons of the best cider vinegar, and set the jar in the hot sunshine for four hours, after which the mixture should be strained, bottled, and sealed. Lay the bottles in a cool cellar. For drinking, stir 2 tablespoons of the mixture into a small glass of ice water.

Raspberry Cordial

Due to popular request we have been able to locate a recipe for 'Raspberry Cordial,' made popular in *Anne of Green Gables*. For this and other Island recipes we recommend *The Anne of Green Gables Cookbook* by Kate MacDonald. Kate is the granddaughter of L.M. Montgomery.

> 1 lb. 3 oz. raspberries, frozen
> $^1/_2$ cups sugar
> 4 cups boiling water
> 2 lemons

In saucepan, add sugar to frozen raspberries and cook for 20–25 minutes, until sugar has dissolved. Then mash the mixture thoroughly. Pour the mixture through a strainer and discard pulp. Add the strained juice of two lemons. Stir. Add the 4 cups of boiling water. Let cool, then refrigerate. Enjoy!

<http://www.island-flower.com/raspberry_cordial.htm>

Pressed Flower Place Card

Place cards will add a delightful touch to the table. They tell each guest where she is to sit; and, after the party, she can take her place card home as a souvenir.

For each card, you will need a piece of heavy paper or card stock about 2 by 3 inches, pressed flowers, and glue.

Fold the card in half so that it measures about 1 by 3 inches. Arrange one or two small pressed flowers on one end of the front of the card. Glue them in place. Draw or paint on extra leaves or tendrils if you wish. Write the guest's name beside the flowers.

Apprentice Worksheet

Write a report based on the answers to the following questions:

1) What do you like most about your job?

2) What is the most difficult part of your job?

3) Could this job be done on a part time basis or at home?

4) How do you balance work and family time?

5) How does your job enable you to influence others for Christ?

6) What type of training did you have to get your job?

7) What skills do you need to do all the aspects of your job?

8) What is your daily schedule?

9) What are the occupational hazards of your job?

———◆◆◆———

Chocolate Mice for a Centerpiece
(Two Recipes)

Chocolate Mice

Prep Time: 20 minutes
Ready In: 2 hours 20 minutes

4 (1 ounce) squares semisweet
    chocolate
1/3 cup sour cream
1 cup finely crushed chocolate
    wafer cookies
1/3 cup chocolate cookie crumbs
1/3 cup confectioners' sugar
24 silver decorating candies
1/4 cup sliced almonds
12 long red vine licorice

1. Melt the chocolate, and combine with sour cream. Stir in 1 cup chocolate wafer crumbs. Mix well. Cover and refrigerate until firm.

2. Roll by level tablespoonfuls into balls. Mold to a slight point at one end (the nose).

3. Roll dough in confectioners sugar (for white mice), or in chocolate wafer crumbs (for dark mice). On each mouse, place silver candy in appropriate spot for eyes, almond slices for ears, and a licorice string for the tail.

4. Refrigerate for at least two hours until firm.

Makes 12 servings

Chocolate Farm Mice
Elise M. of Denver, CO

Make a melt-in-your-mouth mouse.

Here's what you will need to make it:
3/4 cup of dark chocolate
12 chocolate Kisses
12 maraschino cherries with stems (if you can't find cherries with stems
    you can use red licorice for the tails)
some sliced almonds
toothpick
red decorating gel or melted white chocolate
cookie sheet covered with waxed paper

Here's what you have to do:
1. Melt the dark chocolate.
2. Dip the almonds into chocolate and attach to the base of the chocolate kisses at 10 o'clock 2 o'clock position.
3. Dip a cherry into the chocolate and cover it completely, stems and all. This will be the mouse's body and tail.
4. Quickly press the flat end of a chocolate kiss onto the cherry. This will be the mouse's head.
5. Dot Kiss with either white chocolate or red decorating gel to make the eyes.
6. Place on a cookie sheet covered with waxed paper to cool.

Tableau Vivant (Living Portraits)

Overview:
Students borrow a popular 19th-century parlor activity—composing a *tableau vivant*—to learn about artistic conventions used by period portrait painters.

Goal:
Students recognize how music, art, literature, and other cultural forms reflect the cultures and experiences that have produced them.

Objectives:
* Students, using knowledge of an historical character, will create a living model in a style that might have been used by a period portrait artist.
* Students will understand the use of attributes, poses, and facial expressions to convey historical meaning.
* Students will interpret living models in historical context.

New Jersey Core Curriculum Standards:
Social Studies 6.2, 6.3
Visual and Performing Arts 1.1, 1.5

Activity:
1. Have students choose partners. One is the artist and the other is the artist's model. Give students at least one day to plan and another to perform.
2. Explain the term *tableau vivant,* French for "living picture." A *tableau vivant* is a kind of performance art where real people, furniture, and objects are used to recreate a famous painting or scene from history or literature. In this version, the artist will create a living portrait, using the

partner as the model. The portrait may represent the student who is modeling, or it may represent a fictional or historical character.

3. Hang a 5' x 5' sheet of cloth or butcher paper as a canvas. Instruct artists that they must compose their portraits within this space. They may pin background scenery to the canvas (e.g., silk flowers, a cardboard window, paper mountains) and arrange furniture in the foreground. The models may dress in appropriate costume.

4. Discuss some of the possible attributes the artist may give the model, such as a familiar pose or gesture (reading a book, thumbs up) and a particular facial expression. The artist can also have the model hold or pose with a meaningful object that is associated with the person (soccer ball, quill pen).

5. Have partners present their *tableaux vivants* to the class. The other students try to guess who the subject of the "portrait" is. They should support their guesses with meaningful details that they have observed in the portrait.

Discussion:

* What clues tell you the time period represented in this portrait?
* What could be added in the background or foreground to help classmates identify the model in the portrait?
* What attributes could you add to the model to help reveal his or her identity?

Assessment:

Take a photograph of each tableau. Have students write a description of their own tableaux, explaining all the elements they used.

"A Day in Princeton." *The Cotsen Children's Library: Education.* Princeton University. © 1999–2001 <http://www.princeton.edu/~cotsen/education/dip/before.html>.

Christmas Decorations

Lacy Paper Fans

Perfect props for tea party guests, these lacy paper fans are a breeze to make. Use a glue stick to affix a paper doily onto a sheet of colored paper. Fold the sheet accordion style. For a handhold, pinch together one shorter end and secure it with a rubber band.

The size can be decreased by one-fourth and hung on your Christmas tree.

Tissue Paper Flowers

Rose

* Fold tissue paper (8½″ x 11″) or Kleenex once lengthwise, wrap the folded edge tightly around a twig, wrap tightly. Wrap the base of the flower and twig with green florist tape for a long stem rose.

* For a fuller rose, use multiple layers of tissue paper.

Carnation

* Layer 5 pieces of tissue paper (8½″ x 11″) on top of one another, fold accordion style lengthwise. Tie string tightly in the middle of the folded paper.

* Spread each layer of tissue paper gradually apart on both ends until it forms a large carnation. Use excess string to attach to things.

Matthew's Sleigh Bell Door Chimes

Materials needed:

large sleigh bells—check local craft store
strap to sew the bells on
key chain ring

Make strap at least 1½″ wide by 8″ long. Finish edges. Attach key chain ring to the end of the strap. Evenly sew the sleigh bells onto the strap. Hang onto your bedroom door. You will have your own doorbell.

Quiz and Test Appendix

Table of Contents

Unit 1 Quiz
Literature
(37 points)

1. (6 points) Match the name of the punctuation with the punctuation mark.

    _____   ...   A. period

    _____   ,   B. quotation mark

    _____   ;   C. semicolon

    _____   -   D. ellipsis

    _____   "   E. comma

    _____   .   F. hyphen

2. True or False   The American poets serve a positive function in this story.

3. (3 points) Define personification and give an example.

4. (16 points) Capitalize and punctuate the following sentences.

    its time you were dressed she said curtly

    for pitys sake hold your tongue said Marilla you
    talk entirely too much for a little girl

5. (2 points) Rewrite this passage using only the directives and omitting the explanatory phrases. (Hint: use an ellipsis)

Hebrews 13:2–3:
Be not forgetful to entertain strangers: for thereby some have entertained angels unawares. Remember them that are in bonds, as bound with them; and them which suffer adversity, as being yourselves also in the body.

Use an apostrophe to make the following words into contractions:

6. do not

7. could not

8. will not

9. was not

10. I am

11. I will

12. she will

13. it is

14. we will

History
(17 points)

1. (8 points) Give the latitude and longitude of each of the following cities:
   Prince Edward Island

   Charlottetown

   Gulf of Saint Lawrence

   Ephesus, Turkey

Short answer:

2. (2 points) How were orphans an economic factor in the Victorian age?

3. (2 points) Identify one aspect of the child labor laws in your country and the protection it gives.

4. (2 points) What are the worst forms of child labor in today's world?

5. (3 points) From your research, name three countries that currently use child labor.

Health
(10 points)

1. List three effects sugar has on health.

    a.

    b.

    c.

2. Give three examples of cardiovascular exercise.

    a.

    b.

    c.

3. What are four benefits of regular exercise?

    a.

    b.

    c.

    d.

Unit 2 Quiz

History

(35 points)

Mark each statement true or false.

1. ___ The French Revolution started in 1789.

2. ___ Napoleon Bonaparte was King of Italy.

3. ___ Napoleon Bonaparte sold the Louisiana purchase to the U.S. when George Washington was President.

4. Which King and his Queen were beheaded in 1793?

5. (5 points) Name four countries which attacked France after what tragic event?

6. In what battle did Lord Nelson win the battle, but lose his life?

7. (2 points) After many battles, Napoleon was finally defeated at
_____ by English and _____ armies.

8. Napoleon spent his last six years of his life in exile on what island?

9. The Battle of Hohelinden was part of Napoleon's campaign against which European country?

10. Which Polish patriot is celebrated in the poem "The Downfall of Poland"?

    a. Thomas Campbell   b. Duke of Wellington
    c. Kosiuko   d. Archduke John

11. Which poet wrote "The Battle of Hohenlinden" and "The Downfall of Poland"?

12. What historical event occurred at Anne's conception?

13. What historical event occurred at the same time as Anne's birth?

14. Explain why Canada wanted to remain part of the British Commonwealth?

15. In what battle did the Scottish suffer a major defeat and the loss of their King?

    a. Waterloo   b. Flodden   c. Hohenlinden   d. Gettysburg

16. Who was the gallant King?

(9 points) Match each prominent man with three facts from his life.

17. ___, ___, ___ Andrew Carnegie

18. ___, ___, ___ John D Rockefeller

19. ___, ___, ___ John P Morgan

    A. Made his fortune in banking
    B. Made his fortune in steel
    C. Made his fortune in oil
    D. Loaned the United States $62 million to prevent financial collapse
    E. Great private art collection
    F. Vacationed in Scotland while his workers were striking due to low wages
    G. Developed an effective vertical monopoly which ran competitors out of business
    H. Funded the creation of the University of Chicago
    I. Funded the building of libraries

20. How did the Industrial Revolution affect family life?

21. (4 points) King George III reigned 60 years during which many significant events occurred. Name four events which occurred during his reign.

a.

b.

c.

d.

Art
(5 points)

1. Chromos are made by printmaking or

   a. lithography   b. mosaics   c. frescoes   d. petroglyph

2. (3 points) List three characteristics of Impressionistic painting.

   a.

   b.

   c.

3. Draw a color wheel.

Literature
(8 points)

1. (5 points) Write a stanza with four lines. Have the rhyme pattern
   be AABB.

2. (3 points) Write the definition of the following literary terms:

   rhyme:

   rhythm:

   stanza:

Bible
(20 points)

This is an open Bible test.

1. (3 points) Name three specific areas that someone with inattentiveness
   needs to improve.

   a.

   b.

   c.

   Extra credit: Give specific verses which reinforce these qualities.

2. (5 points) From the Bible, demonstrate iniquity being passed down to
   the third and fourth generations.

3. (2 points) Name two results of lack of self-acceptance.

   a.

   b.

4. (4 points) Match the scripture with the Catechism statement.

   ___ What is the chief end of man?

   ___ What rule hath God given to direct us how we may glorify and enjoy Him?

   ___ What does the Scripture principally teach?

   ___ What is God?

   A. Psalm 104:24   B. Revelation 4:11   C. II Timothy 3:15–17
   D. Micah 6:8

5. (6 points) From memory, write the Lord's Prayer.

Health
(5 points)

1. Name five diseases which were epidemic in the later half of the nineteenth century.

   a.

   b.

   c.

   d.

   e.

Unit 3 Quiz

Literature
(17 points)

1. Give an example of a piece of literature which is an allegory.

2. Who wrote the *The Lady of the Lake*?

3. Give an example of personification.

4. Give an example of literature from the Restoration period.

5. Isabella Alden's uncle wrote what song?

6. What did Pansy's father do to develop her writing ability?

7. What did Isabella Alden want to motivate in youth?

8. (4 points) Name four themes in Pansy's books.

   a.

   b.

   c.

   d.

9. (4 points) Did Montgomery share any of these same themes? If so, how?

10. (2 points) What is the essential difference between prose and poetry?

Bible
(22 points)

Proverbs 29:22:

An _____ man stirreth up _____, and a _____ man aboundeth in _____.

Hebrews 12:4–8:

Ye have not yet _____ _____ _____, striving against sin. And ye have _____ the _____ which speaketh unto you as unto _____. My son, _____ _____ thou the chastening of the Lord, nor faint when thou art rebuked of him: For whom the Lord _____ he _____, and scourgeth every son whom he receiveth. If ye endure chastening, _____ dealeth with you as with _____ for what son is he whom the father chasteneth not? But if ye be without chastisement, whereof all are partakers, then are ye bastards, and not sons.

Psalm 139:13–14:

For thou hast possessed my reins: thou hast covered me in _____ _____ _____. I will praise thee; for I am _____ and _____ _____: marvellous are thy works; and that my soul knoweth right well.

History
(3 points)

Mark each statement true or false.

1. ___ King James II wanted to restore Protestantism to the monarchy.

2. ___ King James II was beheaded in the Glorious Revolution.

3. ___ Oliver Cromwell's son was a strong leader.

Unit 4 Quiz
History
(21 points)

1. (3 points) Name three positive characteristics of Napoleon.

   a.

   b.

   c.

2. (3 points) Name three negative characteristics.

   a.

   b.

   c.

3. (3 points) Name three things Napoleon did which were not good.

   a.

   b.

   c.

4. Who was a living lesson that if ambition can raise them from the lowest station, it can also prostrate them from the highest?

5. (2 points) Tell two facts about James V.

   a.

   b.

6. Name the capital of Canada.

7. (5 points) What were some of the arguments for and against woman's suffrage?

8. (2 points) Who were two key figures in the woman's suffrage movement in the United Sates?

9. Who was called the Great Protectorate and ruled England instead of a King?

Bible
(5 points)

1. Name three similarities in doctrinal beliefs between Catholicism and Protestantism. Use the Apostles' Creed.

   a.

   b.

   c.

Health
(6 points)

1. (3 points) Name three long term effects of alcohol use.

    a.

    b.

    c.

2. (2 points) Name two signs of croup.

    a.

    b.

3. When should you NOT use syrup of ipecac for poisoning?

Literature
(2 points)

1. Who wrote *Childe Harold's Pilgrimmage*?

2. To what literary period or category does *The Lady of the Lake* belong?

Fine Arts
(3 points)

1. Who was Napoleon's court painter?

2. What was his painting style?

3. What type of painting is painted on moist plaster?

    a. oil   b. pastel   c. fresco   d. pen and ink

Unit 5 Quiz
Health
(30 points)

1. (3 points) Name three rules necessary for the proper storage of poisons.

    a.

    b.

    c.

2. (3 points) Give three causes of unconsciousness.

    a.

    b.

    c.

3. (3 points) Name three signs of possible spinal cord injury in an injured person.

    a.

    b.

    c.

4. (3 points) What should you NOT do if you suspect spinal cord injury?

    What is the exception?

    What precautions should you take?

5. (4 points) Name four symptoms of food poisoning.

   a.

   b.

   c.

   d.

6. What is the incubation period of food poisoning?

7. (6 points) Name at least six measures for preventing food poisoning.

   a.

   b.

   c.

   d.

   e.

   f.

8. (3 points) Name three things you should do when a person is about to faint or faints?

   a.

   b.

   c.

9. What nutrient is necessary for the healing of bones?

10. (3 points) Name three things you should or should not do when visiting the sick.

a.

b.

c.

Literature
(11 points)

Indicate whether these sentences are similies or metaphors.

_____ 1. Who is that young lady with the "Titian-hair"?

_____ 2. The moon is as big and orange as a pumpkin.

_____ 3. The trees look as if I could blow them away with a breath.

_____ 4. "Come here half-pint," said Pa to Laura.

_____ 5. "I'll be as secret as the dead," assured Anne.

6. "Evelyn Hope" was written by which Romantic poet?

7. (5 points) Write stronger, more colorful words for each of the following:

walk

chair

look

sit

said

Bible
(5 points)

This is an open Bible test.

1. Read Hebrews 9:27. What does this scripture refute and how?

2. (2 points) True or False   Man is naturally good. Give one scripture to support your answer.

3. (2 points) True or False   Pride is a good thing to have. Give one scripture to support your answer.

History
(25 points)

Short answer:

1. Why did Queen Victoria gain the affection and admiration of people throughout the British Commonwealth?

2. What was the Queen's age when she was crowned?

3. (2 points) Whom did she marry?

   When?

4. (2 points) What kingdom was then separated from the British crown?

   Why?

5. What war raged from 1839–1849?

6. (4 points) In what other wars did Great Britain engage during this time?

   Why?

7. What was the result of the war with China?

8. What effect did the repeal of the Corn Laws have in Britain?

9. (2 points) Who took over ruling France after the third Revolution?

   To where did the King of France escape?

10. Who was responsible for the first Great Exhibition?

11. What was the building called once it was moved and reassembled?

12. What war was fought between 1854 and 1856 by England and France against Russia?

13. In what year did Prince Albert die?

   Extra credit: What important U.S. event occurred this same year?

14. (2 points) What event caused 2 million people to leave Ireland due to death or emigration?

   What year did the potato famine occur?

   Extra credit (2 points): From out previous studies where did many of these emigrants later find work in the United States?

15. What did Parliament repeal in order to decrease starvation?

16. (2 points) Name two facts that you learned while studying the Great Exhibition.
   a.
   b.

17. In which country did England suspend the Habeas Corpus Act?

   Extra credit: What is habeas corpus?

Unit 6 Quiz
History
(12 points)

1. Mary, Queen of Scots was executed by whose order?

2. (3 points) Who fought the Crimean War?

   When did the Crimean War begin?

   End?

3. (2 points) Draw the current Canadian flag.

4. (2 points) List two causes of inflation.

   a.

   b.

5. (2 points) True or False According to Uncle Eric the wage/price spiral is a cause of inflation. Why or why not?

6. What previously studied historical event is the poem *Marmion* describing?

7. What does the Consumer Price Index show?

Literature
(12 points)

1. (6 points) What are the three types of irony? Give examples of each.

   a.

   b.

   c.

2. Mary Ann Evans used what pseudonym for her writing?

3. Name a book by this author.

4. For what literary element were Mary Ann Evans' novels known?

5. From this year's reading, giving an example of juxtapostion.

6. (2 points) Name two helpful aides that you can use to understand difficult reading material.

   a.

   b.

Bible
(12 points)

1. Which is the fourth commandment in the Bible?

2. (8 points) Match the facts with the 1800 evangelist. There will not be an even number of facts for each person.

   Dwight Moody   ___, ___, ___

   Charles Spurgeon ___, ___, ___, ___

   Ira Sankey   ___

   A. Compiled Puritain Catechism

   B. Shoe salesman prior to preaching

   C. Read *Pilgrim's Progress* more than one hundred times

   D. Founded the Chicago Bible Institute

   E. Said, "I am only one, but I am one."

   F. Pastored a large church in England

   G. Wrote songs for Dwight Moody's ministry

   H. Sermons were published weekly in the paper, years after his death

3. (3 points) And now abideth _____, _____, charity, these three; but the greatest of these is charity. I Corinthians 13:_____.

Health
(12 points)

1. (3 points) Name three benefits of physical education.

   a.

   b.

   c.

2. What is normal body temperature orally?

3. (3 points) Name three causes of accidental Tylenol overdose.

   a.

   b.

   c.

4. (3 points) Name three functions of the liver.

   a.

   b.

   c.

5. Name one nutrient necessary for healthy hair.

6. Name one enemy of healthy hair.

Unit 7 Quiz
History
(12 points)

1. Define the following terms:
   a. (2 points) vassal:

   b. (3 points) serf:

   c. (2 points) baron:

2. (3 points) Write three facts about Longfellow.
   a.

   b.

   c.

3. Why had Anne not seen any women preachers?

4. What long range effects did Ralph Waldo Emerson's philosophy have on our current education system?

Literature
(10 points)

1. Who is Odin?

2. Find an example of alliteration in *Marmion* from Canto VI.

3. What is the climatic point of Canto VI?

4. Who evaluated Aristotle's teaching on human reason, putting it on equal foothold with Scripture?

5. _____ has its own reward. —Aristotle

6. Give an example of poetic justice.

7. How does the poem "Maidenhood" enhance the theme of *Anne of Green Gables*?

8. Who said, "to err is human; to forgive divine"?

Mark the following statements true or false.

9. ___ Emerson believed that Scripture was the source of Divine revelation.

10. ___ Emerson was a Transcendentalist.

Bible
(10 points)

1. What did Hudson Taylor see as one of the greatest curses of his day?

2. (4 points) Using a technique similar to Montgomery's, write a paragraph utilizing at least three Biblical phrases in the paragraph. (This is not open Bible.)

3. (5 points) And let us not be _____ in well doing: for in due _____ we shall _____, if we _____ not. Galatians __:9

Fine Arts
(9 points)

1. Name two nineteenth century opera composers.

2. Match these opera terms to the correct definition.

score _____

coloratura _____

aria _____

libretto _____

singspiel _____

leitmotif _____

opera buffa _____

A. A summary of action

B. An elaborate vocal solo that usually expresses a character's feeling

C. A form of German opera, usually comic, that has spoken dialogue instead of recitative. Most of the songs are simple and folklike.

D. Written or printed music used by the conductor

E. A flowery, ornamental vocal style generally used by very high soprano voices.

F. An Italian comic opera concerned with humorous situations that occur in everyday life.

G. A short musical passage that identifies certain ideas, places, and characters each time they appear in the drama.

Health
(28 points)

1. (3 points) Name three of the minimum safety requirements for boating safely.

    a.

    b.

    c.

2. Which boats have the highest mortality rates?

3. What heart healthy nutrient does trout contain?

4. (10 points) Draw the heart and label at least 10 parts of the heart
   using correct medical terminology.

5. (4 points) List four things you can do to reduce the risk of having a
   heart attack.

   a.

   b.

   c.

   d.

6. (3 points) List three risk factors you cannot change to decrease your
   change of a heart attack.

   a.

   b.

   c.

Mark each statement true or false.

   7. ___ Vegetable oil has cholesterol.

   8. ___ Your body makes cholesterol.

   9. ___ Hamburgers have cholesterol.

   10. ___ Cholesterol is made by the kidneys.

   11. ___ Your body needs some cholesterol.

   12. ___ Discomfort or a heavy feeling in the chest can signal a heart attack.

Unit 8 Quiz
Literature
(4 points)

1. What would be the meaning of a white lily?

2. Give an example of onomatopeia.

3. What was the purpose of the poem "The Woman on the Field of Battle"?

4. Who wrote the *Aeneid*?

Fine Arts
(7 points)

1. Who is the Madonna?

2. (2 points) Name two of Raphael's paintings.
   a.
   b.

3. (3 points) Name three Pre-Raphaelite painters.
   a.
   b.
   c.

4. Name one Pre-Raphaelite painting.

Bible
(25 points)

1. Fill in the blanks.

According as his _____ _____ hath _____ unto us all things that pertain unto _____ and _____, through the knowledge of him that hath called us to _____ and _____. Whereby are given unto us exceeding great and precious promises: that by these ye might be partakers of the _____ _____, having escaped the _____ that is in the world through lust. And beside this, giving all _____, add to your _____ virtue; and to virtue _____; And to knowledge _____; and to temperance _____; and to patience _____; And to godliness _____ _____; and to brotherly kindness _____. For if these things be in you, and abound, they make you that ye shall neither be _____ nor _____ in the _____ of our _____ _____ _____. II Peter 1:3–8

Unit 9 Quiz

Literature
(7 points)

1. (2 points) Explain what the theme of "The Glory and the Dream" has to do with this Unit.

2. (2 points) "Loss in all familiar things" is a quote from which poet?

3. (2 points) Give an example of a sentence using local dialogue from your area.

4. Name someone who wrote satirical literature?

   Extra credit: Define satire.

Health
(13 points)

1. (3 points) What are the three most common causes of blindness in the United States.

   a.

   b.

   c.

2. (10 points) List the five stages of the loss process. Give an example of what one might say during each stage.

   a.

   b.

   c.

   d.

   e.

History
(7 points)

1. (4 points) Name three causes of bank failures in the past.

   a.

   b.

   c.

2. (3 points) Name three things which a married woman could not legally do in the 1800's.

   a.

   b.

   c.

Bible

1. (11 points) What acronym describes the five points of Calvinism? For what does each point stand?

   a.

   b.

   c.

   d.

   e.

2. Name one famous Calvinist scholar whom we have studied this year.

   Extra Credit: What document opposes the five points of Calvinism?

Final Exam

Crossword Puzzle • Vocabulary

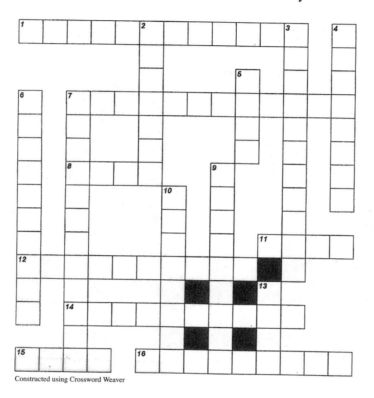

Constructed using Crossword Weaver

Across
1 secret
7 agitation
8 responsibility
11 voluble
12 frequent, repetitive instruction
14 unreasoning passion
15 power
16 strange

Down
2 fate
3 foolishly
4 a challenge
5 absorbed
6 a poisonous substance
7 bias
9 belittle
10 imaginative but impractical
13 saucy

Literature

1. Children are a blessing. Describe the change in Marilla's character as the book progresses.

2. What are Anne's weaknesses?

   How does Marilla help Anne overcome her weaknesses?

3. How does Marilla develop Anne's potential?

4. What role did Matthew play in the family?

5. Tell as many examples as you can of how Diana shows herself a good and true friend.

6. What do you love about the character, Anne?

7. What is in a name? Explain some of the symbolism in the names Montgomery chooses for her characters.

8. Name some of the main themes of Montgomery's *Anne of Green Gables*.

9. Write the definition of each of the following literary terms.

   metaphor:

   foil:

   foreshadowing:

   juxtaposition:

10. Give an example of the following.

    irony:

    poetic justice:

    personification:

    Parthian shaft:

11. Write a sentence using each of the following correctly.

dash:

semicolon:

colon:

12. Has the book *Anne of Green Gables* meant more to you after completing the study *Where the Brook and River Meet?* If so, tell in what way it has meant more to you?

13. Identify the rhyme scheme of the following stanza.

> For thee, who, mindful of unhonored dead,
>   Dost in these lines their artless tale relate,
> If chance, by lonely contemplation led,
>   Some kindred spirit shall inquire thy fate,—

14. Divide the following words into syllables and mark the accented or stressed syllables.

mindful

artless

relate

lonely

contemplation

kindred

15. From your reading during *Where the Brook and River Meet,* give examples of each category of literature, listing title and author.

Restoration Literature (1660–1700)—

Augustan Age or Neoclassical Age (1700–1750)—

Romantic Period (1750–1832)—

Victorian (1832–1901)—

16. List five works of Shakespeare.

a.

b.

c.

d.

e.

History

Essay:

1. What events in England caused John Bunyan to become a political prisoner?

2. What characterized Queen Victoria's reign?

Short answer:

3. In what year did the United States attack Canada?

4. Who fought the Crimean War?

   Extra Credit: During what years was the Crimean War fought?

Mark each statement true or false.

5. ___ The Grand Remonstrance was a document stating grievances against the King and further limiting his power.

6. ___ William of Orange was from France.

7. ___ Charles II led several hundred armed men to the House of Commons to arrest some of the Puritan leaders of Parliament.

8. ___ Charles I was beheaded.

9. ___ Oliver Cromwell was called Lord Protector.

10. ___ Charles II and James II tried to reimpose Catholicism in England.

11. ___ The Glorious Revolution took place in 1688.

Multiple Choice:

12. How many wives did King Henry VIII have?

    a. six   b. eight   c. two

13. In the Restoration those who supported Parliament were
    called _____.

    a. Roundheads   b. Moes   c. Cavaliers   d. Whigs   e. Tories

14. At the conclusion of the English Civil War, Charles I
    fled to _____.

    a. France   b. Scotland   c. Russia

15. The Glorious Revolution was so called because _____.

    a. it was a holy war   c. there was no loss of life
    b. England returned to a monarchy

16. _____ supported the Toleration Act.

    a. Oliver Cromwell   b. Charles II   c. William and Mary   d. James II

17. Match the names and descriptions.

_____ Henry Wadsworth Longfellow	A. A 1700's English satirist
_____ Jacques Cartier	B. Discovered Prince Edward Island
_____ Salmonella	C. Food poisoning common in poultry & eggs
_____ Alexander Pope	D. A Greek philosopher
_____ Robert Browning	E. A popular Victorian poet
_____ Mary, Queen of Scots	F. A beheaded queen
_____ Dwight Moody	G. An American evangelist
_____ Charles Spurgeon	H. Dynamic pastor of a very large church in England
_____ Hudson Taylor	I. Female American satirist
_____ Aristotle	J. Nurse in the Crimean War
_____ James Thomson	K. Famous American poet
_____ Marietta Holley	L. Author of *Winter*
_____ Florence Nightingale	M. Missionary to China

Health

1. Taken orally, what is normal body temperature?

2. List four things you can do to prevent food poisoning from meat.

    a.

    b.

    c.

    d.

3. Draw the heart and label at least ten parts of the heart using correct medical terminology.

4. List four risk factors you can change to decrease your chance of having a heart attack.

    a.

    b.

    c.

    d.

5. List three risk factors you cannot change to decrease your risk of a heart attack.

    a.

    b.

    c.

6. What are the three most common causes of blindness in America? Describe their cause, symptoms, and treatment.

    a.

    b.

    c.

7. By what method of transmission is tuberculosis spread?

8. Name two uses for syrup of ipecac.

   a.

   b.

9. Describe a meal that would be nutritionally helpful to bring to a family if the mother is in a cast.

10. Describe how physical education improves gracefulness and promotes digestion.

Fine Arts

Short Answer:

1. What made Raphael's "Madonna" different from paintings of the Madonna in previous periods?

2. Match these opera terms to their correct definition.

score _____   A. A summary of action.

coloratura _____   B. An elaborate vocal solo that usually expresses a character's feeling.

aria _____

libretto _____   C. A form of German opera, usually comic, that has spoken dialogue instead of recitative. Most of the songs are simple and folk-like.

singspiel _____

leitmotif _____   D. Written or printed music used by the conductor.

opera buffa _____   E. A flowery, ornamental vocal style generally used by very high soprano voices.

    F. An Italian comic opera concerned with humorous situations that occur in everyday life.

    G. A short musical passage that identifies certain ideas, places, and characters each time they appear in the drama.

Bible

1. From Otto Koning's sermons, what are the five weapons of Christian Warfare?

    a.

    b.

    c.

    d.

    e.

2. What is a Calvinist belief system?

3. Write two paragraphs, one explaining the similarities between Catholicism and Protestantism, and the other, the differences.

4. Who is God?

5. Give one example of what a Biblical character said about his unchangeable feature.

6. Write the Lord's Prayer from memory.

7. Is man sinful by nature or inherently good? Use Scripture to support your view.

8. Describe how Anne demonstrates growing in the Lord as described in II Peter 1:2–8.

Answer Appendix

CHAPTER I

Reading Comprehension:

1. How did the positioning of the Cuthbert house differ from the others in Avonlea? *Green Gables was built at the furthest edge of the cleared land instead of being more sociably situated along the main road.* Why? *Matthew's father was the extremely shy and silent type.*

2. How did Marilla keep her yard? *The yard was very green, neat, and precise.* Her kitchen? *Her kitchen floor was so clean one could eat off it.*

3. Why did Marilla agree to adopt Anne despite her misgivings? *It was so seldom that Matthew set his mind to anything that when he did she felt it was her duty to give in.*

4. What effect did Mrs. Lynde's visit have on Marilla? *Marilla felt her doubts and fears reviving.*

5. List at least three of the four community projects in which Mrs. Lynde was involved.
   a. Sewing Circle
   b. Sunday School
   c. Church Aid Society
   d. Foreign Missions Auxiliary

Match the words and phrases with the appropriate character.

6. _C_ deftly
7. _A_ shy
8. _A_ placidly
9. _B_ briskly
10. _C_ disapprovingly
11. _C_ worthy
12. _B_ tall, thin
13. _C_ pessimism
14. _C_ Job's comforting
15. _B_ narrow experience
16. _B_ rigid conscience

Vocabulary Words:

alder* *n*	Lombardies	ferreted
ladies' eardrops* *n*	decorum* *n*	dint
gauntlet	wont	
placidly* *adv*	strychnine* *n*	

Vocabulary: Fill in the blanks using the vocabulary words.

17. *alder*   19. *decorum*   21. *gauntlet*

18. *placidly*   20. *ferreted*   22. *wont*

Activities:

2. a. Why is a semicolon used in the above dictation? *A semicolon is used to separate clauses which contain commas within themselves.*
   b. What is the explanatory phrase in the above dictation? *". . . in Avonlea and out of it . . ."*

3. Is this book fiction or nonfiction? *Fiction. Although there are similarities between the life of Lucy Maud Montgomery and Anne, they are only similarities. Authors write best that which they know best.*

8. Discuss what political and geographic factors differed between the United States and Canada to effect the completion times of each country's transcontinental railway. *In 1867 most British colonies in North America united to form the Dominion of Canada. British Columbia refused to join until 1871 and then only under the condition that a transcontinental railway be established within ten years. The Canadian Pacific railway was a task originally undertaken by the Conservative government of Sir John A. Macdonald. It took fourteen years to build the railroad due to the difficulties of blasting through solid rock and crossing swamps. In the winter there were snow and avalanches, while the summer brought forest fires. During the freezing winter months workers only worked five hour shifts and wore special protective clothing to prevent frostbite. New inventions like powerful dynamite charges for blasting and steam shovels which shifted crushed rocks and other debris enabled the Canadians to cross the Rocky and Selkirk Mountains. In the prairie, 1300 kilometers were laid in 15 months. In the Selkirk Mountains 193 kilometers took 17 months to build. The most difficult section of the track was in British Columbia. Because of the Frazer and Thomson Canyons, it took five years to build 560 kilometers of track. In 1885 the eastern and western tracks met in the Selkirk Mountains. The successful construction of such a massive project, although troubled by delays and scandal, was considered an impressive feat of engineering and political will for a country with a small population and difficult terrain. It was by far the longest railroad ever constructed at the time.*

   In the United States a northern route was chosen because of the Civil War. In the 1700 miles the US intercontinental railroad would cross, the only major city was Salt Lake City, Utah. It would cross desert and mountains as high as 8,000 feet. One river alone would have to be crossed 31 times! Land grants were given to defray the cost of building the railroad, but this was not enough! For both the Central Pacific and Union Pacific, the risks of financial failure and ruin were huge, as was the potential reward. The bulk of the Union Pacific's money came from Oakes and Oliver Ames whose income from a flourishing shovel business during the Gold Rush was further increased by supplying cannons for the Civil War. They invested over a million dollars of their own money. Once again they sold shovels for the project. Money was not the only challenge for the railroad builders. The Union Pacific had to cross the Sierra Nevada Mountains and all of the iron and anything made by heavy industry, including railroad engines, the rail, railroad cars, and wheels, had to be made in the east and shipped around Cape Horn to California. This was a five or six month voyage! Finding wood for ties on Nebraska's nearly treeless prairie and the scarcity of labor were other major problems. Many potential laborers preferred to work the gold mines of the West. The laborers on the Central Pacific were Chinamen while those on the Union Pacific were Irishmen. There was much ill feeling between these two and there were several deaths. Despite all of these challenges, it only took the United States four years to complete its transcontinental railway.

CHAPTER
II

Reading Comprehension:

1. Why did Matthew dread all women except Marilla and Mrs. Lynde? *He had a feeling that they laughed at him.*

2. What was harder than "bearding a lion out of his den" for Matthew? *It was hard for Matthew to ask Anne why she was not a boy.*

3. Did Matthew enjoy Anne's talkativeness? *Like most quiet people, he liked talkative people when they were willing to do the talking themselves.*

4. Matthew dreaded informing Anne she would not have a home with them. To what act did he compare this disclosure? *He likened it to slaughtering an animal.*

Match the words and phrases with the appropriate character.

5. _A_ shuffled

6. _A_ slower intelligence

7. _B_ peculiarly clear sweet voice

8. _A_ long iron-gray hair

9. _A_ ungainly figure

10. _B_ brisk mental processes

11. _B_ freckled

Vocabulary: Fill in the blanks using the vocabulary words.

12. *ludicrously*

13. *alabaster*

14. *eccentric*

15. *vivacity*

16. *rapt*

17. *rapturously*

18. *ruminated*

19. *loquacious*

Activities:

2. *winc-ey*   *al-a-bas-ter*   *cro-cus*   *ru-mi-nat-ed*
   ec-cen-tric   *lu-di-crous-ly*   *vi-vac-i-ty*   *rap-tur-ous-ly*
   rapt   *lo-qua-cious*

CHAPTER III

Reading Comprehension:

1. How did Anne find out about the "mistake" of a girl being sent from the orphanage? *Marilla and Matthew discussed it in front of her.*

2. What were Marilla's three choices for where Anne could spend the night?
   a. a couch in the kitchen chamber   b. spare room
   c. east gable room

3. Who said, "We might be of some good to her"? *Matthew.* What does this statement show about his character? *It shows he loved others as himself.*

Match the words and phrases with the appropriate character.

4. _B_ briskly

5. _C_ meekly

6. _B_ deliberately

7. _C_ depths of despair

8. _C_ odd little figure

9. _C_ stray waif

10. _C_ eager luminous eyes

11. _B_ smile, rather rusty from disuse

Vocabulary: Fill in the blanks using the vocabulary words.

12. *deprecate*

13. *predilection*

14. *romantic*

15. *breach*

16. *perturbation*

Activities:

5. Jacob—*the deceiver*
   Israel—*he struggles with God*
   Ichabod—*no glory*
   Hannah—*grace or prayer*

   Issachar—*reward*
   Hephzibah—*my delight is in her*
   Matthew—*gift of God*

CHAPTER IV

Reading Comprehension:

1. In what season does this chapter take place? *It is late spring.* Write down phrases that illustrate the season. *Some phrases: cherry-tree in full bloom; lilac trees with purple flowers; sprinkled with dandelions.*

2. What did Anne say about sorrows? *"It's all very well to read about sorrows and imagine yourself living through them heroically, but it's not so nice when you really come to have them, is it?"*

3. What did Marilla find more frustrating than a man who would not talk back? *She found a woman who would not talk more frustrating.*

Match the words and phrases with the appropriate character.

4. _B_ curtly

5. _C_ deftly

6. _C_ martyr

7. _B_ distrustfully

8. _A_ looking wistfully

9. _C_ reverie

10. _B_ muttered

11. _B_ grimly

12. _B_ uncomfortable ignorance

Unit 1 Quiz

Literature
(37 points)

1. (6 points) Match the name of the punctuation with the punctuation mark. (Chapter 1, #2; Chapter 2, #2; also see *Topics Covered Appendix*)

   <u>D</u>   <u>F</u>
   <u>E</u>   <u>B</u>
   <u>C</u>   <u>A</u>

2. *True* (Chapter 2, #4)

3. (3 points) Define personification and give an example. *Personification is a literary devise in which the author speaks of or describes an animal, object, or an idea as if it were a person. Examples may vary.* (Chapter 3, #2)

4. (16 points) Capitalize and punctuate the following sentences. (Chapter 4, #2)

   "It's time you were dressed," she said curtly.
   "For pity's sake hold your tongue," said Marilla. "You talk entirely too much for a little girl."

5. (2 points) Rewrite this passage using only the directives and omitting the explanatory phrases: *Be not forgetful to entertain strangers; . . . remember them that are in bonds.*

Use an apostrophe to make the following words into contractions. (See *Topics Covered Appendix*)

6. *don't*   10. *I'm*   *14. we'll*

7. *couldn't*   11. *I'll*

8. *won't*   12. *she'll*

9. *wasn't*   13. *it's*

History
(17 points)

1. (8 points) Give the latitude and longitude of each of the following: (Chapter 1, #4)

Prince Edward	*W 64°25'–W 61°58' / N 47°04'–N 45°56'*
Charlottetown	*W 63°8' / N 46°14'*
Gulf of Saint Lawrence	*W 62° / N 48°*
Ephesus, Turkey	*longitude: 27.3333°; latitude: 37°*

Short answer: (Chapter 3, #12)

2. (2 points) How were orphans an economic factor in the Victorian age? *Orphans were a cheap or unpaid source of labor.*

3. (2 points) Identify one aspect of the child labor laws in your country and the protection it gives. *Answers may vary. Minimum age and limiting the amount of hours worked are two common aspects which protect children.*

4. (2 points) What are the worst forms of child labor in today's world? *Answers may vary. These forms include: forced labor by children; trafficking of children for exploitative labor; forcible recruitment of children for use in armed conflicts; exploitation of children in the commercial sex industry; the use of children for illicit activities such as the trafficking of drugs; and the involvement of children in other hazardous labor that places at risk the health, safety, and morals of children.*

5. (3 points) From your research, name three countries that currently use child labor. *Any three of the following countries would be correct:*

1. Bangladesh	*12. Guatemala*	*23. Pakistan*
2. Benin	*13. Haiti*	*24. Panama*
3. Bolivia	*14. Honduras*	*25. Peru*
4. Brazil	*15. India*	*26. Philippines*
5. Cambodia	*16. Indonesia*	*27. Romania*
6. Costa Rica	*17. Kenya*	*28. South Africa*
7. Dominican Republic	*18. Lesotho*	*29. Tanzania*
8. Egypt	*19. Mali*	*30. Thailand*
9. El Salvador	*20. Nepal*	*31. Togo*
10. Ethiopia	*21. Nicaragua*	*32. Uganda*
11. Ghana	*22. Nigeria*	*33. Zambia*

Health
(10 points)

1. (3 points) List <u>three</u> effects sugar has on health. (Chapter 3, #10)
   a. obesity
   b. decreased immune system
   c. dental caries
   d. empty calories

2. (3 points) Give <u>three</u> examples of cardiovascular exercise. (Chapter 4, #9)
   a. brisk walking
   b. gardening
   c. ballroom dancing
   d. bicycling
   e. running

3. (4 points) What are <u>four</u> benefits of regular exercise? (Chapter 4, #9)
   a. reduces risk of premature death
   b. heart disease
   c. obesity
   d. high blood pressure
   e. type II diabetes
   f. osteoporosis
   g. stroke
   h. depression
   i. colon cancer

CHAPTER V

Crossword Puzzle • Poetry Terms • Activity 12

```
            R     R H Y T H M
    P Y R R H I C         O
            Y         T   N
P   H E X A M E T E R R   O
E   E       E         O   M
N   P           O C T A V E
T   T       O   A   H   E T
A   A       C   N   A Q   E
M   M       T   A   I U   R
E   E       O   P   C A
T E T R A M E T E R   T R
E   E       E   S     R A
R   R       T   T     A
            E   L I M E R I C K
    M E T E R   C         N
```

Reading Comprehension:

1. Of what did Anne's parents die? *Anne's parents died of a fever.* How old was she when they died? *She was three months old.*

2. Describe the different places Anne had lived. *Answers may vary.*

3. What love of her life did Anne reveal in this chapter? *A love for literature, especially poetry.*

4. What fault did Marilla find with Anne? *She thought Anne talked too much.*

Vocabulary: Fill in the blanks using the vocabulary words.

5. *pinion*

6. *confidentially*

7. *reproachful*

8. *asylum*

9. *inculcates*

10. *shrewd*

11. *immigrate*

12. *emigrants*

Activities:

3. *con'-fi-den'-tial-ly*　*in-cul'-cates'*　*re-proach'-ful*　*a-sy'-lum* *'shrewd*　*pin'-ion*　*'em-i-grants*　*'im-mi-grate*

12. What type of foot does a limerick use? *The rhythm can be called an anapestic foot, two short, unstressed syllables and then a long, stressed; the reverse of dactylic rhythm.*

13. a. Which lines rhyme in "The Battle of Hohenlinden"? *The first three lines rhyme.* What is the rhyme scheme for the first stanza? *The rhyme scheme for this stanza is AAAB.*

   b. Is the rhyme scheme of "The Downfall of Poland" the same? *No.* What is the rhyme scheme of "The Downfall of Poland"? *The rhyme scheme is AABBCCDD.*

   c. Look at "The Downfall of Poland." Does it contain couplets? *No, there are more than two lines in each stanza.*

   d. What type of stanza is used in "The Battle of Hohenlinden"? *Quatrain*

15. a. Mark each word with stressed and unstressed syllables. *The stressed and unstressed syllables are:*
   *"On **Lin'**den, **when'** the **sun'** was **low'**, . . ."*
   b. What is the smallest repeated pattern or foot? *The foot pattern is iambic.*
   c. How many feet are in this verse? *There are four feet in this verse, which is called tetrameter.* Check the other verses within the same stanza. Are they the same? *Not exactly, but the overall meter is iambic tetrameter.*

CHAPTER
VI & VII

Reading Comprehension:
Chapter VI

1. Who wanted a girl to help her? *Mrs. Peter Blewett wanted a girl to help her.* What was her reputation? *Mrs. Blewett's reputation was that she was a terrible worker and she drove her servants too hard. She was stingy with a bad temper. Her family had pert, quarrelsome children.*

2. By what attribute was Mrs. Spencer known? *She was quite capable of taking any and every difficulty into consideration and settling it.*

3. Why did Marilla change her mind? *She feared that Anne's look would haunt her the rest of her life. She did not like Mrs. Blewitt.*

4. What did Matthew think of Anne? *Matthew thought she was interesting.* What did Marilla want Anne to be? *Marilla wanted her to be useful.*

5. What was the agreement Marilla made with Matthew? *That she would raise Anne without Matthew's assistance. If she failed then he could help.*

6. Why did Marilla not tell Anne of their decision that night? *She thought she would sleep better not knowing.*

7. What symbolism do you see in Mrs. Blewett's name? *Answers may vary.*

Chapter VII

8. What did Marilla find out about Anne? *She found out that she was almost a perfect heathen.* What was her solution to remedy this situation? *Her solution was to send for* The Peep of Days, *make a dress in which to send her to Sunday School, and teach her a prayer the following day.*

Vocabulary: Fill in the blanks using the vocabulary words.

9. *fractious*

10. *vim*

11. *haunt*

12. *gimlet*

13. *ungraciously*

14. *pert*

15. *qualm*

16. *harrowing*

17. *catechism*

18. *luxurious*

19. *glibly*

20. *obliged*

21. *assented*

22. *irreverence*

23. *infinite*

Activities:

2. What is the reason for the dash? *To set off a parenthetical matter that is very abrupt.*

3. The sentence in your dictation is an example of what figure of speech? *It is a metaphor.*

5. a. What is the rhyme pattern for the first stanza in "Edinburgh After Flodden"? *The rhyme pattern is AABBCCDD.*

   c. What type of stanza is it? *It is an eight-line or octave stanza.*

   d. Mark each word with stressed and unstressed syllables.
      ***News'** of / **bat'tle!** / **News'** of / **bat'tle!** /*
      ***Hark'!** tis / **ring'ing / down'** the / **street'**: . . .*

   e. What is the smallest repeated pattern or foot? *The foot pattern is stressed' unstressed or trochaic.*

   f. How many feet are in this verse? Check the other verses within the same stanza. Are they the same? *There are four feet in the first line of this verse and three in the second line.*

7. a. How many generations are included in Jesus' genealogy in the first chapter of Matthew? *According to Matthew, chapter 1, verse 17, ". . . all the generations from Abraham to David are fourteen generations; and from David until the carrying away into Babylon are fourteen generations; and from the carrying away into Babylon unto Christ are fourteen generations." Note that this scripture counts David and Jechonias each twice, at the end of one set of 14 generations and the beginning of the next 14 generations. Therefore, there are 40 generations from Abraham to Joseph, ". . . the husband of Mary, of whom was born Jesus, who is called Christ."*

   b. Are there any names passed down through the generations? *The name, "Jacob," appears twice: once for the son of Isaac and once for the father of Joseph, Mary's husband.*

14. Why had Anne not said prayers? *She was not fond of God because He had made her hair red.*

Reading Comprehension:

1. What would recall Anne to work? *Only reprimand or catastrophe recalled Anne to work.*

2. Why does one scald a dishcloth? *Scalding kills the bacteria and molds that cause a sour smell in the dishcloth.*

3. What did Marilla think about imagining things to be different than they are? *When the Lord puts us in difficult circumstances He does not mean for us to imagine them away.* What do you think? *Answers will vary.*

4. What did Marilla want Anne to learn about obedience? *She wanted immediate obedience, not discussion.*

CHAPTER
VIII

5. What character qualities did Marilla admire in Diana? *She thought she was pretty, but more importantly to Marilla, good and smart.*

6. At the conclusion of chapter VIII, what does Anne think of herself? *Anne felt she had an identity because now she belonged somewhere.*

7. Do you name inanimate objects? *Answers will vary.* If so, what objects do you name? *Answers will vary.*

Activities:

7. What opinion of Anne did Mrs. Thomas have? *She thought that she was desperately wicked.*

10. According to Marilla, what was Anne's most serious shortcoming? *She let her mind wander.*

13. What is the theme of *Anne of Green Gables? Answers may vary. The answers should include some of the following:*
Conflict between imagination and social expectations
Sentimentality versus emotion
All things happen for good to those that love the Lord
Children are a blessing
Grace versus the Law
Will versus duty
Adolescence and growing up

CHAPTER IX

Reading Comprehension:

1. What did Mrs. Rachel Lynde think of those who are sick? *She had contempt for those who were often sick.*

2. What had Anne done during her free time at Green Gables? *During Anne's free time she had wandered the land about Green Gables.* How long was she allowed to roam? *She was able to roam during odd half hours.*

3. When did Marilla not allow Anne to chatter? *She did not allow Anne to chatter when she found herself becoming too interested in it.*

4. When Marilla spoke of Anne's positive characteristic, to what did she refer? *Anne was intelligent.*

5. What was Anne's response to Mrs. Lynde's unkind remark? *She stamped her foot on the floor and asserted hatred of Mrs. Lynde for her unkindness.*

6. On the way up the stairs Marilla felt condemned about her own feelings. Why? *Marilla was angry at herself for wanting to laugh at Mrs. Lynde's response to Anne's disrespectful remarks.*

7. What event in Marilla's life allowed her to be empathetic with Anne? *She had overheard an aunt refer to her as a dark, homely thing. The memory of that remark continued to sting Marilla for years.* Has this ever happened to you? *Answers will vary.*

8. What are three reasons Anne should have been respectful?
   a. Mrs. Lynde was a stranger.   *c. She was an elderly person.*
   b. She was Marilla's visitor.

9. Why was Marilla "troubled in mind" and "vexed in soul"? *She was upset with herself for chuckling inside when she remembered Mrs. Lynde's dumbfounded look.*

Vocabulary: Fill in the blanks using the vocabulary words.

10. *reprehensible*   14. *empathetic*

11. *vexation*   15. *deprecates*

12. *apology*   16. *fortnight*

13. *grippe*   17. *suppositions*

Activities:

4. What character quality does Marilla have with regard to decisions? *When she makes up her mind, it stays made up.*

5. a. On what quality does Mrs. Lynde pride herself? *She prides herself in speaking without fear or favor.*
   b. How is this good? *She does not have a fear of man and she is not given to flattery.* How is this bad? *Mrs. Lynde is tactless and sometimes unkind.*

6. a. Mark each word with stressed and unstressed syllables.
      "A **sol**'/ *dier* **of**'/ *the* **Le**'/ *gion lay* **dy**'/ *ing* **in**'/ *Al* **giers**' . . ."*
   b. What is the smallest repeated pattern or foot? *The foot pattern is unstressed stressed' or iambic.*
   c. How many feet are in this verse? *There are six feet in this verse.*
   d. Does this happen in this poem? *Yes.* Give an example of enjambment. (Note this further explanation of "enjambment": A line which does not end with a grammatical break, that is, where the line cannot stand alone, cannot make sense without the following line, is enjambed.) *Examples may vary.*
      "And if a comrade seek her love, then ask her in my name
      To listen to him kindly, without regret or shame; . . ."
                                                      —Stanza 4, lines 6–7
   e. Does this poem contain a refrain? *Yes, Bingen on the Rhine.*

Unit 2 Quiz

History
(31 points)

1. *True* (Chapter 5, #8)

2. *True* (Chapter 5, #8)

3. *False* (Chapter 5, #8)

4. *King Louis XVI* (Chapter 5, #8)

5. Name <u>four</u> countries which attacked France after what tragic event? (Chapter 5, #8)
Britain, Holland, Spain, Austria, Prussia;
the assassination of the King and Queen of France

6. *The Battle of Trafalgar* (Chapter 5, #8)

7. (2 points) *Waterloo, Prussian* (Chapter 5, #8)

8. *St. Helena* (Chapter 5, #8)

9. *Austria* (Chapter 5, #8)

10. *c. Kosciuko* (Chapter 5, #9)

11. *Thomas Campbell* (Chapter 5, #4)

12. *The adoption of the Canadian Constitution.* (Chapter 5, #10)

13. *The meeting of the first Canadian legislature.* (Chapter 5, #10)

14. Explain why Canada wanted to remain part of the British Commonwealth? *Answers may vary. They should include some reference to an attachment to the Queen and protection.* (Chapter 5, #10)

15. *b. Flodden* (Chapter 6 & 7, #8)

16. *James IV* (Chapter 6 & 7, #8)

Match each prominent man with three facts from his life. (Chapter 9, #8) (9 points)

17. <u>*B, F, I*</u> Andrew Carnegie

18. <u>*C, G, H*</u> John D. Rockefeller

19. <u>*A, D, E*</u> John P. Morgan

20. How did the Industrial Revolution affect family life? *Answers may vary but should include the separation of parents and children due to working conditions.* (Chapter 9, #8)

21. (4 points) King George III reigned 60 years during which time many significant events occurred. Name <u>four</u> events which occurred during his reign. (Chapter 5, #8)

a. American Revolution
b. French Revolution
c. Napoleonic wars
d. Captain Cook's voyages
e. Mutiny of the British Navy
f. Union of Parliaments
g. First Sunday School
h. First steam vessel
i. Gas street lamps in London
j. Spinning jenny
k. Power loom

Art
(5 points)

1. *a. lithography* (Chapter 8, #12)

2. (3 points) List <u>three</u> characteristics of Impressionistic painting. (Chapter 9, #11)
   a. landscape almost always has a human presence
   b. light and color
   c. broken brushwork
   d. not detailed

3. *See your resource for color wheel.* (Chapter 9, #11)

Literature
(8 points)

1. (5 points) Write a stanza with four lines. Have the rhyme pattern be AABB. *Answers will vary.* (Chapter 5, #12)

2. (3 points) Write the definition of the following literary terms: (Chapter 5, #12)
   rhyme: *similar sounds usually occurring at the end of a line*
   rhythm: *regular periodic beat in a poem*
   stanza: *a division of poetry according to the number of lines it contains*

Bible
(20 points)
This is an open Bible test.

1. (3 points) Name <u>three</u> specific areas that someone with inattentiveness needs to improve. (Chapter 8, #10)
   a. orderliness   *d. listening skill*
   b. subduing desires of the flesh   *e. finishing well*
   c. concentration

   Extra credit: Give specific verses which reinforce these qualities (Chapter 8, #10)

2. (5 points) From the Bible, demonstrate iniquity being passed down to the third and fourth generations. *Answers will vary.* (Chapter 5, #18)

3. (2 points) *a. bitterness*   *b. lack of ability to trust God* (Chapters 6 & 7, #14)

4. (4 points) Match the scripture with the Catechism statement. (Chapter 6 & 7, #11, 12)
   _B_ What is the chief end of man?
   _C_ What rule hath God given to direct us how we may glorify and enjoy Him?
   _D_ What do the Scriptures principally teach?
   _A_ What is God?

5. (6 points) From memory, write the Lord's Prayer. (Chapter 8, #5)
> *Our Father,*
> *Who art in heaven,*
> *Hallowed be thy Name.*
> *Thy kingdom come,*
> *Thy will be done,*
> *On earth as it is in heaven.*
> *Give us this day our daily bread.*
> *And forgive us our trespasses,*
> *As we forgive those who trespass against us.*
> *And lead us not into temptation,*
> *But deliver us from evil.*
> *For thine is the kingdom, and the power, and the glory, for*
> *ever and ever. Amen.*

Health
(5 points)

1. Name <u>five</u> diseases which were epidemic in the later half of the nineteenth century. (Chapter 5, #26)

   a. smallpox   *e. yellow fever*
   b. cholera   *f. polio*
   c. typhus   *g. typhoid*
   d. influenza

Crossword Puzzle • Vocabulary

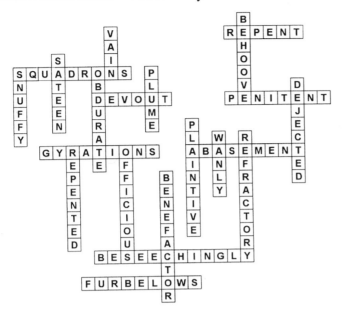

Reading Comprehension:
Chapter X

1. When was the last time Matthew had been upstairs? *Four years ago when he had helped Marilla wallpaper.* What brought him this time? *He thought he could be of help in the stand off between Marilla and Anne.*

2. What did Marilla see in Anne's apology that Mrs. Lynde did not? *Marilla saw that Anne thoroughly enjoyed the valley of humiliation.*

3. What did Mrs. Lynde care for less than one with a temper? *She did not like a sly child.*

4. What effect did Anne holding Marilla's hand have on Marilla? *It was described as an unaccustomed sweetness that made her uncomfortable.*

Chapter XI

5. L.M. Montgomery initially wrote *Anne of Green Gables* as a serial for Sunday School papers. What message did she give in this chapter to teachers and to the girls in the Sunday School class? *Answers may vary. The Sunday School teacher should have the children ask questions about what they do not understand, yet things should be kept in decency and in order. As we see later, Anne is a very loveable child whom the girls shun because she is rumored to be odd. We see the loneliness Anne suffers as a result of their unkindness.*

Worksheet • Who Am I? • Activity 11 • "Winter"

1. *Socrates*
2. *Homer*
3. *Hamlet*
4. *Othello*
5. *Apollo*
6. *Solon*
7. *Lycurgus*
8. *Aristides the Just of Veii*
9. *Cimon*
10. *Camillus*
11. *Cincinnatus*
12. *Scipio*
13. *Cato the Censor*
14. *Brutus*
15. *Pope*
16. *Monimia*
17. *Belvidera*

Reading Comprehension:
Chapter XII

1. How did Marilla keep on track in her discipline of Anne? *Marilla did not allow herself to be drawn from the concrete to the dubious path of the abstract.*

2. Why was Anne so excited to go with Marilla for the skirt pattern? *She was to meet Diana, who she hoped would be a true friend.*

3. Why did Mrs. Barry want a playmate for Diana? *She believed Diana spent too much time reading.*

4. How did Matthew know Anne liked chocolates? *She had mentioned it in a previous conversation and he had paid attention to detail.*

5. What good character quality did Marilla note in Anne? *She noted that Anne was giving rather than stingy.*

6. What did Marilla not like in a man? *She did not like an "I-told-you-so" attitude.*

Chapter XIII

7. What character flaw in Anne needed to be overcome before she could cook? *She needed to be more attentive.*

8. Why did Anne not like patchwork? *She thought there was no scope for her imagination.*

9. In what one way did Anne see Diana as not being perfect? *Anne did not think Diana was as imaginative as herself.*

10. What event was Anne excited about? *She was excited about the church picnic.*

Vocabulary: Fill in the blanks using the vocabulary words.

11. *sarcasm*
12. *dolefully*
13. *dubious*
14. *deprecatory*

Activities:

2. c. Compared to those in the past, authors today usually use clear, succinct sentences. Long sentences can be confusing to read. Rewrite the dictation section with shorter sentences and use formal punctuation for the dialogue with quotation marks and paragraphing. (Each speaker's words should be in a separate paragraph.) *Answers may vary, but an example is included below.*

Then he began to go forward, but Discretion, Piety, Charity, and Prudence, would accompany him down to the foot of the Hill. So they went on together, reiterating their former discourses, till they came to go down the Hill.

Then said Christian, "As it was difficult coming up, so far as I can see, it is dangerous going down."

"Yes," said Prudence, "so it is. For it is a hard matter for a man to go down into the Valley of Humiliation, as thou art now, and to catch no slip by the Way."

"Therefore," said they, "are we come out to accompany thee down the Hill."

So he began to go down, but very warily. Yet he caught a slip or two. —John Bunyan, *Pilgrim's Progress*, "Part the First"

6. What are the two different types of swearing referred to on page 87 (*The Annotated Anne of Green Gables*, pages 139–140)? *One type of swearing is the use of profanity. Another type of swearing is the act of confirming an oath.*

7. c. What makes "Winter" poetry rather than prose? *Unlike prose, poetry generally uses rhyme and rhythm. The exalted language, the personification, the rhythm, and the format all combine to make this poetry.*

Reading Comprehension:

1. What did Anne see as one good thing about herself? *She never made the same mistake twice.*

2. What block did Anne refer to on page 97? *Royal or noble persons going to be executed, especially in the sixteenth century, were "led to the block," or chopping block, to have their heads chopped off by the executioner's axe, whereas common people were usually hanged. Anne Boleyn, Mary Queen of Scots, and Charles I were all beheaded in this manner. This type of execution ceased in 1747.*

3. What did Marilla think was worse than fits of temper? *She thought it was much worse to be a liar.*

4. Who was slow to lose faith in Anne? *Matthew*

5. Why did Marilla feel that she could not go to Mrs. Lynde for advice? *Mrs. Lynde was not supportive of them having Anne. She would say, "I told you so."*

6. What had happened to Marilla's brooch? *Marilla had left it on her shawl.* Why did Anne confess? *She wanted to go to the picnic and Marilla would not believe the truth.*

Vocabulary: Fill in the blanks using the vocabulary words.

7. *retort*   8. *sublime*   9. *scrumptious*

Chapter XV

Reading Comprehension:

1. How long is a generation? *A generation comprises the people living within the same period or a single succession in natural descent, as the children of the same parents; hence an age. Approximately 20–25 years.*

2. Marilla responded sharply to Anne's description of her teacher. What was the tone of Anne's response? *Comfortable.* What does this tell about her? *Answers may vary.* Think of other tones she could have responded with. *Answers may vary, but some possibilities are sharp, rude, kind.*

3. What positive physical characteristic did Anne have? *She had a nice nose.*

4. Tell about Gilbert Blythe. *He was handsome, liked to tease the girls, and he was used to being head of his class.* Why was he behind others that were his age in school? *Gilbert's father had been sick and had to go out to Alberta for his health. Gilbert had gone with his father and had not been able to go to school much for the three years he was there with him.*

5. What did Anne find a little humiliating? *There was no danger of any boy liking her.*

6. What did Anne do wrong in school? *She took vengeance on Gilbert and disrupted the class by yelling at him and cracking her slate over his head.*

7. What was Anne's response to discipline? *She was angry and humiliated, but did not repent.*

8. What was a difference between Anne and Diana? *Diana could never have resisted Gilbert's plea.*

9. From whom did Marilla seek council? *She sought council with Mrs. Lynde.*

10. What amazed Matthew? *The depth of Marilla's laughter amazed Matthew.*

11. Explain the saying: "If you must borrow trouble, for pity's sake borrow it handier home." *Answers may vary. Worry about today, rather than the future.*

Vocabulary: Fill in the blanks using the vocabulary words.

12. *bracken* 15. *drollery*

13. *indignant* 16. *vindictive*

14. *harrow*

Activities:

2. The word "there" has two homophones, words that sound alike but mean something different. Name them. *The two homophones are they're and their.*

Unit 3 Quiz

Literature

(17 points)

1. *Pilgrim's Progress* (Chapter 10 & 11, #7)

2. *Sir Walter Scott* (Chapter 14, #5)

3. Give an example of personification. *Answers will vary.* (Chapter 15, #2)

4. *Pilgrim's Progress* (Chapter 10 & 11, #7 & #8)

5. *"It Is Well With My Soul"* (Chapter 15, #9)

6. What did Pansy's father do to develop her writing ability? *He encouraged her to keep a journal and develop a natural affection for writing.* (Chapter 15, #9)

7. What did Isabella Alden want to motivate in youth? *Following Christianity and the Golden Rule.* (Chapter 15, #9)

8. (4 points) Name <u>four</u> themes in Pansy's books. (Chapter 15, #9)
   a. church attendance
   b. abstinence form alcohol
   c. self-sacrifice
   d. dangers of popular forms of recreation
   e. requirements, tests, and rewards of being a Christian

9. (4 points) Did Montgomery share any of these same themes? If so, how? *Answers will vary.* (Chapter 8, #13)

10. (2 points) What is the essential difference between prose and poetry? (Chapter 12 & 13, #7) *It has irregularity and variety of rhythm and is closer to the patterns of everyday speech.*

Bible

(22 points)

1. Fill in the blanks.

   An <u>*angry*</u> man stirreth up <u>*strife*</u>, and a <u>*furious*</u> man aboundeth in <u>*transgression*</u>. Proverbs 29:22 (Chapter 10 & 11)

   Ye have not yet <u>*resisted unto blood*</u>, striving against sin. And ye have <u>*forgotten*</u> the <u>*exhortation*</u> which speaketh unto you as unto <u>*children*</u>. My son, <u>*despise not*</u> thou the chastening of the Lord, nor faint when thou art rebuked of him: For whom the Lord <u>*loveth*</u> he <u>*chasteneth*</u>, and scourgeth every son whom He receiveth. If ye endure chastening, <u>*God*</u> dealeth with you as with <u>*sons*</u>; for what son is he whom the Father chasteneth not? But if ye be without chastisement, whereof all are partakers, then are ye bastards, and not sons. Hebrews 12:4–8 (Chapter 12 & 13)

   For thou hast possessed my reins: thou hast covered me in <u>*my mother's womb*</u>. I will praise thee; for I am <u>*fearfully and wonderfully made*</u>: marvellous are thy works; and that my soul knoweth right well. Psalm 139:13–14 (Chapter 15)

History
(3 points)

1. *False* (Chapter 10 & 11, #9)

2. *False* (Chapter 10 & 11, #9)

3. *False* (Chapter 10 & 11, #9)

CHAPTER
XVI

Reading Comprehension:

1. What sense was not developed in Marilla? *She had an undeveloped aesthetic sense.*

2. What two things happened because of Anne's inattentiveness while preparing and caring for food? *First she forgot the flour in the cake; then she left the covering off the pudding sauce which allowed a mouse to crawl in and drown.*

3. What did Anne believe God was incapable of doing? *Anne did not believe Him capable of changing such a stubborn woman's heart.*

4. What two changes were occurring in Marilla? *Marilla softened to the point of physically demonstrating love and kissed Anne's cheek. Marilla's heart was lighter and she was able to laugh.*

5. What did Matthew haul to the vessels? *He hauled potatoes.*

6. What made Mrs. Barry suspicious of Anne? *She was suspicious of Anne's big words and dramatic gestures and she thought Anne was making fun of her.*

7. What fault did Marilla see in Diana? *She thought it was greedy of Diana to drink three glassfuls of cordial.*

Vocabulary: Fill in the blanks using the vocabulary words.

8. *nun*
9. *cloister*
10. *aesthetic*
11. *pathetic*
12. *prepense*
13. *mortifications*
14. *wont*
15. *woe*

Activity:

14. Before there were immunizations, how did people attempt to stop the spread of smallpox? *After exposure people were put in quarantine in an attempt to stop the spread of the disease. Those who had previously had smallpox could care for those who were sick because they had developed an immunity to the disease. Interestingly, Edward Jenner created the very first modern vaccine to combat smallpox in 1796 when he inoculated a person with cowpox. Cowpox is a related, but much more benign disease. Still, the inoculation creates immunity to smallpox. Since that time, we have developed many vaccines against many deadly infectious diseases, particularly deadly childhood diseases.*

Reading Comprehension:

1. What did Diana say that surprised Anne? *It surprised Anne that Diana loved her.*

2. What had happened to Katie Maurice and Violetta? *The little dream girls were not as satisfying after having a real friend. The real world had become more interesting than the imaginary.*

3. Had Mrs. Lynde been right about Anne staying out of school? *Yes. Anne returned of her own accord.*

4. What had the other students missed about Anne? *They had missed Anne's imagination in games, her voice in singing, and her dramatic ability in reading books aloud.*

5. What relationship did Anne have with Gilbert? *They were competitors in academics.*

6. Why did Anne progress despite a poor teacher? *Anne was inflexibly determined to learn.*

7. Why did Anne find it hard to stay sad? *It was hard to stay sad because the world was so interesting.*

Vocabulary: Fill in the blanks using the vocabulary words.

8. *tenacity*	11. *ostentation*	14. *effusion*
9. *perquisites*	12. *stanchly*	15. *dolefully*
10. *annexed*	13. *muse*	

Reading Comprehension:

1. What kept Anne studying diligently instead of reading the book she wanted to read? *She had the goal of being the head of her class.*

2. What made the roads red? *The iron in the soil made the roads red.*

3. What was Ruby Gillis' idea of courting? *Answers may vary. See page 140 (The Annotated Anne of Green Gables, page 202).* What do you think about it? *Answers may vary.*

4. What was Anne's approach to resisting temptation? *She gave Matthew the key. She tried to remove the temptation by placing it under the control of somebody with authority over her.*

5. How did Anne heap coals of fire on Mrs. Barry's head? *She saved her daughter's life in spite of Mrs. Barry's unforgivingness.*

6. Anne was not the only person up all night; Matthew was as well. What did he offer to do for Anne? *He offered to do her chores so that she could sleep.*

7. At the same time, what did Anne note about how adults typically treated her? *They laughed at the large words she used and hurt her feelings.*

Vocabulary: Fill in the blanks using the vocabulary words.
8. *buxom*   9. *russets*   10. *indulgently*

CHAPTER XIX

Reading Comprehension:

1. What did Anne use to clean the floor? *She used sand to scour the floor.*

2. What did Anne want to do? *Anne wanted to go to a concert and then spend the night at Diana's house.* What were Marilla's objections to this? *Marilla did not like the idea of Anne going to the concert. She feared Anne would catch cold and have her head filled up with nonsense and excitement. She thought it would unsettle her for a week.*

3. How did Anne do in school the day of the concert? *Gilbert Blythe beat her in both spelling and math.*

4. Why did Carrie Sloan cry? *She cried because she was not allowed to go to the concert as all her peers were.*

5. How did Anne conquer her jealousy of Diana's clothes? *She used her imagination.*

6. What was Anne's response to Gilbert when he quoted one of her favorite poems? *She read a book and appeared bored.*

7. What happened after the concert at the Barry's? *Anne and Diana jumped into bed on top of Diana's Aunt.* What were the repercussions from it? *Answers may vary, but should include scaring the aunt and the aunt becoming dismayed with Diana and deciding not to pay for her music lessons.*

8. After talking to Mrs. Lynde, what did Anne do? *She apologized to Diana's Aunt and made peace with her.*

Vocabulary: Fill in the blanks using the vocabulary words.

9. *contrite*   12. *sagely*   15. *pompadour*

10. *moral*   13. *dire*   16. *pensive*

11. *mortal*   14. *crescendo*   17. *valise*

Activities:

12. On page 214 of *The Annotated Anne,* Marilla states, "I wash my hands of it." See if you can find the Biblical story to which this refers. *Matthew 27:24*

Unit 4 Quiz

History
(21 points)

1. (3 points) Name <u>three</u> positive characteristics of Napoleon. (Chapter 17, #8)
   a. original   *c. independent*   *e. energetic*
   b. bold mind   *d. decisive*

2. (3 points) Name <u>three</u> negative characteristics. (Chapter 17, #8)
   a. worshipped no god but ambition   *c. stern*
   b. knelt at the shrine of idolatry   *d. impatient*

3. (3 points) Name <u>three</u> things Napoleon did which were not good. (Chapter 17, #8)
   a. imprisoned the pope   *c. grasped without remorse*
   b. impoverished the country   *d. persecuted authors, silenced the press*

4. *Napoleon* (Chapter 17, #8)

5. (2 points) Tell <u>two</u> facts about James V. *Answers may vary.* (Chapter 18, #4)

6. *Ottawa* (Chapter 18, #8)

7. (5 points) What were some of the arguments for and against woman's suffrage. *Answers may vary.* (Chapter 18, #15, 16, 17, 18)

8. (2 points) Who were <u>two</u> key figures in the woman's suffrage movement in the United Sates? *Susan B. Anthony and Elizabeth Cady Stanton* (Chapter 18, #17)

9. *Oliver Cromwell* (Chapter 19, #4)

Bible
(5 points)

1. Name three similarities in doctrinal beliefs in Catholicism and Protestantism. Use the Apostles' Creed. (Chapter 16, #18) *Both Catholics and Protestants believe in accord with the statements of the Apostles' Creed: We believe in God the Father Almighty, Maker of heaven and earth. And in Jesus Christ his only Son our Lord; who was conceived by the Holy Ghost, born of the Virgin Mary, suffered under Pontius Pilate, was crucified, dead, and buried; he descended into hell; the third day he rose again from the dead; he ascended into heaven, and sitteth on the right hand of God the Father Almighty; from thence he shall come to judge the quick and the dead.*

Health
(6 points)

1. (3 points) Name <u>three</u> long term effects of alcohol use. (Chapter 16, #11)
   a. cirrhosis of the liver   *c. delirium tremens*   *e. fetal alcohol syndrome*
   b. pancreatitis   *d. osteoporosis*   *f. domestic abuse*

2. (2 points) Name <u>two</u> signs of croup. (Chapter 18, #6)
   a. hoarseness
   b. resonant barking cough
   c. croaking sound called stridor during respirations
   d. obstruction of the upper respiratory tract

3. When should you NOT use syrup of ipecac for poisoning?
   (Chapter 18, #6)
   a. before calling physician or poison control
   b. for caustic (corrosive) solutions

Literature
(2 points)

1. *Lord Byron* (Chapter 17, #11)

2. *Romantic* (Chapter 19, #5)

Fine Arts
(3 points)

1. *Jacques-Louis David* (Chapter 17, #9)

2. *Neoclassical* (Chapter 17, #9)

3. *c. fresco*

Reading Comprehension:

1. What quality did Anne seem to admire the most in people? *Anne admired imagination most of all.*

2. What did Anne discover about imagination? *Answers may vary. She discovered that a person can imagine wrong things to her own detriment.*

Vocabulary: Fill in the blanks using the vocabulary words.

3. *capricious*   5. *sarcastic*   7. *inexorable*

4. *limpid*   6. *reveries*

Reading Comprehension:

1. Who left and who arrived in Avonlea? *Mr. Phillips left and Mr. and Mrs. Allan came.*

2. Why did Mrs. Lynde have several items returned that night? *The new preacher and his wife were at Mrs. Lynde's house and everyone wanted to meet them.*

3. How did the church at Avonlea pick a preacher? *The congregation decided which one they wanted after they had preachers come on a trial basis.*

4. What was special about the way Mr. Allan prayed? *He prayed as if he meant it, not just as if he were in the habit of it.*

5. What change did Mrs. Allan make in Anne's Sunday school class? *She allowed the students to ask questions.*

6. What new kindred spirit did Anne find? *Her latest kindred spirit was Mrs. Allan.*

7. What happened to Anne's cake? *She put anodyne liniment in the cake.* How could this have been prevented? *She could have smelled it or tasted the batter before baking the cake to see if it tasted right.*

8. What made Anne want to be a Christian? *The kindness of Mrs. Allan made Anne want to be a Christian.*

9. What did Anne like about tomorrow? *Tomorrow is a day with no mistakes in it yet.*

Vocabulary: Fill in the blanks using the vocabulary words.

10. *dimples*
11. *dryad*
12. *dissipated*
13. *dyspeptic*
14. *doctrine*
15. *theology*
16. *presentiment*
17. *plaintive*
18. *manse*
19. *adulterated*
20. *inveigle*

CHAPTER
XXII

Reading Comprehension:

1. What was Anne excited about in this chapter? *She was invited to tea at the manse.*

2. Why did Marilla worry about Anne not taking things calmly? *She thought that the ups and downs of life would be hard on Anne.* Why should she not have worried about this? *Because the equal capacity for delight would compensate for the downs.*

3. Anne stated that she wanted to become a minister's wife. Why did she want to become one? *She thought that a minister would be good enough to overlook her red hair.*

4. Can someone be nice and not a kindred spirit? *Yes, they can be.*

5. What did Mrs. Lynde think was a dangerous innovation? *Mrs. Lynde thought a woman teacher was a dangerous innovation.*

Vocabulary: Fill in the blanks using the vocabulary words.

6. *saffron*   10. *demure*

7. *pithy*   11. *deportment*

8. *trebled*   12. *organdy*

9. *seraph*   13. *waif*

Reading Comprehension:

1. Name some small mishaps that have occurred since Anne put the liniment in the cake. *She emptied a pan of skim milk into a basket of yarn balls and walked clean over the edge of the log bridge into the brook while wrapped in imaginative reverie.*

2. What factor led to the girls daring each other? *The girls were bored. They were tired of all their games and ripe for mischief.*

3. What caused Anne's downfall? *Anne's pride was her downfall.*

4. When Marilla saw Mr. Barry carrying Anne, what revelation did she have? *She realized how much she cared for Anne.*

5. What wish of Anne's came true? *Anne had wished that she could faint.* What did she think about it afterward? *She did not think fainting was worth wishing for.*

6. Why would Marilla have stayed on the ground? *Marilla had strength of mind.*

7. What were the consequences of Anne's foolishness? *It was painful when the doctor set Anne's ankle and she had to miss the excitement of the new teacher.*

8. What did Anne think was one good thing about being laid up? *When you are laid up you find out how many friends you have.*

9. What dark burden would Josie have been carrying if Anne had died? *She would have been carrying the dark burden of remorse for being responsible for Anne's death.*

Unit 5 Quiz

Health

(30 points)

1. (3 points) Name <u>three</u> rules necessary for the proper storage of poisons. (Chapter 21, #22) *Answers may vary.*
   a. *Do not store in containers previously used for edible items.*
   b. *Label properly.*
   c. *Do not store in the same place as edible items.*
   d. *Keep out of the reach of children.*

2. (3 points) Give <u>three</u> causes of unconsciousness. (Chapter 23, #3, 5)
   a. head trauma
   b. loss of blood
   c. lack of oxygen
   d. chemical changes due to drugs or diabetic coma
   e. nervous reaction due to fear, hunger, pain, or emotional shock

3. (3 points) Name <u>three</u> signs of possible spinal cord injury in an injured person. (Chapter 23, #4)
   a. severe pain in the neck or spine
   b. tingling, loss of feeling or control of extremities
   c. loss of bowel or bladder control

4. (3 points) What should you NOT do if you suspect spinal cord injury? *You should not move the person.* What is the exception? *If they are in danger where they are at and you are unable to secure the area.* What precautions should you take? *Keep the body in a straight line.* (Chapter 23, #4)

5. (4 points) Name <u>four</u> symptoms of food poisoning. (Chapter 21, #14)
   a. mild to severe diarrhea   *d. fever*
   b. nausea   *e. headache*
   c. abdominal cramping

6. What is the incubation period of food poisoning? *8–48 hours.* (Chapter 21, #14)

7. (6 points) Name at least <u>six</u> measures for preventing food poisoning. (Chapter 21, #14)
   a. At the store, bag your meat separately from other products.
   b. Store at proper temperature (hot foods, 140°F; cold foods, 41°F).
   c. Separate raw meat and poultry from other foods in the refrigerator.
   d. Do not allow blood to drain on other foods.
   e. Work with meat on nonporous surfaces only.
   f. Wash hands, cutting boards, and counter surfaces before and after handling raw meat.
   g. Use disinfectant to clean surfaces.
   h. Never put cooked meat on the same plate on which raw meat was placed without washing it first.
   i. Thaw meat in the refrigerator.
   j. Fully cook the meat; use a meat thermometer, especially for poultry.
   k. Refrigerate leftovers immediately after the meal.

8. (3 points) Name <u>three</u> things you should do when a person is about to faint or faints? (Chapter 23, #5)
   a. Try to control their fall.
   b. Once they are lying down, elevate their legs.
   c. Loosen any tight clothing.
   d. Give them a whiff of ammonia.

9. *Calcium.* (Chapter 23, #6)

10. (3 points) Name <u>three</u> things you should or should not do when visiting the sick. (Chapter 23, #8)

   a. Never sit on the bed; it cramps the patient.

   b. Only stay a few minutes to wish the patient well.

   c. If the nurse or doctor has to do something, be polite and leave the room.

   d. If the patient wants to go for a walk with you, check with the nurse first to see if it is all right. Walking is usually very good for surgical patients, but be sure to watch the patient for any sign of tiredness or dizziness.

   e. Be polite and stand if there are not enough chairs.

   f. If you do take food, even if the patient has asked for it, check with the nurses to see if the patient can eat it.

   g. Be quiet while you are visiting. Others will be sleeping.

Literature
(11 points)

Indicate whether these sentences are similes or metaphors. (Chapter 22, #2)

   M 1. Who is that young lady with the "Titian-hair"?

   S 2. The moon is as big and orange as a pumpkin.

   S 3. The trees look as if I could blow them away with a breath.

   M 4. "Come here half-pint," said Pa to Laura.

   S 5. "I'll be as secret as the dead," assured Anne.

   6. *Robert Browning* (Chapter 22, #3)

   7. (5 points) Write stronger, more colorful words for each of the following: *Answers will vary.* (Chapter 23, #2)

walk	*saunter*	sit	*slouch*
chair	*recliner*	said	*assured*
look	*glance*		

Bible
(5 points)

1. Read Hebrews 9:27. What does this scripture refute and how? *It refutes reincarnation. The Bible says that man dies once and then is judged.* (Chapter 22, #3, 4)

2. (2 points) True or False? Man is naturally good. *False* Give one scripture to support your answer. *Answers may vary. One of the following verses may be used. Psalm 51:5, Romans 5:12–21; and I Corinthians 15:21–22.* (Chapter 22, #8)

3. (2 points) True or False? Pride is a good thing to have. *False* Give one scripture to support your answer. *Answers may vary. One of the following verses may be used. James 4:6 or I Peter 5:5.* (Chapter 22, #5, 6)

History
(25 points)

Short answer: (Chapter 20, #5)

1. Why did Queen Victoria gain the affection and admiration of people throughout the British Commonwealth? *She was hardworking and had true concern for her subjects' welfare.*

2. What was the Queen's age when she was crowned? *She was 19 years old.*

3. (2 points) Whom did she marry? *Her cousin, Albert of Saxe-Coburg-Gotha.* When? *1840*

4. (2 points) What kingdom was then separated from the British crown? *Hanover.* Why? *It was illegal for them to have a female leader.*

5. What war raged from 1839–1849? *The Afghan war*

6. (4 points) In what other wars did Great Britain engage during this time? *A war with Egypt and one with China in 1840.* Why? *1.) Turkey requested assistance in its war with Egypt and to protect British trade in the Black Sea. 2.) Answers on the war with China should tell about the order given by the emperor and the dispute over the importation of opium, a drug which the Chinese love to smoke and chew. The emperor, wishing to put an end to this dangerous habit, ordered that none should be imported, and seized and destroyed many cargoes which British merchants tried to smuggle into the Chinese ports from India, where it is cultivated. He also imprisoned several British subjects.*

7. What was the result of the war with China? *British troops captured several large towns and compelled the Chinese to open four ports to British trade, to pay a large sum of money, and to give up the island of Hong Kong, which has ever since belonged to Britain.*

8. What effect did the repeal of the Corn Laws have in Britain? *It dropped the price of wheat.*

9. (2 points) *Louis Napoleon, England*

10. *Prince Albert*

11. *The Crystal Palace*

12. *The Crimean War*

13. *1861*

    Extra credit: *The Civil War began.*

14. (2 points) *The potato famine, 1845*

    Extra credit: (2 points) From our previous studies, where did many of these emigrants later find work in the United States? *Many of them worked building the railroads.*

15. *The Corn Act was repealed.*

16. (2 points) Name two facts you learned while studying the Great Exhibition. *Answers may vary.*

17. *Ireland*

Extra credit: What is habeas corpus? *In the common law legal system habeas corpus, Latin for "you should have the body," is a prerogative writ requiring the government to produce a prisoner before a court and justify his imprisonment. Its purpose is to release someone who has been arrested unlawfully. Habeas corpus has nothing to do with whether the prisoner is guilty, only with whether due process has been observed.*

Reading Comprehension:

1. How did Anne describe Miss Stacy? *She used the adjectives true, helpful, bright, sympathetic, and young.*

2. What did Anne recite? *Anne recited the poem, "Mary, Queen of Scots."*

3. What did Anne dearly want to be? *Anne dearly wanted to be remarkable.*

4. Why did Anne not see herself as being able to be a foreign missionary? *She believed ". . . one would have to be very good to be a missionary, and that would be a stumbling block."*

5. Why was Matthew glad he did not have to bring up Anne? *He would have worried over frequent conflicts between inclination and duty. This way he would have spoiled Anne.*

6. What did Matthew add to Anne's life? *He appreciated her, which sometimes can have as much value as conscientious upbringing.*

Vocabulary: Classify the words according to their parts of speech.
laudable *adj*　　vivacious *adj*　　gadding *v*

Reading Comprehension:

1. After much consideration, what did Matthew see as different about Anne? *Anne was not dressed like the other girls.*

2. What was a matter of conscience with Matthew? *It was a matter of conscience for him to shop at William Blair's store.*

3. How did Matthew solve the dilemma of purchasing a dress with puffed sleeves? *He went to Mrs. Lynde.*

4. Mrs. Lynde saw Marilla as making what mistake in raising Anne? *Answers may vary. Mrs. Lynde believed it was a mistake to think there is a set formula for raising children; what works to develop a desirable characteristic in one child can be counter-productive in another.*

5. What kind of Christmas were the people in Avonlea looking for. *They looked forward to a green Christmas.*

6. What gift did Diana bring that was providential? *Diana brought a pair of slippers from her Aunt.*

7. What gave Anne courage for the performance? *Anne thought of her puffed sleeves.*

8. How old was Anne? *Anne was twelve.*

9. Was Marilla proud of Anne's performance? *Yes.* Did she tell her? *No.* Did Matthew? *Yes.*

10. What did Matthew think needed a lot of thinking over? *He thought Anne's future needed thinking over. OR: He thought Anne going to Queen's needed thinking over.* What does this say about his personality? *Answers may vary.*

Activities:
10. Find out what ten dollars in Canadian money would be in U.S. dollars. *$1.00 in Canadian dollars equals $.75 in American dollars x $10.00 = $7.50. (Remember this solution works under the false assumption that the exchange rate between the two countries is always the same. The best way to do this would be to change an 1878 Canadian dollar into an 1878 U.S. dollar then change the 1878 U.S. dollar into today's dollar. $7.50 / .057 [Conversion factor for 1878] = $131.58 rounded to the nearest dollar would be $132. The Web site below shows the exchange rates from 1948 until 2002. From 1948–1978 the U.S. and Canadian dollar were almost equal. From 1978 onward the U.S. dollar was stronger with its peak in 2002. In 2004 the rates are similar to what they were in 1995. See The University of British Columbia Sauder School of Business Pacific Exchange Rate Service site at <http:// clk.about.com/?zi=1/XJ&sdn=economics&zu=http%3A%2F%2Fpacific. commerce.ubc.ca%2Fxr%2F>.*

Reading Comprehension:
1. What effect did the concert have on the residents of Avonlea? *There were trifling frictions stemming from jealousy, miscommunication, and rudeness.* Who fought for Anne's reputation? *Charlie Sloan fought for Anne's reputation.*

2. What was Anne's response to people confessing their past sins? *It gave her hope that someday she would be good.* What was Mrs. Lynde's response? *It made her lose confidence in them.*

3. What did Marilla think of the story club? *She thought it was foolishness.*

Activities:
14. Which person in Avonlea emulates Psalm 15? *Mrs. Allan* Who in this chapter fits Proverbs 18:6? *Josie Pye*

CHAPTER XXVII

Reading Comprehension:

1. What were Marilla's expectations upon arriving home? *She thought she was coming home to a nice warm fire and the table set for tea.* What greeted her instead? *Nothing had been done.*

2. Anne was not to let the Italian peddlers in the house, so as not to encourage them. How had Anne followed the rule, while disregarding the intention of it? *She went outside, but the sale encouraged them.*

3. Besides Matthew and Marilla, who knew Anne's fatal secret? *Diana knew her secret.* Did she ever tell? *Diana never told.*

4. What made losing her hair even more tragic for Anne? *It was her mistake, no one else benefited from it, and it was unromantic.*

5. List several consequences of Anne's vanity. *Answers will vary.* What did Anne learn about vanity through this experience? *It is better to be good than beautiful.*

6. Whom did Anne consider to be good? *She considered Marilla, Mrs. Allan, and Miss Stacy to be good people.*

7. What does Marilla now think of Anne's chattering? *Marilla has grown used to it; she likes to hear it.*

Vocabulary: Classify the words according to their parts of speech.

veracity *n*   snood *n*

vexation *n*   implicitly *adv*

Activities:

15. Convert the prices of the dye into U.S. money and then convert them into today's money. *$.75 Canadian is $.56; divided by .057 = $9.82. $.50 Canadian is $.38; divided by .057 = $6.67.* (See Chapter XXV, Activity 10)

Unit 6 Quiz

History

(12 points)

1. *She was executed by Queen Elizabeth's order.* (Chapter 24, #3)

2. (3 points) Who fought the Crimean War? *British, French, and Turkish forces fought against Russian forces.* When did the Crimean War begin? *1853* End? *1856* (Chapter 24, #10)

3. (2 points) See an encyclopedia. (Chapter 24, #11)

4. (2 points) List <u>two</u> causes of inflation. (Chapter 25, #10)
   a. *increased circulation of money*
   b. *removal of the gold standard*
   c. *supply and demand of money, velocity*

5. (2 points) *False* Why or why not? *If the supply of money has not changed, then the only way for one person to have more money is for someone else to have less. The value of the money would not change.* (Chapter 25, #10)

6. *The Battle of Flodden Field.* (Chapter 27, #8)

7. What does the Consumer Price Index show? *It shows how prices have changed over time. It also shows the buying power of the dollar.* (Chapter 25, #10)

Literature
(12 points)

1. (6 points) What are the <u>three</u> types of irony? Give examples of each. *Answers may vary.* (Chapter 25, #5)
   a. dramatic   b. verbal   c. irony of situation

2. *George Eliot* (Chapter 26 #12)

3. Name a book by this author. *She wrote* The Mill on the Floss. (Chapter 26, #12)

4. *Character development* (Chapter 26, #12)

5. From this year's reading, give an example of juxtaposition. *Answers will vary.* (Chapter 27, #6)

6. (2 points) Name <u>two</u> helpful aides you can use to understand difficult reading material. (Chapter 1, #5)
   a. Read an overview of the plot.
   b. Become familiar with the vocabulary.
   c. Understand the historical context.

Bible
(12 points)

1. *Honor the Sabbath.* (Chapter 26, #6)

2. (8 points) Match the facts with the 1800 evangelist. There will not be an even number of facts for each person. (Chapter 26, #3)
   <u>B, D, E</u>   Dwight Moody   <u>G</u> Ira Sankey

   <u>C, A, F, H</u> Charles Spurgeon

3. (3 points) And now abideth <u>*faith*</u>, <u>*hope*</u>, charity, these three; but the greatest of these is charity. I Corinthians 13:<u>*13*</u>. (Chapter 24)

Health
(12 points)

1. (3 points) Name three benefits of physical education. (Chapter 24, #7)
   a. promotes digestion   d. increases flexibility
   b. increases gracefulness   e. increases endurance
   c. increases strength

2. *98.6° F (Chapter 27, #12)*

3. (3 points) Name <u>three</u> causes of accidental Tylenol overdose. (Chapter 27, #12)
   a. *Two people medicating the same child. Always check to make sure no one else has given a child medication.*
   b. *Not realizing Tylenol has several different dosage strengths.*
   c. *Combining two medications with the active ingredient, acetaminophen.*

4. (3 points) Name <u>three</u> functions of the liver. (Chapter 27, #12)
   a. *blood clotting*
   b. *fight disease*
   c. *orchestrate the metabolism of fats, carbohydrates, and protein*
   d. *detoxification*
   e. *break down damaged red blood cells*
   f. *recycle iron*
   g. *store vitamins*

5. Name <u>one</u> nutrient necessary for healthy hair. (Chapter 27, #11)
   a. *Essential fatty acids.*
   b. *Silica provides collagen essential for luxurious hair growth.*
   c. *Lecithin is used by every living cell in the body. It helps purify the system and aids in the absorption of vitamins A, D, E, and K.*
   d. *Choline and inositol are important for hair metabolism.*
   e. *Calcium is important for actively growing hair follicle cells.*
   f. *Vitamin E is an excellent antioxidant particularly good for preventing the oxidization of Vitamins A & C. It maintains cell membranes and the general health of the blood.*
   g. *Zinc keeps hair follicles from atrophying.*
   h. *Copper ensures hair pigment.*
   i. *Manganese and iron are essential for follicle growth.*
   j. *Iodine is essential for optimum hair growth.*
   k. *Biotin has been called "the hair vitamin" because of its growth benefits.*

6. Name <u>one</u> enemy of healthy hair. (Chapter 27, #4, 11)
   a. *chlorine*   d. *permanents*
   b. *sun*   e. *certain drugs like sulfa drugs and birth control pills*
   c. *dyeing*

CHAPTER XXVIII

Reading Comprehension:

1. How was Anne's hair changing? *It was becoming auburn.*

2. What had happened to Idlewild? *Mr. Bell had cut down the circle of trees in his back pasture.*

3. What was more fascinating about the pond? *They could fish for trout and row a boat.*

4. Anne wanted to be the principal character, yet what made her think it was impossible? *She thought it was impossible because she had red hair.*

5. What happened to Anne's boat? *The bottom scraped over a stake and then began to leak.*

6. What limited view of God did Anne have as her boat was sinking? *She thought that all God could do was get her to one of the bridge piles.*

7. Who rescued Anne? *Gilbert rescued Anne.*

8. What did Matthew want Anne to keep a little of? *Matthew wanted her to keep a little of her romance.*

Vocabulary: Fill in the blanks using the vocabulary words.

9. *pall*   12. *samite*   15. *parsed*

10. *jaunty*   13. *procured*   16. *Camelot*

11. *presentiment*   14. *haughtily*

Reading Comprehension:

1. Despite Anne's good imagination, what could she not guess? *Anne and Diana were invited to go with Aunt Josephine to the Exhibition.*

2. Of what did Anne have to repent? *Anne had to repent of being too disappointed to say her prayers.*

3. How was Anne guarding her heart from disappointment? *She wasn't going to think about going to the Exhibition at all until she knew whether or not Marilla would give her permission to go.*

4. Why did Marilla now make Anne's dresses fashionably? *Marilla did not want Matthew to have Mrs. Lynde make any more dresses for Anne.*

5. How did Anne feel in the luxury of Aunt Josephine's house? *She felt uncomfortable.*

6. When did Anne realize how much she liked Mrs. Lynde? *When she saw Mrs. Lynde's face amongst the crowd of strangers at the Exhibition, Anne realized how much she liked Mrs. Lynde.*

7. What did Anne think was the worst part of growing up? *The things you wanted so much as a child do not seem so wonderful to you when you get them.*

8. What was Miss Barry's relationship with most people? *She valued people only as they were of service or amused her.* How was Anne different? *Not only did Anne amuse her, but she was able to love Anne for herself. Anne was enthusiastic, transparent, and had winning ways.*

Activities:

4. Why was Anne glad that Josie Pye took first place in knitted lace? *She thought it was an improvement she could rejoice in Josie's success because Josie had not been kind to her.*

Reading Comprehension:

1. How did Anne deal with Marilla being critical? *She remembered what she owed Marilla.* Why was Marilla so critical? *Her love made her fear being indulgent. She thought it was somehow wrong to care for any human so much and therefore in order to atone, she was more critical.*

2. What was Anne's opinion of thinking about boys all the time? *It does not do well to think about them all the time.*

3. Name the two things Anne had done wrong when she read *Ben Hur* during class time. *She was not doing what she was supposed to be doing and she was being deceitful in trying to hide what she was doing.*

4. Anne had ignored Gilbert for years. What was she finding out now? *She found out she did not like being ignored.*

5. How did Anne pass her days? *Anne studied, read delightful books, practiced for the Sunday School choir, won honors, and went to the manse on Saturday afternoons.*

6. What did Mrs. Lynde admit to being wrong about? *She was wrong in her judgment of Anne and the wisdom of the Cuthbert's taking her in.*

Reading Comprehension:

1. Why did Marilla allow Anne so much freedom during her summer vacation? *The Spencervale doctor had told Marilla to keep Anne in the open air all summer and she envisioned Anne's death by consumption if she did not "scrupulously" heed his warning.*

2. What improved Anne's alertness, spring in her step, and zest? *In her freedom, Anne "frolicked" the entire summer—walking, rowing, picking berries, and dreaming "to her heart's content."*

3. At the end of the summer, what "good friends" did Anne retrieve? *She brought her books down from the attic.*

4. What effect did Rachel have on both Marilla and Anne? *They felt irresistibly tempted to do what Mrs. Lynde did not want them to.* What was good about Rachel? *She was a good Christian woman who never shirked her share of work.*

5. What did Anne find about growing up? *Growing up was a serious thing, with new and perplexing questions to ponder.*

6. What caused Anne to do even better academically? *The threat of the examination made Anne do better.*

7. What did Marilla notice about Anne besides her growth in height? *She noticed Anne talked less. Answers may vary.* What brought forth this change in Anne? *She found it nicer to think pretty thoughts and keep them in her heart like treasures where others could not laugh at them or wonder over them.*

8. Why did Anne expand socially? *Marilla no longer forbid outings because she continued to remember the "doctor's dictum."*

9. What had happened to the story club? *They became too busy for the story club as well as tired of it and the silliness of "writing about love and murder and elopements and mysteries."*

10. What was Anne's stumbling block? *Geometry was Anne's stumbling block.* Moody Spurgeon's? *Moody's was English history.* Who was missing from the list? *Gilbert was missing from the list.*

11. What did Anne think she could not bear? *She could not bear the disgrace of failing the Entrance exams for Queen's.* Is there something that you think you could not bear? *Answers will vary.*

Activities:

6. Skim the chapter to see if you can find these Biblical phrases and then use your concordance to locate at least one reference. *Answers may vary.*
   a. *Anne said she was "rejoicing as a strong man." Read Psalm 19:1–5.*
   b. *The expression "gird your loins" is from the Bible. Read Job 38:3 and Luke 12:35. Probably the most famous "girding" in the Bible is found in Ephesians 6:14.*
   c. *Montgomery used another Biblical phrase when she referred to the "stumbling block" each student had. Read Leviticus 19:14 and I Corinthians 1:23.*

Unit 7 Quiz

History
(12 points)

1. Define the following terms. (Chapter 29, #5)
   a. (2 points) vassal: *Originally the comitatus of German relations where a man would offer his services in return for the protection of a lord. By the 12th century, these contracts had become more formalized and a vassal generally sought to closely define the terms of vassalage and to make the relationship hereditary as a way of providing for offspring. During the Middle Ages a vassal was a free man who voluntarily exchanged his service, sometimes military service, in exchange for protection. A vassal swore an oath of fealty to the liege lord, who swore a return oath to defend the vassal. This contract, enhanced by the personal bond of homage, tied feudal relationships together and insured a measure of continuity and predictability, stability that allowed society to grow and develop out of the feudal age.*
   —*<http://www.chronique.com/Library/Glossaries/glossary-KCT/gloss_v.htm>*

   b. (3 points) serf: *A peasant, the lowest class in the feudal system, belonging to a class who were tied to the land that they worked on behalf of the lord. They were in a very real sense owned by the lord of the manor or property, gradually rising in rights and eventually synonymous to the English villein.*
   —*<http://www.chronique.com/Library/Glossaries/glossary-KCT/gloss_s.htm>*

> villein: *A bondsman, a man bonded to the land that he worked. Villeins lived in villages, attached to a lord's holdings, all but a slave. A lord who owned the land to which a villein was attached could do anything with him he pleased, save mutilation or killing him. Villeins had few rights and only in rare circumstances were released from their bondage. Under Henry I, the releasing ceremony had to be conducted in a public place such as in a church or marketplace. That way many gained knowledge of the release and the villein, now a freeman, was not considered to have fled his feudal contract. A man was a villein if his father was a villein; only by the release of the lord could be ever be free.*
>
>   *Villeins held few rights, unable to fish in the lord's rivers, to hunt or draw firewood from his forests, marry his daughter off without permission (and a fee, generally), or commit his son to Holy Orders.*
>
> —*<http://www.chronique.com/Library/Glossaries/glossaryKCT/gloss_v.htm#villein>*

c. (2 points) baron: *After 1066, the tenants-in-chief who held their lands directly from the king. Gradually, a distinction between the greater and lesser barons emerged, so that by the late 13th century the greater barons began to attend Parliament under summons from the king. The first use of the style "baron" in an individual's name came in 1387. The baron ranks in precedence below a count, carrying the title "your excellency."*

> —*<http://www.chronique.com/Library/Glossaries/glossary-KCT/gloss_b.htm>*

2. (3 points) Write <u>three</u> facts about Henry Wadsworth Longfellow. *Answers may vary.* (Chapter 31, #3, 4)

3. Why had Anne not seen any women preachers? *Answers may vary, but should include some reference to Scripture as a reason.* (Chapter 31, #5)

4. What long range effects did Ralph Waldo Emerson's philosophy have on our current education system? *Answers may vary, but should include reference to defection from the Christian faith.* (Chapter 31 #11)

Literature
(10 points)

1. Who is Odin? *The chief god of Norse mythology.* (Chapter 29, #5)

2. Find an example of alliteration in *Marmion* from Canto VI. *Answers may vary.* (Chapter 29, #5)

> *Did in the dame's devotions share;*
> *Was it that, seared by sinful scorn,*
> *Of such a stem a sapling weak,*
> *For now that sable slough is shed,*
> *When the Dead Douglas won the field,*
> *And send thee forth to fame!*

3. What is the climatic point of Canto VI? *The death of Marmion is the climatic point.* (Chapter 29, #5)

4. *Thomas Aquinas* (Chapter 29, #6)

5. "*Virtue* has its own reward." —Aristotle (Chapter 29, #6)

6. Give an example of poetic justice. *Answers may vary.* (Chapter 30, #2)

7. How does the poem "Maidenhood" enhance the theme of *Anne of Green Gables*? *Answers may vary.* (Chapter 31, #3)

8. *Alexander Pope* (Chapter 31, #7)

9. *False* (Chapter 31, #11)

10. *True* (Chapter 31, #11)

Bible
(10 points)

1. *Novels* (Chapter 31, #1)

2. (4 points) Write a paragraph incorporating at least three Biblical phrases. (Chapter 31, #6)

3. (5 points) And let us not be *weary* in well doing: for in due *season* we shall *reap*, if we *faint* not. Galatians *6*:9 (Chapter 31)

Fine Arts
(9 points)

1. Name two nineteenth century opera composers. *Answers may vary. Verdi and Wagner* (Chapter 29, #13)

2. Match these opera terms to the correct definition. (Chapter 29, #12)

score	*D*	singspiel	*C*
coloratura	*E*	leitmotif	*G*
aria	*B*	opera buffa	*F*
libretto	*A*		

Health
(28 points)

1. (3 points) Name <u>three</u> of the minimum requirements for boating safety. (Chapter 28, #12)
   a. lifejacket or personal floatation device
   b. buoyant heaving line
   c. oar or anchor
   d. bailer or water pump
   e. sound signaling devise
   f. navigation lights

2. *Canoes and kayaks* (Chapter 28, #12)

3. *Omega fatty acids* (Chapter 28, #15)

4. (10 points) Draw the heart and label at least 10 parts of the heart using correct medical terminology. (Chapter 30, #15, 16) *See an encyclopedia for a picture of the heart. The following should be the most commonly identified parts of the heart:*

    a. left ventricle   *h. inferior vena cava*
    b. right ventricle   *i. mitral valve*
    c. left atrium   *j. tricuspid valve*
    d. right atrium   *k. heart muscle*
    e. pulmonary artery, pulmonary vein   *l. septum*
    f. aorta   *m. pericardium*
    g. superior vena cava

5. (4 points) List <u>four</u> things you can do to reduce the risk of having a heart attack. (Chapter 30, #15, 16)

    a. Stop smoking.   *e. Exercise.*
    b. Lower high blood pressure.   *f. Reduce stress.*
    c. Reduce high blood cholesterol.   *g. Improve diet.*
    d. Aim for healthy weight.

6. (3 points) List <u>three</u> risk factors you cannot change to decrease your chance of a heart attack. (Chapter 30, #15, 16)

    a. age   *b. sex*   *c. heredity*   *d. race*

7. *False* (Chapter 30, #16)

8. *True* (Chapter 30, #16)

9. *True* (Chapter 30, #16)

10. *False* (Chapter 30, #16)

11. *True* (Chapter 30, #16)

12. *True* (Chapter 30, #16)

Chapter XXXII

Reading Comprehension:

1. What sage advice did Miss Stacy give for the night before the exam? *Miss Stacy advised her students to go for a walk, not to open a book or think about the exams at all, and to go to bed early.*

2. What unkind words did Josie say to Anne prior to the first day of the exam? *"Josie said I looked as if I hadn't slept a wink and she didn't believe I was strong enough to stand the grind of the teacher's course even if I did get through."*

3. Why was Ruby in hysterics when Anne reached the boarding house? *Ruby had discovered a "fearful mistake" she had made in her English paper.*

4. What was Anne's presentiment? *She did not think she had passed the geometry section of the examination.*

5. For what was the Tory political party blamed? *The lateness of the posting of test scores was blamed on the Tory superintendent of education.*

6. Tell how Diana showed herself to be a true and good friend. *Diana brought Anne the news and truly rejoiced with her.*

Worksheet • Poetry • Activity 4 • "The Highwayman"

Write the definition* and an example from "The Highwayman" for each of the following:

1. Alliteration: *"Over the cobbles he clattered and clashed in the dark inn-yard, . . ."*

2. Metaphor: *"The moon was a ghostly galleon tossed upon cloudy seas, . . ."*

3. Onomatopoeia: *"Tlot-tlot; tlot-tlot!"*

4. Simile: *". . . the hours crawled by like years, . . ."*

5. How does your favorite poetic technique used contribute to the "mental picture" seen by the person reading the poem? *Answers may vary.*

**Note:* The definitions of these terms may be found in* Writers INC.

Reading Comprehension:

1. Describe how the east gable had changed over the past four years? *It was no longer barren, but as "sweet and dainty a nest as a young girl could desire." There was pretty matting on the floor, pale-green art muslin curtains, pictures and "dainty apple-blossom" paper on the walls, fresh flowers; and for furniture, a white-painted bookcase, a cushioned wicker rocker, a toilet table with white muslin, a gilt-framed mirror, and a low white bed.*

2. Where did Anne go and why? *Anne was to give a recitation as part of a benefit at the White Sands Hotel to raise money for the Charlottetown hospital.*

3. What was Diana's reputation? *Diana had a reputation for notable taste in dressing.*

4. Why was Anne forever debarred from wearing wild-rose pink? *Anne did not have a good skin color for wearing wild-rose pink.*

5. What did Diana do for Anne? *Diana used her talents dressing Anne.*

6. Describe Billy. *He was a big, fat, stolid youth of twenty, with a round, expressionless face, and a painful lack of conversational gifts.*

7. What scared Anne? *Everything was so strange; the whole atmosphere was one of wealth and culture.* What helped Anne get over her stage fright? *She refused to fail before Gilbert Blythe.*

8. Why did Anne say they were rich? *The girls were rich because they had lived 16 years, were happy, and had imaginations.*

9. Why was Anne happy with her pearls? *She knew Matthew had given them with love.*

Vocabulary: Fill in the blanks using the vocabulary words.

10. *rustic*

11. *elocutionist*

12. *scrutinized*

13. *stanchly*

14. *lithe*

15. *languidly*

16. *limpid*

17. *dint*

18. *debarred*

19. *unpropitious*

20. *scoffed*

21. *encore*

22. *burnished*

23. *pallid*

24. *conniving*

25. *amateur*

26. *ballads*

CHAPTER
XXXIV

Reading Comprehension:

1. How did Anne demonstrate her affection to Matthew and Marilla? *She told them how kind they were and gave Marilla a butterfly kiss.* What did Marilla wish when Anne did this? *She wished she could put her feelings into words.*

2. What did Matthew see in Anne? *Matthew thought Anne was smart, pretty, and loving.*

3. To what did he attribute Anne's coming to Green Gables? *He attributed it to Providence.*

4. How did Diana and Marilla respond to Anne's leaving? What did each of them do? *Diana cried, then went to the beach. Marilla said good-bye in her practical way, then kept herself busy doing work with the "bitterest kind of a heart-ache."*

5. Why does Anne decide not to board with Miss Josephine Barry? *Miss Barry's home was too far from the Academy.*

6. What did Anne think about having Gilbert in class? *She was glad they were in the same class so the old rivalry could continue.*

7. Anne wondered who would be her friend. From outward appearances, what did Anne think about the girls? *Answers may vary.* What attracted her to each? *One looked vivid and rosy while the other one looked as if she knew something about dreams.* Have you ever done this? *Answers may vary.*

8. Explain the different ways Josie Pye insulted Anne during their visit. *Josie accused Anne of not having self-control because she was homesick and told her she should not cry because she looked "all red." She also said the only reason she came by was because she was "starved" and knew Marilla would have "loaded her up with cake." Then she relates how she told Frank Stockley, Anne was "an orphan the Cuthberts had adopted, and nobody knew very much about what you'd been before that."* Compare Josie's comments with those of Jane's. *Instead of berating Anne, Jane not only confessed she had been homesick, but also told her she felt better knowing she was not the only one who had been homesick. She also said something comforting about the cake.*

9. What did Anne say about ambition? *It is delightful to have ambitions; it makes life so interesting.*

Reading Comprehension:

1. With whom was Gilbert walking home, carrying her satchel? *Gilbert usually walked with Ruby Gillis.* What did Anne think about this? *She did not think Gilbert and Ruby made a good couple. Anne thought it would be pleasant to have a friend like Gilbert.*

2. Which did Anne think were the best and dearest hours in the whole week? *Anne thought that the best time of the week occurred when their friends met them at the railway and they walked over to Avonlea in a merry group.*

3. What positive character qualities did Anne now see in Gilbert? *She thought Gilbert was a "clever young fellow," thoughtful, and with a "determination to get the best out of life and put the best into it."* Why did Ruby not seem Gilbert's kind of girl? *She was not a thoughtful person and did not understand much of what Gilbert said. She was not the type of person with whom one could discuss ambitions.*

4. Were Anne's first impressions of her two female classmates correct? *No, the girls turned out to have characteristics the opposite of what Anne expected.*

5. How did each one at Avonlea make a mark of distinction at Queen's? *Ruby Gillis was the handsomest girl; Jane Andrews carried off honors in domestic science; Josie had the sharpest tongue; Gilbert and Anne were contestants for the medal; and some thought Anne was the prettiest girl in the second year class.*

6. What helped Anne keep the examinations in perspective? *Looking at the big buds swelling on the chestnut trees and the misty blue air made them seem less important.*

7. How did Anne respond to Josie's comment? *She did not allow it to hurt her. She understood the "joy of the strife."*

Unit 8 Quiz

Literature
(4 points)

1. *Purity, virginity, majesty.* (Chapter 33, #5)

2. Give an example of onomatopoeia. *Answers will vary.* (Chapter 33, #4; Chapter 34, #4)

3. What was the purpose of the poem, "The Woman on the Field of Battle"? *Answers will vary.* (Chapter 35, #4)

4. *Virgil* (Chapter 34, #5)

Fine Arts
(7 points)

1. *She is the mother of Christ.* (Chapter 33, #7)

2. (2 points) Name <u>two</u> of Raphael's paintings. *Answers may vary; could include: "The School of Athens" or "The Madonna."* (Chapter 33, #7)

3. (3 points) Name <u>three</u> Pre-Raphaelite painters. (Chapter 33 #8)
      a. Rossetti   b. Hunt   c. Millais   d. Waterhouse

4. Name <u>one</u> Pre-Raphaelite painting. *Answers may vary.* (Chapter 33, #8)

Bible
(25 points)

1. Fill in the blanks.

   According as his <u>*divine power*</u> hath <u>*given*</u> unto us all things that pertain unto <u>*life*</u> and <u>*godliness*</u>, through the knowledge of him that hath called us to <u>*glory*</u> and <u>*virtue*</u>. Whereby are given unto us exceeding great and precious promises: that by these ye might be partakers of the <u>*divine nature*</u>, having escaped the <u>*corruption*</u> that is in the world through lust. And beside this, giving all <u>*diligence*</u>, add to your <u>*faith*</u> virtue; and to virtue <u>*knowledge*</u>; And to knowledge <u>*temperance*</u>; and to temperance <u>*patience*</u>; and to patience <u>*godliness*</u>; And to godliness <u>*brotherly kindness*</u>; and to brotherly kindness <u>*charity*</u>. For if these things be in you, and abound, they make you that ye shall neither be <u>*barren*</u> nor <u>*unfruitful*</u> in the <u>*knowledge*</u> of our <u>*Lord Jesus Christ*</u>. II Peter 1:3–8 (Chapter 35)

Reading Comprehension:

1. What caused Anne to feel a sickening pang of defeat? *She heard the boys crying, "hurrah for Blythe, Medalist!" She believed she had failed and Gilbert had won.*

2. What was Jane to do? *She was to check who won the Avery.* Who won the Avery? *Anne won the Avery.*

3. How did the boys congratulate Gilbert? *The boys carried Gilbert around on their shoulders yelling hurrahs.* How was Anne congratulated? *The girls crowded around, congratulating her: laughing, thumping her shoulders, shaking her hands; pushing, pulling and hugging.*

4. When Anne came home, what did she notice? *Matthew was looking grayer than he had the year before and Marilla looked tired.*

5. What were her plans? *She wanted to take the day off and visit her favorite places.*

6. How did Matthew want to die? *He wanted to be able to work up until the end of his life.*

Reading Comprehension:

1. What sudden shock contributed to Matthew's death? *The Abbey Bank had failed with all their money in it.*

2. What did Anne drop when she grabbed for Matthew? *Anne dropped her flowers.* Do you think this was symbolic? *Answers may vary.* If so, of what? *Answers may vary.*

3. What kind of flowers surrounded Matthew? *He had old-fashioned flowers which his mother had planted in bridal days.* How was this fitting? *Answers may vary.*

4. How did Anne and Marilla respond "out of character" to Matthew's death? *Marilla cried uncontrollably and Anne was tearless.*

5. What did Anne find out about Marilla? *Anne found out that Marilla loved her.* With Matthew's death, what happened to Marilla and Anne's relationship? *Answers may vary.*

6. What did Anne find sad and almost shameful after Matthew's death? *Anne thought it sad they could settle back into the regular routine of life and that it was almost shameful she could still experience joy in the beauty of nature and friendship.*

7. What reminded Marilla of her previous beau? *Gilbert had looked so tall and manly when she had seen him in church, he reminded her of her beau.*

Activities:
8. a. Name the meter of *Snow-bound*. *Snow-bound is written in tetrameter, four feet in each line. Each foot is composed of two syllables, the first unaccented, the second accented. This is called iambic. The meter in* Snow-bound *is therefore called iambic tetrameter.*

Reading Comprehension:
1. Why was Marilla distraught? *The doctor told her she had a good chance of being blind within six months.*

2. What advice and hope did the eye doctor give Marilla? *If she did not do needlework, read, or cry, perhaps her eyes would be saved.*

3. What did Mr. Sadler want? *He wanted to buy Green Gables.*

4. What did Anne decide she would do to help Marilla? *She decided she would not return to college because she would get a teaching job and stay at Green Gables to help Marilla.*

5. What did the people in Avonlea think of Anne's decision? *Most of the people, not knowing the whole situation, thought she was foolish.* Anne cared about Mrs. Allan's opinion. What did Mrs. Allan think about it? *Mrs. Allan and Mrs. Lynde thought she had made the right choice.* What was Mrs. Lynde's reason for agreeing with it? *Mrs. Lynde did not believe girls should go to college with men.* Do you think Gilbert agreed? *He agreed, otherwise he would not have given up his teaching post in Avonlea.*

6. How did Anne find out she had the job at Avonlea? *She found out from Mrs. Lynde.*

7. What was her response toward Gilbert? *She forgave Gilbert and greeted him nicely.*

8. What did Anne think about her future? *She believed her future, like a road, now had a bend in it. While she did not know what would be around that bend, she believed it would be for the best and she found the very mystery fascinating.*

9. Montgomery's writing appeals to the senses. What can be smelled in this chapter? *The following phrases all evoke the sense of smell: "warm, scented summer dusk"; "the odour of mint"; and "a freshness in the air as of a wind that had blown over honey-sweet fields of clover."*

Activities:

5. To which English monarch is she referring? *Queen Victoria*

Unit 9 Quiz

Literature
(7 points)

1. (2 points) Explain what the theme of "The Glory and the Dream" has to do with this Unit. *Answers may vary.* (Chapter 36, #4)

2. (2 points) "Loss in all familiar things" is a quote from which poet? *John Greenleaf Whittier* (Chapter 37, #8)

3. (2 points) Give an example of a sentence using local dialogue from your area. *Answers will vary.* (Chapter 38, #1)

4. Name someone who wrote satirical literature? *Marietta Holley, pen name, Josiah Allen's Wife; Mark Twain.* (Chapter 38, #5)

   Extra credit: Define satire. (Chapter 31, #7) *"A literary work in which human vice or folly is attacked through irony, derision, or wit."*

   —*<http://dictionary.reference.com/search?q=satire>*

Health
(13 points)

1. (3 points) What are the <u>three</u> most common causes of blindness in the United States? (Chapter 38, #9, 10)
   a. macular degeneration   *b. cataracts*   *c. glaucoma*

2. (10 points) List the <u>five</u> stages of the loss process. Give an example of what one might say during each stage. *Examples may vary.* (Chapter 37, #11)
   a. denial   *c. anger*   *e. acceptance*
   b. bargaining   *d. despair*

History
(7 points)

1. (4 points) Name <u>three</u> causes of bank failures in the past.
   (Chapter 37, #5)
   a. managerial weakness
   b. poor internal routines and controls
   c. fraud
   d. economic conditions

2. (3 points) Name <u>three</u> things which a married woman could not legally
   do in the 1800's. (Chapter 38, #5)
   a. sign a will   *d. hold title to property*   *g. establish a business*
   b. testify in court   *e. contract*
   c. sue   *f. sign papers as a witness*

Bible
(15 points)

1. (11 points) What acronym describes the five points of Calvinism?
   T.U.L.I.P. For what does each point stand? (Chapter 37, #8)
   *a. T—Total Depravity or Total Inability. The Calvinists believed man is
   in absolute bondage to sin and Satan, unable to exercise his own will
   to trust in Jesus Christ without the help of God.*
   *b. U—Unconditional Election. The Calvinists believed foreknowledge is
   based upon the plan and purpose of God, and that election is not
   based upon the decision of man, but the "free will" of the Creator
   alone.*
   *c. L—Limited Atonement. The Calvinists believed Jesus Christ died to
   save those who were given to Him by the Father in eternity past. In
   their view, all for whom Jesus died (the elect) will be saved, and all
   for whom He did not die (the nonelect) will be lost.*
   *d. I—Irresistible Grace. The Calvinists believed the Lord possesses
   irresistible grace that cannot be obstructed. They taught the free will
   of man is so far removed from salvation, the elect are regenerated
   (made spiritually alive) by God even before expressing faith in Jesus
   Christ for salvation. If a totally depraved person is not made alive by
   the Holy Spirit, such a calling on God would be impossible.*
   *e. P—Perseverance of the Saints. The Calvinists believed salvation is
   entirely the work of the Lord, and man has absolutely nothing to do
   with the process. The saints will persevere because God will see to it
   that He will finish the work He has begun.*

2. (4 points) Name one famous Calvinist scholar whom we have studied
   this year. (Chapter 26, #3)
   *Calvinism has been known for outstanding scholars, theolo-
   gians, preachers, and reformers, men such as John Owen,
   George Whitefield, William Wilberforce, Abraham Kuyper,
   Charles Hodge, B.B. Warfield, J. Gresham Machen, and
   Charles Haddon Spurgeon.*

   —<http://www.calvarychapel.com/library/smith-chuck/books/caatwog.htm>

Extra Credit: What document opposes the five points of Calvinism? *The document "The Five Points of Arminianism" was a protest against the doctrines of the Calvinists and was submitted to the State of Holland. In 1618, a National Synod of the Church was convened in Dort to examine the teachings or Arminius in the light of Scripture. After 154 sessions, lasting seven months, the "Five Points of Arminianism" were declared to be heretical. After the synod, many of the disciples of Arminius, such as Hugo Grotius, were imprisoned or banished. When John Wesley took up some of the teachings of Arminianism, the movement began to grow, and it affected the Methodist tradition as well as the beliefs of most Pentecostal and Charismatic churches.* —<http://www.calvarychapel.com/library/smith-chuck/books/caatwog.htm>

Final Exam

Crossword Puzzle • Vocabulary

```
C O N F I D E N T I A L     G
    E                 U      A
    S           R     D      U
S   P E R T U R B A T I O N  T
T   R   I       P   T   C    L
R   E   N       T       R    E
Y   D U T Y     D       O    T
C   I       R   E       U
H   L       O   P       S
N   E       M   R   G L I B
I N C U L C A T E S     Y
N   T       N   C   P
E   I N F A T U A T E D
    O       I   T   R
D I N T   E C C E N T R I C
```

Literature

1. Children are a blessing. Describe the change in Marilla's character as the book progresses. *Answers may vary. In the beginning of the book Marilla is rather rigid, decidedly unimaginative, and emotionally reserved. In the end, while no less principled, she is more loving.*

2. What are Anne's weaknesses? *Answers may vary. Anne was flighty.* How does Marilla help Anne overcome her weaknesses? *Marilla helps Anne overcome her flightiness by giving her responsibility in a loving environment. Others had given Anne responsibility, but not in an environment that was emotionally safe or supportive, so she chose to stay in her imaginary world.*

3. How does Marilla develop Anne's potential? *Answers may vary. Marilla teaches Anne character, responsibility, and household skills while letting her use her creative bent decorating and performing in school and community events such as recitations.*

4. What role did Matthew play in the family? *Answers may vary. Matthew was the peacemaker and Anne's intercessor. He rejoiced in Anne the way she was.*

5. Tell as many examples as you can of how Diana shows herself a good and true friend. *Answers may vary. Diana shows herself a true friend by keeping Anne's secrets, not gossiping about her, and not ridiculing her. Diana visits her when she is sick. She gives little advice, but when she does, it is good advice. Diana rejoices with Anne in her successes, even when these achievements do not necessarily mean happiness for herself. For example, when Anne passes her Queen's entrance exam, Diana is happy for her even though this means Anne will be going away and Diana will miss her.*

6. What do you love about the character, Anne? *Answers may vary. I love Anne's imagination and joy of living.*

7. What is in a name? Explain some of the symbolism in the names Montgomery chooses for her characters. *Answers may vary. Mrs. Blewett blew her chance to have Anne. Mrs. Barry had to bury her prejudices about Anne. Diana's name comes from the Greek god Artemis or Diana, the goddess of love.*

8. Name some of the main themes of Montgomery's *Anne of Green Gables*. *Answers may vary. The answers should include some of the following:*
   Conflict between imagination and social expectations
   Sentimentality versus emotion
   All things happen for good to those that love the Lord
   Children are a blessing
   Grace versus the Law
   Will versus duty
   Adolescence and growing up

9. Write the definition of each of the following literary terms.

   metaphor: *A metaphor compares two unlike things without using the words "as" or "like."*

   > *"A green plant is a machine that runs on solar energy."*
   > —Scientific American, April 1988

   foil: *A foil is someone who serves as a contrast or a challenge to another character.*

   foreshadowing: *Foreshadowing is a literary technique which gives clues or hints of what is to come.*

   juxtaposition: *Juxtaposition places two ideas (words or pictures) side by side so that their closeness creates a new, often ironic meaning.*

10. Give an example of the following. *Answers may vary.*

    irony: *The best substitute for experience is being sixteen.*

    poetic justice: *Haman was hung on the gallows he had had built for Mordecai.*

    personification: *The flowers danced in the breeze.*

    Parthian shaft: *As she drove away she yelled, "Don't forget the dishes!"*

11. Write a sentence using each of the following correctly. *Answers may vary.*

    dash: *Technology is wonderful—when it works.*

    semicolon: *My shoe size is 5½ unless I am wearing bowling shoes; then it is 6½.*

    colon: *Ice cream consists of three things: milk, sugar, and flavoring.*

12. Has the book *Anne of Green Gables* meant more to you after completing the study *Where the Brook and River Meet?* If so, tell in what way it has meant more to you? *Answers may vary. I enjoy* Anne of Green Gables *more now because I understand the views, symbolism, and references in the book.*

13. Identify the rhyme scheme of the following stanza. *The rhyme scheme of this stanza is ABAB.*

14. *mind'-ful*
    art'-less
    re-late'
    lone'-ly
    con-tem-pla'-tion
    kin'dred

15. From your reading during *Where the Brook and River Meet*, give examples of each category of literature, listing title and author. *Answers may vary.*

    Restoration Literature (1660–1700)—Pilgrim's Progress *by John Bunyan*

    Augustan Age or Neoclassical Age (1700–1750)—*"An Essay on Criticism" or* Rape of the Lock *by Alexander Pope*

    Romantic Period (1750–1832)—Childe Harold's Pilgrimage *by Lord Byron or "Ode: Intimations of Immortality from Recollections of Early Childhood" by William Wordsworth*

    Victorian Period (1832–1901)—*"Lancelot and Elaine" by Alfred, Lord Tennyson or* Sonnets of the Portuguese *by Elizabeth Browning*

16. List <u>five</u> works of Shakespeare. *Answers may vary.*
    a. *Hamlet*   d. *Romeo and Juliet*
    b. *King Lear*   e. *Much Ado About Nothing*
    c. *Macbeth*

History

Essay:

1. What events in England caused John Bunyan to become a political prisoner? *Answers may vary.*

In 1660 Cromwell's Protectorate came to an end and the monarchy was restored. In the belief that national unity could only be achieved by religious uniformity, the state attempted to restrain the developing Independent congregations by forbidding preaching. Bunyan was arrested in the hamlet of Samsell just after he had begun a meeting. He was held at nearby Harlington Manor overnight and appeared before the local justices there when he was sentenced to three months in prison.

Since Bunyan refused to give an assurance not to preach, he remained in the County Gaol for 12 years from 1661 to 1672. In vain, his wife Elizabeth tried to get his case reopened by pleading with Sir Matthew Hale, the Lord Chief Justice of England, when he stayed in Bedford. Bunyan was allowed several privileges as a prisoner, since he was not a common criminal. The prison was only five minutes from his home so food was brought into his cell, often by his blind daughter Mary. He also received daily visits from friends and had occasional excursions from prison, keeping him in close contact with members of the congregation. He is reputed to have made a wooden flute out of a stool leg in his prison cell. During imprisonment he supported his family by making "long tagged bootlaces" which they could sell.

In 1672 King Charles II issued the Declaration of Religious Indulgence and Bunyan, like other church offenders, was released from prison. He was immediately appointed pastor of the Independent congregation in Bedford, which later bought a barn and orchard in Mill Street as their place of meeting. In 1673 the King was forced to withdraw his Declaration, and early in 1677 Bunyan returned to prison.

—<http://www.museums.bedfordshire.gov.uk/education/Bunyan/Bbiog.html>

2. What characterized Queen Victoria's reign? *Answers may vary.*

"Victorian Times" were a time of great change and growth on a global scale, much like the world today. Foreign trade agreements, cultural exchanges, new technologies, civil unrest, and an abundance of artistic and creative outlets were all characteristics of "Victorian Times." The Victorian period incorporates The Age of Liberalism and Nationalism (1826–1850) and The Age of Imperialism (1875–1900).

Civil unrest and social class battles, as well as strong patriotic bonds among citizens to protect their interests at home characterized the Age of Liberalism and Nationalism in both Europe and America. The emerging middle class sought personal freedoms for the individual and a more democratic government.

The Age of Imperialism, in contrast, was a time of world domination and a desire by governments such as Britain to establish empires. Through Queen Victoria, Britain was able to dominate small countries and control raw materials and world markets.

Despite all this political and governmental turmoil—or, perhaps, because of it—many great minds expressed themselves in the form of invention. Victoria was privileged to reign during a time of great individual achievement. From new colors to cures for deadly diseases to new forms of entertainment, it was a time filled to the brim with change.

—<http://www.liberalartsandcrafts.net/contentcatalog/history/victoria.shtml>

Short Answer:
3. *The War of 1812*

4. *Russia fought England, France, and Turkey in the Crimean War.*

Extra Credit: During what years was the Crimean War fought? *The Crimean War was fought from 1853–1856.*

True or False:
5. *True*

6. *False*

7. *False*

8. *True*

9. *True*

10. *False*

11. *True*

Multiple Choice:

12. *a. six*

13. *a. Roundheads*

14. *b. Scotland*

15. *b. there was no loss of life*

16. *c. William and Mary*

17. Match the names and descriptions.

   _K_   Henry Wadsworth Longfellow

   _B_   Jacques Cartier

   _C_   Salmonella

   _A_   Alexander Pope

   _E_   Robert Browning

    _F_   Mary, Queen of Scots

    _G_   Dwight Moody

    _H_   Charles Spurgeon

    _M_   Hudson Taylor

    _D_   Aristotle

    _L_   James Thomson

    _I_   Marietta Holley

    _J_   Florence Nightingale

Health

1. *98.6°F.*

2. List <u>four</u> things you can do to prevent food poisoning from meat.
   a. At the store, bag meat separately from other products.
   b. Store at proper temperature. Refrigerate food until prior to using.
   c. Separate raw meat and poultry from other foods.
   d. Do not allow blood to drain on other foods.
   e. Thaw meat in the refrigerator.
   f. Work with meat on non-porous surfaces only. Do not use a wood cutting board with meats.
   g. Wash hands, cutting boards, and counter surfaces before and after handling raw meat.
   h. Use disinfectant to clean surfaces.
   i. Fully cook the meat; use a meat thermometer, especially for poultry.
   j. Never put cooked meat on the same plate on which raw meat has been placed without washing it first.
   k. Refrigerate leftovers immediately after the meal. Always store hot foods at a temperature above 60 degrees; cold foods, below 5 degrees. Throw food out after 5 days.

3. Draw the heart and label at least <u>ten</u> parts of the heart using correct medical terminology. *See an encyclopedia for a picture of the heart. The following should be the most commonly identified parts of the heart:*
   a. left ventricle
   b. right ventricle
   c. left atrium
   d. right atrium
   e. pulmonary artery, pulmonary vein
   f. aorta
   g. superior vena cava
   h. inferior vena cava
   i. mitral valve
   j. tricuspid valve
   k. heart muscle
   l. septum
   m. pericardium

4. List <u>four</u> risk factors you can change to decrease your chance of having a heart attack.
   a. Stop smoking.
   b. Lower high blood pressure.
   c. Reduce high blood cholesterol.
   d. Aim for healthy weight.
   e. Exercise.
   f. Improve diet.
   g. Reduce stress.

5. List <u>three</u> risk factors you cannot change to decrease your risk of a heart attack.

   a. age   b. sex   c. heredity   d. race

6. What are the <u>three</u> most common causes of blindness in America? Describe their cause, symptoms, and treatment. *Answers may vary.*

   a. *Macular degeneration, particularly age-related macular degeneration or ARMD, is a leading cause of blindness. Macular degeneration is a degenerative disease that affects the macula, a small spot in the central area of the retina located at the back of the eye. The macula is responsible for sight in the center of the field of vision and is the most sensitive part of the retina. The condition affects central vision.*

      Cause: A tendency to develop Macular degeneration may be seen in some families because of genetic factors. Macular degeneration may also be associated with arteriosclerosis, hereditary factors, eye trauma, or other conditions that are not yet clearly understood.

      Symptoms: As macular degeneration progresses, symptoms will become more and more obvious. If you have macular degeneration, you may notice that straight lines in your field of vision, such as telephone poles, the sides of buildings, and streetlight posts, appear wavy; type in books, magazines and newspapers appears blurry; and dark or empty spaces may block the center of your vision.

      Prevention: The following steps can be taken to help prevent macular degeneration.

      (1.) Eat large quantities of dark green leafy vegetables rich in carotenoids, the yellowish pigments that include precursors of Vitamin A. Two yellow pigments found in the macula known as lutein and zeaxanthin are also found in these vegetables and are thought to filter out visible blue light which might possibly damage the macula. Therefore these two yellow pigments may protect the macula from light damage. A high intake of vitamin C from food may also be beneficial.

      (2.) Protect your eyes from potentially harmful ultraviolet (UV) light. Consumers can be easily confused by misleading claims about certain glasses providing UV protection. A pair of glasses might be labeled UV-absorbent, for example, but the label might not indicate exactly how much of the UVA and UVB rays are blocked.

      (3.) Don't smoke.

      (4.) Eat a low-fat diet.

      (5.) Exercise regularly.

      (6.) Anti-oxidant vitamin supplements may help.

      Treatment: There is no cure for macular degeneration, but treatment may be able to delay its progression or even improve vision. The above preventative measures may be effective for protecting the macula from damage. Research is being done and a number of treatments for macular degeneration are currently being studied.

   b. *Cataracts are a leading cause of blindness among adults in the United States, accounting for one out of every seven cases of blindness in people age 45 and older. Although most prevalent in adults, a cataract can occur in young people, and can sometimes be found in a baby's eyes at birth.*

Cause: A cataract is a clouding of the eye's natural lens. The lens is mostly made of water and protein. The protein is arranged in a precise way that keeps the lens clear and lets light pass through it. As aging occurs, a cataract begins to form if some of the protein clumps together. This starts to cloud a small area of the lens and may grow larger and obscure more of the lens, making it harder to see.

Symptoms: The symptoms of a cataract all revolve around diminished vision—blurred vision, double vision, ghost images, the impression of a "film" over the eyes; problems with light, such as finding lights not bright enough for reading or near work, or being "dazzled" by intense light; and the need for frequent changes of eyeglass prescriptions, which may not improve vision.

Treatment: The treatment for a cataract is surgery, which offers a safe and successful means to restore vision in more than 95 out of 100 cases.

c. *Glaucoma is a leading cause of blindness, accounting for between nine and 12 percent of all cases of blindness.*

Cause: Glaucoma is a group of eye diseases that cause blindness by damaging the nerve cells or the optic nerve located in the back of the eye. Often this damage is thought to be caused in part by increased pressure in the eye called intraocular pressure or IOP. This pressure is a result of a buildup of fluid inside the eye. However, since damage often occurs without increased IOP, many doctors believe glaucoma is better considered as a neurodegenerative disease-caused by damage to and loss of nerve cells-rather than just a disease of high intraocular pressure.

Symptoms: In the vast majority of cases, especially in the early stages, there are few signs or symptoms. At least one-half of all those who have glaucoma are unaware of it. In the later stages of the disease, symptoms can occur that include: loss of side vision; an inability to adjust the eye to darkened rooms; difficulty focusing on close work; rainbow colored rings or halos around lights; and frequent need to change eyeglass prescriptions.

Treatment: Any sight that has been destroyed cannot be restored, but medical and surgical treatment can help stop the disease from progressing.

7. By what method of transmission is tuberculosis spread? *Tuberculosis is spread by droplet.*

8. Name <u>two</u> uses for syrup of ipecac.
   a. *Inducing vomiting in case of non acidic poisoning.*
   b. *May reduce laryngeal spasms as in the case of croup.*

9. Describe a meal that would be nutritionally helpful to bring to a family if the mother is in a cast. *Answers may vary. Look for things high in calcium. A sample menu would be salmon quiche, peas, salad, nettle and horsetail tea, and tapioca pudding for dessert.*

10. Describe how physical education improves gracefulness and promotes digestion. *Answers may vary. Exercise strengthens muscles. Stronger muscles allow one to move with grace. The more one exercises, the more coordination improves. Simple skills such as jumping rope can improve eye hand coordination as well as cardiovascular function. Exercising causes the body's metabolism to speed up, sending freshly oxygenated blood to all parts of the body. It also improves the peristalsis of the gastrointestinal track. (It gets things moving.)*

Fine Arts

Short Answer:

1. What made Raphael's "Madonna" different from paintings of the Madonna in previous periods? *Answers may vary. Raphael made his Madonna very soft and glowing. He paid great attention to detail and scale. Rather than being dwarfed by Mary, the other figures in the picture were all correctly scaled to show they were equally important and Mary was not greater than any of them.*

2. Match these opera terms to their correct definition.

   score   _D_   singspiel   _C_

   coloratura   _E_   leitmotif   _G_

   aria   _B_   opera buffa   _F_

   libretto   _A_

Bible

1. From Otto Koning's sermons, what are the five weapons of Christian Warfare?
   a. rejoice   c. pray   e. meditate
   b. resist   d. love

2. What is a Calvinist belief system? *The Five Points of Calvinism are easily remembered by the acronym T.U.L.I.P. The letters stand for:*

   T—Total Depravity or Total Inability. The Calvinists believed man is in absolute bondage to sin and Satan, unable to exercise his own will to trust in Jesus Christ without the help of God. The unregenerate (unsaved) man is dead in his sins (Romans 5:12). Without the power of the Holy Spirit, the natural man is blind and deaf to the message of the Gospel (Mark 4:11f). That is why "Total Depravity" has also been called "Total Inability." The man without a knowledge of God will never come to this knowledge without God making him alive through Christ (Ephesians 2:1–5).

   U—Unconditional Election. The Calvinists believed foreknowledge is based upon the plan and purpose of God, and that election is not based upon the decision of man, but the "free will" of the Creator alone.

   L—Limited Atonement or Particular Redemption. The Calvinists believed Jesus Christ died to save those who were given to Him by the Father in eternity past. In their view, all for whom Jesus died (the elect) will be saved, and all for whom He did not die (the nonelect) will be lost.

I—Irresistible Grace. Men come to Christ in salvation when the Father calls them (John 6:44), and the very Spirit of God leads God's beloved to repentance (Romans 8:14). The Calvinists believed the Lord possesses irresistible grace that cannot be obstructed. They taught the free will of man is so far removed from salvation, that the elect are regenerated (made spiritually alive) by God even before expressing faith in Jesus Christ for salvation. If a totally depraved person was not made alive by the Holy Spirit, such a calling on God would be impossible.

P—Perseverance of the Saints. The Calvinists believed salvation is entirely the work of the Lord, and man has absolutely nothing to do with the process. The saints (those whom God has saved) will persevere because God will see to it that He will finish the work He has begun. The saints will remain in God's hand until they are glorified and brought to abide with him in heaven (Romans 8:28–39).

3. Write two paragraphs, one explaining the similarities between Catholicism and Protestantism, and the other, the differences. *Answers may vary. This answer is more complete than most students in high school will give.*

Both Catholics and Protestants believe in accord with the statements of the Apostles' Creed:

> *We believe in God the Father Almighty, Maker of heaven and earth. And in Jesus Christ his only Son our Lord; who was conceived by the Holy Ghost, born of the Virgin Mary, suffered under Pontius Pilate, was crucified, dead, and buried; he descended into hell; the third day he rose again from the dead; he ascended into heaven, and sitteth on the right hand of God the Father Almighty; from thence he shall come to judge the quick and the dead.*

Catholics and Protestants are both Christians. The Pope has always taken a strong pro-life stand, even before many Protestants leaders saw any error in the pro-choice movement. However, the Pope presently does not see a contradiction between evolution and Creationism.

There are also many strong differences between the beliefs of the Catholic and Protestant denominations. Historically, especially in the Reformation, many people felt so strongly about the differences they gave up their lives to defend their positions.

There are five Solas of the Reformation:

Sola Scriptura—Scriptures alone: The Scriptures, as the infallible Word of God, are to be our rule for life and doctrine. The Reformers did not see the Church as the final authority. This denial naturally extended to the Pope. Only the Bible, and only because the Bible is God's inspired Word, the Reformers taught, could play the role of final authority in the Church. Therefore, the Reformers maintained, when a matter of dispute arises, regardless of its source or substance, an answer is to be sought in the Scripture where God speaks.

Soli Deo Gloria—to God alone be the glory: God, because of who He is, is to receive all our glory through word, thought, and deed.

Solo Christo—Christ alone: He is the only way to the Father and, through His life and death, the only way we may have eternal life.

Solo Gratia—by grace alone: Salvation is only by the merciful grace of God.

Sola Fide—by faith alone. Salvation is only by the faith God gives and not by any work we may do. The Catholic Church has always taught that we are justified by faith in Christ and in a life of good works lived in response to God's invitation to believe. This teaching is based on two sources: the Holy Bible and Sacred Tradition. The latter pre-dates the Catholic canon of Scripture by nearly 300 years and pre-dates the shorter Reformed canon by nearly 1,500 years. In contrast, the Reformers argued, on the basis of Scripture alone ("sola scriptura"), we are justified by "faith alone" ("sola fide").

Another strongly debated difference between Catholic and Protestant churches is the matter of Transubstantiation. Protestants believe communion is symbolic of the blood and body of Christ while the Catholic church teaches that during the mass, priests have the power to supernaturally turn the bread and wine into the actual and literal body and blood of Jesus Christ.

4. Who is God? *Answers may vary.*

> *God is a Spirit, in and of himself infinite in being, glory, blessedness, and perfection; all-sufficient, eternal, unchangeable, incomprehensible, everywhere present, almighty, knowing all things, most wise, most holy, most just, most merciful and gracious, long-suffering, and abundant in goodness and truth.*
>
> *There is but one only, the living and true God.*
>
> *There be three persons in the Godhead, the Father, the Son, and the Holy Ghost; and these three are one true, eternal God, the same in substance, equal in power and glory; although distinguished by their personal properties.*
>
> —Westminster Larger Catechism, *Answers 7, 8, & 9*

5. Give one example of what a Biblical character said about his unchangeable feature. *Answers may vary. Moses said he was slow of speech and slow of tongue. Jacob's hip muscle shrank. Other examples may be found in Unit 2, Chapter VI & VII, Activity 14.*

6. Write the Lord's Prayer from memory. *Answers may vary slightly.*

The Lord's Prayer

Our Father,
Who art in heaven,
Hallowed be thy Name.
Thy kingdom come,
Thy will be done,
On earth as it is in heaven.
Give us this day our daily bread.
And forgive us our trespasses,

As we forgive those who trespass against us.
And lead us not into temptation,
But deliver us from evil.
For thine is the kingdom, and the power, and the glory, for
ever and ever. Amen.

7. Is man sinful by nature or inherently good? Use Scripture to support your view. *Answers may vary.*

The covenant being made with Adam, not only for himself, but for his posterity; all mankind, descending from him by ordinary generation, sinned in him, and fell with him, in his first transgression.

The fall brought mankind into an estate of sin and misery.

The sinfulness of that estate whereinto man fell, consists in the guilt of Adam's first sin, the want of original righteousness, and the corruption of his whole nature, which is commonly called original sin; together with all actual transgressions which proceed from it. —Westminster Shorter Catechism, *Answers 16, 17, & 18*

Wherefore, as by one man sin entered into the world, and death by sin; and so death passed upon all men, for that all have sinned. Romans 5:12

Wherefore, as by one man sin entered into the world, and death by sin; and so death passed upon all men, for that all have sinned. . . For as by one man's disobedience many were made sinners, so by the obedience of one shall many be made righteous. Romans 5:12, 19

For as in Adam all die, even so in Christ shall all be made alive. I Corinthians 15:22.

And you hath he quickened, who were dead in trespasses and sins; wherein in time past ye walked according to the course of this world, according to the prince of the power of the air, the spirit that now worketh in the children of disobedience: among whom also we all had our conversation in times past in the lusts of our flesh, fulfilling the desires of the flesh and of the mind; and were by nature the children of wrath, even as others. Ephesians 2:1–3

Because the carnal mind is enmity against God: for it is not subject to the law of God, neither indeed can be. So then they that are in the flesh cannot please God. Romans 8:7–8

And God saw that the wickedness of man was great in the earth, and that every imagination of the thoughts of his heart was only evil continually. Genesis 6:5

As it is written, There is none righteous, no, not one: There is none that understandeth, there is none that seeketh after God. They are all gone out of the way, they are together become unprofitable; there is none that doeth good, no, not one.

Their throat is an open sepulchre; with their tongues they have used deceit; the poison of asps is under their lips: Whose mouth is full of cursing and bitterness: Their feet are swift to shed blood: Destruction and misery are in their ways: And the way of peace have they not known: There is no fear of God before their eyes. Now we know that what things soever the law saith, it saith to them who are under the law: that every mouth may be stopped, and all the world may become guilty before God. Therefore by the deeds of the law there shall no flesh be justified in his sight: for by the law is the knowledge of sin. Romans 3: 10–20

Behold, I was shapen in iniquity; and in sin did my mother conceive me. Psalm 51:5

The wicked are estranged from the womb: they go astray as soon as they be born, speaking lies. Psalm 58:3

But every man is tempted, when he is drawn away of his own lust, and enticed. Then when lust hath conceived, it bringeth forth sin: and sin, when it is finished, bringeth forth death. James 1:14–15

8. Describe how Anne demonstrates growing in the Lord as described in II Peter 1:2–8. *Answers may vary.*

giving all diligence: Anne learns to study hard to make top marks in school. The self-discipline she applies to academics also carries through in her study of Scripture as is demonstrated by the increase in quotes from Scripture.

faith: In the book, Anne grows to trust the people around her and at the same time her trust in God grows.

virtue: Anne learns not to meddle or lie. She also learns to love her neighbor.

knowledge: In the book, Anne not only grows in academic knowledge, but also in the knowledge of God and His Word.

self-control: Anne learns to control her impulsiveness and her imagination.

perseverance: Anne learns to persevere and not give up on hard things. She perseveres in her studies to obtain the Avery scholarship.

godliness: Through the book you see Anne growing in godliness. Her respect for God and His laws grows. As the story progresses, she talks less of herself, goddesses, and worldly things and more of God.

brotherly kindness: Anne is kind to Josie, although Josie is self-seeking.

love: Anne is able to love Marilla as much as herself. She gives up her plan to attend school to stay home with Marilla. She does this not out of a sense of duty, but of love.

Appendix of Resources

For the Hard to Obtain Resources

To reduce costs as much as possible, the library and Internet are recommended as the primary sources for materials. Comparable books and sources are fine to use. This list of home school suppliers is not meant to replace your usual retailer. Please check with them first.

Key

**** Books or materials that are used several times or more in this curriculum

*** Books or materials necessary for Contract grade

** Books or materials that contain information for an Activity

* Recommended Latin—different programs (I prefer *Latina Christiana*)

Books that may be of interest for follow-up on a topic

Barbara C. Duncan

<www.barbaraduncanart.com/index.html>

** China painting instructional books and videos

Barbara Jenson Studio

2895 Dorchester
Birmingham, MI 48009
248-649-5718
<www.barbarajensenstudio.com>

** China painting books and supplies

Cadron Creek Christian Curriculum

4329 Pinos Altos Road
Silver City, NM 88061
505-534-1496
<www.cadroncreek.com>

** *American Dictionary of the English Language* (1828 edition) by Noah Webster

**** *Anne's Anthology* compiled and edited by Margie Gray

**** *The Annotated Anne of Green Gables* by L.M. Montgomery edited by Wendy E. Barry, Margaret Anne Doody, and Mary E. Doody Jones

*** *Are You Liberal? Conservative? or Confused?* by Rick Maybury and Richard J. Maybury

**** *The Green Gables Letters from L.M. Montgomery to Ephraim Weber 1905–1909* edited by Wilfrid Eggleston

** *A History of Us, An Age of Extremes 1870–1917,* Book 8, by Joy Hakim

*** *Laurel's Kitchen Caring* by Laurel Robertson

** *Spelling Power* by Beverly Adams-Gordon

** *What in the World's Going on Here?,* Vol. I & II, by Diana Waring

**** *Writers INC* written and compiled by Patrick Sebranek, Dave Kemper, and Verne Meyer

Crown Financial Ministries

<www.crown.org/cartproducts/product.asp?sku=CD970&aid=SCCRN>

** Career Direct Guidance System

Hobby Lobby

1-800-888-0321 Ext. 1275
<www.hobbylobby.com/site3/home2.cfm>

Check your local white pages for the store nearest you.

** Paint and Pretend Mini Tea Set, Creativity for Kids

Home School Digest

Wisdom's Gate
P. O. Box 374-www
Covert, MI 49043
<www.homeschooldigest.com>

** "Pending Notification of the Next of Kin" by Jim and Bonnie Ferguson, *Home School Digest*

** "Journey Through God's Word Concerning Vaccinations" by Alan and Jill Bond, *Home School Digest*

** "When Miss Opinion Comes Calling" by Brook Wayne, *Home School Digest*

Home Life

P. O. Box 1190
Fenton, MO 63026-1190
1-800-346-6322
<www.home-school.com/catalog/>

*** *The Way Home* by Mary Pride

* "Across My Desk" by Mary Pride, *Practical Homeschooling*

Kindred Spirits

Dept. K14
Avonlea, PEI
COB 1MO
1-800-665-2663 • fax 902-436-1787

www. annesociety.org

Kindred Spirits, for Anne fans: The objective of this magazine is to bring together Anne enthusiasts from all over the world, giving them a forum for sharing about L.M. Montgomery's writings and the places she loved and to encourage research on her life, literary work, and its impact.

Wildflowers of PEI

Anne's World, Maud's World: The Sacred Sites of L.M. Montgomery by Nancy Rootland

** *Aunt Maud's Recipe Book* (from the kitchen of L.M. Montgomery) by Elaine and Kelly Crawford

**** *The Green Gables Letters from L.M. Montgomery to Ephraim Weber 1905–1909* edited by Wilfrid Eggleston

* *The Poetry of Lucy Maud Montgomery* selected and introduced by John Ferns and Kevin McCabe

Lacis

3163 Adeline Street
Berkeley, CA 94703
510-843-7178
staff@lacis.com
<www.lacis.com>

* *The Art of Hair Work: Hair Braiding and Jewelry of Sentiment* by Mark Campbell

Mantle Ministries

Richard "Little Bear" Wheeler
228 Still Ridge
Bulverde, TX 78163-1878
830-438-3777
<www.mantleministries.com>

"Pansy" books

*** *A Christmas Surprise* by Isabella Macdonald Alden, "Pansy"

*** *Ester Ried Yet Speaking* by Isabella Macdonald Alden, "Pansy"

CL#26.13

Memoria Press

4103 Bishop Lane
Louisville, KY 40218
877-862-1097 or 502-966-9115
<www.memoriapress.com>

* *Latina Christiana: Introduction to Christian Latin* (for grades 3–9) by Cheryl Lowe

* *Henle Latin* by Robert Henle

Nathhan News

National Challenged Homeschoolers
    Associated Network
P. O. Box 39
Porthill, ID 83853
208-267-6246
<www.nathhan.com>

** "ADHD and the Christian Home" by Rita Jameson, *Nathhan News*

No Thyme Productions

8321 SE 61st Street
Mercer Island, WA 98040
Customer Service: 206-236-8885
info@nothyme.com
<www.nothyme.com/default.cfm>

* Variety of scented geraniums

Truscott Missions

PMB G1
1765 Garnet Ave
San Diego, CA 92109
858-270-5118
<www.truscottmissions.com/>

** *What Does the Bible Teach About Women's Ministry?* by Graham Truscott

Vermont Country Store

<www.vermontcountrystore.com>

** Pastel leather slippers

Vision Forum

4719 Blanco Road
San Antonio, TX 78212
Order Line: 800-440-0022
<www.visionforum.com>

Puritans vs. Witches: Christian Controversies in American History by Paul Jehle, audiocassette or DVD

** *What's a Girl to Do?: How to Wisely Invest Your Daughter's Time* by Doug Phillips, audiocassette or CD

Resources Available in Canada

Both of the following vendors carry the resources listed below.

Canadian Home Resources

7 Stanley Cres SW
Calgary, Alberta CANADA T2S1G1
403-243-9727

Nechako Learning Ladder

P. O. Box 2041
Prince George, B.C. CANADA V2KC8
250-962-2987

** *American Dictionary of the English Language* (1828 edition) by Noah Webster

**** *Anne's Anthology* compiled and edited by Margie Gray

**** *The Annotated Anne of Green Gables* by L.M. Montgomery edited by Wendy E. Barry, Margaret Anne Doody, and Mary E. Doody Jones

*** *Are You Liberal? Conservative? or Confused?* by Rick Maybury and Richard J. Maybury

**** *The Hidden Art of Homemaking* by Edith Schaeffer

**** *How Should We Then Live? The Rise and Decline of Western Thought and Culture* by Francis A. Schaeffer

*** *Laurel's Kitchen Caring* by Laurel Robertson

*** *Mere Christianity* by C. S. Lewis

**** *The Way Home* by Mary Pride

** *What in the World's Going on Here?,* Vol. I & II, by Diana Waring

**** *Writers INC* written and compiled by Patrick Sebranek, Dave Kemper, and Verne Meyer

Topics Covered Appendix

This comprehensive list of topics covered in *Where the Brook and River Meet* is categorized by subject area only. Under each subject area is an alphabetical listing of topics covered in the activities. The chapter in *Where the Brook and River Meet* corresponds directly to the chapter in *Anne of Green Gables*.

You will find your student learns progressively. That is, she is initially introduced to a topic in a general way, and later acquires more in-depth details and understanding of the subject. Still later, she may develop "mastery," a working understanding of a subject and the ability to use the knowledge and explain it to others. This progression in learning (introduction, development, and mastery) is essential for the student to assimilate and build her store of knowledge. Some of the topics in *Where the Brook and River Meet* you may only want to introduce to the student. Other topics may be studied further to develop and master. There are Unit Quizzes and a Final Exam, found in the *Quiz and Test Appendix,* which you may wish to use to measure retention of the material.

Bible

Alcoholic beverages .... Unit 4, Ch. 16, # 9, 13
Ambition .... Unit 8, Ch. 34, # 8
Apostles' Creed .... Unit 4, Ch. 16, # 18
Armor............................... Unit 1, Ch. 2, # 7
Attributes of God .... Unit 2, Ch. 6 & 7, # 11, 12
Beauty .... Unit 1, Ch. 2, # 10
Biblical phrases .... Unit 7, Ch. 31, # 6
Bitterness .... Unit 5, Ch. 23, # 12
                                           Unit 7, Ch. 28, # 8
Brotherly kindness .... Unit 9, Ch. 37, # 13
Calvin, John .... Unit 9, Ch. 37, # 8
Calvinism .... Unit 9, Ch. 37, # 8
Catholicism .... Unit 4, Ch. 16, # 7, 8
Children .... Unit 1, Ch. 1, # 12, 13
Christ............................... Unit 6, Ch. 26, # 7
Christian conversation .... Unit 6, Ch. 26, # 4
Church doctrine .... Unit 5, Ch. 21, # 7
Contentment.................... Unit 5, Ch. 20, # 8
Cults .... Unit 2, Ch. 5, # 20
Daring.............................. Unit 5, Ch. 20, # 12
                                           Unit 5, Ch. 23, # 14
Death .... Unit 3, Chap. 10 & 11, # 10
                                           Unit 9, Ch. 37, # 3
Deeps of affliction .... Unit 5, Ch. 22, # 11
Diligence .... Unit 2, Ch. 5, # 23
Discipline .... Unit 3, Ch. 12 & 13, # 19
Discretion .... Unit 5, Ch. 21, # 20
                                           Unit 9, Ch. 36, # 3
Duty .... Unit 3, Ch. 14, # 10
Emotional quotient .... Unit 9, Ch. 36, # 11
Employer .... Unit 2, Ch. 9, # 9
Faith .... Unit 2, Ch. 6 & 7, # 15
Fear of man .... Unit 2, Ch. 9, # 5
                                           Unit 8, Ch. 33, # 13
Forgiveness...................... Unit 3, Ch. 10 & 11, # 3
Fortune-teller .... Unit 7, Ch. 29, # 10

Friendship .... Unit 2, Ch. 8, # 9
                                           Unit 4, Ch. 18, # 14
                                           Unit 6, Ch. 27, # 13
Gabriel .... Unit 6, Ch. 27, # 5
Gadding about .... Unit 6, Ch. 24, # 9
Gambling .... Unit 7, Ch. 29, # 9
Genealogy of Jesus .... Unit 2, Ch. 6 & 7, # 7
Godliness .... Unit 7, Ch. 31, # 10
Godly leadership .... Unit 5, Ch. 21, # 6
Gossip .... Unit 1, Ch. 1, # 15
                                           Unit 6, Ch. 25, # 6
Guarding the heart .... Unit 7, Ch. 28, # 5, 8
Habits .... Unit 7, Ch. 30, # 8
Haughtiness .... Unit 8, Ch. 33, # 11
Honor .... Unit 5, Ch. 23, # 14
Humility .... Unit 1, Ch. 4, # 3
Idolatry .... Unit 1, Ch. 2, # 9
Impetuousness .... Unit 4, Ch. 19, # 8
Inattentiveness .... Unit 2, Ch. 8, # 10
Iniquity .... Unit 2, Ch. 5, # 18
Job's friends .... Unit 1, Ch. 1, # 11
Joy in the Lord .... Unit 1, Ch. 4, # 4
Leadership .... Unit 5, Ch. 21, # 6
Lord's Prayer .... Unit 2, Ch. 8, # 5, 6
Love .... Unit 2, Ch. 9, # 5
                                           Unit 6, Ch. 24, # 15
                                           Unit 9, Ch. 36, # 11
Love, enemies .... Unit 8, Ch. 34, # 7
Mercy .... Unit 5, Ch. 21, # 21
Mourn .... Unit 9, Ch. 37, # 17
Obedience .... Unit 4, Ch. 17, # 14
Occult.............................. Unit 2, Ch. 5, # 20
Orphans .... Unit 1, Ch. 1, # 12, 14
                                           Unit 1, Ch. 3, # 12
Perseverance .... Unit 3, Ch. 14, # 3
                                           Unit 6, Ch. 25, # 7
                                           Unit 8, Ch. 35, # 6
Pilgrim's Progress .... Unit 3, Ch. 10 & 11, # 7
Pleasing God .... Unit 7, Ch. 30, # 7
Pride .... Unit 3, Ch. 15, # 5, 6
                                           Unit 5, Ch. 22, # 5, 6
                                           Unit 5, Ch. 23, # 11
Protestantism .... Unit 4, Ch. 16, # 7, 8
Reading criteria .... Unit 6, Ch. 26, # 13
Regeneration .... Unit 7, Ch. 29, # 4
Reincarnation .... Unit 5, Ch. 22, # 3, 4
Rejoicing .... Unit 6, Ch. 25, # 3, 7
                                           Unit 8, Ch. 32, # 6
Respect for elderly .... Unit 5, Ch. 23, # 17

Bible Memory

Fine Arts

Health

History, Government, Social Studies, and Geography

Biographies

Literature and Language Arts

Occupational Education

Tea .... Unit 5, Ch. 22, # 12
Teaching............................ Unit 7, Ch. 30, # 19
Visiting
  Cardiac rehabilitation .... Unit 7, Ch. 30, # 18
  Elderly lady .... Unit 4, Ch. 19, # 6
  Florist .... Unit 5, Ch. 21, # 5
  Sick .... Unit 5, Ch. 23, # 8, 19
Volunteering .... Unit 5, Ch. 23, # 18
                     Unit 8, Ch. 33, # 16

Science

Baking powder, rising...... Unit 5, Ch. 21, # 10
Field day: plants, birds .... Units 5–9, Each Friday
Hot air balloons .... Unit 7, Ch. 29, # 19
Jewelweed .... Unit 7, Ch. 30, # 20
Mayflower .... Unit 5, Ch. 20, # 9
Seasons .... Unit 6, Ch. 24, # 12
                     Unit 7, Ch. 28, # 19
Spring signs .... Unit 5, Ch. 20, # 11

Ordering

Placing Orders

Telephone/Fax
  505-534-1496 | *telephone*
  505-534-1499 | *fax*

Electronically
  www.cadroncreek.com
  marigold@cadroncreek.com

Mailing
Cadron Creek Christian Curriculum
  4329 Pinos Altos Rd.
  Silver City, NM 88061

Filling Orders
We will make every attempt to ship your order before the end of the next business day after you place it. During the busy summer months this may extend a day or two. We want to do everything we can to get your order in your hands. We realize that good service will bring you back again.

Back Orders
We make every attempt to minimize the need to back-order. When necessary, we will analyze the likelihood of having all items available for shipment within a week or so. If it is likely we will have all items within a week we may wait to ship all materials at once. Or, we may send a first shipment immediately and wait to ship the remainder until all materials are available for shipment.

Returns
All items purchased from us may be returned within 30 days. Full credit, excluding shipping will be given provided the materials are returned in a resaleable condition.

Group Orders
Having a co-op? Order 5 or more of the same title books published by Cadron Creek and receive 20% off of those books and free shipping on your whole order.

Name

Shipping Address

City   State   Zip

Phone

Email

☐   Visa/MasterCard #

     Exp.Date:M/Y

☐   Check or Money Order made payable to Cadron Creek Christian Churriculum or CCCC

Quantity	Item	Price	Total

*Shipping Costs
Domestic shipping costs are based on the price of the order as follows:

  •$5 minimum
  • less than $100 = 15%
  • over $100 = 10%

Shipments to Canada:
add an additional $5.00 International shipping cost will be calculated per shipment and will include insurance.

Subtotal

Shipping & Handling*

NM residents add 5.9375% sales tax

TOTAL